Counseling and Psychotherapy

Theories and Interventions

David Capuzzi
Portland State University

Douglas R. Gross
Arizona State University

Merrill,
an imprint of Prentice Hall
Education, Career & Technology

Englewood Cliffs, New Jersey   Columbus, Ohio

Library of Congress Cataloging-in-Publication Data
Counseling and psychotherapy : theories and interventions / edited by
   David Capuzzi, Douglas R. Gross
       p.   cm.
   Includes bibliographical references and index.
   ISBN 0-02-319211-9
   1. Counseling. 2. Psychotherapy. 3. Counseling—Case studies.
   4. Psychotherapy—Case studies. 5. Gross, Douglas R. I. Capuzzi, Dave.
   BF637.C6C634   1995
   158'.3—dc20   93-45991
                                                                                    CIP

Cover art: © Marjory Dressler
Editor: Kevin M. Davis
Production Editor: Linda Hillis Bayma
Text Designer: Patti Okuno-Levering
Cover Designer: Patti Okuno-Levering
Production Manager: Pamela D. Bennett
Electronic Text Management: Marilyn Wilson Phelps, Matthew Williams,
   Jane Lopez, Karen L. Bretz

This book was set in Century ITC by Prentice Hall and was printed and bound by R.R. Don-
nelley & Sons Company. The cover was printed by Phoenix Color Corp.

Copyright © 1995 by Prentice-Hall, Inc.
A Division of Simon & Schuster, Inc.
A Paramount Communications Company

Printed in the United States of America

10 9 8 7 6 5 4 3 2 1

ISBN 0-02-319211-9

Prentice-Hall International (UK) Limited, *London*
Prentice-Hall of Australia Pty. Limited, *Sydney*
Prentice-Hall of Canada Inc., *Toronto*
Prentice-Hall Hispanoamericana, S.A., *Mexico*
Prentice-Hall of India Private Limited, *New Delhi*
Prentice-Hall of Japan, Inc., *Tokyo*
Simon & Schuster Asia Pte. Ltd., *Singapore*
Editora Prentice-Hall do Brasil, Ltda., *Rio de Janeiro*

Preface

*C*ounseling and Psychotherapy: Theories and Interventions provides a collection of conceptual frameworks for understanding the parameters of the helping relationship. These parameters can include models for viewing personality development; explaining past behavior; predicting future behavior; understanding the current behavior of the client; diagnosing and treatment planning; assessing client motivations, needs, and unsolved issues; and identifying strategies and interventions of assistance to the client. Theories help organize data and provide guidelines for the prevention and intervention efforts of counselors and therapists. They direct a professional helper's attention and observations and offer constructs, terminology, and viewpoints that can be understood by colleagues and used during supervision and consultation sessions. Theory directly influences the interventions used by counselors and therapists to promote a client's new insight, new behavior, and new approaches to relationships and problem solving. The greater a counselor or therapist's awareness of the strengths and possibilities inherent in numerous theoretical frames of reference, the greater the potential for understanding the uniqueness of a particular client's life space.

This book is unique in both format and content. All the contributing authors are experts who provide state-of-the-art information about theories of counseling and psychotherapy (see pages vii to xiii for their backgrounds). In addition, each chapter discusses applications of a theory as it relates to one particular case study: a hypothetical client named John, whom we are introduced to on pages 109 to 116. The book also includes information that is sometimes not addressed in other counseling and psychotherapy textbooks, such as a chapter that focuses on the importnce of achieving a personal and professional identity before beginning work with clients, a chapter on developmental stages and individual counseling and psychotherapy, and a chapter on alternative approaches to counseling and psychotherapy. The book's unique approach enhances its readability and should increase reader interest in the material.

This book is designed for students who are beginning their study of individual counseling and psychotherapy. It presents a comprehensive overview of each of the following theories: psychoanalytic, Jungian, Adlerian, existential, person-centered, Gestalt, transactional analysis, rational-emotive, cognitive-behavioral, reality, ecosystems, developmental, and nontraditional approaches. Each theory is addressed from the perspective of history, human nature, major constructs, the process of change, intervention strategies, supporting research, a case study, and limitations consistent with the theoretical model under discussion.

We know that one text cannot adequately address all the factors connected with a given theory; entire texts have been written discussing each of the theories in this book. We have, however, attempted to provide readers with a consistent approach to analyzing each theory and have included examples of how to apply a theory in a case study.

OVERVIEW OF THE TEXT

The format for this text is based on the contributions of the coeditors, who conceptualized the content and wrote the first four chapters, as well as the contributions of 23 authors selected for their expertise in various theories. Each chapter contains theoretical and applied content. The text is divided into the following three parts: "Foundations for Individual Counseling and Psychotherapy," "Theories of Counseling and Psychotherapy," and "Additional Perspectives for Counseling and Psychotherapy."

Part One, "Foundations for Individual Counseling and Psychotherapy" (chapters 1 through 4), begins by offering general information about the helping relationship and individual counseling. That foundation is followed by chapters titled "Achieving a Personal and Professional Identity," "Developmental Stages and Individual Counseling and Psychotherapy," and "Ethical and Legal Issues in Counseling and Therapy."

Part Two, "Theories of Counseling and Psychotherapy" (chapters 5 through 16), presents information on the 12 theories selected for inclusion in this portion of the text. These chapters—"Psychoanalytic Theory," "Jungian Analytical Theory," "Adlerian Theory," "Existential Theory," "Person-centered Theory," "Gestalt Theory," "Transactional Analysis Theory," "Rational-Emotive Theory," "Cognitive-Behavioral Theories," "Reality

Therapy Theory," "Ecosystems Theory," and "Developmental Counseling and Therapy: Integrating Individual and Family Theory"—each present a theory and then apply the theory to the case study of John.

Part Three, "Additional Perspectives for Counseling and Psychotherapy" (chapters 17 through 19), includes "Nontraditional Approaches to Counseling and Psychotherapy," "Counseling and Psychotherapy: Multicultural Considerations," and "Counseling and Psychotherapy: An Integrative Perspective."

We the coeditors and the 23 other contributors have made every effort to give the reader current information and content focused on both theory and application. It is our hope that *Counseling and Psychotherapy: Theories and Interventions* will provide the foundation that students need to make decisions about follow-up study of specific theories as well as development of their own personal theory of counseling and psychotherapy.

ACKNOWLEDGMENTS

We would like to thank the other 23 authors who contributed their time and expertise to the development of this textbook for professionals interested in individual counseling and psychotherapy. We also thank our families, who supported and encouraged our writing and editing efforts, as well as the counselor education faculties at Portland State University and Arizona State University. Thanks go out to our editors and the other staff members at Prentice Hall for their collaborative and competent approach to the editing and production of this textbook. We would like to give special recognition to Nancy Crain, secretary to the assistant dean of the School of Education at Portland State University, who worked so diligently to make this publication possible. Thanks also to Karen Hafner, graduate assistant and student in the community counseling specialization of the counselor education program at Portland State University, for her assistance in meeting publication deadlines. Without the dedicated efforts of this group of colleagues, we know this book could not have been published.

In addition, we would like to thank the following colleagues for their comments and suggestions about the book: Virginia Allen, Idaho State University; Martin Gerstein, Virginia Tech; Samuel T. Gladding, Wake Forest University; Larry Golden, University of Texas at San Antonio; Richard J. Hazler, Ohio University; Don C. Locke, North Carolina State University; Don W. Locke, Northeast Louisiana University; Donald L. Mattson, University of South Dakota; Eugene R. Moan, Northern Arizona University; and Nancy L. Murdock, University of Missouri at Kansas City.

Meet the Authors

MEET THE EDITORS

David Capuzzi, Ph.D., N.C.C., L.P.C., is past president of the American Counseling Association (formerly the American Association for Counseling and Development) and is assistant dean for academic development and research and professor of counselor education for the School of Education at Portland State University in Portland, Oregon.

From 1980 to 1984, Dr. Capuzzi was editor of *The School Counselor*. He has authored a number of textbook chapters and monographs on the topic of preventing adolescent suicide and is coeditor and author, with Dr. Larry Golden, of *Helping Families Help Children: Family Interventions with School Related Problems* (1986) and *Preventing Adolescent Suicide* (1988). In 1989 he coauthored and edited *Youth at Risk: A Resource for Counselors, Teachers and Parents*; in 1991, *Introduction to Counseling: Perspectives for the 1990s;* and in 1992, *Introduction to Group Counseling* with Douglas R. Gross. He has authored or coauthored articles in a number of ACA and related journals.

A frequent speaker and keynoter at professional conferences and institutes, Dr. Capuzzi has also consulted with a variety of school districts and community agencies interested in initiating counseling and intervention strategies for adolescents at risk for suicide. He has facilitated the development of suicide prevention, crisis management, and postvention programs in communities in 24 states.

Douglas R. Gross, Ph.D., N.C.C., C.P.C., has been a faculty member in the counseling program at Arizona State University in Tempe for 26 years. His professional work history includes public school teaching, counseling, and administration. He has been president of the Arizona Counselors Association, president of the Western Association for Counselor Education and Supervision, chairperson of the Western Regional Branch Assembly of the American Counseling Association (formerly the American Association for Counseling and Development), president of the Association for Humanistic Education and Development, and treasurer and parliamentarian of ACA.

Dr. Gross has contributed chapters to four texts: *Youth at Risk: A Resource for Counselors, Teachers and Parents* (1989), *Foundations of Mental Health Counseling* (1986), *Counseling: Theory, Process and Practice* (1977), and *The Counselor's Handbook* (1974). His research has appeared in *The Journal of Counseling Psychology*; *The Journal of Counseling and Development*; *The Association for Counselor Education and Supervision Journal*; *The Journal of Educational Research, Counseling and Human Development*; *The Arizona Counselors Journal*; *The Texas Counseling Journal*; and *The AMHCA Journal*.

Dr. Gross also serves as a consultant to several alcohol and drug programs in the state of Arizona.

MEET THE CONTRIBUTORS

Ellen S. Amatea, Ph.D., is licensed in Florida as a marriage and family therapist and as a psychologist. She earned her doctorate from Florida State University and is currently a professor of counselor education at the University of Florida, teaching in the marriage and family therapy and mental health counseling programs. Dr. Amatea is a clinical member and approved supervisor of the American Association for Marriage and Family Therapy. She was editor of the Florida Family Therapy News from 1985 to 1987 and has presented workshops and published numerous articles and books on the application of family systems concepts and techniques in the school setting.

G. Miguel Arciniega, Ph.D., is an associate professor in the Division of Psychology in Education at Arizona State University in Tempe. Dr. Arciniega has been director of minority counseling projects and institutes, teacher corps, and centers for bilingual and bicultural education. He has consulted extensively with federal, state, and local agencies about counseling minorities and has also consulted with Aid for International Development (AID) in Central and South America. He has published several articles concerning multicultural counseling.

Loretta J. Bradley, Ph.D., is a professor of counselor education in the Department of Educational Psychology at Texas Tech University. She teaches counseling practicum, counseling theories, dysfunctional behavior, and careers courses. Dr. Bradley received her Ph.D. from Purdue University. She has written more than 30 articles published in professional journals and has authored or coauthored four books. Dr. Bradley was the corecipient of the 1987 ACA Research Award, the 1985 ACES Research Award, and the 1990 ACES Best Publication Award. In addition to serving as chairperson of the ACA Media Committee, she has served on the editorial boards of *The American Counselor*, *The Journal of Counseling and Development*, *Counselor Education and Supervision*, and *The Journal of Humanistic Education and Development*. She is currently president-elect of the Association for Counselor Education and Supervision (ACES).

Leonard R. Corte, Ph.D., is a psychoanalyst in private practice. He is a member of the Los Angeles Institute and Society for Psychoanalytic Studies and is an associate member of the International Psychoanalytic Association. In addition, Dr. Corte is the president of the Southwest Center for Psychoanalytic Studies and a member of the teaching faculty at the center. He is also an adjunct faculty member at the Arizona State University School of Social Work.

Mary Lou Frank, Ph.D., has been trained in family therapy and psychology. At Arizona State University in Tempe, she coordinated the eating disorders program, co-coordinated practicum training, and concurrently taught in the counseling department. She contributed a chapter to *Introduction to Group Counseling* and has published in the *Journal of Counseling and Development* and *Psychological Reports*. Dr. Frank received a Distinguished Service Provider Award in counseling for 1989–1990 and was listed in *Who's Who in America* in 1993 and *International Who's Who of American Women* in 1991. She has been a consultant and speaker at several eating disorders programs, private hospitals, and universities. Currently, she is the assistant academic dean and an associate professor of psychology at Clinch Valley College of the University of Virginia.

Oscar F. Gonçalves, Ed.D., is currently a professor and director of training in the Department of Psychology, University of Minho, Portugal. He has held visiting positions at the University of Massachusetts and at the University of California in Santa Barbara. Dr. Gonçalves holds a doctorate in counseling psychology from the University of Massachusetts in Amherst. He has written six books and numerous articles and has been published internationally, mainly in the domain of cognitive approaches to counseling and psychotherapy. During the last few years he has been developing an innovative therapeutic model known as cognitive narrative psychotherapy.

L. J. Gould, M.A., is a doctoral candidate in counseling in the Department of Educational Psychology at Texas Tech University. Ms. Gould's previous publications include coauthoring three book chapters and two journal publications. She has served as the ACES program committee student chairperson. Her major research interests include gender bias and stereotyping, human development, and multicultural counseling.

Richard J. Hazler, Ph.D., is a faculty member in the counselor education program at Ohio University. Previously he worked professionally as an elementary school teacher, school counselor, prison counselor, counselor in the military, and counselor in private practice. Dr. Hazler is editor of *The Journal of Humanistic Education and Development* and the *Student Focus* column for the American Counseling Association's (formerly the American Association for Counseling and Development's) *Guidepost*, in addition to other professional writing roles. Dr. Hazler earned his doctorate at the University of Idaho. He was a leader in the development of numerous youth programs, including gifted and remedial education programs and the Youth Conservation Corps. He lives in Athens, Ohio, with his wife, Kitty, and two daughters, Shannon and Erin.

Allen E. Ivey, Ed.D., is currently a professor in the counseling psychology program at the University of Massachusetts, Amherst. He received his doctorate in counseling from Harvard University. Dr. Ivey served as a Fulbright scholar at the University of Copenhagen and as a Fulbright lecturer at Flinders University. His research and writing have focused on preventive and developmental concepts for well over 20 years. Dr. Ivey is also well known as the originator of the microskills framework. In the 1980s, he turned his attention to constructing the developmental counseling and therapy model. He is now directing most of his energies toward examining the model's special applications in multicultural thought and in the construction of systemic treatment plans for specific client diagnoses.

Cynthia R. Kalodner, Ph.D., is associate professor of counseling psychology in the Department of Counseling, Rehabilitative Counseling, and Counseling Psychology at West Virginia University. She received her doctorate in counseling psychology from Pennsylvania State University in 1988. Previously, she was an assistant professor in the counseling psychology program at the University of Akron. Dr. Kalodner spent a year in a postdoctoral fellowship studying public health at Johns Hopkins University. She currently studies the interface between psychology and health. Dr. Kalodner's present research focuses primarily on cognitive-behavioral approaches to understand and treat women with eating disorders.

Henry A. Lewis is a doctoral candidate in counselor education at the University of North Carolina at Greensboro. He holds a master's degree in public administration from North Carolina State University. In 1993 Mr. Lewis received the outstanding doctoral student award from Chi Sigma Iota, the academic and professional honor society for counseling. He is a member of the American Counseling Association, the American College Personnel Association, the American College Counseling Association, and the Society for Human Resource Management.

Mr. Lewis has an appointment as lecturer at the Bryan School of Business and Economics at the University of North Carolina at Greensboro. He also serves as a feedback consultant in leadership development with the Center for Creative Leadership. Mr. Lewis has 14 years' experience in the public and private sector as a human resource professional and has expertise in organization development, assessment center theory, and management training. He has developed training programs using transactional analysis theory, which have been widely used in government and corporate settings.

Hanoch Livneh, Ph.D., is associate professor for counselor education and coordinator of the rehabilitation counseling specialization in the counselor education program at Portland State University in Portland, Oregon. He received his B.A. in psychology from Hebrew University in Jerusalem (1971) and his M.A. (1973) and Ph.D. (1976) degrees in rehabilitation counseling psychology from the University of Wisconsin at Madison. Before joining the faculty at Portland State University in 1988, Dr. Livneh served as the director of the rehabilitation counseling program and as professor of counseling and educational psychology at Rhode Island College.

Mary Finn Maples, Ph.D., a former president of the American Counseling Association (formerly the American Personnel and Guidance Association), is a professor of counseling and educational psychology at the University of Nevada, Reno. Her specialties are organizational development, strategic planning, team building, and spirituality in adult development. She is also a consultant to the National College of Juvenile and Family Law and to various businesses and organizations throughout the country.

Betty J. Newlon, Ed.D., is an associate professor and head of the counseling and guidance program at the University of Arizona in Tucson. Dr. Newlon is responsible for training and supervising graduate students in the mental health and community counseling program at the university.

Gerald Parr, Ph.D., is an associate professor of counselor education at Texas Tech University. He received his Ph.D. from the University of Colorado in 1974. His experience includes secondary school teaching and counseling. Dr. Parr currently teaches group counseling, child counseling, and theories of counseling; and he has received a President's Excellence in Teaching Award during his tenure at Texas Tech University. He was corecipient of the 1988 Texas Association of Counseling and Development's Professional Writing Award.

John M. Poidevant, Ph.D., is a former assistant professor and coordinator of school counseling at the University of North Carolina at Greensboro, and he is currently a school psychologist with Rockdale County Schools in Conyers, Georgia. He completed his graduate study at the University of Florida where he earned a master's and specialist degree in school psychology and a doctorate in counselor education. He is a licensed professional counselor, a national certified counselor, a nationally certified school psychologist, and a certified school psychologist in the state of Georgia. An active writer, he has published numerous articles in journals such as *Elementary School Guidance and Counseling, Counselor Education and Supervision, The Journal for Specialists in Group Work,* and *The School Counselor*. He is currently affiliated with Children's Evaluation and Counseling Associates, a private-practice group that specializes in mental health services for children in the Atlanta area.

Sandra A. Rigazio-DiGilio, Ph.D., is currently an assistant professor of human development and family relations in the School of Family Studies' marriage and family therapy program at the University of Connecticut, Storrs. In addition, she is a clinical assistant professor at the University of Connecticut School of Medicine in the Department of Psychiatry, a consultant to the Bristol Hospital Family Therapy Training Institute, and a private practitioner. Dr. Rigazio-DiGilio received her doctorate in counseling psychology at the University of Massachusetts at Amherst. She is a licensed psychologist and a certified and licensed marital and family therapist. Her scholarly activities focus on clinically and empirically extending the developmental counseling and therapy model to family developmental theory and therapy, to specific clinical populations, and to marriage and family therapy training and supervision.

Susan E. Schwartz, Ph.D., is a Jungian analyst trained at the C. G. Jung Institute in Zurich, Switzerland; she also has a doctorate in clinical psychology. She is a training analyst and teacher at the C. G. Jung Institute of Santa Fe, New Mexico and a member of the International Association of Jungian Analysts. Dr. Schwartz has given lectures and workshops on various aspects of Jungian analytical psychology in the United States, Europe, and Canada and has a private analytical practice in Scottsdale, Arizona, and Las Vegas, Nevada.

Peter A. D. Sherrard, Ed.D., is an associate professor of counselor education at the University of Florida, where he teaches in the marriage and family therapy and mental health counseling programs. He is licensed as a marriage and family therapist and mental health counselor in Florida. Dr. Sherrard holds the diplomate in counseling psychology from the American Board of Professional Psychology and the diplomate in marriage and family therapy from the American Board of Family Psychology. He is a clinical member and approved supervisor of the American Association for Marriage and Family Therapy.

Dr. Sherrard graduated from the University of Massachusetts in Amherst. Before accepting his current position, he was director of the Kansas State University counseling center, visiting assistant professor of psychology at the University of Missouri in Columbia, and training director of the Southern Illinois University counseling center's APA-approved doctoral internship program. Dr. Sherrard completed postgraduate training in marriage and family therapy at the Menninger Foundation in Topeka, Kansas.

Dr. Sherrard was associate editor for practice of *The Journal of Mental Health Counseling* (1987–1993), president of the North Central Florida Association for Marriage and Family Therapy (1991), and corecipient of the 1992 AMHCA Research Award.

Ardis Sherwood-Hawes, M.S., is an academic counselor and a mental health and group therapist at Clark College in Vancouver, Washington. She also has a private practice in Beaverton, Oregon. Her training includes a B.S. in psychology and an M.S. in counselor education at Portland State University in Portland, Oregon. Ms. Sherwood-Hawes has published articles covering a wide range of topics, including teenage pregnancy, counseling and therapy for children and adolescents, and issues related to suicide. She works primarily with women who experience economic, academic, or societal barriers. Her work includes group counseling for women who are survivors of sexual abuse; parenting skill education; self-esteem, self-empowerment, and assertiveness training; and issues that concern gay and lesbian populations, women, and single teenage parents.

Thomas J. Sweeney, Ph.D., L.P.C.C., has been an adherent of the work of Alfred Adler and Rudolph Dreikurs for more than 20 years. He has written *Adlerian Counseling*, which is in its third edition, and is the author of the award-winning telecourse *Coping with Kids*, which reached thousands of laypeople and professionals, both nationally and internationally, on public broadcast and film. He has researched and published articles about the application of Adlerian psychology to various populations. Professor emeritus of counselor education at Ohio University, Dr. Sweeney is also an adjunct professor and special assistant to the dean of the School of Education at University of North Carolina at Greensboro. He is past president of the American Counseling Association and the Association for Counselor Education and Supervision, and he was founding president and is now executive director of Chi Sigma Iota Counseling Academic and Professional Honor Society International. In addition to holding a variety of leadership positions, Dr. Sweeney has received numerous state, regional, and national awards. He has presented keynote addresses and workshops nationally and internationally.

Peggy E. Wright received her B.S. in home economics education from Oregon State University in Corvallis and is a certified teacher in the state of Oregon. Ms. Wright holds a graduate assistantship and is a master's candidate in the rehabilitation specialization in the counselor education program at the School of Education, Portland State University, Portland, Oregon.

Robert E. Wubbolding, Ed.D., received his bachelor of arts degree from the Athenaeum of Ohio and his doctorate in counseling from the University of Cincinnati. As director of training for the Institute for Control Theory, Reality Therapy, and Quality Management, he monitors the 18-month reality therapy training program. He is also assistant director and full professor in the counselor education department at Xavier University as well as the director of the Center for Reality Therapy in Cincinnati. Author of seven books on reality therapy, Dr. Wubbolding has taught reality therapy in North America, Europe, and the Pacific Rim. He currently studies cross-cultural applications of reality therapy.

Brief Contents

Contents

CHAPTER EIGHT
Existential Theory

Mary Lou Frank

CHAPTER NINE
Person-centered Theory

Richard J. Hazler

CHAPTER TEN
Gestalt Theory   267

Mary Finn Maples

CHAPTER FIFTEEN
Ecosystems Theory   425

Peter A. D. Sherrard and Ellen S. Amatea

CHAPTER SIXTEEN
Developmental Counseling and Therapy: Integrating Individual
and Family Theory   471

Sandra A. Rigazio-DiGilio, Oscar F. Gonçalves, and Allen E. Ivey

CHAPTER NINETEEN
Counseling and Psychotherapy: An Integrative Perspective   **589**

Loretta J. Bradley, Gerald Parr, and L. J. Gould

Counseling and Psychotherapy

Theories and Interventions

Foundations for Individual Counseling and Psychotherapy

■ ■ ■ CHAPTERS

Counseling and psychotherapy encompass a number of relationship modalities in which the counselor or therapist needs to be proficient. Achieving a personal and professional identity is also interrelated and fundamental to being able to facilitate the process of counseling and psychotherapy. In addition to being able to create some essential core conditions that are prerequisite to change on the part of the client, the counselor or therapist, before choosing a particular frame of reference from which to operate, must possess knowledge about human development across the life span as well as ethical and legal issues. This section of the text provides foundational information pertinent to individual work with clients.

The helping relationship is the foundation on which the process of counseling and psychotherapy is based. It is not possible to use the concepts and associated interventions of a specific theory unless such applications are made in the context of a relationship that promotes trust, insight, and behavior change. Chapter 1, "Helping Relationships in Counseling and Psychotherapy," is designed to aid students in both the development and delivery of the helping relationship. To achieve this purpose, the helping relationship is presented in terms of definitions and descriptions, stages, core dimensions and personal characteristics, and helping strategies. A brief case study is also presented.

Chapter 2, "Achieving a Personal and Professional Identity," discusses why the personal and professional identity of the helping professional must be addressed before and during the process of studying and applying individual approaches to counseling and psychotherapy. The chapter addresses the importance of health and wellness for the helping professional, recognition of values and cultural bias in theory and practice, awareness of the daily world of the practitioner, and achieving perspective and balance between the individual as a person and the individual as a professional. Brief comments about the importance of developing a personal theory are also provided.

Chapter 3, "Developmental Stages and Individual Counseling and Psychotherapy," is based on the belief that the content of subsequent chapters in this book, which focus on specific theories and associated interventions for individual work with clients, can best be understood and applied when supplemented by awareness of human development across the life span. Although each client is unique, it is also true that each client can be expected to bear similarities to other clients who are in the same stage of development. Infancy and early childhood, later childhood, adolescence, the early adult years, the midlife years, and the final decades comprise the age-and-stage approach of this chapter. Developmental patterns and concerns and typical presenting problems are discussed in subsections of the chapter.

For both the novice and the experienced practitioner, determining what is or is not ethical behavior is often a perplexing dilemma. While the numerous specialties that comprise the helping professions have provided practitioners with a plethora of guidelines and codes of ethical behavior, confusion still exists. The purpose of chapter 4, "Ethical and Legal Issues in Counseling and Psychotherapy," is to discuss the definition and rationale for ethical codes, dimensions of ethical behavior, and legal issues. No counselor or therapist should initiate individual work with a client, from any theoretical frame of reference, prior to becoming familiar with the information in this chapter.

As these chapters indicate, practitioners must achieve high levels of competence, effectiveness, and expertise to create a helping relationship beneficial to clients. They must also develop the ability to know themselves from both personal and professional perspectives, apply their knowledge of human growth and development, and understand the ethical and legal aspects of working with clients prior to adopting, modifying, or integrating the theory and intervention options for individual counseling and psychotherapy. We have made every attempt to introduce the readers to these topics in the chapters included in this section of the text. Readers are encouraged to do additional reading and follow-up course work and to commit to personal counseling or therapy to achieve the purposes we have outlined in these chapters.

CHAPTER ONE

Helping Relationships in Counseling and Psychotherapy

Douglas R. Gross
Arizona State University

David Capuzzi
Portland State University

The following scenario depicts a student, much like you, who has taken the preparatory classes leading up to enrollment in practicum. Jane has completed course work in testing, analysis, careers, groups, human development, personality theory, ethics, cultural diversity, and counseling strategies. In her work with clients in practicum, she will be asked to integrate the knowledge gained from this course work with both her personal dynamics and life experiences. Such integration is the foundation on which the process of counseling and psychotherapy rests—a foundation defined for our purposes as the *helping relationship*. The information contained in the scenario serves as an introduction to our discussion of this helping relationship.

■ ■ ■

Jane maneuvered her car through the heavy traffic at the entrance to the university parking area. She was annoyed that it was taking her so long to park this morning. She had left home early so that she would have plenty of class time to prepare to meet her first client in practicum. Already 10 minutes behind her schedule and concerned that she would not have time to review all the material before beginning her first client meeting, she parked her car and caught the tram into the main part of the campus. She was oblivious to the various classroom buildings she passed and to the other people on the tram. Her thoughts centered on the fact that she would see her first client this morning. Would she be able to work effectively with this person?

Jane's supervisor had reviewed basic helping conditions and strategies such as empathy, respect, genuineness, rapport building, active listening skills, session planning, and a myriad of other operational procedures during the early meetings of her practicum group. He then asked members of the practicum group to explain their theoretical approach to working with clients. During her time, Jane discussed the appeal of the Gestalt approach and also her fear that she would not be able to translate this into action once she sat down face to face with another person. The supervisor assured her that he would work with her in helping translate knowledge into action steps. The supervisor had cautioned all members of the practicum group to remain open to other theoretical approaches. He said that the purpose of practicum was to experiment with various approaches and to see what worked best for both the student and the client. Jane thought the supervisor's cautions made sense. She had practiced other approaches in role-playing sessions, but none felt as comfortable to her as the Gestalt approach. She remembered that she had received a good deal of positive feedback the day she had presented this particular role play. Today, however, was not a role play. She would meet a client, not a peer; and she had many reservations, not about the theory, but about her ability to apply it. She was frightened because she knew that people would be watching from the adjoining room and that she would be evaluated directly after the session. Jane was a good student, and she wanted to be a good practitioner. She was not sure that the two necessarily went together. This was the first time she had been called upon to demonstrate her knowledge and skill in what she saw as a "real" setting.

When the tram reached the stop closest to her building, Jane raced to the fourth-floor practicum training center. Carolyn, the center receptionist, told her that her client had arrived early and was completing the necessary paperwork. Jane was instructed to get the room ready and then return to the waiting area to meet her client. She felt her heart beat a little faster as she returned to the waiting room. She had checked in with her supervisor, arranged the chairs in the room where she would meet the client, put a tape in the recorder, and made sure that nothing was blocking the two-way-vision mirror. She was ready for the most exciting yet frightening experience of her educational program.

This scenario plays itself out each semester when students are confronted with their first client contacts in either practicum or internship. All of the classes you have taken up to this point have been preparing you for this encounter. It is often the first time you are called upon to integrate the learned knowledge and skills into a counseling or therapeutic relationship—a helping relationship. The fact that you must demonstrate this untried relationship for both peers and supervisors in the fishbowl environment called practicum/internship adds both excitement and anxiety. The excitement stems from being able to put your knowledge and skills to a practical test. The anxiety stems from a lack of experience in trying this relationship outside the safety of the role-play situations in structured classes. You should expect such personal reactions, and perhaps they are necessary as you move from a position of inexperience to one of experience.

This chapter will aid you in understanding the various factors that impact the helping relationship: definitions and descriptions, stages, core dimensions, strategies, and conclusions. We hope the information presented in this chapter will help you realize that your excitement and anxiety can be natural and productive. We also hope you will be able to incorporate this information into effective models of the helping relationship.

HELPING RELATIONSHIPS: DEFINITIONS AND DESCRIPTIONS

The helping relationship appears to be the cornerstone on which all effective helping rests (Delaney & Eisenberg, 1972; Dixon & Glover, 1984; Purkey & Schmidt, 1987; Terry, Burden, & Pedersen, 1991). Words such as *integral, necessary* and *mandatory* are used to describe this relationship and its importance in the ultimate effectiveness of the helping process. Even though different theoretical systems use different words to describe the relationship (see chapters 5 through 17), each addresses the significance of the helping relationship in facilitating client change. Kottler and Brown (1992), in their book *Introduction to Therapeutic Counseling*, made the following comments regarding the significance of this relationship:

> Regardless of the setting in which you practice counseling, whether in a school, agency, hospital, or private practice, the relationships you develop with your clients are crucial to any progress you might make together. For without a high degree of intimacy and trust between two people, very little can be accomplished. (p. 64)

In further support of the significance of the helping relationship, Terry et al. (1991) said:

> Most people find themselves engaged in some type of helping relationship nearly every day. Some helping occurs informally while other helping happens in a more formal way. Friends and family usually help one another in a reciprocal, informal way, while helping professionals such as counselors, psychologists, or social workers help their clients within a formal, unidirectional relationship. (p. 44)

The ideas expressed in these two statements describe the essential value of the helping relationship in the process of counseling and psychotherapy and the significant role that the counselor or therapist plays in developing this relationship. Through this relationship, client change occurs. Although the creation of the relationship is not the end goal of the process, it certainly is the means by which other goals are met. It serves as the framework within which effective helping takes place.

Although agreed-upon definitions and descriptions should be easy to find, such is not the case. Despite the importance of the helping relationship in the overall helping process, a perusal of textbooks and articles dealing with counseling and psychotherapy shows the lack of a common definition. Rogers (1961), for example, defined a helping relationship as one "in which at least one of the parties has the intent of promoting the growth, development, maturity, improved functioning and improved coping with life of the other" (p. 39). Purkey and Schmidt (1987) described the helping relationship as an "inviting relationship" and defined it as "the incorporation of compatible theories, systems, and techniques of human service into a therapeutic 'stance' for professional helping" (p. 3). A third definition of the helping relationship, provided by Hansen, Stevic, and Warner (1982), concluded that "the counseling relationship is an alliance formed to help the client move toward a goal: more appropriate behavior" (p. 200).

It is easy to see the difficulty in categorically stating an accepted definition or description of the helping relationship, regardless of which of these statements you choose to embrace. Each carries with it directions and directives aimed at a single goal, the enhancement and encouragement of client change. The following definitive characteristics of the helping relationship embrace this goal and describe our conceptualization of this relationship:

- A relationship initially structured by the counselor or therapist but open to cooperative restructuring based upon the needs of the client
- A relationship that begins with the initial meeting and continues through termination
- A relationship in which all persons involved perceive the existence of trust, caring, concern, and commitment and act accordingly
- A relationship in which the needs of the client are given priority over the needs of the counselor or therapist
- A relationship that provides for the personal growth of all persons involved
- A relationship that provides the safety needed for self-exploration of all persons involved
- A relationship that promotes the potential of all persons involved

The major responsibility for creating this relationship rests initially with the counselor or therapist, with increasing demands for client involvement and commitment. It is a shared process, and only through such shared efforts will the relationship develop and flourish. This development evolves in stages that take the relationship from initiation to closure. The stages in this evolving process are the subject of the following section.

HELPING RELATIONSHIPS: STAGES

The helping relationship is a constant throughout the counseling and psychotherapeutic process. The definitive characteristics we have already presented indicate that the relationship must be present from the initial meeting between the client and counselor or therapist through closure.

Viewing the helping relationship as a constant throughout the helping process leads to visualizing this process from a developmental perspective. This development can best be viewed in terms of a narrow path whose borders are limited by the client's fear, anxiety, and resistance. Such client reactions should not be seen as lack of commitment to change; they need to be understood in terms of the unknown nature of this developing alliance and the fact that this may be the first time the client has experienced this type of interaction. These reactions are often shared by the counselor or therapist, depending on the experience level of the person involved. The path broadens through the development of trust, safety, and understanding as the relationship develops. The once narrow path becomes a boulevard along which two persons move courageously toward their final destination—change.

The movement along this broadening path is described by various authors in terms of stages or phases. Osipow, Walsh, and Tosi (1980), in discussing the stages of the helping relationship, stated:

> Persons who experience the process of personal counseling seem to progress through several stages. First, there is an increased awareness of self and others. Second, there is an expanded exploration of self and environment (positive and negative behavioral tendencies). Third, there is increased commitment to self-enhancing behavior and its implementation. Fourth, there is an internalization of new and more productive thoughts and actions. Fifth, there is a stabilization of new behavior. (p. 73)

Brammer (1985) divided this developmental process into two phases, each with four distinctive stages. Phase 1 is called "Building Relationships" and includes the following stages: preparing the client and opening the relationship, clarifying the problem or concern of the client, structuring the process, and building a relationship. Phase 2 is called "Facilitating Positive Action," and it involves the stages of exploration, consolidation, planning, and termination.

Purkey and Schmidt (1987) set forth three stages in relationship building, each containing four steps. Stage 1 is called "The Preparation Stage," and it includes these steps: having the desire, expecting good things, preparing the setting, and reading the situation. Stage 2 is known as "The Initiating Responding Stage," which includes choosing caringly, acting appropriately, honoring the client, and ensuring reception. The third stage is called "Follow-up" and includes interpreting responses, negotiating positions, evaluating the process, and developing trust.

Authors such as Gilliland, James, Roberts, and Bowman (1984), Brown and Srebalus (1988), Baruth and Robinson (1987), and Ivey and Simek-Downing (1980) provide other models of the developmental nature of the stages of the relationship. Although the terms used to describe these stages may differ, there seems to be a consistency shared by all these models: the reader moves from initiation of the relationship through a clinically based working stage to a termination stage.

The following developmental stages show our conceptualization of this relationship-building process and are based on the consistency found in our research and our clinical experience:

- *Stage 1: Relationship development.*   This stage includes the initial meeting of client and counselor or therapist, rapport building, information gathering, and goal determination.

- *Stage 2: Extended exploration.*   This stage builds on the foundation established in stage 1. Through selected techniques, theoretical approaches, and strategies, it explores in depth the emotional and cognitive dynamics of the person of the client, problem parameters, previously tried solutions, decision-making capabilities, and a reevaluation of the goals determined in stage 1.

- *Stage 3: Problem resolution.*   This stage, which depends on the information gained during the previous two stages, is characterized by increased activity for all parties involved. The counselor or therapist's activities include facilitating, demonstrating, instructing, and providing a safe environment for the development of change. The client's activities focus on reevaluating emotional and cognitive dynamics, trying out new behaviors both inside and outside the sessions, and discarding those behaviors that do not meet goals.

- *Stage 4: Termination and follow-up.*   This stage is the closing stage of the helping relationship and is cooperatively determined by all persons involved. Methods and procedures for follow-up are determined prior to the last meeting.

It is important to keep in mind that people do not automatically move through these identified stages in a lockstep manner. The relationship may end at any one of these stages, based upon decisions made by either the client, the counselor or therapist, or both. Nor is it possible to identify the amount of time devoted to any of these stages. With certain clients, much more time needs to be devoted to specific stages. Brown and Srebalus (1988), in addressing the tentative nature of these relationship stages, have the following caution for their readers:

> Before we describe a common sequence of events in counseling, it is important to note that many clients, for one reason or another, will not complete all the stages of counseling. The process will be abandoned prematurely, not

because something went wrong, but because of factors external to the counselor-client relationship. For example, the school year may end for a student client, or a client or counselor may move away to accept a new job. When counseling is in process and must abruptly end, the participants will feel the incompleteness and loss. (p. 69)

Viewing the helping relationship as an ongoing process that is composed of developmental stages provides counselors or therapists with a structural framework within which they can function effectively. Inside this framework fit the core conditions and strategies that serve the goals of movement through the relationship process and the enhancement and encouragement of client change. These core conditions and strategies are discussed in the following two sections.

HELPING RELATIONSHIPS: CORE CONDITIONS

The concept of core or basic conditions related to the helping relationship has its basis in the early work of Rogers (1957) and the continued work of such authors as Carkhuff and Barenson (1967), Truax and Carkhuff (1967), Patterson (1974), Egan (1982), Combs (1986), and Ivey (1988). The concept incorporates a set of conditions, which, when present, enhance the effectiveness of the helping relationship. These conditions vary in terminology from author to author but generally refer to the following: empathic understanding, respect or positive regard, genuineness or congruence, concreteness, warmth, and immediacy. We also add cultural awareness to this list. Our rationale for this inclusion stems from our belief that counselors or therapists must be culturally aware, culturally sensitive, and appreciative of cultural diversity in order to provide the other six core conditions. Support for this belief is found in Newlon and Arciniega (1992), Sue and Sue (1990), and Wehrly (1991).

It should be obvious from the list that the concept of core or basic conditions relates directly to various personal characteristics or behaviors that the counselor or therapist brings to and incorporates into the helping relationship. It is difficult to pinpoint with any exactness how such characteristics or behaviors develop. Are they the result of life experiences, classroom instruction, or a combination of both? Our experience in education favors the last explanation: a combination of both life experiences and classroom instruction. Core conditions or behaviors must already be present to some degree in our students for our instruction to enhance or expand them.

The remainder of this section deals with core conditions and relates them directly to personal characteristics or behaviors of counselors or therapists, which should enhance their ability to effectively use these conditions in the process of helping. Although definitions, emphases, and applications of these conditions differ across theoretical systems, there appears to be agreement about their effectiveness in facilitating change in the overall helping relationship (Baruth & Robinson, 1987; Gazda, Asbury, Blazer, Childers, & Walters, 1977; Ivey & Simek-Downing, 1980; Kagan, 1971; Rogers, 1957).

Empathic Understanding

Empathic understanding is the ability to feel *with* clients as opposed to feeling *for* clients. It is the ability to understand feelings, thoughts, ideas, and experiences by viewing them from a client's frame of reference. The counselor or therapist must be able to enter the client's world, understand the myriad aspects that make up this world, and communicate this understanding so that the client perceives that she has been heard accurately.

Egan (1982), in discussing empathy, discussed both primary and advanced levels of empathic understanding. At the primary level, it is the ability to understand, identify, and communicate feelings and meanings that are at the surface level of clients' disclosures. At the advanced level, it is the ability to understand, identify, and communicate feelings and meanings that are buried, hidden, or beyond the immediate reach of clients. Such feelings and meanings are more often covert, rather than overt, client expressions.

Personal characteristics or behaviors that enhance counselors' or therapists' abilities to provide empathic understanding include, but are not limited to, the following:

- The knowledge and awareness of their own values, attitudes, and beliefs and the emotional and behavioral impact they have on their life
- The knowledge and awareness of their own feelings and emotional response patterns and how they manifest themselves in interactive patterns
- The knowledge and awareness of their own life experiences and their personal reactions to those experiences
- The capacity and willingness to communicate these personal reactions to clients

Respect and Positive Regard

Respect and positive regard are defined as the belief in the innate worth and potential of clients and the ability to communicate this belief in the helping relationship. This belief, once communicated, provides clients with positive reinforcement relative to their innate ability to take responsibility for their own growth, change, goal determination, decision making, and eventual problem solution. It is an empowering process that delivers a message to clients that they are able to take control of their lives and, with facilitative assistance from the counselor or therapist, foster change. Communicating and demonstrating this respect for clients takes many forms. According to Baruth and Robinson (1987), it "is often communicated by what the counselor does not do or say. In other words, by not offering to intervene for someone, one is communicating a belief in the individual's ability to 'do' for himself or herself" (p. 85).

Personal characteristics or behaviors that enhance counselors' or therapists' abilities to provide respect and positive regard include, but are not limited to, the following:

- The capacity to respect themselves
- The capacity to view themselves as having worth and potential
- The capacity to model and communicate this positive self-image to clients
- The capacity to recognize their own control needs and the ability to use this recognition in a manner that allows clients to direct their own lives

Genuineness and Congruence

Genuineness and congruence describe the ability to be authentic in the helping relationship. The ability to be real as opposed to artificial, to behave as one feels as opposed to playing the role of the helper, and to be congruent in terms of actions and words are further descriptors of this core condition. Boy and Pine (1982), in discussing the importance of genuineness on the part of the counselors or therapists, stated:

> The counselor's genuineness is imperative if the client is to achieve genuineness. If the counselor is truly genuine, he or she engages in counseling attitudes and behaviors that influence clients to be genuine. The authentic counselor feels compelled to be involved in facilitative behaviors that have meaning and relevance for clients rather than to adopt superficial and mechanical behaviors that have little or no value. (p. 8)

Inherent in the preceding statement is the idea of the ability to communicate and demonstrate this genuineness, not only for relationship enhancement but also to model this core condition so that clients can develop greater authenticity in their interactions with others.

Personal characteristics or behaviors that enhance counselors' or therapists' abilities to provide genuineness and congruence include, but are not limited to, the following:

- The capacity for self-awareness and the ability to demonstrate this capacity through words and actions
- The understanding of their own motivational patterns and the ability to use them productively in the helping relationship
- The ability to present their thoughts, feelings, and actions in a consistent, unified, and honest manner
- The capacity for self-confidence and their own ability to communicate this capacity in a facilitative way in the helping relationship

Concreteness

Concreteness is the ability not only to see the incomplete picture that clients paint with their words, but also to communicate to clients the figures, images, and structures that will complete the picture. In the process of exploring problems or issues, clients often present a somewhat distorted view of the actual situation. Concreteness enables counselors or therapists to help clients identify the distortions in the situation and fit them together in such a way that clients are able to view the situation in a more realistic fashion. This concreteness helps clients clarify vague issues, focus on specific topics, reduce degrees of ambiguity, and channel their energies into more productive avenues of problem solution.

Personal characteristics or behaviors that enhance counselors' or therapists' abilities to provide degrees of concreteness include, but are not limited to, the following:

- The capacity for abstract thinking and the ability to "read between the lines"
- The willingness to risk being incorrect as they attempt to fill in the empty spaces
- The belief in their own competence in analyzing and sorting through the truths and partial truths in clients' statements
- The ability to be objective as they work with clients in arriving at the reality of clients' situations

Warmth

Warmth is the ability to communicate and demonstrate genuine caring and concern for clients. Using this ability, counselors or therapists convey their acceptance of clients, the desire for the well-being of clients, and their sincere interest in finding workable solutions to the problems that clients present. The demeanor of counselors or therapists is often the main avenue for communicating and demonstrating warmth, for it is often through nonverbal behaviors—a smile, a touch, a tone of voice, a facial expression—that genuine caring and concern are communicated. A counselor's or therapist's capacity for transmitting concern and caring to clients, either verbally or nonverbally, enables clients to experience, often for the first time, a truly accepting relationship.

Personal characteristics or behaviors that enhance counselors' or therapists' abilities to demonstrate warmth include, but are not limited to, the following:

- The capacity for self-care and the ability to demonstrate this capacity through both actions and words
- The capacity for self-acceptance, basing this acceptance on their assets as well as their liabilities
- The desire for their own well-being and the ability to demonstrate this desire through both words and actions
- The desire to find, and successful personal experience in finding, workable solutions to their own problems and the ability to communicate this desire through words and actions

Immediacy

Immediacy is the ability to deal with the here-and-now factors that operate within the helping relationship. These factors are described as overt and covert interactions that take place between counselors or therapists and clients. A client's anger at a counselor or therapist, the counselor's or therapist's frustration with a client, and the feelings of clients and counselors or therapists for each other are all examples of factors that need to be addressed as they occur and develop. Addressing such issues in the safety of the helping relationship should help both participants gain insight into personal behavioral patterns, which may be conducive or not conducive to growth, and use this insight in relationships outside the helping relationship.

Dealing with these factors can be threatening because it is often easier to deal with relationships in the abstract and avoid personal encounters. Counselors or therapists need to be able to use this factor of immediacy to show clients the benefits that can be gained by dealing with issues as they arise. According to Egan (1982), immediacy not only clears the air, but is also a valuable learning experience.

Personal characteristics or behaviors that enhance counselors' or therapists' abilities to use immediacy effectively include, but are not limited to, the following:

- The capacity for perceptive accuracy in interpreting their own feelings for, thoughts about, and behaviors toward clients
- The capacity for perceptive accuracy in interpreting clients' feelings for, thoughts about, and behaviors toward counselors or therapists
- The capacity for and willingness to deal with their own issues related to clients on a personal as opposed to an abstract level
- The willingness to confront both self and clients with what they see happening in the helping relationship

Cultural Awareness

Cultural awareness addresses counselors' or therapists' openness and motivation to learn more about their own cultural diversity as well as the cultural diversity that clients bring to the helping relationship. Such understanding is the cornerstone on which all the core conditions rest. This understanding, based upon both education and life experiences, should enable culturally aware counselors or therapists to increase their sensitivity to the issues that confront clients. It should enable them to develop insight into the many variables that impact clients and should enable them to place clients' issues, problems, and concerns in their proper perspective. The key word in these last two statements is *should*. Experience indicates that the key factor in the development of cultural awareness is the individual's receptiveness, openness, and motivation to gaining such awareness. Without these characteristics, education and experience will have little value. The combination of these characteristics with both education and experience enhances the chances of changing the *should* to *will*.

Personal characteristics or behaviors that enhance counselors' or therapists' ability to become culturally aware include, but are not limited to, the following:

- The need and the personal motivation to want to understand their own cultural heritage as well as that of others
- The need to seek out both education and life experiences that will afford them the opportunity to gain greater cultural awareness
- The need to be open to new ideas and differing frames of reference as they relate to cultural diversity
- The need for self-assurance to admit what they do not know about the cultural diversity of clients and the willingness to learn from clients
- The need to be aware of their cultural stereotypes and biases and be open to changing them through education and experience

HELPING RELATIONSHIPS: STRATEGIES

The previous section identified the core conditions that need to be present for the effective development of the helping relationship. The difference between these core conditions and the strategies are the subject of this section.

The core conditions relate to specific dynamics present in the personality and behavioral makeup of counselors or therapists, which they are able to communicate to clients. The term *strategies* refers to skills gained through education and experience that define and direct what counselors or therapists do during the relationship to attain specific results and to move the helping relationship from problem identification to problem resolution.

Various terms have been used to address this aspect of the helping relationship. Some authors prefer the word *strategies* (Combs, Avila, & Purkey, 1978; Cormier & Cormier, 1979; Gilliland et al., 1984; Hackney & Cormier, 1988); others prefer *skills* (Hansen et al., 1982; Ivey, 1971; Terry et al., 1991); while others prefer *techniques* (Belkin, 1980; Brown & Pate, 1983; Osipow et al., 1980). The terms, however, are interchangeable.

We have decided to use the term *strategies*. The term denotes not only deliberative planning, but also action processes that make the planning operational. We feel that both factors are necessary. We have grouped the strategies, for discussion purposes, into the following categories:

- Strategies that build rapport and encourage client dialogue
- Strategies that aid in data gathering
- Strategies that add depth and enhance the relationship

Note that specific strategies, such as those stemming from various theoretical systems, are not included in this section. They will be presented in chapters 5 through 17, which deal with specific theories. It is also important for you to understand that there is much overlap between these arbitrary divisions. Strategies designed to build rapport and encourage client dialogue may also gather data and enhance relationships. With this caveat in mind, we present the following strategies.

Strategies That Build Rapport and Encourage Client Dialogue

This group of strategies includes the active listening strategies that enhance the listening capabilities of counselors or therapists. When used effectively, these strategies should provide an environment in which clients have the opportunity to talk and share their feelings, thoughts, and ideas with the assurance that they will be heard. By using such strategies, counselors or therapists enhance their chances of providing such an environment.

This set of strategies includes attending and encouraging, restating and paraphrasing, reflecting content and reflecting feeling, clarifying and perception checking, and summarizing. The following paragraphs present explanations and examples of these strategies.

Attending and Encouraging.   These strategies use counselor or therapist posturing, visual contact, gestures, facial expressions, and words that indicate to clients not only that they are being heard but also that counselors or therapists wish them to continue sharing information.

Example:

Encouraging   Counselor/Therapist: (smiling) Please tell me what brought you in today.
                         Client: I am having a difficult time trying to put my life in order. I am very lonely and bored and I am not able to maintain a lasting relationship.

Attending/   Counselor/Therapist: (leaning forward) Please tell me more.
Encouraging   Client: Every time I think I have a chance of developing a relationship, I screw it up by saying or doing something dumb.

Encouraging   Counselor/Therapist: (nodding) This is helpful; please go on.

Restating and Paraphrasing.   These strategies enable counselors or therapists to serve as sounding boards for clients by feeding back the ideas, thoughts, and feelings that clients verbalize. Restating involves repeating the exact words used by clients. Paraphrasing repeats the ideas, thoughts, and feelings of clients, but the words are those of the counselor or therapist.

Example:

        Client: I don't know why I do these dumb things. It's almost as if I didn't want a relationship.

Restating   Counselor/Therapist: You don't know why you do dumb things. It may be that you don't want a relationship.
Client: But I do want a relationship, but each time I get close, I seem to do everything in my power to destroy it.

Paraphrasing   Counselor/Therapist: You are very sure that you want a relationship, but each time you have the opportunity, you sabotage your chances.

Reflecting Content and Reflecting Feeling.   These strategies enable the counselor or therapist to provide feedback to the client regarding both the ideas (content) and the emotions (feelings) that the client is expressing. When they reflect content, counselors or therapists share their perceptions of the ideas or thoughts that clients are expressing, either by using the clients' words or by changing the words to better reflect the counselors' or therapists' perceptions. When they reflect feelings, counselors or therapists go beyond the ideas and thoughts expressed by clients and respond to the feelings or emotions behind those words.

Example:

        Client: Sabotage is a good word. It's like I see what I want and instead of moving toward it, I take a different path that leads me nowhere.

Reflecting content   Counselor/Therapist: You have a good idea of what you want but when you see it developing, you turn and walk the other way.
Client: I am not sure *walk* is the right word. Run is more descriptive of what I do, and all the time I look back to see if anyone is following.

Reflecting feeling   Counselor/Therapist: You are afraid of getting close to someone, so you put as much distance as possible between the other person and yourself. I also hear that you are hoping that someone cares enough about you to run after you and stop you from running away.

Clarifying and Perception Checking.   These strategies enable counselors or therapists either to ask clients to define or explain words, thoughts, or feelings (clarifying) or to request confirmation or correction of perceptions they have drawn regarding these words, thoughts, or feelings (perception checking).

Example:

>Client: If what you say is true, I am a real jerk. What chance do I have to be happy if I run away every time I get close to someone else?

Clarifying

>Counselor/Therapist: You say you want to be happy. What does happy mean to you?
>
>Client: (long pause) I would be happy if I could let someone care for me, get to know me, want to spend time with me and allow me just to be me and stop pretending.

Perception checking

>Counselor/Therapist: Let me see if I understand you. Your view of happiness is having someone who cares enough about you to spend time with you and to allow you to be yourself. Am I correct?

Summarizing.   This strategy enables counselors and therapists to do several things. First, it allows them to review verbally various types of information that have been presented up to this point in the counseling or therapeutic session. Second, it allows them to highlight what they see as significant information, based on everything that has been discussed. Third, it provides clients with an opportunity to hear the various issues they have presented. Therefore, summarization provides both counselors or therapists and clients with the opportunity not only to review and determine the significance of information presented, but also to use this review to establish priorities.

Example:

>Client: Yes, I think that is what I would like to have happen. That would make me happy. I would be in a relationship, feel cared about, and yet be able to be myself without having to run or pretend.

Summarizing

>Counselor/Therapist: We have talked about many things today. I would like to review some of this and make plans for our next meeting. The parts that stick out in my mind are your loneliness, boredom, desire to have a lasting relationship, behaviors that drive you away from building such a relationship, and need for caring and the freedom to be yourself. Am I missing something?
>
>Client: Only that I want someone who wants to spend time with me. I think that is an important factor.

Summarizing   Counselor/Therapist: So now we have a more complete picture, which includes loneliness, boredom, desire for a relationship, desire for someone to spend time with, desire for someone who cares, and the need to be yourself. On the other side of the picture, we have your behaviors, which keep this from happening. Where do you think we should begin next week?

Strategies That Aid in Data Gathering

This group of strategies includes all the active listening strategies plus two strategies designed to extract specific information and gain greater depth of information in areas that are significant in the statements of clients. As with active listening strategies, counselors or therapists who use the following strategies enhance their chances of gaining significant information. This set of strategies includes questioning, probing, and leading. The following paragraphs present explanations and examples of these strategies.

Questioning.   This strategy, when done in an open rather than a closed manner, enables counselors or therapists to gain important information and allows clients to remain in control of the information presented. Counselors or therapists, using open questioning, design their questions to encourage the broadest client responses. Open questions, as opposed to closed questions, generally cannot be completely answered by either a yes or a no, nor can they be answered nonverbally by shaking the head. This type of questioning places responsibility with clients for the information shared and allows them a degree of control over what information is shared.

Example:
                     Client: I have thought a lot about what we talked about last week, and I feel I have to work on changing my behavior.

Open questioning   Counselor/Therapist: Would you tell me what you think needs to be done to change your behavior?
                     Client: (short pause) I need to stop screwing up my chances for a relationship. I need to face whatever it is that makes me run away.

Open questioning   Counselor/Therapist: Would you please talk more about the *it* that makes you run away?
                     Client: (long pause) I can't tell you what it is. All I know is that I hear this voice saying, "Run, run."

Probing and Leading.   These strategies enable counselors or therapists to gather information in a specific area related to the clients' presented concerns (probing) or to encourage clients to respond to specific topic areas (leading). Each of these strategies enables counselors or therapists to explore in greater depth areas that are seen as important to progress within the session.

Example:

Probing   Counselor/Therapist: I want you to be more specific about this voice. Whose voice is it? What does it say to you?
Client: (very long pause) I guess it's my voice. It sounds like something I would do. I'm such a jerk.

Leading   Counselor/Therapist: You told me whose voice it is, but you did not tell me what the voice says. Would you talk about this?
Client: (raising his voice) It says, "Get out or you are going to get hurt. She doesn't like you, and she will use you and drop you just like the rest."

Strategies That Add Depth and Enhance the Relationship

This group of strategies is used to enhance and expand the communicative and relationship patterns that are established early in the counseling or therapeutic process. When used effectively, these strategies should open up deeper levels of communication and strengthen the relationship patterns that have already been established. Counselors or therapists using these strategies model types of behaviors that they wish their clients to emulate. Such behaviors include, but are not limited to, risk taking, sharing of self, demonstrating trust, and honest interaction. This set of strategies includes self-disclosure, confrontation, and response to nonverbal behaviors. The following paragraphs present explanations and examples of these strategies

Self-disclosure.   This strategy has implications for both counselors or therapists and clients. In self-disclosing, counselors or therapists share with clients some feelings, thoughts, and experiences that are relevant to the situation presented by clients. Counselors or therapists draw upon situations from their own life experiences and selectively share these personal reactions with clients. Clients who use counselors or therapists as models increase their ability to self-disclose. Gains are made by all persons involved, and the relationship moves to deeper levels of understanding and sharing.

Example:

Self-disclosure   Counselor/Therapist: (aware of the client's agitation) The anger I hear in your voice and words triggers anger in me as I think of lost relationships in my life.
Client: (smiling) I *am* angry. I am also glad you said that. I sometimes feel I am the only one who has ever felt this way.

Self-disclosure   Counselor/Therapist: (smiling) I have been where you are and probably will be again. The anger I feel is generally directed at me, not at the other person.

Confrontation.   This strategy enables counselors or therapists to provide clients with feedback in which discrepancies are presented in an honest and matter-of-fact manner. Counselors or therapists use this strategy to indicate their reactions to clients, the observed differences between clients' words and behaviors, and a challenge to clients to put words and ideas into action. This type of direct and honest feedback should provide clients with insight about the way they are perceived and indicate the degree of counselor or therapist caring.

Example:

Client: (smiling) I feel angry at myself a great deal. I want so much to find a person and develop a relationship that lasts.

Confrontation   Counselor/Therapist: You have said this several times in our sessions, but I am not sure I believe you based on what you do to keep it from happening. Make me believe you really want this to happen.
Client: What do you mean you don't believe me? I just told you, didn't I? What more do you want?

Confrontation   Counselor/Therapist: Yes, I heard your words, but you have not convinced me. I don't think you have convinced yourself either. Say something that will convince both of us.

Responding to Nonverbal Cues.   This strategy enables counselors or therapists to go beyond the words of clients and respond to the messages that are being communicated by the physical actions of clients. Care is needed not to overgeneralize about every subtle body movement. Counselors or therapists are looking for patterns that either confirm or deny the truth in the words clients use to express themselves. When such patterns become apparent, it is the responsibility of counselors or therapists to share these patterns with clients. It becomes a client's responsibility to confirm or deny the credibility of the perception.

Example:

> Client: (turning away) Yes, you are right. I am not con-
> vinced that this is what I want. (smiling) Maybe I was just
> never meant to be happy.

*Nonverbal
responding*

> Counselor/Therapist: What I said made you angry, and I
> suspect it hurt a little. Did you notice you turned away
> before you began to speak? What were you telling me when
> you turned away?
> Client: (smiling) What you said did hurt me. I was angry,
> but I'm also embarrassed about not being able to handle
> this part of my life. I don't like you seeing me this way.

*Nonverbal
responding*

> Counselor/Therapist: I've noticed that on several occasions
> when you talk about feelings such as your anger, embarrass-
> ment, or hopelessness, you smile. What does the smile
> mean?
> Client: (long pause) I guess I want you to believe that it isn't
> as bad as it sounds or that I'm not as hopeless as I think I am.
> Counselor/Therapist: It *is* bad or you wouldn't be here, and
> hopeless is your word, not mine. Our time is up for today.
> Between now and next week I want you to think about what
> we have discussed. See you next week?

The strategies we have outlined in this section enable counselors or therapists to achieve more effectively the process and outcome goals related to counseling or psychotherapy. Choosing which strategy to use, when to use it, and its impact on the helping relationship is based upon the education, experience, and personal dynamics that counselors or therapists bring to the helping relationship.

CONCLUSIONS

The helping relationship is the foundation on which the process of counseling or psychotherapy rests. It is best viewed in terms of developmental stages, the first of which begins with the initial meeting of the client and counselor or therapist and is characterized by rapport building, information gathering, and goal determination. Building on the foundation established in the first stage, later stages address extended exploration and problem resolution. They lead to the final stage in this process, termination and follow-up.

The helping relationship, when viewed from this developmental perspective, progresses from stage to stage due to the presence of certain components that counselors or therapists bring to the relationship. The first of these are the core conditions of empathic understanding, respect and positive regard, genuineness and congruence, concreteness, warmth, immediacy, and cultural awareness. These conditions are personality characteristics of counselors or therapists that they are able to incorporate into the helping relationship.

The second component is a set of strategies aimed at building rapport and encouraging client dialogue, data gathering, and relationship enhancement. These conditions are skills and techniques that counselors or therapists gain through education and experience and are able to use effectively within the helping relationship. In combination, the developmental nature of the helping relationship, the presence of the core conditions, and the implementation of the various strategies create a facilitative environment in which both clients and counselors or therapists have the strong potential for positive growth. *The potential exists; guarantees do not*. Achieving the true potential of the helping relationship depends upon what counselors or therapists and clients bring to the relationship and what each takes from it.

In closing, the authors return to Jane as she begins her practicum experience. She appears to have concern for the client and the desire to be an effective counselor or therapist. These qualities should aid her as she attempts to provide the core conditions. Her education has provided her with both a theoretical foundation and some practice in the helping process. This background should assist her as she begins to apply helping strategies. Her practicum experience should allow her to reduce her anxiety and fear by enhancing her ability to apply both the core conditions and the strategies in a theoretical system of her choosing. Her excitement should increase as she enters the complex and challenging arena of the helping relationship.

REFERENCES

Baruth, L. G., & Robinson, E. H. (1987). *An introduction to the counseling profession*. Englewood Cliffs, NJ: Prentice-Hall.

Belkin, G. S. (1980). *An introduction to counseling*. Dubuque, IA: Brown.

Boy, A. V., & Pine, G. J. (1982). *Client centered counseling: A renewal*. Boston: Allyn & Bacon.

Brammer, L. M. (1985). *The helping relationship: Process and skills* (3rd ed.) Englewood Cliffs, NJ: Prentice-Hall.

Brown, J. A., & Pate, R. H. (1983). *Being a counselor: Direction and challenges*. Monterey, CA: Brooks/Cole.

Brown, D., & Srebalus, D. J. (1988). *An introduction to the counseling profession*. Englewood Cliffs, NJ: Prentice-Hall.

Carkhuff, R. R., & Barenson, B. G. (1967). *Beyond counseling and psychotherapy*. New York: Holt, Rinehart, & Winston.

Combs, A. W. (1986). What makes a good helper? A person-centered approach. *Person-centered Review, 1*, 51–61.

Combs, A. W., Avila, D. L., & Purkey, W. W. (1978). *Helping relationship: Basic concepts for the helping profession.* Boston: Allyn & Bacon.

Cormier, W. H., & Cormier, L. S. (1979). *Interviewing strategies for helpers: A guide to assessment, treatment, and evaluation.* Belmont, CA: Wadsworth.

Delaney, D. J., & Eisenberg, S. (1972). *The counseling process.* Chicago: Rand McNally.

Dixon, D. N., & Glover, J. A. (1984). *Counseling: A problem solving approach.* New York: Wiley.

Egan, G. (1982). *The skilled helper: A model for systematic helping and interpersonal relating* (2nd ed.). Monterey, CA.: Brooks/Cole.

Gazda, G. M., Asbury, F. R., Blazer, F. J., Childers, W. C., & Walters, R. P. (1977). *Human relations development: A manual for educators* (2nd ed.). Boston: Allyn & Bacon.

Gilliland, B. E., James, R. K., Roberts, G. T., & Bowman, J. T. (1984). *Theories and strategies in counseling and psychotherapy.* Englewood Cliffs, NJ: Prentice-Hall.

Hackney, H., & Cormier, L. S. (1988). *Counseling strategies and interventions* (3rd ed.). Englewood Cliffs, NJ: Prentice-Hall.

Hansen, J. C., Stevic, R. R., & Warner, R. W. (1982). *Counseling: Theory and process.* Boston: Allyn & Bacon.

Ivey, A. E. (1971). *Microcounseling: Innovations in interviewing training* (2nd ed.). Springfield, IL: Charles C Thomas.

Ivey, A. E. (1988). *Intentional interviewing and counseling: Facilitating client development.* Monterey, CA: Brooks/Cole.

Ivey, A. E., & Simek-Downing, L. (1980). *Counseling and psychotherapy: Skills, theory, and practice.* Englewood Cliffs, NJ: Prentice-Hall.

Kagan, N. (1971). *Influencing human interaction.* East Lansing: Michigan State University, CCTV. Mimeographed.

Kottler, J., & Brown, R. (1992). *Introduction to therapeutic counseling* (2nd ed.). Pacific Grove, CA: Brooks/Cole.

Newlon, B. J., & Arciniega, M. (1992.) Group counseling: Cross cultural. In D. Capuzzi & D. Gross (Eds.), *Introduction to group counseling* (pp. 285–306). Denver: Love.

Osipow, S. H., Walsh, W. B., & Tosi, D. J. (1980). *A survey of counseling methods.* Homewood, IL: Dorsey.

Patterson, C. H. (1974). *Relationship counseling and psychotherapy.* New York: Harper & Row.

Purkey, W. W., & Schmidt, J. J. (1987). *The inviting relationship: An expanded perspective for professional counseling.* Englewood Cliffs, NJ: Prentice-Hall.

Rogers, C. R. (1957). The necessary and sufficient conditions of therapeutic personality change. *Journal of Consulting Psychology, 21,* 95–103.

Rogers, C. R. (1961). *On becoming a person: A therapist's view of psychotherapy.* Boston: Houghton Mifflin.

Sue, D. W., & Sue, D. (1990). *Counseling the culturally different: Theory and process.* New York: Wiley.

Terry, A., Burden, C., & Pedersen, M. (1991). The helping relationship. In D. Capuzzi & D. R. Gross (Eds.), *Introduction to counseling: Perspectives for the 1990s* (pp. 44–68). Boston: Allyn & Bacon.

Truax, C. B., & Carkhuff, R. R. (1967). *Towards effective counseling and psychotherapy: Training and practice.* Chicago: Aldine.

Wehrly, B. (1991). Preparing multicultural counselors. *Counseling and Human Development, 24,* 1–23.

CHAPTER TWO

Achieving a Personal and Professional Identity

David Capuzzi
Portland State University

Douglas R. Gross
Arizona State University

"**H**ow well do I really know myself and how effective will I be with clients? Do I really understand my chosen profession and the stressors involved?" Those are just two of the questions we believe each of you should continually ask as you progress through your graduate education and clinical supervision experience. Some careers can be pursued without a high level of self-awareness, but the profession of counseling or psychology is not one of them. Knowledge of theory and research and expertise in translating that knowledge into strategies and interventions can only be delivered through the being and personhood of the provider. Each member of the helping professions is given an enormous amount of responsibility every time client interactions occur. This responsibility can only be upheld if each counselor or therapist maintains a sense of health and wellness to assure that the understanding and support, assessment and treatment planning that a client receives are the best they can possibly be. The more a counselor or therapist has developed, integrated, and accepted an identity as a person and as a professional, the better that individual is at giving the incredible gift of helping another human being develop a unique sense of self.

Personal and professional identity must be addressed before and during the process of studying and applying individual approaches to counseling and psychotherapy. It is not easy, for example, for the beginning graduate student to be receptive to peer and supervisor feedback as it relates to individual work with clients. The student must have a great enough sense of well-being and self-awareness to be receptive to suggestions for changes that are needed to maximize therapeutic effectiveness. As we noted in chapter 1, on-site observations of individual sessions and required videotaping and playback for supervisory purposes escalate the stress level of any graduate student. If students can develop high levels of self-acceptance and understanding, they will receive more benefit from the supervision process and have greater potential for developing clinical skills.

Many students are enrolled in graduate programs that require participation as a client in either individual or group counseling for the purpose of facilitating continued personal growth. This requirement helps students avoid the confusion that arises when client issues are similar to unresolved personal issues.

Faculty in counseling and psychology departments are becoming more definitive and assertive about expectations for the wellness and functionality of potential counselors and therapists because of the stresses and complexities of the helping professions. Many educators and clinical supervisors are stressing the postdegree expectation that counselors and therapists will involve themselves in counseling or psychotherapy and consultation to maintain personal growth, wellness, and treatment-planning ability. Many experienced professionals stress the importance of involving significant others in ongoing couples or family counseling so that as the counselor or therapist grows and changes, friends and family members can participate in and understand that process of change.

This chapter addresses the importance of health and wellness for the counselor or therapist, as well as the importance of recognizing values and cultural bias in theory and practice, becoming aware of the daily world of the practitioner, and achieving perspective and balance between personal and professional roles. It also includes some brief comments about developing a personal theory and provides a summary of the chapter as a whole.

THE IMPORTANCE OF HEALTH AND WELLNESS

The personal qualities, traits, and characteristics of the counselor or therapist have long been recognized as an extremely important component of the helping relationship (Carkhuff & Berenson, 1977; Egan, 1975; Rogers, 1961). As noted by Okun (1987), a continually increasing data base supports the concept that counselors and therapists are only effective if they are self-aware and able to use themselves as the instruments through which change occurs. One way of conceptualizing this role in the relationship is to compare the contribution the counselor or therapist makes to a client's growth and maturation to that of a painter working on a canvas, an architect designing a building, or a sculptor chiseling a statue. The client presents possibilities and options, which are much like the raw materials of canvas and paint, building site and construction materials, or chisels and stone. The artist approaches the task with a data base of information and the expertise to translate a concept or mental image into something beautiful or functional. Whether the data base and expertise of the artist can be fully accessed most often depends on the mental, emotional, physical, and spiritual sensitivities with which the artist approaches the work. Creativity can be compromised or never actualized if the being of the creator is impaired, tired, or dysfunctional because everything the artist has to contribute is conveyed through the person of the artist.

The counselor or therapist is the conveyer of possibilities and potentials to the client. If the being or personhood of the counselor or therapist is impaired at the time of an encounter with a client, it may be difficult to see the potential and use the possibilities for engaging in a mutually rewarding relationship to achieve desirable outcomes. The health and wellness of the counselor or therapist have much to do with the art form inherent in the helping relationship.

Approaches to Health and Wellness

There are a number of approaches to health and wellness that are described, researched, and prescribed by those wishing to sensitize counselors and therapists to the importance of self-care as a prerequisite to caregiving. We have identified three commonly discussed models for presentation: the personal characteristics model, the psychological health model, and the multidimensional health and wellness model.

The Personal Characteristics Model.   Person-centered counseling theory offers a well-researched analysis of how counselors and therapists might work with clients. The person-centered school identifies accurate empathy, nonpossessive warmth, positive regard, and genuineness as the "necessary and sufficient conditions" for therapeutic change (Rogers, 1957; Truax & Carkhuff, 1967). *Empathy*, often defined as the capacity to view and understand the world through the client's frame of reference (Egan, 1975), is one of the most extensively studied personal characteristics or variables in process-outcome research. Most reviews of studies that analyze the relationships between empathy and outcome show positive relationships in half to two-thirds of the research under scrutiny (Orlinsky & Howard, 1978, 1986). *Genuineness*—described as consistency in values, attitudes, and behaviors on the part of the counselor or therapist—is also the focus of therapeutic process research and is generally related positively to therapeutic outcomes (Orlinsky & Howard, 1986).

Counselor or therapist *affirmation*—the ability to communicate positive regard, warmth, and acceptance to the client—is also significantly associated with positive therapeutic outcomes (Orlinsky & Howard, 1978). In addition, Carkhuff and his associates have stressed the importance of concreteness or specificity of expression (Carkhuff & Berenson, 1977). As we noted in chapter 1, *concreteness* means that the practitioner's response serves to clarify the meaning the client is communicating so that the client's self-understanding is actually enhanced.

The personal characteristics model for addressing the health and wellness of the counselor or therapist has been addressed from perspectives other than those of Carl Rogers. Combs and his colleagues conducted a series of studies resulting in the conclusion that the personal beliefs and traits of the counselor or therapist differentiated between effective and ineffective helping (Combs, Soper, Gooding, Benton, Dickman, & Usher, 1969). Effective helpers seem to perceive others as able, rather than unable, to solve their own problems and manage their own lives. Effective helpers also perceive others as dependable, friendly, worthy, able to cope, and able to be communicative and self-disclosing. In general, effective helpers maintain a positive view of human nature and approach family, friends, colleagues, and clients in a trusting, affirming way. A composite model of human effectiveness was suggested by George and Cristiani (1990) as a means of analyzing the personal characteristics of effective helpers. The elements of this composite model included openness to and acceptance of experiencing, awareness of values and beliefs, ability to develop warm and deep relationships with others, willingness to be seen by others as they actually are, willingness to accept personal responsibility for their own behaviors, and development of realistic levels of aspiration.

The literature about the personal characteristics model that is available to counselors or therapists is voluminous. Characteristics such as assertiveness, flexibility, tolerance of ambiguity, honesty, emotional presence, goal directedness, self-respect, and so on have all been addressed to the point that the beginning counselor or therapist may find the suggested profile somewhat overwhelming and threatening. The important thing to remember is that it would never be possible to achieve the perfection that such idealized models suggest. All of us have flaws and imperfections that can obstruct our ability as helpers, just as all of us have unique strengths and capabilities that enable us to influence others positively. We believe that effective counselors and therapists are able to maintain a sense of personal well-being and happiness despite flaws or inadequacies and stress the importance of a perspective that ensures that personal issues do not diminish the capacity to engender personal growth on the part of clients.

The Psychological Health Model.   The following provocative scenario can be used to introduce some of the dilemmas inherent in suggesting criteria for psychological health:

> Imagine a psychological health contest between the John Wayne persona of the 1950s silver screen and the Leo Buscalia persona of the 1980s lecture circuit. Which persona would win? Among John Wayne's celluloid traits were his stoicism and his readiness to fight. He rarely displayed any weaknesses or "shared his feelings" with anyone. In contrast, Leo Buscalia's most salient public traits have been his readiness to cry and "share his feelings" with everyone. Is "strong and silent" healthier than "vulnerable and expressive?" For males? For females? Does the answer depend entirely upon the biases of the judges and the context of a specific time and place? (Kinnier, 1991, p. 25)

To cope with dilemmas such as the one posed by Kinnier, the majority of mental health practitioners have focused upon identifying symptoms of psychopathology instead of criteria for mental health. It has been easier to identify undesirable behaviors and emotions than it has been to identify and agree upon behavior and emotions indicative of mental health. Cross-cultural differences have added to the complexity of attempting to delineate the traits of a psychologically healthy client. It is difficult to establish acceptable criteria for psychological health because such criteria are intricately woven into a particular cultural and temporal background. Nevertheless, a number of theoreticians and practitioners have emphasized psychological health models as approaches to promoting the health and wellness of clients.

More than three decades ago, Jahoda (1958) proposed six mental health criteria: a positive attitude toward self, continual movement toward self-actualization, purpose or meaning in life, the ability to function independently and autonomously, an accurate perception of reality, and mastery in the environment. Basic self-esteem was viewed as essential by luminaries such as Allport (1961), Erikson (1968), Jung (1954), Maslow (1970), Rogers (1961), and Sullivan (1953). Personal autonomy and competence were emphasized by Fromm (1955), Horney (1950), Maslow (1970), and Rogers (1961). The capacity to give and receive love as a criterion for psychological health has also been endorsed by Adler (1978), Allport (1961), Erikson (1968), Freud (1930), Fromm (1955), Maslow (1970), and Sullivan (1953).

Kinnier (1991) proposed nine criteria for psychological health, which were developed by surveying psychological literature to determine what criteria had been identified by theoreticians and researchers. We believe these criteria apply to counselors and therapists as well as to their clients.

1. *Self-love (not self-infatuation).*   Self-esteem seems to be a prerequisite for developing other important components of psychological health. Psychologically healthy individuals experience strong feelings of self-acceptance and self-love but are not self-obsessed. Individuals who love and respect themselves have the capacity to love and respect others and the foundation for becoming self-actualized.

2. *Self-knowledge.*   The importance of self-exploration and self-knowledge cannot be overemphasized. Psychologically healthy individuals know themselves well and stay aware of feelings, motivations, and needs. They are introspective and committed to understanding themselves.

3. *Self-confidence and self-control.*   Individuals who are psychologically healthy have confidence in themselves and can function independently

of others. They have appropriate skills for assertive behavior but do not unnecessarily impose their views or will on others. Such individuals have an internal locus of control, believe that they can exert reasonable control over their lives, and feel capable of achieving their goals.

4. *A clear (though slightly optimistic) perception of reality.*   Perceptions of the people, events, and objects around us are always subjective, but there is usually enough societal consensus about the nature of reality to provide beneficial comparisons with our own point of view. Psychologically healthy individuals have a clear perception of reality and an optimistic view of life. They view themselves, their present circumstances, and their futures accurately and positively, which enhances possibilities and potentials.

5. *Courage and resilience.*   Danger and risk surround the daily lives and decision-making opportunities of most individuals; therefore, failures, crises, and setbacks are inevitable. Psychologically healthy individuals are aware of this reality, adapt well to challenges and changed circumstances, and can bounce back from disappointments and setbacks. As noted by Kinnier (1991), "psychologically healthy individuals courageously confront their fears and accept their responsibility. They are prepared to take risks when appropriate. They accept setbacks and failures as part of life and, as the popular song says, after a fall they 'pick themselves up, dust themselves off, and start all over again'" (p. 34).

6. *Balance and moderation.*   The theme of balance and moderation is one that recurs in psychological literature. Psychologically healthy individuals work and play, laugh and cry, enjoy planned and spontaneous time with family and friends, and are not afraid to be both logical and intuitive. They are rarely extremists or fanatics and usually do not do anything in excess.

7. *Love of others.*   The capacity to care deeply about the welfare of another person or the condition of humanity in general is another characteristic of the psychologically healthy person. Mental health professionals from a number of theoretical orientations believe that the need to belong to another person, family, or group; the ability to give and receive love; and the desire to develop close ties to another person or persons are fundamental to mental health. Psychologically healthy individuals are not reticent about loving and caring for others. They need to experience close interpersonal relationships and are intimate with at least one other person.

8. *Love of life.*   The psychological benefits of humor, spontaneity, and openness have been touted by numerous professionals. People who are

active, curious, spontaneous, venturesome, and relaxed have traits that promote their capacity to enjoy and partake of life. Psychologically healthy people embrace the opportunities that life presents, do not take life too seriously, and look forward to the unexpected with the vitality to cope, problem-solve, and move on to the future with a positive perspective.

9. *Purpose in life.*   Individuals vary in their choice of the most meaningful aspects of life. Work, love, family, intellectual or physical accomplishment, or spirituality may become the primary focus for one individual or another. While variation among individuals is bound to exist, the important achievement for each person is to develop a purpose, an investment, that creates a sense of meaning and satisfaction. The joy and sense of exhilaration and accomplishment that result from finding meaning and purpose in life are prime factors in the maintenance of psychological health.

The Multidimensional Health and Wellness Model.   As noted by Myers (1991), several different wellness models have been proposed for use by counselors and therapists. One of the most common models defines wellness holistically by considering it from spiritual, mental, and physical aspects of functionality. Other models describe dimensions such as spirituality, physical fitness, job satisfaction, relationships, family life, nutrition, leisure time, and stress management (Ardell, 1988). In 1984 Hettler's six dimensions of intellectual, emotional, physical, social, occupational, and spiritual wellness were proposed as components of a lifelong paradigm to promote health and wellness. Health has been defined as the absence of illness; wellness goes far beyond the absence of illness and incorporates a zest and enthusiasm for life, which results when the dimensions of wellness (intellectual, emotional, physical, social, occupational, spiritual, etc.) have been addressed, developed, and integrated. "With a holistic focus, wellness incorporates not just the whole person, but the whole person throughout the totality of the life span" (Myers, 1991, p. 185). A person can be "well" even when undergoing treatment for physical illness because the physical dimension is just one dimension of the wellness model.

The importance of this brief discussion of the multidimensional health and wellness model should be understood by all those undertaking the study of theories of counseling and psychotherapy. Some of the theories and approaches included in the second section of this book do not encourage the counselor or therapist to approach clients from a multidimensional perspective, nor do they encourage the practitioner to engage in personal care from a holistic frame of reference. One of the tasks of a beginning counselor or therapist is to think about developing a theory or approach to the helping relationship. This may entail the adoption of one of the theories presented in this textbook, the development of an integrated model, or the conceptualization of a personalized theory or approach based on the study of theory and research as well as experience with clients. We encourage you to consider a number of perspectives before conceptualizing a personal theory of counseling and psychotherapy, for no single theory provides a perspective that could be described as multidimensional.

VALUES AND CULTURAL BIAS IN THEORY AND PRACTICE

As you read the theory chapters in the second section of this book, you should think about the way the values and cultural biases of the chief proponents of each theory may have influenced the development of the theory. In addition, you should assess personal values and understandings of cultural differences. In this section of the chapter, we introduce you to a discussion of values and cultural bias in theory and practice. After presenting chapters 5 through 17, we reintroduce the topic of cultural differences and further refine the subject in chapter 18.

Values in Theory and Practice

Everyone has a set of beliefs that guides decisions, determines one's ability to appreciate the people and things in the environment, governs conscience, and influences perceptions of others (Belkin, 1984). Because the counselor's or therapist's values are an integral part of what is brought to a relationship with a client, we think it is important to consider the role that values play in theory and practice and in achieving a personal and professional identity.

One of the key issues to consider is whether or not counselors or therapists can avoid conveying their values to the clients they see during the process of counseling and psychotherapy (George & Cristiani, 1990). Some maintain (especially professionals associated with the orthodox psychoanalytic point of view) that counselors or therapists must remain neutral with clients and avoid communicating value orientations. In such circumstances counselors or therapists would strive to appear nonmoralizing, ethically neutral, and focused on the client's values. If topics such as pro choice versus pro life, religion, euthanasia, gay or lesbian orientation, and so on were to arise during the counseling and psychotherapy process, the counselor or therapist would not take a position. The reason for such neutrality is the belief that it is important for clients to move from an external to an internal locus of control during the counseling and psychotherapy process. Values introduced by the counselor or therapist would be detrimental to such an objective.

As early as 1958, however, Williamson voiced an opposing position and promoted the idea that counselors and therapists cannot avoid letting clients know about their values and should be open and explicit about the nature of those values. Williamson reasoned that counselor or therapist neutrality may be interpreted by clients to mean that the professional is supporting client behavior that is not acceptable by social, moral, or legal standards. Samler (1960) went further and encouraged counselors and therapists to develop an awareness of their own values and how these values relate to and influence the development of client values. He further believed that assisting clients to change their values is a legitimate goal and a necessary component of the helping relationship. As early as 1958 and as recently as 1989, Patterson pointed out that the values of the counselor or therapist influence the ethics of the helping relationship and the goals, techniques, and interventions employed in the context of helping.

We believe it is imperative for counselors and therapists to be aware of their own values and to consider the influence that the values of the professional have upon the client. The following questions may prove useful to the helper in the process of examining values issues:

- Am I completely cognizant of my own values?
- Do my values influence my preference for particular theoretical frameworks (such as rational-emotive therapy or Jungian concepts) and associated techniques and interventions?
- How will I resolve dilemmas that arise when my values and those of my client are opposed?
- What is my belief about whether a counselor or therapist can remain neutral and avoid communicating value orientations to clients?
- What is my role in helping clients delineate their values more clearly?

Cultural Bias in Theory and Practice

In 1962, C. Gilbert Wrenn was one of the first to suggest that practitioners were providing counseling and psychotherapy from a narrow cultural perspective. He encouraged counselors and therapists to broaden their monocultural perspectives and be more responsive to clients from different cultural backgrounds. By the mid-1970s, more emphasis on the issue of cultural bias in theory and practice began to appear in the literature. Today, it is widely acknowledged that current theories are derivatives of Western culture and really are not universally applicable to crosscultural counseling and psychotherapy situations (McFadden, 1988; Vontress, 1988). Because the United States is becoming increasingly diversified, recognition of the cultural bias that exists in theories and techniques of counseling and psychotherapy becomes even more important in the process of achieving a personal and professional identity.

Claire Hamilton Usher (1989) provided some helpful guidelines for assessing the cultural bias inherent in theories of counseling and psychotherapy. We include those guidelines here to extend the discussion of cultural awareness that we began in chapter 1 and to alert the reader to some of the pitfalls associated with attempts to apply Western frames of reference to all clients irrespective of their cultural identity and experience. We do not intend to discourage counselors and therapists from making appropriate use of current theory; rather, we want to sensitize practitioners to the importance of cultural differences as determiners of approach selection and the development of a personal theory of counseling and psychotherapy.

Assumptions About Normal Behavior.   A very real source of cultural bias is the assumption that *normal* means the same thing to members of various social, political, economic, and cultural backgrounds. Although some clients may believe that being reasonably assertive or responsibly individualistic is a normal goal, such traits may be considered inappropriate in cultures different than our own. Pedersen (1987) argued that "what is considered normal behavior will change according to the situation, the cultural background of a person or persons being judged, and the time during which a behavior is being displayed or observed" (p. 16). He pointed out the danger of diagnostic errors when using definitions of normality as defined from the perspective of the culture in which a particular theory or conceptual frame of reference was developed.

Emphasis on Individualism.   A number of theories (for example, person-centered and rational-emotive therapy) emphasize the welfare and centrality of the individual and de-emphasize the importance of obligation and duty to family, organizations, and society. Because such themes are central to some cultures' value systems, it would be a mistake for the counselor or therapist to promote individualism on the part of a client for whom such a focus would be contrary to cultural or ethnic identity. For example, an Asian-American client might not return to a counselor or therapist who did not respect what the client communicated about deference to the wishes of parents or other experienced members of the extended family.

Fragmentation by Academic Disciplines.   Many theories of counseling and psychotherapy have been developed without considering the potential contributions of other academic disciplines such as sociology, anthropology, theology, and medicine. When counselors or therapists use a theory that has been developed from a narrow perspective, they may be handicapped in attempts to facilitate the helping relationship with a client who is culturally different. It is important for all counselors and therapists to take courses or participate in training experiences offered by other disciplines or by those who maintain a different cultural perspective.

Dependence on Abstract Words.   Counselors and therapists with a Western frame of reference live in a low-context culture and may depend on abstract words associated with theory and practice and assume that these abstractions will be understood by others, including clients, in the same way they are understood by the professional. Such abstractions may have little meaning or take on different meanings when used outside the cultural context in which they were initially developed. For example, would all clients understand the concepts of self-actualization or fictional finalism? Many clients are not receptive to abstractions or conceptualizations, which seem removed from the reality of life in a culture not based on Western values, world views, or protocols.

Overemphasis on Independence.   Usher cited Pedersen (1987) who criticized theories and practices that devalue necessary dependencies inculcated by certain cultures. Because most counselors or therapists in this country view the independence of the client as desirable and neglect the function of healthy dependencies in some cultures, many of the theories used by counselors and therapists do a disservice to clients who have grown up and continue to function in a different cultural context. There are many cultural groups that value a person's capacity to subjugate individual desire for preference to the overall welfare of the family, community, or organization. It is important for counselors and therapists to be both sensitive to and respectful of such a perspective.

Neglect of Client Support Systems.   Many theoretical orientations do not recognize the role that family and peers play in providing support for a troubled client to the same extent as they recognize the role of the professionally prepared counselor or therapist. (Neither do the proponents of many approaches to counseling and psychotherapy.) It may be necessary for counselors and therapists to incorporate the client's natural support system into a treatment plan. In some cultures, talking with family members or friends may be more acceptable than talking with a trained professional who is usually a total stranger.

Dependence on Linear Thinking.   Most theories make the assumption that clients relate to linear thinking. Linear thinking emphasizes cause-and-effect relationships. In contrast, the nonlinear or circular thinking characteristic of some cultures does not separate cause and effect, does not follow a singular stream of thought, and invites free association. It is important for counselors and therapists to realize that for some clients, conversation about topics seemingly unrelated to counseling and psychotherapy may be an essential element of a productive helping relationship.

Focus on Changing the Individual Rather Than the System.   Quite often, counselors and therapists who use Western theory as the sole basis for practice assume that their role is to make the client more congruent with the system. They do not question whether the system should be changed to fit the individual. Such an assumption should be questioned. If counselors or therapists do not question whether the system is in the best interests of a culturally different client, are they simply serving as agents of the status quo?

Neglect of History.   Some counselors and therapists minimize the relevance of a client's personal and cultural history, focusing more intensively on present behavior, the current problem, and immediate events. Clients from some cultures, such as native American cultures, see themselves as closely connected to their ancestors. Their current problems cannot really be fully understood without consideration of past history. Such clients might not return to a counselor or therapist who did not provide opportunity to explore the present in terms of past experience as well as present needs.

Cultural Encapsulation.   It is important for counselors and therapists to guard against the possibility of becoming culturally encapsulated by the mainstream group with which they are associated. When such encapsulation occurs, assumptions and beliefs may not be questioned, and clients from diverse cultural backgrounds may not be treated effectively because of the operation of certain biases on the part of the professional. The more counselors and therapists can experience and learn about other cultural groups, the less likely they will be to approach clients with biases that prevent effective helping.

THE DAILY WORLD OF THE PRACTITIONER

There is no doubt that there is a complex relationship between elements of the therapeutic process and the demands experienced by the counselor or therapist on a daily basis. The clients with whom one works, the setting, the expectations of colleagues and supervisors, one's personal life, and significant others are constantly interacting and, at times, reciprocally influencing outcomes. We believe that an important part of developing a personal and professional identity is becoming as aware as possible of the daily world of the practitioner and the stresses that sometimes impede the counselor or therapist's well-being and the services provided to clients.

The demands inherent in just about any work environment (school, college, university, mental health center, hospital, private practice, rehabilitation clinic, and so on) are tremendous. Concerns about having enough clients, students, supervisees, research funds, publications, involvements in professional and community organizations, collected fees, malpractice and liability insurance are just a few examples of the kinds of demands that converge on counselors and therapists. As Freudenberger (1983) notes, the very nature of the therapeutic personality often makes it difficult to say no; and many people engaged in counseling and psychotherapy find themselves overextended, tired, and overly involved with work. For some professionals the drive to develop a reputation for excellence coupled with the needs for success must be monitored carefully to avoid chronic discontent and eventual burnout.

The demands that clients place upon counselors and therapists are a significant factor in a practitioner's daily world. In the span of just a few days, many counselors and therapists find themselves confronted with the problems of the chronically mentally ill, the terminally ill, the physically or sexually abused, the suicidal, the eating disordered, the substance abuser, and clients with a host of other concerns and issues. Most research to date (for example, Hellman & Morrison, 1987; Pines & Maslach, 1978) indicates that counselors and therapists in settings that serve large numbers of seriously disturbed clients experience higher rates of personal depletion, less career satisfaction, and more impaired working relationships with colleagues. This information is quite pertinent for those planning to place themselves in settings in which there is a high probability of working with challenging clients.

The ominous shadow of malpractice hovers all too often over the daily world of the practitioner. Rates for liability insurance have risen as clients have become more litigious and counselors and therapists have become fair game. Because many clients enter the counseling or psychotherapy process with expectations about becoming better, perhaps in an unrealistically short period of time, counselors and therapists are vulnerable to having client disappointments or frustrations worked out in court rather than in a therapeutic environment. More and more lawyers have chosen to specialize in personal injury and malpractice cases and actively seek clients who are discontent with the results of counseling and psychotherapy (Kaslow & Schulman, 1987). Even when the counselor or therapist is innocent, the insurance carrier or one's own legal counsel may suggest an out-of-court settlement in order to avoid the trauma of a trial, the possibility of a guilty verdict, the accompanying censure of professional organizations, and the possibility of losing required state licensing. To the beginning and even to the experienced counselor or therapist such a settlement can seem like an admission of guilt, yet preparing for and going through a trial can pose an even greater ordeal and create a high level of stress. In addition, such trials in small communities may attract a great deal of unwelcome media attention. Because counselors and therapists believe in the sanctity and privacy of the therapeutic encounter, such public exposure can be a bitter experience, with negative impacts on personal well-being as well as on the lives of family members.

More than any other professional, the counselor or therapist must continually deal with the reality of terminations. Whether the treatment process has been successful or not, the ending of a helping relationship may be experienced as another separation and, quite often, as a permanent loss. Despite the fact that counselors and therapists are prepared during their educational and supervisory experiences for the inevitability of terminating with clients, endings may be difficult and force the counselor or therapist to deal with unresolved personal losses (departure of adult children, death of significant others, divorce).

Terminations can also become transformations when clients appear in different roles in the life of the counselor or therapist. Examples of these roles include former clients who may later reenter as trained mental health professionals or, as is often the case in small communities, become part of the social milieu of the counselor or therapist. The reality of termination or transformation can be a source of satisfaction or stress depending upon how the counselor or therapist views the nature of the posttreatment void or the posttreatment relationship.

In many ways the daily world of the counselor or therapist may threaten relationships outside the workplace. For example, in the process of striving to improve working relationships with cotherapists, colleagues, and supervisors, counselors or therapists may share much of their inner selves and, in so doing, develop satisfying relationships built on trust, respect, and mutual understanding. These relationships may supplant or replace other significant relationships outside the workplace. As a result, a marriage or long-term relationship may begin to seem less interesting and rewarding unless some steps are taken to prevent this from happening.

In addition to the impact that relationships with colleagues may have on the personal life of a counselor or therapist, the expression of admiration by clients, trainees, and colleagues may also result in some unexpected fallout. Significant others outside the workplace may begin to resent the attention that the counselor or therapist receives from clients and colleagues, or the counselor or therapist may begin to expect the same level of admiration from significant others. In either situation, resentment, frustration, and anger may result. Again, counselors and therapists need to take steps to prevent this from occurring.

Finally, the basic principle of confidentiality may create problems for the counselor or therapist in relationships outside the workplace. Counselors and therapists cannot talk about their clients except in the context of receiving supervision or consultation or in situations when the best interests of the client or society are at stake. Significant others may feel shut out, especially when they know that others have access to information unavailable to them.

ACHIEVING PERSPECTIVE AND BALANCE

Our previous discussion of the daily world of the counselor or therapist is necessarily limited in scope, yet we believe the discussion does convey the fact that counselors and therapists deal with demands and stresses that can place them at risk for burnout and personal depletion. Because it is important to maintain a high level of personal health and wellness, we think the following guidelines may prove useful to individuals in training as well as to other members of the profession.

Know the Warning Signs for Burnout

How do graduate students or practicing counselors or therapists know they are heading for difficulty when striving to develop and maintain a high level of professional competence? Kaslow (1986) lists some of the signs of burnout:

- Not wanting to go to work
- Constantly complaining about disliking practice or feeling overwhelmed by it
- Experiencing a sense of foreboding or imminent doom
- Viewing life as dull, heavy, and tedious
- Experiencing an increasing number of negative countertransference reactions to patients or students
- Being extremely irritable, withdrawn, depressed, or intolerant at home
- Suffering frequent illnesses of inexplicable origin
- Wanting to run away from it all or having periodic suicidal ideation

Kaslow (1986) notes that when two or more of these indicators appear periodically and with gradually increasing frequency, intensity, and duration, counselors or therapists have entered a warning zone and should seek personal counseling and psychotherapy, take a vacation, cut back on obligations, and so on until they reexperience perspective and balance.

Consider Networking Options

It is not always necessary to enter a counseling or psychotherapy relationship to achieve balance and perspective. Counselors and therapists have a number of beneficial protections that they can use to renew and revitalize their ability to function in a positive way. They can establish a network of professional contacts to provide different options for support and continued professional development. For example, working with a cotherapist, asking a colleague to view a client session through a one-way mirror and then offer feedback, or seeking clarification and assistance from a supervisor can provide invaluable support and ideas for treatment options when working with a difficult client. Any one of these networking options can help a counselor or therapist share the burden of providing counseling and psychotherapy or break through an impasse in a client/practitioner relationship (Kaslow & Schulman, 1987).

Most communities provide opportunities for professionals to join a support group to share personal or professional concerns. Often there are local opportunities to attend workshops and training sessions to enhance expertise or develop new skills. Such workshops also allow practitioners to meet and talk with other counselors and therapists who share similar interests. It is always important to participate in some combination of local, state, regional, or national professional organizations such as the American Counseling Association, the American Psychological Association, or the American Association of Marriage and Family Therapists. Professional organizations provide a myriad of opportunities for continued learning and networking with other members of the helping professions. An excellent source for graduate students is involvement with a local chapter of Chi Sigma Iota, an international honor society for students, alumni, and supporters of counselor education programs and departments.

Refer Clients When Appropriate

Another way to maintain perspective and balance is to be amenable to the possibility of referring clients who are difficult or chronic or whose issues fall outside your ability to provide adequate care. A referral can be done in a positive way from the vantage point of a client and will be viewed by colleagues as a sign of professional integrity and wisdom. Sometimes, when a client is struggling with issues too close to those of the counselor or therapist, referral of the client is preferable to undertaking or prolonging work in which one becomes overly involved.

Disengage from the Professional Role

The experienced counselor or therapist knows how to disengage from the role of being a professional so that time with friends and family members, social engagements, vacations, avocational interests, and so on can be enjoyed. Disengaging provides opportunities for rest, relaxation, and rejuvenation while relieving the practitioner from obligations. It is important for counselors and therapists to experience nurturing interpersonal relationships, just as it is important for clients to spend time with significant others. At times, counselors and therapists can become so enmeshed in the demands of the profession that it becomes difficult to let go and enjoy opportunities for fun and relaxation.

Consider Possible Options for Renewal

We began our careers in the 1960s as members of the profession of counseling and human development. At that time the daily world of the practitioner was quite different from the way it is today. Standards for credentialing, education, and supervision, although reasonably demanding, were not as specific, time consuming, and exacting as they are currently. As the profession has matured, the expectations for graduate work, credentialing, practice, and continuing education have become decidedly more demanding and stress producing. Because of these demands, many professionals develop a pattern of overload that can be traced back to graduate education and, quite often, to some inherent needs and predispositions that make overload seem acceptable as a way of life.

We do not believe that it is possible to continue indefinitely as an effective counselor or therapist unless options for renewal are considered and pursued. These options are uniquely different for each counselor or therapist and can only be identified on an individual basis. Exercise, time with friends, participation in a choral group, leaves of absence or sabbaticals, travel, gardening, white-water rafting, massages, time with significant others, and time alone are examples of the hundreds of options, and combinations of options, that may have appeal as well as potential for practitioner renewal. It is not possible to nurture others unless we provide the self-nurturance and renewal that maintains and restores our capacity as helpers. As we have already mentioned, the health and wellness of the helper has much to do with the art form inherent in the helping relationship.

THE IMPORTANCE OF A PERSONAL THEORY

After you finish reading the next two chapters of this book, you will begin a fascinating exploration of theories of counseling and psychotherapy. Some theories will have more personal appeal than others; all of them will present some stimulating perspectives about human nature and about providing help to those seeking assistance. In addition, each will suggest a variety of theory-congruent strategies or applications designed to help the client achieve desired changes in behavior, outlook, motivation, and so on. We want the contents of this book to help you continue to think about a personal theory of counseling and psychotherapy.

What theory you may decide to adopt or develop will be gradually identified as you accumulate knowledge about theory, research, and practice and build experiences with clients through practicum, internships, and volunteer and paid positions. A personal theory will also relate to values, culture, experience with diverse client populations, and a view of human growth and development throughout the life span. We encourage readers to begin thinking about the conceptual frame of reference with which they plan to approach clients, but we discourage them from adopting a position until they carefully explore possibilities and participate in a variety of clinical opportunities with associated one-to-one and group supervision experience.

As you read chapters 5 through 16, notice that each theory is consistently addressed in terms of a nine-point paradigm: history, human nature, major constructs, process of change, intervention strategies, supporting research, a diagnosis and treatment plan relating to a case study, limitations, and summary. These nine elements may form the basis for beginning to formulate a personal theory. It is important to realize, however, that there are other paradigms that could be developed with additional elements or components. In addition, it is beneficial to read the last three chapters of this book, which address theories of counseling and psychotherapy from alternate, crosscultural, and integrative perspectives, before formulating perspective on working therapeutically with others.

CONCLUSIONS

This chapter has stressed the importance of achieving a personal and professional identity as you begin to study theories of counseling and psychotherapy and gain experience in translating theory into practice. We believe personal identity and professional identity are interrelated and fundamental to being able to understand, evaluate, and apply the theories presented in this text. Because the health and wellness of the counselor or therapist is a prerequisite to effectiveness, we addressed this topic through descriptions of personal characteristics, psychological health, and multidimensional health and wellness models.

The values and cultural biases of each counselor or therapist does impact the use and application of theory as well as the structuring of the helping relationship. We hope readers will make personal assessments of their values and sensitivity to culturally diverse client populations as well as evaluate the values and cultural biases upon which the theories presented in subsequent chapters are based.

At times, students enroll in college and university programs for preparing counselors and therapists without being totally aware of the demands they will encounter. By describing the daily world of the counselor or therapist and the importance of achieving perspective and balance, this chapter provided an initial overview of the stresses and expectations as well as the importance of learning how to cope with professional demands. We believe each person needs to develop a realistic understanding of the profession and that this knowledge is an essential component for the development of personal and professional identity.

Finally, this chapter stressed the importance of thinking about the conceptual frame of reference with which clients are approached. Although some practitioners may adopt an existing theory, many will develop integrative or other perspectives based upon a number of professional and life experiences. We want our readers not only to obtain the benefits provided by the information in this book, but also to develop the analytic and evaluative skills that will enable them to apply this information effectively to client populations. Effective application will result when a practitioner is able to find a compatible balance between theoretical tenets and the personal and cultural characteristics that serve as a basis for the person's uniqueness. At that point the counselor or therapist will have answers to the two questions that began this chapter.

REFERENCES

Adler, A. (1978). Cooperation between the sexes. In H. L. Ansbacher & R. R. Ansbacher (Eds.), *Writings on women, love, and marriage, sexuality and its disorders*. Garden City, NY: Doubleday.

Allport, G. W. (1961). *Pattern and growth in personality*. New York: Holt, Rinehart, & Winston.

Ardell, D. B. (1988). The history and future of the wellness movement. In J. P. Opatz (Ed.), *Wellness promotion strategies: Selected proceedings of the eighth annual National Wellness Conference*. Dubuque, IA: Kendall/Hunt.

Belkin, G. (1984). *Introduction to counseling* (2nd ed.). Dubuque, IA: Brown.

Carkhuff, R. R., & Berenson, B. G. (1977). *Beyond counseling and therapy* (2nd ed.). New York: Holt, Rinehart, & Winston.

Combs, A., Soper, D., Gooding, C., Benton, J., Dickman, J., & Usher, R. (1969). *Florida studies in the helping professions*. Gainesville: University Press of Florida.

Egan, G. (1975). *The skilled helper*. Monterey, CA: Brooks/Cole.

Erikson, E. H. (1968). *Identity: Youth and crisis*. New York: Norton.

Freud, S. (1930). *Civilization and its discontents*. (J. Strachey, Trans. & Ed.). New York: Norton.

Freudenberger, H. (1983). Hazards of psychotherapeutic practice. *Psychotherapy in Private Practice, 1*(1), 83–89.

Fromm, E. (1955). *The sane society*. New York: Rinehart.

George, R. L., & Cristiani, T. S. (1990). *Counseling theory and practice* (3rd ed.). Englewood Cliffs, NJ: Prentice-Hall.

Hellman, I. D., & Morrison, T. L. (1987). Practice setting and type of caseload as factors in psychotherapist stress. *Psychotherapy, 24*(3), 427–432.

Hettler, B. (1984). Wellness: Encouraging a lifetime pursuit of excellence. *Health Values, 8*(4), 13–17.

Horney, K. (1950). *Neurosis and human growth*. New York: Norton.

Jahoda, M. (1958). *Current concepts of positive mental health*. New York: Basic Books.

Jung, C. G. (1954). *The development of personality*. Princeton: Princeton University Press.

Kaslow, F. W. (1986). Therapy with distressed psychotherapists: Special problems and challenges. In R. R. Kilburg, P. E. Nathan, & R. W. Thoreson (Eds.), *Professionals in distress: Issues, syndromes and solutions in psychology* (pp. 187–210). Washington, DC: American Psychological Association.

Kaslow, F. W., & Schulman, N. (1987). How to be sane and happy as a family therapist or the reciprocal impact of family therapy teaching and practice and therapists' personal lives and mental health. *Journal of Psychotherapy and the Family, 3*(2), 79–96.

Kinnier, R. T. (1991). What does it mean to be psychologically healthy? In D. Capuzzi & D. R. Gross (Eds.), *Introduction to counseling: Perspectives for the 1990s* (pp. 25–43). Boston: Allyn & Bacon.

Maslow, A. H. (1970). *Motivation and personality* (2nd ed.). New York: Harper.

McFadden, J. (1988). Cross-cultural counseling: Caribbean perspective. *Journal of Multicultural Counseling and Development, 16*, 36–40.

Myers, J. E. (1991). Wellness as the paradigm for counseling and development: The possible future. *Counselor Education and Supervision, 30*(3), 183–193.

Okun, B. F. (1987). *Effective helping: Interviewing and counseling techniques* (3rd ed.). Monterey, CA: Brooks/Cole.

Orlinsky, D. E., & Howard, K. I. (1978). The relation of process to outcome in psychotherapy. In S. L. Garfield & A. E. Bergin (Eds.), *Handbook of psychotherapy and behavior change* (2nd ed.) (pp. 283–330). New York: Wiley.

Orlinsky, D. E., & Howard, K. I. (1986). Process and outcome in psychotherapy. In S. L. Garfield & A. E. Bergin (Eds.), *Handbook of psychotherapy and behavior change* (3rd ed.) (pp. 311–381). New York: Wiley.

Patterson, C. H. (1958). The place of values in counseling and psychotherapy. *Journal of Counseling Psychology, 5*, 216–223.

Patterson, C. H. (1989). Values in counseling and psychotherapy. *Counseling and Values, 33*, 164–176.

Pedersen, P. (1987). Ten frequent assumptions of cultural bias in counseling. *Journal of Multicultural Counseling and Development, 15*, 16–22.

Pines, A., & Maslach, C. (1978). Characteristics of staff burnout in mental health settings. *Hospital and Community Psychiatry, 29*, 233–237.

Rogers, C. R. (1957). The necessary and sufficient conditions of therapeutic personality change. *Journal of Consulting Psychology, 21*, 95–103.

Rogers, C. R. (1961). *On becoming a person*. Boston: Houghton Mifflin.

Samler, J. (1960). Change in values: A goal in counseling. *Journal of Counseling Psychology, 7*, 32–39.

Sullivan, H. S. (1953). *The interpersonal theory of psychiatry*. New York: Norton.

Truax, C. B., & Carkhuff, R. R. (1967). *Toward effective counseling and psychotherapy: Training and practice*. Chicago: Aldine.

Usher, C. H. (1989). Recognizing cultural bias in counseling theory and practice: The case of Rogers. *Journal of Multicultural Counseling and Development, 17*, 62–71.

Vontress, C. (1988). An existential approach to cross-cultural counseling. *Journal of Multicultural Counseling and Development, 16*, 73–83.

Williamson, E. (1958). Value orientation in counseling. *Personnel and Guidance Journal, 36*, 520–528.

Wrenn, C. G. (1962). The culturally encapsulated counselor. *Harvard Educational Review, 32*, 444–449.

CHAPTER THREE

Developmental Stages and Individual Counseling and Psychotherapy

David Capuzzi
Portland State University

Douglas R. Gross
Arizona State University

Course work in human development across the life span is considered essential to the education and supervision of counselors, psychologists, social workers, psychiatrists, psychiatric nurses, and other members of the helping professions. Our rationale for this chapter is based on the belief that the approach used during an individual session with a client is, to some extent, based on the counselor or therapist's beliefs about the nature of development. Such development includes the client's motives, capacities, responsibilities, stresses, and perceptions (Ivey, 1991; Thomas, 1990).

We also believe that the content of subsequent chapters in this book, which focus on specific theories and associated interventions for counseling and psychotherapy with clients, can be best understood and applied when supplemented by an awareness of human development across the life span. As noted by Thomas (1990), most counselors and therapists assume that every client is unique and that it is the responsibility of the counselor or therapist to understand this uniqueness and develop a treatment plan that best enhances the positive growth and development of the client. Although each client is unique, it is also true that each client can be expected to bear similarities to other clients who are in the same stage of development. The counselor's or therapist's prior knowledge of human development across the life span can assist in the anticipation of decisions, stresses, and capacities that are paramount in the life of a client. Such knowledge can also provide guidelines for deciding whether a particular client is likely to benefit from a series of interactive sessions based on specific theoretical concepts and interventions.

There are two major approaches to studying human development across the life span: the topical approach and the age-and-stage approach (Hughes & Noppe, 1985). In the topical approach, biological influences, processes of intellectual development, and socioemotional aspects of development become the focal points for insight into human development. In the age-and-stage approach, infancy and early childhood, later childhood, adolescence, early adult years, midlife years, and the final decades of life may be viewed along with age-related normative data as a means of providing information about the kinds of questions and issues a client may bring to an individual session. Both approaches have merit; however, the focus of this chapter will be to present the age-and-stage approach, particularly as described by Thomas (1990), as a paradigm for human development across the life span. Developmental patterns and concerns and typical presenting problems will be discussed in conjunction with each stage.

INFANCY AND EARLY CHILDHOOD: THE PRENATAL PERIOD THROUGH AGE 5

As noted by Lerner (1986), the most dramatic developmental changes of the entire life span occur during the first half decade of life: sperm and egg unite and develop from a single cell into a physically independent kindergarten child who speaks, sings, remembers, runs, plays, experiences emotions, and develops social skills. When a counselor or therapist is asked to assist with difficulties related to infants and young children, she must recognize that she will be dealing with more than one client; the child and the child's guardian(s) or parent(s) will also be involved (Thomas, 1990). Unless the child is at least three years of age, most of the counselor's or therapist's time will likely be spent with the adult caregiver(s).

Developmental Patterns and Concerns

Physical Size and Normality.   Most parents of newborns are initially concerned about whether the baby is physically normal. They ask for reassurance that the baby's organs are functioning properly and that the baby is free of disfigurements and disabilities of any kind. Parents of infants with disabilities will have many concerns about the future and need accurate information about future development, resources, and so on, which the counselor or therapist may be called upon to provide. Parents of infants and young children also may seek information that helps them assess physical growth and what present growth characteristics suggest for the child's future size, strength, and mobility.

Normative data about the way present growth characteristics predict future characteristics are available but should be used with considerable caution and restraint (Tanner, 1978). For example, predictions of adult height, which are based on an infant's length, are not very accurate during the first two years of life; however, when the child reaches age three, the correlation with adult height reaches +.8 (Tanner, 1978). A three-year-old who is taller than his classmates will likely be taller than other men during adulthood, but it is important to remember that estimates based on a +.8 correlation leave a substantial possibility for error or variation. When this child reaches adulthood, he could be as much as three inches above or below the earlier predicted height. It is important for counselors and therapists to use available predictive data with caution; it is also important for counselors and therapists to help parents prepare for probable outcomes. For example, parents may be concerned about a child who is well below the norm in height for her age group, and it is quite possible that this child will not grow up to be an adult of average height. The counselor or therapist may need to encourage such parents to prepare for the future by helping the child develop high self-esteem and an inherent sense of self-worth.

Cognitive and Language Development.   Sometimes parents think that the naive thoughts expressed by children are a result of children's lack of experience and information (Thomas, 1990). Parents may feel frustrated and disappointed when their attempts at instruction fail because they do not realize that children's thinking progresses through successive stages and that each stage has its own characteristics. Young children think differently from older children, adolescents, and adults.

Counselors and therapists can help parents most if they are knowledgeable about stages of children's mental growth. Swiss psychologist Jean Piaget (1896–1980) depicts cognitive development as progressing through four main stages, which take place from birth to adolescence (Piaget, 1972). The first two stages, sensorimotor (birth to age two) and preoperational thought (age two to age seven), take place during infancy and early childhood. It is important for counselors and therapists to be conversant with models that conceptualize cognitive development so they can be helpful to parents who may have concerns and questions or need information.

There are a number of additional characteristics of young children's thought processes that are also important to recognize (Lerner, 1986). For example, in counseling situations involving parent-child conflicts, an important element of such conflicts can be the failure of adults to understand the egocentric character of a preschooler's thinking. Young children are highly self-centered and interpret the world entirely from their own point of view. They do not understand that others may see things differently or that sharing and taking turns may be necessary. Parents who argue or reason with a very young child may need to be taught that the child may best be guided by learning to understand whether a particular behavior results in a reward or in the withdrawal of privileges. Young children also have difficulty distinguishing reality from fantasy, dealing with ideas that are not easily represented by concrete objects or events, understanding relationships and classifications, and using words and sentence structures accurately. The more background that counselors and therapists have in such areas, the more helpful they can be to families seeking assistance.

Social Relations.   During the first few years of a child's life, parents, siblings, and other family members are the people with whom the child has most contact. The manner in which the child learns to conduct personal-social interaction is very dependent upon what the caregivers model. Counselors and therapists often are faced with the challenge of helping parents recognize that their complaints about a child's socialization cannot be addressed without recognizing that the home environment they create and the behaviors they exhibit affect their child's behavior in social situations (Thomas, 1990). It is also necessary at times to help parents understand that a young child may have difficulty identifying characteristics of different social situations that may require adjustments in behavior. Parents may be feeling angry and disappointed with the behavior of their four-year-old in church and need encouragement and information to realize that the child must be taught that different social environments require adjustments in social interactions and other behaviors; a young child does not automatically have such insight. Counselors and therapists can also recognize that extreme delays in social development may be strong cues that the child is being raised in a home environment of abuse or neglect.

Sexuality.   Both Sigmund Freud (1938) and Erik Erikson (1963) have provided members of the helping profession with data relating to the fact that from the time of birth children exhibit sexual drives. Professionals generally agree that the way in which parents and other adults respond to young children's oral, anal, and genital interests has an important impact on the child's psychosocial adjustment as well as inherent feelings of self-worth. Parents who do not understand early psychosexual development may develop unrealistic expectations or destructive reactions to normal sexual curiosity or experimentation. Working with parents may involve teaching them parenting skills that help them avoid making children feel guilty or uncomfortable about their sexuality yet provide proper guidelines for self-expression that is not publicly offensive.

Perception of Self.   An important psychological component of infancy and early childhood is the process through which a child differentiates self from the environment to develop a perception of self in relation to others. Thomas (1990) notes:

> The newborn apparently has no notion of self in the adult sense of the term. However, by trial and error, the infant gradually recognizes that his or her fingers and toes are part of him or her, while the toy dog and baby bottle are not. Furthermore, how adequately young children meet parental expectations—the rewards and punishments they receive, the attention and neglect they experience—helps them to define who they are in relation to the world. (p. 114)

Such a process of self-identification and differentiation is extremely important during early formative years because by the time a child enters nursery school a distinctive self-concept has evolved. Counselors and therapists often work with parents of young children to help them maximize their ability to provide affection and protection, age-appropriate expectations, and a stable, predictable home environment so that opportunities to develop a positive, healthy perception of self are maximized.

Typical Presenting Problems

What a counselor or therapist knows about human development during infancy and early childhood can be extremely helpful in conjunction with the counseling or psychotherapy of one or both parents of a young child. The practitioner's expertise can also provide perspective for individual work with the preschooler. It is not uncommon for parents to seek some parent education because they want to know more about development during early childhood. Such knowledge will give them realistic expectations as well as ideas for how to relate to the child as he or she exhibits cognitive abilities different from those of adults or social skills that need to be redefined. Often, the counselor or therapist may need to refer parents to a parent-education group after a few individual sessions have provided some needed reassurance, information, or disciplinary guidelines. Counselors and therapists can anticipate some of the concerns of parents of young children by knowing in advance some of the issues parents typically raise as they cope with parenting an infant or young child.

Parents who do not agree about the way to relate to children, role-model for them, and provide standards of conduct or discipline often seek assistance when the family constellation becomes tense and conflictual. Counselors and therapists may be called upon to do some rather intense work with such parents to help them get in touch with the parental modeling they received in their respective families of origin. It may also be necessary to help such parents identify differences in child-rearing practices as modeled by their own parents and arrive at some sort of consensus about their own parenting styles and expectations. Such couples may also need to be tutored about new parenting concepts that they never experienced or observed during the years when they lived with parents and siblings.

Many parents present concerns about the physical development of a young child. As we discussed previously, cautious interpretation of age-related normative data may be quite helpful to parents who have not accessed such data in the past. Parents of children who have a physical disability also have questions and issues that catalyze the need for personal counseling. Many such couples need help first with the guilt they experience for conceiving a child with a disability and feel inadequate and guilty for having done so. They might also be grieving for the loss of a physically normal child or be emotionally or physically abusing the child because of their own anxiety about having brought such a child into the world.

The older the child, the greater the probability that the counselor or therapist will also conduct sessions with the child. There may be a number of issues to address during the process of working with a child with a disability. The first issue often relates to whether the counselor or therapist has the education and supervised clinical experiences to assist the child in overcoming the disability (for example, a speech or hearing impairment). If the counselor or therapist does not have special education preparation, then she will need to facilitate a referral for that purpose while focusing work with the child on accepting and coping with the disability in a positive way.

LATER CHILDHOOD: AGES 6 TO 12

As with children who are infants or preschoolers, it is unusual for an elementary-aged child to self-refer. It is more likely that a child in this stage will be referred by a parent or guardian or by a concerned member of the elementary school faculty or staff. In the case of referral by school personnel, it is possible that the school counselor will be called upon simultaneously to serve the child, the child's parents, and the child's teacher or teachers. Much of this work may be done on an individual basis, and it may involve some classroom or playtime-with-peers observation as well.

Developmental Patterns and Concerns

Physical Size and Appearance.   Later childhood is a period of time during which there is a reduction in the pace at which height, weight, and musculature increase (Hamill, 1977). Later childhood is a period of refinement and development of muscular coordination and strength in both large and small muscles (those used for running, jumping, and catching and those used for drawing, writing, and handling small utensils).

During this period, the growth rate of girls begins to exceed that of boys. At times, the fact that girls are taller and more mature than boys by the time they are 11 or 12 requires the counselor or therapist to provide both information and support to girls, who may feel out of place or self-conscious about their physical development, and to boys, who may feel awkward around their female peers and anxious about how and when they will progress into the next stage of physical maturation.

Cognition and Language Development.   Later childhood marks a critical period for intellectual development. When teachers and parents assist in their development by posing tasks that are manageable and interesting, children's cognitive and language abilities are nurtured in a way that promotes an enhanced sense of self-esteem and feelings of accomplishment. By the same token, if children become frustrated and discouraged or are bored by the structure and expectations of the educational environment, they may experience lowered self-esteem, less curiosity, and anger about demands of parents and other significant adults.

As we noted earlier, counselors and therapists can be more helpful to parents and teachers if they are knowledgeable about the stages of children's mental growth. Understanding development during the concrete-operations stage (ages 7 to 11) and during the formal-operations stage (beginning about age 12), as outlined by Piaget (1972), is critical for counselors employed in upper elementary or middle school settings or therapists working with families in clinical or private practice settings. In addition, it is important for counselors and therapists to have studied other models of childhood psychosocial development, such as those proposed by Erikson (1964) and Vygotsky (1962), so that expectations for children's learning can be challenging and achievable rather than disheartening and failure prone.

Social Relations.   Entering school is one of the most significant events that occurs during middle and later childhood. For children who have been in nursery school or kindergarten before entering first grade, the transition from home to school may be less upsetting than for children who have been at home full time with parents and few or no siblings. When children experience full-time student status for the first time, they are introduced to expectations and situations that may be very different from their at-home experience. For example, they may be introduced to different rules of conduct, tasks, or social groups. They may be asked to cooperate, share, and negotiate more than they have had to do at home. They may be introduced to racial, ethnic, and cultural diversities they feel unprepared for, and they may not know how to respond and interact comfortably. Counselors and therapists may be challenged not only by problem solving in relation to acting-out behaviors catalyzed by children's changed routine and new environment, but also by attitudes of parents who themselves may not have had opportunities to interact within a diverse social situation.

Sexuality.   As we noted earlier, there is a difference between boys and girls in the rate of physical maturation during later childhood. Girls typically begin to experience pubertal development one or two years before boys, and later childhood is a period during which children tend to spend the most time with peers of the same gender (with whom they have the most in common). Counselors and therapists can provide invaluable information and support to parents who may tend to push their children into activities with members of the opposite sex and worry that their child's preference for companions of the same gender is an indication of sexual orientation rather than a normal stage of human development (Thomas, 1990).

Perception of Self.   During early childhood, children have a tendency to remain egocentric and to have difficulty understanding that they cannot always be the center of attention and that others may not perceive a situation as they do (Thomas, 1990). However, throughout later childhood with its increasing, often school-related, opportunities for social interaction, children experience a variety of options for developing self-identification. Exposure to television, books, teachers, and other nonparental adult role models all provide perspective for children and help them experience an increasing sense of individuality and a vocabulary to describe "who I am." Counselors and therapists should encourage children's searches for self-identity and be alert to signs that indicate that such differentiation is not occurring.

Typical Presenting Problems

Counselors and therapists may be called upon to assist children, their teachers, and their parents with a variety of school-related concerns during the period of later childhood (Thomas, 1990). Unsatisfactory mastery of basic reading, vocabulary, writing, and mathematical skills may precipitate concern about present and future educational achievement. Shyness, competitiveness, crying, temper outbursts, unmanageable behavior in the classroom, truancy, and so on may cause concern at home or at school and become the basis for the presenting problem with which a counselor or therapist is called upon to assist. Counselors or therapists may need to serve simultaneously in individual and family counseling or psychotherapy, teacher consultation, and learning-specialist roles.

Family tensions and issues may also be the impetus for individual counseling or psychotherapy with a child in the 6- to 12-year-old age range. Tensions experienced by one or both parents may create marital discord that negatively impacts the child both at home and at school. Such tensions may be a result of career difficulties, financial pressures, or communication problems between parents. The assumption should not be made that a child in need of individual counseling or psychotherapy because of family problems comes from a traditional two-parent family in which each spouse has been married to the other since the marital dyad was formed. Blended families and single-parent families make up a large portion of the family constellations in North America; each creates unique adjustment challenges, and each is very likely to be formed when the child is in the developmental stage labeled as later childhood. In addition, adoptive families and families parented by gay or lesbian couples present a variety of other questions and concerns to a child old enough to recognize differences and ask questions but without enough experience to have developed needed coping strategies. Besides the individual needs created by family discord, families usually require counseling or psychotherapy in addition to any individual work done with the child or a specific member of the family. It behooves all counselors and therapists, whether in educational, mental health, private practice, or other settings, to obtain the education and supervised practice to work with families and to have a readily accessible referral network when caseloads are too high or families present problems beyond a practitioner's expertise.

This brief overview and discussion of typical presenting problems would not be complete without mentioning presenting problems connected with developmental delays. A developmental delay or lag refers to the fact that the child is behind other children of the same age and sex with respect to cognitive, emotional, physical, or social growth. Because such a delay may be caused by genetic endowment, environment, or the integration of both, counseling and psychotherapy require expertise in diagnosis and treatment planning and may present special challenges to the helping professional.

ADOLESCENCE: AGES 12 TO 24

Adolescence is a time of rapid change and, quite often, frequent turmoil. On the one hand, young people appreciate the stability of a home with parents who provide consistency, expectations, and structure; on the other hand, adolescents often perceive the home situation as presenting barriers to their developing independence and identity. As the peer group becomes more and more important during the period of adolescence, the teenager may feel pressure to live up to the expectations of parents and other family members at the same time she is encouraged by peers to experiment, resist conformity, and venture into uncharted terrain. Counselors and therapists who provide assistance to adolescents may be expected to deal with a number of concerns that are stressful not only for the adolescent but also for family members. Issues connected with educational achievement, developing sexuality, drugs, gang membership, and suicide may exert intense pressure on adolescents and their families to seek solutions and answers to problems and situations that even the most mature and experienced individual would find difficult to solve.

Developmental Patterns and Concerns

Physical Size and Appearance.   Adolescence is a period of rapid physical change, the timing of which can be influenced by nutrition, exercise, medical care, and education about health practices. Although the pattern and sequence of changes in adolescent men and women are the same, the time at which puberty occurs varies. In general, pubertal changes in girls occur one to two years earlier than in boys. During early adolescence it is common for girls to be taller and heavier than boys, who for a time may seem childish and immature to female peers of the same age (Roche & Davila, 1972). The timing of development, height, weight, body hair and configuration, and musculature varies. For example, in girls menstruation may begin as early as 9 or as late as 16; penis growth in boys can start as early as 11 or as late as 14 or 15. Whether the physical maturation of an adolescent is early or late can have an effect on such characteristics as self-esteem, personal and social skills, and anxiety (Jones, 1965; Peskin, 1973). However, as the individual becomes older, early or late development seems to have less of an effect. By the age of 30 or 40 most differences between early and late maturing individuals have disappeared (Thomas, 1990).

Cognitive Development.   In Piaget's stages (1972), the highest level of cognitive development, the formal-operations stage, is achieved during adolescence. This is the stage in which the individual can develop abstract thinking ability, the capacity to apply generalizations, and the comprehension to identify relationships that are not usually operative during early and later childhood. During this stage, the study of history, mathematics, language, biology, physics, literature, and so on can be approached less literally and concretely. Such advanced cognitive abilities are not achieved suddenly or uniformly. Some adolescents may excel in abstract thinking ability as it is applied in mathematics and simultaneously experience extreme difficulty with abstractions as they relate to history or literature classes (Thomas, 1990).

Counselors and therapists may find that some adolescents need more time to develop the sophisticated and complex thought patterns often demanded in secondary or postsecondary education. Adolescents who begin experiencing academic difficulties because of a slower rate of cognitive development or because of a cognitive disability may respond by becoming depressed or truant or by creating classroom management problems. Diminished self-esteem and lowered aspiration levels for the future may be the result of an unsuccessful academic career. To minimize the possibility that a school experience could effect emotional damage and less-than-optimal learning opportunities, it is important for counselors and therapists to know how to assess an adolescent's cognitive development so that educational and treatment planning can be accomplished in a way that supports the individual during the adolescent period of human development. Some theorists, such as Klaus Riegel (1973), propose that cognitive abilities continue to develop beyond the ages and stages suggested by Piaget. Such alternative models for understanding cognitive development may provide insight for counselors and therapists working with adolescents who appear to be developing cognitive capacities differently from many of their peers.

Social Relations.   The period of adolescence is one in which acceptance by and popularity in peer groups is of extreme importance (Hughes & Noppe, 1985). Studies show that adolescents identify a number of traits as desirable and as a prerequisite for popularity (Rice, 1981; Snyder, 1972). Being nice looking, outgoing, involved in athletics and school or community activities; having the right friends, clothes, and cars are all examples of what many adolescents aspire to in order to achieve acceptance by peers. Parental social and moral values, which usually exert a strong influence during early, middle, and late childhood, diminish in importance during adolescence as peers and images furnished by various media (television, films, radio, magazines) become increasingly important models for adolescents' behavior (Thomas, 1990). The unisex groups of later childhood gradually become heterosexual groups; heterosexual groups eventually break down into couples when dating begins, which can be as early as 12 for some adolescents (Hughes & Noppe, 1985). A rather obvious function of dating is selection of a partner, but many adolescents do not see dating as preparation for marriage. Rice (1981), for example, cited recreation, companionship without marriage, status and achievement, and opportunity for sexual experimentation as reasons adolescents give for dating.

The search for identity becomes a major developmental task as adolescents are presented by ever-expanding options for role models, education, and career choices. Many adolescents overidentify with cliques or well-known personalities to the point of losing, for a period of months or years, any identity of their own. A major task for many if not most adolescents is to resolve the identity crisis so that they can enter adulthood with a clear set of values and a positive concept of their appearance, abilities, potentials, and plans for the future.

Sexuality.   The issue of how to manage the sexual drives that escalate with the arrival of puberty is of great concern to most adolescents. The initiation and extent of heterosexual exploration during adolescence often depends upon peer pressure, the need to prove one's desirability to members of the opposite sex, and a society that encourages adult experience at earlier and earlier ages. Most studies since the 1950s have provided evidence that increasing numbers of adolescent men and women have been sexually intimate; the most dramatic reported increases have taken place among adolescent women (Dreyer, 1982). As noted by Thomas (1990), the confusion, guilt, and disappointment that may arise during this process of sexual exploration may bring many adolescents to counseling or psychotherapy. Problems connected with teenage pregnancy, venereal disease, and AIDS may also contribute to the need for assistance from a counselor or therapist.

Heterosexual exploration is not the only issue connected with adolescent sexuality that causes dissonance and discomfort. When adolescents become oriented to members of the same gender and begin to deal with the identity issues, societal prejudices, and myths connected with gay and lesbian life-styles, they may find it very difficult to handle inherent desires for sexual intimacy and questions about self-worth. Depression and suicidal ideation are extremely high among the gay and lesbian adolescent population (Capuzzi & Gross, 1989). We cannot overemphasize the need for counseling and psychotherapy opportunities facilitated by counselors or therapists who understand the importance of assisting such adolescents with questions connected to self-acceptance, self-esteem, honesty, and so on.

This brief overview of adolescent sexuality would not be complete without noting that masturbation is an almost universal practice during adolescence, particularly among males (Hughes & Noppe, 1985). Because some ethnic and religious groups continue to promote the concept that masturbation is sinful, many adolescents experience guilt and confusion about what is acceptable as a means of expressing and managing powerful sexual urges.

Typical Presenting Problems

There are numerous ways in which adolescents and their families present their problems to school and mental health professionals. Completion of secondary education and graduation from high school is generally considered a rite of passage and a transition from total dependence on the family to eventual separation from the family and independence. Therefore, questions, issues, and problems relating to secondary education and career planning may be the focus of much concern. The high-achieving, ambitious student may have questions about options for postsecondary education. The concerned parents of a potential school dropout may need support and reassurance. The gifted yet rebellious adolescent may need to vent emotion related to parental demands and expectations. The undecided student may need assistance provided by career information, aptitude testing, or assessment of interests. The high school years are a time of accelerated academic demands and increased interest in educational achievement and planning for the future.

The identity issues experienced by adolescents may precipitate the initiation of counseling or psychotherapy in a variety of ways. For example, adolescents concerned about body image may develop eating disorders in a frantic attempt to achieve the "ideal" body contours and image promoted by the media or to maintain a weight category for athletic competition, dance, or a potential career as a model. Often the young person experiencing difficulty with acceptance by positively focused peers may identify with a gang to simulate feelings of belonging and a sense of purpose (even if gang members engage in illegal activities or brutalize other members of society). Many adolescents experiment with, use, and eventually abuse alcohol and other substances in an effort to overcome feelings of low self-worth or affiliate with peers who engage in drug-related activities and socialization. Depression also afflicts adolescents struggling with identity issues, and suicidal ideation has escalated to the point that suicide is the second leading cause of death among the adolescent population (Capuzzi & Gross, 1989).

Many teenagers who have been sexually active are faced with decisions related to terminating a pregnancy, placing an infant for adoption, or parenting; increasing numbers of adolescents are HIV positive or diagnosed with AIDS. As we noted earlier, gay or lesbian adolescents are often confused and guilt-ridden or suffering from lowered self-esteem.

THE EARLY ADULT YEARS: AGES 21 TO 40

The two decades spanning the 20s and 30s represent a busy developmental period for most individuals as they progress from the more carefree days of youth to choosing a partner, establishing a career, and perhaps raising a family. This is the period of life during which the individual is expected to become fully independent; for many, it is a period of high stress and concern about making it in a competitive society. This is also a period of time during which the ideals of youth must be adjusted to meet the demands of reality.

Developmental Patterns and Concerns

Physical and Psychophysical Growth. Although genetic endowment and growth experiences from childhood and adolescence account for many differences among individuals' physical condition during early adulthood, there are other variables that must be taken into consideration. Nutrition, exercise, and communicable disease; use, abuse, or avoidance of drugs; stress, type of occupational environment (including pollution level and noise), and forms of leisure and recreation can all affect the young adult's physical condition (Thomas, 1990). From the mid-20s until the end of life, individuals experience a decline in muscle strength, stamina, reaction time, visual and auditory perception, and skin elasticity (Troll, 1982). Weight can easily increase because many young adults fail to alter their eating habits even though the calorie intake required for rapid physical growth and development during childhood and adolescence is no longer needed. It is important to realize that the style of life the individual adopts influences the degree of physical fitness, stamina, and energy experienced during the period of early adulthood. Many young adults seek support for initiating diets and exercise programs to lose weight and enhance their sense of well-being only to find that weight returns and stress escalates once the regime has been completed and established patterns are again followed. Many young adults experiencing distress over their physical appearance and condition must face the prospect of making permanent life-style changes or accepting an altered body image and general level of energy.

Intellectual Development. As noted by Thomas (1990), evidence about the increase and decline of mental abilities during the adult years has been derived from three main sources: biographical accounts of people's productivity in the sciences and the arts, analyses of adults' test scores of aptitude and intelligence measures, and people's work performance. According to the histories of numerous well-known scientists, writers, artists, and historians, the general pattern of achievement indicates that the decade of the 30s is the time of peak performance for most individuals. Studies of adult performance on intelligence tests show a general pattern of increase until the early 20s, a stable period until around age 30, and a decline thereafter. It should be noted, however, that the decline after age 30 occurs principally on measures of response speed, memory span, and nonverbal reasoning. It should also be noted that these skills depend more on the efficiency of the body's perceptual-neural system rather than experience and education. Investigations of work performance indicate that for jobs that have advanced education or training requirements, people's scores on intelligence tests are not related to job success. (Advancement has more to do with motivation, personality traits, or other special abilities.) The research on memory and other aspects of cognitive capacities during the early adult years is too complex and conflicted to include in a single chapter on human development across the life span. Readers should refer to textbooks such as Hughes and Noppe (1985) and Lerner (1986) for more complete information.

Social Development.   During the early adult years, social relationships usually occur in four settings: the family, the occupational setting, the location of recreation and avocational pursuits, and locations related to daily routines (grocery stores, traveling to and from work, etc.) (Thomas, 1990). Each of these locations presents unique options and challenges for the young adult.

Today, more so than 15 or 20 years ago, young adults are free to establish any one of a number of life-styles with respect to family living arrangements. The traditional family with married spouses who parent and support their biological children until they launch their own careers and families is just one of many possibilities. Young adults may live together as unwed companions with members of the opposite or the same gender; the relationships may be platonic or sexual. Married couples are free to have their own children, remain childless, or adopt. Marriages can be ended, and custodial parents can remarry to create blended families. It is not at all unusual or unacceptable for young adults to remain single by choice and to prefer solitary life-styles more than companionship with another individual. Gay and lesbian couples often decide to parent biological or adopted children. The roles connected with these possible life-styles can be quite complex. Young adults may find themselves faced with social constraints, obstacles, or prejudices from those around them (whether from similar, older, or younger age groups) who do not understand or accept a particular life-style chosen by a young adult.

Occupational settings present different social expectations and challenges. Many 20- to 40-year-old adults view this period of time as the point at which they must establish themselves in a career field, often after completing extensive educational preparation, and begin an upward climb to positions of greater responsibility and financial remuneration. Expectations for extra unpaid hours at work, entertaining, and collaboration with colleagues who may or may not share similar value systems can create conflicts, stresses, and questions about initial career decisions. Often adjustments have to be made in the domestic setting as job demands take time away from a partner, spouse, or children. This is a period in which career mobility may require relocation to a new community or reentry into additional educational or vocational training in order to retain a current position, adapt to a changing occupational scene, or become eligible for better positions. Such changes and transitions usually present new social expectations and roles as individuals relocate into new communities or adapt to student status.

Choices of recreational and avocational pursuits require young adults to enter social networks in which the expectations of others are focused on diversion from family or occupational settings in order to lower stress, obtain exercise, or develop a new skill or hobby. Acquaintances that are made and friendships that are established may introduce individuals to a network of adults completely separate from family, extended family, immediate neighbors, and colleagues at work. Social amenities may be more connected with the setting (local bowling alley versus a country club) or with the activity (deep-sea fishing versus duplicate bridge). Young adults may acquire a completely new circle of acquaintances and circulate in a different social stratum requiring different interpersonal skills and social amenities than those required at home and work.

Finally, young adults must adjust to simultaneous networks that they contact during daily or weekly routines. Child-care providers in nursery or day-care facilities, clerks in grocery stores, mechanics in automotive repair shops, and home repair and maintenance personnel all introduce separate sets of social expectations and demands. Certainly, young adults are faced with a variety of new social expectations as they move from the home of a parent or guardian to an independent living situation in the community.

Sexuality.   The dissolution of marriages and cohabitation without marriage has become common; yet there are many members of the North American culture who view divorce, serial marriage, cohabitation without marriage, living alone, or living with a person of the same gender as an unacceptable departure from tradition (Thomas, 1990). As a result, numerous young adults seek counseling or psychotherapy for resolution of problems created by living arrangements or sexual expression. In addition, earlier laws governing marriage and sexual behavior remain in effect while a widening range of options for sexual expression and habitation are practiced. In many communities attempts are being made to remove constitutional rights from individuals or couples whose life-styles do not conform to expectations established by past generations. Given this juxtaposition of traditional and alternative life-styles and legislative frameworks, many young adults find themselves the brunt of discrimination, whether they follow a traditional, couples-parenting-children life-style; one that is single and living alone; one that includes divorce with plans to remarry; or one of gay or lesbian commitment. Issues relating to choosing a partner, deciding to separate and divorce, child rearing, sexual orientation, sexual dysfunction, and so on are common to the caseload of any counselor or therapist working with this age group.

Typical Presenting Problems

The decades of the 20s and 30s present demands and expectations for independence and inner directedness that in many ways can be as stressful and confusing as those experienced during adolescence. Issues related to the family and whether and how to establish one can take on many forms, directions, and parameters. A young man and woman considering marriage, for example, may come for premarital counseling to identify compatibilities upon which to build the relationship or to examine differing styles of decision making or communicating that need to be better understood. Recently married couples may need assistance with money management, sexual adjustment, or conflict resolution. Child-rearing practices may need clarification, or career decisions may need to be discussed. Couples who have divorced and blended families that were originally established in a prior marriage, two men or two women involved in a long-term relationship, adults or couples considering abortion or adoption, dual-career couples stressed by escalating work demands, and upwardly mobile individuals faced with relocation requirements are all examples of the kinds of situations that may be brought to the counselor or therapist whose clientele includes young adults.

Occupational pursuits become so closely linked with the self-identity of the working adult that career-related issues may become a primary focus for young adults seeking the assistance of a counselor or therapist. Questions about career choice, vertical and horizontal moves within a career field, work-related demands that diminish time or quality of time with family members, or the importance of additional education for changing occupational opportunities are all examples of career-related questions posed by adults in the second and third decades of life. It behooves every counselor and therapist to be well grounded in theories of career development, sources of educational and occupational information, and appraisal instruments designed to help clients assess career-related interests, aptitudes, and abilities.

Because life in the last decade of the twentieth century has become complex, competitive, and linked by mass-communication systems to customs and events in other countries, it is important for the counselor or therapist to be able to help young adults develop interests in recreational and avocational pursuits in order to lower stress and maintain perspective. Many young adults who present problems that have a psychosomatic component need help with learning how to relax and enjoy leisure time in the fullest sense. The key to maintaining physical and emotional health is very much linked to the ability of the individual to follow a pace that presents opportunities for new learning and achievement as well as time for relaxation with family and friends.

THE MIDLIFE YEARS: AGES 40 TO 60

Some of the terminology often applied to the middle years, such as midlife crisis, the empty-nest syndrome, and the declining years, imply that this period in life is one of stress, adjustment, and loss. Such implications are unfortunate because many factors can make an individual's middle years productive, positive, and rewarding. For example, the experience accumulated during the first decades of life can compensate for declines in physical strength, stamina, and agility. A chosen life-style, which may be a combination of choice and luck, can result in a person of 60 who looks and functions like someone who is 40 or 45 years of age. For example, the life-style of a chronic alcoholic is different than that of someone who is careful about diet and exercise, and a high school dropout attempting to support several children will experience a different quality of life than two high-salaried executives with one child. A person's genetic endowment also governs many of the events connected with the normal aging process, such as weight gain, reduction in strength or auditory acuity, and ability to understand stress.

Developmental Patterns and Concerns

Physical Changes.   When the years of early adulthood come to an end, a number of physical functions typically become less efficient. The heart and lungs do not work as well, food is not metabolized as efficiently, muscles do not readily increase in strength, and the kidneys do not filter waste products as efficiently. When individuals take relatively good care of themselves and have regular physical examinations and assessments, these changes in bodily functions do not significantly impact their ability to lead a normal life. It is often difficult, however, for middle-aged people to admit that their physical abilities are on the decline and that they may need to alter physical and emotional demands or activities, which they are not as well equipped for as they were during earlier periods. Some middle-aged adults may ignore their increasing susceptibility to fatigue, extremes of heat and cold, stress, physical competition, or demands on the job. A physical crisis, such as a heart attack, the need for surgery, or the development of hypertension, can come as a surprise and result in the need for counseling or psychotherapy and mandated life-style changes. Counseling or psychotherapy may need to include such topics as information about physical changes during midlife and the need to alter health practices, opportunities for emotional catharsis, and a reassessment of goals so that a transition to a new life-style can be accomplished.

Mental Abilities.   In general, it is expected that middle-aged people have a little more difficulty adopting new viewpoints and learning new material than they did during adolescence and early adulthood. It should be noted, however, that the special skills and wisdom that middle-aged adults have gained through experience, and their capability of applying such knowledge to familiar situations and types of problems, will most likely remain intact (Rybash, Hoyer, & Roodin, 1986).

An understanding of intellectual functioning in middle age is useful to counselors and therapists assisting clients who are considering midlife changes in their careers. Such clients will probably be more successful in areas relating to past experience than in ones that require different kinds of learning. It is extremely important, however, to be careful when assuming that normative trends can be generally applied; there are decided differences in how individuals bring intellectual capacities to bear on new learning situations during middle age.

Social Relations.   Middle-aged adults with children typically find themselves launching their children into young adulthood. For the first time in years, adults may find themselves unfettered with the daily responsibilities connected with parenting. Couples may be alone again for the first time in well over 20 years. For some middle-aged adults this adjustment is made easily, and new opportunities for freedom, recreation, and socializing with friends are welcomed and enjoyed. Other couples, however, may find these changes difficult and grieve for the loss of their children or find spending time with each other more stressful than anticipated. When children select partners or careers or decide to relocate, parents may readily adapt or resist such decisions, depending on their own levels of self-esteem, how much they respect and trust the judgment of their adult children, and the degree to which children still remain dependent on parents for emotional or financial support. Midlife is also a time during which adults become grandparents; such an addition to the individual's self-concept may or may not be readily or happily integrated.

Career settings may provide opportunities for either an enhanced sense of well-being and feelings of increased productivity or deteriorating collegial relationships and declines in job adjustment capacity. Some middle-aged adults are stimulated by change and interested in the new perspectives brought to the work setting by younger employees. Other experienced employees are stressed by expectations, policies, and philosophy changes; new employees may be viewed as threats to job security. Sometimes middle-aged employees have advanced to positions of administrative and supervisory responsibility; some individuals may find such positions challenging and exciting, while others may find them too demanding in terms of interpersonal relationships, conflict resolution, and evaluation of subordinates. Changes in physical capacity (such as those resulting from heart problems or other serious illnesses) may create havoc with career self-concept when changes in physical status necessitate a move to a less demanding position.

Sexuality.   The term *climacteric*, or change of life, identifies the marked decrease in reproductive capacity in women and men. The average age for the end of menstruation in women is about age 50 in industrial societies such as ours; however, the event can occur as early as the late 30s or as late as the middle to late 50s (Notman, 1980). As noted by Thomas (1990):

> A set of characteristics traditionally, associated with "the change of life" comprise what has been called *the menopause syndrome.* Physical conditions within the syndrome include hot flushes, night sweats, and accelerated loss of calcium from the bones (osteoporosis). Some women also report painful coitus (dyspareunia) resulting from the vagina becoming shorter and narrower, accompanied by a decline in the vagina's ability to lubricate and expand. All of these symptoms appear related to reduced activity of the ovaries and to diminishing estrogen levels. In other words, the evidence suggests that such conditions are directly caused by alterations in body chemistry that occur with the cessation of menstruation. (p. 288)

A psychophysical effect usually included in the syndrome is insomnia. Until the past 20 or 30 years, a widespread conviction in the psychiatric community was that the climacteric, particularly in women, often precipitated a type of psychotic depression referred to as involutional melancholia. As a consequence, members of the general public came to anticipate menopause with great apprehension. More recent studies, however, suggest that this earlier conceptualization was in error and should not be accepted as fact.

Compared with younger men, almost all older men need more time to achieve an erection, have erections that never reach the maximum levels of their younger counterparts, and find that their erections are slower to rebound after a partial loss (Belsky, 1984). Among men of middle age, sexual adequacy can lessen because of mental or physical fatigue, boredom, preoccupation with their jobs or other concerns, and apprehension that their sexual performance will diminish. Many men feel unattractive when their hair begins to thin and grey and weight accumulates in their midsection.

Typical Presenting Problems

Middle-aged adults experience numerous anxieties, problems, and questions that may lead them to the counselor's or therapist's office:

- Individuals who have experienced interpersonal conflicts with neighbors, partners, and colleagues may find that they are experiencing escalating difficulties with those around them and seek to understand and alter what may be a long-standing pattern of communication.
- Mothers who have dedicated two or three decades to parenting may now find their lives without meaning or occupation since children have left home.
- Individuals may experience career dissatisfaction because hopes have not been realized, demands have become too stressful, or the job market has changed.
- Individuals who are distressed because of the death of a spouse or friends of long standing may experience difficulty with the grieving process.
- Individuals may be concerned about entry into the final decades of life.
- Individuals may worry about retirement planning or feel concerned about the impending loss of a career identity.

These presenting problems are typical, but the list is by no means exhaustive. Any one of the concerns in the above list could form the basis for numerous one-to-one sessions. For example, a woman who finds herself at a loss once her youngest child has left home to pursue additional education or become established in separate living quarters may need help redefining purpose and focus for day-to-day life. She may wish to explore educational or vocational training options or need encouragement and direction in the process of initiating and completing a job search. She may be in the position to explore volunteer options in the local community or even consider the possibility of becoming a foster parent. In any event, she will need support, empathy, and information to partially redefine her role in a way that is meaningful to her.

Both men and women may need assistance if they find during midlife that they have been unable to realize career goals established at an earlier date. They may experience feelings of frustration, disappointment, or depression and need help to become more aware of accomplishments, strengths, and past contributions. They may be able to identify other reasonably attainable career objectives that they had not previously considered and would find challenging and satisfying.

Individuals who are distressed because of the death of a spouse or friends may find the opportunity to work with a counselor or therapist beneficial. They may need time with a professional who can help them experience the stages of grief and loss so they can adjust to their losses and move forward in their own lives, making new connections with other people or focusing more energy on an established relationship. They may need reassurance that the stages of grief they are experiencing are to be expected and are part of the healing process.

Concerns about aging, diminished or altered sexual capacity, and impending retirement all create issues and generate the need for decision making and integration of new information. Such presenting problems can be expected from clients in the midlife period of the life cycle, and exploration of such areas can help clients lead happier, more productive lives.

THE FINAL DECADES: AGE 60 AND BEYOND

We realize that identifying age 60 as the age at which individuals progress into the final decades of life is an arbitrarily chosen demarcation. The task of identifying the point at which one becomes an older adult is difficult because of individual differences in genetics, life-style, and attitude. Botwinick (1984) proposed four categories as phases of the final decades: the young-old (55–64), middle-old (65–74), old-old (75–84), and very old (85 and over). As both men and women survive to more advanced ages, the need for counselors and therapists interested in working with older adults becomes even more important.

Developmental Patterns and Concerns

Physical Changes.   Studies in the 1980s indicated that heart disease was the leading cause of death among the elderly (Botwinick, 1984). This was followed by malignant neoplasms (such as cancer), cerebrovascular diseases (such as strokes), influenza and pneumonia, arteriosclerosis, diabetes mellitus, and accidents. Although the immediate cause of death in the elderly is usually listed as heart disease, cancer, and so on, it should be noted that the more basic cause has to do with the gradual failure of the individual's immune system (Thomas, 1990). In addition, the natural healing mechanisms for repairing damaged parts—such as broken bones, torn muscles, and kidney infections—do not operate as well, resulting in longer recoveries or partial recoveries. The body's mechanism for controlling cellular growth can also malfunction; cancer is a prime example of cellular malfunction, as are prostate disorders in men.

Numerous other physical problems bring pain to the elderly and make it more difficult to pursue activities that bring enjoyment. Visual and auditory acuity diminish as cataracts or glaucoma interfere with vision and the delicate bones that convey sound to the ear's receptor nerve deteriorate and cause deafness. The flexibility of the spine diminishes as cartilage between the bones of the spine becomes depressed; joints of the limbs undergo changes that result in arthritis and bursitis, and bladder malfunctions create discomfort and embarrassment. As time passes, older adults await two inevitable conditions: decline in abilities they once had, and eventually death. When earlier dreams of future accomplishment and pleasure become less tenable, many elderly adults experience loss of enthusiasm, depression, and frustration that requires counseling assistance.

Mental Abilities.   There is a substantial body of knowledge about changes in the mental abilities of the elderly (Belsky, 1984; Salthouse, 1982). It should be emphasized, however, that there are large differences among elderly individuals of the same age in respect to how well they have maintained earlier intellectual and psychomotor skills. Changes in cognitive skills have been identified through experiments on reasoning and decision making, memory, spatial ability, and the way the aged view themselves. Often the perception of others helps determine both the older adult's self-concept and behavior. As noted by Thomas (1990), there are at least three implications of stereotypical thinking about the elderly:

1. Generic stereotypes can influence the way in which older people are treated.

2. If older adults accept stereotypes as valid, they may behave in a manner that is not in their own best interest.

3. Counselors' and therapists' approaches to working with the elderly can be affected by the way typical stereotypes influence the practitioners.

It should be obvious to the reader that stereotypical thinking about the elderly, if accepted without question, can contaminate the process of counseling or psychotherapy with the older adult. We refer you to a more thorough discussion of the topic by Thomas (1990) in his chapter on the final decades of life.

Social Relations.   The personal and social adjustment of older adults seems to be linked to daily living arrangements, which influence the older adult's sense of emotional and material support and control and the availability of assistance when it is needed. By the mid-1980s, people over 65 formed about 12 percent of the total U.S. population (Kovar, 1986). An estimated 94 percent of these older adults lived in the community rather than in nursing homes or other facilities. One-third of these older adults lived alone; two-thirds, mostly women, lived with others. Interestingly, even most of the elderly population that lived alone were leading happy, productive lives if they had access to adequate social support through friends, family, social-service agencies, and the telephone.

Understanding the social support systems of the elderly can enhance the ability of the counselor or therapist to suggest changes in an individual's network of social support that might improve the mental and physical health of clients. In some studies, for example, it has been found that access to a telephone on a regular basis is associated with greater life satisfaction, self-esteem, and reduced mental health problems (Revicki & Mitchell, 1986). Another study suggested that older adults who had no nearby family used the hospital emergency room 7 to 30 times more often than older adults who resided in close proximity to family members (Coe, Wolinsky, Miller, & Prendergast, 1985). Yet another study indicated that with respect to home care provided to elderly who are chronically disabled, assistance provided by friends and relatives was usually preferred to that provided by social service agencies (Soldo, 1985). In a rather extensive study with over 2,500 respondents from the northwestern part of the United States, Lee and Ishii-Kuntz (1987) discovered that increased social interaction with friends served to enhance morale and decrease feelings of loneliness. Interaction with family members, to whom the study participants were connected because of family ties, had no influence. One possible implication for counselors and therapists is to realize that the elderly benefit from interacting with friends they have chosen and that support and contact with family members alone may not be enough.

An overview of the large body of research that is available on this topic is beyond the scope of a single subsection of one chapter. It is important for counselors and therapists to have enough education and background relating to this aspect of human development across the life span to know how to intervene in positive and constructive ways with older adult clients.

Typical Presenting Problems

Counselors and therapists working with elderly clients can expect to encounter clients who present problems such as the following:

- Depression due to feelings of loneliness and loss of purpose. Without the structure provided by the responsibilities of day-to-day work and family responsibility, many elderly adults, who do not build other meaning through hobbies, volunteer work, or time with friends, begin to lose initiative and energy. They may need support to overcome tendencies to sit idle, withdraw, and remain uninvolved.

- Discontent and discouragement because of poor health, impaired mobility, and lack of previous levels of stamina and energy. Such adults may dwell on their physical complaints and actually exacerbate certain physical conditions because of lack of interests and involvements upon which to refocus. They, too, may need encouragement to network and establish meaningful ways to structure time.

- Suicidal ideation because of feelings of loss and grief when long-term partners, spouses, and friends die. These individuals may find it difficult to attempt to initiate new friendships and easier to simply give up on life.

- Severe financial problems resulting from a steadily increasing cost of living combined with a fixed or nearly fixed retirement income. Basic nutritional and medical needs may be rapidly neglected. The cost of heating and cooling during cold and hot weather may also become problematic, and subsequent health risks may develop.

- Distress over a change in cognitive abilities. Sometimes the elderly forget where they put things, can't remember to keep appointments or to take medications, or repeat stories they just told a few minutes ago or several times during a period of a few days.

- Concern over the loss of sexual interest, especially if a partner continues to show a desire to be intimate.

- Worry about the cost of impending surgery and concern about recovery if the assistance of nearby friends and family is not available.

As with previous subsections in this chapter that overview typical presenting problems of a specific age group, it is not possible to provide a complete list. The important point is that the well-prepared counselor or therapist must be cognizant of typical developmental concerns and issues. Many counselors and therapists, particularly those interested in working with an elderly population, specialize in this life stage and develop a clientele on that basis.

IMPLICATIONS FOR THEORY AND APPLICATIONS

Part 2 of this book presents overviews of current approaches to counseling and psychotherapy. In conjunction with each approach, both the theory and applications are described. Each of these approaches introduces the reader to a framework around which to view the client and to develop a diagnosis and treatment plan. Each approach has strengths, and each, if appropriately applied, will effect constructive growth and development.

It is important to remember, however, that use of a particular model is dependent not only upon the expertise and preparation of the provider of counseling or therapy, but also upon the suitability of the approach for a particular client. Familiarity with human development across the life span assists the practitioner in determining applicability. For example, a Gestalt approach might be suitable for a cognitively able adult, but it would not be suitable for a child whose mental capacities are in an early stage of cognitive development. A person-centered model might be extremely effective with an adult client sorting through some issues related to careers or relationships, but it might not provide all that is necessary to assist an adolescent confused by issues of developing sexuality or questions about improving communication skills with parents or peers.

Knowledge of human development across the life span also provides counselors and therapists with a method of determining which presenting problems are appropriately associated with a particular stage of life and which ones have been left unresolved for so long that they have become chronic and debilitating to the health and wellness of the client. It is not unusual for a parent to experience a feeling of loss after the youngest child establishes an independent life-style separate from the family home; it *is* unusual for that same parent not to have established new meaning and focus after a reasonable period of months or years.

We believe in the value of the models available to the practitioner for use with clients. Use of these models must be tempered, however, with the needs and capacities of clients at various stages of the life cycle.

REFERENCES

Belsky, J. K. (1984). *The psychology of aging*. Monterey, CA: Brooks/Cole.

Botwinick, J. (1984). *Aging and behavior* (3rd ed.). New York: Springer.

Capuzzi, D., & Gross, D. R. (Eds.). (1989). *Youth at risk: A resource for counselors, teachers and parents*. Alexandria, VA: American Association for Counseling and Development.

Coe, R. M., Wolinsky, F. D., Miller, D. K., & Prendergast, J. M. (1985). Elderly persons without family support networks and use of health services. *Research on Aging, 7*(4), 617–622.

Dreyer, P. H. (1982). Sexuality during adolescence. In B. B. Wolman (Ed.), *Handbook of developmental psychology*. Englewood Cliffs, NJ: Prentice-Hall.

Erikson, E. H. (1963). *Childhood and society* (2nd ed.). New York: Norton.

Erikson, E. H. (1964). *Insight and responsibility*. New York: Norton.

Freud, S. (1938). *An outline of psychoanalysis* (1973 ed.). London: Hogarth.

Hamill, P. V. V. (1977). NCHS growth curves for children. In *Vital and health statistics: Series II, no. 165, data from the national health survey*. Washington, DC: U.S. Government Printing Office.

Hughes, F. P., & Noppe, L. D. (1985). *Human development across the life span*. St. Paul, MN: West.

Ivey, A. E. (1991). *Developmental strategies for helpers: Individual, family, and network interventions*. Belmont, CA: Brooks/Cole.

Jones, M. C. (1965). Psychological correlates of somatic development. *Child Development, 29*, 491–501.

Kovar, M. G. (1986). Aging in the eighties, age 65 years and over and living alone, contacts with family, friends, and neighbors. In *NCHS advance data, no. 116* (pp. 1–5). Washington, DC: U.S. Department of Health and Human Services.

Lee, G. R., & Ishii-Kuntz, M. (1987). Social interaction, loneliness, and emotional well-being among the elderly. *Research on Aging, 9*(4), 459–482.

Lerner, R. M. (1986). *Concepts and theories of human development* (2nd ed.). New York: Random House.

Notman, M. T. (1980). Changing roles for women at mid-life. In W. H. Norman & T. J. Scaramella (Eds.), *Mid-life: Developmental and clinical issues* (pp. 85–109). New York: Brunner/Mazel.

Peskin, H. (1973). Influence of the developmental schedule of puberty on learning and ego functioning. *Journal of Youth and Adolescence, 2*, 273–290.

Piaget, J. (1972). *Psychology and epistemology*. London: Penguin.

Revicki, D. A., & Mitchell, J. (1986). Social support factor structure in the elderly. *Research on Aging, 8*(2), 232–248.

Rice, F. P. (1981). *The adolescent: Development, relationships, and culture* (3rd ed.). Boston: Allyn & Bacon.

Riegel, K. F. (1973). Dialectic operations: The final period of cognitive development. *Human Development, 16*, 346–370.

Roche, A. F., & Davila, G. H. (1972). Late adolescent growth in stature. *Pediatrics, 50*, 874–880.

Rybash, J. M., Hoyer, W. J., & Roodin, P. A. (1986). *Adult cognition and aging*. Oxford: Pergamon.

Salthouse, T. A. (1982). *Adult cognition: An experimental psychology of human aging*. New York: Springer.

Snyder, E. E. (1972). High school student perceptions of prestige criteria. *Adolescence, 6*, 129–136.

Soldo, B. J. (1985). In-house services for the dependent elderly. *Research on Aging, 7*(2), 281–304.

Tanner, J. M. (1978). *Fetus into man: Physical growth from conception to maturity.* Cambridge, MA: Harvard University Press.

Thomas, R. M. (1990). *Counseling and life-span development.* Newbury Park, CA: Sage.

Troll, L. E. (1982). *Continuations: Adult development and aging.* Monterey, CA: Brooks/Cole.

Vygotsky, L. S. (1962). *Thought and language.* Cambridge, MA: MIT Press.

CHAPTER FOUR

Ethical and Legal Issues in Counseling and Therapy

Douglas R. Gross
Arizona State University

David Capuzzi
Portland State University

The following scenario depicts students much like you, who are enrolled in a required course entitled "Ethics and Legal Issues in Counseling and Psychotherapy." Courses such as this are now required in all educative programs for counselors or therapists and are one of the core requirements for national and state certification or credentialing of counselors or therapists. This chapter is intended to increase your knowledge of ethical and legal issues related to counseling or psychotherapy, and the information contained in the following scenario serves as our way of introducing you to the subject.

■ ■ ■

As Dr. James ended her class for the evening, she said, "Keep in mind that the codes of ethics we are reviewing are only guidelines and offer directives rather than hard-and-fast answers for situations that arise in counseling or therapy. The answers rest with you as you review the situation and attempt to apply the guidelines and directives. We will discuss this more fully next week."

While she gathered her materials and erased the board, she noticed that several students were huddled together in the back of the room. The voice level of the participants indicated that they were involved in a heated discussion. When Dr. James crossed to the door, one of the students asked if she could spare a moment to answer a question.

"I will if I can," she said as she approached the group. "What is the question?" She drew up a chair to join the group.

John, the student who had stopped her, explained that he and some other students were very concerned because all they were getting in class were guidelines and directives. They had hoped for answers regarding what should and should not be done ethically in counseling or therapy. He explained that the students wanted the type of information that would enable them to behave ethically, information they would need when they took professional positions.

Dr. James thanked John for asking her to join the group. "You raise an issue that has been raised in every section of this course I have taught," she said. She explained that she saw it as a very important issue and that the group should compliment itself.

"It usually takes students longer to voice this concern," she said. "Ethical codes seldom provide specific answers for specific situations. They are designed to guide practitioners as they evaluate the various aspects of the helping relationship and enable them to make decisions regarding appropriate behaviors. I know it would be nice to have specific answers for the situations that each of you will face as you assume professional positions, but neither I nor the codes of ethics presented in this class will provide those answers. As a professional, it will be your responsibility both to interpret and apply the information contained in these codes to assure that your behaviors in the helping relationship are ethical. This class cannot give you the answers you seek, but it should equip you to interpret and apply the ethical guidelines more effectively."

As she stood up and moved toward the door, she asked, "Will one of you bring up this issue at next week's class? I feel that all the students in class could benefit from this discussion."

After Dr. James left the room, the group asked John if he would bring up the issue at the next class. He agreed; and after gathering up their materials, the students left the classroom.

■ ■ ■

We hope that you are able to identify with the concerns of the class members as they attempt to translate ethical principles into operational procedures that they will be able to apply. Ethics, as an area of professional investigation, is both confusing in definition and frustrating in application. The confusion stems from the generalized terminology used in established codes to cover a broad professional population. The frustration stems from attempting to translate this generalized terminology into specific behaviors that are operational within the helping relationship.

Determining what is or is not ethical behavior often creates a perplexing dilemma for both the novice and the experienced practitioner. While the helping professions have offered practitioners a plethora of guidelines and codes of ethical behavior, confusion still exists (Gross & Robinson, 1987). These codes include *Code of Ethics* (1989) published by the National Board of Certified Counselors (NBCC); the *AAMFT Code of Ethics* (1991) adopted by the American Association for Marriage and Family Therapists; *Code of Ethics for Mental Health Counselors* (1987) adopted by the American Mental Health Counselors Association (AMHCA) and supported by the National Academy for Certified Clinical Mental Health Counselors (NACCMHC); *Ethical Guidelines for Group Counselors* (1989) approved by the Association for Specialists in Group Work (ASGW); *Ethical Principles of Psychologists and Code of Conduct* (1992) adopted by the American Psychological Association (APA); *Ethical Standards* (1988a) adopted by the American Association for Counseling and Development (AACD) (now ACA, the American Counseling Association); and *Ethical Standards for School Counselors* (1984) adopted by the American School Counselors Association (ASCA).[1]

Not only have these national professional groups provided ethical guidelines for their members, but many state counseling and psychological associations have also adopted their own versions of ethical standards.

Although intended to be helpful, these codes, standards, principles, and guidelines result in more questions than answers. This is particularly

---

[1]The American Counseling Association is currently reviewing for formal adoption a new code of ethics, which will be published either in the fall of 1994 or the spring of 1995.

true if one examines the documents for parameters of ethical conduct in light of the various roles and functions that practitioners perform. According to Gross and Robinson (1987):

> Most counselors consider direct service to individuals, to groups, or to families as their primary role. Secondary role responsibilities might include consultation, supervision of counselor trainees or subordinates, and research attempting to evaluate service or to answer clinical questions. Regardless of the role being performed, counselors must be cognizant of ethical responsibilities to the client or client system and to the profession. (pp. 5–6)

The variety of codes and the diversity of practitioner roles add directly to the confusion inherent in definition and the frustration involved in application. This chapter addresses these problems in relation to the following topics: the definition and rationale of ethical codes, guidelines for ethical decision making, dimensions of ethical behavior, and legal issues. We place major emphasis on the *Ethical Standards* (1988a), developed by the American Counseling Association, and the *Ethical Principles of Psychologists and Code of Conduct* (1992), developed by the American Psychological Association. We selected these sets of standards because they are widely used in educational coursework for counselors or therapists.

ETHICAL CODES: DEFINITION AND RATIONALE

As an area of inquiry, ethics is a branch of philosophy that focuses on morals and morality as they relate to decision making. Studies in this area concentrate on the standards of morality found in various cultures, societies, and professional groups and how these standards translate into directives aimed at regulating the behaviors of members of these various groups.

According to *Webster's Ninth New Collegiate Dictionary* (1988), the word *ethic* means "the discipline dealing with what is good and bad and with moral duty and obligation; . . . a set of moral principles or values; . . . the principles of conduct governing an individual or a group" (p. 392). Of the three definitions, the one that most closely captures the subject of this chapter is the one dealing with principles of conduct governing an individual or a group. The other two definitions, which address concepts of good and bad, moral duty and obligation, and values, are inherent in these "principles of conduct" and provide the context around which professional codes of ethics were developed. Ethical behavior, therefore, deals with the application of concepts of morality, values, and good versus bad to situations that individuals encounter in life. Ethical behavior related to counseling or therapy deals with the application of these same concepts to situations that counselors or therapists encounter in the context of the helping relationship.

The terms *ethics* and *ethical behavior* can be addressed from both an individual and a group perspective. It is obvious that areas such as morality and values are best understood in terms of the attitudes and behaviors of the individual. People develop their moral and value orientations based upon a wide array of impacting variables. These orientations often govern not only the interactive patterns of people, but also their view of the world. Human diversity would make it extremely difficult for people to develop agreed-upon standards of ethical behavior for each individual in every part of the world. But such standards are possible for specific cultures, societies, and professional groups when they are based upon shared values, views of morality, and accepted concepts of good and bad. These shared beliefs and the group's desire to have its members behave according to these beliefs are the foundation on which codes of ethics are developed. According to Allen (1986):

> One of the beliefs of every professional organization is that its members must perform their professional duties according to an established code of ethics. Without an established ethical code, a group of people with similar interests cannot actually be considered a professional organization. (p. 293)

This statement provides a rationale for the development of codes of ethics by professional groups and indicates that such codes are one of the unifying factors that designate disciplines such as medicine, psychology, and counseling as professional organizations. Support for this proposition can be found in the writings of Biggs and Blocher (1987); Corey, Corey, and Callanan (1993); Mabe and Rollin (1986); and Tennyson and Strom (1986).

Besides providing a professional identity, what other purposes do such codes serve? Van Hoose and Kottler (1985) identified the following:

1. Codes provide guidelines for ethical decision making.
2. They regulate the behavior of members of the profession.
3. They demonstrate the willingness of an organization to police itself and provide a method of self-regulation.
4. They regulate intermember interactions such as referral of clients, consultation, and client recruitment.
5. They protect the profession by setting standards of practice that are used in the adjudication of liability suits.

We support all of those purposes as appropriate rationales for the development of codes of ethics. Each attempts to provide the profession, its members, and its public with guidelines and directives aimed at assuring the group that basic ethical standards will be practiced. Such assurance also serves a protective function for each group. The profession itself is protected because it is able to police its membership and suspend members who are in violation of the code; members who operate within these ethical standards are protected to some degree from malpractice adjudication; and the public is served when the profession provides a degree of protection, through legal recourse, against violations of these standards.

The importance of codes of ethics to professional groups and their various publics seems obvious. We would present an unbalanced picture, however, if we did not also discuss various limitations of these codes (Corey et al., 1993; Ibrahim & Arredondo, 1990). One such limitation deals with the general nature of the codes and the fact that the types of situations encountered by members attempting to operate within them are seldom as clear-cut as those addressed in the codes. This leaves the final determination of ethical versus unethical behavior with an individual and his ability to make the correct decision.

A second limitation stems from the lack of adequate coverage for certain areas within the codes. Examples include consultation and group work. The codes of ethics of the American Counseling Association and the American Psychological Association deal with these topics in a cursory sense. Members must seek out special codes of ethics, developed by associations who specialize in these areas, to be aware of all of the ethical parameters that surround them.

A third limitation stems from conflicting differences that exist among codes of ethics. This limitation exists when an individual is a member of more than one professional group. If such a situation exists (and it often does with members of both the American Counseling Association and the American Psychological Association), which code do members follow? How do they decide which code best governs their behavior? In addressing this limitation, Kitchener (1986) stated:

> The ambiguity of codes is further complicated because professionals may belong to more than one association with an ethical code. . . . These codes may not always be in agreement. Therefore, compliance with the ethical code of one association may be judged as unethical by another association. (p. 306)

A fourth limitation exists when ethical codes are in conflict with institutional policies and procedures. If a person is a member of a professional association and an employee of an institution, she may discover that the policies and procedures supported by the two are in conflict.

A fifth limitation exists due to the cultural diversity of the public and the need for adaptation when dealing with specific cultures.

There are no easy answers to the questions posed by these limitations. If answers do exist, they will be found in the members' ability to interpret the information presented in the codes and to make appropriate decisions. To aid you in this interpretive and decision-making process, we have developed guidelines for approaching professional situations that may present ethical and legal concerns. These guidelines apply to a wide range of situations and should help you answer the question, "What should I do if I think a legal or ethical issue exists because of my behavior or the behavior of others?"

GUIDELINES FOR ETHICAL DECISION MAKING

The following guidelines may be helpful:

- *Guideline 1.*   When confronted with a situation that may have ethical or legal ramifications, review the ethical standards of your professional group to determine if the situation is addressed and if guidelines and directives exist. If not, review codes of ethics of professional groups that may deal more specifically with the special situation you face.

- *Guideline 2.*   If you cannot find answers or if you need more information, review the *Ethical Standards Casebook*, fourth edition, written by Herlihy and Golden (1990), which was designed to clarify the intent of the American Counseling Association's *Ethical Standards*. Also review the *Casebook of Ethical Principles of Psychologists* (1987), published by the American Psychological Association. In addition, it might be helpful to review the *Policies and Procedures for Processing Complaints of Ethical Violations* (1988b), published by the American Counseling Association.

- *Guideline 3.*   If you cannot find satisfactory answers, talk with colleagues and ask them for assistance in both interpretation and decision making. The decision must be yours, but make that decision only after you have investigated all possible sources of information.

- *Guideline 4.*   If you feel the situation has legal parameters, review the legal statutes that have implications for counseling or psychotherapy, not only within your state but also from a national perspective.

- *Guideline 5.*   To better understand the legal parameters, talk with members of the legal profession who have expertise in the area of member-client rights. Review the material presented in *The Counselor and the Law*, third edition, by Hopkins and Anderson (1990), which explores the permissible bonds of conduct within which counselors or therapists can perform their job legally. Also review the material in *The ACA Legal Series* (1992). This is a seven-volume monograph series edited by Remley covering a wide range of ethical and legal issues for counseling or psychotherapy.

■ *Guideline 6.*   If the situation stems from differences between organizational and professional requirements, review the various policies and procedures that operate within your work environment. In most settings, these policies are available in printed form; and you are responsible for understanding them and operating within them. If questions arise, please check with your supervisor to gain appropriate clarification.

■ *Guideline 7.*   If the situation stems from questions of professional competence or personal issues that may negatively affect the counseling or therapeutic relationship, review the situation with a colleague or supervisor. Based upon the results of this review, either continue with the client or make an appropriate referral.

These guidelines are designed to help you initiate the interpretive and decision-making processes of ethical behavior. We will refer back to them later in this chapter.

DIMENSIONS OF ETHICAL BEHAVIOR

Codes of ethics are composed of both general and specific categories that describe the various dimensions of ethical behavior. These categories or major topical areas establish the ethical dimensions or parameters within which members of a profession operate. We illustrate these dimensions or parameters using the two ethical codes that are the primary focus of this chapter. The *Ethical Standards* of the American Counseling Association (1988a) includes the following categories: general, counseling relationship, measurement and evaluation, research and publication, consulting, private practice, personnel administration, and preparation standards. The *Ethical Principles of Psychologists and Code of Conduct* (1992) includes the following categories: general principles; general standards; evaluation, assessment, or intervention; advertising and other public statements; therapy; privacy and confidentiality; teaching, training supervision, research, and publishing; forensic activities; and resolving ethical issues. Each category discussed in the codes contains specific principles that not only explain and define the category, but also show the differing degrees of emphasis that the two professional groups place on the category. These differences, for the most part, are based on the fact that each code was developed to address a specific professional population. Therefore, each professional association places its emphasis on what is most appropriate for its members.

Regardless of differences in terminology and emphasis, there are also similarities in the two codes. For example, the content in the section titled "General" in the *Ethical Standards* (1988a) of the ACA relates directly to the content presented in the section titled "General Principles" in the *Ethical Principles of Psychologists and Code of Conduct* (1992) of the APA. Both deal with counselors' or psychologists' ethical responsibilities to both the profession and the client, their integrity, their competence to perform stated services, their attention to client welfare as it relates to relationship variables, their use of assessment and research, their respect for human rights and dignity, their need for continued education and growth, their willingness to confront unethical behavior in others, and their need to avoid dual relationships. Each of these principles carries with it behavioral directives for the counselor or therapist.

Because this book deals with theories related to individual counseling and therapy, this chapter will focus on specific dimensions in the two codes that have the greatest similarity as they apply to the individual counselor or psychologist operating in a one-to-one counseling or therapeutic relationship. These dimensions include member responsibility, member competence, and member-client relationships. Basing our decision on the language of the codes and the fact that they deal with both counselors and psychologists, we have chosen the term *member* to designate either a counselor or a psychologist.

Member Responsibility

Member responsibility is at the core of all ethical behavior. Members are responsible for determining what ethical conduct means both philosophically and behaviorally and for incorporating this meaning into their professional practice. Members are responsible for continually evaluating not only their own behaviors but also those of their colleagues. All of the principles in the codes hold members responsible for understanding the principles and the ethical application of the intent of the principles. Even though the codes address the tenets of ethical behavior, the responsibility for putting those tenets into practice rests squarely in the hands of the member.

The breadth of members' responsibility is obvious: they are expected to understand and apply the behaviors outlined in the codes. This would not seem like a difficult task if the member were responsible only to self and client. In reality, however, a member's responsibility goes beyond self and client.

After reviewing five sets of ethical standards, Gross and Robinson (1987) discovered that members

> are found to be responsible not only to the client but also to society, the community in which the service is provided, the institution which employs the counselor, the referral agency, the parents of the client, the more extended family of the client, colleagues and professional associates, state statutes which impact on counseling practices as these relate to working with minors, professional boards which set counseling policies, and self. (p. 6)

The list clearly mentions a larger public to or for whom members are responsible. Even if one were to discuss major and minor degrees of responsibility or to prioritize according to "most responsible for, least responsible for," the answer remains confusing.

Even more confusion exists when the member works with a multiple-client system. In discussing member responsibility, the *Code of Ethics* (1989) of the National Board of Certified Counselors (NBCC) states:

> The primary obligation of certified counselors is to respect the integrity and promote the welfare of a client, regardless of whether the client is assisted individually or in a group relationship. In a group setting, the certified counselor is also responsible for taking reasonable precautions to protect individuals from physical and/or psychological trauma resulting from interaction within the group. (p. 1)

The area of marriage and family counseling presents yet another dimension in the complex issue of member responsibility. According to Margolin (1982), "Yet difficult ethical questions confronted in individual therapy become even more complicated when a number of family members are seen together in therapy" (p. 788). The area of multiple-client systems brings into play a myriad of issues that are addressed only superficially in the two sets of ethical standards that serve as the primary focus for this chapter. Even the *AAMFT Code of Ethics* (1991) lacks specificity. According to this code, "marriage and family therapists are dedicated to advancing the welfare of families and individuals, including respecting the rights of those persons seeking their assistance, and making reasonable efforts to ensure that their services are used appropriately" (p. 1).

What are the answers to these complex issues? Where do members turn to find the direction and guidance that will lead them through this ethical maze? To paraphrase the words of Dr. James, our hypothetical instructor in the opening scenario, the helping professionals have the responsibility both to interpret and to apply the information contained in the established codes of ethics to assure that their behaviors in the helping relationship are ethical. In other words, they must gain knowledge regarding acceptable ethical standards, develop the ability to interpret these standards in light of the situations that they face, and develop decision-making skills that will allow them to put these standards into practice. Moreover, members' responsibility does not end with an awareness of the many publics or the ability to interpret, make decisions, and apply the codes. They must also take responsibility for their own mental health to assure that personal difficulties do not negatively impact on the client or the helping relationship.

Although specific answers do not exist to questions surrounding responsibility, we direct your attention to the guidelines presented earlier in this chapter. You should also be aware of the following "red flags," which should help you identify areas where member responsibility may be an issue:

1. Age of the client
2. Individual versus multiple-client systems
3. Legal statutes that address member responsibilities
4. Policies and procedures of the employing agency or institution that address member responsibilities
5. Ethical standards of the profession that address member responsibilities
6. Referral sources that require member responsibility not only to the client but also to the referral source
7. Client rights that prescribe member responsibilities

When in doubt, follow the directives of the guidelines we presented earlier in the chapter and seek answers from those who can assist you. Both the client(s) and your professional welfare depend on your appropriate use of decision-making skills.

Member Competence

Member competence—the provision of only those services and techniques for which the member is qualified by training or experience—is also central to all ethical behavior. In reviewing the ethical codes that serve as the main focus of this chapter, we identified such competence as encompassing five basic areas:

1. Accurate representation of professional qualifications

2. Professional growth through involvement in continuing education

3. Provision of only those services and techniques for which one is qualified

4. Maintenance of accurate knowledge and expertise in specialized areas

5. Assistance in solving personal issues that impede effectiveness

In addition, Robinson (1991) adds the following:

> I would add your responsibilities as counselors-in-training to learn basic skills, to integrate academic study with supervised practice, to develop self-understanding, to seek continual evaluation and appraisal, and to become intimately familiar with ethical guidelines. (p. 451)

A review of these areas and the fact that they consistently appear in statements of professional standards leads one to assume that this area of ethical behavior has been clearly defined and that evaluation of member competence is a relatively simple task. In reality, however, this is not the case. Ethical review boards and licensing committees spend a large percentage of their time and financial resources attempting to determine the degree of competence of the practitioner.

It is interesting to note that of the six areas defining member competence only four are subject to formal review and evaluation. The fifth and sixth, which deal with the personal aspects of the member, are seemingly left to the member's discretion. If the member has personal issues that impede effectiveness or if she does not integrate study and practice, develop self-understanding, seek continual evaluation, or become familiar with ethical guidelines, the ethical standards recommend that she seek assistance in solving these issues. Such a directive seems somewhat weak when compared with the strong evaluative measures for the other areas of competence.

The concept of member competence must be viewed from both an internal and an external frame of reference. From an internal perspective, members do all they can to gain the skills and knowledge basic to the profession. Each member takes full responsibility for adhering to the rules and regulations of the profession, which address the concepts of proper representation of professional qualifications, for providing only those services for which he has training and experience and for making every effort to seek assistance with personal issues that stand in the way of providing effective service.

From an external perspective, it is important for members to realize that processes such as reviewing, evaluating, examining, and screening will continue to be handled by external forces such as licensing boards and professional groups. The best advice that can be given to members in dealing with this situation is to exercise the responsibilities and controls from an internal perspective, to develop confidence in their own degree of competence, and to be alert to the established criteria used in external evaluations. If members conscientiously attend to these aspects of competence, the end result should be positive.

Specific answers to questions surrounding competence do not exist. Guideline 7, mentioned previously in this chapter, may aid you in this decision-making process. The following list can also alert you to situations when member competence may be an issue:

1. Statements made in advertising your services

2. Not keeping current in your field

3. Dealing with client problems about which you have little information

4. Legal statutes dealing with required competencies

5. Ethical standards dealing with required competencies

6. Agency or institutional requirements related to required competencies

7. Personal problems that impede the effective use of competencies in the helping relationship

8. Lack of familiarity with the existing codes of ethics

Member-Client Relationships

A third central factor related to ethical behavior deals with relationship dynamics between the member and the client. This is a broadly defined area and includes provision for or prohibition of such relationship variables as client freedom of choice; client accessibility regardless of ethnicity, race, religion, disability, and socioeconomic group; confidentiality; informed consent; dual relationships; sexual involvement; other professional relationships; and technology. Due to the interrelatedness of these variables, we will discuss them in terms of their applicability to the more generic term *client welfare*.

Client welfare serves as the focal point around which all codes of ethics revolve. It is present both overtly and covertly in the various sections and principles that make up the codes. It serves as the goal of the helping process, and the developers of the codes of ethics designed the codes to meet this goal through their emphasis on the maintenance and protection of the welfare of the client. Section B, article 1 of the *Ethical*

Standards of the ACA (1988a) makes the following statement regarding client welfare:

> The member's primary obligation is to respect the integrity and promote the welfare of the client(s), whether the client(s) is (are) assisted individually or in a group relationship. In a group setting, the member is also responsible for taking reasonable precautions to protect individuals from physical and/or psychological trauma resulting from interaction within the group. (pp. 4–5)

In principle E, "Concern for Others' Welfare," in the general principles of the *Ethical Principles of Psychologists and Code of Conduct* of the APA (1992), the following statement relates to client welfare:

> Psychologists seek to contribute to the welfare of those with whom they interact professionally. In their professional actions, psychologists weigh the welfare and rights of their patients or clients, students, supervisees, human research participants, and other affected persons, and the welfare of animal subjects of research. When conflicts occur among psychologists' obligations or concerns, they attempt to resolve these conflicts and to perform their roles in a responsible fashion that avoids or minimizes harm. (p. 1600)

Whether a member is a counselor or a psychologist, the directive regarding the promotion and protection of client welfare is central to the helping relationship. To comply with this directive, the member must pay special attention to the following issues.

Freedom of Choice.   Members must recognize the need for clients to be free to choose as that choice relates to the helping relationship. Such choices include but are not limited to the following:

- Counseling or therapy as a treatment modality
- Counselor or therapist selection
- Treatment selection
- Types of information provided by the client
- Testing procedures
- The involvement of others in the treatment process
- Length of treatment
- Access to client records and information
- Sharing client information with others

Under those circumstances where freedom of choice may not be possible–for example, involuntary treatment, working with minors, agency or institution rules and regulations, and state statutes—members must apprise clients of the restrictions that may limit their freedom of choice. For further information regarding freedom of choice, read section B, introduction, of the *Ethical Standards* of the ACA (1988a) and principle D, "Respect for People's Rights and Dignity," of the general principles of the *Ethical Principles of Psychologists and Code of Conduct* (1992).

Client Accessibility.   Members must do all they can to ensure that the services they provide are available to all clients regardless of ethnicity, race, religion, sex, sexual orientation, disability, or socioeconomic status. If the member finds that such barriers exist within the work setting, she must take steps to alleviate such barriers. For further information regarding client accessibility, read principle D, "Respect for People's Rights and Dignity," and principle F, "Social Responsibility," of the general principles of the *Ethical Principles of Psychologists and Code of Conduct* (1992) and section A(10), section B(19), and section C(12) of the *Ethical Standards* of the ACA (1988a).

Confidentiality.   According to Schwitzgebel and Schwitzgebel (1980), confidentiality is a professional concept that protects the client from unauthorized disclosures of information given in confidence without his expressed consent. The concept of confidentiality has been used by professional associations to establish parameters applied to information shared by the client(s) during the helping process.

It is important to distinguish confidentiality from the term *privileged communication*, which is a legal term that indicates that the client's communications cannot be disclosed in a court of law without the client's consent. This privilege belongs to the client, not the member, and under most circumstances only the client can waive the privilege. Privileged communication is usually granted by states to clients of legally certified mental health professionals such as psychologists, certified professional counselors, or certified marriage and family counselors.

The term *confidentiality* is best viewed as a client right. Codes of ethics assure clients that the information they present in the helping relationship will not be shared with others. Exceptions to this right do exist, as stated in section 5.05, "Disclosures," in the *Ethical Principles of Psychologists and Code of Conduct* (1992) of the APA:

> (a) Psychologists disclose confidential information without the consent of the individual only as mandated by law, or where permitted by law for a valid purpose, such as (1) to provide needed professional services to the patient or the individual or organizational client, (2) to obtain appropriate professional consultations, (3) to protect the patient or client or others from

harm, or (4) to obtain payment for services, in which instance disclosure is limited to the minimum that is necessary to achieve the purpose. (p. 1606)

A statement in section B, article 4 of the *Ethical Standards* of the ACA (1988a) also addresses this issue of disclosure.

Confidentiality has application to more than just the verbal communication between the member and the client. It also applies to client records. Section B, article 5 of the *Ethical Standards* of the ACA (1988a) includes the following statement:

> Records of the counseling relationship, including interview notes, test data, correspondence, tape recordings, electronic data storage, and other documents are to be considered professional information for use in counseling, and they should not be considered a part of the records of the institution or agency in which the counselor is employed unless specified by state statute or regulation. Revelation to others of counseling material must occur only upon the expressed consent of the client. (p. 5)

Similar statements appear in section 5.04, "Maintenance of Records," of the *Ethical Principles of Psychologists and Code of Conduct* of the APA (1992).

Informed Consent.   The term *informed consent* does not appear in either set of the ethical standards but is inferred based upon the nature of the two documents. Informed consent has a direct relationship to client freedom of choice, as discussed earlier. The choices that clients have relative to the helping process are based, first, on the fact that clients are provided with all significant information relative to the helping process and, second, that they are provided with the opportunity to agree or to consent based upon this information. Such information includes the procedures to be used in the helping relationship, the member's responsibilities, and the client's rights. Such consent may be given orally, but it is a much better practice in certain situations to have the client's written consent. Robinson (1991) instructed the member to take these steps:

> If you are asked by the client to disclose to a third party information revealed in therapy, have the client sign an informed consent form for disclosure. On this form the exact information to be disclosed, to whom, for what purpose, the name of the client, the name of the person and the date, event, or condition that will revoke the consent for disclosure should be clearly specified. (p. 459)

In discussing the legality of informed consent, Everstine, Everstine, Geymann, True, Frey, Johnson, and Seiden (1980) propose the following three conditions that must be present for informed consent to be legal. First, the individual granting the consent must be competent to engage in rational thought. Second, the individual must be supplied with all relevant information so that the consent is based in fact, not fiction. Third, the client must give the consent voluntarily without the presence of coercion.

As with other ethical standards, there are exceptions. If the client is under the age of 18, informed consent must be secured from the parent or legal guardian. Even in such situations, however, it is still suggested that consent also be secured from the client.

Dual Relationships.   Dual relationships have reference to the member's involvement with the client in a capacity other than that of a professional helper. These relationships may impair the member's judgment and his ability to work effectively with the client. Such relationships are found when the member has an administrative, supervisory, instructional, or evaluative relationship with an individual seeking his services for counseling or therapy. The codes caution against such a dual relationship and suggest referral of the individual to another professional. Only in situations where such an alternative is unavailable and where delaying counseling or therapy could be harmful to the individual should the member enter into or maintain such a relationship.

Another example of a dual relationship that reduces the member's ability to be objective and in turn may be harmful to the client deals with providing counseling or therapy to family members or friends. Such dual relationships are discouraged by the codes for obvious reasons.

For further information on this issue, read section B, article 13 of the *Ethical Standards* of the ACA (1988a) and section 1.17, "Multiple Relationships," of the *Ethical Principles of Psychologists and Code of Conduct* of the APA (1992).

Sexual Involvement.   There is strong agreement between the two sets of ethical standards under discussion in this chapter that sexual involvement with a current client or any form of sexual harassment emanating from the member is unethical. The *Ethical Standards* of the ACA (1988a) states, "The member will avoid any type of sexual intimacies with clients. Sexual relationships with clients are unethical" (p. 5). The *Ethical Principles of Psychologists and Code of Conduct* of the APA (1992) states, "Psychologists do not engage in sexual intimacies with current patients or clients" (p. 1605). The latter code adds two dimensions not found in the *Ethical Standards* of the ACA (1988a): members should not accept as clients persons with whom they have been sexually intimate, and a member should place a time limit of at least two years after the termination of professional services before she engages in sexual intimacies with a former client.

For further information relating to sexual involvement, read sections A(8) and A(9) and section B(14) of the *Ethical Standards* of the ACA (1988a) and sections 1.11, "Sexual Harassment"; 4.05, "Sexual Intimacies with Current Patients or Clients"; 4.06, "Therapy with Former Sexual Partners"; and 4.07, "Sexual Intimacies with Former Therapy Patients," in the *Ethical Principles of Psychologists and Code of Conduct* of the APA (1992).

Other Professional Relationships.   The member may find that the client seeking his service is currently in another helping relationship. In such cases, the member is instructed not to initiate a relationship without first contacting and receiving the approval of the other professional involved. If such a discovery is made after the relationship has been initiated, the member must gain the consent of the other professional or terminate the relationship unless the client elects to terminate the other relationship. For further information, read section B(3) of the *Ethical Standards* of the ACA (1988a) and section 4.04, "Providing Mental Health Services to Those Served by Others," of the *Ethical Principles of Psychologists and Code of Conduct* of the APA (1992).

Technology.   Because computer use in the fields of counseling and therapy is a growing phenomenon, it is important that members be aware of the possible impact it may have on assuring client welfare. Electronic data storage of client files, assessments, and test results place such information at the disposal of any person who can tap into such storage systems. When comparing the *Ethical Standards* of the ACA's 1981 and 1988 editions, we found that the term *computer* appeared in 6 of the 20 articles under section B, "Counseling Relationship," in the 1988 edition. This was not the case in the earlier edition. The 1988 edition, section B, article 6 of these standards provides the following directive for members:

> In view of the extensive data storage and processing capacities of the computer, the member must ensure that data maintained on a computer are: (a) limited to information that is appropriate and necessary for the services being provided, (b) destroyed after it is determined that the information is no longer of any value in providing services, and (c) restricted in terms of access to appropriate staff members involved in the provision of services by using the best computer security methods available. (p. 5)

The member-client relationship is very complex and, as with other issues addressed by the standards, guidelines—not answers—exist. The guidelines for ethical decision making, which were presented earlier in this chapter, should aid you. In addition, the following client situations may help you identify areas in which the member-client relationship may be an issue:

■ Clients have no choice regarding what is taking place in the helping relationship

■ Clients have difficulty availing themselves of the service due to issues of ethnicity, race, religion, sex, sexual orientation, disability, or socioeconomic status

■ Client information, presented in the privacy of the individual or group relationship, is known outside the relationship

■ Clients are not asked either orally or in writing to agree to certain aspects of the treatment process

■ Parents of clients who are under the age of 18 are not given the opportunity to consent to the treatment

■ Clients are involved in relations with the member outside the professional helping relationship

■ Clients are being approached sexually or are being sexually harassed by the member

■ Clients are in helping relationships with other professionals who are providing the same type of service

■ Client information in the electronic data storage system is not protected by the best computer security methods available

LEGAL ISSUES

Legal issues have become a major concern for today's practitioner and are closely allied with issues of ethical behavior already discussed in this chapter. According to Brown and Srebalus (1988):

> Twenty-five years ago this chapter would have been unnecessary. Today, legal concerns stand as one of the most serious issues confronting counselors. The dramatic rise in the importance attached to legal concerns can be attributed to two factors: the status of the counseling professional and the "legalizing" of American society. Even the most casual observer of current news events is aware that civil liability is of great concern to professionals, corporations, municipalities, and private citizens. This is primarily because juries have awarded increasingly larger sums of money to plaintiffs when physicians, psychologists, or others have been found liable for damages in malpractice cases. (p. 210)

Dealing with the developing importance of legal issues for the practitioner, Robinson (1991) stated:

> Because the relationship between a counselor and a client is a fiduciary relationship, one which fosters great trust and confidence, the legal system becomes involved when this trust is violated and the client does not receive what he or she believes is a reasonable standard of care. (p. 465)

These two statements emphasize the need for practitioners to be aware of the legal ramifications of their behaviors. It is difficult to discuss with great specificity such ramifications due to the complexity of state laws. The information that follows was selected, not because it encompasses all of the areas in which legal issues play a part, but because it is representative of the growing impact that legal interpretations have on professional practice. We present information about the following topics: duty to warn and due care.

Duty to Warn

According to the codes of ethics we have already discussed, counselors and psychologists have a duty to maintain confidentiality and not to disclose matters unless there is clear and imminent danger to the client or others or if they are required to do so by law. It is the second part of this statement that speaks directly to the concept of duty to warn. *Tarasoff v. Regents of the University of California* (1976) is perhaps the most well-known example. In this situation, legal action was taken regarding the responsibility of a university psychologist to warn the Tarasoff family regarding the possible actions of Prosenjit Poddar, a client at the University of California Hospital. The client informed the psychologist that he planned to kill an unnamed girl, readily identifiable as Tatiana Tarasoff, when she returned home after spending the summer in South America. The psychologist informed the university police department and requested that the client be detained. The client was taken into custody but was soon released after he promised to stay away from Ms. Tarasoff. Shortly after her return from South America, the client went to her home and killed her. Her parents brought suit against the university regents, the police, and doctors in the university hospital, charging that they had not been warned of the danger.

The lower court decided in favor of the defendants. Following that decision, the Tarasoff family filed an appeal; and the Supreme Court of California reversed the judgment and found the defendants guilty of negligence. The supreme court held that "once a therapist does in fact determine, or under applicable professional standards reasonably should have determined, that a patient poses a serious danger of violence to others, he bears a duty to exercise reasonable care to protect the foreseeable victims of that danger. (*Tarasoff v. Regents of the University of California*, 1976).

We agree with Biggs and Blocher (1987), Corey et al. (1993), and Robinson and Gross (1986) when they advise practitioners, through the use of informed consent forms, to tell clients before the beginning of the helping relationship that confidentiality does not exist in certain situations. The client is then able to make informed decisions regarding the type of information she is willing to share. We also recommend that practitioners inform clients of the action that they will be taking, in order to protect the client and others before taking the action. This step tries to involve the client as much as possible in the process.

Due Care

Due to the special relationship that exists between practitioners and clients, practitioners must do everything within their power to place the care of the client foremost on their list of priorities. This demonstration of care is exemplified in the provision of skilled services and treatment and by not placing the client in compromising situations that will either detract from the treatment or cause physical or psychological harm to the client. The concept of due care is inherent in the various standards of the codes of ethics we have discussed, and it serves as a major directive governing the ethical behavior of members.

A legal interpretation of the principle of due care is exemplified in the case of *Roy v. Hartogs* (1975). Client Julie Roy sought damages through a malpractice suit from her therapist, Dr. Hartogs, claiming she had experienced deleterious effects from a sexual relationship lasting several months that had developed between the two during therapy. In defending himself, Dr. Hartogs claimed that their sexual relationship had nothing to do with the therapeutic process. He said it was outside their professional relationship; therefore, he was not guilty of malpractice. The court, in deciding the case, ruled in favor of Ms. Roy and gave the opinion that Dr. Hartogs had not used due care in his professional relationship with the client.

Van Hoose and Kottler (1985), in discussing due care as it relates to the helping relationship, have this advice for the practitioner:

> The courts seem to be saying to the helping professions that close relationships involving trust and mutual caring between therapist and client are

understood and are, in fact, necessary for effective treatment. Such intimacies are permitted as long as the therapist does not use the relationship for personal advantage and as long as he maintains due regard for professional propriety and community conscience. (pp. 55–56)

Most areas of counseling and psychotherapy have witnessed the involvement of the law and its interpretation as they relate to ethical practice. Public laws such as P.L. 94-142, "Education of the Handicapped," and P.L. 93-380, "Family Educational Rights and Privacy Act," both of which were passed in the 1970s, are further examples of this involvement. To close this section, we suggest that guidelines 4 and 5, mentioned earlier in this chapter, may help you make decisions about legal issues.

CONCLUSIONS

This chapter has discussed the ethical and legal aspects that impact the helping relationship. It has addressed the complexity of the issues involved and provided the reader with guidelines, not answers. Dr. James, the professor in the opening scenario, may wish to offer her students the guidelines for ethical decision making as well as the information that follows. This should aid them in the difficult process of ethical interpretation and decision making.

■ *Ethical standards of the profession.*   Review the ethical standards of your professional group to determine if the responsibility issue in question is addressed and if guidelines and directives exist. If not, review codes of ethics of professional groups who may deal more specifically with the special situation you face. Review the *Ethical Standards Casebook*, fourth edition, by Herlihy and Golden (1990), which was designed to clarify the intent of the American Counseling Association's *Ethical Standards*. Review the *Casebook of Ethical Principles of Psychologists* (1987), published by the American Psychological Association. It might also be helpful to review the *Policies and Procedures for Processing Complaints of Ethical Violations* (1988b), published by the American Counseling Association. If you cannot find satisfactory answers, talk with colleagues and ask them for assistance in both interpretation and decision making. In the last analysis, the decision must be yours, but make that decision only after you have investigated all 41 possible sources of information.

■ *Legal statutes.*   Become familiar with the legal statutes that have implication for counseling and therapy, not only for your state but also from a national perspective. Talk with members of the legal profession who have expertise in the area of member-client rights. Review the material presented in *The Counselor and the Law*, third edition, by Hopkins and Anderson (1990), which explores the permissible bounds of conduct within which counselors and therapists can perform their job legally, and *The ACA Legal Series* (1992), edited by Remley, which covers a wide range of ethical and legal issues.

■ *Agency's or institution's policies and procedures.*   Be knowledgeable about the various policies and procedures that operate within your work environment. They are usually available in printed form, and it is your responsibility to understand them and operate within them. If questions arise, please check with your supervisor for clarification.

Even though Dr. James's hypothetical students do not have the specific answers they had hoped for, the information, guidelines, directives, and situations in this chapter should enable them to enter the professions of counseling and psychotherapy feeling more assured of their ability to make informed and intelligent ethical decisions.

REFERENCES

Allen, V. B. (1986). A historical perspective of the AACD Ethics Committee. *Journal of Counseling and Development, 64*(5), 293.

American Association for Counseling and Development. (1981). *Ethical standards.* Alexandria, VA: Author.

American Association for Marriage and Family Therapy. (1991). *AAMFT code of ethics.* Washington, DC: Author.

American Counseling Association. (1988a). *Ethical standards.* Alexandria, VA: Author.

American Counseling Association. (1988b). *Policies and procedures for processing complaints of ethical violations.* Alexandria, VA: Author.

American Counseling Association. (1992). *ACA legal series.* (T. Remley, Ed.). Alexandria, VA: Author.

American Mental Health Counselors Association. (1987). *Code of ethics for mental health counselors.* Alexandria, VA: Author.

American Psychological Association. (1987). *Casebook of ethical principles of psychologists.* Washington, DC: Author.

American Psychological Association. (1992). Ethical principles of psychologists and code of conduct. *American Psychologist, 47*(12), 1597–1611.

American School Counselors Association. (1984). *Ethical standards for school counselors.* Washington, DC: Author.

Association for Specialists in Group Work. (1989). *Ethical guidelines for group counselors.* Alexandria, VA: Author.

Biggs, D., & Blocher, D. (1987). *Foundations of ethical counseling.* New York: Springer.

Brown, D., & Srebalus, D. J. (1988). *An introduction to the counseling profession.* Englewood Cliffs, NJ: Prentice-Hall.

Corey, G., Corey, M. S., & Callanan, P. (1993). *Issues and ethics in the helping professions* (4th ed.). Monterey, CA: Brooks/Cole.

Everstine, L., Everstine, D. S., Geymann, G. M., True, R. H., Frey, D. H., Johnson, H. G., & Seiden, R. H. (1980). Privacy and confidentiality in psychotherapy. *American Psychologist, 35*(9), 828–840.

Gross, D. R., & Robinson, S. E. (1987). Ethics in counseling: A multiple role perspective. *TACD Journal, 15*(1), 5–16.

Herlihy, B., & Golden, L. (1990). *Ethical standards casebook* (4th ed.). Alexandria, VA: ACA Press.

Hopkins, B. H., & Anderson, B. S. (1990). *The counselor and the law* (3rd ed.). Alexandria, VA: ACA Press.

Ibrahim, F.A., & Arredondo, P. M. (1990). Ethical issues in multicultural counseling. In B. Herlihy & L. B. Golden (Eds.), *Ethical standards casebook* (4th ed.) (pp. 137–145). Alexandria, VA: ACA Press.

Kitchener, K. S. (1986). Teaching applied ethics in counselor education: An integration of psychological processes and philosophical analysis. *Journal of Counseling and Development, 64*(5), 306–310.

Mabe, A. R., & Rollin, S. A. (1986). The role of a code of ethical standards in counseling. *Journal of Counseling and Development, 64*(5), 294–297.

Margolin, G. (1982). Ethical and legal considerations in marital and family therapy. *American Psychologist, 37,* 788–801.

National Board of Certified Counselors. (1989). *Code of ethics*. Alexandria, VA: Author.

Robinson, S. E. (1991). Ethical and legal issues related to counseling: Or it's not as easy as it looks. In D. Capuzzi & D. Gross (Eds.), *Introduction to counseling: Perspectives for the 1990s* (pp. 445–468). Boston: Allyn & Bacon.

Robinson, S. E., & Gross, D. R. (1986). Ethics in mental health counseling. In A. J. Palmo & W. J. Weikel (Eds.), *Foundations of mental health counseling* (pp. 309–327). Springfield, IL: Charles C Thomas.

Roy v. Hartogs, 366 N.Y. S.2d 297 (1975).

Schwitzgebel, R. L., & Schwitzgebel, R. K. (1980). *Law and psychological practice.* New York: Wiley.

Tarasoff v. Regents of the University of California, 551, Cal. P.2d 334 (1976).

Tennyson, W. W., & Strom, S. M. (1986). Beyond professional standards: Developing responsibleness. *Journal of Counseling and Development, 64*(5), 298–302.

Van Hoose, W. H., & Kottler, J. A. (1985). *Ethical and legal issues in counseling and psychotherapy* (2nd ed.). San Francisco: Jossey-Bass.

Webster's Ninth New Collegiate Dictionary. (1988). Springfield MA.: Merriam-Webster.

■ PART TWO

Theories of Counseling and Psychotherapy

■ ■ ■ CHAPTERS

5   Psychoanalytic Theory

6   Jungian Analytical Theory

7   Adlerian Theory

8   Existential Theory

9   Person-centered Theory

10 Gestalt Theory

11 Transactional Analysis Theory

12 Rational-Emotive Theory

13 Cognitive-Behavioral Theories

In part 1 of this text, we examined four basic areas that are significant to the individual counseling process and to the person of the counselor or therapist. We discussed the helping relationship, ethical and legal issues, developmental stages, and the issues surrounding the counselor or therapist's personal and professional identity. We believe that this foundation was necessary before introducing you to the theories of counseling and psychotherapy that are the subject of part 2.

Part 2 contains 12 chapters, each of which addresses a selected theoretical system that has direct application to the counseling or therapy process. We selected the theoretical systems based upon their current use in the field of counseling and therapy, and we chose the chapter authors based upon their expertise and their current application of the theoretical system in their work with clients. To provide the reader with a consistent format, each chapter contains information dealing with the following areas:

- *History.* The background information related to the development of the theoretical system.
- *Human nature: A developmental perspective.* The process of individual development over time, as defined by the theoretical system.
- *Major constructs.* The structural components that compose the theoretical system.
- *The process of change.* The factors that bring about change in the individual as addressed by the theoretical system.
- *Intervention strategies.* The methods used to translate the theoretical system into practice.
- *Supporting research.* The current research studies that form the basis for continued use of the theoretical system.
- *Case study.* The application of the theoretical system in the diagnosis and treatment of a client. The same case study information was used by all authors.
- *Limitations.* The applicational limitations, based upon the personal experience of the authors.
- *Summary.* A summary of the chapter.

The first three chapters in part 2 deal with the theoretical systems, often classified as *analytical,* which were developed by Sigmund Freud,

Carl Jung, and Alfred Adler. Chapter 5, "Psychoanalytic Theory," provides background information relative to counseling and therapy within a psychoanalytic framework and emphasizes current use of this framework for individual counseling and therapy. Chapter 6, "Jungian Analytical Theory," takes the reader from the development and definition of the major constructs of Jungian psychology to their application in the case of John, the subject of our hypothetical case study. We think readers will find this journey both intriguing and enlightening. Chapter 7, "Adlerian Theory," highlights the contributions of Alfred Adler and demonstrates the application of his major constructs in current approaches to counseling and psychotherapy.

The second three chapters in part 2 deal with the theoretical systems, often classified as *humanistic*, which were developed by the following theorists: Binswanger, Boss, Bugental, Frankl, Maslow, May, Tillich, Yalom, Rogers, and Perls. Chapter 8, "Existential Theory," sets forth the philosophical underpinnings of existential counseling and psychotherapy and demonstrates how this philosophy translates into approaches that can be used by the counselor or therapist in working with clients. Chapter 9, "Person-centered Theory," deals specifically with the work of Carl Rogers and highlights the continual development of this theoretical system from Rogers's work in the early 1940s to the last years of his life, when he traveled to the most troubled places in the world and used his person-centered approach to promote peace among warring groups. Chapter 10, "Gestalt Theory," emphasizes the pioneering work of Frederick Perls and his development of Gestalt counseling and psychotherapy. Major concepts and interventions are presented in combination with their current use in counseling and therapy.

The next four chapters in part 2 deal with the theoretical systems, often classified as *behavioral* or *cognitive-behavioral*, which were developed by the following theorists: Berne, Harris, Karpman, the Gouldings, Ellis, Beck, Meichenbaum, and Glasser. Chapter 11, "Transactional Analysis Theory," presents the early work of Eric Berne in the development of the major constructs of transactional analysis and emphasizes the current counseling and therapeutic practice derived from this frame of reference. Chapter 12, "Rational-Emotive Theory," highlights the work of Albert Ellis and emphasizes the basic assumptions, major constructs, and the application of rational-emotive therapy from both a past and current perspective. Chapter 13, "Cognitive-Behavioral Theories," provides the reader with a general background about both the behavioral and cognitive-behavioral theoretical views and discusses how the cognitive-behavioral approach developed from the behavioral point of view. Emphasis is given to the work of both Aaron Beck and Donald Meichenbaum. Chapter 14, "Reality

Therapy Theory," highlights the work of William Glasser and places special emphasis on a system he developed to provide a delivery system for reality therapy in helping others remediate deficiencies, make better choices, and become more fully self-actualized.

The last two chapters of part 2 deal with theoretical systems that are not easily classified into one of the standard categories for theory differentiation. Chapter 15, "Ecosystems Theory," provides a history of the development of the systemic approach to working with families, highlighting not only the theorists and practitioners who aided in its development but also the impact played by such factors as epistemology and cybernetics. Chapter 16, "Developmental Counseling and Therapy: Integrating Individual and Family Theory," presents an approach for integrating developmental theory into the practice of counseling and therapy. This approach, developed by the chapter's authors, provides an integrative assessment and treatment model for individuals and families.

We think that the theoretical systems included in part 2 provide the reader with a comprehensive and current review of major counseling and psychotherapy approaches to working both with individuals and families. Our conviction is strengthened by our selection of authors, who not only have expertise in the specific theoretical systems, but also practice these approaches in working with clients and families.

We asked each author or set of authors to address the following case study information in the development of a diagnosis and treatment or counseling plan that is consistent with the theoretical system. This approach gives readers the opportunity to view the theoretical systems from a comparative perspective as they search for the theoretical system that is most appropriate for their future work as counselors or therapists.

■ ■ ■

CASE STUDY INFORMATION

Presenting Information

John was examined by a specialist in internal medicine and then referred to a clinical psychologist for further evaluation. The client complained of a long-standing problem of severe cramps and diarrhea whenever he ate highly seasoned foods or encountered any type of stressful situation. This problem was diagnosed as an irritable colon when the client was a child. Since that time, he had been treated by a series of physicians, all of whom confirmed this diagnosis. The client reported that the medications prescribed for him had varied in effectiveness, and he had recently been in severe discomfort.

John is 40 years old, married, and the father of a 6-year-old boy and a 2-year-old girl. He is a college graduate with a degree in library science and has been a librarian in the same city library since he graduated from college. John stated that he began having unusually severe gastrointestinal symptoms at the time that a new director was appointed to the library 7 months ago. Recently, he has been sexually impotent on occasion, and this problem also concerns him.

John was neatly dressed in a conservative grey suit, and his demeanor indicated that his appearance was important to him. He spoke rapidly; and when inquiries were made regarding his feelings, he reported degrees of anxiety, depression, fear, and a sense of hopelessness. He reported his inability to sleep through the night and the recent occurrence of dreams in which he was being pursued by a myriad of faceless individuals whom he viewed as determined to harm him. The first of these dreams occurred about a month ago and involved his racing through a maze of rooms chased by two large males. Escape seemed impossible, and he awoke in a panic after being cornered in a room without exits. As the interview continued, he seemed to calm down, as measured by the reduced speed of his speech.

Childhood History

John was an only child. His parents were working-class, first-generation Americans of German origin. Their formal education concluded at the grade school level, and both were employed in factories. John's father had worked on the night shift for many years; and throughout John's childhood, the boy had little contact with his father except on weekends. John portrayed his father as a well-meaning but gruff person who usually let his wife handle disciplinary matters. He occasionally spanked John for misbehaving; but if he intervened at all, it usually involved shouting at his son. If John continued the negative behavior, his father did not follow through with any further disciplinary action. John's father generally stayed around the house when he was not working, but from time to time he took his son to a sporting event. John said that he felt affection for his father, but they never had common interests nor had there been much communication between them.

John described his mother as a tender and affectionate person. She was usually quite cheerful, and she spent a great deal of time with her son when she was home. She was very pleased when John helped her with the household chores, and she was extremely solicitous to him when he was ill. John felt that his parents were able to establish a good marital relationship. They sometimes had loud arguments, but these incidents did not last for long and there was no carryover of negative feelings.

John attended Catholic parochial schools until he went to college, and his parents were very pleased with the good grades he received. He particularly enjoyed reading, preferring this activity to playing with other youngsters. If his parents got into a dispute with each other or with him, he habitually withdrew to his room to read. John related that he had had numerous occurrences of intestinal difficulties ever since childhood. These episodes were associated with circumstances such as his mother's or teacher's insisting that he do something he did not want to do. He also became ill when he had to make a public appearance such as participating in his first communion or in a play at school. His mother tended to be quite concerned about making him comfortable when he had intestinal symptoms, although she always told him that it was just a nervous stomach. She said that she knew how he felt because she was also troubled with a nervous stomach when she was anxious or upset.

When John was 9 years old, his mother took him to her physician because he was in severe discomfort. He was in the midst of an episode of cramps and diarrhea that lasted for about a week. The onset of the symptoms was associated with his complaints that his new teacher was too strict and forced him to keep going over material he had already mastered. John stayed home from school during the latter part of that week, and the physician prescribed some medication that relieved a great deal of the discomfort. John's mother pleaded with the doctor to call the school principal and explain the reason for John's symptoms. This was done, and John reported that his teacher became somewhat more flexible in relation to his school activities. He had other occurrences of cramps during that school year, but none as severe as the earlier occasion.

John also had periodic intestinal problems while he was growing up, but these attacks usually lasted for just a few hours at a time. In high school, he experienced another prolonged occurrence of intestinal symptoms during a final examination period. He generally received good grades in school, but he was always quite anxious before a test because he was afraid that he would not do well. He was very anxious during these particular examinations because he had received lower grades than he had expected on some of his previous tests. Therefore, he studied a great deal and ignored his mother's assurances that he would do well on the exams.

John began having intestinal symptoms during the examination period, and the symptoms did not subside, even with medication, until 10 days later, when he went to a physician. He was given a complete medical examination, including a number of specialized tests of the gastrointestinal tract. These tests revealed no structural defects or damage, and the problem was again diagnosed as a chronic irritable colon. He was given a new medication to take when he felt that the symptoms were about to recur.

Early Adult Years

John lived at home while he attended a city college. The first friends he ever had were some students he met at college. He had always been shy and somewhat detached from others, and before college, he had never met any persons his age with whom he felt comfortable. Because of his interest in books, he decided to major in library science, and he eventually got to know some of the other students majoring in similar fields. There were relatively few males in most of his classes, but he did meet two or three young men with whom he became friends. They sometimes went to movies or concerts, and occasionally they went out together with some girls they knew from school.

Although John found it pleasant to be part of a group that included females, he was a senior in college before he decided to go out alone with just one girl. At that time, he met a girl he was attracted to, and he eventually asked her out. John said that he enjoyed being with Carol, and they spent a great deal of time together over the next several months. Carol was also Catholic, and they sometimes went to church together. John's mother told him that Carol was a nice person, but he felt that his mother did not really encourage or discourage his friendship with Carol.

John had not had much sexual experience before he met Carol. He had begun masturbating before adolescence, but he felt this activity was sinful and would harm him. He recalled that he tried to control this urge as best he could, but he was not always successful. John's physical approach to Carol was tentative and unsure. Carol told him that she believed it was wrong to engage in premarital sexual activity, and John stated that he felt the same way. He said that they lost interest in each other after only five months, and they eventually drifted apart to other friendships.

John met Betty, a college sophomore, two months before he graduated. As John phrased it, "We got used to spending our time together." Betty had also been brought up as a Catholic, and she and John began to attend church together on Sundays. Betty's immediate family was quite large, and each time John went to her house, there were a number of persons at home. John said that he did not feel at ease with Betty's family, but he made an effort to converse with whoever happened to be at home.

After they had known each other for about a year, Betty and John decided to get married. They agreed that it would be best to postpone marriage until John was more financially secure in his position at the library. John said that both his parents and Betty's were pleased that they were going to get married, and they approved of the plan to wait until they had saved some money.

Betty told John that she felt they should wait until they were married before having any sexual relationship, and John said that he respected this wish. He related that his sexual relationship with his wife proceeded from a stage of mutual inexperience to one of satisfaction. However, he still felt that the sexual drive was a reflection of man's baser instincts. They decided that it would be best to delay having children for a few years, and they followed the rhythm method of birth control.

John reported that he had not been greatly troubled with irritable colon symptoms during college and when he first started to work at the library. He expected that he would have a nervous stomach during examination periods, and he took medication accordingly to keep these symptoms to a minimum. Betty knew of these problems, so she tended to go out of her way to maintain John's good humor during these episodes. She watched the food that he ate when they were together, and she encouraged him to rest rather than to be with her. John also had some difficulty with intestinal symptoms during the period before their wedding. However, he recalled that he was able to function reasonably well and that he did not have to miss any of the social activities planned as long as he took the prescribed medication.

Marital and Employment History

John stated that reading was one of the most gratifying activities that he could think of. Betty had seemed pleased with his interest in books before their marriage, but her attitude later changed. She indicated to him that she had come to feel that his constant reading was a means of avoiding interactions with her and others. Especially after the children were born, she repeatedly told John that it was important for him to spend less time reading and more time with his family.

John said that he had never really been with other children for any length of time when he was young because he was an only child. He revealed that he did not feel any more comfortable interacting with his own children than he had trying to relate to other youngsters during his childhood. He left disciplinary matters to his wife, and generally spent his time at home reading. John sometimes played ball with his son, Michael, but he engaged in this activity very infrequently and only after his wife had asked him for some time. His daughter, Karen, was 2 years old, and

John commented that she was more verbal than Michael had been at the same age. He occasionally interacted with Karen by teaching her to say new words.

John described his marriage as "reasonably good." Betty was on good terms with John's parents, and she and John's mother joined together in their efforts to prevent him from having episodes of intestinal difficulties. John said that Betty was a good homemaker, and she tried hard to please him. When they were first married, Betty did not seem to mind spending most of their evenings at home. She was very proud of the vocational advances John had made at the library, and she accepted his statements that he could not participate in various social events because the reading he did at home helped him with his work. They presently had some friends they saw from time to time, but they generally did not attend as many social activities as his wife would have liked.

John indicated that his relationship with his wife seemed to deteriorate after the children were born. He felt that he and Betty did not communicate with each other as much as they used to, and he recognized that many times he purposely withdrew from social interactions by reading. It appeared to him that most of his wife's time was spent taking care of the children or nagging him about them, and she did not seem as interested in his work as she used to be. He also realized that he was not sharing with her as many of the events that happened at work as he once had. John said that he did not agree with his wife's belief that it was important for a father to interact with his children. He pointed out that his own father had spent very little time with him, but he cared for his father nonetheless and felt this lack of companionship had not hurt him.

John described his vocational situation as quite satisfactory until a number of months ago. He enjoyed working with books, and he found it gratifying to aid persons in finding the materials they were looking for. He eventually advanced to the position of head of the reference department, and two female librarians worked under his supervision. He stated that he had no difficulty interacting with them, and he generally ignored any attempt either of them made to influence the way he ran his department. He always avoided open confrontations. He typically listened without comment to what others said and then went ahead and did what he thought was best. John said that he generally behaved in this manner with his wife whenever they had a difference of opinion on some matter.

A new library director had been hired a few months previously, and John found it extremely difficult to get along with this woman. The director tended to issue statements to the library staff about policy changes without consulting with them first. John said that he was not able to ignore these orders and continue doing whatever he wanted to do, as had been his practice with the previous administrator. Further, he felt that he should have been offered the director's position, and he found it especially difficult to take arbitrary orders from a person whom he felt was not as qualified as he was.

Over the past few years, John's intestinal difficulties had gradually become more severe and incapacitating, and there was a marked intensification of his problems during the previous year. The medication prescribed for him had been reasonably effective in controlling his symptoms, but lately he found it necessary to stay home in bed whenever he had an episode of bowel spasms. The intestinal cramps had become extremely painful, and he often had spells of diarrhea lasting for almost a week. These bouts came on suddenly, with little advance warning, and were generally associated with negative events that had occurred at work or at home.

John stated that his wife continued to be very solicitous and helpful, encouraging him to rest at home when he was in discomfort. He said that she went out of her way to see that he was not disturbed by the children or upset by outside events. John indicated that his mother also became greatly concerned when he was ill and brought over special foods that she had found through her own experience to be good for "settling your stomach."

John related that there had been a number of instances since his marriage when he was impotent. He stated that his wife was very understanding during these infrequent occurrences, and he noted that each occasion had followed a prolonged period of intestinal difficulties. During the past several months, the episodes of impotence had increased in frequency; and John said that there were times when he wanted to have sexual intercourse, but he was not sure whether he could have an erection. He felt that his wife was also becoming more concerned about this problem, but she was purposely not saying anything for fear of making the situation worse.

In order to make sure that the irritable colon disorder had not developed into something more serious, John heeded the pleas of his wife and mother and made an appointment for a complete medical examination. He also hoped that the doctor would prescribe a stronger medication to control the distressing bowel symptoms. While in the process of the medical evaluation, John told the physician about the occasions of impotence.

Medical Evaluation

The physical examination and blood tests were all within normal limits. X rays of the gastrointestinal tract revealed an irritability and hyperactivity of the bowel, but there were no indications of obstructions, ulcerations, or other organic changes.

The diagnosis of chronic irritable colon made at this time was consistent with earlier diagnoses of John's condition. His problem was viewed as psychophysiological in nature: that is, changes in bodily function were associated with emotional stress. The internist referred the client for psychological consultation in order to explore further the problems with interpersonal relationships and to learn more about the episodes of impotence. He continued to prescribe antispasmodic medication.

■ ■ ■

CHAPTER FIVE

Psychoanalytic Theory

Leonard R. Corte
Southwest Center for Psychoanalytic Studies

This chapter provides a brief outline of psychoanalytic theory and technique. It has been written for the beginning clinician and is intended as an introduction to a complex psychotherapeutic process. Its goal is to interest the student in further exploring psychoanalysis as a treatment option.

Beginning with the work of Sigmund Freud, the chapter reviews a history of psychoanalysis and then divides and presents the psychoanalytic movement from the perspective of three historical periods. The first period is dominated by Freud and covers his early work through the end of World War I. The second period, which follows the end of World War I, is dominated by the establishment of training institutions and the emergence of the American Psychoanalytic Association. The third period begins with the end of World War II, continues into the present, and deals with the expansion of psychoanalysis worldwide.

Building on this historical background, the chapter presents a developmental perspective of human nature that emphasizes unconscious dynamics and the process involved in change. These dynamics include psychic determinism or causality, consciousness as an exceptional rather than a regular attribute of the psychic process, displacement, condensation, psychosexual stages, and defense mechanisms. The developmental theory espoused by Freud is used to explain not only the etiology of human behavior but also the etiology of human neuroses and psychoses. This developmental perspective explains both client dynamics and the intervention strategies used by the counselor or therapist.

Material from John's case study is woven into an explanation of theoretical concepts, and I've invented a session involving dream material in order to demonstrate a clinical application of psychoanalytic theory and technique. The chapter ends with a discussion of the limitations of the psychoanalytic approach and a summary of the significant material presented.

HISTORY

The history of psychoanalysis begins with Sigmund Freud (1856–1939). Before Freud, the field of psychology was considered a speculative philosophy, and the study of the human mind was limited to religious and magical thought. With psychoanalysis, psychology took a definite first step in the direction of scientific thinking. As Fenichel (1945) observed, "An understanding of the multiplicity of everyday human mental life, based on natural science, really began only with psychoanalysis" (p. 4).

Fine (1979) divides the history of psychoanalysis into three periods. The first period is dominated by Freud and covers his early work through the end of World War I. During this period Freud drew adherents to his cause, many of whom became the early pioneers of the psychoanalytic movement. The first psychoanalytic society was formed in Vienna; and later, with international recognition, the International Psychoanalytical Association was founded. This period led to the emergence of psychoanalysis, which has since evolved into a dynamic psychology and a philosophy of great cultural importance.

The second period, which dates from 1918–1939, is dominated by the establishment of training institutions and the emergence of the American Psychoanalytic Association. With the organization of many new psychoanalytic societies in democratic countries, specific regulations were adopted for the training of psychoanalysts. The training system that is now almost universally standard involves a tripartite model, the foundation of which includes the candidate's personal analysis. "It may be assumed that since about 1930 every practicing analyst has been through a training analysis" (Fine, 1979, p. 3). The training also includes theoretical instruction that lasts about four years and control analyses in which the candidate in training is supervised in the conduct of several analyses. Candidates are typically drawn from the mental health professions, especially in the United States, which has the largest membership of psychoanalysts belonging to the International Psychoanalytical Association.

The significance of this second historical period is marked by not only the proliferation of psychoanalytic education worldwide, but also the expansion of psychoanalytic thought through the creation of a great body of scientific literature.

The third period begins with the end of World War II and continues into the present. This period is marked by the further expansion of psychoanalysis worldwide. The 1992–1993 roster of the International Psychoanalytical Association lists 8,197 members, 45 component and provisional societies, and one regional society (the American Psychoanalytic Association). The roster includes 18 societies in Europe; 16 in Latin America; three in the Middle and Far East; one in Australia; and eight in North America. This third historical period is also marked by the expansion of psychoanalytic theory beyond classical Freudian metapsychology. Pine (1985) enumerates four distinct psychoanalytic psychologies that have developed within psychoanalytic metapsychology: Freud's drive theory, and the newer theories of ego, object relations, and self-psychology.

Recent developments in American health care are also affecting the perception of modern psychoanalysis. The contemporary psychotherapeutic scene has been greatly influenced by modern health care marketing. Rising health care costs have engendered the development and proliferation of a variety of abbreviated psychotherapeutic strategies. Managed care programs such as health maintenance organizations, preferred provider agreements, and employee assistance programs typically rely on interventions designed to keep costs to a minimum. Accordingly, the field of psychotherapy has become a veritable "convenience market" in which reducing the total number of contacts between the counselor/therapist and the subscriber/client is a priority. Similarly, the choices available to the average person who decides to get help are limited by the health care option to which she subscribes. It is not surprising, therefore, that a precise definition of psychotherapy has been further obscured by rapidly expanding methods designed to limit costs. Wolberg (1977) lists no fewer than 36 definitions that "generally do not agree on the techniques employed, the process included, the goals approximated or the personnel involved" (p. 14).

In the midst of these "innovations," psychoanalysis has lost favor as a treatment option, except perhaps in a few urban areas. Because it is recognized as a depth psychology and the analytic method involves multiple sessions over an extended period of time, it has little economic advantage in the contemporary marketplace of managed health care. Nevertheless, despite the predicted demise of psychoanalysis, due in large measure to these changes, new training institutes continue to form in major metropolitan areas, which indicates a continued interest in psychoanalysis on the part of professional counselors and therapists. In part, this may be the result of a dedication to dynamic theory, which seeks to understand psychopathology as well as the forces operative in the therapeutic process. It may also reflect the counselor or therapist's dissatisfaction with technique-oriented strategies and a wish to increase the use of self as a tool in the therapeutic process. (Personal analysis is a requirement for psychoanalytic training.)

What distinguishes psychoanalysis as a psychotherapeutic theory and method? Wolberg (1977) divides the varieties of psychotherapy into three main groups: supportive therapy, reeducative therapy, and reconstructive therapy. His schema depicts a gradation from lesser to greater complexity in the perceived objectives of each therapeutic strategy. For example, whereas the "object in supportive therapy is to bring the patient to an emotional equilibrium as rapidly as possible" (p. 68), reeducative therapy attempts to achieve more extensive goals through an "actual remodeling of the patient's attitudes and behavior in line with more adaptive life integration" (p. 101). The difference is in the specific therapeutic technique employed. In supportive strategies, reassurance, suggestion, relaxation, and persuasion may be used. In contrast, reeducative approaches rely more on reconditioning. The counselor or therapist introduces behavioral reinforcers or the therapeutic relationship to modify, liberate, or promote self-growth.

The objectives of reconstructive therapies offer the greatest complexity. The goal of reconstructive psychotherapy is to bring the client to an awareness of crucial unconscious conflicts and their derivatives. In contrast, supportive efforts toward this kind of insight are minimal, and the reeducative emphasis is less on searching for unconscious causes than on promoting new and better forms of conscious behavior through conscious action. Counselors or therapists who direct their efforts toward reconstructive changes within the client have typically turned toward psychoanalytic methods and theories because the techniques employed in bringing unconscious conflicts to awareness were originally developed by Sigmund Freud, the founder of psychoanalysis.

HUMAN NATURE: A DEVELOPMENTAL PERSPECTIVE

The Freudian Unconscious

In the late nineteenth century, medically oriented approaches assumed that neuroses were due to some unknown organic factor, and therapeutic measures were limited to electric shock and hypnotism (Fine, 1979). Freud isolated himself from this mainstream position, as Fine observes, and in the process made his first major discovery: "The key to neuroses lies in psychology, and all neuroses involve a defense against unbearable ideas" (Fine, 1979, pp. 21–25). In an attempt to understand clinical data, Freud arrived at two fundamental hypotheses concerning mental development and functioning, which can apply to normal as well as pathological activity. According to Brenner (1974), these two hypotheses, "which have been abundantly confirmed, are the principle of psychic determinism or causality, and the proposition that consciousness is an exceptional rather than a regular attribute of psychic processes" (p. 2).

The first principle observes that mental activity is not meaningless or accidental; nothing happens by chance or in a random way. All mental phenomena have a causal connection to the psychic events that precede them. An example of this principle can be drawn from the case study of John. The presenting information and the client's childhood history are organized in such a way as to develop a context of continuity between early psychic experiences and the symptoms we assume to be a consequence of these experiences. We ask ourselves, "What caused this?" and we organize our data around this question because we are confident that a coherent answer exists that is connected to the rest of the client's psychic life. We assume that each neurotic symptom is caused by other mental processes, despite the client's protestation that the symptom is foreign to his whole being. For example, John complains of gastrointestinal distress and is convinced that it is a physical illness that has invaded his body. As counselors or therapists, however, we presume psychological causes outside of the client's conscious awareness.

Freud first noted the principle of psychic determinism in relation to dreams. He discovered that "each dream, indeed each image in each dream, is the consequence of other psychic events, and each stands in coherent and meaningful relationship to the rest of the dreamer's psychic life" (Brenner, 1974, p. 3). This principle contrasts with the notion that dreams are products of random brain activity during sleep, an idea popularly held by neurologists and psychiatrists seventy years ago and by some organic theorists today.

The second principle, that of unconscious mental processes, is closely linked to psychic determinism. This principle accounts for the apparent discontinuities in the client's perception of symptom and cause, for the causal connection has become part of the unconscious process. In the case study, John has repressed his mental conflicts into the unconscious, thereby causing his symptom. It follows, then, that if the unconscious cause or causes can be discovered through the therapeutic process, the causal sequence becomes clear and the client's insight leads to cure. It should be noted that this brief explanation is a rather simplified version of what in actuality is a long and complex treatment process in which the client examines through free association a variety of unconscious mental processes. This simplified explanation also ignores the role of interpersonal influence as a mutative factor in psychoanalysis.

Freud (1938/1940) argued that "the governing rules of logic carry no weight in the unconscious; it might be called the Realm of the illogical" (pp. 168–169). He also declared:

> We have found that processes in the unconscious or in the Id obey different laws from those in the preconscious ego. We name these laws in their totality the primary process, in contrast to the secondary process, which governs the course of events in the preconscious ego. (p. 164)

In other words, Freud called attention to the fact that a portion of the mind, which is particularly active in our dreams, our emotional life, and our childhood, works within a framework of timelessness, spacelessness, and the coexistence of opposites. For example, timelessness is implied in our clinical work when we take for granted the simultaneous presence of an adult client and his expressions of infancy. Freud's notions of *displacement* (an idea's emotional emphasis becomes detached from it and is superimposed on some other ideas) and *condensation* (several ideas are expressed through a single idea) exemplify spacelessness. We recognize in clinical work that feelings expressed toward an uncaring employer may be an unconscious replication of childhood feelings felt toward a parent in the past or the counselor/therapist in the present. They are displaced onto the employer as a defense against a painful memory or onto the counselor/therapist against the threat of awareness. Freud and his followers identified a number of defensive strategies unconsciously employed by the mind; these defy normal logic but act to protect the subject from awareness.

In her definitive study, *The Ego and the Mechanisms of Defense* (1966), Anna Freud specified 10 such defensive mechanisms: regression, repression, reaction formation, isolation, undoing, projection, introjection, turning against the self, reversal, and displacement. Repression and projection, commonly seen in clinical practice, are unconscious defensive processes. *Repression* refers to "an operation whereby the subject attempts to repel, or to confine to the unconscious, representations (thoughts, images, memories) which are bound to an instinct" (Laplanche & Pontalis, 1973, p. 390). *Projection* is an "operation whereby qualities, feelings, wishes or even 'objects,' which the subject refuses to recognize or rejects in himself, are expelled from the self and located in another person or thing" (Laplanche & Pontalis, 1973, p. 349). The other mechanisms operate similarly by unconsciously protecting the subject from awareness of repressed conflict and subsequent anxiety.

Freud's Development Theory

"In psychoanalytic treatment, the client regresses and recapitulates, in a modified form, early developmental phases. Both neuroses and psychoses are based on a series of fixations on and regressions to these past ego stages and orientations" (Giovacchini, 1987, p. 87). Freud postulated the psychosexual stages of infantile sexuality as oral, anal, and phallic, which linked developmental theory with sexual impulses. This meant that Freud believed sexual expression went beyond what is ordinarily considered sexual, for he postulated infantile activities as erotic.

In essence, psychosexual stages refer to a sequential acquisition of progressively sophisticated modes of gratification from various bodily zones that are necessary for growth and development. The term *libido* describes instinctual energy that belongs to the sexual drive. The discharge of this energy leads to pleasure, and the part of the body that leads to such pleasure is referred to as an erogenous zone.

Erikson (1963) elaborated on these erogenous zones: oral-sensory, which includes the facial apertures and the upper nutritional organs; anal, or the excretory organs; and the genitalia (p. 73–74). He posited modes of functioning within each zone. These included modes of incorporation, retention, elimination, and intrusion. The following examples show how modes may interplay with each zone.

Orality represents a method of relating to the external world. The infant's smiling is an indication of ability to recognize objects in the external world as separate from the self. The first mode of approach in the oral zone is incorporation: that is, to "take in" in a dependent fashion what is offered by the mother. Modes of incorporation dominate this stage, yet other modes are also expressed. According to Erikson (1963):

> There is in the first incorporative stage a clamping down with jaws and gums; there is spitting up and out (eliminative mode); and there is a closing up of the lips (retentive mode). In vigorous babies even a general intrusive tendency of the whole head and neck can be noticed, a tendency to fasten itself upon the nipple and, as it were, into the breast (oral intrusive). (p. 73)

In clinical work, one might refer to orally dependent clients. This indicates that extreme dependence is the result of a predominance of oral elements in adult functioning. This functions as a metaphor to describe a fixation at the oral stage of development, wherein the overly dependent adult client tends to relate to the world in terms of a need to be nurtured. While the child actually requires this nurturing to survive, the adult client is seen as wanting to be taken care of, to be soothed and nurtured in a psychological sense. A client described as an oral character may use any or all of the modes described previously: spitting out what the counselor/therapist offers or intrusively penetrating into the counselor/therapist's space, demanding to be "fed." Erikson saw the nuclear conflict at this level as one of developing the sense of basic trust versus the sense of mistrust.

To Freud, control of the anal sphincter initiates the anal stage of development and is seen as an important contributor to adult structure. Control of the sphincter, which is part of the total muscle system activated at this stage, places an emphasis on the duality of rigidity and relaxation, flexion and extension. As noted by Erikson (1963):

> The development of the muscle system gives the child a much greater power over the environment in the ability to reach out and hold on, to throw and to push away, to appropriate things and to keep them at a distance. This whole stage, then, which the Germans called the stage of stubbornness, becomes a battle for autonomy. For as he gets ready to stand more firmly on his feet the infant delineates his world as "I" and "you", "me" and "mine." Every mother knows how astonishingly pliable a child may be at this stage, if and when he has made the decision that he wants to do what he is supposed to do. (p. 82)

Accordingly, the conflict at this stage involves the antithesis of letting go and holding on, of autonomy versus shame and doubt.

The Oedipus complex, which is one of the most controversial and best known of Freud's theories, dominates the phallic stage. At this stage, the child has moved away from a two-person system of mother-child interaction to a triangular relationship with both mother and father. The Oedipus legend, based on Greek mythology, assumes the child's wish to possess the parent of the opposite sex, which creates a conflict with the parent of the same sex. In more graphic terms, and truer to the original legend, incestuous feelings are combined with patricidal impulses.

In the case of the boy who wishes to possess his mother, he fears retaliation by the father and fantasizes the father's revenge of castration. That is, the father's retaliation will be directed at the boy's penis, resulting in castration anxiety. This complex is necessary for later development because the threat of castration leads the child to internalize, as a permanent part of his psychic structure, a prohibiting, controlling superego that is the foundation of morality. In the case of a girl, the unconscious wish is to marry the father and to take care of him in a much better way than she imagines the mother is capable of doing. While these theories remain controversial today and are seriously questioned by modern developmental theorists, they continue to be used as important metaphors in understanding clinical material.

Major Constructs and the Process of Change

The assumptions upon which the system of psychoanalytic theory rest are referred to as *metapsychology* (Rapaport & Gill, 1959). As noted by Greenson (1967), "The clinical implications of metapsychology intimate that in order to comprehend a psychic event thoroughly, it is necessary to analyze it from six different points of view—the topographic, dynamic, economic, genetic, structural and adaptive" (p. 21).

The *topographic* point of view is the first major concept. It contrasts unconscious versus conscious mental processes. The deeper layer of the mind, the unconscious, has only the aim of discharging impulses. Both conscious and unconscious expressions are present in clinical material and can be described as manifest and latent. In order to illustrate this concept, we will use the dream material noted in John's clinical study. The client reports recent occurrences of dreams such as the following:

> He was being pursued by a myriad of faceless individuals whom he viewed as determined to harm him. The first of these dreams occurred about a month ago and involved his racing through a maze of rooms chased by two

large males. Escape seemed impossible, and he awoke in a panic after being cornered in a room without exits.

In psychoanalytic clinical work, it is essential to have the client's association to a dream in order to verify our assumptions about the latent, or unconscious, meaning of a symbol or the dream itself. To interpret the meaning of a dream without these associations would be to impose our own thoughts onto the client, a process derogatorily called wild analysis. Because we do not have John's associations in this case, we will guess at some possible associations in order to illustrate the metapsychological points of view. We might assume, for example, that the manifest symbol *maze* would unconsciously represent (in other words, have a latent meaning of) a library, with all its rows and shelves of volumes carefully ordered and numbered. While the conscious representation of library represents order and control, the unconscious representation stands for chaos without exit. Both stand in topographical relation to the other: one conscious, the other unconscious. A further elaboration, and much more presumptive, is that the maze is not only symbolic of library but also at a deeper level of intestine and bowel. We might assume that at this level John's gastrointestinal conflict is about control versus chaos, a desperate holding onto or an involuntary letting go of his internal contents, as represented by his symptoms of cramping and diarrhea.

Dynamic and *economic* points of view are the second and third major concepts of psychoanalytic metapsychology. In order to understand these two points of view, it is necessary to explore Freud's idea of the psychoeconomic hypothesis. This hypothesis requires a concept of psychic energy, much like physical energy, with principles of pleasure-pain and constancy. The idea of psychic energy will be explained briefly before we define the dynamic and economic points of view.

For Freud, the development of instincts necessitated conflict. For example, when instincts such as sexual and aggressive drives strive toward expression, they clash with the reality principle, leading to states of pent-up tension. As noted by Giovacchini (1987):

> Psychoanalysis requires a concept of psychic energy to explain the various movements of the psychic apparatus, those involved in action, problem solving, reestablishment of emotional equilibrium, and growth. A hypothesis of psychic energy must be based on certain general principles that dictate the distribution and production of energy and how it is to be used. (p. 62)

Giovacchini further noted:

Freud relied on two principles on which he built his concepts of psychic energy, the *principle of constancy* and the *pleasure principle*, more specifically, the *pleasure-pain principle*. The constancy principle is based on the hypothesis that the function of the nervous system and the psychic apparatus is to keep the level of excitation at its lowest point. The pleasure principle is related to the constancy principle in that it asserts that lowering the level of excitation, which connotes release and relief, leads to pleasure, whereas increased excitation creates tension and disruption and is experienced as pain. (p. 63)

This tension-discharge hypothesis supports the dynamic point of view, which assumes that mental phenomena are the result of the interaction of psychic forces seeking discharge. Greenson (1967) tells us that "this assumption is the basis for all hypotheses concerning instinctual drives, defenses, ego interests, and conflicts. Symptom formation, ambivalence, and over-determination are examples of dynamics" (p. 23).

The way in which psychic energy is distributed, transformed, or expended defines the economic point of view. To illustrate these points of view, we might assume that John was in a state of dammed-up instinctual tension before the recent outbreak of his gastrointestinal symptoms. However, his ego was still able to carry out defensive operations so that he could function without obvious symptoms. These operations seemed to be consistent with a compulsion for order, as exemplified by his appearance, manner, and vocation. We would expect that his need for order was bolstered by a variety of stereotypical rituals and repetitions, not only as they concerned himself (that is, his thoughts and his body) but also as they involved his interpersonal interactions. This obsessive-compulsive style would be necessary to contain instinctual forces, such as intense rage, from explosive expression. The client's hostility toward the new director precipitated the most recent outbreak of symptoms.

John's ego could not cope with this influx of anger seeking discharge. The impulse to rage broke through in his severe intestinal cramps and diarrhea, expressive of the conflict of painfully, intentionally holding onto and involuntarily letting go of something from within. In this instance the something within happens to be feces, which unconsciously are equated with rage.

This brings us to the fourth major concept of psychoanalytic metapsychology, the *genetic* point of view, which concerns an understanding of the origin and development of psychic phenomena. It explains how the past is being brought to the present and why a certain specific compromise solution has been adopted. To return again to our case example, John's history and associations in analytic sessions would no doubt highlight the importance his mother played in his adopting a defensive style as well as those psychic conflicts already noted.

The fifth major metapsychological concept is the *structural* point of view, which assumes that the psychic apparatus can be divided into several persisting functional units. "The concept of the psychic apparatus as consisting of an ego, id and, superego is derived from the structural hypothesis" (Greenson, 1967, p. 25). The id is the agency from which all instincts derive, while the ego is the agency that mediates these drives with the external environment. Based on a signal of anxiety, the ego brings a number of defensive operations into play. It works as an agency of adaptation with functions such as control over perception, voluntary motility, and the setting up of affective memory traces, to name just a few. The superego is the agency of the personality within which develops a framework of conscience, self-observation, and the formation of ideals. It acts as a judge or censor for the ego.

To illustrate the structural point of view as it applies to John, we could assume that the ego's defensive functions have weakened under the pressure of the appointment of the new director. Her unconscious signification as mother mobilizes John's conflict over the expression of hostility. We might further assume that as he progresses in analysis he will no longer regress in this way when confronted with similar situations, for his ego functions will have replaced inadequate defenses with new insight.

Thus far, all the examples we have used from the case study reflect attempts at *adaptation*, the last major metapsychological construct. A person's relationship to his or her environment, objects of love and hate, and society are based on the adaptive point of view.

INTERVENTION STRATEGIES

Freud's technique for uncovering hidden psychic processes evolved over a period of several years, and despite some relatively minor variations it is still in use today. The classical technique entails a process of *free association* (letting thoughts drift over events of daily life, past history, and dreams) on the part of the client, who is typically in a recumbent position with the counselor or therapist sitting behind and out of sight. The practitioner maintains a position of neutrality, referred to as the rule of abstinence, based on denying the client's wish for gratification of instinctual demands. These techniques minimize the actual presence of the counselor or therapist and allow the client to focus more freely on intrapsychic matters such as fantasies, dream analysis, childhood-based conflicts, and defensive or resistive operations that block awareness of unconscious processes. More important, they facilitate the development of the *trans-ference*, defined by Laplanche and Pontalis (1973) as

> infantile prototypes that re-emerge and are experienced with a strong sensa-tion of immediacy and are directed toward the analyst within the analytic sit-uation. This is the terrain on which all the basic problems of a given analysis play themselves out: the establishment, modalities, interpretation and reso-lution of the transference are in fact what define the cure. (p. 455)

In other words, transference is reliving in the presence of the counselor or therapist the client's repetitious and rigid defenses of the past. It is the analysis of these defenses within the transference that makes change pos-sible.

The aim of the analytic technique, primarily through the analysis of transference, is to increase the client's insight into herself. The analysis also seeks to strengthen ego functions, which are required for gaining understanding. The most important analytic procedure is *interpretation*—making an unconscious phenomena conscious. Interpre-tation is considered the most decisive procedure.

Empathy, intuition, and the counselor/therapist's own unconscious and theoretical knowledge all contribute to the construction of an inter-pretation. Other analytic procedures include confrontation, clarification, and working through. This latter procedure is of great significance because it involves the continued analysis of resistances brought about after an insight has been achieved. It refers to the broadening and deepen-ing of insight that leads to permanent change.

SUPPORTING RESEARCH

Psychoanalysis shares with other fields of study in the social sciences the problem of demonstrating itself as scientific. In addition, because it is a method of therapy, research limitations are imposed upon it that do not exist in other fields. For example, a simple research design of treating one person analytically while using a similar person as a control would be unethical. Therefore, the empirical value of psychoanalysis has to be founded on clinical investigations. That is to say, the empirical testability of psychoanalytic theory must be demonstrated in the treatment situation. Grunbaum (1984) notes:

> The naturalistic setting or "psychoanalytic situation" is purported to be the arena of experiments in situ., in marked contrast to the contrived environ-

ment of the psychological laboratory with its superficial, transitory interaction between the experimental psychologist and his subject. (p. 100)

The following information is a cursory review of research findings from studies of the psychoanalytic theory and method.

In their book *The Scientific Credibility of Freud's Theories and Therapy* (1977), Fisher and Greenberg compiled a synthesis of almost 2,000 individual studies on the scientific status of psychoanalysis. They concluded that Freudian theory had been subjected to more scientific appraisal than any other theory in psychology and that results had borne out Freud's expectations. Similarly, Luborsky and Spence (1978) emphasize that the psychoanalytic session has epistemic superiority over experimentally obtained validation and supports Freud's general theory of unconscious motivation.

Despite these affirmations, particularly as they relate to the clinical observation of the major motivational forces of mental life, current criticism of psychoanalysis focuses on its use of multiple sessions and overall length of treatment. Opponents of psychoanalysis point to the efficacy of briefer models of treatment, especially practical in contemporary health care settings where cost of care is a concern. They argue that brief, technique-oriented psychotherapy may be just as effective in alleviating a specific symptom without uncovering unconscious dynamics. This debate is not so much about the empirical testability or value of psychoanalysis as it is about the economics of treatment.

Although this brief review is limited to empirical studies before 1979, it should be noted that research in psychoanalysis is ongoing, with researchers using the naturalistic setting of the psychoanalytic situation as the field of study. Fenichel (1945) observes:

> Psychoanalysis began as a therapeutic method and even today secures material principally because of the happy circumstance that its psychological research method and the medical therapeutic method coincide. What Freud observed during the treatment of his patients he could apply later to an understanding of the mental phenomena of healthy persons. When psychoanalysis then went on to study the conscious phenomena and the various mental functions, it could do this in a way different from that of other psychologies, for it had previously studied the unconscious and the instincts. It conceives of all these "surface manifestations" as structures that have been formed out of deeper instinctual and emotional sources through the influence of the environment. Of course it should not be claimed that except for the Freudian findings there is no scientific psychological knowledge; but it should be asserted that all psychological knowledge gains new light when considered from the psychoanalytic point of view. (p. 85)

■ ■ ■

THE CASE STUDY OF JOHN: THE PSYCHOANALYTIC APPROACH

In order to continue to illustrate the psychoanalytic method and theory outlined in the preceding pages, it is necessary to invent a session as we might imagine it unfolding. As we have already noted, the research material of psychoanalysis is drawn from the productions of clients in therapeutic settings—that is, free association, dream analysis, and so on. This material is used to substantiate psychoanalytic theories regarding mental functions. Accordingly, this section provides clinical material as it might unfold in order to serve as an example as well as to explain our ideas about unconscious processes.

We begin by assuming that the client, John, has been in analysis for several months and is being seen for four sessions weekly. The counselor or therapist is using a classical technique (John is in a recumbent position with the practitioner out of sight), after it had been determined that the client was capable of working in the psychoanalytic situation.

Before the session begins, the counselor or therapist recalls that the client had reported a dream in the previous session. The dream involved the client's being at a library or a bookstore, he wasn't sure which. In the dream he knew that whichever it was, it was his; that is, he owned it. A faceless person, a woman or a man, was there rearranging the order of the books. John concluded that this person was critical of his arrangement. He was afraid.

His associations to the dream took him to his need for order and the somewhat ritualized way in which he followed directions. He recalled being an overly compliant child who felt that if he didn't follow directions exactly as given, his impulse would be not to follow them at all. He thinks the person in the dream could be his mother. Here is an excerpt from the session following the dream.

Client: I went to the doctor and he said my stomach is not getting any better. I need to take my medication regularly, yet I don't want to be dependent on it. I agreed to take it, though, and I guess I'm taking it because someone said I should. My stomach feels awful; it's always bloated. It makes me think of a water tank that could explode under pressure. I shouldn't fight it because it could get much worse. Sometimes I imagine I have stomach cancer. Something in the back of my head says "I told you so," as if the doctor were saying it. For some reason I think of coming here. I've had thoughts of ending therapy, but I've made a commitment to do this. It's like unless I make a strong commitment to someone else, I won't do it on a regular basis. I guess I need the structure. If I stop doing something over and over, I won't do it at all. Like there is a destructive part of me.

Counselor/Therapist: You need to imagine that I am making you do this; otherwise, you feel you wouldn't do it at all.

The dream and the clinical material reflect the developing transference, in which the counselor or therapist is seen as both the doctor and the critical mother or father inside his library. The library possibly signifies the inside of the client's body, which incorporates the faceless person, both man and woman, who is critical of his arrangement. His anxiety in the dream is assumed to be a reaction to his growing rage at the critical parent/practitioner that he has internalized and on whom he feels dependent.

In the session, he continues with this theme. Here he imagines that he must do something according to formula or repetition or his initiative would fail him. This compulsion suggests that he cannot derive pleasure from an acquired control during the anal phase because he is not the initiator of action: that is, he is not in control of what is inside of him. It also suggests a defensive measure to block explosive expression of his anger. The defense is his compulsive adherence to repetition. The conflict of holding on to or letting go of his anger is experienced somatically as severe cramps and diarrhea, the latter being a somewhat involuntary, out-of-control discharge of internal contents.

In order to be a "good boy," he must depend on his absolute commitment and dependency on someone else's regimen. The result is a somatic experience of pressure mounting within, along with a fantasy of permanent physical damage—that is, a growing cancer. His need for the parent/practitioner to provide structure, however, thereby defending himself and the counselor or therapist from his anger, seems evident, even though he experiences this as bloating, damaging to him physically, and provocative of explosion.

The counselor or therapist chooses to interpret within the transference, calling attention to the general nature of the client's defense. We might assume that the counselor or therapist selected this alternative over other possible interpretations because the client is still in the early months of the analysis and is learning to think in terms of displacing thoughts and feelings onto the counselor or therapist. Other aspects of the dream or the clinical material are open to interpretation, such as the unconscious connection between mother and director, between anger and stomach contents, between library and bowel, and between medication and the counselor/therapist's prescription of words and sessions. The latter interpretation would be of particular importance because the material reflects the client's growing anger at the counselor or therapist (analogous to the doctor), whose medication does not seem to be effective. In fact, the client feels that it is provoking discomfort, and his thoughts turn to retreat from his therapy. In other words, the very conflict that we imagine brought John to therapy—holding on to or involuntarily letting go of his anger—is now being mobilized in his analysis and directed at the counselor or therapist. Although the client is as yet unaware of this development, it is nonetheless surfacing in his dreams and in his associations.

LIMITATIONS

Psychoanalysis in the United States has traditionally been limited to the educated, middle- to upper-class client who is able to afford the cost of treatment. Likewise, counselors or therapists using psychoanalysis have tended to practice mainly in areas of large urban populations. Therefore, the urban and rural poor, as well as the rural middle and upper class, have not had access to psychoanalytic services. Even if this limitation were alleviated by a national health care plan, the overall cost of educating a counselor or therapist as well as the personal sacrifices involved in analytic training automatically tend to limit the availability of counselors or therapists certified in psychoanalysis. It is a rigorous training method that severely taxes interested candidates both financially and emotionally. The unfortunate outcome of this last limitation is that it restricts the pool of psychotherapists, whose training includes—in fact, mandates—personal therapy of considerable duration.

It is not surprising that counselors or therapists, on occasion, harbor disturbing feelings toward their clients. These strong passions of both love and hate can skew how well the therapy is conducted. Sometimes counselors or therapists are aware of these strong emotions, but sometimes they are buried in the unconscious, making an understanding of the source and usefulness of these feelings unavailable to the practitioner as a means of improving the therapeutic process. In this regard, psychoanalytic training provides an advantage that could be offered to any counselor or therapist who wishes to go beyond a method of brief or technique-limited therapy. Those practitioners who do not have an understanding of the source and rationale for emotions experienced in therapeutic situations may be shortchanging themselves and their clients.

The limitations of psychoanalytic methods, as applied to large populations of both rural and urban poor, may never be alleviated. Yet greater strides may be made toward offering counselors and therapists, through psychoanalytic training, a sound procedure for better understanding them-selves and their clients, thereby improving their overall therapeutic skill.

SUMMARY

This chapter attempts to condense in a few brief pages a great body of psychoanalytic literature on theory and technique. It began with a review of the historical development of psychoanalysis, which was followed by Freud's metapsychology, developmental theory, and technique. An imaginary session was also included in order to illustrate key elements of both theory and technique.

The theoretical summary, admittedly, is a simplified version of what constituted Freud's formulations, which to some degree, have been expanded upon in modern psychoanalytic thought. Pine (1985), for example, enumerates four distinct psychoanalytic psychologies: drive, ego, object relations, and self. He points out that in ego psychology, greater emphasis is given to reality, drive, conscience, and a strong "theory of the ego, its development, and its functions; a conception of autonomy, and adaptation" (p. 58). In contrast, object relations emphasizes the "object seeking, (rather than pleasure seeking)" nature of the libidinal drives, and self psychology leads to "formulations centering on a 'self' and to a developmental theory heavily weighting the confirming/mirroring/rewarding inputs of the other" (pp. 59–60). The limitations of space prohibited a more complete discussion of recent theories of ego psychology, object relations, and self psychology. This chapter also focused on classical psychoanalysis as opposed to psychoanalytic psychotherapy because the fundamental theories and techniques of psychoanalysis are essential for the practice of counseling or therapy within a psychoanalytic/psychotherapeutic framework.

One final note. To reiterate an earlier statement, it was necessary to invent a session and a dream to demonstrate a clinical application of psychoanalytic theory and technique. This invention was the result of my clinical experience and was based on clues to the possible unconscious conflicts underlying the client's presentation of history. It shows, at best, my own projections and should be read only as an attempt to illustrate theory and technique. Working from a case history, no matter how inclusive and definitive the material, limits the potential for drawing analytic assumptions or conclusions. The working material of an analysis must be provided not only by the history, but also, and more importantly, by the client's associations in clinical sessions. This is what brings the analysis to life for both the client and the counselor or therapist.

REFERENCES

Brenner, C. (1974). *An elementary textbook of psychoanalysis*. New York: Doubleday.

Erikson, E. (1963). *Childhood and society*. New York: Norton.

Fenichel, O. (1945). *The psychoanalytic theory of neurosis*. New York: Norton.

Fine, R. (1979). *A history of psychoanalysis*. New York: Columbia.

Fisher, S., & Greenberg, R. (1977). *The scientific credibility of Freud's theories and therapy*. New York: Basic Books.

Freud, A. (1966). *The ego and the mechanisms of defense*. New York: International Universities Press.

Freud, S. (1940). *An outline of psychoanalysis* (Vol. 23), Standard Edition. Translated by James Strachey. London: Hogarth Press. (Original work published 1938)

Giovacchini, P. (1987). *A narrative textbook of psychoanalysis*. London: Aronson.

Greenson, R. (1967). *The technique and practice of psychoanalysis*. New York: International Universities Press.

Grunbaum, A. (1984). *The foundations of psychoanalysis: A philosophical critique*. Berkeley: University of California Press.

Laplanche, J., & Pontalis, J. B. (1973). *The language of psychoanalysis*. New York: Norton.

Luborsky, L., & Spence, D. P. (1978). Quantitative therapy. In S. L. Garfield & A. E. Bergin (Eds.), *Handbook of psychotherapy and behavior change* (2nd ed.). New York: Wiley.

Pine, F. (1985). *Developmental theory and clinical process*. New Haven: Yale University Press.

Rapaport, D., & Gill, M. M. (1959). The points of view and assumptions of metapsychology. *International Journal of Psychoanalysis, 40,* 153–162.

The roster of the International Psychoanalytical Association. (1992–1993). London: Broomhill's.

Wolberg, L. (1977). *The technique of psychotherapy*. New York: Harcourt Brace Jovanovich.

CHAPTER SIX

Jungian Analytical Theory

Susan E. Schwartz
C. G. Jung Institute of Santa Fe, New Mexico

Everything good is costly, and the development of personality is one of the most costly of all things. It is a matter of saying yea to oneself, of taking oneself as the most serious of tasks, of being conscious of everything one does, and keeping it constantly before one's eyes in all its dubious aspects—truly a task that taxes us to the utmost. (Jung, 1967, p. 18)

Years ago I attended a lecture by a Jungian analyst educated at the Jung Institute in Zurich, Switzerland.[1] Part of the presentation was a fairy tale. In the process of telling the tale, the analyst described the thunder of giants. Just as he reached that point in the story, there was an actual resounding thunderclap outside. At that moment I realized I wanted to be a Jungian analyst and to study in Zurich. A month later I began analysis as the first step toward reaching those goals.

The fairy tale reached some psychological opening inside me. I remembered the love I had for fairy tales as a child. When I read them, a world opened that took me out of my own, that transported me to the archetypal level portrayed by the symbols and images in the tales. The personal world was transcended; and at the same time it was united with the larger psychological culture of stories and experiences extending beyond a circumscribed time and space.

The thunder in the tale represented an intuitive feeling: I was struck by the unconscious and synchronistically given direction from an inner message. During a synchronistic event, inner and outer situations come together in a meaningful way. The analyst, who was a man, was important because my masculine side (my animus) found a goal for the productive use of energy. Going to Zurich was a journey to a distant land—part of my psyche that was foreign and unfamiliar. Little did I know at the time where this journey would take me and how much it would require to surrender to the unknown. My life was going to be radically transformed, as if struck by giants hurling thunder. Thunder comes from heaven and is associated with spiritual communication from the gods. Giants are large, primitive, and instinctual with powerful energy that is different from the intellect. My psychological quest was to unite spirit and matter, heaven and earth, father (or the sky) and mother (or the earth).

---

[1]Because of the requirements of this book, I will generally use the terms *counselor* and *therapist*. In Jungian psychology, however, the term *analyst* is more common, and *analysand* is used rather than *client*.

Although this small vignette does not mention personal life events that are crucial for analytical work, it does show that Jungian analytical psychology is an endeavor of the soul that involves a process of deep self-examination. One's problems attain significance for finding life meaning, and their resolution reaches beyond the personal world.

HISTORY

Jungian analytical psychology was originated by the Swiss psychiatrist Carl Gustav Jung, who was one of the early pioneers in the Freudian psychoanalytic circle. Although he was chosen as Freud's heir apparent, it gradually became clear to Jung that he could not agree with Freud concerning the primacy of the sexual trauma theory or the solely reductive and personalistic approach of psychoanalysis. The difference in their perspectives solidified with Jung's book *Symbols of Transformation*, for which he was subsequently ostracized by Freudians.

After this realization, Jung quit his teaching position at the University of Zurich and resigned from his post at the Burgholzli Psychiatric Clinic. He spent the next six years without publishing anything, because he was intensely immersed in the unconscious. However, he continued his private analytical practice while devoting his energy to working on the psychological crisis and his resulting aloneness, which the break with Freud had precipitated. Through intense inner work involving playing and building as a child in the sand, writing and dialoguing with dream figures, drawing, and chiseling with stone, Jung discovered many of the later concepts that appear in his writings as well as the methodology of personality transformation that he was formally to call the process of individuation.

In the early 1900s Jung worked at the Burgholzli Psychiatric Clinic in Zurich under Dr. Eugen Bleuler, who was known for his studies in schizophrenia. Jung's contributions included his discovery of the word association test, which revealed the existence of complexes and their archetypal core and confirmed the influence of the unconscious on the conscious life. Through these researches he and Freud became connected, for both were unearthing evidence of the powerful forces residing in the unconscious. Jung also discovered what was later to be termed the collective unconscious, an idea he developed through listening to schizophrenic patients who used images and symbols paralleling ancient religions, alchemy, myths, and fairy tales. According to Jung:

> At a time when all available energy is spent in the investigation of nature, very little attention is paid to the essence of man, which is his psyche,

although many researches are made into its conscious functions . . . yet deciphering these communications seems to be such an odious task that very few people in the whole civilized world can be bothered with it. Man's greatest instrument, his psyche, is little thought of, if not actually mistrusted and despised. "It's only psychological" too often means: "it is nothing." (1964, p. 102)

The basic premise of his approach resounded with the reality of psychic phenomena.

Jung was born in 1875. He was descended from a long line of ministers, and his father was also a minister in a small town outside of Basel, Switzerland. Early in life Jung was dismayed by his father's loss of faith and his inability to experience spirituality with personal meaning. During studies for his own confirmation at age 13, Jung was struck by the banality and lack of direction that his father provided. This spiritual lacuna later led to Jung's search for the spiritual aspects of the psyche. It also contributed to an initial projection of the father image onto Freud, who was 20 years Jung's senior. In their discussions, Freud would not share his dreams with Jung and interpreted Jung's dreams in personalistic modes that Jung resented; this caused him to lose faith in Freud. Their later severance of friendship guided Jung to a different path of self-discovery, and it also depicts the necessary juncture for personality growth when the son separates from the father.

Jung was also influenced by his mother, whom he observed to have two personalities—one that complied with the conscious societal rules and the other that complied with the unconscious underpinnings that seemed to express her real self. It was these two personalities that Jung later developed into the theoretical distinction between the personal and collective unconscious. Mother and father, whose relationship was emotionally distant, represented the polarized concepts of spirit and matter, anima and animus, persona and shadow, ego and self, and they added to the shaping of Jung's theories.

Jungian analytical psychology derived from the personal life struggles Jung found applicable to general psychological development. He said, "My life is what I have done, my scientific work; the one is inseparable from the other. The work is the expression of inner development" (1963, p. 211). According to him, this work began in childhood and was prefigured there. Jung searched for verification of what he had experienced and theorized and found similar processes paralleled in religion, the medieval science of alchemy, and the mythological legends and tales of the world. All supported Jung's discovery of the collective unconscious and the psychological process of individuation.

HUMAN NATURE: A DEVELOPMENTAL PERSPECTIVE

The psyche is made up of conscious and unconscious elements with continually shifting borderlines of contact. The unconscious is the matrix out of which consciousness arises.

Ego

The ego is central to the personality because it is the subject of consciousness that maintains relations with other psychological contents. The ego is the point of reference for the field of consciousness; and as one among many complexes, it possesses a high degree of continuity and identity—is part of the personality but not the whole of it. In a situation in which the ego is assimilated by the unconscious components of the personality, as when a complex takes over, the ego becomes greatly altered. This occurs in a state of "abaissement du niveau mental" (the diminution or extinction of consciousness), which refers to the loss of energic value by the ego and a corresponding dip into the unconscious.

Consciousness refers to the type of knowledge that is felt through the realization that "I am a being who has a world." The ego is personal, and

TABLE 6.1
Jungian Vocabulary

Anima:	the psychological feminine component in a man
Animus:	the psychological masculine component in a woman
Archetype:	collective image expressing material from the collective unconscious; an inherited pattern of organization
Complex:	psychic entities that have escaped and split off from the control of consciousness and may help or hinder conscious life
Ego:	the subject or center of the field of consciousness
Persona:	the mask or adapted appearance or stature that may or may not reflect individuality
Psyche:	the totality of all psychic processes; the conscious and unconscious
Self:	the subject of the total psyche, including the unconscious; also embraces the ego; the source and ultimate foundation of our psychic being
Shadow:	symbolizes the other or dark side that is an invisible but inseparable part of the psychic totality; has both positive and negative forms and can be manifest in both personal and collective figures

---

individuality is one of its main characteristics as the seat of subjective identity. It is reflected in the personal unconscious and composed of the forgotten, repressed, and subliminally perceived events and reactions in one's life. The process of individuation or transformation of the ego entails a relationship to the self, which is the representative of the objective or archetypal psyche. The creatively active aspect of the psychic nucleus comes into play when the ego gets rid of purposive and wishful aims and tries to establish a meaningful form of existence. How the self becomes integrated depends on whether or not the ego can listen to its messages, for only if the ego notices can the inner gifts be brought into reality. The ego cannot function when overwhelmed by the self.

The individuated ego is the part of the self that we know. The first half of life involves ego separation from self, as psychological development proceeds to detach the ego from the unconscious matrix. In the second half of life, ego and self reunite to break out of a state of personality alienation. The ego must be capable of expanding without losing creative contact with the unconscious. The process of individuation is one that requires giving up the ego position for the emergence of a different and more fluid relationship with the self. Becoming human is a sacrifice of the ego, which entails a surrender to the feared loss of control and involves flexible movement between the personal sphere and the more encompassing transcendent self. This does not mean loss of consciousness or retreat from the world.

Persona

In Jungian psychology the word *persona* (from Latin, meaning "sounding through") denotes the presentation one puts forth to others in the world, be it through job, dress, or societal position. The outer cover is what gives protection and provides acceptance and participation in the world. It is possible that the genuine nature of a person can come through the public face; however, exclusive reliance on the persona is a defensive attempt to hide the complete personality and can be used to control what others think.

The differentiation of the ego from identity with the persona opens up the multiple nature of the psyche and is indispensable for psychological development. Counseling and psychotherapy separate the persona from the collective standards and foster perception of the individual personality. There are problems when the particularity of a person is suppressed or neglected in order to fit the collective ideals. If external values are artificially adopted and pasted on, the person acts in false and mechanical conduct to himself and others without a sense of natural-ness.

The persona is the skin mediating between the inside and outside. It functions in dynamic and compensatory relation to the shadow and to the anima and animus to reveal rather than conceal their qualities. The persona serves to widen the personality when a person can divest herself of the wrappings that do not fit so that the creative aspect of the personality can bring liberation and growth. The more narrow the persona, the more the ego lacks adaptation and energy instead will go into shadow forma-tion. When it is used as an indispensable cover-up, the persona becomes rigid, stiff, and phony; dependence on this mask reflects distrust in the substance of the personality. The masks and illusions stave off being real and foster inauthenticity because this use of the persona prevents inner conflicts and insecurities from attaining visibility.

Shadow

The shadow and its differentiation from the ego are part of the movement towards wholeness of the personality. Jung wrote:

> The shadow, as we know, usually presents a fundamental contrast to the con-scious personality. This contrast is the prerequisite for the difference of potential from which psychic energy arises. Without it, the necessary ten-sion would be lacking. Where considerable psychic energy is at work, we must expect a corresponding tension and inner opposition. The opposites are necessarily of a characterological nature: the existence of a positive virtue implies victory over its opposite, the corresponding vice. One is flat and boring when too unsullied and there is too much effort expended in the secret life away from the eyes of the others. Without its counterpart virtue would be pale, ineffective, and unreal. The extreme opposition of the shadow to consciousness is mitigated by complementary and compensatory processes in the unconscious. Their impact on consciousness finally pro-duces the uniting symbols. (1963, p. 707)

In the shadow resides the dilemma of how to separate the individual self-regulatory conscience from that of the collective. The shadow includes both personal and collective, or archetypal, attributes. It causes reflection on human nature, and its uncovering reveals the deepest and most intrinsic values for the fulfillment of individuality. The shadow spans the realms of the personal by appearing in dreams personified as a figure with unpleasant or unknown qualities and the collective as expressed by a devil, a movie star, Hitler, and so on. Living one's shadows implies taking responsibility for oneself as well as for others in the owning of both talents and problems. With the moral obligation to self-development, figures appear in the shadow that represent positive possibilities of one's nature or the potentialities not yet given a chance.

Dissonance and harmony, opposition and concordance, balance and imbalance are conceivable through the polarity inherent in the concept of the shadow, for without this polarization there is no energy, no process, and no movement. One cannot help but be ambivalent about the shadow because it contains all that is worst and best in the personality: the Mr. Hyde and Dr. Jekyll. The dark side gains in strength when there is movement away from one's potential toward a secretive withdrawal into oneself. Affects and emotions occur where adaptation is weakest and there is an inferiority in the yet-to-be-developed aspects that remain unconscious. It is bitter to accept the shadow, for it is the black, the chaos, the melancholia, the start of the work. This is sometimes the first complex to personalize in Jungian counseling or psychotherapy because it contains material relating to the problem as well as holds the potential for healing.

A rude awakening comes with the discovery of the shadow because it brings one down to basic human nature. The shadow is difficult to confront and assimilate due to the ease we have in unconsciously projecting it onto others. We much prefer to entertain idealized images of ourselves rather than acknowledge personal weakness or areas of shame, and the recognition of the shadow means moving away from the ideal and the perfect. The shadow contains those qualities we would rather not admit as ours and makes its appearance in the dream as figures of the same sex as the dreamer. When the shadow is not brought to light, it gets projected onto others; the inner images are externalized, undermining the capacity to form honest relationships. By taking back the projections, the personality attains definition, style, and unity. Owning one's shadow makes it easier to help solve marital and family problems rather than project the unwanted or rejected contents onto others.

Integration of the shadow and the realization of the personal unconscious marks an initial stage in this counseling or psychotherapeutic process. It provides a bridge from the ego to the contrasexual part of the personality. In Jungian psychology, this contrasexual part is called the anima as feminine soul for a man and the animus as masculine spirit for a woman. According to Jung:

> The disciple will have every opportunity to discover the dark side of his personality, his inferior wishes and motives, childish fantasies and resentments, etc.: in short, all those traits he habitually hides from himself. He will be confronted with his shadow, but more rarely with the good qualities, of

which he is accustomed to make a show anyway. He will learn to know his soul, his anima. . . . He attains this knowledge with the help of the spirit, by which [is] meant all the higher mental faculties such as reason, insight, and moral discrimination. (1963, p. 473)

Anima

In Jungian psychology *anima* is a word connoting the constellation of feminine qualities that a man carries inside his personality and that personifies his relation to the unconscious feminine psyche—the image of woman in man's interior world as well as the image projected onto outer women. The anima is a psychic factor, an inner guide with a role as mediator between the ego and the self. It is influenced by the personal and archetypal experience of the feminine, and conscious knowledge of "her" is considered essential for the attainment of completeness as a person.

The anima refers to the images of the soul and functions best when there is receptivity and absence of prejudice in order to foster belief in oneself. It, like all archetypes, can never be totally known. The man discovers the feminine aspect of his soul coincidentally with the psychological movement into himself. It is "her," as a part of the anima mystery, that draws a man to himself and results in the development of a more complete life.

If a man does not know his feminine nature, he can become uneasy and uncommitted as well as avoid conflict and drift. When he remains distant from the feminine and from his emotions, he pays too little attention to the psyche. A narrow representation constricts inner and outer freedom, and life cannot emerge from the flat and monotonous moods of neglect. Anima moods cause dullness, impotence, and even suicide. When out of touch with this essence, a man does not experience wholeness, and he turns to accomplishment or performance when he cannot get an inner reflection of himself. Due to fear of the feminine, a man becomes distant from inner and outer relationships, and the bridge is not established between the anima to the ego and subsequently to the core of the self. Becoming conscious of the inward sexual polarity promotes wholeness and motivates participation in those aspects lying beyond the personal.

The anima image becomes conscious and tangible through actual contact with women, with the first and most important experience coming from mother. The image of mother occurring in the child is colored by the innate capacity to produce an image of woman through the archetype of the anima. In different eras the image changes and is modified. The anima psychologically implies the existence of a semiconscious psychic complex with partial autonomy of function. The anima is expressed in a man's life through projection upon women and in creative activity, and it also functions as a mirror to reflect fantasies, moods, emotional outbursts, and presentiments. The inward feminine personality becomes known through images arising from the unconscious and is associated with the instinctual part of life, the flow of emotion, the rhythm of nature, and the physicality of pleasure. Only as the anima becomes increasingly differentiated can a man assume an active rather than a passive role in relation to women. In reference to this, Jung describes the anima as "that from which consciousness arises. It lives of itself, makes one live, and cannot be fully part of consciousness" (1959, p. 57). This statement refers to the transcendent and archetypal psychological aspects that allow one to stretch beyond the narrower world of the ego.

Animus

The animus in woman is the counterpart of the anima in man. It is derived from three roots: the collective image of man that a woman inherits, her experience of masculinity from contact with the men in her life, and the latent masculine principle within herself. The animus signifies woman's feeling relationship to man, to men in general, to culture. This Greek word originally meant "breath or spirit," and it connects a woman to the spiritual aspects of the psyche. Activating the masculine principle is likened to knowing one's goal and doing what is necessary to achieve it with courage and determination, force and authority, using the qualities that further a woman to be effective, powerful, and competent in a feminine way in the world.

The masculine principle is encountered through the direct experience of relating to the father as the first and primary example of a male. There are problems when the father figure has no limits and is either all-giving or a rigid disciplinarian encased in a distant and foreboding authority structure. In this case, the woman may not be personally touched by him in a positive way. When his emotion is absent or when he is physically unavailable or abusive, no guidance is imparted but rather a vacuum of bewilderment is formed. The void is often negatively filled under such conditions. A woman is passionless when held by the animus in a negative father complex, for he has her energy and cuts off her life force.

When the animus is undeveloped and has not had sufficient room for expression or growth, it hounds and hinders the feminine through castigations and sufferings and effectively undermines entry into adult life. The negative animus manifests in a voice of critical comments or issues commands and prohibitions that are obeyed in slavish servility. As the feminine nature is overwhelmed and pushed into the background by an animus, creating depressions, general dissatisfactions and loss of interest in life arise. The animus in its destructive aspect cuts off a woman's participation in life, and she feels separated, tortured, and unable to go on. When drawn to a negative fascination with the animus or taken over by inertia, she severs contact with the world.

The animus problem includes self-alienation because the woman does not listen to herself or take herself seriously. There is a melancholy passivity in avoidance of the life of the spirit, and she gives up her soul. A woman may be dreamy and unfocused or even very assertive, but she suffers from a chronically latent depression that keeps her in a fragmenting despair without satisfaction while she is constantly driven by a life hunger to do more. The loneliness and hunger arise from aptitudes remaining dormant. The negative animus is self-destructive and destructive of relationships. The woman eventually must go through some form of psychological sacrifice to escape the mastery of the animus, turn its energy to beneficial use, and regain her spirit.

Self

Behind all psychological patterns lies the self, which is the blueprint of life unfolding from the center of the personality as a guide. The self contains awareness of the uniqueness of each person and embodies intimate relationship with the entirety of life—human, plant, animal, and even inorganic matter and the entire cosmos. The self is a synthesis from which the personality emerges and is a cohesive force establishing a sense of balance and well-being. It represents one's essence and gives support to the personality.

The empirical symbols of the self possess a distinct numinosity, or powerful emotional value, and appear in dreams, myths, and fairy tales in the figure of supraordinate personalities such as the hero or heroine or in the symbol of an animal, an egg, a hermaphroditic figure, the "treasure hard to attain," a jewel, a flower, or as geometrically or concentrically arranged totality figures known as mandalas. *Mandala* is a Sanskrit word meaning "magic circle," and it is one of the world's oldest religious symbols. Jung found the mandala symbol appearing spontaneously in the dreams of many of his patients, which revealed the directive function of the self as the creator and preserver of individual development striving toward the potential of wholeness. The question is not of the self's being created during the course of life, but the extent of its attaining consciousness.

The self is a *temenos*—a container providing holding from the interior environment as the source and ultimate foundation of our psychic being—and it transcends personal vision. The self contains the harmony of the archetypes and the multiplicity of the instincts, and it is supraordinate to the conscious ego. While the self is the center of the personality, the midpoint that embraces the conscious and the unconscious psyche, it is also the whole circumference. "The beginnings of our whole psychic life seem to be inextricably rooted in this point and all our highs and ultimate purposes seem to be striving toward it" (Jung, 1967, p. 67). There are no bounds to the self, which is not limited to the individual psyche, but its limits lie in the illimitable and indeterminable unconscious where one is simultaneously wholly oneself yet unknowable and connected beyond oneself. Because the self is both able to experience and also includes the not-yet-experienced, it is a transcendental concept characterizing an entity that can be described only in part.

At the more encompassing level, the self is a metapsychological concept referring to the entirety of the psyche as the object of the process of individuation that contains the whole range of psychic phenomena. We are born with the self as the matrix of all the potential faculties waiting to be actualized. Jung says, "In the last analysis every life is the realization of a whole, that is, of a self, for which reason this realization can also be called individuation" (1953b, p. 330). The self is paradoxical, as are all archetypes, containing both positive and negative polarities for the organizing and uniting of experiences from within, operating in the service of the ego, and endowed with the capacity to experience continuity throughout time.

MAJOR CONSTRUCTS

The structure of the psyche is a dynamic, self-regulating system governed by opposition and built on complementary or compensatory factors. *Enantiodromia*, a Greek concept borrowed from the philosopher Heracleitus, means the flow into the other side of the psyche to bring a revaluation to appreciate its opposite aspects. The idea is not to convert from one side to the other but to conserve the old values together with the cognizance of a renewed way of regarding and using them. The psychic energy or libido pulsing through all psychological forms, when lost to consciousness, passes into the unconscious through repression and activates its contents through the archetypal images and the complexes.

Psychological Types

We are all familiar with the terms *introvert* and *extravert*, which were originated by Jung as the two attitudes or ways in which people inherently perceive the world and themselves in relation to it. The extravert looks at the world and then refers to himself, while the introvert first checks the perspective of her own eyes and then looks out to the world. The extravert is oriented by outward collective norms and the introvert by subjective factors. It has been noted that Jungian analysts are predominately introverts, as are those who come for this type of counseling or psychotherapeutic treatment. This is not a requirement, but the work does emphasize the inner world and the reactions and observations of the psyche, which is easier for those who are naturally oriented in this way.

In addition to the two attitudes, there are four functions determining a person's psychological characterization of orientation to the world. They are *thinking*, which gives meaning and understanding; *feeling*, which weighs and values; *sensation*, which is perception through the senses; and *intuition*, which intimates future possibilities.

Thinking tells us what a thing is, and this function can be recognized when a person is ruled by intellectual motives and conclusions that are based primarily on objective data. Contents of ideation are brought into conceptual connection with one another when logic and order are preferred. The corresponding repression of emotion and feeling means the person tends to appear cold and has some difficulty understanding human relationships.

In contrast, feeling is especially concerned with human relationships. This particular function is not to be confused with emotion because any of the functions can lead to emotion. Feeling is distinguished from affect because it produces no perceptible physical ennervations. Feeling hierarchically weighs and values psychological contents in a subjective process based on internal judgments of acceptance or rejection.

The person who functions primarily through sensation takes everything as concrete, calling a spade a spade and using an insistence on facts as a way to mediate the conscious perception of physical stimuli. Sensation conveys to the mind the perceptual image of the external object, just as it brings bodily changes to consciousness.

Intuition, like sensation, is an irrational function, for both lack the logic associated with the rational functions of thinking and feeling. Intuition is the opposite of sensation and entails a perception of those realities not known to consciousness, which emerge via the unconscious in an active and creative process that has the capacity to inspire. Intuitive types are able to tell the possibilities of what something might become, but they can be so removed from the present and the senses that they often forget the physical body.

One of these functions, called the *superior function*, predominates in each person's personality and takes on particular forms depending on the influence of social, intellectual, and cultural factors. Another, called the *inferior function*, is closest to the unconscious and remains the least formulated. The functions are limited to four because Jung determined that they are not further reducible; within them all the possibilities are contained. Furthermore, the number four has been regarded throughout time as designating wholeness, completeness, and totality.

The main or superior function becomes fully available as the most developed, and the two accessory functions are reasonably so. This leaves the fourth or inferior function remaining undifferentiated, primitive, impulsive, and out of one's control. Because human nature is not simple, one rarely finds an absolutely pure type. The superior function is what one does with most ease and confidence, and its development can be influenced by the family values. All functions can change, depending on how one is engaged at different life stages. The attitudes do not change but become more truly realized as the individual proceeds in life. For example, a child may learn to be an introvert in a quiet and withdrawn family. Later, he may discover that this was an adaptation, that he is actually more comfortable being an extravert.

Each attitude can be paired with each function, making eight psychological combinations in all. Relationships become clearer as people understand their typology and the concept that those around them have a compensatory typology, in accordance with the old adage that opposites attract. The complementary or compensatory relation between the opposite functions is a structural law of the psyche. In the second half of life, the opposite function of the conscious existence calls attention to development, often to the point of inner conflict, and causes the psychological situation to alter.

Complex

The complex is composed of energic entities of psychic dynamism functioning at varying levels of dependence and independence, with some even operating like separate personalities. A complex has varying degrees of autonomy, from hardly disturbing functioning to being strong enough to rule the personality. Because it presents as a well-organized but split-off part of the personality, the complex feels like an independent source of energy at work within the psyche. Complexes occur where the repressed energy is blocked and the nucleus of the complex draws psychological energy with its magnetic quality.

The particular makeup of the complex contains the images pertaining to the unconscious psychological situation colored with a specific emotional tone, but it can be difficult to reconcile with the conscious mind.

The unconscious complexes assist in the unfolding of the personality and are productive to psychological knowledge through their appearance in dreams. The conscious observation of formerly unconscious contents brings awareness through reflection on the images. Although the complex is a normal part of the psychic life, when it is unconsciously projected, there can be a contagious effect exerted upon others; thus, one's destiny can be controlled by the complex, and the problem can go unresolved through the family for generations. Part of the work in counseling or psychotherapy is to understand and clarify the complexes through the intensely compelling attention of their emotional components.

Archetype

The personal unconscious consists for the most part of complexes, and the collective unconscious consists essentially of archetypes. The archetype is the nucleus of the complex imbued with a tendency to form and reform images rich in emotional content with infinite possibilities for analysis. Jung called the repetitions of the archetypes *motifs*. The archetype is a formless structure that is enmeshed in history and changes shape over time. It is specific to, yet broader than, each era because there are a definite number of archetypes that are more or less pertinent to a time or place in the evolution of the psyche. Jung states, "No archetype can be reduced to a simple formula. It is a vessel which can never empty and never fill. It has a potential existence only, and when it takes shape in matter it is no longer what it was. It persists throughout the ages and requires interpreting anew. The archetypes are imperishable elements of the unconscious, but they change their shape continually" (1959, p. 179).

We all inherit the tendency to structure experience through psyche and body in certain typical and predictable ways. An archetype is a basic form expressive of the structure of the human psyche defining a psychological pattern of development that gives a coordinating and coherent meaning to inner perceptions. These are the essential building blocks of the psyche in the form of basic psychological instincts and behavioral patterns that are counterparts of the biological instincts.

In Jungian psychology, *archetype* means that which is universally present in the human psyche and common to entire peoples or epochs. Jung says that the archetype "represents or personifies certain instinctive data on the dark, primitive psyche, the real but invisible roots of consciousness" (1959, p. 271). The archetype cannot be described but can be circumscribed. It encompasses the opposite sides of the spectrum while oscillating between both. The archetypes are of an impersonal nature personifying human potential. They lead one to follow the deeper currents of life and carry an energy that fascinates the individual and causes the images in dreams, mythology, religions, and fairy tales to strike a responsive inner chord.

Symbol

The Jungian perspective is differently oriented from other psychological approaches because the symbols in the psyche connect one not only to the personal situation but also to the collective unconscious, wherein reside powerful images containing information reaching back through historical time. A living symbol is different from a sign because it formulates essential unconscious factors with profundity and is pregnant with significance. Jung described this as a numinous feeling capable of giving meaning and depth to life.

Every symbol inherently has two sides—one related to the conscious ego and one turned toward the unknown contents of the collective unconscious from which the archetypes arise. The unconscious produces answers to psychological problems through the images emerging compensatory to the conscious mind. These images are spontaneous manifestations of the process of individuation pertinent both to the individual and society. A symbol functions by taking energy or libido from the unconscious dimension, often considered as the irrational and mysterious, and transforms it for conscious use. By pointing toward the resolution of psychic conflict, the symbol embodies a creative dynamism that channels self-expression from the wellspring of the life force.

One of the ways in which the archetype is expressed and comprehended is through mythological images. Jung spent time studying myths, for he considered them to be fundamental symbolic expressions of human nature representing typical psychic phenomena. Because the myth is a projection from the unconscious, we come upon similar themes in all cultures. Jung comments:

> It is only possible to come to a right understanding and appreciation of a contemporary psychological problem when we reach a point outside our own time from which to observe it. This point can only be some past epoch that was concerned with the same problems, although under different conditions and in other forms. (1954, p. viii)

The archetypes reveal the essence of their immortal character, which is refashioned anew in sacred images. The archetypes are ever-present in their dominance and are woven into the symbolic patterns of mythologies that reflect the distinctive life of the psyche of any given culture or religion. They not only explain natural events but also express how humans experience them. Religion, poetry, folklore, and fairy tales all exhibit central figures that are archetypal in nature. The attention to mythology gives a fullness to existence, for these age-old parables explore the purpose and meaning of life and are reflective of the eternal depths of the psyche. The spirit of the myth, the creative urge it represents, and the feelings it expresses and evokes come from the realm of the collective unconscious.

The figurative languages of both the mythological and the psychological—as apparent through the dream life—clarify, amplify, and explain each other. Dream thinking, a symbolic kind of thinking and expression, is similar to that of mythology. Signals in the form of symbols are received from the unknown part of the psyche every night. Dreams are real experiences, scenes from the play of life that address the blind spots of the personality. The dream images reverberate from within as an involuntary psychic process not controlled by the will. Their images stimulate us to think in paradoxes; from interaction with them, we gain insights and begin to transform through the subjective feeling aroused by the symbolic world.

The word *symbol* derives from the Greek *symbolon*, which means "coming together." This process happens when one concentrates and values the unconscious parts of the personality as they come together in the conscious life. A symbol arises from a state of conflict or disorientation, joins two separate elements, and thereby mobilizes energy. Symbols are spontaneous products of the collective unconscious and transform the unconscious psyche into conscious experience, giving life energy to the ego. The unconscious is full of the germs of the future psychic situations and ideas. It is timeless while also being pertinent to the particular moment. The transmutation of the libido or energy through symbols, referred to by Jung as the *transcendent function*, has been going on since the beginning of time and is deeply rooted in human nature.

To the extent that one is unaware of the symbolic dimension of existence, one experiences the problems of life as symptoms. They become more intolerable when they are perceived to represent meaninglessness, which is the great threat to humanity. It is the ability to recognize the symbolic image behind the symptom that transforms the experience into the meaningful.

Collective Unconscious

This is a pivotal concept encompassing all the previous ones, and it most distinguishes Jungian analytical psychology from other theories. However, to endeavor to define the collective unconscious is to attempt the impossible, for there is no knowledge of its boundaries or its true nature. All we can do is to observe its manifestations and try to understand them as much as possible.

By collective, Jung referred to psychic contents belonging not to one individual but to many. The collective part of the unconscious does not focus on the individual ego but is the inherited psychic functioning of the brain. It is revealed through religions, myths, and images that spring up independently of historical tradition and that appear in the dreams, drawings, active imagination, dance, or other creative work of individuals.

The collective unconscious carries the heritage common to all humans and is the foundation of every individual psyche. It contains the deposit of human reactions to universal situations that have occurred since primordial times. It seems understandable that if people are biologically related, then they must also be psychologically related through the collective and archetypal level.

The collective unconscious is felt, often on a visceral level, when a very important and moving dream is experienced. This psychic layer is deeper than the personal unconscious and is the unknown material from which consciousness emerges. Jung called the tendency to apprehend and experience life in a way conditioned by past history *archetypal* in order to designate the collective image or symbol from the personal. The archetype is a content that is the psychological counterpart of instinct. Instinct defined as impulses to action without conscious motivation gives reality to the archetypal image, just as the image gives meaning to the instinct. Instinct is essentially collective and universal; it is a regularly occurring phenomenon that has nothing to do with individuality. Although some archetypes are personal as well as collective, both archetypes and instincts are considered to have a collective nature.

THE PROCESS OF CHANGE

The uneasy ambiance of the current age has heightened a pervasive aimlessness and inner alienation that is manifested in a frantic search for fulfillment. The illnesses of society, the boredom, joylessness, and inability to love penetrate everyone to a greater or lesser degree and cause havoc in interpersonal and intrapersonal relationships. Jungian analytical psychology attempts to relieve modern isolation and confusion through the search to find one's particular place and meaning in the stream of life.

According to Jung, the psyche is a dynamic system that is in constant movement and at the same time self-regulating. This approach gives the inner psychic process a value equal to the outer one by demonstrating the unconscious as a force to be acknowledged, fostering its expression, and helping to find a channel for the repressed libido. The development of individual consciousness and the integration by the individual of unconscious contents are safeguards against blind possession by the archetypes. The archetype can present as an aspect of good or evil, destructive or constructive, depending on the conscious attitude and capacity for understanding.

During the analytic session, one discusses dreams, active imagination, personal relationships, current problems, childhood developmental issues, transference, synchronous occurrences, and so on. All of these are worked on additionally outside the sessions through the journaling of feelings, emotions, and thoughts and through any creative endeavors that become a means to observe the inner life and bring the unconscious to consciousness. The presenting problems vary, and the direction that treatment takes usually goes beyond the initial issues presented. People naturally become intrigued with themselves and through the unconscious material awaken to their purpose and meaning in life.

The transformation of the character and the course of the interior drama arises naturally because the potential for growth is inherent in the human psyche. The individuation process or the way in which people come into their own uniqueness is at the core of all experiences and reflects the archetypal process of psychological rebirth. The spontaneous spiritual and religious activities of the psyche use the natural production of symbols timelessly occurring in the unconscious in a language universally understood through age-old images crossing all cultures.

This form of counseling or psychotherapy is a method of education, rebirth, and transformation that shows its effects gradually over time. The process reveals where developmental difficulties have arisen and where growth needs to take place. Individuality is found through embarking on this lonely yet guided inner journey. Self-knowledge makes people look at and question what has been taken for granted, rouses their sense of moral and ethical values, and releases the creative powers. For example, the integration of the anima and animus into conscious life leads to the possibility of a new kind of relationship between men and women rather than a blind fulfillment of stereotypical roles.

Jung discovered historical validation for the individuation process in many places, but the one he researched most extensively was alchemy, a medieval science and a precursor of modern-day chemistry. The alchemical symbols and the goal of symbolically turning lead into gold parallels the psychological journey—for example, the stages of nigredo, or darkness and melancholia; calcinatio, or burning in destruction; albedo, or whitening and purifying. Jung used the alchemical symbols to amplify dreams and understand transference and countertransference, for alchemical work also often entailed a helper.

A person goes along, often until midlife, functioning sufficiently well but with a certain part of the personality undeveloped and lying dormant. When creativity has atrophied and one is unable to move on, a crisis develops: a person wonders who she is. Relationships alter and life becomes tumultuous if she is not living according to the truth of her being. The second half of life is significant; the energy stored in the unconscious pushes forward to be acknowledged and to bring fulfillment through the assimilation of unconscious contents. Jung's personal crises and his psychological work with many people confirmed that the inner turn of the personality during adulthood promotes unused creative aspects. Broadening of the personality occurs by confronting the unconscious on its own terms and synthesizing the conscious and unconscious material—taking it apart and bringing it together in an altered form. The raw material from the unconscious is used to refashion the personality. By modeling the counselor or therapist's listening and participating attitude, a person is taught to regard herself psychologically and to comprehend the reality of the psyche with its link between the inner and outer worlds.

Currently, Jungian counselors or therapists use a chair or a couch. Clients are seen at least weekly, preferably two or more times a week. Frequent sessions are necessary because this form of counseling or psychotherapy searches deeply into the psyche, and the concentration of energy encourages emergence of elements from the unconscious. The process of true change is not quick or easy, and each person embarks on this path in a unique way, deriving meaning from the suffering and psychic pain of the past to live fully in the present. This approach is applicable to people of all ages, including children.

INTERVENTION STRATEGIES

Dreams

Dreams are the most natural way to discover and unravel the inner workings of the personality. They are more than just bizarre images that come with sleep. Dream work takes one to the unexpected core issues and even becomes a source of inspiration. The belief that dreams are a means of divine communication or an occult way of discerning the future was pervasive in the ancient Near East. In biblical times, dreams were considered to be the agents of God's word by announcing his will to the dreamer. Dream interpretation was an important part of the spiritual life of the ancient Greeks and Egyptians, whose word for dream was derived from the verb "to awaken." In all races and at all times, dreams have been regarded as truth-telling oracles because the world of dreams is as natural and real as the waking and conscious life.

Attention to the dream world is a way to obtain information about areas that are unknown and untapped but that carry useful messages. The external universe is duplicated in the dream world and demonstrates the various roads to the psyche. No dream books suffice as a ready-made guide for dream interpretation; nor can the dream symbol be separated from the person who dreams it, as standard interpretations can negate the individual. The value of the dream information is that the day world becomes enhanced with unacknowledged qualities and contents repressed into the unconscious, which have robbed the individual of full vitality and participation in life. Following the dreams leads to recovery of oneself and brings return through the recall of past phenomena as a bridge connecting one inward. In unique and creative ways, dreams weave the current experiences with those from the past.

Dreams keep one from straying from the truths of the body when the concrete life coincides with the psychic image in a symbolic portrayal of the actual situation in the unconscious. A dream is like an X ray that depicts the current condition of the inner world, and its potency is brought to life in a way that affects the fundamental layers of the personality through the triggering of various emotional reactions. The physical disorders in dreams express a psychic situation and may even serve as a sort of early-warning system for illness or a certain vulnerability. Dreams often give more than expected by suggesting treatment and providing guidance for the conduct of life. They contain methods and tools for psychological healing and practical problem solving by crystallizing a problem into something workable and understandable.

Jung wrote, "One should never forget that one dreams in the first place, and almost to the exclusion of all else, of oneself" (Jung, 1964, p. 312). What the dream has to say is always seen in light of the attitude of the conscious mind of the dreamer. The dream and its timing has bearing on current life. When the inner potential is negated or ignored, pathology appears; when the gold of the personality has become stuck and repressed into the unconscious, things go badly. The dream mediates between the still invisible potentials and the experienced outer reality, making them compensatory rather than oppositional. Through the personal associations, the dreamer is opened to the deeper nature of the psyche paralleled by the motifs in religions, cultural myths, and fairy tales. It is no wonder that children are so easily in touch with their dreams, for they are psychologically closer to the world of the unconscious. For adults, work is needed to get back to this state. Too often the rational world has taken over, and the spontaneity of inner life has been sorely negated.

To concern oneself with dreams is a way of reflecting on one's real nature. The dream is comprised of truths couched in a language of wisdom that conveys the knowledge necessary to help free the complexes surrounding the personality. It is not the ego reflecting on itself; rather, attention is turned to the actuality of the dream as a communication from the unconscious that is beyond, yet in relation to, the ego.

The dream is like a play with an opening scene, the statement of a problem, the development to the climax, and finally a resolution. The dream characters represent the various expressions of the personality, and the awareness of the projection of one's qualities onto the dream figures is a way to reclaim them when the material that was once unconsciously projected out returns with conscious effort. On the subjective level, the figures in dreams are personified features of the dreamer's own personality. On the objective level, they represent an actual person or a close relation such as a partner, a child, a parent. It is worth noting in the dream where the dreamer stands, or the position and action of the dreaming "I," and whether one is an observer, a participant, or not even present. There is no accident involved in the sequential order of events, the people who appear, or those named or unnamed. The physical place of the dream in a foreign or familiar country or not even on earth gives information about the distance of the psychological information from conscious awareness. Definition comes through things being named, but the dream retains its mystery and yet-to-be-plumbed nature by keeping some answers hidden.

Dreams are more or less synchronous with daily life; and when they parallel or anticipate actual occurrences, they may be met with unbelieving surprise. This relates to the concept of *synchronicity*, a term Jung used to refer to acausal meaningful coincidences imparting the profound order in the world and opening the way to experiencing the self. This element can be discomfiting, but eventually when understood it reinforces trust in the deeper layers of the psyche and in the essential wisdom operating from within.

In working with the dream, one stays consonant with the facts and does not distort or change the information. The dream has its own rationale and specifically orders the material. When one stays with the dream images, the reasons for psychological blocking and resistance gradually emerge through the way the image portrays the problem. Not everything in a dream can be analyzed at the time; it becomes clearer through the addition of later material. In dreams nothing is certain but uncertainty, which means one should be careful about application of theory so it does not ossify or distort the truth of the dream.

Dreams are self-regulating to the personality and depict the psyche's forward and regressive movements. The process of psychological change relies upon the compensatory interventions of the unconscious to correct conscious functioning that has become worn out or too narrowed. By holding the tension of the opposites, the living relation between the conscious and unconscious helps sustain and organize the personality. The field of consciousness is enlarged by pursuing the "treasure hard to attain" lying in the unconscious.

Dreaming is a growth process wherein new aspects from internal data of the personality are synthesized. The dreamer's attitude of serious attention stimulates the constructive activity of the unconscious. If dreams are listened to, not only the individual but also others benefit from the process of opening and respecting the existence of the personal and collective unconscious. As concentration and value are placed on the dream world, the unconscious parts of the personality come into the conscious life through the process of self-reflection, which takes one to the origins of the personality and energizes its healing powers. The recognition of uniqueness and individuality brings strength to the personality and provides emotional energy. A healthy pride is developed and credence given for one's own specialness. Through dreams one gains a self-portrait of the constructive forces for personality integration and individuation.

Transference/Countertransference

The focus of Jungian analytical psychology is on reweaving the personality through the holding container, or the temenos of the counseling or therapeutic relationship in which the personality develops. In the encounter with the personality of one's counselor or therapist, one learns to do the work through which psychological transformation occurs. In the relationship with another, the unconscious and conscious material are explored.

The analytic art requires timing and sensitivity from the counselor or psychotherapist, with attention to psychological and physical signals of both people involved. Transference reveals the inner situation, expectations, complexes, fantasies, and feelings of the client, who experiences his internal personality in and through the counselor or psychotherapist. The practitioner psychologically carries, by means of the transference projection and until integration occurs, the elements of the family, the unused aspects of the personality, and the potential of the person.

Transference is a phenomenon of projection, or the seeing of oneself in the other. It is an unconscious process in which the split-off or unintegrated parts of the client are put onto or into the counselor or psychotherapist. The material, feelings, and reactions are transferred at the unconscious level from one to the other during the counseling or psychotherapeutic process. This is not an intellectual sharing of facts but an experience of the unconscious forces through and within the mutuality of encounter. The relationship changes the inner and outer world, offering the opportunity to work out the problems obstructing personality development that have arisen when the client is not truly living her own myth. The counselor or psychotherapist who asks and interprets becomes an essential technical and methodological resource in the process of learning. The instrument used throughout is the totality of both psyches and includes conscious and unconscious material.

The transference/countertransference relationship is an enactment of the unconscious drama in which the client has been held prisoner. The counselor or psychotherapist must be able to have sufficient emotional clarity to differentiate the projections and to know what issues from the past contribute, what archetype colors the person, and what hints at solution are present in the dreams and fantasies. Countertransference reflects the counselor's or psychotherapist's feelings in relation to the client. There is a correspondence between the counselor or therapist's own personality and the internalized picture from the personal and collective unconscious of the client, which affects the unconscious space between them both. Each counselor or psychotherapist must ask if what is felt in relation to the client stems from his own unconscious and unintegrated conflicts or if it is a reaction to the unconscious drama the client is reenacting. The mutual transformation through this process demands honesty and perseverance from both participants.

The transformative process—the death of the old way of living—occurs through psychological renewal and results in redemption of the personality. Jung says, "I have no ready made philosophy of life to hand out. . . . I only know one thing: when my conscious mind no longer sees any possible road ahead and consequently gets stuck, my unconscious psyche will react to the unbearable standstill" (1954, p. 84). Jung often described the counselor or psychotherapist as a wounded healer, reminiscent of the shaman in various cultures who functions in the role of activating healing powers for the sick person. This form of counseling or psychotherapy is an experience that encourages one to be involved with life rather than isolated on a mountain top. Part of the journey is to bring the inner work out to the world.

SUPPORTING RESEARCH

There has been little traditional research done in Jungian analytical psychology because it is nonreplicable and highly individual. One must also consider the crucial issue of confidentiality. No tests are necessarily administered, and the material cannot be generalized in a scientifically measurable way from one individual to others. However, clinical results gleaned from a heuristic (related to the process of discovery) and empirical (or experiential) approach are important in this transformative process, which is not verified through laboratory research or with statistics. Jung used proof from his extensive empirical research into the myth themes, world tales, primitive cultures, religious ceremonies, and symbols to substantiate the existence of the unconscious processes that form his theories of the path of individuation.

The growing popularity of Jungian psychology relates to the need in the culture for ways to probe the unconscious in order to provide the connection for which the psyche naturally yearns. The numerous case examples used by Jung and his followers reiterate this need and demonstrate a means of substantiation for the effects of the theory.

■ ■ ■

THE CASE STUDY OF JOHN: THE JUNGIAN ANALYTICAL APPROACH

We see from John's example how important midlife is for the unfolding of the personality. Because the process of individuation is differently played out for each person, there are no technical tools per se in Jungian analytical psychology. No formal treatment goals per se are set by the counselor or psychotherapist, nor does the practitioner categorize a client in classically psychopathological ways. Problems are perceived to be due to an ossified, one-sided approach to life that has become devoid of emotional connections. Thus, disunity with oneself eventually builds to discontent. The psychological disorder is seen as a force that contributes to the formation of the personality. The problem is not in having difficulties, for they are necessary for health, but an excessive amount of difficulties or the way in which they are handled. The symptomatology of an illness is at the same time a natural attempt at healing and serves as a warning that the personality is in need of broadening.

John needs security, routine, and control because he fears being out of control. This is demonstrated by his presentation of a careful and conservative persona that could fit anyone; it is without individual markings. He is probably hiding anxiety and stress under this cover and simultaneously feels an apprehension about being seen. We can also surmise that his ego is not well enough connected to the self, as signified by the extent of his panic. A damaged ego-self axis negatively affects the confidence and ability to function in relationships and work and to find comfort with oneself. According to the generally recognized categories in the diagnostic statistical manual, this man fits the narcissistic personality disorder with psychosomatic features.

Because one develops an image of self also through the body, the Jungian counselor or therapist explores with John his childhood and the situation between his parents when his physical symptoms began. There are, no doubt, issues of letting go and holding in; and one wonders about the dynamics between John and his parents during the toilet-training years. The personal experience reflects the myth the person is unconsciously repeating. For example, John is caught in the body of the mother and aligned with the Christian mother-son myth repeated from the Egyptian Isis-Osiris and the Greek Hera-Hephaestus myths.

The medical problems are the body symbolically speaking through the symptoms. Psychic contents not yet conscious express themselves in symbolic actions. Jung says:

> But if we can reconcile ourselves with the mysterious truth that the spirit is the life of the body seen from within, and the body an outer manifestation of the life of the spirit—the two being really one—then we can understand why the striving to transcend the present level of consciousness through acceptance of the unconscious must give the body its due, and why recognition of the body cannot tolerate a philosophy that denies it in the name of the spirit. (1967, p. 242)

If the body is rejected one cannot live; but once returned to, it can promote new life.

The psyche is considered as real as the body. Together they encompass the realms of the spiritual and biological. Although John's symptoms need to be addressed, it is the psychological meaning of his problem that is significant in counseling or therapy. The unconscious is the matrix out of which psychogenic symptoms arise when the conscious and unconscious are not working in harmony. The focus of psychic energy or libido on the belly relates to the primordial and instinctive center. Throughout history the renewal of a person has been represented as childbirth, a transformation occurring in the belly as a symbol for the locus of emotions and the place of all vegetative functioning. The colon represents the digestive process involving the transformation and elimination of waste material. Psychologically John holds in his waste, does not put out to others, and suffers the pain by retaining the toxicity of his anger and frustration in a self-destructive manner.

It is worthwhile to learn about John's early childhood dreams, those occurring at the time of the original illness, and any recurrent dreams or dream themes. The dream is an emanation from the unconscious that does not obey our will and stands in opposition to conscious life to produce adjustment or rectification as well as to give answers to psychogenic problems. Dreams provide indicators concerning objective causality and tendencies in their self-portrayal of psychological processes.

John's emotional reaction while telling his dream shows that the unconscious is asking him to pay attention. We don't know if he has any associations with the dream characters or what meaning he makes of them after awakening. Taken alone, a dream is ambiguous and contains a multiplicity of meanings. However, a series of dreams shows a circular arrangement around a particular problem and kaleidoscopes a number of different perspectives. Dreams need the associations of the dreamer; if there are few or no associations, the material has been repressed far into the unconscious and becomes difficult to access due to resistance. The point is to attend to the resistance rather than forcefully break it down. The wisdom gleaned from the dream can be cultivated by listening intently to oneself, by valuing the inner world.

A dream should not be analyzed without first hearing the person's own associations with its contents. In this case, the counselor or psychotherapist sensitively asks John for his associations and feelings. John is not to provide "brilliant" associations; rather, the test of a correct interpretation is that it works for the dreamer. The practitioner wants to honor John's way of accessing the unconscious. He might naturally begin to dialogue with the dream figures, draw them and his feelings, or write about his reactions. One wonders if this is the first dream of the work with the counselor or therapist, for the initial dream depicts the prognosis for the counseling or psychotherapy and is usually correct in its prognostication.

Because we do not have John's associations, we will hypothetically enhance the dream with some of its archetypal meanings. The males in the dreams represent the masculine shadow aspects that are in pursuit and are cornering him. The shadow is the guardian of the threshold of the path leading to the world of transformation and renewal. As the dream warns, captivity by the shadow is released through facing it. The shadow sets one free from repression through symptoms thrown up by the unconscious. When the shadow is obfuscated and laden with repressed guilt and shame, a person has betrayed himself; and the energy creates intense inner pain and darkening of the spirit as the unconscious assumes a devouring nature to force attention inward. Destructive powers from the energy of the unrecognized shadow turn against the personality and negatively affect creativity and the urge for life. In the shadow, John's true face is laid bare without a mask. The shadow gives dimensionality to life, for only if one casts a shadow is one real. It creates the immediacy of situations and plunges one into humanness.

The faceless males are the yet-to-be-known parts of John, and the counseling or therapy process requires looking at them to help John get in touch with his masculinity, which is not yet evolved. The male shadow figures show that he must deal with them before encountering the female aspects of his personality. There are three characters in the dream, which is a masculine number of dynamism and energic movement. Jung often refers to its properties as signifying the next movement on to the fourth, which represents wholeness and totality.

The dream maze of rooms is like the labyrinth in the Greek myth of the minotaur, in which Theseus had to find his way as an initiatory test of his qualities. Although we have lost the formal rites of initiation, men have a great need to be introduced to the male mysteries and myths or stories of ways to gain not only the fight but also the spirit of masculinity. This process can be observed through the dreams and fantasies that store in the unconscious the psychological heritage of initiation.

When a man is too close to his mother and has a distant father, he is not initiated psychologically to the masculine world and cannot feel its energy. The father and mother teach and model the concepts of the masculine and feminine principles, and the inner contrasexual principle is influenced by both parents. A hole in the psyche of the son is formed if there is no emotional or physical father, and it fills with psychological splits and confusions that destructively affect work, relationships, and self-regard. The reverse of this situation is equally disruptive: an overpowering or threatening father creates anxiety in the son and makes the emotional approach toward him forbidden.

A strong and authentic sense of self is rooted in a well-developed sexual identity based on identification with the parent of the same sex, hence the important influence in a son's early years of the presence of a father. Many psychological problems can be traced to a father who was physically absent, emotionally aloof, or rejected by the son for being brutally authoritarian or violent. A father's absence suggests to the boy that men cannot be trusted, and the void fills with a loneliness in the son. The confusion about the reasons for separateness from the father coalesces into the son's question, "Why doesn't he love me?"

A father's lack of attention to the son leads to discord between the inborn archetype of the father, who remains unknown yet unconsciously desired, and the behavior of the actual father, who has aroused disappointment, anger, and feelings of emptiness in the son. A father's physical involvement contributes to the son's sense of identity because males also need to be touched in order to know they exist; otherwise, they develop a distance between themselves and the world. Instead of familiarizing themselves with the full range of their senses, body parts, and movements, boys are taught to focus only on a few gestures and to speak in certain predictable ways. Vast numbers of men learn to steel themselves against their feelings and are so desensitized that they lose touch with themselves unless they experience some crisis or continual excitement. Emotions become separated from sexuality so that the psyche and the body remain in disharmony.

John, who was brought up primarily by his mother, took a feminine attitude to the masculine and saw his father through his mother's eyes. However, this approach creates a distortion because masculinity cannot be learned through the animus or male side of the woman. Eventually John must begin to discover his father and masculinity and, in the process, direct energy away from pleasing his mother and toward the search for his own male instincts. John has to take back the power from his mother and psychologically get away from the force field of her bed; but she may not easily let go, for she will lose her boy in the bargain. The psychological possessiveness that some mothers exercise on sons cannot be overestimated in its damaging effect on sons' ability to function in harmony with themselves and their relationships and to establish a stance in the world. A man with this sort of mothering experience will feel that any interference on the part of his wife is an invasion or engulfment. It takes a long time for a man to overcome his absorption with his mother until, rather naturally, the psyche calls out for a man to turn toward the world of his father.

The journey into oneself involves going back to the mother psychologically and then consciously separating from her. In childhood John took the role of being close to his mother, functioning as an emotional surrogate constellating the Jungian diagnosis of a mother complex. In the process he has tied himself to her and she to him through the cocoon of stomach problems, learning that the way to attention is through the ill body. The cramps may be an attempt at identification with the feminine, but in a painful way. It is psychologically incestuous when mother and wife become so closely aligned and undifferentiated, as shown by the fact that the case presents little material about anyone other than John's mother and wife. This psychological situation has affected John's relationship to his wife because she takes over the role of his mother and sexuality suffers. The bed has become increasingly used for illness rather than for sex.

Marriage as a psychological relationship is limited and not based on free choice when unconsciousness exists in the corresponding mesh of ego identity between the partners. Progressive mental development brings the extension of consciousness into the distinction between instinctive reactions and the differentiated personality. John's initiative has been crippled by the memory of the idyllic world with his mother, and he has avoided growing up and owning himself. He feels the power of the feminine over him, which can take the overwhelming form of the devouring Terrible Mother, as in the fairy tale "Hansel and Gretel," when Hansel was almost eaten by the witch. The world makes demands on the masculinity of a man, his courage, and his resolution; and he needs Eros, or the feeling of relatedness, to be capable of relinquishing his mother's love. Until a man has found love through the inner anima figures, he will not be able to connect outwardly or will regress to being a boy, stay out of relationships altogether, and never leave his mother.

The immaturity of the psyche prevents one from adapting to reality, which makes itself apparent in crisis situations. The problem becomes acute for John at times of ending or completion, when the lack of internal solidity becomes more perceptible. For example, staying home during college represented a decision to remain within the triangle of his parents. The powerful unconscious pull of the family mitigated against leaving; in other words, John was affected by *participation mystique*, a phrase Jung used to denote a person's unconsciously staying within the family dynamics. Symbolically John has not had the fundamentals to rely on or the inner structures to deal with psychological growth.

John has remained cut off from feelings and prefers to live through books or the intellect and away from the passions of life, separating the mind and body in a defensive attempt to contain anxiety. The relation to his wife is stuck, and the children are held at a distance. He acts unconsciously like his father, from whom he was emotionally distant. These factors demonstrate the characteristics of an introverted, thinking, sensation typology. Adaptation to the environment fails when there is a one-sided focus on the superior function, which in this case is the thinking function, and a damming up of libido that causes the unconscious and inferior feeling function to be activated by regression. Regression is an adaptation to the conditions of the inner world, one that responds to the vital need to satisfy the demands of individuation. As Jung says:

> Over against the polymorphism of the . . . instinctual nature there stands the regulating principle of individuation. . . . Together they form a pair of opposites . . . often spoken of as nature and spirit. . . . This opposition is the expression, and perhaps also the basis, of the tension from which psychic energy flows. (1960, p. 58)

Jung's phrase *canalization of libido* refers to the process of energic transformation of psychic intensities or values from one psychological content to another. The solution to the principle of progression and regression is portrayed in the many myths of the night sea journey, when entry into the darkness is symbolic of the effort of the hero to face the conditions of the psychic inner world. Overcoming the monster from within brings emergence of the hero from the monster's belly and symbolizes the progression recommencing.

The psychological treatment includes transference and countertransference, which will be affected by the sex of the counselor or psychotherapist, especially because of the internal conflict John has with women and with his identity as a man. There will no doubt be problems of trust and intimacy in the counseling or psychotherapeutic relationship due to the strength of John's defenses and fears. As in handling dreams, the counselor or psychotherapist does not have a preconceived plan but follows the direction of the unconscious.

No captivity is so terrible and so impossible to break as that which the individual imposes on himself. When the human relation to reality is not let in, then life is shut out. Any natural part turns negative when rejected and then assumes overwhelming power and control. The part of the personality that is not loved and respected goes out from a person in hostility, but a conscious and responsible attitude turns the shadow into a friend. The partial assimilation of the shadow, which like any archetype cannot be totally assimilated, allows the ego some control over its fate. The process of psychological healing and the uncovering of self-deceptions occurs with knowledge of the various aspects of the personality, especially when there is protestation against their presence.

Distress, blackness of feeling, and wishes and motives from the unconscious side of the personality require the reconciliation of the warring elements to bring conscious differentiation of the psyche. Jung says:

> Evidently it [our rational philosophy] still does not know that we carry in ourselves a real shadow whose existence is grounded in our instinctual nature. No one can overlook either the dynamism or the imagery of the instincts without the gravest injury to himself. Violation or neglect of instinct has painful consequences of a physiological and psychological nature for whose treatment medical help is required. (1959, p. 57)

The path to health involves turning to the voice of the unconscious to glean the resources of creativity, relationship, and knowledge. Consciousness is a unique act wrenching one from the blind clutches of assimilation with the collective. A relationship with oneself and with others rests on the dynamism of the psyche pressing onward the quest for individuality and identity. Emergence of the personality is fraught with distress in the struggle to separate from the chaos at the beginning of any psychological endeavor. Through its suffering the soul reveals the meaning of personal destiny, and life can develop as a creative experience. Growth is a process of differentiation through integration of unconscious contents, and the broadening of consciousness means the continuation and deepening of this pattern throughout life, an undertaking that entails taking the totality of oneself seriously. With increasing consciousness, possession is taken of the personality, and light emerges from the confrontation with the opposite forces operating from within.

LIMITATIONS

Jungian analytical psychology has limitations in the sense that most people who embark on this path are of an intellectual bent, have achieved a certain level of accomplishment, and are looking not only for crisis intervention but to enhance the meaning of life. Their outer functioning may look sufficient to others, but they know they are living below their level of satisfaction and have to plumb the depths to stretch their personality further. This is not an elitist approach, but some people have more need for psychological development.

Those who choose this journey are willing to devote much time, money, and personal effort. It requires more than a cursory look at oneself, and the psyche is rigorous in its demand for attention once it is discovered. So although the approach is useful for all ages and backgrounds, the internal desire and the ability for strenuous work are requirements and set the limitations. Often people do not know at the beginning what is entailed in this process, yet some part of their psychological makeup agrees to take a long and arduous internal look. Sometimes it is surprising to discover who remains in the work and who finds it inappropriate.

Essentially, this approach is useful for those who want to invest in themselves over time and not for the short term; those who wish to go beyond the symptom and into the psyche; those who have an amount of wonder and fear and need to work out their underlying malaise, depression, anxiety, or other presenting problem through the world of the unconscious and discover what lies in the unknown. Jung often said that many are called and few are chosen; we might say that those whom this approach fits will choose this way.

SUMMARY

Jungian psychology is an analytical procedure to deal with the complications of psychic disease. The earlier stages of this type of counseling or psychotherapy deal largely with personal problems and, therefore, with the personal unconscious. As one progresses, however, the individual begins to find a place in the life of the generations from the dialectical interchange with the realm of the collective unconscious. It leads the individual to the knowledge and fulfillment of his own personality, an aim that has always been integral to all striving for depth.

Jungian analytical psychology is a system of personality education and spiritual guidance, and this distinguishes it from other psychological approaches. People embark on Jungian psychology who have come to a dead end. They know many of the answers that consciousness can give but are dissatisfied and unable to find comfort in the usual way. They turn to this work when the ordinary psychotherapeutic processes that focus on the ego personality are insufficient. Rational solutions and collective norms cannot replace the individual path without loss to the person who has a standpoint differently oriented but not antagonistic to the collective norm. The goal is not cure because there can be no change that remains valid over a long period of time. Instead, the goal is to attain new orientations for the whole personality to retain viability. The aim is to explore latent possibilities, find out what kind of a person one is, and to live the creative process that has been set in motion. In Jung's words:

> As far as we can discern the sole purpose of human existence is to kindle a light in the darkness of mere being. It may even be assumed that just as the unconscious affects us, so the increase in our consciousness affects the unconscious. (1963, p. 326)

REFERENCES

Jung, C. G. (1953a). *Collected works 7: Two essays on analytical psychology.* New York: Pantheon.

Jung, C. G. (1953b). *Collected works 12: Psychology and alchemy.* New York: Pantheon.

Jung, C. G. (1954). *Collected works 16: The practice of psychotherapy.* New York: Pantheon.

Jung, C. G. (1956). *Collected works 5: Symbols of transformation.* New York: Pantheon.

Jung, C. G. (1959). *Collected works 9: The archetypes and the collective unconscious.* New York: Pantheon.

Jung, C. G. (1960). *Collected works 8: The structure and dynamics of the psyche.* New York: Pantheon.

Jung, C. G. (1963). *Memories, dreams, reflections.* New York: Pantheon.

Jung, C. G. (1964). *Man and his symbols.* Garden City, NY: Doubleday.

Jung, C. G. (1967). *Collected works 13: Alchemical studies.* New York: Pantheon.

■ CHAPTER SEVEN

Adlerian Theory

Thomas J. Sweeney
Ohio University

Alfred Adler created not only a psychology of human behavior, but also a social movement to correct the methods of child rearing and human interaction that foster conflicts and individual discouragement. Adler was born in Vienna in 1870 and died in 1937 in Scotland while on a lecture tour. A middle child reared in a Jewish merchant family, he was subject to sickness and injury as a child. The fact that he pursued medicine as a vocation is not surprising to Adlerians. Energetic and fun-loving, he was known to enjoy parties, singing, the theater, and time with friends and colleagues. He was a refugee from Nazi Germany, and he lived in the United States long enough to help establish what has become the North American Society of Adlerian Psychology. While he is probably best remembered for his work here and in Europe with families and children, his theory and work have been extended by followers, most notably Rudolf Dreikurs, to include every dimension of counseling and therapy: individuals, couples, families, groups, and organizations.

Adler's theory is based on a phenomenological understanding of individual motivation and behavior. He rooted his interventions in the values and philosophy of social democracy. Dreikurs was an articulate spokesman, a consummate teacher, and a clinician of Adlerian thought and practice. His books on parenting, marriage, and classroom management have become classics translated into several languages.

Even a casual reading of Adler's and Dreikurs's works will reveal the visionary nature of their insights into both individual behavior and societal needs. The practical applications of their insights, however, are what has given their work its greatest impact. Followers have added new dimensions to the theory and new techniques to the methods. Yet the foundation in philosophy and values remains essentially the same, and research across disciplines continues to corroborate the soundness of these ideas.

HISTORY

Individual psychology was born in Vienna at the turn of the twentieth century. Its creator, Alfred Adler, has been historically overshadowed by his contemporary, Sigmund Freud, although the two pioneers of psychological theory and practice were collegial in their initial relationship. That relationship changed, however, as the differences between their ideas became more evident. In fact, the differences between them were so significant that they eventually became antagonists.

Adler's interest in why people respond differently to similar life events is reflected in his early attention to the study of organ inferiority (1907). His later lectures, books, and articles illustrated even more clearly his conviction that individuals create their own evaluations and choices of how to respond to life events.

In 1935, when the Nazis began their oppression of Europe, Adler had to flee to the United States with his radical and politically unacceptable ideas about a society of social equals. Although he taught and lectured extensively in the United States before his death in 1937, there was great resistance to his ideas from people who had adopted the tenets of Freud's psychoanalysis. In addition, the United States was far from practicing the egalitarian principles upon which individual psychology is based.

Adler's most prolific advocate, Dr. Rudolf Dreikurs, published a number of books, monographs, and articles that are still widely read today. Dreikurs's book on marriage (1946) forecast the social revolution between men and women that we have experienced since World War II. His books *Children: The Challenge* (Dreikurs & Soltz, 1964) and *Maintaining Sanity in the Classroom* (Dreikurs, Grunwald, & Pepper, 1971) are classics in this country and abroad. Ridiculed and rejected by many of his peers in medicine and psychiatry, Dreikurs lived long enough to see his books become best-sellers among lay persons and professionals alike. Equally important, his work continues through his students and colleagues such as the Ansbachers, Sadie Dreikurs, Harold Mosak, Bob Powers, the Pews, the Dinkmeyers, Gary McKay, Jon Carlson, Len Sperry, and Tom Sweeney.

HUMAN NATURE: A DEVELOPMENTAL PERSPECTIVE

Early Development

Adler and Dreikurs are probably best known for their work with children and the adults in their lives. Adler never considered the child totally dependent at birth. He believed that infants begin training adults far better than many adults train their children. There is now, of course, research that demonstrates that infants are far more responsive and capable of modifying adult behavior than previously believed.

Adler firmly believed that love and parental interest are important ingredients to healthy personality development. Unfortunately, too much of what some parents consider to be love results in pampering or overprotecting. Pampered children may perceive that they are not able, that others must take care of them, or that terrible things may happen when their parents are away. If corrective training is not instituted during their early years, such notions may become a part of what Adler referred to as one's unique, private logic. *Private logic* is his term for an individual's unique pattern of thoughts, feelings, and attitudes that guides understanding, predicting, and managing life experiences and behavior.

In most instances, children begin developing a sense of their strengths and weaknesses while attempting mastery over those aspects of life that seem within their reach. They also begin to make observations about their place in events around them. As they grow in size and ability, others' expectations for them change. Then they must decide if and how they will respond. If they are convinced of their security in the family and assess their capabilities as adequate, they will require less attention, service, and outward encouragement from those around them.

On the other hand, many children make inaccurate assessments about being loved, appreciated, and secure within their family. These children likewise behave according to their assessments. Adler noted that children usually are excellent observers of others, but they often are poor evaluators and interpreters of their experiences. As a consequence, he believed that feelings of inferiority are common because of children's initial experiences as dependent, small, and socially inferior persons. Feelings of inferiority are not inherently good or bad. Individuals, for example, often move toward mastery and competence to compensate for these feelings. Through social interaction, they become persons whom Adler described as high in social interest and empathy (Adler, 1938). Children's responses to early experiences within the family unit, then, have importance for how they approach their basic life tasks, such as school, friendships, and family participation.

Family Constellation

Adler placed considerable importance upon the family constellation. Shulman and Nikelly (1971) define the term as follows:

> Family constellation is a term used to describe the socio-psychological configuration of a family group. The personality characteristics and emotional distance of each person, age differences, order of birth, the dominance or submission of each member, the siblings, and the size of the family are all factors in the family constellation and affect the development of the personality. . . . certain behavior types can be characterized by examining the individual's place in the constellation. Thus, the first born, the second born, and the only child have certain characteristics which render their personality predictable in terms of attitudes, personality traits and subsequent behavior. (p. 35)

Individuals' perceptions of their family position has special significance for understanding their outlook on life. While much is said about birth order or ordinal position in relation to the family constellation, Adlerians are aware that it is the individual's psychological position that must be studied. For example, two children born six or more years apart may perceive themselves as only children—that is, not as one who is the older and another who is second or younger.

Adlerians typically list five ordinal positions: oldest, second, middle, youngest, and only child. Each ordinal position is associated with certain common characteristics, but these characteristics are nomothetic impressions that should be quickly set aside when idiographic data about a given individual refute the validity of the classical characteristics. The general principle is that each child makes a unique place for herself. Whatever characteristics distinguish a child from the other children in the family are singularly embraced as the child's very own. However, Adlerians also use these nomothetic characteristics as a way of uncovering an individual's uniqueness: for example, how she is different from other oldest or youngest children.

Oldest children are literally the first child of the family, most often the cause of glad tidings and happily the center of attention. Then one day a new child appears in the family. Considering the proximity in months or years, parental attitudes, sex, and other such variables, oldest children evaluate the threat to their position in the family. On the average, they learn to take the younger newcomer in stride, especially if the parents provide encouragement for the oldest child to recognize his place as secure within the family.

Oldest children generally are able to relate well to adults, subscribe more readily to adult expectations and values, help with the younger children, assume social responsibility, and develop socially acceptable ways of coping with life's tasks. A tendency of oldest children is to strive for perfection as a goal, which can have negative consequences. When they assert their independence from parental dominance, they tend to do so covertly: that is, they do not "hear" instructions or "forget" things.

The second child arrives to find someone already ahead of her. Second children born within six years of the older child, and again depending upon age and similar variables, typically will be less responsible, more independent, and more interested in whatever the oldest does not pursue or master. Second children often strive to be first in something. Sibling rivalry can be quite intense in families that encourage comparisons between children.

The middle child must compete with an older and younger sibling. Middle children often feel squeezed in their position. They perceive themselves as singularly disadvantaged. They believe that they have few, if any, of the privileges of the oldest youngster nor the advantages of the youngest. What's more, the oldest children often help take care of the youngest, thereby establishing for themselves an ally and leaving the middle children to fend for themselves. In this way, too, the oldest children acquire a reputation among the other children as bossy.

Middle children will most likely establish their uniqueness in directions opposite to their older sibling. They may be more independent, rebellious, and sensitive, and they may overtly seek assurances of their place with their parents. As is true with each position in the family, children can transcend these early perceptions through compensatory behavior that eventually works to their benefit. Each child, however, often perceives his position as the most burdensome to bear.

Youngest children enjoy a position that they perceive as the center of attention. They have both parents and older siblings to entertain them and provide them service. While the youngest children might be troublesome at times, they also have protectors to care for them. In fact, as youngest children get a little older, it is even fun to start something with the middle child and watch the older ally and the parents run to save the "baby." A youngest child is often described as cute, a charmer, and the family's baby, no matter how old she becomes. She may choose to use her manipulative ways to just get by and enjoy life's many pleasures. On the other hand, with parental values on achievement, the youngest might be the hardest runner and greatest achiever of them all if she perceives that approach as a way to make her unique place.

Only children may have the perceptions of the oldest child with one important exception. They are never dethroned and are less likely to feel the pressure of a close competitor. Only children may be perceived as precocious for their age, comfortable with adults, responsible, and cooperative. Unlike other youngsters, they may have little or no intimate give and take with other children. This can make early school experiences more difficult as these children begin coping with new life situations involving a peer group.

MAJOR CONSTRUCTS

Socio-Teleo-Analytic

Adler perceived humans as social beings with a natural inclination toward other people. Developmentally, human beings are among the most dependent of all creatures at birth. They must be cared for if they are to survive. As a consequence, they can be understood best through their early interactions with others. Through their early impressions they develop rules about life that they use to understand, predict, and manage their unique perceptions of themselves, others, and the world. They develop a private logic that becomes a part of their unconscious, guiding principles for daily living. They live life as if their unique perceptions were fact or irrefutable reality. Through selective perceptions, these fictive notions tend to go unchallenged and often are self-fulfilling prophecies that only serve to reinforce themselves.

Socio.   Adler believed that human beings have a basic inclination toward *Gemeinschaftsgefuhl*—that is, a striving to feel belongingness, a willing-ness to serve the greater good for the betterment of humankind. The clos-est interpretation of this German word in English is "social interest." An expression of this inclination is observed in each person's striving to make a place for himself and to feel belongingness. Understanding individuals' striving becomes a significant factor in helping them to overcome self-defeating behaviors.

Adler was a phenomenologist who believed that human motivation was understood through the eyes of the beholder. He referred to the basic notions that guide us through life as our style of life or, as more commonly referred to now, life-style. He characterized life-style as "unity in each indi-vidual—in his thinking, feeling, acting; in his so called conscious and unconscious, in every expression of his personality. This (self-consistent) unity we call the style of life of the individual" (Ansbacher & Ansbacher, 1967, p. 175).

Life-style is not determined by heredity or environment, but both are important antecedents. Individuals decide how they think, value, and feel about their gender, family position, or ethnicity. Each life-style is unique. Each is developed by individuals according to its usefulness in coping with other people and the world. Through an understanding of these unique perceptions, individuals also come to understand the consistency in their behavior.

Obviously, a psychology of personality that revealed no general or nomothetic rules of behavior upon which to base practice would be of little use. As I will show in subsequent sections, Adlerian principles do indeed provide many useful guidelines. Adler believed that individuals can be understood best within the social context of their transactions with others; and through this insight, the importance of a person's family constellation, early role models, and early recollections take on signifi-cance.

Teleo.   *Teleo* denotes the goal-striving nature of human beings. Behavior is purposive even though this facet may be obscure to the observer. Indi-viduals choose to act or not act because it is useful to them. They are not victims of instincts, heredity, environment, or experience. As Ansbacher (1969) writes:

> The science of Individual Psychology developed out of the effort to understand that mysterious creative power of life—that power which expresses itself in the desire to develop, to strive and to achieve—and even to compensate for defeats in one direction by striving for success in another. This power is teleological—it expresses itself in the striving after a goal. (p. 1)

This teleological orientation has an optimistic and encouraging nature. As Rudolf Dreikurs (personal communication, June, 1970) once said, "Tell a person what they are, schizophrenic, so what? Tell a person how they feel, sad or bad, so what? But, tell a person what they intend! Now that is something they can change!"

Because goals of behavior can be understood and anticipated, they can be changed. Individuals may choose to change the valuing of their goals or the behavior they use in their striving. Individuals, therefore, are not victims of circumstances beyond their control in any absolute way.

Analytic.   Individuals frequently report that they do not understand their behavior or motives. Closer inspection reveals that individuals often understand more than they willingly admit. The analytic aspect of individual psychology is derived from the observation that most behavior is based upon what is unconscious or not understood (Mosak & Dreikurs, 1973). In a helping relationship, however, individuals more readily accept direct confrontations about the purposes of their behavior, including purposes of which they were not consciously aware.

Adler was influenced by Vaihinger's *The Philosophy of "As If"* (1965). He concurred with Vaihinger that individuals behave "as if" circumstances were absolutely true: for example, life is threatening, I am inadequate, or others are more able than me. While some notions of individuals are stated clearly and believed beyond reproach, other notions are far more subtle yet powerful in their influence upon behavior. Adler referred to these as *fictive notions*.

So long as individuals function fairly well in their daily life, their fictive notions remain unexamined. When their notions are challenged or proved ineffective at maintaining feelings of belonging or adequacy, an emotional crisis develops. At these times clients most often seek counseling or psychotherapy.

Individuals learn new or different behavior due to varying circumstances, including age, cultural milieu, and similar factors. Life-style is not believed to change, however, except through psychotherapy, personally powerful life experiences, or other causes such as brain injury, diseases, and drugs.

Life Tasks

Adler believed that everyone is confronted by at least three major life tasks: work, friendship, and love (Dreikurs, 1953). In addition, Mosak and Dreikurs (1967) have identified a fourth and fifth task only alluded to by Adler. The fourth task is one's dealing with the spiritual self in reaction to the universe, God, and similar concepts. The fifth task concerns the individual's success in coping with the self as subject (I) and as object (me).

Equipped with their unique rules or guidelines about life, themselves, and others, individuals move from childhood to preadolescence, adolescence, and adulthood with a societal expectation that they will become more responsible, cooperative, and able to cope with life situations. Lack of success in the work task characterizes the most discouraged people in society. Although this task does not require gainful employment, persons who find difficulty sustaining employment are in all probability individuals who lack confidence in their worth and ability.

In the school situation, failure and dropping out are tantamount to demotion and unemployment—that is, loss of confidence and a sense of worth. Dreikurs (1968) believed that children who failed were not bad or lazy but instead discouraged. To face and fulfill one's life tasks requires the courage to be imperfect, to make mistakes, to fail occasionally but to try again. For too many children, school becomes a confirmation of their private assessment: they are not adequate. In later life, many of these individuals will be consistently unemployed, welfare recipients, or institutionalized. Although it appears difficult for persons to change in later life, Adler believed that we always have that capability.

Dreikurs (1953) indicated that discouragement generally was not limited to one life task area. For example, most individuals can cope with the daily requirements of work whether by gainful employment or through services to others; and doubts, reservations, and fears may reveal themselves only at times. Friendship and intimate love relationships tend to demand cooperation, give and take, and respect. If an individual has persistent difficulties in either or both of these life tasks, discouragement is present that probably can be noted in the other areas as well. Obviously not all life task difficulties can be traced to psychosocial origin. However, Dreikurs (1946) stated that whenever individuals persistently complain, blame, make excuses, report fears, or reveal disabilities, they are disclosing discouragement.

Of the life tasks, love relationships require the greatest courage and faith in self and the other party. Individual weaknesses, concerns, and peculiarities come under closer scrutiny than in most other life situations. Adlerians have noted that the very characteristics that attract individuals to one another also contribute to their friction in marriage. Changing attitudes about the roles of men and women notwithstanding, the private logic of partners in their selection of a mate means getting more of those specific qualities than you like! A man may select a woman because, among other attributes, she is intelligent, interested in many areas, and admired by others for her competence. She may have liked him because of his fun-loving nature, his laid-back, "smell the roses" enjoyment of life, and his appreciation of her positive qualities. As their relationship unfolds, friction can develop if there is not a balance in these qualities: he needs to be sufficiently serious, competent, and successful; and she needs to appreciate his attributes, be able to slow down, and initiate some of the fun in their relationship.

Adler demonstrated that once individuals understand their own movement through life, they can decide to change their attitudes and behavior with renewed respect for themselves and one another. For example, through marriage enrichment groups as well as counseling, couples can learn to appreciate one another's private logic and to develop mutual respect on the basis of a deeper, more intimate knowledge of one another.

Function of Emotions and Feelings

Adler perceived emotions as tools necessary to the execution of behavior. Emotions are not considered entities unto themselves; love, joy, anger, sadness, guilt, and fear do not come to us out of a vacuum. We must perceive, value, feel, and then act.

Much of our valuing in regard to life, ourselves, and others is a blueprint already stored in our unconscious thought processes. Therefore, much of what is attributed to instant love, fear, or anger can be traced back to one's life-style data bank. This is the stuff of which self-talk is made.

Many clients wish to discredit this concept of emotions because it places responsibility on them for their present decisions and actions. Adlerians are very much interested in emotions but more as signposts to the understanding of an individual's mistaken notions and intentions. As Dreikurs (1967) explained, the messages we send ourselves build the energy we use to act. We do not fall in love because we were struck by Cupid's arrow. Rather, we experience, value, and then emotionally commit to action to achieve our desired relationship.

Observers of the Adlerian counselor or therapist might conclude that he is insensitive to the anger, complaining, blaming, tears, or affection expressed in a counseling or therapy session. If the emotions are tools used by clients to distract or otherwise manipulate the counselor or therapist from the goals for counseling and psychotherapy, the practitioner may indeed seem unimpressed by their presence. It is the less visible feelings and attitudes that the Adlerian will pursue: for example, isolation, lack of confidence, and insecurity. This deeper level of human empathy must be touched if genuine change and positive growth are to be realized.

Holistic View

The indivisibility of a person is a fundamental belief of individual psychology. At a time when holistic approaches to medicine, mental health, and rehabilitation are coming into the forefront, a practitioner will find the usefulness of this view apparent.

Adlerians recognize the interaction between physical and psychological well-being. Biofeedback research and its application in stress management has helped to corroborate Adler's assumption that what one thinks can produce physiological symptoms similar to those that stem from a more physical origin. Infection, disease, and other injuries to the body are potentially mood modifying. Fatigue, particularly due to distress, is symptomatic of the interaction of mind and body. In short, even personal experience suggests the validity of such a position. Adlerian practitioners also are aware that samples of an individual's behavior can help counselors and therapists understand a more global life plan and direction of movement. Such behaviors, however, are only an approximation of the total and must be kept in proper perspective.

Holism from an Adlerian perspective is a point of view from which to understand others as dynamic and self-directed. It also presents the concept of an interrelated mind and body moving through life with a unique plan for having significance in relation to others. Helping clients change how they think and feel in their relationships with others, for example, can result in better physical health, greater satisfaction with their work, and increased joy and interest in other aspects of their life.

THE PROCESS OF CHANGE

Adlerians note that the life-style of the individual is a unique, unconscious, cognitive "map" that facilitates her movement through life (Mosak & Dreikurs, 1973). Life-style is a unifying set of convictions that permits individuals to evaluate, manage, and predict events within their experiences. Adlerian counseling and psychotherapy involve uncovering and using our understanding of these combinations of beliefs to reorient thoughts and goals related to self, others, and the world upon which individuals' expectations are based. These self-determined notions become the source of direction and movement through which the individual establishes his place in the world. By consciously examining them, change is possible.

In many instances, behavior change can take place with little more than an insight as to how one's goals can be met more effectively by a modest change. For example, parents and children learn quickly that the use of natural and logical consequences—that is, negative results from children's poor choices in behavior—can win cooperation and peace for the family within as little as one counseling session. One illustration of this technique is letting a child who persistently forgets to take lunch to school experience hunger as a consequence. Without any punitive reaction of the parent, the child can learn more responsible behavior.

Also, within each individual's life-style is latitude for behavioral choice: that is, one's convictions may result in a variety of behaviors. For example, the belief that "life is a test that only the strong survive" may result in a person's choosing the vocation of special-forces commando or martial arts black belt. If that belief is combined with "I am a fragile person," the conviction may result in someone who is a submissive individual. The potential for pursuing socially useful or useless life activities, therefore, lies within the same life-style convictions.

Adlerians make a distinction between counseling and psychotherapy processes. In the case of counseling, behavior change within the existing life-style is the goal. In psychotherapy, a change in life-style is the desired outcome. While this distinction can be construed as moot, considering the differences is valid. Adlerian success in psychotherapy requires motivation modification. Dreikurs (1963) stated:

> We do not attempt primarily to change behavior patterns or remove symptoms. If a patient improves his behavior because he finds it profitable at the time, without changing his basic premises, then we do not consider that as a therapeutic success. We are trying to change goals, concepts, and notions. (p. 79)

I have experienced instances in which this distinction with behavior modification was clearly justified. An illustration can be found in the life-styles of some individuals in professions related to counseling and psychotherapy. For some people, the motivation for being a helper was intimately intertwined with their concept of self-worth. When unsuccessful as a helper, some developed feelings of discouragement and disappointment. A change in behavior was not necessary, but they benefited from an examination of why they wished to help, which allowed them to determine how such notions were self-defeating.

Many youngsters strive daily to please their parents, teachers, and others. They are rewarded for being "good" children. Although a change in behavior may not be necessary, the motivation for doing well deserves serious examination. The child striving for perfection is a discouraged person whose goal can never be attained. Encouragement for simply participating in life, including acceptance of their mistakes, can be one objective for helping such youngsters.

On the other hand, changes in behavior can open new alternatives to behavior and attitude change. For example, the counselor's or therapist's knowledge of the goals of disruptive behavior—that is, excessive attention seeking, personal power, revenge, and inadequacy—can help to suggest alternative behaviors to the youngsters without conducting a life-style analysis. Similarly, Dreikurs's (1971) four steps for problem solving can be implemented in establishing a new agreement between marriage partners without changing basic life goals.

Therefore, for the purposes of this chapter, Adlerian counseling includes those methods and techniques used within the helping relationship that encourage situational, attitude, or behavior changes. This counseling frees individuals to function more fully as self-determining, creative, and responsible equals within their environment. By contrast, Adlerian psychotherapy results in fundamental changes in motivation as evidenced by changes in early recollections and the guiding themes of one's life-style.

INTERVENTION STRATEGIES

The number and types of interventions used by Adlerians are those common to most professional counselors and therapists today. What follows are interventions that have uniquely Adlerian aspects or are central to Adlerian intervention. Adler, Dreikurs, and those who followed them have been in the forefront of community mental health in this country and abroad. In fact, Dreikurs was criticized by Americans early in his career for his radical practices of group work, family counseling, and individual therapy demonstrations. Because this work is no longer seen as radical, neophytes could miss the significance of his contributions. Among them are methods of encouragement, parent and teacher education, and life-style assessment with individuals and couples.

Encouragement

Methods of encouragement prompt one to act with responsibility, deliberation, and conviction. Courageous actions involve acting responsibly despite uncertainties or fears for the outcome. Equally important, they free one to live fully as an active participant each moment of each day. The essential element in the concept of encouragement is courage. As Gandhi said, "Courage is the one true foundation of character. Without courage there can be no truth, no love or religion. For one subject to fear can pursue neither truth nor love" (Nehru, 1958, p. i).

Actions that tend to encourage include:

1. Bringing attention to *what* someone is doing more so than *how* he is doing—that is, evaluating performance

   Example: That's a beautiful shine on the floor. What did you do to get it that way? (invites more explanation)

   Versus: I'll bet you take better care of your house than anyone else in town. (compares)

2. Focusing on present behavior more than the past or the future

   Example: It's really obvious that you're enjoying this project. I can tell by the effort and enthusiasm you have for it.

   Versus: I sure wish you would work this hard all the time!

3. Acknowledging the deed rather than praising the person

   Example: I really appreciate your help. Thanks!

   Versus: You're such a good kid. You always do the right thing!

4. Emphasizing the effort rather than the product or outcome

   Example: That was fun! As I learn to be more patient and not rush the ball, I should be able to give you a better match! (emphasis on progress, what to do, and the enjoyment of increased competence)

   Versus: I ordered a new racket that's going to give me the advantage I need to beat that guy! (it's winning that counts)

5. Promoting intrinsic motivation (i.e., satisfaction, enjoyment, challenge) as preferable to extrinsic motivation

   Example: No matter how long it takes, nothing gives me more pleasure than capturing a moment in time that reflects the beauty in life.

   Versus: What do I get for doing it? What's in it for me?

6. Bringing attention to what is being learned rather than what is not being learned

   Example: You've just about mastered nouns and pronouns. That will be very helpful to you in learning to construct sentences. Now let's look at a couple of problems that gave you difficulty and help you master them.

   Versus: You need to get help at home or the rest of this term is going to be hard for you.

7. Attending more to what is being done correctly rather than to what is not being done correctly

>   *Example:*   You got 84 out of 100 correct. With just a little more effort, I
>   know you'll be able to go on to the next lessons, too.
>   *Versus:*   You missed 16 out of 100.

In short, a major emphasis of encouragement is helping individuals establish goals, attitudes, and competencies needed to cope with life as they
experience it.

Effective verbal communication is also important. It involves the following considerations:

1. Reflective listening, which reveals an awareness of the kind and intensity of feelings expressed
2. Nonjudgmental attitudes, which show respect for the individual even
   though the counselor or therapist may not like what the person has
   done
3. Accepting responsibility for feelings and avoiding blaming, complaining, and nagging
4. Understanding the purpose of behavior and how it may be self-defeating to the other person or ourselves as we try to find solutions to life
   circumstances

However, limiting one's attention to verbal methods of encouragement is not sufficient. For example, Adlerians stress the significance of
action, not words, when coping with discipline problems. The same principle can be espoused for encouragement. All of us look for evidence that
what others say is revealed also in their behaviors. Nonverbal encouragement can be as simple as smiling or as involved as coordinating a surprise
birthday party specifically designed to reflect love, respect, and genuine
caring for another person. At such times, the recipients may not remember exactly what was said or what was given to them, but they will remember the manner in which it was given.

Acts of encouragement may include the following (Sweeney, 1989):

1. Help someone do a job that might otherwise be done alone.
2. Listen to someone describe a hobby, a vacation, or an event that he
   wanted to share.
3. Keep busy and remain patient while someone else completes a task
   that she found difficult.
4. Complete or do another's task in order to let him have more leisure
   time.
5. Share a book or a recording that has value to you.

6. Offer to do a favor without being asked.
7. Send letters of appreciation, thanks, or remembrance, especially when such a gesture might easily be overlooked.
8. Intervene on another's behalf to help others appreciate her capabilities or contributions.

Encouragement is multifaceted. It is an essential part of helping others cope, change, and meet life's challenges. Mastering the art of encouragement is a continuing process that Adlerians incorporate into everything that they do.

Parent and Teacher Education

The following list summarizes Adlerian thought as it concerns adults who guide children:

1. Free oneself of the mistaken notion that one should control a child's behavior.
2. Accept responsibility for changing one's behavior first.
3. Respect the child or adolescent for making the best choices, as he perceives them, under the circumstances.
4. Realize that children are attempting to make a place for themselves by whatever means seem available—that is, by employing socially useful or useless behavior.
5. Understand that when children misbehave, their misbehavior is an outward sign of their internal discouragement as participating members of the class or family.
6. Commit oneself to helping children learn self-discipline and cooperation by friendly participation in the daily tasks that everyone must fulfill.

As a consultant to adults who are working and living with young people, you may find the following four steps helpful in summarizing what is required of you (Sweeney, 1989). You can remember these steps easily by using the acronym CARE.

1. Catch yourself; don't act impulsively.
2. Assess goals. What goals are served by the behavior?
3. Respond with consequences and encouragement.
4. Execute with consistency, friendliness, and respect.

Dreikurs believed that before an adult can begin doing something correctly, he must stop doing what is incorrect. Parents and teachers alike tend to behave toward their children and students the way their own parents and teachers behaved toward them. These old methods are not appropriate today because they were based on an authoritarian system. As a consequence, the following recommendations are offered.

Catch Yourself.   Behavioral research on conditioning affirms the Adlerian conviction that what most adults do impulsively when they respond to misbehavior is incorrect. Stopping what the adult has been doing opens the possibility for change by both the child and adult.

A comment on talking too much deserves special note. Adults tend to talk when annoyed by misbehavior, even though the children rarely listen. In fact, we have nonverbal agreements with the children about when they should listen. Counseling and consultation with parents, teachers, and children reveal that such factors as the number of times instructions are repeated, pitch of voice, and voice inflection convey more to children than what is said. In such situations, silence becomes an adult's ally.

New rules can be established: for example, the adult gives instructions once and after that they are repeated only under exceptional circumstances or when it is convenient. Action, not words, becomes the principal means of conveying intentions.

Assess Goals.   Adlerians have been teaching adults about the goals of children's misbehavior as a means of redirecting the motivation and behavior of such children toward more cooperative, responsible self-discipline. Being aware of the goals can help adults understand children better and avoid inadvertently reinforcing the misbehaviors they wish to correct. The goals of children's misbehavior before the age of 12 (the age is approximate) are excessively seeking attention, pursuing personal power, seeking revenge, and withdrawing through inadequacy. To identify the goals and begin anticipating corrective action, the counselor or therapist should ask the adults four questions:

1. What did the youngster do?
2. What did you do?
3. How did she respond to your action?
4. How did you feel?

An example will help to illustrate. The following excerpt is from a discussion between a teacher and a counselor/therapist.

Teacher: Samantha is constantly passing notes, talking to other children, raising her hand at inappropriate times, or just blurting out her thoughts. She's really driving me crazy!

Counselor/Therapist: In your most recent encounter, what did she do? Then what did you do?

Teacher: Well, just this morning I gave instructions for everyone to remain quiet while one of the children read from a book he had brought from home. Not two minutes later, Samantha was giggling and pointing at the boy across from her and passing a note to her friend behind her. When I told her to stop, she did; but a short time later she was doing something else.

Counselor/Therapist: In this case, would you say you were more annoyed than angry?

Teacher: Well, yes. Most of the time she gets right back to work, but I just wish she'd stop bugging me.

In this case, we see a child who is seeking attention. We understand this goal because of two pieces of information. First, when the teacher corrects Samantha, she stops what she was doing. Second, the teacher feels more annoyed by Samantha's behavior than anything else. This feeling is significant because children seeking power usually will not stop their behavior until they have clearly challenged the adult and provoked anger to some degree. Children seeking revenge will do what is necessary to elicit hurt, disappointment, or similar feelings. Children wishing to withdraw through inadequacy will have succeeded when the adult finally says, "I give up. I can't do anything with her!" The feeling most often expressed by the adult is one of defeat.

Assuming that a mistaken conviction or notion about how they can make their place motivates children's behavior, Adlerians note that children with a goal of misbehavior usually believe the following (approximately):

- *Attention.*   I only really count when others notice or serve me.
- *Power.*   I only really count when others know I can do what I want to do.
- *Revenge.*   I can't be liked, but I can hurt others and then they'll know I count, too.
- *Inadequacy.*   I'm stupid, inadequate, really hopeless, so why try? Don't expect anything from me. Trying will only prove it to everyone.

Children generally are not aware of the purposes of their actions. Many will stop their disruptive behavior when made aware of its purpose by a counselor or therapist. Teachers and parents, however, are cautioned to refrain from confronting children with observations about goals to avoid the appearance of labeling. Still, understanding the purposiveness of the children's behavior frees the adults to redirect the child's behavior toward more positive goals through the use of consequences and encouragement.

Respond with Consequences and Encouragement.   Responding with consequences and encouragement often involves the use of natural and logical consequences. A *natural consequence* is the result of an ill-advised action that brings about a negative result to the actor: for example, locking keys in the house or car, or damaging necessary items by using them carelessly. In a classroom example, children who persistently forget their pencils may not participate in certain writing activities for the day.

Logical consequences, however, result in negative social consequences to the actor: for example, others withhold service, cooperation, or invitation to participate in activities. Pupils who miss the teacher's instructions may be expected to wait until everyone else has started their lessons before having them repeated. The concept behind the effectiveness of natural and logical consequences is the logical order and pressure of reality. There are literally hundreds of examples of these methods that have been found effective in homes and classrooms (Dreikurs & Grey, 1968). Methods for creating new consequences are also available (Sweeney, 1989).

Adults of all generations have tended to present rules and regulations without helping new generations understand or discover the logic of social living. Some rules are illogical and arbitrary, and children perceive this quickly. These rules are fair game for conflicts in a power struggle. Patience in helping children and adolescents learn to experience the natural and logical order of daily living, however, is the keystone of effective helping.

With social democracy as the basis for training methods, adults can extricate themselves from the arbitrary exercise of power. Consequences that work effectively seem to be associated with the following general guidelines (Sweeney, 1989):

1. Natural consequences are sought first, before an adult considers a logical consequence.

2. New class or family rules are generally presented or discussed before implementation.

3. New rules apply to everyone, including the adults, who are excused only when parental responsibilities logically supersede an agreement.

4. Alternatives are always open to the individual: for example, "You can stop crying, or go to your room and return when you have finished crying."

5. Consistency in implementing either the rules or consequences is maintained with action, not words.

6. Logical consequences are avoided when power struggles are in process: that is, angry feelings, evidence of power's being exerted or challenged.

7. If consequences ensue from ill-advised acts of a family or class member, friendliness prevails before, during, and after. That is, "I told you so" comments do not precede or follow, either verbally or nonverbally.

8. Encouragement is highlighted for the many positive ways individuals share, participate, and cooperate. Everyone is made to feel and know that they have a place and belong, particularly when they reveal discouraged behavior.

9. Time for having fun together is an important part of the planning that takes place.

Through parent and teacher study groups, these methods can be learned in such a manner that new attitudes and behaviors can be mastered and shared with others.

Life-style Assessment

Adlerians have used both observation and interview techniques to derive insight into the motivation of their clients. A variety of techniques may be used to conduct what is referred to as a life-style assessment. Adler characterized life-style as the "unity in each individual—in his thinking, feeling, acting; in his so called conscious and unconscious, in every expression of his personality. This (self-consistent) unity we call the style of life of the individual" (Ansbacher & Ansbacher, 1967, p. 175). Life-style analysis or assessment is an effort to make explicit the attitudes, beliefs, and convictions that one uses in approaching or avoiding life's tasks. An example of life-style assessment techniques will be found later in this chapter, in "The Case Study of John."

SUPPORTING RESEARCH

In the past, Adlerian theory and practice were validated primarily by use and incorporation into several other systems or approaches to counseling

FIGURE 7.1
Wheel of wellness and prevention

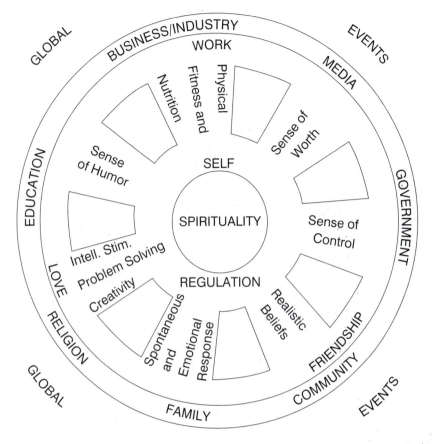

Source: Copyright 1990, J. Melvin Wittmer and Thomas J. Sweeney, Ohio University. Reprinted by permission.

and psychotherapy. While some authors have credited Adler with holding ideas similar to their own or have considered him to be a foundation for certain of their practices, others seem unaware of his works or at least do not acknowledge them (Ellenberger, 1970). More recently, research in other disciplines has served to validate many of Adler's constructs (Witmer, 1989).

A new model (see figure 7.1) of human development over the life span uses Adlerian theory for integrating the data from other theorists and disciplines (Sweeney & Witmer, 1991; Witmer & Sweeney, 1992). In this new model the five Adlerian life tasks interact dynamically with one another and the life forces. Spirituality and self-regulation are central to all other dimensions in relation to personality and human development.

While the model components appear to be uniform, proportional, and unidimensional, the model is more accurately depicted as dynamic, multidimensional, and continually shifting in proportions as human beings cope within their individual life space. As an illustrative paradigm, however, wholeness seems to represent this configuration well and has been selected for this reason.

Adlerians also characterize individuals as in a dynamic state of "being and becoming" (Sweeney, 1989). Movement is emphasized whenever lifestyle is presented. Social embeddedness and striving to make one's place are characteristic of the human condition. Within the outer bands of the model, called life forces, the individual is touched and touches each of the institutions that represent avenues for expressing self through the life tasks. Outside of the wheel are the global forces, which touch each of us through the institutions represented within the outer circle. Illustrative of the support for Adlerian concepts are those dealing, for example, with sense of worth, sense of control, and realistic beliefs.

The spiritual life task is our creative energy source for purposiveness in life. Optimism, inner harmony, and values for character development are associated with cooperation, social participation, and contribution—not only to self, but also to others and the common good (Witmer & Sweeney, 1992).

The literature on self-esteem tends to blend or combine sense of self-worth and sense of control. Accepting oneself as a person of worth and having a sense of competence or control corresponds to Adler's emphasis upon striving for significance. Maslow's research (1970) suggests that persons with a strong acceptance of themselves and their own nature are those who are most healthy. Likewise, a study by Campbell (1981) on satisfaction with life found that those who scored highest on satisfaction with self had extraordinarily high positive feelings of well-being. In addition, the satisfaction with self seemed to have little to do with objective circumstances such as education, income, or place of residence. Persons with positive self-esteem also have been found to cope better with stress (Witmer, Rich, Barcikowski, & Mague, 1983). In fact, poor copers have lower self-esteem and a greater amount of anxiety and physical symptoms.

Control is sometimes described in the literature as competence, locus of control, or self-efficacy. Adler (1954) identified the goal of superiority with power—that is, overcoming inferiority in a compensatory manner. There is much evidence accumulating to support the potency of power with wellness. Beliefs about personal control have to do with feelings of mastery and confidence. Studies have confirmed that persons who perceive themselves as having a high degree of control over their lives are more likely to feel good about themselves mentally and physically, report fewer ailments, and manage stress more effectively (California Department of Mental Health, 1979; Witmer et al., 1983).

Supporting the concepts of holism and mind-body interaction, behavioral medicine, psychosomatic medicine, and psychoneuroimmunology have established a relationship between thoughts, feelings, and illness (Witmer, 1985). When negative emotions become chronic or are suppressed, they can be destructive to our well-being. Orstein and Sobel (1987), for example, found that hostility appears to be the most likely characteristic that contributes to high blood pressure, coronary artery disease, and death among competitive, hard-driving personalities. There are also findings that suggest that anxiety, loneliness, and depression are associated with suppressing the immune system, thus increasing the chances for illness (Locke, Kraus, Leserman, Hurst, Heisel, & Williams, 1984). By contrast, relaxation and positive emotional states appear to enhance immune function (Dillon, Minchoff, & Baker, 1985; Kiecolt-Glaser, Garner, Speicher, Penn, Holliday, & Glaser, 1984; McClelland, Ross, & Patel, 1985). Indeed, responses to daily events influence internal bodily functions. Of special interest to Adlerians are findings showing that a negative mood results in lower antibody response and a positive mood is associated with a higher antibody response (Stone, Cox, Valdimarsdottir, Jandorf, & Neale, 1987). Private logic is the Adlerian conceptualization of personal beliefs that guide the feelings and behavior of individuals. It is a biased apperception about self, life, and others. Because it is a uniquely subjective view of reality, it is very much open to error with respect to objective reality: for example, how others may experience an event. The greater the discrepancy between one's private logic and reality, the greater the probability for inappropriate behavior in response to life events.

Research and clinical evidence have documented that negative thoughts causing emotional turmoil nearly always contain gross distortions or unrealistic expectations (Beck, 1976, 1984; Ellis, 1962). In addition, research by Witmer et al. (1983) indicated that those persons with more positive outlooks and who scored lowest on five of Ellis's irrational beliefs were less anxious and had fewer physical symptoms. Kobasa's (1979) findings also suggest that executives who perceive change as a challenge rather than a threat are more hardy and half as likely to experience illness. In the latter case, losing a job is stressful for most people. The healthier individuals, however, tend to perceive changes as a challenge rather than a threat. Persons with unrealistic beliefs tend to expect stability or constancy; change is the enemy to be dreaded.

Krumboltz (1988) made the following observation after a review of related literature concerning internal and external locus of control characteristics among young people:

So what have we learned? We know that internals achieve more and have fewer discipline problems than externals. We know that persons with good self-concepts tend to exhibit a strange inconsistency: They are responsible for their successes but not failures. We know that external beliefs can be changed to internal beliefs by persuasion, exhortation, goal setting exercises, cognitive restructuring, and telling the children, "you're good at this." We cannot be sure that changing beliefs changes academic achievement. (p. 41)

While research has not yet demonstrated that achievement will be affected by deliberate intervention to restructure the thinking of young people, this seems to be a likely byproduct of such a change, from an Adlerian/cognitive point of view.

Adlerians base many of their recommendations upon the merits of cooperation in all human relationships. Likewise, they promote cooperative activities through which all youngsters can learn not only about academics but also about life. There are data to support such a position in the schools.

Johnson (1981) reported a meta-analysis based on 122 studies dealing with the influence of cooperative, competitive, and individualistic goal structures on achievement. Johnson stated:

Cooperation promotes higher achievement than does interpersonal competition. These results hold true for all subject areas (language arts, reading, math, science, social studies, psychology, and physical education), for all age groups (although the results are stronger for pre-college students), and for tasks involving concept attainment, verbal problem solving, categorizing, spatial problem solving, retention and memory, motor performance, and guessing-judging-predicting. (pp. 56–57)

In addition, Johnson noted that cooperation promotes higher achievement and productivity than individualistic efforts. While these results are less conclusive, due to the number and types of studies conducted, there is some indication that cooperation without intergroup competition promotes higher achievement and productivity than cooperation used in conjunction with intergroup competition (as in team sports). In conclusion, Johnson recommends, "Given the general dissatisfaction with the level of competence achieved by students in the public school system, educators may wish to considerably increase the use of cooperative learning procedures to promote higher student achievement" (p. 58).

Slavin (1980) found that in 14 of 17 studies, student achievement was highest under a team-learning approach as compared to an individualistic control group. In the remaining three studies, there were no signifi-

cant differences between groups on achievement. In another study involving over 400 fourth- and fifth-grade students and 17 teachers, Slavin and
Karweit (1981) found that students who spent most of the day in a cooperative classroom environment liked school more than the control-group
students did, named more friends in school, and significantly increased
their self-esteem. They also achieved significantly more on three academic
tests of reading vocabulary, language mechanics, and language expression. There were no differences on four other tests of academic achievement. In short, the gains for the cooperative groups took place in both
academic and social-personal variables.

In light of the findings related to internally versus externally oriented students, Nowicki (1982) sought to determine if a cooperative
learning environment favored one type of student over another. He found
that both internals and externals achieved their best under the cooperative learning condition. However, when individuals were competing
against themselves or other individuals, internals tended to improve more
than externals.

When addressing the topic of encouraging teachers to experiment
with forming cooperative classroom teams, Krumboltz (1988) went so far
as to say:

> If we were to take these [research] findings seriously, we would drastically
> alter the way in which American education is conducted. Each student
> would be assigned to a team in every class, members would be expected to
> help each other, and the performance of the whole team would determine
> the grade of each individual member. (p. 55)

In addition, a number of studies related to effective elementary and
secondary school applications of Adlerian methods have been reported, as
well as those related to birth order, early recollections, life-style assessment, and teacher and parenting programs (Burnett, 1988; Kern, Matheny,
& Patterson, 1978; Sweeney, 1989). For example, based on a review of the
literature that documents the usefulness of parent study-consultation
groups, Burnett (1988) concluded, "The research studies . . . strongly support the effectiveness of Adlerian parenting programs. Changes in a positive direction were noted on measures of children's behavior, children's
self-concept, parental behavior, and parental attitude. The studies were, on
the whole, methodologically sound" (p. 74).

In addition, the evaluation of multimedia approaches has been added
to the more traditional study-group methods (Kerney, 1980; Kibler, Rush,
& Sweeney, 1985). One of the promising aspects of these study-group
methods is the capability of assisting parents or others in child care without the requirement that adults must read in order to understand the

methods. Films, audiotapes, and poster illustrations supplement the leader's materials.

There is still a need for much more research to explore new areas of Adlerian psychology. Crandall (1991) has sought to develop an instrument to measure social interest and reports some success in this validation. Likewise, Wheeler (1991) has noted promise for an inventory to assist with life-style assessment. As with any approach to understanding human behavior, there are always more questions than answers, no matter how much data are collected. For the clinician, however, validity is seen in its application to real clients. In this respect, Adlerian practitioners agree with others who have used Adler's methods and philosophy of human relationships in any number of settings. This is a pragmatic, commonsense approach that grows in both depth and breadth over time.

■ ■ ■

THE CASE STUDY OF JOHN: THE ADLERIAN APPROACH

The stages in Adlerian counseling or therapy include establishment of rapport, psychological investigation, interpretation, and reorientation. These are dynamic in nature, as opposed to lockstep; that is, relationship issues are essential throughout the process. Likewise, interpretation of life-style insights may take place throughout the process.

In *Problems of Neurosis* (1929), Adler noted that many ways are available to detect indications of another's life-style. Among his early observations were those revealed through organic problems. Suggested in recent stress research is that individuals tend to respond to similar stressful circumstances with particular physiological reactions unique to their coping skills. When some individuals say, "I can't stomach this situation," they literally mean it! In John's case, intestinal problems have persisted throughout his life. While we do not know why he has had these particular problems, we might reasonably hypothesize that they serve a purpose for him in his approach to his life tasks. To ascertain the accuracy of such a hypothesis, we ask clients early in the identification of the presenting problem, "How would life be different if this were not a problem for you?"

The counselor or therapist with insight about the purposiveness of human behavior will be listening to the client's responses as a story that reveals either organic origin (such as injury or infection), social (an excuse to avoid meeting responsibilities), or a combination of both as indicative of internal versus external locus of control. In the case of suspected organic origin, a referral for medical diagnosis would be in order as well.

In the case of John, of course, he has been under medical treatment for some time and more recently has been diagnosed with chronic irritable colon with a psychophysiologic origin. In short, his condition seems related to his coping (or lack thereof) with home and work responsibilities and relationships. His response to the question of how life would be different would include increased and consistent sexual potency, ability to go to work without intestinal distress, and greater harmony with his wife regarding his relationship with her and the children. He would most likely perceive events external to him as causing his problems, and among them include his new library director.

Following a format similar to that developed by Dreikurs (1967), the counselor or therapist collects information helpful in uncovering the private logic and motivation of the client (Sweeney, 1989). This information is based upon perceptions of early childhood, usually before the age of 8. It includes summarizing data from the family constellation (psychological position in the family); comparisons on personal attributes (such as intelligence, sense of humor, sensitivity, pleasing others); perception of relationships with siblings or peers; perceptions of mother and father (for example, characteristics, their relationship, problem or conflict resolution techniques); and early recollections (such as memories of specific events and the feelings associated with them before the client was 6 to 8 years of age).

John grew up as an only child who was pampered by an affectionate, well-meaning mother who intervened with others on his behalf when circumstances did not suit him. Father and mother were of first-generation German origin with old country expectations for roles and responsibilities, including an obedient boy. While the father was distant and somewhat gruff in his manner, he only occasionally spanked John. More important, John learned that by ignoring orders, he could have his own way; his father did not follow through.

John also learned early that illness was a cause for solicitousness from his mother. In fact, she sympathized with him because she, too, had a nervous stomach. While John characterized his mother as usually cheerful and affectionate, we might guess that her stomach problems were not unlike the proverbial, "I have a headache; not tonight, dear!"—a statement that humorously depicts the symptoms of a troubled marital relationship. This is not to say that the marital relationship was negative; rather, we can guess that the mother used her stomach problems as a buffer for unpleasant relationship circumstances.

In relation to children his age (if he were not an only child, comparisons would have been made to siblings), John described himself as intelligent and hardworking. He said he performed well in school subjects and helped around the house (when he wanted his mother's favor). He was obedient but strong willed (covertly disobeying elders), critical of others who tried to tell him what to do (especially those of his own age or station in life), sensitive, and easily upset (especially regarding his performance to meet expectations); he held high standards of achievement, behavior, and morals. Both at home and at parochial school, these achievement standards were reinforced.

Equally important, John did not describe himself as rebellious, particularly considerate of others, prone to temper tantrums, particularly materialistic or idealistic, athletic, strong, handsome, or masculine. In short, he is not inclined to "stick up for himself" and prefers to maintain a low profile rather than draw attention to himself. These descriptors of himself as a child are consistent with his present behavior as well. He also does not rate himself high with respect to his sense of humor, compared to others his age. Indeed, for John, life is serious business!

John felt that he was special to his mother. In a family with siblings, he might have described himself as the favorite. However, he most closely identified his characteristics with his father's: that is, distant, private, serious-minded, responsible. He could not understand why his wife, Betty, persisted in trying to engage him more with the children. They were her responsibility, just as he as a child was his mother's responsibility in his parents' home.

He remembered that his parents occasionally had loud arguments, but they did not carry on for long. Usually they ended with his father's leaving the room or house. He remembered one incident in particular (an early recollection) in which he heard them arguing over whether they would accept an invitation to dinner with some other people. His mother wanted to go very much and kept asking his father why he did not want to go. His father repeated, "Because I don't want to!" Finally, she insisted too much, and his father left the house and slammed the door. He never slammed the door otherwise. John thought his father had a perfect right to not go if he did not want to go. His initial feeling associated with his recollection was fear: his parents were arguing loudly. Then he was curious about why they were arguing, and he came to believe that his father was perfectly right in his position. Finally, he felt relief when his father left and they stopped arguing. He was not sure, but he does not think that his parents accepted the invitation.

We do not know without verifying it with John, but we might guess what thoughts he saved for use in future situations. They might include:

- No one should go where they don't want to.
- Disagreements are scary.
- When the going gets tough, it's time to get going.
- Women can be unreasonable.
- No women can tell me what to do.
- A man has a right to what he wants.

John's other early recollections are equally revealing of his motivation and movement through life. I recommend recording or writing them down verbatim; the choice of words, descriptors, and what is said or not said are all a part of the self-talk that forms the private logic of the individual. Leaving out or changing John's language will directly affect the discovery of his unique logic and its meaning. In fact, it is in collaboration with the client that the precise words and meaning are discovered. Therefore, such statements developed apart from the client are only the stimulus for the interpretive stage.

The following are examples of what John's early recollections may have been like:

- *At 4 years of age.*   I was in bed sick waiting for my mother. Then she came into the room and smiled at me. She brought me something to eat. I felt safe, loved, good. Life is best in a supportive, loving environment.

  A woman is a source of nourishment and emotional support.

  Being sick has its advantages.

  If I wait, good things will come to me.

- *At 5 years of age.*   My mother took me shopping. I started looking around away from her. Another boy scared me while she was busy with the clerk. My mother scolded the other boy and picked me up. I felt relieved and comforted. Bad things can happen when you venture away from safety. Boys can be mean and scary.

  It's important to have someone female to "pick me up" when life gets scary.

  New places can be unsafe.

- *At 4 or 5 years of age.*   I was someplace where there were a lot of kids. I think it was the church hall, and everyone else seemed to be playing or doing something. I was looking at pictures in a book by myself. I felt OK. Nothing special. I like doing my own thing without company. Books make good companions. I prefer my own place—quiet, secure, comfortable.

■ *At 6 years of age.*   I remember my confession before my first communion. Reverend Father asked me if I played with myself for pleasure. I
was embarrassed because I did, but I didn't know anyone would ever
know. He told me that it was a mortal sin and that I wasn't to do it any-
more. If I did, I was to come to confession before the next communion.
I felt awful and embarrassed. I wondered if I was going to go to hell for
playing with myself. (Try as I would, every once in a while, I'd wake up
at night physically excited and scared because I couldn't seem to control myself.)

Sexual pleasure can be sinful, even when you don't know it.

Sin is really bad.

Sinful people are bad.

If sex is pleasurable, it may be bad.

God knows I sin, even if I don't tell anybody.

I have to try hard to avoid sinning and still I sometimes fail.

Heroes, favorite childhood stories, and even current preferences in
hobbies, avocations, and reading material are helpful in understanding
how clients strive to "master that which they suffer." If John was asked
about his hero, he might have said St. Thomas Aquinas. His reason:
"Because St. Thomas was a good and moral man who discovered God's
plan for him through his reading and the reasoning of the Bible." John's
anxiety has greater roots in existential issues than the intake data may
suggest. G. K. Chesterton was one of his very favorite authors. Principally,
he liked Chesterton "because he thinks rightly and conveys his meaning in
wonderful ways." Indeed, spirituality is a central but unspoken concern of
John's.

At the time in the process when the possible meaning of the life-style
data are interpreted, the counselor or therapist is interactive and dynamic,
with an attentiveness that conveys, "Let us see what we can discover
together" as compared to "Let me tell you about yourself." Depending
upon the client's concerns and the purpose of the life-style assessment,
the counselor or therapist may suggest focusing only on those guiding
thoughts and convictions that are most related to the presenting problem.
As clients validate the accuracy and usefulness of the observations, they
are directly related to the most obvious presenting problems. As the counseling or psychotherapy process unfolds, the data can be revisited for
additional insights or as a reminder of themes that are applicable to
another life task. In the case of John, the presenting problems relate to
both work (relationship with the new woman director) and love (wife's
desire for more companionship and John's impotency). To address the

relationship with his wife fully, both John and Betty would be invited to participate in joint sessions involving life-style assessments and couples counseling to help them understand the guiding convictions of the other and to enhance the marriage relationship (Sweeney, 1989). Naturally, the relationship with the children, his mother, colleagues at work, and friends of his wife are relevant as well; and these, too, could be addressed in time. While they had not been disclosed in the initial session, issues related to religion and spirituality would eventually emerge. Attention to physical fitness and general good health would be encouraged in order to correct mistaken notions and also encourage optimum well-being. The irritable colon is being treated medically but should be inquired about periodically, especially if psychotropic drugs are prescribed. Naturally, the initial interview would include an assessment for severity of the anxiety, depression, fear, and hopelessness, with continuing observation of the progress toward amelioration of these symptoms.

The life-style assessment is discussed following the initial session, which allows John to tell his story about the nature of his physical problems and the physician's report and recommendations. These life-style data are compiled in a narrative, personalized manner, including personal attributes as they relate to work, friendships, and the marital relationship. The counselor or therapist typically formulates what appears to be the main guiding convictions about self, others, and life, from which are derived those situations that constitute security, belonging, and adequacy versus those that do not. The latter are consistently related to the presenting problem.

John's life convictions clearly illustrate the connection to his current crisis. His library supervisor is a woman whose directives he cannot ignore. His source of support is his wife and, more particularly, his mother. In both cases, these women are most solicitous when he has stomach problems. At other times, his wife is a source of stress because of issues of friendships and sex. While he has not stated his concerns as such, his anxiety associated with his rather rigid religious upbringing seems to underlie much of his health problems as well. He truly needs help in order to reorient his motivation from goals related to avoiding unsafe places, uncomfortable relationships, and unacceptable behavior. His guiding thoughts and goals are associated with avoiding the unpleasant, the unsafe, and the sinfulness of life. The price he pays to attempt to achieve this is found in his symptoms.

Assuming that this analysis is basically accurate, the counselor or therapist asks John if he wants to change his circumstances. Even if John says that he does, the counselor or therapist suggests that this may not be true. Attention is brought to the fact that these thoughts, feelings, and behaviors have served John's purposes for a long time. Giving them up will not be easy. John is asked to speculate on how he will think and feel in future situations that have caused him problems before. In fact, he may even fall back on feeling unworthy and anxious as he regresses in the process of change. On the other hand, he may well embrace new ways of thinking, feeling, and behaving. This introduction to the process of change creates a paradox for the client. Adlerians refer to it as "spitting in the client's soup." John may choose to continue his old ways, but he will no longer be innocent with respect to his purposes for avoiding his responsibilities or blaming others for his predicaments.

At this point, the counselor or therapist develops a plan with homework assignments; possible bibliotherapy (such as finding new heroes, becoming informed about sexuality and parenting); relaxation techniques (coping with stress); potential imagery for rehearsing new ways of thinking, feeling, and behaving (such as coping with conflict, intimacy, communication); and eventually couples and family counseling, including the mother at some point as needed.

Adlerians measure success in such a case in a variety of ways. Clearly, some of those ways are client and spousal reports of more satisfying marital and family relations, greater ease and satisfaction with work, and evidence of greater empathy and interest in others outside of the family. Clinically, another useful index is change in the life-style convictions, as revealed through new or significantly revised early recollections. Some or all of the recollections that John reported may be "forgotten" as though they never existed. In such a case, he will recall recollections that reflect a reorientation to life in keeping with a goal of engaging life, meeting adversity, and celebrating its joys. In short, he will emerge healthier and more able to cope and enjoy his participation in life without inhibiting fears.

■ ■ ■

LIMITATIONS

Limitations to individual psychology theory and practice are principally in the eye of the beholder. The philosophy and methods associated with Adler's approach to understanding and redirecting human behavior do not constrain the practitioner or researcher. Naturally, there is much to be learned by the study and adaptation of other approaches within an Adlerian perspective. For example, the systemic approaches to counseling couples and families are relevant and quite compatible with Adlerian methods. In fact, so many theorists and practitioners have borrowed liberally from Adler that it is not surprising to realize they have similarity and overlap.

If Adler were alive today, he would be gratified by the kinds of research across disciplines that have corroborated his insights and assumptions. However, he would not have been concerned so much with proving the validity of his approach as he would with demonstrating its usefulness. Therein lies a limitation of the movement and its advocacy for his approach. Those who follow Adler, including Rudolf Dreikurs, often have a zeal and commitment to teaching this healing art as a way of life, which requires no validation except in the hearts and minds of those who can benefit from it.

Adlerians such as Harold Mosak, Bob Powers, Don Dinkmeyer, Jon Carlson, Len Sperry, and myself have done much to go beyond the typical Adlerian advocacy for the approach. However, there is still much to be done. Adler and Dreikurs were teaching human relations methods for a democratic society where social equality would be the norm. Many of the abuses of persons and substances today are indicative of a society that has not realized these lofty goals. In fact, we have our priorities completely misaligned. Even as we strive to multiply the number of mental health workers needed to provide therapy to the sick and wounded in our society, our politicians debate how to pay for a system that continues to fail us.

At this point, the reader may wonder, What does this discussion have to do with the limitations of Adlerian counseling? The answer is simple, but it may not be understood. Adlerians have not succeeded in helping to prevent the problems that they and others seek to repair. Adler and, most particularly, Dreikurs were striving not so much to teach a therapy as to teach a philosophy of living through which we all validate one another's social equality and promote one another's "pursuit of happiness." Social equality as a political, economic, social, psychological, and spiritual reality requires a kind of revolutionary movement within our institutions that surpasses anything known to us yet.

To the extent that Adlerians have failed to become effective in the mainstream of institutions that educate, serve, and manage the affairs of this country, Adler and Dreikurs have not realized their dream. Their work was dedicated to a holistically healthy society that invests more in education and enrichment of its citizenry's quality of life than in repair and remediation of preventable dysfunctions. For those who share this dedication, there is still much to be done.

SUMMARY

The individual psychology of Alfred Adler is based upon a phenomenological, holistic understanding of human behavior. It espouses a philosophy of human relations based upon social equality. The practice of individual psychology has been characterized as "common sense," yet it is still not commonly practiced as Adler intended and modeled. While the fundamental principles have remained the same, new techniques and applications and the evolution of theory continue into the 21st century.

While Adlerians have been unconcerned with research per se, the research of others continues to reveal the validity of Adler's fundamental concepts. As is true of any effective practitioners, Adlerians adopt techniques from other theoretical approaches that work within the Adlerian construct. As a consequence, they are pragmatists who judge what is worthy by its usefulness in realizing the goals for the client.

Anyone may borrow from Adlerian techniques and have them serve a specific purpose. To be an Adlerian, however, is to embrace the philosophy and values that are the foundation of this approach. It is to these values and their philosophy that Adlerians adhere when they practice individual psychology.

REFERENCES

Adler, A. (1907). *Study of organ inferiority and its contribution to clinical medicine* (S. E. Jelliffe, trans.). New York: Moffat-Yard.

Adler, A. (1929). *Problems of neurosis.* London: Kegan Paul, Trench, Truebner & Co.

Adler, A. (1938). *Social interest.* London: Faber & Faber.

Adler, A. (1954). *Understanding human nature* (W. B. Wolf, trans.). New York: Fawcett. (Original work published in 1927.)

Adler, A. (1964). *Problems of neurosis.* New York: Harper & Row.

Ansbacher, H. L. (Ed.). (1969). *The science of living: Alfred Adler.* Garden City, NY: Doubleday.

Ansbacher, H. L., & Ansbacher, R. R. (Eds.). (1967). *The individual psychology of Alfred Adler.* New York: Harper & Row.

Beck, A. T. (1976). *Cognitive therapy and the emotional disorders.* New York: New American Library.

Beck, A. T. (1984). Cognitive approaches to stress. In R. L. Wollfolk & P. M. Lehrer

(Eds.), *Principles and practice of stress management* (pp. 255–305). New York: Guilford.

Burnett, P. C. (1988). Evaluation of Adlerian parenting programs. *Individual Psychology, 44,* 63–76.

California Department of Mental Health, Office of Prevention. (1979). *In pursuit of wellness.* San Francisco: Author.

Campbell, A. (1981). *The sense of well-being in America: Recent patterns and trends.* New York: McGraw-Hill.

Crandall, J. E. (1991). Life style can be measured. *Individual Psychology: Journal of Adlerian Theory, Research, and Practice, 47,* 229–240.

Dillon, K. M., Minchoff, B., & Baker, K. H. (1985). Positive emotional states and enhancement of the immune system. *International Journal of Psychiatry in Medicine, 15*(1), 13–18.

Dreikurs, R. (1946). *The challenge of marriage.* New York: Hawthorne.

Dreikurs, R. (1953). *Fundamentals of Adlerian psychology*. Chicago: Alfred Adler Institute.

Dreikurs, R. (1963). Psychodynamic diagnosis in psychiatry. *American Journal of Psychiatry, 119*, 1045–1048.

Dreikurs, R. (1967). *Psychodynamics, psychotherapy, and counseling*. Chicago: Alfred Adler Institute.

Dreikurs, R. (1968). *Psychology in the classroom* (2nd ed.). New York: Harper & Row.

Dreikurs, R. (1971). *Social equality: The challenge of today*. Chicago: Regnery.

Dreikurs, R., & Grey, L. (1968). *Logical consequences*. New York: Hawthorne.

Dreikurs, R., Grunwald, B. B., & Pepper, H. C. (1971). *Maintaining sanity in the classroom*. New York: Harper & Row.

Dreikurs, R., & Soltz, V. (1964). *Children: The challenge*. New York: Hawthorne.

Ellenberger, H. (1970). *The discovery of the unconscious*. New York: Basic Books.

Ellis, A. (1962). *Reason and emotion in psychotherapy*. New York: Lyle Stuart.

Johnson, D.W. (1981). Effects of cooperative, competitive, and individualistic goal structures on achievement: A meta-analysis. *Psychological Bulletin, 89*, 47–62.

Kern, R., Matheny, K., & Patterson, D. (1978). *A case for Adlerian counseling: Theory, techniques and research evidence*. Chicago: Alfred Adler Institute.

Kerney, E. J. (1980). *The efficacy of an Adlerian child guidance study group on changing teachers' attitudes toward students' behavior*. Unpublished doctoral dissertation, Ohio University, Athens.

Kibler, V. E., Rush, B. L., & Sweeney, T. J. (1985). The relationship between Adlerian course participation and stability of attitude change. *Individual Psychology, 41*, 354–362.

Kiecolt-Glaser, J. K., Garner, W., Speicher, C., Penn, G. M., Holliday, J., & Glaser, R. (1984). *Psychosomatic Medicine, 46*, 7–14.

Kobasa, S. C. (1979). Stressful life events, personality and health: An inquiry into hardiness. *Journal of Personality and Social Psychology, 37*, 1–11.

Krumboltz, J. (1988). The key to achievement: Learning to love learning. In G. R. Waltz (Ed.). *Proceedings on building sound school counseling programs*. Alexandria, VA: American Association for Counseling and Development Press.

Locke, S. E., Kraus, L., Leserman, J., Hurst, M. W., Heisel, J. S., & Williams, R. M. (1984). Life changes, stress, psychiatric symptoms, and natural killer cell activity. *Psychosomatic Medicine, 46*, 441–453.

Maslow, A. H. (1970). *Motivation and personality* (2nd ed.). New York: Harper & Row.

McClelland, D. C., Ross, G., & Patel, V. (1985). The affect of an academic examination on the salivary norepinephrine and immuninoglobulin levels. *Journal of Human Stress, 11*, 52–59.

Mosak, H. H., & Dreikurs, R. (1967). The life task III, the fifth life task. *Individual Psychologist, 5*(1), 16–22.

Mosak, H. H., & Dreikurs, R. (1973). Adlerian psychotherapy. In R. Corsini (Ed.), *Current psychotherapies*. Itasca, IL: Peacock.

Nehru, J. (1958). *Toward freedom*. Boston: Beacon.

Nowicki, S., Jr. (1982). Competition-cooperation as a mediator of locus of control and achievement. *Journal of Research in Personality, 16*, 157–164.

Orstein, R., & Sobel, D. (1987). *The healing brain*. New York: Simon & Schuster.

Shulman, B. H., & Nikelly, A. G. (1971). Family constellation. In A. G. Nikelly (Ed.), *Tech-*

niques for behavior change. Springfield, IL: Charles C Thomas.

Slavin, R. E. (1980). Cooperative learning. *Review of Educational Research, 50,* 315–342.

Slavin, R. E., & Karweit, N. L. (1981). Cognitive and affective outcomes of an intensive student team learning experience. *Journal of Experimental Education, 50,* 29–35.

Stone, A. A., Cox, D. S., Valdimarsdottir, H., Jandorf, L., & Neale, J. M. (1987). Evidence that lg A antibody is associated with daily mood. *Journal of Personality and Social Psychology, 52,* 988–993.

Sweeney, T. J. (1989). *Adlerian counseling: A practical approach for a new decade* (3rd ed.). Muncie, IN: Accelerated Development.

Sweeney, T. J., & Witmer, J. M. (1991). Beyond social interest: Striving toward optimum health and wellness. *Individual Psychology, 47*(4), 527–540.

Vaihinger, H. (1965). *The philosophy of "as if"*. London: Routledge & Kegan Paul.

Wheeler, M. S. (1991). A scale for social interest. *Individual Psychology: Journal of Adlerian Theory, Research and Practice, 47,* 106–114.

Witmer, J. M. (1985). *Pathways to personal growth*. Muncie, IN: Accelerated Development.

Witmer, J. M. (1989). Reaching toward wholeness. In Sweeney, T. J. (Ed.), *Adlerian counseling: A practical approach for a new decade* (3rd ed.). Muncie, IN: Accelerated Development.

Witmer, J. M., Rich, C., Barcikowski, R. S., & Mague, J. C. (1983). Psychosocial characteristics mediating the stress response: An exploratory study. *The Personnel and Guidance Journal, 62,* 73–77.

Witmer, J. M., & Sweeney, T. J. (1992). A holistic model for wellness and prevention over the life span. *Journal of Counseling and Development, 71*(2), 140–148.

CHAPTER EIGHT

Existential Theory

Mary Lou Frank
Clinch Valley College of the University of Virginia

The primary confrontation with death was addressed by the existential philosophers and has found life in the existential therapies. May (1969a), in examining the roots of existential thought, indicated that the term *existentialism* derived from *exsistere*, meaning "to stand out" or "to emerge." The theory of existentialism is an emergent part of the third force of psychology, attempting to look at the deeper meanings of our lives.

Existentialism addresses issues of death, freedom, isolation, and meaninglessness (Yalom, 1980). Despite the universal nature of these core struggles of life, existentialism is not the prevailing force in psychology today (Maslow, 1968). The emphasis on the rational and scientific techniques of behavioral, cognitive, and cognitive-behavioral counseling and therapy often relegate existentialism to a complementary existence. Existentialists were the "homeless waifs who were not permitted into the better academic neighborhoods" (Yalom, 1980, p. 21). However, contemporary thought points to an awakened need for existential answers. Current trends reflect an emphasis on health and wellness (Thauberger, Thauberger, & Cleland, 1983; Travis, 1981); loss and death (Kubler-Ross, 1975; Viorst, 1986); religiosity or spirituality (Wilber, 1986); and process issues in counseling and therapy (Bugental, 1978). Each area has directly or indirectly indicated the emerging importance of existential concerns.

Psychological theories are an intimate reflection of the real people creating the theories, their values, and biases. Existentialists are no exception. Whereas a behavioral approach reflects a theorist to whom science and logic are the organizing factors for existence, an existentialist is a theorist to whom science is complementary to meaning, for whom relationships are as important as the scientific advancement of a theory and who is involved as much in the process as in the product (May, 1983). For an existentialist, the journey is as important as the destination (Bugental, 1978); and the existential journey is not superficial.

> To explore deeply from an existential perspective does not mean that one explores the past; rather it means that one brushes away everyday concerns and thinks deeply about one's existential situation. It means to think outside of time, to think about the relationship between one's feet and the ground beneath one, between one's consciousness and the space around one; it means to think not about the way one came to be the way one is, but that one is. . . . The future-becoming-present is the primary tense of existential therapy. (Yalom, 1980, p. 11)

Unlike the psychoanalytic and psychodynamic theorists, existentialists are not deficiency focused. Instead, they concentrate on potentialities. Existentialists hope to aid individuals in developing schemata to understand and cope with their lives. Likewise, existentialists represent a diverse population. In as many ways that meaning can be gleaned from life, there are as many avenues to describe the process of finding meaning. Just as some existentialists are more psychodynamic in their orientation (Yalom, 1980) others are more humanistic (Bugental, 1978; Maslow, 1968). The newest wave in psychology, transpersonal theory (Wilber, 1977), also seems to flow from existentialism.

For some individuals, a meaning emerges from the struggle with life and death, destiny and freedom, isolation and connection. Anticipated by an existential founder (Maslow, 1971), transpersonal psychology offers a haven for those individuals finding meaning in the spiritual realm. The existential philosophers Buber (1970) and Tillich (1987), as well as the psychological theorists Wilber (1977) and Maslow (1968), were explicit that from an existential quest, a spiritual awakening could unfold. For some, hope emerges from despair. However, not all existentialists find meaning through spirituality. Some find that the quest for meaning is always filled with the anxiety of ultimate death (Yalom, 1980). Regardless, transpersonal psychology is a framework for examining the process of spiritual development that may surface after scratching the existential veneer.

The purpose of this chapter is to develop a historical basis for existentialism, explore the developmental nature of the quest for meaning, examine the major constructs of existential thought, describe the change process, list intervention strategies, and examine supporting research. The final analysis is a case discussion. I hope that in the process of understanding a theory about existence, you will gain a deeper sense of yourself, your own life, and humanity.

HISTORY

Existentialism is rooted in the philosophical thought of post-World War II Europeans, where it found form and voice. Emerging from the atrocities of war, vanquished idealism, and fragmented family life, the philosophers of this period developed a perspective reflecting the realities of existence. In the midst of the destruction, the ultimate loss occurred: God was also dead (Nietzsche, 1967). People saw death as the core experience permeating their existence. These experiences reflected a new perspective; and although not always optimistic, it was full of realism. Kierkegaard (Bretall, 1951) was one of the first existential philosophers before World War II, and he was a primary influence on other existentialists such as Heidegger, Buber, and Nietzsche. Kierkegaard (1944) pursued scientific truth from the landscape of our humanness. Our greater problems were not due to lack of knowledge or technology, but lack of passion and commitment (May, 1953). Kierkegaard (1944) was convinced that the goal of pure objectivity was not only impossible, but was also undesirable and immoral; these beliefs foreshadow recent findings in the new physics (Bohm, 1973). Kierkegaard was clear that except when examined in a relational context, science alone does not produce truth (Bretall, 1951). The objective, detached examination is an illusion because a subject can never be truly separated from the object. No small wonder that Kierkegaard (1944) was not favored among the more objective, cognitive, and behavioral theorists who were influenced by Descartes.

Descartes was so influential that he has been called the father of modern psychology (MacLeod, 1975). According to Descartes, an objective, rational examination was crucial to the development of empirical science. Consistent with Descartes was the prevailing thought of Copernicus, who provided the scientific model of a detached observer that we see embodied in current scientific research methodology. From Descartes emerged a mechanistic theory of mind and body only causally interacting.

In the midst of a Cartesian mind-set, Heidegger (1949) developed an alternate paradigm. Building on Kierkegaard, Heidegger continued to develop existential thought. Heidegger's concept was antimechanistic and antitheoretic in a Cartesian sense. To Heidegger (1962), theories and humans were imperfect, and an objective reality is not reality at all. Existence can only be understood in terms of being in the world through subjective participation and involvement. Heidegger (1962) noted that in striving for exactness, the Cartesian system was missing reality.

Heidegger's (1962) notions of choice also impacted the existential psychologists. Reasoning that each choice represented the loss of an alternative, the past becomes important in terms of lost opportunities. Future choices are limited due to past choices and the finite time remaining to fulfill them. By encountering these limitations, we may experience nothingness, guilt, and anxiety. Existentialism provided a path of expression for many others as well. The field of literature was ripe for existential development (for example, Dostoyevsky, Tolstoy, Kafka, Sartre, Camus, Hemingway, Eliot, Fitzgerald, Stein, Ellison, Faulkner, Wolfe, Pound, Blake, Angelou, Rand, and Frost). Both in the United States and Europe, the best literary minds echoed the existential rumblings.

North American psychologists initially reflected the focus on universal concerns through humanism. The third force (the first force was scientific behaviorism; the second was analytical Freudian theory) arose as an answer to the limitations of the first two schools. The positive aspects of humanness (such as love, freedom with responsibility, self-actualization, potential, transcendence, uniqueness, choice, and creativity) were missing from Freudian and behavioral theories. The development of the Association for Humanistic Psychology spawned a positive model for change. The humanistic element focused on human capacities and potentialities (Bugental, 1978). Demonstrating the natural evolution from humanistic to existential, many of the initial humanistic theorists moved into an existential position (for example, Maslow, Bugental, Buber, and May). Although humanism was the initial paradigm, existentialism built on the existing tenets and added the dimension of ontology, experiential awareness, and responsibility.

Existentialism also has roots in contemporary religious thought. Religion's differing perspectives kindles a conflict. The disagreement is one of essence (representing scientific, objectivity, and facts) over existence (representing what is real for each individual). In Western culture, essence has triumphed over existence (May, 1983). However, this battle takes place on holy ground, as indicated by Tillich (1987):

> The story of Genesis, chapters 1–3, if taken as myth, can guide our description of the transition from essential to existential being. It is the profoundest and richest expression of man's awareness of his existential estrangement and provides the scheme in which the transition from essence to existence can be treated. (p. 190)

The quest for knowledge and understanding is what eventually separates humanity from the safety of objectivity. Descartes may have won the battle, but Tillich would contend that the war is not yet over.

Existential questions themselves have a religious flavor. Some existentialists would say that religion is a superficial defensive against the ultimate reality of death (Yalom, 1980). They indicate that religion has nothing to do with the worldly questions of meaninglessness, anxiety, and existence (Tillich, 1987). However, the dichotomy may be more one of semantics than substance. As Tillich (1987) wrote:

> Whenever existentialists give answers, they do so in terms of religious or quasi-religious traditions which are not derived from their existential analysis. . . . The answers . . . come from hidden religious sources. They are matters of ultimate concern or faith, although garbed in a secular gown. . . . Existentialism is an analysis of the human predicament. And the answers to the questions implied in man's predicament are religious, whether open or hidden. (pp. 187–188)

Tillich contends that the existential dilemmas are religious questions in secular terms.

In similar form, Buber (1970) also emphasizes the religious lineage within existential ancestry through the reverence implicit in some relationships. When "a man addresses with his whole being the You of his life that cannot be restricted by any other, he addresses God" (Buber, 1970, p. 124). When an individual no longer relates to another as an object, as an extension of herself or as a means to an end, she enters a relationship expressed by "I to Thou" (Buber, 1970). The essence of the ideal existential encounter embodies respect, honor, and divinity.

The religiosity that develops from the existential quest is developmental (Frankl, 1975). From an individual's struggle with consciousness and responsibility, and from unconscious existential choices, the third stage of development emerges as a "spiritual unconscious" (Frankl, 1975). Unconscious religiosity is intrinsic to our ability to transcend. Whether the spiritual dimension is labeled, inherently perceived, or ignored, it is an element of an existential development.

HUMAN NATURE: A DEVELOPMENTAL PERSPECTIVE

Isolation

The universality of existential concerns is evident in children as well as adults. From a number of studies, Yalom (1980) examined the development of existential concerns with death. The findings indicate that existential concerns, first expressed as death anxiety, are found at a very early age (five to eight years or before). The anxiety produced by awareness of nonexistence is overwhelming, even to a young child. From ages 9 to 12, children cope with death by denying it. Denial is fostered by parents and adults in the first phase of life. By the time of adolescence, denial becomes ineffective. The initiation into adulthood reintroduces the reality of death and isolation and necessitates a search for new meaning.

Despite the contemporary focus on commercial fulfillment, many people still search for existential meaning. A public opinion poll in France indicated that 89 percent of people felt that a purpose was needed to give meaning to life (Frankl, 1984). In a group from a leading hospital training facility, 78 percent of students surveyed indicated that "finding a meaning in life" was their first life goal (Frankl, 1984, p. 122).

Yalom's (1985) survey of group clients also suggests that existential factors are very important to client growth. One question emerged as central to individual development in a group context. "Learning that I must take ultimate responsibility for the way I live my life no matter how much guidance, identification, and support I get from others" was ranked fifth out of 60 curative factors (Yalom, 1985, p. 85). Gaining understanding about the meaning of life and taking responsibility for it serves to influence and inspire our development.

Self-awareness

The process of development, whether spiritual or secular, is characterized by anxiety. Death seems to be the primary cause (Frankl, 1984; May, 1979; Yalom, 1980). Although existential issues can arise in childhood, most existential concerns become salient in adulthood (Bugental, 1978; Wilber, 1986; Yalom, 1980). The developmental necessity of examining the issues of death may be coming to terms with nonbeing (Heidegger, 1949, 1962); ontological anxiety (Tillich, 1987); loss of the world (Bretall, 1951; Nietzsche, 1967); or realizing the fear of loss of self (Yalom, 1980). "To venture causes anxiety, but not to venture is to lose one's self" (May, 1979, p. 55). Facing death is critical in coming to terms with life (Kubler-Ross, 1975):

> Death is the key to the door of life. It is through accepting the finiteness of our individual existences that we are enabled to find the strength and courage to reject those extrinsic roles and devote each day of our lives to growing as fully as we are able. It is the denial of death that is partially responsible for people living empty, purposeless lives. (p. 164)

Whether one transcends (Maslow, 1971), develops heightened awareness (Yalom, 1980), or is shaken by the struggle (May, 1953), individuals are forever changed by the confrontation with death.

Psychopathology

Psychopathology is always a potential consequence of confronting or not confronting existential questions. The manifestations of pathology represent the loss of a potential within an individual. In the confrontation with life and death, some people develop a desperate sense of isolation (May, 1983). They have literally lost their world and their community. The separation of self from the individual's inner world creates a detached, unaffected person who covers up problems with intellectualization. Instead of being in the world, the individual feels hopeless, shattered, and alone.

Another pathological reaction that might develop from the existential crisis is depression. Depression is a last attempt to hold on to the defenses against anxiety (Bugental, 1978). Yalom (1980) reported that studies on dying patients indicate that death anxiety is inversely proportional to life satisfaction. Critically ill patients with meaningless lives were more anxious and subsequently more depressed than those whose lives were satisfying. Despite the depression, studies support Nietzsche's contention that "what has become perfect, all that is ripe—wants to die. . . . All that is unripe wants to live" (Yalom, 1980, p. 208). Even though depressed, the person really is not prepared for the emotional confrontation with death. The fear of approaching the universal questions is as strong as the fear of not approaching them. The individual is estranged in a chasm of existential depression.

In discussing the need for authenticity, Heidegger (1962) described the authentic person as having awareness of existence, not just of life's characteristics. The lack of *dasien*, or of "being there," implies that the person is avoiding presence, accessibility, and expression (Bugental, 1978). By increasing our awareness of life itself, we become more authentic, more present (Bugental, 1978). For instance, the counselor or therapist who treats clients as individuals and not just as diagnoses is at one level living authentically. Conversely, the inauthentic person pathologically resists being known. It is impossible to experience a veiled life. Everything that makes the person alive and allows the individual freedom remains imprisoned behind the mask of inauthenticity.

Maslow's (1954) seminal work with self-actualizers provided additional insight into the psyches of creative individuals who were unable to fulfill their true potential. Not everyone with capability becomes self-actualized. Maslow (1968) cites three reasons that people do not rise to their potential: lower instinctive pressure to self-actualize, cultural institutions that control or inhibit creativity, and tendencies toward fear and regression. Without these constraints, Maslow suggests that actualization is a natural process. But individuals who do not actualize experience shame, anxiety, and defeat. Remorse may be a guide back to actualization; but if the warning is not taken, individuals live knowing they did not reach their potential. In our culture, members of minority classes and women represent repressed groups; these groups have often been discouraged to self-actualize and encouraged to self-doubt (Bepko, 1989; Gerardi, 1990; Horner, 1972; Parham & Helms, 1985). Although taking responsibility is ultimately the solution (Yalom, 1980), oftentimes it is not deemed worthy of effort. Once self-actualization is aborted, individuals see their lives as meaningless.

Before the final stage of transcendence that seems to characterize most existential breakthroughs (Maslow, 1968; May, 1979; Tillich, 1987), some people get bogged down with existential guilt.

> Life is marked by ambiguity, and one of the ambiguities is that of greatness and tragedy. This raises the question of how the bearer of the New Being is involved in the tragic element of life. What is his relation to the ambiguity of tragic guilt? What is his relation to the tragic consequences of his being, including his actions and decisions, for those who are with him or who are against him and for those who are neither one nor the other? (Tillich, 1987, p. 228)

On the verge of understanding meaning in one's life, guilt may prove the ultimate undoing. Heidegger (1949) described the guilt flowing from heightened awareness and questioned the right of anyone to let himself be killed for the truth. "He who does so must know that he becomes tragically responsible for the guilt of those who kill him" (Tillich, 1987, p. 229). Existential guilt prohibits the individual from joining in the awareness of reality. Instead, the individual is left with the consequences of unremitting shame and responsibility.

Of all the pathologies discussed thus far, possibly the most unsettling is a loss of self in the world, or existential isolation. Yalom (1980) describes existential isolation as failing to develop an inner strength, worth, and identity. The person instead internalizes anxiety and searches for any available sanctuary. Yalom (1980) describes two coping styles that provide security to the existentially isolated individual: existing through others, and fusing with others. For some people, safety lasts only as long as their existence is perceived. Being alone means being forgotten. The other defense that individuals use to seek protection from existential isolation is fusion. By living in and for others, they lose their boundaries and, in essence, their personhood. Under the popular label of codependence, women have been stereotypically described as using this defensive mode (Hogg & Frank, 1992). In the despair of existential isolation, the individual has lost hope of finding a place in the world.

A World View

Unique among the theorists, existentialists have conceptualized their philosophy in context. They suggest that all theories have a place in the world. Bugental (1978) was the first to see the theories in perspective. According to Bugental, there are six levels of helping goals, extending from behavioral change to spiritual development. Corresponding to the six goals are six different types of helping, from behaviorism to transpersonal.

Wilber (1986) also offers a broader viewpoint, incorporating other theoretical orientations into a developmental schema. Wilber's theoretical model is transpersonal and more reflective of Eastern religion than Tillich's (1987) focus on the Western perspective. For Wilber (1986), an individual's pathology is seen as a matter of degree, beginning with psychotic symptoms and advancing to enlightened awareness. Like Bugental, Wilber sees each theory as subtly answering the questions raised at various levels of dysfunction. The physiological interventions (psychiatry) are more effective for psychotic symptoms. Psychodynamic and existential therapies are the bridge to transpersonal techniques. Each theory is seen as having a contribution, but none has the answer for all people or all issues.

MAJOR CONSTRUCTS

Existentialism embodies differing perspectives and approaches. For the purposes of this discussion, Yalom, Maslow, and Bugental provide the major divisions within existentialism (see figure 8.1). Each theorist addresses the key existential constructs of death, meaning, isolation, and freedom in very different ways. Common to all theories is the nature and quality of the existential relationship.

Dynamic Existentialism

Yalom's (1980) perspective is representative of the dynamically oriented existentialists. Yalom coined the term *existential psychodynamics* to describe a change in emphasis. The existential dynamic approach emphasizes security over conflict and existential questions instead of anxiety. Sexual drives are replaced by drives to understand the existential questions, but anxiety and defense mechanisms are still the outgrowth of the conflict (see figure 8.2). The paradigm hasn't changed, only the source of anxiety. Confrontation with death, freedom, isolation, and meaninglessness offers the potential for hope or the possibility of despair.

Yalom (1980) lists four roles of death in counseling/therapy and psychopathology:

1. The fear of death plays a major role in our internal experience.
2. Children at an early age are pervasively preoccupied with death, and their major developmental task is to deal with terrifying fears of obliteration.

FIGURE 8.1
Approaches to existential counseling

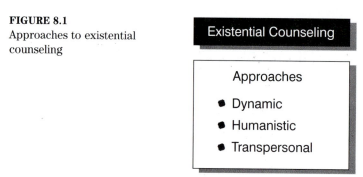

FIGURE 8.2
Conceptualization from a
dynamic existential perspective
(Yalom, 1980)

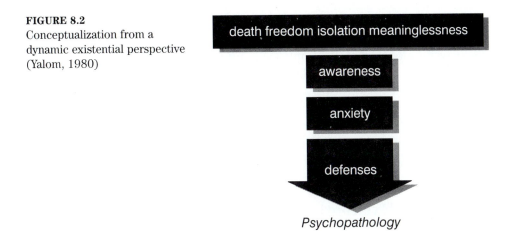

death freedom isolation meaninglessness

awareness

anxiety

defenses

Psychopathology

3. To cope with these fears, we erect defenses against death awareness, defenses that are based on denial. They shape character structure and, if maladaptive, result in clinical syndromes.

4. A robust and effective approach to counseling or psychotherapy may be constructed on the foundation of death awareness.

Ego development and defense structure provide the framework for understanding death anxiety. The personality structure is viewed in light of an awareness of death.

Freedom has a similar meaning. To Yalom (1980), it includes freedom of choice, action, and change. Included in freedom is the concept of individual responsibility and the courage to act. Decisions to change take time and patience and involve exploring the future's potential as well as the past's history. Although freedom offers unlimited potential, we are ultimately alone. Yalom focuses on the notion of differentiation as being part of the process of separation and inherent in our fear of loneliness. Relationships cannot displace isolation, but they are the only bridge that can connect people and provide comfort. In Yalom's most recent book, *Love's Executioner and Other Tales of Psychotherapy* (1989), love is described as antitherapeutic. When people fall in love, they no longer understand their existential isolation in the same way or to the same depths. The existential confrontation with isolation is meaningless to a person who does not feel alone.

Meaninglessness is the dreaded answer to the existential questions "What is the meaning of life?" "What difference do I really make?" "What is the purpose of the struggles?" Yalom (1980) implies that the problem is implicit in the two known truths of existence. First, we need to understand the meaning of our lives. Second, despite our need for meaning, we live in a meaningless universe. The dilemma for the counselor or therapist is to help the client address the challenge but not provide answers. As implied, discovering meaning also involves staying engaged in the helping relationship. The goal is to help the client find meaning in meaninglessness. Counselors and therapists continually need to acknowledge the existential struggle. They are most effective when they help clients find meaning as it evolves through counseling or therapy. "The question of meaning in life is, as the Buddha taught, not edifying. One must immerse oneself in the river of life and let the question drift away" (Yalom, 1980, p. 483).

Humanistic Existentialism

Humanistic existentialism represents the blending of two forces within existential theory. Exemplified by Bugental (1978), the humanistic existentialists have a confident respect for the individual. Their view of death, freedom, isolation, and meaninglessness shows a similar inclination.

Death is encountered in all therapeutic experiences from the humanistic-existential perspective. In working through resistance to authenticity, clients watch as part of themselves die. Suicidal and homicidal feelings are common during this period. Drawing from Horney's notion of idealized and despised images of self, Bugental (1978) asserts that both images are false and must die for the real person to emerge: "But there is a fearful wrenching involved in that relinquishment. The nakedness seems, and indeed is, so terribly vulnerable and so truly mortal. Usually the 'killing' of the old self occurs in some kind of break out experience" (p. 79). A confrontation with death signals the rebirth of a more aware and more authentic being.

Freedom comes after our confrontation with our inaccurate representation of ourselves. It only emerges after we realize that the world is an arbitrary construction of our awareness. Hence, we can make each moment the way we wish, and make our future different from any moments in our past. Although we can choose each thought we have, there are costs and benefits for each decision. Freedom is silhouetted by responsibility.

Isolation, according to humanistic existentialism, is more a separation from oneself than from others. But the isolation from our true self, as described earlier, keeps us from connecting and contributing to the larger social order in more productive ways. We are isolated and defended by our own identities. Out of our own fears, we erect walls to prohibit the connections we most desire. As Bugental (1978) says, "When I begin to realize that my truest identity is as process and not as fixed substance, I am on the verge of a terrible emptiness and a miraculous freedom" (p. 133).

The world from a humanistic-existential perspective is full of meaningfulness as opposed to meaninglessness. Out of our will to love and live, we arrive at meaning in our lives (May, 1969b). In gaining a deeper awareness of ourselves, we also gain a deeper sense of others. Our efforts to gain understanding involve confronting aspects of ourselves before we develop a heightened sense of meaning of the world.

Transpersonal Existentialism

Maslow was an originator of both existential and transpersonal theory, and his description of existentialism (1968) has a flavor of both disciplines. Whereas the first two forces of psychology offer us an understanding of illness, Maslow's force advances a conceptualization of health. Maslow describes health as intrinsic in each individual and a part of our natural development. Destructive tendencies are not natural; they are "violent reactions against frustration of our intrinsic needs, emotions, and capacities" (Maslow, 1968, p. 3). People actualize when nurtured and given sufficient space.

The dynamic existential focus on death and awareness of the ultimate realities of existence may induce despair (Yalom, 1980). The transpersonal existential approach perceives death as an opportunity for the individual to transcend and rise above the given circumstances. Most people experience tragedy; but in equal proportion, they experience joy (Maslow, 1968). Health is the ability to transcend the environment, drawing from the joyful aspects of existence (see figure 8.3). The capacity of individuals to stand out from their given situations and emerge is the key to understanding our potential (May, 1983). Frankl's (1984) example of finding

FIGURE 8.3
Development from the
transpersonal existential
approach

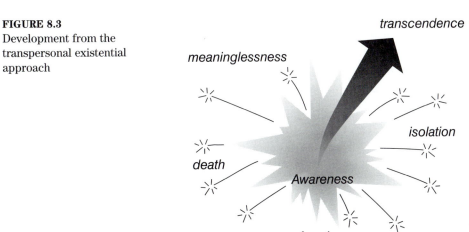

meaning and love of life through a concentration camp experience is a testament to the innate human capacity to transcend.

Freedom is similar for Yalom and Maslow. However, it is mediated because our inner nature is not strong and overpowering and unmistakable like the instincts of animals. It is weak and delicate and can be easily overcome by habit, culture pressure, and wrong attitudes (Maslow, 1968). Even though our creativity never disappears, it may struggle to surface. Because of external pressures, we may not be totally free to actualize because of our own restraints.

Central to transpersonal existentialism is a notion of universal connection rather than isolation (Maslow, 1954). Looking to find our real self includes being conscious of our biological needs, but it also involves experiencing our commonness with all other beings. Connection is almost paradoxical in application. "The more eager we are to make a diagnosis and a plan of action, the less helpful do we become. The more eager we are to cure, the longer it takes" (Maslow, 1968, p. 184). The more we attempt to connect, the further apart we are. The more we struggle to understand our feelings, the more they will elude our realization. By letting go and accepting, we can begin to connect with others and, most important, with ourselves.

The meaninglessness that is described by Yalom (1980) and meaningfulness described by Bugental (1978) is answered by Maslow (1971) with transcendence. We transcend, find meaning in our world, by fully being ourselves. Truly being oneself involves being more integrated within and without. The observing and experiencing functions of self are united; the individual is able to join with the world. Paradoxically, as people become more wholly themselves, they are better able to join with others and be one with the world. The person is more able to love. Through transcendence, the person also becomes more capable. When a person is most truly herself, she is also more creative, aware, and productive. Life is not a struggle. People are more aware of the potentialities in their lives and within themselves. As for the humanistic existentialists, life is not meaningless. The transpersonal existentialists add worldly scope to understanding. Meaning is implicit in discovering ourselves and our awareness of others.

Existential Relationships

The outcome research indicates that the relationship is the most important aspect of the helping process (Yalom, 1980). Across all of the factions within existential thought, the form and quality of the relationship are consistent. There is a sense of relational truth embedded in the encounter (May, 1983). Bugental (1978) describes the relationship as professional,

FIGURE 8.4
Buber's relationship levels
(1970)

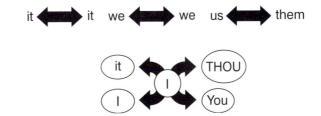

dedicated to healing and growth, and sensitive. Although skilled, the counselor or therapist is present with the client in a very real and immediate existence. But these only describe the functions, not the substance of the encounter.

The diversity and substance of relationships were probably best described by Buber (1970). According to Buber, relationships may be experienced at several levels or at a combination of differing levels. He describes the ways people relate to each other (see figure 8.4). Some individuals relate to the world and to others as "I to I." Because other people are not seen as objects or individuals, these relationships are characterized by indirectness. People speak at or about others, seldom to them. These individuals take and never give.

"I to it" relationships depict an individual relating to another as an object. These relationships do not persist. The individual generally moves to another level of relating, but it more intimate or more detached.

Another level of relationship is among people who relate to others and the world as "it to it." For these individuals, *I* has little meaning, for they don't have much sense of self. Buber (1970) calls this the "community of solid scholars—so solid that there is no room at the center for any core" (p. 13). People relating to others at the it-it level have no room for any "I"-ness.

The next relationship level is called "we to we." These people also have no sense of *I*. This relationship is generally seen in young children. No one has any individuality nor any objectivity.

"Us to them" describes a relationship between the chosen few and the damned. Some people will triumph, and others will fail. The lesser individuals are not even heard by the chosen because they represent *them*. All the good attributes are wrapped up in *us*; all the negative are represented by *them*.

The "I to You" relationship implies treating the other individual as a person. The encounter involves two rather than one to an object or one to a despised part. There are more possibilities for understanding within an "I to You" relationship.

The profound meeting, the core of the existential relationship, is the "I to Thou." As discussed earlier, this relationship involves an encounter with God and deeper respect for the individual. The notion of transcendence is a part of the connection at the "I to Thou" level. The most potent form of help is being present in a respectful, honoring encounter (Dass & Gorman, 1985). In the final analysis, "I to Thou" relationships provide hope for genuine understanding.

In the "I to Thou" relationship, the counselor or therapist is merely a guide on a journey (Bugental, 1978). He offers respect for the client but is also a traveler on the same road. In *How Can I Help?* (Dass & Gorman, 1985), counselors and therapists are given vignettes illustrating the power of a helping relationship for all involved. Relationship may reflect several levels of encounter at a given time for the client and the counselor or therapist. Whatever the level, the counselor or therapist impacts and is impacted by the helping process.

Hazards on the Journey

The journey through the "dark night of the soul" can be difficult for counselors and therapists (Bugental, 1978, p. 77). They must take some time to protect against psychological and physical intrusion into their private lives (Bugental, 1978). Making several such painful journeys with clients is bound to affect practitioners at a very personal level.

> Doing therapy is like remembering all the time that you are going to die. Because the therapy hour has a definite beginning and ending, we are kept aware of its being temporary. There is only me, and you, and here, and now. We know in advance that it will not last, and we agree to this. (Kopp, 1972, p. 42)

Being an existential counselor or therapist means being open to continued learning and awareness because existential helping operates at an intense level of involvement.

If we are to listen to Freud's warning, truly being with clients may be harmful to the helping process. The counselor or therapist may be ineffective by engaging in an authentic encounter. Yalom (1980) argues that the relationship needs to achieve a balance, but the counselor or therapist should not be afraid of contact with another person or of being known. It is a delicate balance, a journey that is uncharted and unlike other therapeutic approaches.

Additionally, May (1979) suggests that there is a potential for losing the scientific focus when working with people at an existential level. In rebelling against the rationalistic tradition of contemporary psychology, existential counselors and therapists might be detached from philosophical or technical realities. The trend toward transpersonal theory only underscores the danger. Ignoring the present need to delineate therapeutic interventions, the existential counselor or therapist may be professionally vulnerable.

Despite all the concerns and warnings, there is value in taking the risk to encounter another person at the existential level. For the field, existentialism is an alternative and the only viewpoint solidly grounded in theory (May, 1983). Most significantly, clients find this approach very helpful (Yalom, 1980).

THE PROCESS OF CHANGE

The existential process of change is "tragically optimistic" (Frankl, 1984, p. 161). Existential assistance promotes change in the following ways (Frankl, 1984):

1. It turns suffering into a human achievement and accomplishment.
2. It derives from guilt the opportunity to change oneself for the better.
3. It derives from life's transitoriness an incentive to take responsible action.

Although steeped in philosophy, however, these guideposts hardly provide a working primer for the budding existential counselor or therapist.

The existential change process resembles the title of a book by Yalom and Elkin (1974): *Every Day Gets a Little Closer*. Existential change is a true process. The product seems to emerge from the mist rather than spring forth at a specific juncture in counseling or therapy. Clients transform through a courageous and subtle encounter with aspects of their humanness.

Change evolves from a client's willingness to participate in counseling or therapy, confront loneliness, experience individuality, encounter true connection, and develop the inner strength to transcend this difficult situation (May, 1953). But the process of change begins much earlier. By reaching out to be with another person authentically, the client begins the process of transformation. Anxiety loses its power, and clients change as their fears melt into vital energy. Tillich (1980) indicates that courage to be oneself evolves out of one's own anxiety.

The process of existential change is an awakening from anxiety to freedom. Through increased awareness of self and experience of the world, clients are able to experience their potential more fully. Instead of a veiled existence, they are living consciously and responsibly; they are connecting with others as well as with aspects of themselves. The actual process of change may move very rapidly: clients may bloom into creative, energized self-actualizers. The process may also unfold more gradually. Regardless, the "arena of change" is the relationship facilitating the development of awareness, acceptance, and authenticity in the individual (Yalom & Elkin, 1974, p. xviii).

The change process discussed thus far has been in the context of individual counseling or therapy. But as indicated by the numerous citations in a recent text for group counseling and therapy (Capuzzi & Gross, 1992), many people have found Yalom's (1985) existential model useful for understanding and implementing group process. The multiple relationships provided by the group can promote a change toward greater awareness and genuineness through an awareness provided by the relationships. Additionally, existential counseling or therapy can facilitate change in counselors and therapists themselves. Dubin (1991) relates that "in all my years of graduate school, internship, and psychoanalytic training, I never had direct supervision on how to be with a patient" (p. 65). By receiving training in authenticity, counselors and therapists learn to be genuine. Supervisors promote change by not only "being" with their supervisees, but also training the supervisee in the "I to Thou" encounter. The exact nature of the meeting may vary, but the helping relationship remains the most potent change agent available for the existential counselor or therapist (Bugental, 1978; May, 1983; Yalom, 1980).

INTERVENTION STRATEGIES

Although supported by a fully developed theory, existentialism offers no set of techniques (May, 1983). As you read about the interventions, you will notice that traditional techniques do not exist in this approach. In most theories, understanding follows technique, but the existential counselor or therapist allows the approach to flow from the clients rather than forcing a circumscribed intervention upon them. Existential theory is steeped in phenomenological awareness. Therefore, the following intervention strategies flow from a respectful understanding of clients.

Understanding the Client's History

History is of varying importance to counselors and therapists, depending on how much they lean toward the dynamic end of existentialism. The intervention of canvassing a client's history is articulated by Binswanger and Boss (1983). The client's history is gathered but is not explained or categorized. Instead, the existential intervention "understands this life history as modifications of the total structure of the patent's being in the world" (Binswanger & Boss, 1983, p. 284). The practitioner is viewing the client's history through the client's being and awareness rather than focusing on pathological development.

Sharing Existence in the Moment

The existential relationship is the primary therapeutic intervention, and the client is an existential partner. Viewed with compassion, the client is not met with pity or sympathy (Dass & Gorman, 1985). The counselor or therapist must be genuinely present on the "sharp edge of existence in the world" (Binswanger & Boss, 1983, p. 285). As Bugental (1978) asserts:

> Presence is the quality of being in a situation in which one intends to be as aware and as participative as one is able to be at that time and in those circumstances. Presence is carried into effect through mobilization of one's inner (toward subjective experience) and outer (toward the situation and any other person in it) sensitivities. . . . Presence is being there in the body, in emotions, in relating, in thoughts in every way. (pp. 36–37)

Emerging from the intervention is a deep sense of relatedness, which Heuscher (1987) calls love.

Included in the relatedness and therapeutically significant, the counselor or therapist must be able to use himself as an indicator of what is occurring within the client. "It is not possible to have a feeling without the other having it to some degree also. . . . The use of one's self as an instrument requires a tremendous self-discipline on the part of the therapist" (May, 1979, p. 122). Being implies not only presence but also restrains the counselor's or therapist's own distortions, thoughts, and feelings as she participates in the client's world.

Centered Awareness of Being

Existential counselors and therapists help the client become more centered, more aware. The key is becoming clear and authentic. "Analysis and confrontation of one's various inauthentic modes . . . particularly extrinsically oriented, non-autonomous, or death denying . . . seems to be the key therapeutic technique on this level" (Wilber, 1986, p. 137). By eliminating the extrinsically focused aspects of themselves, clients can become more focused. The subjectivity gained in centering (Bugental, 1978) can lead to other levels of understanding or transcendence (Kopp, 1972; Maslow,

1968; Wilber, 1977). Only by looking inward does the client develop insight and a keener awareness of personal problems (May, 1983). The most important first step is becoming more conscious of reality and authentically examining the various aspects called self.

Self-responsibility

Taking responsibility for growth is important, but taking responsibility for what we do to ourselves is not easy. This intervention involves helping clients take responsibility for their lives. First, they must take responsibility for their choices. Equally important is letting go of the responsibility that others own in the process of relating (Wilber, 1986). Being accountable acknowledges that responsibility can be assumed, shared, and owned by others.

Dream Work

Counselors and therapists working in a variety of approaches have seen dreams as the window to the unconscious. In existentialism, dreams have a different place. The focus is on the client's "dynamic, immediately real and present" existence viewed through the dream rather than the set of dynamic mechanisms at work (May, 1983, p. 152).

> In the dream we see the whole man, the entirety of his problems, in a different existential modality than in waking, but against the background and with the structure of the a priori articulation of existence, and therefore the dream is also of paramount therapeutic importance for the existential analyst. (Binswanger & Boss, 1983, p. 285)

Through dream work, the counselor or therapist is better able to help the client see the pattern of being in the world and know the possibilities of existence through the dream (Binswanger & Boss, 1983). Dreams are like insight. They provide a reflection of inner vision, and the dreamer must discover their meaning.

Disclosing and Working Through Resistances

Addressing resistances to awareness requires a sensitive intervention, and the counselor or therapist is most effective when addressing issues supportively. This intervention creates both anxiety and joy for the client (May, 1983). Bugental (1978) suggests that counselors and therapists use comments such as "You can feel how much that way of being has cost you all of your life," and "You have wanted so much to be loved that you have often forgotten to take care of your own needs" (p. 90). The client owns the responsibility and the power to address the issues blocking awareness and authenticity. The counselor or therapist serves as the midwife in the birth of an authentic being.

Confronting Existential Anxiety

Probably the most important intervention is being aware of the client's existential issues. Few counselors or therapists even acknowledge the anxiety or fears of death and being (Yalom, 1980). It takes courage to discuss the forbidden subject of death. As Yalom (1980) says, "If we are to alter therapeutic practice, to harness the clinical leverage that the concept of death provides, it will be necessary to demonstrate the role of death in the genesis of anxiety" (p. 59). By not denying the ultimate losses (such as relationships, life, and self) and by being present through the anxiety, counselors and therapists have a powerful tool to help clients work through fear.

Sustaining Changes in Being

When clients relinquish their old selves by stepping into the unknown, they place an inordinate amount of faith in their counselor or therapist guide. The guide needs to answer with faith in the client. Bugental (1978) offers guidance to the counselor or therapist for this most critical period. Bugental suggests that the practitioner should provide support by transferring power back to the client. Counselors and therapists may constantly be attuned to unresolved issues in therapy. As part of supporting the new ways of being, they must also address the paradigm shift from the objective to the subjective reality (Bugental, 1978). By mourning the disillusionment and years of unnecessary struggle, the client maintains growth.

Separating

Facing the end of the helping relationship is the final confrontation with reality. It is expected that additional issues will arise to delay the inevitable ending. The intervention of termination requires continued authenticity and willingness to be present. The counselor or therapist and the client may never meet again. It is critical that the practitioner help the client by processing the ending of therapy, by creating a good parting. The difficulty with this intervention is that it exposes the reality of ending that is present in all relationships.

Using Testing to Measure Existential Conflict

Several tests have been constructed that can also be used as interventions in counseling or therapy. The use of these instruments depends on the needs of the counselor or therapist and that person's comfort with assessment in an existential relationship. Each test offers additional information that may be helpful for the counselor or therapist and the client. Additionally, the assessment information might also be useful in the continued efforts toward understanding, building, and substantiating the theory of existentialism.

The "purpose of life" test, which measures meaninglessness, was developed by Crumbaugh and Maholic (Yalom, 1980). This instrument is one of the few measuring existential concerns, but it lacks the validity that would make it more applicable.

A second pair of scales was developed to measure avoidance of the ontological confrontation of death (the AOC scale) and avoidance of existential confrontation (the AEC scale). They are used to look at differences between those who avoid and those who confront the existential dilemmas. The reliability of both instruments has been high, but subsequent studies indicate that there are advantages and disadvantages associated with different strategies of gaining awareness (Thauberger et al., 1983).

The LRI ("life regard" index), developed by Battista and Almond, examines meaning in life (Yalom, 1980). Although theoretically sophisticated, it has not been used (Yalom, 1980). The LRI is another effort of little consequence.

The "experienced levels of emptiness and existential concern" questionnaire developed by Hazell (1984a, 1984b) is another existential instrument. It examines the issues of meaninglessness and existential fear. But like other tests, the questionnaire would benefit from further study.

All of the instruments would benefit from increased validity, sensitivity to cultural differences, and awareness of societal gender pressures. One recent study points to the deficit. When Yalom and Lieberman (1991) were examining awareness and bereavement, they resorted to interviews because of the "poor construction" (p. 336) of existing instruments.

New instruments for therapeutic intervention need broader use. Ibrahim (1985) suggests that effective crosscultural counseling or therapy requires an examination of existential concerns. The emphasis on authenticity within gender (Baker-Miller, 1976) also would seem to benefit from the ontological perspective. Still, an instrument has not been developed that addresses the world view that existential theory advances.

SUPPORTING RESEARCH

Most of the existential research falls into two categories: research that further develops existential concepts, and research that applies existentialism to specific populations. Unfortunately, existentialists tend to be congruent. The theory that focuses on existence over essence is more centered on theory and counseling/therapy than on scientific analysis (Binswanger & Boss, 1983; May, 1969a).

The first section of research sets out to develop an understanding of existential behaviors. In the following conclusions, Yalom (1980) synthesizes the research in existential theory before 1980 (p. 459):

1. A lack of a sense of meaning in life is associated with psychopathology in a roughly linear sense: that is, the less the sense of meaning, the greater the severity of pathology.
2. A positive sense of meaning in life is associated with deeply held religious beliefs.
3. A positive sense of life meaning is associated with self-transcendent values.
4. A positive sense of meaning in life is associated with membership in groups, dedication to some cause, and adoption of clear life goals.
5. Life meaning must be viewed in a developmental perspective: the types of life meaning change over an individual's life; other developmental tasks must precede development of meaning.

Unfortunately, Yalom indicates that all of the statistical relationships are associational and not causal. More studies are necessary, or the meaningless struggles of existential thought will also apply to the research.

Several other studies add to the investigation of existential theory. Bereavement, health and social behavior, religiosity, and emotional behavior have been explored in relationship to existential concerns. Yalom and Lieberman (1991) discovered that grief over a deceased spouse offered important information in studying existential reactions. In one study, Blyski and Westman (1991) found that existential anxieties were separate from religious concerns. Health and social behavior were studied by Thauberger et al. (1983). They discovered that people confronting death and those avoiding it experience advantages and disadvantages associated with their coping style.

Hazell (1989, 1984a) conducted two studies examining levels of emotional development within existential concern. Existential development was "correlated directly with religious interest and emotional development" (Hazell, 1984a, p. 967). Hazell (1989), while studying a group of men, found that emotional development and emptiness were positively correlated. Emotional development was associated with consciousness about emptiness.

Efforts to apply existentialism to specific populations have been significant, but the lack of research is equally frustrating. Ibrahim (1985) made an excellent case for a theory of cultural existentialism. No subsequent studies have answered that need. Attinasi (1992) proposed a rationale for examining outcomes assessment for crosscultural students that includes phenomenological interviews. Existentialism appears to be the important variable that may determine persistence in education. But again, more work is needed.

Single or group case studies have proved helpful in examining existential concerns. A schizophrenic was studied and found to have core existential concerns (Schmolling, 1984). Lantz and Pegram (1989) studied several clients and cited the importance of the "will to meaning" across all cases.

All studies indicate the need for further investigation. Among the studies surveyed, some lack the ability to be generalized (Hazell, 1989), and others address association only (Hazell, 1984b; Blyski & Westman, 1991). Much work needs to be done to understand and apply existential theory fully.

■ ■ ■

THE CASE STUDY OF JOHN: THE EXISTENTIAL APPROACH

Diagnosis

John's issues reflect an existential struggle with isolation and meaninglessness. Confronting a loss of self in the world, John experiences existential isolation. To find meaning or to escape from finding it, he withdraws from others. He ultimately seems to lose himself. The life John has constructed is fragile, as shown by the considerable impact of his new supervisor. He has coped by living through the people he has helped in the library and through his marriage. The new supervisor threatens that brittle existence by imposing structure on John's reality. She also seems to represent a part of John's self because she, too, is oblivious to others' needs. In facing the very real part of himself, John withdraws further and fears any connection with others. He is left alone and afraid.

Treatment/Intervention Plan

John's desire to work on these issues is paramount. Because his current defense of withdrawal is not working, he seems to be motivated to change. The goal of treatment will be to help increase John's awareness of his fear in relationships and his fear of hopelessness (meaninglessness). Ultimately, he will gain freedom by confronting his fears. Because there is a pervasive pattern to his behaviors, his actions and reactions are ingrained and habituated into his sense of self in the world.

The first phase of treatment will be developing a therapeutic relationship. Because John has some anxiety about interpersonal connections, developing trust and groundwork for the "I to Thou" relationship is important. A concurrent component is helping him to reframe the paradigm for a cure. In the past, interventions by physicians have allowed him to survive, but the new paradigm is that John will become instrumental in helping himself gain power in his life situation.

The dream seems to be a sign of positive prognosis for John. Understanding that the ideal and final interpretation will be made by John, the following discussion emerges from an existential interpretation. At a deep level, his real self is confronting his isolation from others ("faceless individuals"). The two large males may very well be aspects of himself that he is facing (possibly aspects of his despised and idealized self) for the first time.

The counselor or therapist will need to help John confront the anxiety of death. By meeting his fears and encountering the aspects of himself that are frightening, John will develop a stronger sense of self. He will also be able to find a place in the world that is not bound by an exitless room. By continuing to flee anxiety-provoking situations, John avoids being and living. Therapy will involve staying with John on his journey as he encounters the fears embodied by the room, the faceless individuals, and the two large men. In essence, providing a context of relating to others in a real sense will help him learn that his sanctuary (escaping through reading) only perpetuates anxiety. By facing his defenses, John will gain a sense of inner strength, awareness, and individuality. By taking responsibility, he can have the freedom he wants to be himself.

LIMITATIONS

Existentialism is not for everyone. It proposes a world view in which each theoretical approach has a place with optimal effectiveness. Systemic concerns by their nature deserve a family approach. Likewise, individuals with serious ego deficits will benefit from the psychoanalytic model. Each theoretical model reflects different levels of goals and needs of the client.

Existentialism faces the world with a subjective perspective. Because subjectivity runs counter to much of today's thought, it is understandable that existentialism may not answer the client's perceived needs. For example, upon encountering existentialism, Szasz (1987) was struck by the fantasy of this relative world. Understandably, some clients may also be skeptical of the lack of defined steps involved in treatment. Existentialism is not for the client who wants a quick fix. Whether or not counseling or therapy is brief, the existential search tends to go beyond four or five sessions.

Existentialist counseling or therapy relies heavily on the verbal encounter. The underlying assumption of healing for existentialists is rooted in the relationship. Individuals who avoid contact with others will find existentialism intrusive. Silence has its uses in existentialist counseling or therapy (Dass & Gordon, 1985), but most existentialist counselors and therapists rely on the verbal exchange.

Probably the most evident challenge for existentialism is the lack of scientific exploration. While cognitive behaviorists are churning out research to validate their theory, a lack of research permeates every aspect of the existential domain. Existentialists are left defenseless in a battle of science. Not only is the lack of validation of the theory problematic, but individuals without a solid sense of integrity are attracted to a model lacking a sequence of techniques and guidelines. Encounter groups are only one example of an early experiential existential model lacking the scrutiny of validation. Until existentialists address this issue (which runs against their subjective grain), existentialism will be a haven for unusual and fanciful approaches with no substance.

Because most strengths also embody weaknesses, the underlying faith in a client's potential for growth may appear shallow and unprofound. Met at a concrete level, the question of "Who am I?" appears inconsequential. Existentialism's strength in honoring the person may be comprehended as a cursory gesture.

SUMMARY

The existential perspective is not simplistic or technique driven. Existential theorists and counselors or therapists explore themselves when they look at the concerns of others. The emphasis is on existence, not essence. From this perspective, it is more important to understand and experience the person in the moment rather than examine the essential parts. We all experience ontological insecurities, existential anxieties, and fear of ultimate meaninglessness. Existential theory provides a theoretical basis from which to address these basic concerns. Whether we are more present in the world or transcend our given situations, we are more aware, alive, and connected. We emerge from a confrontation with ultimate reality with a renewed sense of purpose, understanding, and hope. Embodying the original intent of "psyche"-ology (MacLeod, 1975), existentialism is most truly a study of the individual's soul.

REFERENCES

Attinasi, L. (1992). Rethinking the study of the outcomes of college attendance. *Journal of College Student Development, 33*, 61–69.

Baker-Miller, J. (1976). *Toward a new psychology of women*. Boston: Beacon.

Bepko, C. (1989). Disorders of power. In M. McGoldnick, C. Anderson, & F. Walsh (Eds.), *Women in families* (pp. 406—426). New York: Norton.

Binswanger, L., & Boss, M. (1983). Existential analysis and Dasienanalysis. In T. Millon (Ed.), *Theories of personality and psychopathology* (3rd ed.) (pp. 283—289). New York: Holt, Rinehart, & Winston.

Blyski, N., & Westman, A. (1991). Relationships among defense style, existential anxiety, and religiosity. *Psychological Reports, 68*, 1389–1390.

Bohm, D. (1973). Quantum theory as an indication of a new order in physics. Part B: Implicate and explicate order in physical law. *Foundations of Physics, 2*, 139–168.

Bretall, R. (Ed.). (1951). *A Kierkegaard anthology*. Princeton, NJ: Princeton University Press.

Buber, M. (1970). *I and thou*. New York: Scribner.

Bugental, J. (1978). *Psychotherapy and process: The fundamentals of an existential humanistic approach*. Reading, MA: Addison-Wesley.

Capuzzi, D., & Gross, D. (Eds.). (1992). *Introduction to group counseling*. Denver: Love.

Dass, R., & Gorman, P. (1985). *How can I help?* New York: Knopf.

Dubin, W. (1991). The use of meditative techniques in psychotherapy supervision. *Journal of Transpersonal Psychology, 23*, 65–80.

Frankl, V. (1975). *The unconscious god*. New York: Simon & Schuster.

Frankl, V. (1984). *Man's search for meaning*. New York: Washington Square Press.

Gerardi, S. (1990). Academic self-concept as a predictor of academic success among minority and low-socioeconomic status students. *Journal of College Student Development, 31*, 401–407.

Hazell, C. (1984a). Experienced levels of emptiness and existential concern with different levels of emotional development and profile of values. *Psychological Reports, 55*, 967–976.

Hazell, C. (1984b). Scale for measuring experienced levels of emptiness and existential concern. *Journal of Psychology, 117,* 177–182.

Hazell, C. (1989). Levels of emotional development with experienced levels of emptiness and existential concern. *Psychological Reports, 64,* 835–838.

Heidegger, M. (1949). *Existence and being.* South Bend, IN: Regnery.

Heidegger, M. (1962) *Being and time.* New York: Harper & Row.

Heuscher, J. (1987). Love and authenticity. *The American Journal of Psychoanalysis, 47,* 21–34.

Hogg, A., & Frank, M. L. (1992). Toward an interpersonal model of codependence and contradependence. *Journal of Counseling and Development, 70,* 371–375.

Horner, M. (1972). Toward an understanding of achievement related conflicts in women. *Journal of Social Issues, 28,* 157–175.

Ibrahim, F. (1985). Effective cross-cultural counseling and psychotherapy: A framework. *The Counseling Psychologist, 13,* 625–637.

Kierkegaard, S. (1944). *The concept of dread* (W. Lowrie, trans.). Princeton, NJ: Princeton University Press.

Kopp, S. (1972). *If you meet the Buddha on the road, kill him.* New York: Bantam.

Kubler-Ross, E. (1975). *Death: The final stage of growth.* New York: Simon & Schuster.

Lantz, J., & Pegram, M. (1989). Casework and the restoration of meaning. *Social Casework: The Journal of Contemporary Social Work,* 549–555.

MacLeod, R. (1975). *The persistent problems of psychology.* Pittsburgh: Duquesne University Press.

Maslow, A. (1954). *Motivation and personality.* New York: Harper & Row.

Maslow, A. (1968). *Toward a psychology of being* (2nd ed.). New York: Van Nostrand.

Maslow, A. (1971). *The further reaches of human nature.* New York: Viking.

May, R. (1953). *Man's search for himself.* New York: Dell.

May, R. (1969a). *Existential psychology.* New York: Random House.

May, R. (1969b). *Love and will.* New York: Norton.

May, R. (1979). *Psychology and the human dilemma.* New York: Norton.

May, R. (1983). *The discovery of being.* New York: Norton.

Nietzsche, F. (1967). *The will to power* (W. Kaufmann & R. Hollingdale, trans.). New York: Random House.

Parham, T., & Helms, J. (1985). Relation of racial identity attitudes to self actualization and affective states of black students. *Journal of Counseling Psychology, 32,* 431–440.

Schmolling, P. (1984). Schizophrenia and the deletion of certainty: An existential case study. *Psychological Reports, 54,* 139–148.

Szasz, T. (1987). Discussion by Thomas Szasz. In J. Zeig (Ed.), *The evolution of psychotherapy* (pp. 210–211). New York: Brunner/Mazel.

Thauberger, P., Thauberger, E., & Cleland, J. (1983). Some indices of health and social behavior associated with the avoidance of the ontological confrontation. *Omega, 14,* 279–289.

Tillich, P. (1980). *The courage to be.* New Haven: Yale University Press.

Tillich, P. (1987). Systematic theology. In M. Taylor (Ed.), *Paul Tillich: Theologian of the boundaries.* San Francisco: Collins.

Travis, J. (1981). *Wellness workbook* (2nd ed.). Berkeley, CA: Ten Speed Press.

Viorst, J. (1986). *Necessary losses.* New York: Fawcett.

Wilber, K. (1977). *The spectrum of consciousness*. Wheaton, IL: Theosophical Publishing House.

Wilber, K. (1986). The spectrum of psychopathology. In J. Engler, K. Wilber, & D. Brown (Eds.), *Transformations of consciousness* (pp. 65–159). Boston: New Science Library.

Yalom, I. (1980). *Existential psychotherapy*. New York: Basic Books.

Yalom, I. (1985). *Theory and practice of group psychotherapy* (3rd ed.). New York: Basic Books.

Yalom, I. (1989). *Love's executioner and other tales of psychotherapy*. New York: Basic Books.

Yalom, I., & Elkin, G. (1974). *Every day gets a little closer*. New York: Basic Books.

Yalom, I., & Lieberman, M. (1991). Bereavement and heightened existential awareness. *Psychiatry, 54*, 334–345.

CHAPTER NINE

Person-centered Theory

Richard J. Hazler
Ohio University

Carl R. Rogers's person-centered theory is one of the most popular in the fields of psychology, counseling, and education. His perceptions of people and of how a supportive environment can assist in their development have had an immense impact on a wide variety of professions and parenting. This approach to people was a major deviation from the psychoanalytic and behavioral models for working with people that were predominant in the early part of the 20th century.

Person-centered theory offered a new way to look at individuals and their development as well as how people can be helped to change. From this frame of reference, people were viewed as fully in charge of their lives and inherently motivated to improve themselves. The responsibility for personal behaviors and the ability to choose to change them were also seen as belonging fully to the individual. Here was a way to view and deal with human beings that did not rely on other people (counselors or therapists, psychologists, parents, teachers, and so on) as the primary directors of change. People could now control their own change if the right conditions were offered.

Rogers saw all individuals as having inherent qualities that made nurturing possible; attempting to change basic personality characteristics or behaviors was not necessary. He believed people saw the world from their own unique perspective, which is referred to as a phenomenological perspective. No matter what that phenomenological view of the world was, it was further assumed that everyone is continually attempting to actualize her best and most productive self. This positive and optimistic view of human beings is often challenged by those who call attention to the unlimited opportunities for observing people as they think and act in ways that are harmful to themselves and others. But Rogers believed these thoughts and actions were primarily reflections of a distorted view of oneself and the world, which were caused by trying to meet the expectations of others rather than trying to actualize one's own self.

The origins of these beliefs, their development into a major helping process, and an examination of the essential ingredients of that process will serve as a foundation for this theory. Information on the counselor's or therapist's role in providing interventions and the methods used to carry out that role will then provide the practical base for beginning to implement the process.

HISTORY

Carl R. Rogers

Person-centered theory began to make an impact on psychology in the 1940s. Carl R. Rogers was the individual behind the theory, and his influence was so great that it is commonly referred to as Rogerian theory. The major concepts of the autonomous self, reliance on one's own unique experiences, the desire and ability to make positive personal changes, and movement toward the actualization of potentials are all observable in Rogers's personal development.

Carl Rogers was born in 1902 into a morally and religiously conservative family that was strictly religious, devoted to its children, and committed to the concept of hard work. Activities such as dancing, movies, smoking, drinking, or anything that vaguely suggested sexual interest were clearly forbidden, although little was said about them. The family was able to convey its directions in subtle ways that were generally unsaid but very clear to everyone.

The family was very self-contained, and the young Rogers had few friends. He became a loner of sorts, spending most of his time working, thinking, and reading. His early life-style caused him to pay close attention to his personalized experience of the world. In later years, this concept would become better known as a phenomenological approach to counseling or psychotherapy.

The Rogers family moved from Chicago to a farm when he was 12. It was here that his work ethic was reemphasized; he also developed an interest in science and experimentation. He spent much of his time studying the variety of insects and animals that were now available to him. A scientific approach to all issues was further emphasized by his father, who insisted that all farming should be as scientific and modern as possible. These concepts of scientific study, experimentation, and evaluation would later set Rogers apart from other theorists: he was the first to intentionally and creatively expose experientially recognized human development and therapeutic processes to rigorous scientific study. This rigorous experimentation aspect of his work is often overlooked by those interested in his theories, but it is, in fact, a major contribution to the development of professionalism in counseling and psychotherapy.

Rogers left home to study agriculture in college but later turned to religious studies and eventually to clinical psychology as he became more interested in people, beliefs, and values. His religious beliefs, like those of his parents, were strong. However, the more he studied and discussed the issues, the more his views diverged from his parents. A six-month trip to China as part of the World Student Christian Federation Conference emphasized his change to a more liberal rather than fundamentalist viewpoint.

Explaining these changes to his parents was extremely difficult and often disappointing for all concerned. However, Rogers reported great growth in his intellectual and emotional independence from these open conflicts. The experience left him much more confident in himself, his beliefs, and his ability to deal with difficult situations. This idea that individuals must and can rely on themselves for direction and strength was to become another major emphasis in his theory as well as his own life.

Rogers graduated from the University of Wisconsin, married, and began to study for the ministry in 1924 at the Union Theological Seminary in New York City. His focus of attention changed during his two years at Union as he became more and more interested in psychology and education. Consequently, he transferred to Columbia University to study psychology and eventually earned his Ph.D. there in 1931.

Following graduation from Columbia, Rogers worked with children in Rochester, New York, for 12 years and later was on the faculty at Ohio State University, the University of Chicago, and the University of Wisconsin. His final stop was at the Center for Studies of the Person at La Jolla, California, beginning in 1963. This period of time until his death in 1987 was extremely productive. It included work in education, individual counseling and psychotherapy, and group work. The last years of his life were spent traveling in the most troubled places in the world, using his person-centered approach to promote peace among warring groups.

Theory Background

The field of counseling or psychotherapy in the 1920s and 30s relied on techniques that were highly diagnostic, probing, and analytic as well as unsupported by scientific research. Rogers's first major work, *Counseling and Psychotherapy* (1942), was a clear reaction to this situation and to his work with children: "So vast is our ignorance on this whole subject [counseling and psychotherapy] that it is evident that we are by no means professionally ready to develop a definitive or final account of any aspect of psychotherapy" (p. 16). He presented nondirective counseling and psychotherapy in this work along with a clear call for a more scientific approach to research on both his nondirective and other more directive techniques.

Client-centered Therapy (Rogers, 1951) was a culmination of a decade of practice and research in which Rogers expanded his concepts and renamed his approach. This new emphasis changed the role of the counselor or therapist from an individual who only reflected the content of client statements to one who identified the client's underlying emotions in client words and through the helping relationship. The effect of this new work was to expand the dimensions of accurate empathy with the client and to force the counselor or therapist to go beyond simple reflection of client words.

Rogers moved to the University of Wisconsin in 1957, where his efforts at research on his theory increased and broadened. Here, he was testing his ideas on hospitalized schizophrenics as opposed to the primarily normal population he had been working with at the University of Chicago. His research confirmed the view that the conditions present in the helping relationship did have a significant effect on both the progress of counseling or psychotherapy and the outcomes for clients (Rogers, 1967). Rogers's work with client populations ranging from normal to extremely disturbed encouraged him to broaden the use of his ideas to include all people.

Person-centered is the current term used to emphasize the personal nature of counseling or psychotherapy and other relationships in education, business, and government agencies. The therapeutic or helping relationship is now envisioned as one of person to person rather than healthy counselor or therapist to unhealthy client. Person-centered theory developed out of a close examination of individual helping relationships. However, a common misconception is that this theory does not apply well to groups. In fact, Rogers focused more on groups during the 70s and 80s than on individuals. He was a major promoter of personal-growth groups where individuals worked together for the purpose of self-actualizing growth rather than toward a more limited goal of overcoming psychological illnesses (Rogers, 1970). Another group adaptation saw Rogers using person-centered concepts in a group-process format to deal with critical world conflicts. He traveled to areas with major social conflicts such as Central America (Thayer, 1987), South Africa (Rogers & Sanford, 1987), Northern Ireland (Rogers, 1987b), and even the Soviet Union (Rogers, 1987a) to run growth groups with leaders and nonleaders who had fought but never tried to understand each other. His accounts of these encounters make it clear that a person-centered orientation can be promoted in groups as well as in individual relationships.

HUMAN NATURE: A DEVELOPMENTAL PERSPECTIVE

The person-centered approach to counseling or psychotherapy implies great confidence in each client. This confidence arises out of a belief that all people have innate motivation to grow in positive ways and the ability to carry out such a growth process. The view of a highly positive human being varies widely from other theories that view human nature as evil, negative, or a nonissue. Such a positive view of human nature is essential for the person-centered practitioner because of the major role clients are given in the direction, style, and content of the helping profession. The person-centered perception of people has four key characteristics: a belief that people are trustworthy, a belief that people innately move toward self-actualization and health, a belief that people have the inner resources to move themselves in positive directions, and a belief that people respond to their uniquely perceived world. The interaction of these characteristics with a person's external environment brings about the most desirable aspects of development.

People Are Trustworthy

Person-centered counselors or therapists must treat their clients as trustworthy, or there will be no reason to allow them to take a leadership role in the helping relationship. Words such as *good, constructive,* and *trustworthy* are natural characteristics of human beings from this point of view, although people also appear to take actions that demonstrate the opposite. These inappropriate actions are taken when the individual's ideal view of self does not match the real self. Individuals use defensive thoughts and actions to protect themselves from having to observe that they are not living the lives they believe they should. Such actions are not deceitful as much as they are direct actions based on conflicting perceptions of a person's world. All individuals are trying to improve and to act in the world as they see it in as honorable a manner as possible.

Consider the teenage boy who skips school and has been arrested for the fourth time for robbery. Many in society will judge this individual to be a bad person or one who cannot be trusted, and the boy knows this. The person-centered counselor or therapist must believe that the boy will be trustworthy in their relationship if and when he is convinced that he has a meaningful relationship with a genuine counselor or therapist. A major part of that relationship will be the counselor's or therapist's conveying trust through words and actions. Anything less than this trusting relationship will serve to convince the boy that this is just another person who will not trust him. The result is that there will be little reason for the individual to work on his potential for trustworthiness.

Movement Toward Actualization

Human beings are viewed by the person-centered theory as always striving to obtain the maximum amount from themselves. They seek any means to develop all their abilities "in ways that maintain or enhance the organism" (Rogers, 1959, p. 196). This is the driving force in the positive development of the individual. It clearly moves the individual away from control by others and toward autonomy and self-control. Unlike some other theories, the movement towards actualization provides individuals rather than outside persons (parents, counselors, therapists, teachers, and so on) with the primary motivational strength behind development. This energy source is also seen as potentially more influential than environmental factors such as socioeconomic status, hunger, or danger, even though these often impact how the individual perceives or seeks self-actualization.

The problem teenage boy discussed previously would likely be seen by many to have inadequate self-control and little desire to overcome his problems. The result is that individuals and society as a whole will probably seek to control him and force him to grow in ways deemed appropriate by others. The person-centered view, however, emphasizes the concept that the boy is actually working toward making the most out of himself and that he will continue to do so regardless of what others do. What others can do is provide a safe environment where the boy can lower his defenses and antisocial behaviors without fear of failure and nonacceptance. When this occurs, the boy can be expected to continue to pursue self-actualization but now in ways that are more appropriate and socially acceptable.

Inner Resources

The actualizing tendency provides the motive for positive development in people. A related question is, Do individuals have the capacity to carry out this motivation? Person-centered theory presumes that individuals have that capacity as well as the motivation (Rogers, 1961).

The fact that persons have the motivation to grow in positive directions does not mean that they have the ability to do so. The person-centered approach emphasizes a belief that this ability is available to them. Certainly some of the most heartwarming stories told throughout the ages have demonstrated how people can overcome tremendous odds to become successful. These same stories also cause people to question why it happens for some and not others. Person-centered theory emphasizes that these potential differences in degree of ability to overcome are not as important as persons' beliefs that they can accomplish what they set out to do. In many ways, it presumes a fairly well accepted principle of human dynamics, which states that people always have much more potential than they use most of the time. Person-centered counselors or therapists must believe in this principle if they are to help clients recognize and accept their own abilities.

The person-centered counselor or therapist must have the confidence that the troubled boy we have been discussing has the inner resources as well as the motivation to grow. Without this recognition the boy might very well feel that the ideals are reasonable but that he is doomed to failure due to his lack of ability. The counselor or therapist must recognize that this doubting attitude in the boy will most likely cause him to give up his efforts far short of his potential.

Individually Perceived World

The person-centered view of people recognizes that events seen by any two people will be perceived differently (Rogers, 1961). Two armies fight, two adults argue, and relationships often break down because each side perceives what is "right" to be different from the other side's perceptions. The person-centered view of these examples is that individuals or groups relate to the world and their own actions from a unique context. Therefore, words, behaviors, feelings, and beliefs are selected to match the specialized view of the world held by each individual. The same concept causes each person to develop in a manner that is somewhat different from every other individual.

The idea that no two people perceive the world in exactly the same way explains much of the variation we see in the previous three concepts. Our troubled boy surely does not perceive the world as the safe and kind place that another boy who is successful in school and has a comfortable family life does. Neither will he perceive it as the rational world that the counselor or therapist is likely to see. It is quite possible that the boy is stealing, in part, because of a different perception of the world. Perhaps he sees this behavior as the only one available for him to help feed himself, his mother, and his infant sister. Person-centered counselors or therapists must recognize these differently perceived worlds, work hard to understand them, and seek to help clients grow through their personally perceived world rather than that perceived by the counselor, therapist, or some other individual.

Interaction with External Factors

A person-centered view of human development gives attention to external factors that impact psychological development in addition to critical internal forces. Even as infants, people make choices that induce growth and actualize potential. They reject experiences that are recognized as contrary to their perceived well-being. However, these naturalistic ways of making choices become confused as the developing person recognizes that other individuals may provide or withhold love based on how well the child assimilates values and actions set by others. This recognition can move individuals away from using their own best judgment to make personal choices and can provide a second method that requires taking actions based on the presumed desires of others. The two theoretical concepts used to explain this aspect of development are *unconditional positive regard* and *conditions of worth* (Rogers, 1959).

Individuals who are given unconditional positive regard by significant people in their lives receive recognition of their positive nature, including their motivation and ability to become increasingly effective human beings. The worth and value of the individual are never questioned in this case, although specific behaviors or beliefs can be rejected as inappropriate. Individuals who are given and can recognize unconditional positive regard that is provided to them feel permitted to continue trusting themselves as positive human beings. The belief is conveyed that they will make errors of judgment and behavior but that as positive individuals they will also strive to examine themselves continually and be able to take actions for their own improvement. Being provided with unconditional positive regard helps individuals to continue seeking their own development with the confidence that they will become increasingly effective human beings.

Many times the regard and love offered by others has strings attached. For example, children might come to believe that they are only good, loved, cared for, fed, or valued if they do just as their parents say. These conditions of worth pressure developing persons to devalue inherent potential for choice making and growth. They begin looking for directions and decisions to originate from external sources instead of their more natural internal ones. They begin to see themselves as having conditions placed upon their worth, and they may understand that these conditions of worth are set by others rather than themselves. This process moves developing individuals away from confidence in their ability to run their own lives and pushes them to seek validation based on the lives of other people who appear to be more positive than they are.

MAJOR CONSTRUCTS

The core of person-centered theory is a set of beliefs about people and relationships rather than a set of behavioral counselor or therapist techniques. Counselors or therapists interested in implementing this theory must look first to themselves and their perceptions of others rather than to what specific behaviors ought to be performed. This is a challenging task, particularly for new practitioners who are seeking to find out what they should "do" and to what extent they "do things well." The following constructs are essential beliefs involved in person-centered theory. Practitioners must have a clear perception of them before they can implement a person-centered approach effectively.

No Two People See the World Exactly Alike

The phenomenological approach to dealing with individuals means that no two people can be expected to see things as happening in exactly the same way. Counselors or therapists must recognize that whatever they personally believe reality to be will be different from the client's perspective and that each client will have a different perspective. Therefore, asking the client to believe or act in a way that "everyone knows is right" becomes the counselor's or therapist's opinion, based on her own phenomenological view rather than a fact. Because helping someone from a person-centered approach emphasizes the phenomenological concept, it becomes imperative to understand the client's perspective as thoroughly as possible.

Empathic Understanding

Empathic understanding is critically important to the person-centered approach. It reflects the belief that individuals respond to a phenomenologically perceived world. Empathy refers to the understanding of the client's world from the client's point of view. This is no easy task because it is hard for counselors or therapists to set aside their own biased view of the world in an attempt to see things through the client's eyes. All other actions they take will be inappropriate without empathy because these actions will be based upon inaccurate perceptions of the client. This construct allows practitioners to respond effectively and assures clients that their confidence in the counselor or therapist is justified.

Empathic understanding has two equally important dimensions that make it a useful construct: understanding, and accurately conveying that understanding. The most obvious of these dimensions is that counselors or therapists must set aside their own beliefs and enter the client's world so that they can understand. However, this understanding will not be effective by itself. The client must also be aware of the degree to which the counselor or therapist understands. This second dimension is crucial in order for the empathic understanding to be useful. Just as human development is impacted by the type of regard others demonstrate to the individual, this dimension is a major construct for interaction with clients.

Unconditional positive regard provided to the client is essential for creating an atmosphere that will foster growth.

People Make Simple Mistakes in Judgment

People make simple mistakes in judgment. They also make choices that appear to be right to them but are ineffective because they are made to match the perceived world of others rather than an individual's own best judgment. People are attempting to act as they believe others would have them act (conditions of worth) rather than trusting their own positive, growth-oriented nature (tendency to actualize). Counselors or therapists who demonstrate faith in the whole person rather than denigrating clients for mistakes of behavior allow their clients the freedom to explore their inner world without fear of rejection. Lacking such unconditional positive regard, clients may try to do what they believe the counselor or therapist wants in order to achieve a better life. Unfortunately, these actions will only increase clients' belief that they cannot personally make effective choices. They may find some more socially acceptable ways of behaving, but they will not have gained confidence in their own ability to seek more changes as needed.

Confidence in the Client

Person-centered theory places tremendous confidence in the client in comparison to other theories. This confidence is based on the construct that people are innately good and continually seeking a fully functioning experience in the world. Their tendency to actualize personal potential in positive ways is the force that the person-centered practitioner recognizes and seeks to free from self-induced constraints. Clients are treated as effective human beings who will succeed regardless of the nature of their difficulties. This contrasts with other views of the individual that do not allow counselors or therapists to trust clients because client difficulties are seen as weaknesses or deficiencies that will stand in the way of personal progress unless the counselor or therapist corrects them.

The Perceived World of the Client May Not Approximate the World Sought

Individuals come to counseling or psychotherapy for help because of difficulties evolving from the fact that the world they perceive is not in close proximity to the world they naturally seek. The natural, growth-oriented, self-trusting nature of these people has been pushed into conflict with their chosen world, where they continually look outside their true selves for decisions. They act based on perceptions of what others think is right, and the results of their actions are not personally fulfilling or effective. This conflict is termed *incongruence*.

Congruent Individuals Trust Their World View

Congruent persons are the individuals who trust their view of the world and their ability to act on their basic positive nature. They feel confident about reacting in the present moment because of their belief in their organism's ability to determine appropriate from inappropriate behaviors. This self-trust is then generally verified by those around them because their actions tend to be beneficial both personally and socially. Where human fallibility causes errors in reactions, the congruent individual also has a view of the world that allows for the reactions of others to be evaluated and appropriate adaptive responses taken. Congruent people are not infallible but instead have the ability to recognize and use their errors to grow without devaluing themselves.

The concept of congruence versus incongruence is critical to person-centered theory, for it identifies the essential goal for people who are having psychological or sociological difficulties. They are attempting to perceive more accurately their own positive nature and learn to use it more effectively in their everyday lives. As this occurs, they will better accept both their strengths and weaknesses as legitimate parts of their positive nature. This knowledge will reduce the distortions in their view of the world. The congruence versus incongruence construct also helps explain the concept of anxiety in person-centered theory. Low personal anxiety occurs when the perceived self is in line with actual experiences (congruence). The degree to which the individual's perception of himself does not match the way he actually is (incongruence) is conversely related to higher levels of anxiety. It is significant for the counselor or therapist to recognize that in person-centered theory, efforts are made to increase congruence in the client rather than directly reduce anxiety.

THE PROCESS OF CHANGE

The concept of a growth-oriented and competent individual in need of counseling or psychotherapy presumes a scenario analogous to the growth of a simple garden bean. The bean seed has all the potential to grow but must be provided with the proper climate in order for it to achieve its full potential. It will develop as expected if placed in fertile ground where adequate warmth, sun, and water are available. Human hands do not need to touch it under the ground, nor should those hands help pull it out of properly prepared ground. In fact, such human attempts to directly manipulate will almost surely kill the bean's development. The effective gardener knows that arranging correct conditions and leaving the actual plant alone as much as possible is the best way to allow it to reach its greatest potential.

This process of change is similar in people and is viewed in much the same way by the person-centered counselor or therapist. The client is provided with the essential growth conditions of a genuine human relationship, acceptance and caring, and a deep understanding of the person. These conditions are the ingredients that allow the person to develop to her greatest potential.

> Studies with a variety of clients show that when these three conditions occur in the therapist, and when they are to some degree perceived by the client, therapeutic movement ensues, the client finds himself painfully but definitely learning and growing, and both he and his therapist regard the outcome as successful. It seems from our studies that it is attitudes such as these rather than the therapist's technical knowledge and skill, which are primarily responsible for therapeutic change. (Rogers, 1961, p. 63)

The first of these three conditions is the genuineness of the counselor or therapist. Clients must perceive that this individual is a real person who has feelings, thoughts, and beliefs that are not hidden behind facades. This genuine nature allows clients to trust that whatever specifics of the relationship emerge, they can be recognized as both personal and honest. It also allows the client to see that being open and genuine, which includes revealing one's fallibilities, is not a condition from which competent human beings must hide. Most of our daily relationships are not highly genuine but are instead controlled by facades and roles that cause us to doubt the information we receive from people.

The second condition is acceptance and caring provided by the counselor or therapist, which allows clients to be less anxious about their perceived weaknesses and the prospect of taking risks. The weaknesses we perceive in ourselves generally become those things we least want to be seen by others. We try to hide our weaknesses whenever possible. Limitations often result in some degree of embarrassment with an accompanying tendency to work even harder at hiding them. Persons needing assistance are working hard to hide their perceived weaknesses both from others and from themselves. Often they will even identify a less threatening weakness as the problem in order to avoid examining a more personally threatening one. Counselor or therapist acceptance and caring, if consistently felt by the client as unconditional positive regard, offers the opportunity to reduce the degree of stress caused by these fears in the relationship. This in turn will increase the chance that the client can recognize, talk of, and work on these problem areas rather than hiding from them.

The third condition for change is empathic understanding of the client. This is a deep recognition of the client's internal frame of reference that is effectively communicated to the client. In other words, a counselor or therapist who has empathic understanding of the client has nothing until the exact nature of that understanding is effectively communicated to the client. Neither counselors nor therapists nor clients can ever fully understand the client. However, the degree to which they can explore the client's world together with common understandings will improve the client's ability to understand and therefore take action about his life.

These three basic conditions provide the necessary environment that allows individuals to implement their actualizing tendencies. They arrive in counseling or psychotherapy questioning their abilities and ideas, afraid of the weaknesses they recognize, and even more afraid of those they expect are unknown to them. They have been seeking answers from other people, whom clients believe "must clearly have better answers." All of these conditions make them fearful of letting their true selves be seen by others or even themselves, so they wear a variety of masks to present a "better" picture than what they believe is there. The basic therapeutic conditions provided allow clients to relax, explore themselves and their fears, and experiment with new ways of thinking and behaving.

Finding attention and support from a genuine individual who can be trusted allows clients to explore themselves in areas and ways they cannot do in less therapeutic situations. Having another person closely and consistently listen helps clients begin observing and listening to themselves better: "You're right, I am angry. And now that I think of it, I've been angry for a long time." They begin to drop their masks as they recognize aspects of themselves to be not quite as bad as they thought: "I do have the right to be angry even when someone else doesn't want me to be that way. I'm not comfortable with that idea, but I believe it." Self-recognition and self-acceptance are key first steps in the growth process.

As individuals become open to their true experiences and begin to trust their own organism, they begin to see the blocks to growth that have burdened them. They also gain the confidence needed both to recognize and deal with their problems on their own. These new levels of self confidence allow them to begin dropping their protective masks and accepting their strengths and weaknesses as aspects of themselves that are both real and changeable over time. Internal loci of control develop when clients take control of their lives rather than seek "shoulds and oughts" from others who have been running their lives.

A major part of the development process in clients is a recognition that they are fallible human beings in a process. This is very different from the belief that one must be perfect in order to be good or loved. Acceptance of this position allows people to view themselves as continuing to learn and grow throughout their lives and to see success as improvement rather than perfection.

Clients' confidence in their own ability to evaluate themselves, decide how to change, actually change, and accept their errors reduces anxiety and the dependence on others for directing their lives. A quality perception of the real world and their part in it will continue to give importance to the reactions and beliefs of others, but this information will now be seen as more equal in significance to their own views. Consequently, clients will take more responsibility for their own existence and need external intervention less.

INTERVENTION STRATEGIES

The counselor or therapist looking for a specific list of things to say, actions to take, or diagnoses to make will not find them in this theory. Person-centered theory is much more related to who a counselor or therapist is rather than to what he does. The actions of this person are focused around providing the conditions of genuineness, unconditional positive regard, and empathy in the relationship. No book can say how this individual should be genuine because each of us is different. Likewise, how one genuinely shows unconditional positive regard or empathy is also be dictated to some degree by the type of person she is. This section suggests two general concepts regarding therapeutic intervention techniques: some thoughts on how to be genuine, and some specific behaviors that have most consistently been identified with the core conditions.

Being Genuine

To be genuine, counselors and therapists need to look closely at themselves before deciding how to be or what to do. Obviously one cannot be genuine by looking to someone else for the way to be. Knowing oneself, then, becomes very important: it allows actions and words to be congruent with the way a counselor or therapist really is while at the same time helping the practitioner match the client's needs. Person-centered counselors or therapists need to be knowledgeable about themselves and reasonably comfortable with this information. They must be more congruent than their clients, or the likelihood is that more will be taken from the client than is given. One clear way to deal with these issues is for practitioners to seek quality helpful relationships, including counseling or psychotherapy, for themselves and work at their own continued growth just as they would have their clients do.

Being genuine does not mean sharing every thought or feeling with the client. Such a tactic would simply take the focus off the client and put it on the counselor or therapist, which is not a part of person-centered helping or any other type of helping. What is appropriate is being a helpful, attentive, caring person who is truly interested in the client and being able to demonstrate that interest. Everyone has experienced the type of situation in which an acquaintance says, "I know how you feel," and you know very well the words coming from this near stranger are nothing more than words. Not only do you reject the words, but you also lose faith in the person's honesty. The same person might have said, "I hardly know you, but if it is anything like my own loss it must hurt a great deal." The second statement recognizes the reality of the two people rather than trying to indicate more understanding than is reasonable to believe. There are as many genuine statements or nonstatements as there are people and situations. The right one matches the person you are with the unique situation you have with the client at a given time.

Active Listening

The first basic technique emphasized in person-centered theory is active listening and its reflection of content and feelings. Demonstrating empathy for the client requires highly attentive and interactive listening skills. Counselors or therapists must first show that they are paying attention. The physical steps most common to this are facing the clients, leaning toward them, and making good eye contact. This position and the use of facial and body expressions that relate to the clients' comments will at least initially put counselors or therapists and clients in observable contact. After putting themselves in the best possible position to listen, practitioners must hear and see what is communicated. Both the words and the actions of the client are used to develop an understanding of the content and feelings being presented.

Taking in information is only the first part of active listening. Counselors or therapists must then reflect the content and feelings of clients back to them. "I hear you saying . . . ," "So you are feeling . . . ," "You seem to be feeling . . . because of . . . " are samples of the ways counselors and therapists attempt to explore with the client how accurate their empathy truly is.

It is to be expected that the counselor or therapist will not always have a full understanding of the client's world and will make varied degrees of mistakes trying to reflect it. The process of active listening helps both parties clarify the content and feelings of a situation and is a learning process for each participant. Counselors or therapists who can treat their own mistakes and growth in this learning process in a genuine manner as a natural part of life will also help clients accept their own uncertainties and weaknesses.

Reflection of Content and Feelings

The first steps in this empathy exploration process tend to be the recognition and reflection of the actual words stated and the feelings that are most obvious. As the counselor or therapist and client get to know each other better, effective counselors or therapists will become better able to see behind these surface interactions. They will begin to see and convey feelings clients do not even recognize they are expressing. For example, a client may be distracted or become more quiet periodically during the session. Initially, these reactions may appear to be related to the specific topic at hand. However, over time, the counselor or therapist may be able to tie those reactions to some general concept that pulls the different discussion topics together. Describing to the client what has been recognized may actually be little more than extended listening, observing, and reflecting of the person's world. However, it can also bring together complex elements of the client's world that draw a much more accurate picture of the client as a whole than the individual elements provided separately.

Appropriate Self-disclosure

A truly genuine relationship lets the client see relevant parts of the counselor's or therapist's phenomenological world as well as the client's world. Appropriate self-disclosure allows clients to compare their views of the world with another individual whom they have come to trust and value as a significant human being. Under nonthreatening circumstances, these comparisons give clients the chance to review and revise their views based on information they might otherwise not have had available or that has been too threatening to accept. The supportive relationship developed further allows the client to try out new thoughts and behaviors based on the new information. Much like the growth of the bean mentioned earlier in the chapter, the client is allowed to use the supportive atmosphere to develop at the rate and in the manner most appropriate for her.

Immediacy

Many of the most powerful interactions are those in which the content and feelings involved relate directly to the immediate situation between counselor or therapist and client; in other words, they depend on immediacy. Recognition, understanding, and use of feelings are seen as a major problem for clients from the person-centered perspective. Immediacy takes a here-and-now approach to the relationship in general and feelings in particular. The relationship between client and counselor or therapist is seen as the most important therapeutic factor. Therefore, the feelings that both client and counselor or therapist are currently experiencing are seen as the most beneficial ones to use. Statements that receive primary emphasis are ones like "How are you feeling now?" and "This is how your statements make me feel." On the other hand, statements seen as less clinically useful might be "Why did you feel that way?" "What did the other person think?" or "What did you believe then?"

A major reason for the emphasis on the here and now of person-centered theory is that reactions between the client and counselor or therapist can be verified, checked, and explored immediately by both participants. Statements or feelings from the past make use of only the client's perspective, thus giving the counselor or therapist a more reduced opportunity to be a current part of the client's experience.

Personalized Counselor or Therapist Actions

Recent person-centered theorists have expanded on this model in a variety of ways. Many theorists now use Rogers's model as the basic concept for starting a relationship. They see it as the foundation on which to build other cognitive, behavioral, or emotional approaches. Boy and Pine (1990) have taken person-centered theory itself a step further. They see additional stages in person-centered theory in which counselors or therapists use their own creative methods for helping clients recognize and deal with problems after the essential relationship elements have been established. They also argue that because each client is different, person-centered counselors and therapists must adjust their methods as much as possible to fit the specific preferred mode of the client. Their view is that a true person-centered approach will have a consistent foundation, but that the full range of the relationship must be built upon the unique aspects of the counselor or therapist, the client, and their personalized relationship together.

Non-client-centered Intervention

It is also important to note the kind of techniques that will not be used in the relationship. Diagnosis and treatment planning have become significant parts of the mental health field today. Increasingly, insurance companies and government agencies require clear-cut statements of the client's so-called illness, its severity, and the estimated length of time it will take to be corrected. Individuals using a person-centered approach can have a great deal of trouble with these requirements because they do not tend to look at clients in an ill-versus-well context. Instead, they view clients as individuals who are growing and seeking their most actualized selves. It is a theory much better suited to helping people progress than it is for getting them over some designated condition. Person-centered practitioners who find themselves in situations where they needing to design extensive diagnosis and treatment models will need to give close attention to how and to what degree they can integrate these relatively diverse processes.

Many new counselors and therapists identify with a person-centered approach because it fits what they want to do and what has helped them grow in other positive relationships. However, when they attempt to use this approach, they often get caught up in many non-person-centered techniques. For example, there is little need for extensive questioning in the person-centered approach, for the task is to follow the client rather than to suggest continually what issues need to be explored. However, new practitioners sometimes question clients more than is necessary. They also find themselves seeking information in clients' pasts rather than from talking about current interactions. Finally, they tend to find themselves over-analyzing client comments and reactions to develop elaborate rationales for why clients do what they do. These reactions may come in part from the fact that student trainees have completed many years of education where these tactics are highly effective methods for finding success. These new counselors or therapists are faced with the pressure of helping clients in need and having doubts about their own ability to use the skills they have been taught. This lack of confidence and experience often causes them to fall back on the questioning, directing tactics of the academic community rather than the responding and following tactics of the person-centered approach. Just as clients need time and proper conditions to learn to trust in their organism, it takes time for those new to the person-centered approach to trust in their developing helping organism.

SUPPORTING RESEARCH

Carl Rogers's perception of people, counseling, and psychotherapy as highly personal and individualized often gives newcomers to the field a sense that he and his theory de-emphasize research over personal interaction. This perception could not be further from the truth. Rogers was a major innovator in the development of research techniques for counseling/therapy and person-centered theory. He recognized that for any theory or technique to remain credible and become more effective, solid research is a necessity (Rogers, 1986).

Rogers pioneered the use of taped transcripts (Cain, 1987) and other clinical measures of interacting to broaden the scope of psychological research (Hjelle & Ziegler, 1992). These techniques, along with the use of the Q-sort method, helped bring the more subjective aspects of people, counseling, and psychotherapy into respectability. Among his earliest significant publications were books on extensive research studies with standard mental health center populations (Rogers & Dymond, 1954) and schizophrenics (Rogers, 1967). All this work demonstrated his commitment to research on his theory and established his basic concepts as valid and reliable sources of client progress.

The Q-sort method of data collection became a major influence in the acceptance of Rogers's theory. It was developed by William Stephenson (1953), who was a colleague of Rogers's at the University of Chicago. The Q-sort method employs many different formats for people to sort attributes of themselves into various categories and levels. Generally, when the method is used in person-centered research, subjects are asked to perform the task once for self-description and another time for ideal self-description. These two sortings are then compared to see how well their perceived and real selves match. The theory follows that the closer the match of the real and perceived selves in a person, the more congruent the person is. Because congruence is theorized to increase during effective person-centered interaction, researchers can look for increasingly closer matches between these two measures as interaction continues. This procedure enabled Rogers to validate many of his theoretical constructs and procedures.

Most research on the person-centered approach has continued to focus on the necessary and sufficient conditions for successful counseling or psychotherapy (Cain, 1987). It motivated major amounts of research in its early years, but recently the momentum for such research has declined significantly (Combs, 1988). This may be due in part to the general acceptance of Rogers's basic concepts based on extensive research in the 1950s and 60s. This acceptance is so widespread throughout the thinking and practice of the profession that we no longer consider many of his concepts "Rogerian" (Goodyear, 1987). They are more often now referred to as basic essentials to the helping relationship.

Potential weaknesses in person-centered research have not been ignored by the profession. The methodological aspects of these studies in particular have been questioned by some researchers. Questions of sophistication and rigor have been raised (Prochaska, 1984), and similar comments have led others to ask whether these problems raise doubts about the validity of the theory (Watson, 1984). These concerns may deserve particular attention when considered alongside the fact that less person-centered research is being conducted and the core conditions are so widely accepted.

Person-centered theory has remained relatively unchanged over the last 30 years, according to some authorities (Cain, 1986). Combs (1988) suggested that this lack of development of the basic theory is the reason for a lessening of research in the area. Whether or not a lack of theory development has brought about less research in this area, it is clear that for the theory to grow, both new ideas and additional research will be necessary in the future.

■ ■ ■

THE CASE STUDY OF JOHN: THE PERSON-CENTERED APPROACH

The use of a client case study to view person-centered theory raises several problems. To begin with, the standard case study concept suggests that a collection of historical, behavioral, and psychological factors will be used to describe and diagnose a given situation. However, person-centered theory places more emphasis on clients' perceptions of their world as opposed to observable facts. Additionally, the relationship with the counselor or therapist is much more critical in the success of therapy than the client's specific historical case development. Many person-centered counselors or therapists might, therefore, choose to ignore the concept of a clinical case history or presenting problem altogether and discuss only the progress of the relationship of client to counselor or therapist.

The problem with this approach is that it may convey to the learner that the person-centered counselor or therapist does not seek understanding of clients' perceived historical experiences or expect to observe specific progress outside the therapeutic relationship. The fact is that person-centered practitioners attend closely in order to understand the clients' perceived experiences precisely. They then use that understanding within a therapeutic relationship that is unique to the particular phenomenological worlds of the client and the counselor or therapist. Like all good counselors and therapists, person-centered practitioners also must evaluate the progress of their clients both inside the therapeutic relationship and in the outside world. Therefore, this chapter presents a modified case study to examine potential phenomenological aspects of the client's development prior to counseling. We will also look at John's relationship with the counselor or therapist and suggest potential directions for John's growth in a context that should make the case study presentation somewhat comparable to other theories.

The focus of the "initial assessment" portion of this case study will be on the potential factors that could have moved John toward the directions he has taken. They will not be verifiable factors that can be translated to all other clients with problems similar to John's. Instead they are possible factors in John's phenomenological world that could have influenced his thoughts and actions. Also, no attempt will be made to tie past experiences to specific therapeutic techniques. This background is offered only as an example of potential understandings that person-centered counselors or therapists might acquire in the development of a relationship with John, which would have an impact on the potential content and the directions that the relationship might take.

The "counselor's or therapist's role" portion of the case study will emphasize the relationship with John. This part of the case study most closely parallels the essence of person-centered theory.

"Expectations for John's progress" is another area that is highly speculative and more clinical than the standard person-centered practitioner would like. However, it does offer some ideas about the potential positive directions a person in John's situation might take.

Initial Assessment

John has been working very hard to build a life and style of interaction that is positive and useful and that meets everyone's needs. The ways he chooses to reach these goals, however, are based on his phenomenological view of the world, which is frequently out of line with the world that actually affects him. This causes John great anxiety. He looks outside himself for ways to act, only to find that what seems to be the "right" way does not satisfy himself or others. He knows that who he is and what he does are not working, but he cannot identify other ways to look at the situation.

John has lost faith in his ability to share and interact with others and has for many years made most of his decisions in isolation. He got into this position based on his perception that the ways to think and act that most help him to get along are the ones most appreciated by other important people in his life (conditions of worth). He is able to accept those decisions by others that match his perceived world, such as his mother's or wife's requests for him to rest, see a doctor, and, in general, do what they ask of him. His infrequent attempts to make independent decisions generally include avoiding input from others or ignoring it when given. This is the case in his relationships with the library workers he supervises and his past supervisors. This isolationist model makes John overly dependent on a rigid view of the world. This further reduces the opportunities for his view to be modified by seeing the differences between it and the actual world in which he lives.

John is working hard to actualize his most appropriate self, but his success is frustrated due to his limited view of the world and the masks he wears to keep himself isolated. These masks stop him from perceiving other alternative views that could potentially lead him to much greater self-actualization. He needs to gain confidence in his ability to interact in a world that does not match the one in which he has learned to live. This can only happen if John takes exploratory risks into uncharted waters. Such risk taking is frightening and not easily undertaken.

The Role of the Counselor or Therapist

The role of the person-centered counselor or therapist is to provide the therapeutic conditions that John needs in order to help him on his path to actualization. He needs a feeling of security in his own worth (unconditional positive regard) so that the fear associated with the necessary risk taking is approachable. He needs someone to pay close attention to his thoughts, actions, and feelings in order to understand fully the way he is experiencing the world (accurate empathic understanding). This condition will help John both to clarify the intricacies of his own feelings and to see that it is possible to share this view accurately with another person. John also needs to be in close contact with a counselor or therapist who is not burdened by false fronts so that he can trust the information as legitimate human information (genuineness). This will show John that outer expressions can match internal feelings in effective human beings.

Providing unconditional positive regard for John can be conveyed in part by showing confidence that he is a competent person who can choose effective ways to think and act. The counselor or therapist will not lead John to specific topics; suggest ways to act; identify his problems for him; or direct, reward, or punish him. Showing both attention and active listening without placing judgments on the information will help demonstrate this condition.

The person-centered counselor or therapist will listen to and observe closely in order to grasp all verbal and emotional aspects of John. This listening and observing will be regularly clarified by the practitioner's attempts to convey what he sees, hears, and feels. Mistakes, underestimations, and overestimations are common in this process of developing accurate empathic understanding. There is no reason to believe that the counselor/therapist or John will quickly and accurately recognize all the dimensions that John has been masking for years. Accurate empathic understanding should be viewed as a learning process for both parties involved rather than a set of correct statements made by the counselor or therapist. It becomes a negotiating process in which the client presents ideas and the counselor or therapist tries to reflect them and possibly tie them into other previously recognized concepts. Then both parties can negotiate to reach some mutual agreements. It is only from such struggle that accurate understanding can be fully achieved.

Unconditional positive regard and accurate empathic understanding begin to look false and misleading to the client unless genuineness is also conveyed. John needs to see himself in a relationship that is open and honest. It must be made clear that what the counselor or therapist thinks, does, and says are consistent and that taking on the role of counselor or therapist does not mean one cannot be one's real self. Such consistency will allow John to trust the relationship as well as the ideas, skills, and behaviors that seem to develop from it. He will learn to use the counselor or therapist as a model for the idea that he, too, can develop such congruence. As progress continues, John will recognize that because this is a real human relationship with genuine people, the ideas and actions can be transferred to his life outside the relationship. The relationship, therefore, will be viewed as a real and dependable experience. This natural aspect of the relationship will help John to see that similar positive relationships can be sought outside the helping relationship.

The person-centered practitioner is often considered to be caring and kindly, but it must also be recognized that the core conditions offer a great deal of challenge to the client. John will not always want to hear how the counselor or therapist is reacting to him. Many of the ways John reacts to himself and to the counselor or therapist will not be things he wants to accept. Only the truly empathic counselor or therapist, who is also very genuine, can approach such difficult issues. There are many challenging times and confrontations in this person-centered approach that are to be expected in any genuine human relationship.

Expectations for John's Progress

The person-centered counselor or therapist who adequately and consistently provides the necessary therapeutic conditions can expect John to progress in some general ways. It should be made clear, however, that

John may not change in the ways that others deem to be best. John is seeking himself. Although that self is affected by certain other people, progress in counseling or psychotherapy will likely reduce the control these others have over John. Such control will be replaced by increasing trust in his organism so that John will begin to see his personal ability to control his own life while still considering the needs of others.

The process begins as John starts to trust his relationship with the counselor or therapist. He becomes more free to talk of difficult issues and recognize that this person will still think well of him, no matter how inappropriate certain aspects of his feelings, thoughts, and actions appear to be. These issues appear in a different light compared to what John had envisioned previously. Generally, this new view offers the problems in a manageable form that is not nearly as terrible or insurmountable as John had believed. Excitement about finding potential ways to see the world will likely be followed by struggles to understand his new world and how he will need to relate to it differently.

John will soon find a need to explore his new ways of looking at and acting in the world outside of the helping relationship. He will want to know how his wife, children, boss, and mother would respond if he chose to look at and act differently with them. Such issues will likely be explored in the therapeutic relationship before trying them out. John will want to discuss both the good and bad results after they have been tried in real life. Each new idea, observation, and attempted behavior in each new situation will expand John's view of the world and likely bring him back to the counselor or therapist for help in integrating the information.

There will be pleasures, fears, successes, and disappointments in John's development just as in everyone's. But he will come to recognize that he can learn from each experience and that each time he learns he increases the confidence in his own ability to direct himself. Eventually, he may learn to have enough confidence in his own immediate reactions so that he will not need to hide from them or other people. He will be better able to use both his own ideas and those of others to develop positive outcomes. He will also recognize that even when things do not work out as planned, he is effective enough as a human being to overcome mistakes.

LIMITATIONS

Person-centered theory may suffer most from the fact that it appears so simple to learn. The concepts are relatively few, there is not a great list of details to remember, and one does not need to recall a specific tactic for each problem a client might have. The counselor or therapist can be lulled into a feeling of security by this apparent simplicity. For example, simple listening and reflecting of words and surface feelings are usually beneficial at the very beginning of a session. However, continued surface-level inter-actions that do not attend to the many dimensions of both the client and counselor or therapist will quickly be seen as repetitive, nondirectional, and trite.

The reality is that the few basic concepts in person-centered theory have a virtually unlimited complexity because counselors and therapists must be fully aware of both their clients' and their own phenomenological worlds. They must respond to the interactions between these worlds in ways that best fit the genuine natures of the client and the counselor or therapist. This is a difficult task that requires an excellent understanding and continuing awareness of self and the client. New counselors and ther-apists in particular have a difficult time with this complexity. Anyone who is working hard and feeling under pressure to remember and do a "new thing" or a "right thing" will naturally find it very difficult to be natural and aware of all that is happening around and within themselves and oth-ers. Acting on what they recognize adds yet another level of difficulty to the task at hand.

The supportive nature of person-centered theory is often misinter-preted to mean that one should not be confrontational with clients. Coun-selors and therapists often need to do more than listen and reflect. Effec-tively functioning people confront themselves all the time, and counselors and therapists must recognize that appropriate confrontation is a natural part of an effective helping relationship. Person-centered theory makes room for such confrontation, but it gives few specific guidelines as to where, when, and how it should occur.

Person-centered theory requires a great deal of trust in the positive motivation and abilities of oneself and the client. Without this trust, many of the other person-centered concepts lose their true value, and a thera-peutic interaction can become little more than polite conversation. Such trust in people and a process is not necessarily easy to provide in all cir-cumstances. Human beings have difficulty suspending their mistrust because fears, previous experiences, and preconceived notions are a nat-ural part of the human condition that impacts everyone. The more extreme the negative experiences and reactions are, the more difficult it is to act fully on the person-centered belief system. The result is that most counselors or therapists can place confidence in a bright, college-edu-cated, law-abiding, depressed client but have more difficulty maintaining a similar confidence in a depressed rapist or murderer.

Person-centered practice requires a great deal of personal knowledge, understanding, and awareness. The counselor or therapist must also be willing to act on this information. There are few techniques or activities to fall back on if the counselor or therapist does not have or cannot act on this information about the helping relationship. Many other theories provide more activities or tactics that allow the therapist or counselor to give the process a boost when the relationship is not all it could be.

SUMMARY

Person-centered theory has become one of the most popular theories of counseling and therapy since it developed in the 1940s. It was first labeled *nondirective* by its originator, Carl Rogers. The theory offered a distinct alternative to the behavioral and psychoanalytic theories that dominated psychology at the time. Rogers later broadened the concepts of the process and renamed it *client-centered* to de-emphasize the nondirective nature and emphasize a full understanding of all the client's dimensions. The *person-centered* concept evolved as issues relating to equality of participants in the relationship and a focus on the positive health of people as opposed to a more unhealthy client status became significant issues.

Person-centered theory makes possible the expansion of helping situations. Originally developed as an individual process, it has since become a major group theory. This group focus has expanded into concepts popular in education. Rogers's most recent work emphasized the same concepts as ways of dealing with international conflict resolution in an emphasis on promoting world peace.

Person-centered theory places great emphasis on the individual's ability to move in positive directions. Practitioners of the theory have a belief in the trustworthiness of individuals and in their innate ability to move toward self-actualization and health when the proper conditions are in place. Tied to these beliefs is the confidence that individuals also have the inner resources to move themselves in such positive directions. Finally, a core concept in the theory states that individuals perceive the world in a unique phenomenological way so that no two people's perceptions of the world are the same.

The perception of clients as competent, trustworthy, and forward-moving people who have their own unique view of the world places great confidence in the individual's ability to control her own positive change. This confidence in the client directs the counselor or therapist to provide the conditions for that change. Specifically, there are three basic conditions needed to support an individual's natural inclination for positive growth: a genuine relationship with a relatively congruent individual, acceptance and caring from the counselor or therapist, and an accurate understanding on the part of the counselor or therapist of the client's phenomenological world.

Clients who are provided with these growth conditions will realize their actualizing tendencies for growth. They will explore their difficulties and natural competencies in this productive environment, which will then lead to a clearer picture of themselves and their potential. As clients' pictures of themselves become more accurate, they become better able to act in ways that are most in line with their true self (congruence). This in turn will lead to more self-confidence, self-understanding, and better choices.

The role of the counselor or therapist in person-centered theory is primarily to promote the conditions for change rather than do things to bring about specific changes. Counselors and therapists are expected to maintain a genuine human relationship in which they provide unconditional positive regard to their clients. This demonstrates their faith in clients and support of the process. Much of the work of the person-centered counselor or therapist revolves around developing an accurate empathic understanding of a client, conveying that understanding to the person, and working with him to expand and clarify the understanding and its impact on the client's choices and actions.

Rogers's work initiated much research on the helping relationship and client gain. The use of taping and transcriptions to evaluate the necessary conditions of counseling and psychotherapy received emphasis from research on this theory. A great deal of innovative research in the area of clinical growth was also produced in the development of this theory. However, much of this theory has been integrated into the overall body of the theory, and relatively little research is currently being done in the area. Calls are being made for potential expansion of the theory and research into its future development. Person-centered counseling and psychotherapy has given much to the field, and professionals continue to emphasize the need for growth of the theory rather than a stagnant use of the theory's many positive contributions.

REFERENCES

Boy, A., & Pine, G. (1990). *A person-centered foundation for counseling and psychotherapy*. Springfield, IL: Charles C Thomas.

Cain, D. J. (1986). Editorial: A call for the "write stuff." *Person-centered Review, 1*(2), 117–124.

Cain, D. J. (1987). Carl R. Rogers: The man, his vision, his impact. *Person-centered Review, 2*(3), 283–288.

Combs, A. W. (1988). Some current issues for person-centered therapy. *Person-centered Review, 3*(3), 263–276.

Goodyear, R. (1987). In memory of Carl Ransom Rogers. *Journal of Counseling and Development, 65,* 523–524.

Hjelle, L. A., & Ziegler, D. J. (1992). *Personality theories.* New York: McGraw-Hill.

Prochaska, J. O. (1984). *Systems of psychotherapy: A transtheoretical analysis* (2nd ed.). Pacific Grove, CA: Brooks/Cole.

Rogers, C. (1942). *Counseling and psychotherapy.* Boston: Houghton Mifflin.

Rogers, C. (1951). *Client-centered therapy.* Boston: Houghton Mifflin.

Rogers, C. (1959). A theory of therapy, personality, and interpersonal relationships, as developed in the client-centered framework. In S. Koch (Ed.), *Psychology: A study of a science.* New York: McGraw-Hill.

Rogers, C. (1961). *On becoming a person: A therapist's view of psychotherapy.* Boston: Houghton Mifflin.

Rogers, C. (Ed.). (1967). *The therapeutic relationship and its impact: A study of psychotherapy with schizophrenics.* Madison: University of Wisconsin Press.

Rogers, C. (1970). *Carl Rogers on encounter groups.* New York: Harper & Row.

Rogers, C. (1986). Carl Rogers on the development of the person-centered approach. *Person-centered Review, 1*(3), 257–259.

Rogers, C. (1987a). Inside the world of the Soviet professional. *Counseling and Values, 32*(1), 47–66.

Rogers, C. (1987b). Steps toward peace, 1948–1986: Tension reduction in theory and practice. *Counseling and Values, 32*(1), 12–16.

Rogers, C., & Dymond, R. (1954). *Psychotherapy and personality change.* Chicago: University of Chicago Press.

Rogers, C., & Sanford, R. (1987b). Reflections on our South African experience. *Counseling and Values, 32*(1), 17–20.

Stephenson, W. (1953). *The study of behavior: Q-technique and its methodology.* Chicago: University of Chicago Press.

Thayer, L. (1987). An interview with Carl R. Rogers: Toward peaceful solutions to human conflict. Part I. *Michigan Journal of Counseling and Development, 18*(1), 58–63.

Watson, N. (1984). The empirical status of Rogers' hypotheses of the necessary and sufficient conditions for effective psychotherapy. In R. F. Levant & J. M. Shlien (Eds.), *Client-centered therapy and the person-centered approach: New directions in theory, research, and practice* (pp. 17–40). New York: Praeger.

CHAPTER TEN

Gestalt Theory

Mary Finn Maples
University of Nevada—Reno

Many of the texts on Gestalt counseling and therapy have focused almost exclusively on the contributions of Fritz Perls to the theory. This chapter will also explore the works of the German contributors who were fundamental to his background and writings. Although many of Perls's writings were influenced by the psychologists Köhler, Koffka, and Wertheimer, little reference to their work appears in his work. The notion that behavior is best understood by considering the entire person and the entire situation—sometimes known as the "wholes"—was a major reaction against the reductionism apparent in early behaviorism but also against the formulations of Freud. Gestalt psychology, then, provided a framework for Gestalt counselors and therapists to focus on the whole person. By understanding the contributions of Wertheimer, Köhler, and Koffka, the student of Gestalt theory can enjoy a broader picture of the breadth and depth of the theory. Wertheimer's work on motivation and perception, Koffka's introduction of the term *Gestalt*, and Köhler's reputation as a humane and patient researcher all provided valuable insight to Perls's more popular and practical applications in counseling and therapy.

HISTORY

Frederick Salomon (Fritz) Perls (1893–1970) is credited with being the foremost practitioner of Gestalt counseling and psychotherapy. However, he was influenced by Gestalt psychologists who preceded him. Psychological theorists Max Wertheimer, Wolfgang Köhler, and Kurt Koffka initiated the Gestalt movement in the United States when they immigrated to this country after the rise of Nazism in Germany (Rock & Palmer, 1990). Perls's biographer, Martin Shepherd (1975), wrote that "the traditional Gestalt psychologists claim him [Perls]" (p. 198). Perls, however, stated, "The academic Gestaltists, of course, never accepted me. . . . I certainly was not a pure Gestaltist" (1969a, p. 62).

The Austrian philosopher Christian von Ehrenfels may be credited with the initial use of the term *Gestalt*, which appeared in his essay "On Gestalt Qualities" in 1890. This publication ignited a current of thought which created a strong position in both philosophy and psychology during the first half of the 20th century. Yet it was the psychologists of the Berlin school, which included Wertheimer, Koffka, and Köhler, who laid the psychological groundwork for Perls's application of Gestaltism in counseling and psychotherapy.

Perls first used the term *Gestalt therapy* in his 1947 text, and readers have had conflicting reactions to this early work. Yontef (1981) stated that while the roots for Gestalt therapy were established in Gestalt psychology, there were doubts as to whether "the Gestalt therapy system has much to do with Gestalt psychology" (p. 1). Yet Emerson and Smith (1974) wrote that "no one can understand Gestalt therapy well without an adequate background in Gestalt psychology" (p. 8). Mary Henle concluded in 1978 that "the two approaches, Gestalt psychology and Gestalt therapy have nothing in common" (p. 26). Cadwallader (1984) stated that Gestalt therapy "has, in my opinion, rather little to do with Gestalt psychology" (p. 192).

Emerson and Smith (1974), Kogan (1976), and Yontef (1981) believe that Perls moved from psychoanalysis to Gestalt therapy in 1947. Perls confirmed this in his *Ego, Hunger and Aggression: The Beginning of Gestalt Therapy* (1947). The modern Gestalt counselor or therapist who learns theory, research, and practice from the writings and demonstrations of Fritz Perls may understand his ideas more thoroughly and appreciate his works after learning more about his predecessors.

Max Wertheimer

Max Wertheimer (1880–1943) was one of the Berlin psychologists who influenced Perls's ideas. His works on motivation and perception were particularly influential. They contributed to one of Perls's most important constructs, that of awareness in the client. Wertheimer's effect on Perls was initiated by his study *Perception of Apparent Movement* (1912), which led to Wertheimer's reputation as the founder of Gestalt psychology (Hartmann, 1935). It was also at this time that Wertheimer gathered around him a group of brilliant young disciples, among them Kurt Koffka and Wolfgang Köhler, who were active human subjects in several of his experiments, including the seminal one in 1912 (Smith, 1976).

Kurt Koffka

Kurt Koffka (1886–1941) was concerned with the definition of *Gestalt*. He asserted:

> The term gestalt is a short name for a category of thought comparable to other categories like substance, causality, and function. But gestalt may be considered more than simply an addition to pre-existing conceptual princi-ples; its generality is so great that one may ask whether causality itself or even substance does not fall legitimately under it. (1935, p. 16)

Koffka and other Gestaltists who contributed to the study of percep-tion described Gestalt as "a pattern or shape"; but in psychology, and particularly in counseling and psychotherapy from Perls's perspective, the word means "configuration" (Rock & Palmer, 1990). Perls used the word *Gestalt* to mean a specific type of patterning (configuration) where parts can be integrated into perceptual wholes. This wholeness concept is used extensively in counseling and therapy, in education, and in social psychology (Passons, 1975).

Koffka was passionate in his belief in Gestaltism. He said, "I wanted to present a system of psychology that was not a dead or finished system but a system in the making, a system in a state of growth" (Koffka, 1935, p. ix). Perls continued to nurture that growth by extending it into therapy and counseling.

Wolfgang Köhler

The writings of Wolfgang Köhler (1887–1967), like those of Koffka, Wertheimer, and others, contributed much "humanness" to Perls's work. Of the three precursors to Perls's work in Gestalt counseling and therapy, Köhler was probably the most humane. His friends and colleagues described him as an affective and sensitive person, "one who could see beyond what others could" (Henle, 1971, p. 89). He "show[ed] us what a man is capable of being" (Hormann, 1967, p. 202).

Köhler's sensitivity to others is often a help to beginning students of Gestalt counseling and therapy. Henle (1971) felt that this sensitivity was reflected in both Köhler's life and his writings. Those writings, however, also emerged as a result of disintegration, disenchantment, and even disbelief in the favored psychological theories of the 1920s and 1930s: structuralism and behaviorism. Köhler wrote in *The Mentality of Apes* (1927), "The subject matter I have tried to present, resembles in 1928 a promising start, more than a complete achievement" (p. vii). His greatest challenge in that publication, as he was to state many times, was converting his simple and almost crude concepts to the English language. He was quite careful with this text, having given it to Mortimer Adler for literary criticism and finally to Kurt Koffka for final revision.

Frederick (Fritz) Perls

Frederich, later spelled Frederick, (Fritz) Salomon Perls was born in 1893, the middle child and only son of middle-class Jewish parents in Berlin. His childhood experiences were much like those of most American children who became adults in the middle of the 20th century. He recalled that his childhood was fairly happy, although he related more positively to his younger sister than his older. He did well in primary school, but by the seventh grade his spirit of rebellion began to assert itself. However, he persevered, tolerated the mediocrity of those years, and received a medical degree in 1920 after a brief stint as a medical corpsman during World War I, a practical and personally important experience.

His early training in psychoanalysis took place in Austria and Germany, and he became associated with the famed neurologist Kurt Goldstein. While working as Goldstein's assistant at Frankfurt am Main's Institute for Brain Injured Soldiers in 1926, Perls became interested in the transforming of Gestalt psychology into Gestalt therapy (Perls, 1969b). Goldstein's work significantly affected Perls's later counseling and psychotherapy interventions (Wheeler, 1991). Perls's early works make it apparent, however, that he disagreed with psychoanalysis, behaviorism, and structuralism. It was time for him to move on.

That moving on may have been rooted in his own human nature: he was always seeking the free spirit (Perls, 1969b). Mary Henle (1978) believes that Perls viewed most of his differences with Gestalt psychology as insurmountable discrepancies because he regarded himself as an organismic psychologist or a viewer of humankind in its holistic sense. According to Henle (1978), "Gestalt psychology deals primarily with perception and cognition, while Gestalt therapy (counseling) is concerned with personality psychopathology and psychotherapy" (p. 29). Perls particularly admired the work of Kurt Lewin because of his holistic approach to human nature (Perls, 1969b).

When Hitler came to power, Perls and his wife, Laura, relocated to Johannesburg, South Africa, and he shed the Freudian influence of psychoanalysis. In 1946, he immigrated to the United States, where he published *Gestalt Therapy: Excitement and Growth in the Human Personality* (1951). Following the successful publication of this text, he established several Gestalt institutes throughout the country, the first one in New York in 1952. His work at the Esalen Institute in Big Sur, California, established him as a prominent practitioner of Gestalt counseling and therapy. For a more intimate portrait of Fritz Perls, the man and the practitioner, you may be interested in reading his *In and Out of the Garbage Pail* (1969b).

It is important to consider the time in history in which a particular theorist was living and working in order to understand and appreciate that person's work and views of life more clearly. The language of the time and the way people lived and loved, worked and played are crucial to understanding counseling theorists and practitioners decades later. Consider Perls's 1969 statement in *Gestalt Therapy Verbatim* (1969a): "It took us a long time to debunk the whole Freudian crap. We are entering the phase of the quacks and the con-men who think if you get some breakthrough, you are cured" (1969a, p. 1). He had a negative experience with Sigmund Freud in 1936 when the two engaged in a brief conversation at a psychology convention in Vienna. Perls felt humiliated by Freud. Because of the humiliating experiences he also had with his father while growing up, this interchange may have contributed to his desire to prove Freud's theories obsolete (Perls, 1969a).

Perls was a product of the decades of work done before him; he was also influenced by the works of Wertheimer, Koffka, and Köhler. However, his most memorable representations, translations, extensions, and practice occurred at a time of unsettlement and unrest, a questioning of authority, the rejection of traditional customs, and the opening of the free spirit: the decade of the 60s, when Perls himself was in his 70s. According to him, that time of the century, which included the years in which he was strengthening his theory, helped him make this discovery: "The meaning of life is that it is to be lived; and it is not to be traded and conceptualized and squeezed into a pattern of systems. We realize that manipulation and control are not the ultimate joy of life" (1969a, p. 3). But was he *reflecting* the growing freedom of the human spirit at that time or was he *advancing* it? There is no answer in his works.

From a historical perspective, Gestalt counseling and psychotherapy is now in the third generation of a holistic approach to helping. It is noteworthy that the first generation began with the philosophical underpinnings of Ehrenfels (1890). That generation then opened the door to the psychological works of Wertheimer, Koffka, and Köhler (from 1912 through 1960), each of which dealt with the mental aspects of the human being: cognition (thinking), perceiving, motivation. In the second generation, building on the first, Perls extended the research into the physical and emotional aspects of the human being (from 1947 to 1969) to include the medical model of psychotherapy. As the third generation, Gestalt counseling and psychotherapy recognizes the importance of the counselor or therapist in the counseling and psychotherapy process (Gilliland, James, & Bowman, 1989; Polster & Polster, 1973a; Zinker, 1978). Gestalt counseling and psychotherapy is intended to bring more meaning to the value that counseling has for individuals, families, and work groups who are in relatively good health, psychologically and physically, but who are experiencing roadblocks or difficulty adjusting to an increasingly complex, diverse, and problematic world.

HUMAN NATURE: A DEVELOPMENTAL PERSPECTIVE

Perls had a passionate belief in the holistic nature of humankind: that human beings had the capacity and strength to grow, develop, and become the persons that they desired. That belief led to his ultimate disassociation from the traditional Gestaltists, who were still connected to cognition, perception, and motivation and not to the wholeness of the organism.

According to Perls (1969a), Lewin made a prominent impact on Perls's view of human nature. In his chapter "Education and Reality," from *A Dynamic Theory of Personality* (1935), Lewin discussed a holistic view of a child educated in a Montessori setting. The Montessori educational system was developed by Maria Montessori in Italy as an alternative to educating children by parts: that is, breaking education down into arithmetic, spelling, language, and the like. She believed in the education of the whole child, much in the manner that John Dewey proposed in the United States. Discussing Montessori's method, Lewin wrote that the "extension of psychological life space and time and the demand for a life in the present is realized to an extreme degree in the young child" (1935, p. 172). He said that the child has "levels of reality and unreality from kindergarten and perhaps even before" (p. 174) and that even "in the infant the forces of psychological environment are determined essentially by his own needs" (p. 175).

Lewin's influence on Perls's view of human nature is particularly valuable because the holistic approach in Gestalt theory can be applied effectively to children in a school or family counseling and psychotherapy setting. Other theories or systems are often ineffective because their success is limited to adults (family systems theory) or children (play therapy) but not to both.

Perls's views of Gestalt counseling and psychotherapy focus more on *how* and *where* in the body the process of behavior takes place, rather than *why*. Smith (1976) contends that Gestalt counseling and therapy has also been expanded and honed by the influence of Jung in at least three ways: first, the Jungian facilitation of growth through self-realization; second, the Jungian position of personality development through wholeness; and third, the Jungian illumination of the transpersonal realm in counseling. These influences contributed to Perls's belief in the wholeness and completeness of life. Centered in the present, according to Kempler (1973), the person in Gestalt counseling or therapy is always in the process of being what she is in the here and now, not, as Rogers and Maslow believed, in the process of striving to become the person that she can be. Further, Perls believed in the ability of persons to change and to be responsible for their behavior and, inevitably, the directions they take in their lives. A valuable aspect of the Gestaltist's view of human nature is that persons gain more from experiences and involvement in activities than in talk.

Perls was seen by his contemporaries as a consummate actor (Shepherd, 1975). That is, they saw him as successful in eliciting behaviors from his clients that traditional psychoanalysts, behaviorists, and structuralists may not have been able to accomplish. Perls, Hefferline, and Goodman (1951) commented on the psychoanalytical belief that the ego confines itself to perceiving and is otherwise otiose. When writing about human awareness in Gestalt counseling and psychotherapy, they stated that "awareness is not otiose," implying that the client is active, dynamic, and involved in the counseling and psychotherapy process (Perls et al., 1951, p. 71).

Perls (1969a), describing his view of human nature, spoke of an organism—in this case, the human being—by noting that it always works as a whole. "We *have* not a liver or a heart. We *are* liver and heart and brain and yet, even this is wrong—we are *not* a summation of parts but a *coordination* of the whole. We do not have a body, we *are* a body, we *are* somebody" (1969a, p. 6). He admired Goldstein's belief in the organism as a whole but broke with him because Goldstein thought of the organism as *having* a heart, a liver, and so on (1969a).

Perls was enthralled by the value of Gestalt counseling and psychotherapy because "we see the whole being of a person right in front of us—Gestalt counseling is being in touch with the obvious, the human being, the wholeness of his/her frailties, strengths, weaknesses, joys, and sorrows" (Perls, 1969a, p. 14). An example of a client's coming to believe in the wholeness, the simplicity, the individual responsibility for her own behavior as a worthwhile human being was demonstrated by Swanson (1984) in a videotaped session with a woman client using the Gestalt belief system of the wholeness of human nature. The client had come to obtain assistance because she was unable to express herself in an honest manner. She felt that she always had to "hide [her] true feelings so as not to make others angry at [her]" (Swanson, 1984). In a series of six sessions, Swanson facilitated her "response-ability" and her worth as a person (Perls, 1969a, p. 29). He worked with her entire being throughout this session (Swanson, 1984).

MAJOR CONSTRUCTS

The structure of Gestalt counseling and psychotherapy is contained in Perls's belief in the holistic system of humankind, of the organism's (individual/figure) relationship to its environment (ground). Perls first called his Gestalt therapy "concentration therapy." He spoke of "end gains" and "the means whereby" neurotic and paranoid disturbance can be cured (1947, p. 268). Later, he modified the idea of concentration as an end gain in counseling or therapy to *awareness*, one of the present-day major constructs of this theory. The following components are important aspects of Gestalt counseling and psychotherapy.

Experience and Activity

Because Perls believed that awareness was curative (1969a), he also believed that to become aware, the client needs to be more involved in the experience of counseling and psychotherapy instead of simply talking about becoming aware. This awareness represents itself through *contact*, another major construct. The individual becomes more aware by reaching out and touching, not necessarily physically but by words or looks. An example of awareness through contact can be seen in a videotape of family counseling and psychotherapy in which the counselor/therapist demonstrates the constructs of awareness and contact by charging each member of the family to communicate and act out their frustrations *with* and *to* each other and not to talk *about* their frustrations to the counselor/therapist (Nevis & Harris, 1988).

Figure-Ground (Bound)

According to Perls et al. (1951), the model of contact is figure-bound: that is, the analysis of the contact process (awareness or experience) is incomplete without direct consideration of organized features or structures of ground, enduring, in some cases, across situations and over time. Counseling or psychotherapy, or any change-induction process, is always a matter of reorganization of these structures of ground over time. This figure-ground (bound) construct is used in Gestalt as "unfinished business" (Passons, 1975, pp. 18–19). Unfinished business can be an issue as simple as an adult's resenting a childhood nickname without knowing the reason for his parent's choice of the nickname. The business remains unfinished until the adult is able to confront his parent and resolve the issue. The unfinished business—figure-ground—may be a part of the larger Gestalt, a problem of adult child and parent relationships.

Here-and-Now Orientation

In *Gestalt Therapy Verbatim* (1969a), Perls wrote that the purpose of Gestalt counseling and psychotherapy is to "promote the growth process and develop the human potential" (p. 2). The terms, *promote* and *develop* imply a current nature to the counseling process. Perls further stated that "nothing exists but the here and now. The past is no more, the future is not yet" (p. 41).

In working with clients to keep them in the here and now, Perls often spoke of the two legs upon which Gestalt therapy walks: the *now* and the *how*. *Now* includes the balance of being here—the client experiencing, involving, and becoming aware. *How* relates to the structure, the behavior, its changes and fluctuations—all that is actually happening, the ongoing process. Many clients who bring problems related to anxiety in family, marital, or other relationships can be helped with activities that will keep them in the here and now. Perls saw anxiety as the gap between now and then. In counseling and psychotherapy, the client usually does not experience anxiety in the now because she is engaged in spontaneous and creative activities suggested by the counselor or therapist in which she becomes certain of her place in the activity. Gestalt counselors and therapists believe that uncertainty plays a significant role in the development of anxiety. Perls suggested that "anxiety causes the excitement of life, (the 'elan vital' that we carry with us), to become stagnated, if we are unsure of the person we are, or our place in a particular situation" (1969a, p. 3).

Ego Boundaries and Polarities

Perls described *ego boundary* as "the organism's (the human being's) definition in relation to its environment, that this relationship is experienced both by what is inside the skin and what is outside the skin, but it is not a fixed thing" (Perls, 1969a, p. 7). The two phenomena of ego boundary are *identification* and *alienation*. An example of these phenomena might be the mental obsession in this country with physical thinness. For many men and women to identify positively with society, they must be thin; whereas, if one is obese, then one is alienated from society. In other words, the more obese a person is, the greater the alienation. Another Gestalt term, *polarities*, may describe the same client as top dog/underdog (Simkin, 1975). The client wants to be thin, often feeling like the underdog because everyone picks on him.

This underdog sees a certain thin person as a model (top dog) that he has chosen or has been in conflict with, a person to whom "thinness is natural" or who "doesn't like food anyway, so I can never achieve that goal." The model, often a relative, parent, or associate, may use the ploy, "But you must do this. I know what is best for you, and you'll be a happier person," thereby actually encouraging the ego boundary and the polarity "I can't; therefore, I won't try." The attempt is for identification with (underdog) but results in alienation from (top dog). Recognizing ego boundaries and polarities and integrating them are the work of the counselor or therapist. This recognition and integration are accomplished by facilitating client awareness through experiencing them in contact during therapy (Simkin, 1975).

Appreciating, as Perls did, that Gestalt therapy is an extension, outgrowth, or fruit of Gestalt psychology, I feel it is appropriate to close this section with a reminder that

> the basic premise of Gestalt psychology or counseling structure is that human nature is organized into patterns or wholes, that it is experienced by the individual in these terms, and that it can only be understood as a function of the patterns of wholes of which it is made. (Perls, 1969b, pp. 3–4)

THE PROCESS OF CHANGE

> Reality is nothing but
> The sum of all awareness
> As you experience here and now. (Perls, 1969a, p. 30)

While this statement may appear oversimplistic and perhaps even idealistic, it is Perls's dismissal of the mind-body dichotomy in favor of monism, and it presents a challenge to the student of Gestalt counseling or therapy (1969a). Understanding the process of change from a Gestalt perspective calls for an appreciation of Perls's goal for the process:

> The Gestalt approach attempts to understand the existence of any event through the way it comes about, which is to understand becoming by the *how* and not the *why*; through the all-pervasive gestalt formation; through the tension of the unfinished situation (business). (Perls, 1966, p. 361)

One of the major differences between the process of change in Gestalt counseling/therapy and Freudian psychoanalysis, for example, is that in the Gestalt approach, it is crucial that the counseling/therapy process recognize and encourage clients, consider family systems, and work within stages and tasks in human development. The methods of recognition, consideration, and working within are unique to Gestalt practitioners. "There are specific skills, techniques and knowledge that should not be overlooked by the Gestalt counselor" (Shepherd, 1975, p. 196). Another aspect of the process of change in Gestalt counseling/therapy is the excitement that is generated when the organism (client) contacts something new, leading to the creation of a new Gestalt or a new experience. The Swanson tape noted earlier demonstrated the client's excitement: "It's all so simple—all I have to do is to say what I really am feeling, be honest about it, and be willing to be responsible for the results" (Swanson, 1984).

Specifically, the process of change in Gestalt counseling and therapy consists of the identification and working through of a variety of blocks or interferences that prevent the organism from achieving a balance (Wallen, 1970). Perls (1969a) described clients who block:

1. Those who cannot maintain eye contact, who are unaware of their own movements
2. Those who cannot openly express their needs
3. Those who use repression, examples of which are insomnia and boredom

If awareness is a main focus in the process of change, the student of Gestalt counseling/therapy must understand the challenge of achieving this goal, which can often be met by attempting some of the activities suggested by Gestaltists but that are not always familiar to the practitioner (Yontef, 1981).

Change in the client requires that the counselor or therapist create an atmosphere that will encourage exploration by the client necessary for client growth. According to Polster and Polster (1973b), this process mandates that counselors and therapists be exciting, energetic, and full of life. Obviously, this is demanding on the practitioner. According to Levitsky and Perls (1970), the process of change, which is aimed at helping clients become more aware of themselves in the here and now, involves several precepts, including but not necessarily limited to the following:

1. *A continuum of awareness.* Clients focus constantly on the how, what, and where in the body, in contrast to the why.
2. *Statements rather than questions.* Many theorists and practitioners have found the establishment of response-ability to be more helpful and respectful than expecting answers to questions (Gazda, 1986).
3. *Use of the first person pronoun "I" rather than "it" or "they."* The reference to the here and now, even in the use of dreams (one of Perls's intervention strategies), requires that counseling or psychotherapy deal with the role that the client is presently enacting in the dream rather than the interpretation, in the Freudian sense, of the dream.
4. *The contact issue of addressing someone directly.* This approach relates to the client's presenting problem rather than tells the counselor or therapist *about* the problem.

As I stated earlier, the process of change in Gestalt counseling or psychotherapy involves experience and activity. Yontef (1981) believes that all Gestalt techniques are a means of experimentation. He further states that experimentation in the change process can be used to study any phenomenon that the client has experienced.

Contributing to the process of change are Perls's five layers of neurosis, which the client passes through in this experience. Perls defines *neuroses* as "growth disorders" (1969a, p. 29).

- *The cliché layer*:   one of noncontact with others; the "Hello, how are you?" "Fine, how are you?" routine
- *The phony layer*:   the role-playing layer; the boss, the victim, the good boy/bad girl layers; the superficial and pretend layers; Perls believed that people devote much of their active lives to this game-playing layer
- *The impasse layer*:   described by the Russians as the "sick patient" or the place between dependence on outside support (parents, for example) and the ability to be self-supportive; an avoidance process
- *The implosive layer*:   all the previous roles in the process are exposed, stripped, and seen for what they are—roles; this layer involves "pulling oneself together, contracting, compressing, and imploding" (p. 60)
- *The exploding layer*:   the final process; the "death layer comes to life and this explosion is the link-up with the authentic person who is capable of experiencing and expressing his emotions" (Dye & Hackney, 1975, p. 89)

The layers in this process, particularly from impasse to explosion, are often difficult for the client to comprehend. Yet most people have at one time or another reached that soul-searching depth that leads to getting in touch with values and self-perceptions that form the core of existence. The process, according to Dye and Hackney (1975), is best understood "only after it has been experienced" (p. 40).

Finally, the process of change in Gestalt counseling and psychotherapy contains a crucial feature that is both a valuable asset and a critical handicap: its open-endedness. Gestalt counselors and psychotherapists rarely use techniques or tools that can be quantified from a "proof of theory" perspective. However, this open-endedness is the very quality that encourages creativity, inventiveness, response-ability, and outcome resolution on the part of the client in the process of change.

INTERVENTION STRATEGIES

Most theories value the personhood of the counselor or psychotherapist. In Gestalt counseling or therapy, however, practitioners are particularly important as persons because of the active nature of the client and counselor or therapist relationship.

The following views about counseling and therapy are particularly appropriate to Gestalt practitioners. "The most important element in counseling is the personhood of the counselor. The most powerful impact on the client may be that of observing what the counselor is and does" (Gilliland et al., 1989, p. 7). Zinker (1978) focuses on the importance of the counselor or therapist as a creative agent of change who must be both caring and compassionate as a human being. Polster and Polster (1973a) see the "therapist as his own instrument" (p. 19). Further, Yontef and Simkin (1989) stress that *who* the counselor is as a person is more important than *what* she is doing to or with the client.

During his life, Perls believed that counseling and therapy are a means of enriching life (Dye & Hackney, 1975). From his perspective, it is clear that "well people can get better" (Bates, Johnson, & Blaker, 1982). Intervention strategies suggested in this section are for clients who are fundamentally well, in the existential sense, but who need assistance in "making it" in a complex world. The main purpose, then, of intervention with persons who are seeking counseling or psychotherapy is to "simply sit down and start living" (Enright, 1970, p. 112). Dye and Hackney (1975) see that the aim of Gestalt counseling or therapy is to take advantage of all dimensions of humanness by "achieving an integration of the thinking, feeling and sensing processes. The goal is to enable *full experiencing* rather than merely a cognitive understanding of certain elements" (p. 44).

Given the goal of completeness, wholeness, integration, and fulfillment of the essentially healthy but needy individual (in the sense of an incomplete Gestalt), the following intervention strategies might be employed.

Breathing and Relaxation

Unfortunately, many counselors or therapists mistakenly believe that when the client enters the therapy room, he is completely ready to be helped. This is not the case with most clients. The practitioner's role is to help the client get in touch with how he is feeling in the here and now. Most of the time, the client will be nervous, apprehensive, uncertain of what is going to take place. Relaxing the client is crucial. This process begins with a

5-minute deep-breathing session, which readies the client for relaxation. Empathizing with the client helps the counselor or therapist get in touch with him; it enables both to begin from the same base line.

Locating Feelings

Instead of asking the client, "What are you feeling?" the Gestaltist encourages her through statements such as "Show me where you are feeling this anxiety, apprehension, nervousness" (Swanson, 1984). This helps the client to understand that she is not alone in the process and that the counselor or therapist is inviting herself into the client's space.

Enactment and Confrontation

Because the client must be involved in the change process, the new behaviors call for confronting old behaviors and acting out new ones. Confronting the self is a very important strategy in which the client must be involved. The confronting of self and then the enacting allows the client to discover how change is possible (Polster & Polster, 1973b). An example of this is demonstrated in the following session between a counselor or therapist and a female client who is, but does not want to be, pregnant (Maples, 1992).

Counselor/Therapist: Show me where you are feeling this anger at being pregnant.
Client: In my heart. (points to heart)
Counselor/Therapist: In your heart, rather than where you're carrying the child.
Client: I think it means that I'm sorry that I don't want to be pregnant, but I know that I should feel wonderful.
Counselor/Therapist: Should.
Client: My husband and my family. They think it's great that we're having a baby.
Counselor/Therapist: And you don't.
Client: Oh, no, I really do. I just don't think I'm ready.
Counselor/Therapist: But you want to be ready.
Client: My goodness! I really do—but I've been living with this "putting off pregnancy" for so long that I guess if I wasn't pregnant now, I could put it off forever.

By enacting her feelings, the client begins to see that things aren't as bad as she thought.

Empty-chair or Two-chair Strategy

An extension of confrontation and enactment—the empty-chair (Perls, 1966) or two-chair (Clarke & Greenberg, 1986; Greenberg, 1980) strategy—allows the client a clearer view of how his behavior may be affecting the behavior of others. Using this strategy, the counselor or therapist asks the client to play one or more roles in addition to his own real self. This is accomplished by providing the necessary number of chairs. The client is then asked to speak the part of each of the people connected with the problem by moving back and forth from chair to chair. For example, in the case of the reluctantly pregnant young woman, she is asked by the counselor or therapist to respond from the perspective of people who may be part of the presenting problem—her husband, a parent, or a friend—by physically moving to the designated chair. This contributes to the client's awareness that she is not isolated, that others are or may be there for her and may see the situation from a different perspective.

Greenberg (1980) has experimented and researched the empty-chair or two-chair technique, turning it into an art used to resolve decisional conflict. His results appear to reinforce Perls's (1966) premise that the empty-chair technique results in an awareness of the disparate aspects of experience and contact among these experience aspects and leads to integration and conflict resolution. Greenberg and Webster (1982) contend in their research that the two-chair intervention is more effective than traditional problem-solving techniques in counseling and psychotherapy. They use the two-chair technique effectively in resolving decisional conflict as it relates process to outcome. The authors believe that the use of the two-chair technique supports the validity of Greenberg's interpersonal conflict resolution model, which uses the empty-chair or two-chair technique effectively.

Dream Work

Instead of using of the Freudian concept of dream interpretation, the Gestaltist uses dreams to help the client in the present, to understand what may be going on in the here and now. Perls (1966) believed that dreams are the projections of the person, that certain parts of a person's dream display certain aspects of that person's life. The client is asked to reenact the dream in the present tense and then asked to play out the parts of the dream as if it were happening now. This allows the counselor or therapist to help the client come into contact with, own, accept responsibility for, or empower himself to interact in a different or similar way with the persons in the dream.

Homework

In the counseling and psychotherapy process, homework allows the counselor or therapist to bring closure to a session and to establish contact with the client for a future session. For the client, homework helps make a commitment to action. According to Polster and Polster (1973b), "homework contributes to the client's insights, possibilities and meanings" (p. 279). It is important that the homework be directly related to the client's presenting problem and be economical enough to be accomplished. For example, in the case of the reluctantly pregnant woman, it would be futile for the counselor or psychotherapist to say, "Next week I want you to come back with 10 reasons that explain why having a baby is great for you." Instead, the counselor or therapist might suggest more economically, "Next week let's explore the pros and cons of your pregnancy. In the meantime, can you reflect on one or two positives or negatives?"

In these intervention strategies, both the counselor and the client are active, involved, and committed. The action takes place in the present. The goal is to heighten the client's awareness so that the entire person of the client is active throughout the process.

SUPPORTING RESEARCH

One of the most valuable compliments that can be paid to a theorist is the extension, stretching, and re-creation of a theory that does not destroy the essence of the theory itself. In Gestaltism, this may be easier to accomplish than in other theories. The main reason is that Gestaltism is evolutionary. As I stated earlier, the theory began in philosophy (Ehrenfels), was extended into psychology (Wertheimer, Koffka, and Köhler), was put into practice in psychotherapy (Perls), and has since evolved into modern counseling and therapy practice (Maples, 1992; Nevis & Harris, 1988; Swanson, 1984). In 1979, Rainwater suggested experiences and activities to enhance self-awareness from a Gestaltist perspective. She encourages the use of a personal journal, the writing of autobiographies, the practice of living in the here and now, and the possibilities of dream work.

The Cleveland School

The Gestalt Institute of Cleveland was founded in 1953 and continues to enhance the work of Gestaltism. The survival of the Cleveland Institute, as compared with the more prominent New York Institute (established in 1952) and Esalen Institute (established in 1958), is credited to the Cleveland Institute leaders' commitment to publish and remain active in the field (Wysong & Rosenfeld, 1982).

Recent research on the Gestalt concept of the here and now suggests that the past and future are important and admissible for discussion. They are, according to Polster and Polster (1973b), used as commentary on or clarification of the present interaction or organization, which is the issue under consideration. Experienced leaders in Gestaltism promulgated in the Cleveland school a refocusing on the importance of the interpersonal dimension between client and counselor or therapist. This was a major digression from Perls's (1973) statement, which contended that anything interpersonal is less important than anything autonomous, a view that stresses the organism's (human being's) response-ability for self and surroundings.

Gestalt Group Counseling or Psychotherapy

In recent years, much has been done to extend Perls's individual approach to group work (Frew, 1984; Gladding, 1992; Yontef & Simkin, 1989). Applying Gestalt principles to families, Nevis and Harris (1988) highlight and reinforce the three constructs of *awareness, contact* and *withdrawal.* For example, in one videotape, the counselor or therapist demonstrates the pattern she has in mind: how the family arranges itself physically, how they talk to each other, and what theme emerges in the counseling process. In this case, the theme involves the family members' abilities to provide clean, clear, positive messages of support for each other.

Maintaining safety for the client while creating enough of an emergency to enable fruitful exploration of uncharted emotions and behaviors is an area studied by Swanson (1984). This aspect of Gestalt counseling or therapy is crucial in the group setting. Greenberg (1980) states that Gestalt counseling skills should be taught to more advanced students, those who have previously mastered the basic intervention skills. These cautions are valuable for the beginning supervisor to remember. In his 1980 article, Greenberg suggests an effective method by which to teach the empty-chair technique.

Research on Gestalt continues into the 90s. Wheeler (1991) made a significant contribution in his *Gestalt Therapy Reconsidered.* Three further recent applications of Gestalt therapy are cited by Alexander and Harman (1988), Enns (1987), and Dolliver (1991). Alexander and Harman used Gestalt therapy as a means of dealing with the surviving classmates of a student who committed suicide. Through the task process of enhancing students' awareness of their feelings, the choices for how they would respond both to Jason's death and their own feelings, and the experiences that would keep them in the present and not the past, the authors contended that the students experienced a more long-lasting and effective healing process. The authors believe, however, that this contention cannot be easily measured beyond self-report. They further caution that using a Gestalt approach with traumatic events such as suicide should be done only with "support of comparable theory, knowledge and skill" (1988, p. 283).

In her 1987 study, Enns suggested a proposal for integrating the Gestalt goals of self-responsibility with a feminist perspective that places value on the web of relationships in women's lives and focuses attention on the "environmental constraints and socialization that affect women's lives" (p. 93). Her use of Gestalt therapy included the empty-chair technique and the exploration of polarities or fantasy journeys.

In a review of Perls's (1980) film interview with Gloria, Dolliver (1991) identifies discrepancies between his description of Gestalt therapeutic processes and his interview behavior. Dolliver had first reviewed the film in 1981 and apparently missed the conclusion that he arrived at in this 1991 review: that "Perls was an unreliable guide to Gloria about her perceptions of the world" (p. 304). However, the author did arrive at a new understanding of Perls's use of Gestalt techniques.

■ ■ ■

THE CASE STUDY OF JOHN: THE GESTALT APPROACH

If John were to seek counseling or psychotherapy from Fritz Perls, he would hear, "You are 'living lopsided'" (Perls, 1973, p. 118). The following quotation from Perls's last work (1973) serves as a good introduction to John's case study:

> To make the whole man of our time come to life and to teach him to use his inborn potential to be, let's say, a leader without being a rebel, having a center instead of living lopsided, is a big mouthful. (p. 118)

Centeredness (wholeness) is a key construct for Gestalt counselors and psychotherapists to facilitate in clients. Perls's view of Gestalt counseling and psychotherapy (1948) also provides a goal for John:

> A treatment is finished when the patient has achieved the basic requirements: a change in outlook, a technique of adequate self-expression and

assimilation, and the ability to extend awareness to the verbal level. He has then reached that state of integration which facilitates its own development and he can safely be left to himself. (p. 585)

Finally, in developing a Gestalt plan of action, the counselor or therapist might keep in mind the nine valuative elements developed by Naranjo (1970, p. 285):

- Live now.
- Live here.
- Stop imagining.
- Stop unnecessary thinking.
- Express rather than manipulate, explain, justify, or judge.
- Give in to the pleasure, just as to unpleasantness and pain.
- Accept no should or ought other than your own.
- Take full responsibility for your actions.
- Surrender to being who you are.

With this background for dealing with John, the Gestalt counselor or therapist might follow the intervention strategies described previously in this chapter.

Breathing and Relaxation

Because John's presenting problem over the years has been his "nervous stomach," "irritable colon," "intestinal difficulties," it is important for the counselor or therapist to be certain that John is at ease, physically and mentally, with himself and with the counselor or therapist. The first session might begin this way:

Counselor/Therapist: I understand, John, that you have had some stomach problems over the years. Please share with me how you feel right now.
John: I'm quite upset. I always thought my problems were in my stomach. It's hard to believe that they might be in my head. That's why the doctor told me to see you, isn't it?
Counselor/Therapist: I believe, John, that the body and mind might work together, not separately. Let's begin getting to know each other by responding to this tape that I'd like to play. It will relax both of us. (plays a tape called *Mountain Stream* [1988])
John: That sounds okay.

Locating Feeling

John's presenting problem appears to be "How do I get rid of this lifelong stomach trouble?" He was referred by the specialist in internal medicine because there was no apparent physical cause for his difficulty. The counselor or therapist, constantly cognizant of the necessity to see John's problem holistically and to bring John to an awareness of the situation, moves to locate the feelings that John may be able to express as a result of the relaxation tape.

Counselor/Therapist: Now, John, how do you feel?

John: I feel more relaxed than when I came in; but because I'm not certain what will happen next, I'm not completely relaxed.

Counselor/Therapist: I'm glad to hear that, John. It suggests that you may be willing to take some responsibility for what happens next without leaving it all to me. Tell me, *where* are you feeling?

John: Where? I'm not sure I know what you mean.

Counselor/Therapist: Feeling means that it's happening somewhere other than your head. That would be thinking. Take a deep breath, relax, and then share where that uncertainty about what is going to happen is occurring in your body.

John: (points to his stomach)

Counselor/Therapist: You're pointing to your stomach. It feels . . . ?

John: Queasy.

Counselor/Therapist: So uncertainty about what is happening causes queasiness?

John: Yes.

Confrontation and Enactment

Counselors and psychotherapists who have been trained to be facilitative and accommodating often do not realize that confrontation can be gracious and necessary (Bates & Johnson, 1988; Maples, 1991). When considering Perls's confrontational nature (1969a, 1969b), the counselor or therapist may confuse the strategy with the person. In this case, confrontation that is necessary to achieve awareness occurs in the manner in which the counselor or therapist is able to deal with it. According to Passons (1975), if confrontation is approached in a challenging yet gentle (gracious) manner, the client may not even realize that he has been confronted.

Counselor/Therapist: John, there seems to be a connection between the manner in which you interact with your children and the way your father behaved with you. For example, you engage sometimes with Michael by playing ball with him—somewhat like when your father took you to athletic events. How do you feel now about my bringing up that comparison?

John: There's no connection! (clenching fists, folding arms, and frowning)

Counselor/Therapist: Interesting. John, I note that you've been quite relaxed since hearing the tape, that you have smiled a great deal, and now I notice some tension in your body. Explain your clenched fists.

John: I feel the same way I did when my father would try to talk to me. My stomach would begin to churn, and I'd close down the conversation and escape to my room and my books. (enactment)

Counselor/Therapist: And how did that escape work?

John: Great! Within a half hour, I'd forget all about what was going on.

Counselor/Therapist: So then and now, whenever tough or challenging things come into your life, either family or work, you still escape. (enactment)

John: Yes, I guess it seems like I've never really grown up. I'm still escaping into books.

Empty Chair

The empty chair is a valuable strategy designed to remove the counselor or therapist from the necessity of prescribing a solution and passing it on to the client. The Gestaltist operates from the premise that the client possesses the necessary components to solve the problem, to achieve awareness, and to accomplish complete wholeness as a person.

Counselor/Therapist: John, it's easy to blame yourself for things that have happened in the past. But our concern is the here and now. I'd like to try something that might help. In front of you in that empty chair is John. With the understanding that you are trying to reach at this point, what might you say to John (yourself) if he were in that chair right now?

The dialogue between the two Johns in each chair goes on for another half hour. Ultimately, John returns to the counselor.

John: It really is quite simple, isn't it? I've always been so afraid of telling people how I really feel, so I've accommodated and then gotten sick over it. My mother and my wife have cooperated, trying to make me feel better, but in the end, I often feel worse.

Dream Work

Several sessions have brought John to a place where he now appears to work fairly effectively, yet one area remains to be explored: the dreams that seem to plague him. The Gestalt counselor or therapist, instead of interpreting the dreams in the Freudian sense, uses the dreams as a "play within a play." John is assigned a role in the dream, and then he reenacts the dream with the counselor or therapist. John may be asked to play several roles in order to make contact with himself through this enactment. Dream work is a valuable strategy to help the client achieve one of the primary goals of Gestalt counseling or psychotherapy: self-awareness.

Homework

Homework is assigned and agreed to at the close of an interaction. It is then used as a beginning strategy for the next session. The Gestalt counselor or therapist assigns homework for two reasons: to involve John in the relationship as an active participant or partner, and to assess John's commitment to solving his problems and his willingness to take response-ability (Perls, 1969a).

Homework may consist of several assignments during the counseling or psychotherapy experience. For example, because of John's difficulty with authority figures (his father, his female boss), he rehearses a discussion with one or both of them. He then comes to the next session and acts out this discussion through the strategy of the empty chair. The counselor or therapist also asks John to keep a written journal throughout the counseling experience, writing in at will or at planned times between sessions. In addition, John works on "staying with feeling," particularly as he interacts with his son, Michael.

Before assigning homework, the counselor or therapist uses the empty-chair technique, encouraging John to reenact discussions between himself and his father, and then himself and Michael. This helps John to see that he is carrying over his father's behaviors and can take response-ability for his own.

The Gestalt intervention strategies used with John are directed towards facilitating the following abilities:

1. John will come to understand the relationship between his mind and body in order to achieve a sense of wholeness.

2. He will take responsibility for what happens in the here and now and for his own actions through a more direct and assertive response-ability. If he responds honestly and assertively in the present, his stomach difficulties, which seem to build up to a crescendo, may be relieved over time.

3. He will move within the polarities of identification and alienation—not always needing to experience the former, and not always experiencing the latter, but achieving a balance between the two.

4. He will become aware of himself in the here and now and remain that way in order to maintain a holistic balance among his mind, his body, and his emotions.

LIMITATIONS

The following limitations apply to Gestalt counseling and therapy:

1. Perls's work, although credited to Gestalt psychology, is seen by many as a potpourri of theories—a little of Freud, a little of Jung (Smith, 1976), and a lot of Wertheimer, Koffka, and Köhler—yet Perls seldom credited them for their contributions.

2. If one views Perls as the model practitioner of Gestalt counseling and psychotherapy, it seems unclear if the therapy or his acting ability is really effecting growth or change in the client (Shepherd, 1975).

3. The holistic nature of Gestalt counseling or psychotherapy flies in the face of today's specialization process in the medical field—an excessive list of symptoms leading to a specialist—although this holism may be a significant asset as well.

4. With only a limited understanding of Perls's application of Gestalt counseling and psychotherapy, the neophyte counselor or therapist can become confused. That is, Perls's early description (1947) of Gestalt therapy as "concentration therapy" and its "end gains" and "means whereby" approaches to neuroses and paranoia can seem unclear (p. 268).

5. Perls's here-and-now orientation could limit the freedom that a counselor or therapist might like to use in exploring the issue, problem, or concern fully. This exploration is often demonstrated by a client's reflecting on childhood experiences and early relationships while in the rapport-building aspect of the client-counselor/therapist relationship.

6. The emphasis suggested by Polster and Polster (1973b) on the counselor or therapist's being exciting, energetic, and full of life can be misleading. A high energy level is valuable for a counselor or therapist, regardless of her theory. But there are many counselors or therapists

who are described by clients and others as cool, calm, collected, or low-key in their demeanor. Yet they are extremely effective in their work, and their clients become self-sufficient and function quite well as a result of the counseling or psychotherapy.

7. The need for balanced mental health in practitioners may appear to be a given. However, because they exert active participation in the helping process, it is important to reiterate that they be well balanced physically, emotionally, and mentally.

8. The use of dream work in Gestalt counseling or psychotherapy is an art. Too often it can be confused by the beginning practitioner with a Freudian interpretation of dreams. The client can often snare the neophyte with the all-encompassing and oft-repeated question "What do you think that means?"

9. Perhaps one of the most cogent limitations related to Gestalt counseling and therapy has little to do with the theory itself, but with Perls. Korb, Garell, and Van De Riet (1987) state the case well: "The intervening years since 1980 have shown that the history and theory of Gestalt therapy is more complex and involves more individuals [than Perls]" (p. viii). The reliance on the workshop format developed during the 60s seemed to lead to a reliance on the man himself as a sort of guru who could answer any problem by demonstrating Gestaltism in a workshop, almost like an actor with an adoring audience. According to Polster (1987), "We, as Gestalt therapists, often became identified with burlesques of our principles with no possibilities of clarification [other] than [what] is available in any spread of rumor" (p. 34).

Despite the potentially serious limitations that may exist in Gestalt counseling or psychotherapy, it is crucial to consider that the holistic nature of Gestaltism is one of its most appealing features. Contrasted with more scientific approaches such as behaviorism (that is, with clearly measurable outcomes), it offers a wide variety of opportunities to take the client on a journey toward effective mental health.

SUMMARY

Gestalt counseling or psychotherapy is simultaneously simple and complex. Its simplicity is inherent in its evolutionary nature, making it easy to understand. The theory began as a philosophy with Ehrenfels's work in 1890 and was expanded into psychology by Wertheimer, Koffka, Köhler, and Lewin.

Fritz Perls is credited with applying the Gestalt theory of counseling and therapy to the mentally ill. His followers in the United States have adapted his approach to work with clients who may not be mentally ill but who are temporarily dysfunctional and need assistance. Gestalt counseling or psychotherapy is complex because the student or practitioner must have mastered basic skills and simple interventions before moving on to such skills as empty chair and dream work. The complexity of Gestalt counseling and psychotherapy is enhanced by its position as an existential theory as well as a directive practice. Because many theorists believe that existentialism is philosophical in nature, they find it difficult to practice it in counseling and psychotherapy (Henle, 1978).

The personhood of the counselor or therapist is extremely important, even crucial, to the effectiveness of the relationship. The Gestaltist needs to be balanced physically, mentally, and emotionally before a therapeutic encounter in order to be fair to the client. However, a major strength of Gestalt counseling and psychotherapy is that the Gestaltist's role is to facilitate the client's response-ability to help solve his own problems (Resnikoff, 1988).

The Cleveland Institute for Gestalt Therapy continues and expands upon the work of Perls. *The Gestalt Journal* is published twice a year, and practitioners are extending and enhancing Gestalt counseling and psychotherapy in creative ways. For example, they have applied the theory to videotaped sessions, which lend themselves well to demonstration of the technique with an experienced practitioner's supervision.

An enjoyable aspect of Perls's work is the fact that it became recognized in the United States when he was more than 70 years old but behaving like a child of the 60s decade, a time that celebrated the free spirit. His attitude in those days serves as an appropriate conclusion to this chapter:

> Junk and chaos come to halt!
> 'Stead of wild confusion.
> Form a meaningful gestalt
> At my life's conclusion. (1969b, p. 11)

REFERENCES

Alexander, J., & Harman, R. (1988). One counselor's intervention in the aftermath of a middle school student's suicide: A case study. *Journal of Counseling and Development, 66*, 283–285.

Bates, M., & Johnson, C. (1988). *Group leadership: A manual for leaders* (2nd ed.). Denver: Love.

Bates, M., Johnson, C., & Blaker, J. (1982). *Group leadership*. Denver: Love.

Cadwallader, E. (1984). Values in Fritz Perls' Gestalt therapy: On the dangers of half-truths. *Counseling and Values 4*, 192–201.

Clarke, K., & Greenberg, L. (1986). Differential effects of the Gestalt two chair intervention and problem-solving in resolving decisional conflict. *Journal of Counseling Psychology, 33*(1), 11–15.

Dolliver, R. (1991). Perls with Gloria reviewed: Gestalt techniques and Perls' practices. *Journal of Counseling and Development, 69,* 299–304.

Dye, A., & Hackney, H. (1975). *Gestalt approaches to counseling.* Boston: Houghton Mifflin.

Ehrenfels, C. (1890). Vierteljahrsschrift fur wissenschaftliche Philosophie. Richard Avenarius (ed). in *Journal of Scientific Philosophy* as quoted in Smith, B. (1988) Foundations of Gestalt Theory. Berlin: Philosophic Verlag Munchen Wien.

Emerson, P., & Smith, E. (1974). Contributions of Gestalt psychology to Gestalt therapy. *Counseling Psychologist, 4,* 8–13.

Enns, C. (1987). Gestalt therapy and feminist therapy: A proposed integration. *Journal of Counseling and Development, 66,* 93–95.

Enright, J. (1970). An introduction to Gestalt techniques. In J. Fagan & I. Shepherd (Eds.), *Gestalt therapy now: Theory, techniques and applications.* Palo Alto, CA: Science & Behavior Books.

Fagan, J., & Shepherd, I. (Eds.). (1970). *Gestalt therapy now: Theory, techniques and applications* (1970). Palo Alto, CA: Science & Behavior Books.

Frew, J. (1984). Enlarging what is not figured in the Gestalt group. *Journal for Specialists in Group Work, 8,* 175–181.

Gazda, G. (1986). *Human relations development: A manual for educators.* Boston: Allyn & Bacon.

Gilliland, B., James, R., & Bowman, J. (1989). *Theories and strategies in counseling and psychotherapy.* Englewood Cliffs, NJ: Prentice-Hall.

Gladding, S. (1992). *Group work: A counseling specialty.* New York: Merrill/Macmillan.

Gloria. (1980). Comments on the interview with Perls. *Psychotherapy: Therapy, Research and Practice, 17,* 140–141.

Greenberg, L. (1980). An intensive analysis of recurring events from the practice of Gestalt therapy. *Psychotherapy: Therapy, Research and Practice, 17,* 143–152.

Greenberg, L., & Webster, M. (1982). Resolving decisional conflict by Gestalt two chair dialogue relating process to outcome. *Journal of Counseling Psychology, 29*(5), 468–477.

Hartmann, G. (1935). *Gestalt psychology: A survey of facts and principles.* New York: Ronald Press.

Henle, M. (Ed.). (1971). *The selected papers of Wolfgang Köhler.* New York: Liveright.

Henle, M. (1978). Gestalt psychology and Gestalt therapy. *Journal of the History of Behavioral Sciences, 14,* 23–32.

Hormann, H. (1967). Wolfgang Köhler zum gedenken. *Psychologische Forschung, 31,* xvii.

Kempler, W. (1973). Gestalt therapy. In R. Corsini (Ed.), *Current psychotherapies* (pp. 251–286). Itasca, IL: Peacock.

Koffka, K. (1935). *Principles of Gestalt psychology.* New York: Harcourt, Brace, & World.

Kogan, G. (1976). The genesis of Gestalt therapy. In C. Hatcher & P. Hililstein (Eds.), *The handbook of Gestalt therapy* (pp. 255–257). New York: Aronson.

Köhler, W. (1927). *The mentality of apes.* New York: Harcourt Brace.

Köhler, W. (1969). *The task of gestalt psychology.* Princeton: Princeton University Press.

Korb, M., Garell, J., & Van De Riet, V. (1987). *Gestalt therapy: Theory and practice* (2nd ed.). New York: Pergamon.

Levitsky, A., & Perls, F. S. (1970). The rules and games of Gestalt therapy. In J. Fagan & I. Shepherd (Eds.), *Gestalt therapy now* (pp. 140–149). Palo Alto, CA: Science & Behavior Books.

Lewin, K. (1935). *A dynamic theory of personality*. New York: McGraw-Hill.

Maples, M. (1991). *Motivation in the workplace*. Workshop presentation for General Motors Acceptance Corporation, Lansing, MI.

Maples, M. (1992). *Gestalt counseling session with pregnant female client* [Videotape]. Reno: University of Nevada, Instructional Media Center.

Mountain Stream. (1988). [Cassette Recording]. Duluth, MN: Whole Person Associates.

Naranjo, C. (1970). Present-centeredness: Techniques, prescriptions and ideals. In C. Hatcher & P. Hililstein (Eds.), *The handbook of Gestalt therapy* (pp. 320–321). New York: Aronson.

Nevis, S., & Harris, V. (1988). *A session of Gestalt therapy with families* [Videotape]. Cleveland: Gestalt Institute of Cleveland.

Passons, W. (1975). *Gestalt approaches in counseling*. New York: Holt, Rinehart, & Winston.

Perls, F. (1947). *Ego, hunger and aggression: The beginning of gestalt therapy*. New York: Random House.

Perls, F. (1948). Theory and technique of personality integration. *American Journal of Psychotherapy, 2*, 563.

Perls, F. (1951). *Gestalt therapy: Excitement and growth in the human personality*. New York: Julian Press.

Perls, F. (1966). *The meaning of Gestalt therapy*. Workshop presented in Atlanta, GA. (cited in Fagan & Shepherd, 1970, pp. 360–362)

Perls, F. (1969a). *Gestalt therapy verbatim*. Lafayette, CA: Real Person Press.

Perls, F. (1969b). *In and out of the garbage pail*. Lafayette, CA: Real Person Press.

Perls, F. (1972). *The Gestalt approach*. Ben Lomand, CA: Science & Behavior Books.

Perls, F. (1973). *The Gestalt approach and eyewitness to therapy*. New York: Bantam.

Perls, F., Hefferline, N., & Goodman, P. (1951). *Gestalt therapy*. New York: Dell.

Polster, E., & Polster, M. (1973a). *Gestalt therapy integrated*. New York: Vintage.

Polster, E., & Polster, M. (1973b). *Gestalt therapy integrated: Contours of theory and practice*. New York: Brunner/Mazel.

Polster, M. (1987). Gestalt therapy: Evolution and application. In J. K. Zeig (Ed.), *The evolution of psychotherapy*. New York: Brunner/Mazel.

Rainwater, J. (1979). *You're in charge: A guide to becoming your own therapist*. Los Angeles: Guild of Tutors Press.

Resnikoff, J. (1988). Gestalt therapy revisited. *Journal of Counseling Psychology, 36*(3), 260–269.

Rock, I., & Palmer, S. (1990). *The legacy of Gestalt psychology*. Springfield, IL: Charles C Thomas.

Shepherd, M. (1975). *Fritz*. New York: Saturday Review Press.

Simkin, J. (1975). An introduction to Gestalt therapy. In F. Stephenson (Ed.), *Gestalt therapy primer* (pp. 9–10). Springfield, IL: Charles C Thomas.

Smith, E. (1976). *The growing edge of Gestalt therapy*. New York: Brunner/Mazel.

Swanson, J. (1984). *Gestalt counseling with an adult client* [Videotape]. Corvallis: Oregon State University, Communications Media Productions.

Wallen, G. (1970). Gestalt therapy and Gestalt psychology. In J. Fagan & I. Shepherd (Eds.), *Gestalt therapy now: Theory, tech-*

niques and applications (pp. 116–117). Palo Alto, CA: Science & Behavior Books.

Wertheimer, M. (1912). *Perception of apparent movement*. New York: Harper.

Wheeler, G. (1991). *Gestalt reconsidered: A new approach to contact and resistance*. New York: Gardner.

Wysong, J., & Rosenfeld, E. (1982). *An oral history of Gestalt therapy*. Highland, NY: The Gestalt Journal Press.

Yontef, G. (1981). *Gestalt therapy: Past, present and future*. Paper presented at the International Council of Psychologists conference, London.

Yontef, G., & Simkin, J. (1989). Gestalt therapy. In R. Corsini & D. Wedding (Eds.), *Current psychotherapies* (4th ed.) (pp. 323–361). Itasca, IL: Peacock.

Zinker, J. (1978). *Creative process in Gestalt therapy*. New York: Vintage.

CHAPTER ELEVEN

Transactional Analysis Theory

John M. Poidevant
Rockdale County Schools, Conyers, Georgia

Henry A. Lewis
University of North Carolina—Greensboro

Transactional analysis is a theory of personality that allows counselors and therapists to view clients within a cognitive, emotional, and behavioral framework. The purpose of this chapter is to consider the development of transactional analysis at both theoretical and practical levels. To accomplish this goal, we will provide a brief biographical sketch of Eric Berne, the founder of transactional analysis (TA), and then organize the remainder of the chapter around seven sections: the history of transactional analysis, human nature, major constructs, the process of change, intervention strategies, supporting research, and a case study with a diagnosis and treatment plan.

Eric Berne (1910–1970) was born in Montreal, Canada. His father was a physician who died when Berne was nine years old, and the boy was raised by his mother. Like his father, Berne became a physician. In 1935 he received his degree from McGill University and then moved to the United States to begin a psychiatric residency. During this time, he became very interested in the neurosurgical research of Wilder Penfield, whose experiments with electrical stimulation of certain parts of the brain led him to believe that patients were able to reexperience previous thoughts and feelings in a vivid manner (Penfield & Roberts, 1959). Such findings served as an initial catalyst for Berne's later model, which was based on the three ego states of parent, adult, and child.

In 1941, Berne began training as a psychoanalyst, but he interrupted this training to serve in the army medical corps as a psychiatrist during World War II. Upon release from the army in 1946, he continued his psychiatric training under Erik Erikson, began a private practice, and in 1947 published his first book, *The Mind in Action*, which was later revised in 1957 as *A Layman's Guide to Psychiatry and Psychoanalysis*.

Other publications followed, including a series of professional journal articles that addressed the nature of intuition, work that was the basis of the ego-state theory (parent-adult-child) of personality. Berne argued that traditional psychoanalytic theory was too complex for the ordinary layperson, creating an inequality in the therapeutic relationship.

Berne's first work outlining this ego-state theory was *The Nature of Intuition*, which was published in 1949. His theory was further defined by his clinical experience with a variety of patients with psychological maladies. Most noteworthy in this respect was his work with a patient who proclaimed that he was "not a lawyer but just a little boy" during one of his sessions.

At age 46, Berne was rejected for membership in the Psychoanalytic Institute, which gave him further impetus to develop a new approach to psychotherapy using terminology that both the counselor/therapist and patient could understand, thus allowing equal participation in the therapeutic process. Berne continued to develop TA theory and eventually began practicing TA with his patients. In 1961 he published his first book devoted entirely to TA, *Transactional Analysis in Psychotherapy*. At this point in his career, he began to develop a following of clinicians. Clinical seminars in his hometown of San Francisco were heavily attended. In 1964, *Games People Play* became a best-seller, and the ideas and language of TA began to capture a larger audience.

One of the major components of TA is the *script*, an unconscious life plan made in early childhood to live a life in a predetermined manner based on early messages from emotionally significant others (usually parents). In his book *Scripts People Live*, Steiner (1971) suggests that Berne's life was influenced by his own life script, which called for an early death. Steiner (1971) further believed Berne's death was the result of conflicting parental messages about loving and accepting others' love and being an independent and detached individual. Like his parents, Berne was committed to helping others and suspicious of any physician more interested in financial gain. When not engaged in private practice with patients, he wrote books about his works. Because Berne was a shy person, he allowed little time for fun and intimacy with others. Like his mother, he died of coronary heart failure at age 60.

Before his death in 1970, Berne published eight books and 64 articles. The transactional analysis model is still widely used and is the focus of an international organization with more than 10,000 members.

HISTORY

Most proponents of TA suggest that the theory has gone through four separate and distinct phases (Dusay, 1977). The first phase, from 1955–1962, can be conceptualized as the discovery and delineation of ego states. Ego states are defined as overt sources of behavior, phenomenological in nature, that are based on one's early life experiences. Berne developed his notion of states as a result, in part, of his work with mentally ill patients in a state psychiatric hospital. During this period, Berne observed patients with a variety of disorders and theorized that people behaved differently according to their unique ways of thinking, behaving, and feeling. From these experiences Berne's theory of three distinct ego states emerged, including the parent, adult, and child. He considered each ego state to be different, conscious, and observable. Berne's view of ego states differs from Freud's psychoanalytic theory because ego states are conscious and observable rather than unconscious and not observable.

The second phase of Berne's theory (from 1962–1966) involved transactions and games. This phase centered on the transactions that occur between individuals. Berne defined a transaction as a system of communication that consists of a stimulus and response between two persons' ego states. Likewise, he defined games as a series of transactions that often lead to a predictable outcome. His research and writing in this area led to the publication of *Games People Play* (1964), arguably his most significant contribution to the helping professions.

Script analysis (1966–1970) is the third phase of transactional analysis. Berne (1972) defined a script as "a life plan based on a decision made in childhood, reinforced by the parents, justified by subsequent events, and culminating in a chosen alternative" (p. 162). Thus, a person's script is analogous to a plan for life, complete with personal and professional goals. By examining a client's script, Berne believed it was possible to discern a clearer picture of the past, present, and future of the individual.

Since Berne's death in 1970, the status of TA has remained relatively stable, although it has been refined. For example, changes occurred to help make TA more practical and helpful for practicing professionals. These included incorporating Gestalt and psychodrama techniques into TA. Such developments allowed TA to gain more widespread popularity, including applications in corporate settings with major airlines and utility companies.

HUMAN NATURE: A DEVELOPMENTAL PERSPECTIVE

Transactional analysis does not posit a set of rigid developmental stages that all individuals' personalities proceed through in a set manner. According to TA theory, the personality is divided into three ego states: parent, adult, and child. We will explain development of the personality from a TA perspective using Klein's (1980) eight-stage model of personality development.

Stage 1: Birth to Age 1

In an infant, the only part of the personality that is intact is the *natural child*, an egocentric being who is lovable, honest, spontaneous, and dependent. During the first six months of life parents provide strong strokes to meet the basic physiological and emotional needs of the child. After about six months of age, another ego state starts to emerge, which is known as the *adult in the child* or the *little professor*. As a precursor to the adult ego state, the little professor prompts the child to explore the environment actively. Such activity serves as the basis for creating a healthy, inquisitive, and intuitive child.

Stage 2: Age 1 to Age 3

During this phase the child becomes increasingly interested in the environment, particularly in social interactions. At the same time, parents are required to impose restrictions on behavior. These restrictions serve as a catalyst for the development of other components of the personality, such as the *parent* and *adult* states, which remain malleable until about age six. Basic social skills are developed during this phase, such as the use of "please" and "thank you." More important, (at least from the parents' perspective!), children learn to meet their needs through methods other than tantrums. During this phase of development, often known as the "terrible twos," children need positive strokes to ensure healthy development of their emerging personality.

Stage 3: Age 3 to Age 6

Parental stroking remains vital for the development of the adult and parent ego states. The parent ego state further develops by the child's exposure to values and morals of significant others in the child's life. The adult ego state continues to develop as the child acquires basic life skills such as bathing, toileting, table manners, and so on.

Stage 4: Age 6

By the time a child reaches age six, the parent, adult, and child ego states are developed and ready for use. Most TA theorists suggest that the basic personality structure of the child is strongly developed by age six. For example, the parent ego state of the six year old may say, "My dad knows more than anybody else." The adult state may ask, "Why is the grass green?" The compliant child stage may say, "Yes, sir."

Stage 5: Age 6 to Age 12

Stage 5 is characterized by disproportionate development of the adult ego state because education exposes children to academic and social skills that benefit the objective and nonfeeling adult ego state. In fact, the development of the adult state outpaces development of other ego states by a considerable margin. The child tends to deal with the world in a matter-of-fact manner that may serve as a pleasant reprieve for parents before the onset of puberty. Theorists suggest that this stage of development is when children are most capable of dealing with traumatic events such as the death of grandparents or the divorce of their own parents.

Stage 6: Age 13 to Age 16

The onset of puberty creates a surge of anxiety about sexual development that affects the child ego state. Conflict also occurs with other ego states, most notably the parent state with its emphasis on values and morality. For example, parents are often confused during this stage, finding it difficult to temper their own parent states and perhaps exhibiting judgmental and harsh attitudes toward their children. During this stage, parents attempt to instill a strong sense of responsibility in their children. They may say, "You may take the car tonight, but you must be home by 11:00 P.M." Such efforts usually result in negative reactions from the child, while parents are held accountable for the child's difficulties. Concurrently, the rapid development of the child ego state serves as a catalyst for rebellious behavior that results in much blame and guilt on the part of parents and children.

Stage 7: Late Adolescence

During this stage the personality becomes more balanced than it was in stage 6. The adult ego state has developed through the educational process and is now able to temper the needs of the child state. The collaboration of ego states also occurs: the adult, parent, and child states work in concert in order to meet the needs of specific ego states or the entire personality.

Stage 8: Maturity

The personality is now balanced, and the individual assumes a mature stance toward life. The various ego states remain in constant interaction yet with a greater sense of purpose and function.

MAJOR CONSTRUCTS

Counselors and therapists who wish to use transactional analysis in therapeutic settings need to be knowledgeable of the key components of the theory. In this section, the major constructs of TA are discussed under the following headings: structural analysis, an explanation of ego-state theory; transactional analysis proper, the analysis of what people do and say to one another; game analysis, including stamp collecting and racket feelings; script analysis, or the individual's plan to live life in a predetermined manner based on early parental messages; and basic life positions, the attitudes and behaviors of individuals stemming from previous transactions and life scripts.

Structural Analysis

Like many other theories, transactional analysis has its roots in Freud's psychoanalytic theory. Although some commonality exists, TA is comprised of unique constructs that include the three ego states of parent, adult, and child (see figure 11.1).

Unlike Freud's theory, which suggests that the id, ego, and superego are largely driven by unconscious forces, Berne's three ego states are viewed as conscious or preconscious components of the personality. Each of the three ego states—parent, adult, and child (P-A-C)—has a distinct source of behavior that is active, dynamic, and observable. Klein (1980) offered the following explanation:

> All of us in our waking lives are in one or another of three possible ego states. These are not roles but different real parts of our being. Nor are they synonyms or near synonyms for the psychoanalytic Superego, Ego and Id, which are concepts that refer to forces in the Unconscious. Ego states, by contrast with these concepts, are all contained within the [psychoanalytic] Ego. (p. 11)

The parent state is derived primarily from external influences, including parents and parentlike figures from childhood such as grandparents and teachers. It is not uncommon for clients to suggest that they have become their parents, a notion that may have both negative and positive connotations. The parent state is instilled at an early age and serves as a major component of the personality. It also may assume a nurturing or critical role, depending on the situation; thus, it is split into two entities. The nurturing parent state comforts, praises, and helps. In contrast, the critical parent state disapproves, admonishes, and advises when neces-

FIGURE 11.1
The ego state model

sary. In essence, the parent state tends to control and act with authority while also providing respect and love for the child state (see figure 11.2).

The adult state is the most objective of the three ego states, and it operates in a logical and nonemotional manner. It is not age-related except during early childhood, when the adult and parent states are not yet fully developed. It is objective and reality oriented and tends to process information and produce the best solution to any given situation. The adult is functional and rational, serving the other ego states by appraising and evaluating the reality of a situation.

The child state is the first part of the personality to develop and is most concerned with the affective state of the individual. The need for freedom and spontaneity are rooted in the child state of the individual. It

FIGURE 11.2
Analysis of ego states

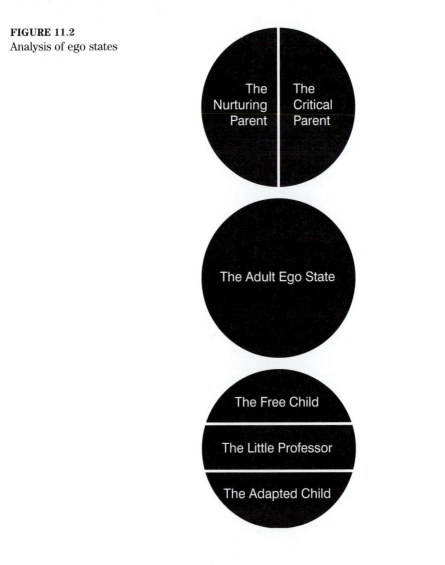

is characterized as impulsive, spontaneous, and fun-loving. This state may also be differentiated into two parts: free ("little professor") and adapted. The free child state is curious, playful, eager, intuitive, and spontaneous. In contrast, the adapted child state is compliant, conforming, compromising, easy to get along with, and occasionally rebellious.

Thompson and Rudolph (1992) suggested that healthy functioning persons are able to balance their ego states effectively and choose the state most amenable to the situation. Persons who are unable to maintain a balance may experience an array of problems. For example, the constant parent may prove boring to others, and the constant child may not be mature enough to handle the difficulties of everyday life.

Transactional Analysis Proper

TA proper is characterized as the communications patterns that occur between individuals. Whenever two or more people encounter one another, sooner or later one of them will speak or give some indication of acknowledging the presence of the other. This is called a *transactional stimulus*. Another person will do or say something that in some way is related to this stimulus. This is called a *transactional response*. The unit of social interaction, transactional stimulus, and transactional response is called a *transaction*. Simple transactional analysis is concerned with the analysis of transactions between people. The P-A-C model is used in the analysis of transactions.

In TA there are three different types of transactions: complementary, crossed, and ulterior:

1. *Complementary transaction*:   A complementary transaction is one in which the lines (vectors) of communication are parallel. In other words, the response comes from the same ego state as the stimulus, or the ego state that is addressed is the one that responds. Figure 11.3 shows a complementary transaction from the adult ego states.

   David: Where is my belt?
   Laura: It is in the closet.

2. *Crossed transaction*:   A crossed transaction is one in which the lines (vectors) of communication are crossed. In other words, the stimulus comes from one ego state and the response from another ego state, or the ego state that is addressed is not the one that responds. Figure 11.4A shows a crossed transaction using the adult and child ego states. Figure 11.4B shows a crossed transaction using the parent and adult ego states.

FIGURE 11.3
Complementary transactions
(parent-parent; adult-adult)

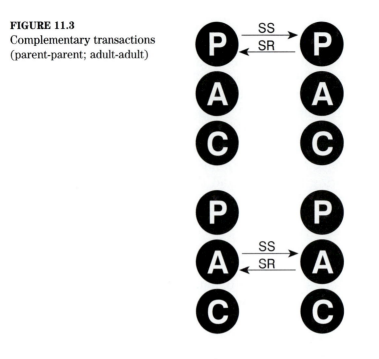

> *David:*   (matter of factly) Have you seen my belt?
> *Laura:*   (whining) Can't you see I'm getting ready to go to work?
> *David:*   (angrily) Where is that report I asked you to do?
> *Laura:*   (matter of factly) I put it on your desk.

3. *Ulterior transaction:*   An ulterior transaction is one in which two messages (or levels of conversation) take place at the same time. One message, the social level (SS and SR) of the conversation, is the audible conversation heard by the parties involved in the communication. The other message, the psychological level (PS and PR) of the conversation, is the real or hidden meaning in the conversation. In other words, in an ulterior transaction, the parties in the communication are saying one thing, but they really mean something else.

For example, David and Laura go to a party, leaving their children with a 14-year-old baby-sitter. At the party David and Laura find themselves very bored and figure out an excuse to leave. The host of the party approaches them, at which time David and Laura have the following conversation: (see figure 11.5A):

SS: Sweetheart, I think we'd better go home and relieve the baby-sitter. (parent to parent on the social level)

SR: Yes, I did tell her mother that we would have her home before 10:00 P.M. (parent to parent on the social level)

FIGURE 11.4
(A) Crossed transactions (adult-adult; child-parent); (B) Crossed transactions (parent-child; adult-adult)

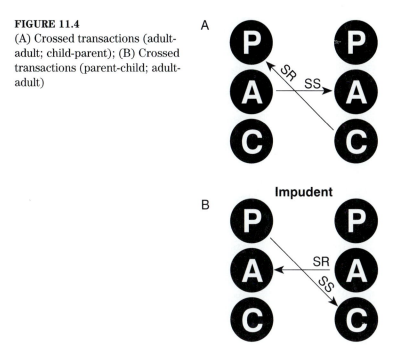

PS: This party is really boring. Let's get out of here. (child to child on the psychological level)

PR: Yeah, let's get out of here. It's no fun. (child to child on the psychological level)

Here's another example. After a nice evening of dinner and the theater, a young man asks his date if she would like to come over to his apartment for a social drink (see figure 11.5B):

SS: I know it's late, but to top off a perfect evening, would you like to come over to my place for a glass of wine? (adult to adult on the social level)

SR: Sounds like a nice idea. (adult to adult on the social level)

PS: I'm interested in getting to know you better. (child to child on the psychological level)

PR: I'm really interested in you. (child to child on the psychological level)

Strokes are an integral part of all transactions and are defined as a unit of recognition to the person. There are generally three types of strokes: physical, verbal, and nonverbal. Physical strokes include touching, whereas verbal strokes are received through oral communication. Nonverbal strokes occur through the subtleties of body language. All strokes may be positive, negative, conditional, or unconditional. Strokes are given and received in order to gain attention and recognition. In each family, members learn the importance of giving and receiving strokes, and

FIGURE 11.5
(A) Ulterior transaction
(social level: parent-parent;
psychological level: child-child);
(B) Ulterior transaction (social
level: adult-adult; psychological
level: child-child)

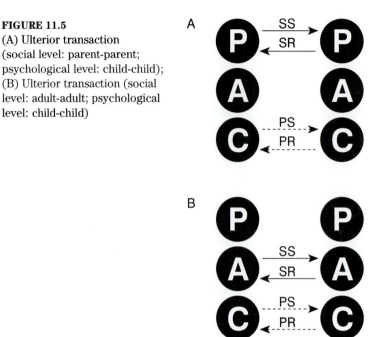

these interactions serve to shape the personality. Berne (1964) emphasized the importance of giving and receiving strokes early in life. Positive
strokes are viewed as better than negative ones, but negative strokes are
seen as better than no strokes.

Game Analysis

Games are viewed as ongoing transactions, a way to support early decisions made in life, and are part of the early life script. Games often end
with negative feelings for at least one person, and they may intentionally
prevent intimacy. For example, players transact on an open (overt) level
and, at the same time, transmit a hidden agenda (covert) or ulterior
transaction. One type is the "poor me" or martyr game. For example, a
secretary may accept more responsibility than he can handle (overt
behavior) and complain about being overworked (covert behavior).
Another example is the wooden leg game. In this game, clients feign a disability as a way of avoiding work or responsibility. Children often play this
game with parents as a means of avoiding age-appropriate tasks or
chores.

Karpman's (1968) drama triangle illustrates the ways in which clients
play games (see figure 11.6).

FIGURE 11.6
The drama triangle

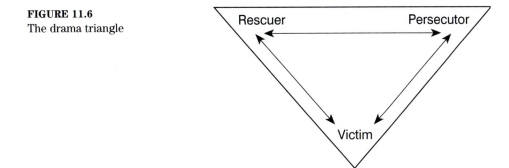

Each corner of the triangle contains a distinct role of persecutor, victim, and rescuer. For example, Jim may be doing poorly in school, which essentially prompts his playing the "kick me" game. His father is quick to condemn Jim for his grade, thereby prompting his mother to rescue him. When roles change—that is, when Jim tells his mother to back off—each participant assumes a new role and the cycle continues.

Berne (1964) differentiated by degree the seriousness of game play. First-degree games are physically safe with most action being verbal. Second degree-games are more likely to be physical and include altercations. Third-degree games are of a very serious nature and may include major life adjustments or even lethal consequences.

Counselors and therapists need to be cognizant of the games and rackets played by clients. Games are viewed as ongoing transactions, a way to support early decisions made in life that become part of the early life script. Games often end with negative feelings for at least one person, and counselors and therapists need to assess the way in which games may adversely affect their clients. These games may include "I'm only trying to help you"; "yes, but"; and "look what you made me do." Counselors and therapists need to actively challenge clients to examine and take responsibility for games being played.

Rackets may be defined as the emotional aftermath of games. Not surprisingly, rackets are often carried with us from an early age as a result of games learned from our parents. Such rackets are built into our life script. Sample rackets include the anxiety racket, the depression racket, and the suicide racket. Rackets are typically used over and over again, regardless of their appropriateness.

James and Jongeward (1971) equated rackets with *stamp collecting*, in which clients save enough negative experiences until it is possible to cash them in on a psychological payoff such as a nervous breakdown, divorce, or worse. Likewise, individuals are also able to collect positive stamps in order to justify relaxation and other leisure pursuits.

Script Analysis

An individual's life script is influenced by messages known as injunctions that are received from the child ego state of parents. Sample injunctions include messages such as "don't want," "don't think," "don't do well," and "don't be close." Such injunctions may lead to individuals' early decisions aimed at receiving strokes, which ultimately determine the individuals' perception of themselves as OK or not OK.

Life scripts are analogous to a drama stemming from an early life plot. The life script serves as a personal gyrocompass that guides the person on both a conscious and unconscious level. Berne suggested that people are born OK but that negative life scripts learned as a child may cause problems in the future. For example, a child is physically abused at an early age and learns that severe physical beatings are acceptable to bring about changes in behavior. When the child eventually becomes a parent, the abuse cycle continues and more negative life scripts are formed.

Basic Life Positions

The four basic life positions serve as a cornerstone of TA. By exploring previous transactions and life scripts, clients learn the importance of their current life positions. The four life positions (see figure 11.7) are defined by Harris (1967) as follows:

I'm OK–You're OK.   This is the healthiest of the four life positions. Persons with this life position tend to have healthy development of parent, adult, and child ego states, which leads to appropriate expectations of themselves and others. Problems are solved in a constructive manner, and personal relationships are valued and nurtured. This life position is indicative of the "winner," the person who is able to function effectively on personal and professional levels.

I'm OK–You're Not OK.   The client with this life position will tend to exercise an external locus of control and play the role of victim. Children who are physically, sexually, or emotionally abused tend to adopt this life position. Criminals often accept this life position and believe that they are OK and the rest of the world has the problem. Clients with more serious psychopathological disorders such as antisocial personality disorders may also adopt this life position.

I'm Not OK–You're OK.   Persons who adopt this life script typically feel powerless, insecure, and depressed. Other persons may choose to with-

FIGURE 11.7
The four life positions

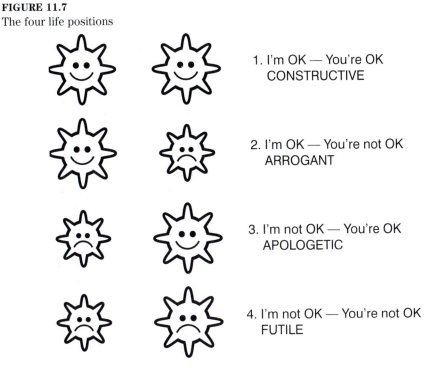

1. I'm OK — You're OK
   CONSTRUCTIVE

2. I'm OK — You're not OK
   ARROGANT

3. I'm not OK — You're OK
   APOLOGETIC

4. I'm not OK — You're not OK
   FUTILE

draw and limit social opportunities with others. Children often express this life position as they search for their own identity. Adults with this life position may place too much reliance on the adapted child of the personality and yearn for acceptance.

I'm Not OK–You're Not OK.   Clients who adopt this life position tend to be suspicious and insecure in their personal relationships. As the most negative of life positions, clients may exhibit suicidal or homicidal urges as a way of coping with ongoing failures. A conflict between the parent and child ego states occurs, and the adult state is largely excluded. Counselors find clients with this life position to be resistant to effective change.

THE PROCESS OF CHANGE

A plethora of factors are used by counselors and therapists to initiate change in their clients. In the context of TA, change is defined as helping clients gain new insights to effect positive changes in affect, cognition, and behavior. To accomplish this, counselors and therapists may initiate change in their clients through the use of simple vocabulary and contracting. Such techniques are instrumental in assisting clients in assuming autonomy and responsibility in their lives.

Vocabulary of TA

A strength of the TA model is that its concepts are easily conveyed using common terminology. Key concepts such as parent, adult, and child states; strokes; scripts; and games are readily understood by adults, adolescents, and children. This facilitates the helping process because counselors and therapists need not spend time explaining more complex theoretical concepts. The majority of the effort and time spent in counseling and psychotherapy is geared toward assuming responsibility and gaining autonomy. Although the simplistic nature of the vocabulary belies a more complex overall structure, counselors and therapists need to be wary of allowing the helping process to appear too gimmicky. Instead, they need to emphasize the many practical and useful techniques associated with the TA.

The Use of Contracts

The use of contracts is one of the ways in which change is initiated within a TA framework. Like reality therapy, transactional analysis emphasizes the use of contracts to bring about effective change with clients. Such an approach serves as a road map, a specific and concrete agreement between counselor or therapist and client to expedite the therapeutic process by mutually involving both parties. The following four guidelines for TA treatment contracts are offered by Dusay and Dusay (1979):

1. *Mutual assent*:   Both client and counselor or therapist agree to the goals and objectives of therapy, an agreement ideally made between the adult ego states of the two parties. Nevertheless, games are often played during this phase, and counselors and therapists need to assess the types of transactions that occur between ego states from the onset of the counseling or psychotherapy relationship.

2. *Competency*:   An effective TA counselor or therapist needs to provide only those services that can be dispensed in the realm of a professional helping relationship. Concomitantly, it is important that the client also be made cognizant of the realistic nature of outcomes associated with therapy. Counselors and therapists should be viewed by clients as facilitators for change, not as persons with the ability to prescribe changes geared toward improvement.

3. *Legal object*:   The contract should have an objective that both parties agree to as a common goal. The goal must be reasonable and within the ethical limits of the relationship.

4. *Consideration*:   A foundation of the TA approach is that it actively encourages clients to participate in the counseling and psychotherapy process. Counselors should encourage their clients to commit to the process through whatever means are feasible. For example, clients should pay an appropriate fee when possible or contribute some other form of compensation if fees are not required in the setting.

The contractual agreements between counselor or therapist and client serve to facilitate growth and commitment to the helping relationship and bring about change on the part of the client.

INTERVENTION STRATEGIES

One of the significant advantages of using transactional analysis is that it provides the professional counselor or therapist with many therapeutic strategies to assist clients. The theory and its related techniques are easy to understand and apply in both individual and group settings. The intervention strategies that follow represent some of the ways in which counselors or therapists can assist clients using the principles of TA and related therapeutic applications.

There are three closely aligned schools of thought connected to the practice of transactional analysis. These include reparenting, redecision therapy, and the Berneian approach. Reparenting was developed by Schiff (1969) and others primarily for severely disturbed and psychotic patients. Redecision therapy was developed by Robert and Mary Goulding (1979), and it incorporates the use of Gestalt techniques with TA. The Berneian or pure TA approach includes the use of structural analysis, game analysis, life-script analysis, and other related techniques. Each of the schools will be delineated, and strategies specific to each will be explained. Other noteworthy intervention strategies associated with TA include family counseling, family modeling, analysis of rituals and pastimes, analysis of games and rackets, and the use of egograms. They will also be discussed in this section.

Reparenting

One of the more controversial approaches related to the use of TA is reparenting (Schiff, 1969). Essentially, the approach involves having clients regress to their childhood and reexperience key developmental events. A client receives positive reparenting from the counselor or therapist who serves as a surrogate parent. This is typically done in a residential setting and may require a long-term commitment. Critics charge that reparenting is not effective and requires an excessive time commitment. Counselors and therapists should exercise caution when using this strategy with clients.

Redecision Therapy

Goulding and Goulding (1979) integrated the use of Gestalt techniques into the theoretical framework of TA. Such an integration gave TA practitioners a combination of affective and cognitive strategies to provide a strong catalyst for clients to change.

The basic premise of redecision therapy is that early life decisions are reversible if clients are able to reexperience those decisions both intellectually and emotionally. Thus, the practitioner assists the client in returning to a childhood state and reexperiencing early life scenes. He serves as a catalyst for the client to develop new, healthier decisions about living. Once new decisions are made in the therapy sessions, the counselor or therapist and the client work jointly to implement new beliefs and actions into the client's everyday existence. Such strategies permit the client to achieve more autonomy and excitement in his life (Goulding, 1987).

The Berneian Approach

Berne's traditional TA model includes four intervention strategies for counselors and therapists to consider. These include structural analysis, transactional analysis, game analysis, and life-script analysis. Although these strategies were previously mentioned in the constructs section, our focus now shifts to the therapeutic application of the traditional Berneian approach.

First, structural analysis is a means by which clients become aware of their parent, adult, and child ego states. Clients are taught how to identify and change their ego states in order to realize more effective ways of behaving. By recognizing faulty behavior and its related ego states, clients are more readily able to change behavior.

Berne offered two types of problems associated with the way personalities develop. *Exclusion* is best characterized as a rigidly held belief system or an overreliance on a specific ego state. Generally, most people have an ebb and flow between ego states. When movement between these states is inhibited, exclusion occurs. Persons may focus on one ego state exclusively, such as the constant parent who becomes a workaholic. A constant adult can be described as an overly objective, nonfeeling, mechanized person who is hardly the life of the party. A constant child is the type of person who is reluctant to assume responsibility for her actions, is dependent on others, and, at an extreme level, may exhibit sociopathic tendencies.

When parts of two ego states become mixed, *contamination* has occurred. All three ego states are equally likely to contaminate another. For example, when a person declares that he only wishes to work on a seasonal basis in order to pursue recreational activities, the child has most likely contaminated the adult ego state. Counselors and therapists can address this problem by the use of boundary work—the differentiation of each of the respective ego states. By actively exploring the degree of influence of each of the ego states, counselors and therapists can help clients achieve a more balanced personality.

The transactions between persons result in what Berne called games (1961). Whenever two persons communicate, a transaction occurs. A transaction may take one of three different forms. Complementary transactions occur when a stimulus and a response are made between the same two ego states. Crossed transactions occur when the stimulus is made from one ego state and the response comes from another. For example, a man who tells his wife that he is going body surfing at the beach (child) and is rebuffed by her for not acting his age (parent) is an example of a crossed transaction. The child ego state of the man is not pleased with the parent ego state response from his wife.

Ulterior motives are more complicated and may involve more than one message or ego state. The student who requests additional help after class (adult ego) may also wish to spend more time with the teacher for personal reasons (child ego). Such messages contain an explicit as well as an implicit message. The explicit message may be disguised as a socially appropriate transaction whereas the implicit message may have a more devious intent. Regardless, counselors and therapists need to assist their clients in recognizing ego state behaviors and, more important, the way in which transactions occur between ego states.

A life-script analysis evaluation permits counselors and therapists to assess the impact of early life experiences on the client's here and now. Life patterns are often established at an early age, and the life process to date can be better understood if counselors and therapists are able to analyze the client's script.

The process of redecision is largely dependent on the ability to discern the client's life script accurately and encourage redecision. Through emotional awareness and rational decision making, it is possible to redecide healthier ways of living; and script evaluation serves as the first step in this process.

Family Counseling and Psychotherapy

The principles and techniques of TA are especially compatible with family counseling or therapy. The combination of affective and cognitive strategies enable those who work with families to address problems using a number of practical strategies associated with TA.

McClendon (1977) created a three-step family counseling and psychotherapy model based on TA principles. In stage 1, the counselor or therapist assesses the dynamics of the family from a systemic perspective. Each member of the family is given an opportunity to share how he may be impacting the family structure. Needed changes are identified, and contracts are made with each of the family members. Counselors and therapists avoid focusing on the problems of just one person, the "identified patient." Instead, they encourage each family member to speak directly with the others and to state explicitly what she wants from the family structure.

In stage 2, the counselor or therapist works with each of the members in the context of the family structure. Counselors or therapists usually begin this process with the person who wields control or power within the family structure. For example, fathers with rigid rules may be a good place to start the helping process. The counselor or therapist assists the father in exploring early life decisions, life scripts, and injunctions so that the other family members are able to see how the father's early life experiences influenced his actions in the current family structure. During stage 2, counselors and therapists receive information that may necessitate a return to stage 1 to explore with various family members details, events, and circumstances that continue to influence family structure.

In stage 3, counselors and therapists work toward reintegration of the family structure. This is accomplished through remediation of difficulties associated with each family member's life scripts, rackets, and early injunctions. The intent is to set the groundwork for stage 4, where the goal of the counselor or therapist is to instill a more harmonious family structure.

In stage 4, counselors and therapists attempt to ensure that individual family members have their needs met while simultaneously providing a harmonious family structure. The goal of stage 4 is to instill a sense of interdependence so that family members are able to work together for self and group improvement.

Family Modeling

This group technique is a form of structural analysis that enables clients to re-create past events using other group members. The re-creation serves as a catalyst for insight as the client reexperiences the specific situation. The counselor or therapist can then assist the client and other group members to discuss and evaluate what they have just experienced. This type of approach is particularly useful for clients who are troubled by a specific ego state.

Analysis of Rituals and Pastimes

The way in which clients choose to spend time is an important therapeutic consideration. The script of the client serves as a guide for the pursuit of strokes. Clients who choose to spend time engaged in ritualistic behaviors and pastimes are more likely to suffer from stroke deprivation. Such behavior may lead to depression, boredom, loneliness, and apathy.

Egograms: Shifting the Energy

The shifting of energy between ego states is another way in which counselors or therapists can bring about change with clients. Generally, clients have differing amounts of energy in each of their three ego states (see figure 11.8). This state of disequilibrium initiates a need by clients to strengthen weaker ego states (Dusay & Dusay, 1979). Counselors and therapists can assist clients in creating egograms as graphic illustrations

FIGURE 11.8
The egogram

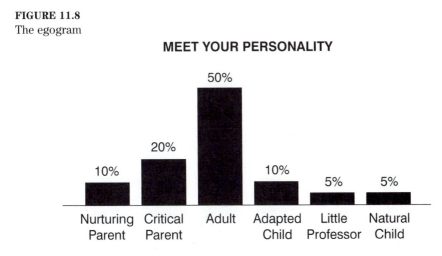

of their ego. For example, a client who is harsh and demeaning toward his kids may need to reduce his critical parent state and enhance his nurturing parent state. This may be accomplished by using a variety of therapeutic interventions including script evaluation, redecision counseling, family modeling, and game analysis.

SUPPORTING RESEARCH

This section discusses current research that forms the basis for continued support and refinement of TA. We emphasize the settings and populations where TA has been effective, including wellness and family/parenting practices.

Wellness

Allen and Allen (1989) found that deprivation of strokes was linked to depression, poor health, and the failure of individuals to live to full potential. Likewise, Horwitz (1982) found a positive relationship between stroking and overall wellness. Subjects who reported receiving adequate positive strokes had fewer back pains and headaches and a more positive affective state. The authors also proposed further study into the physiological effects of strokes on the well-being of individuals.

Hazell (1989) blended TA with interventions based on rational-emotive therapy to create an effective stress reduction model. Cognitive self-talk strategies were blended with TA-based interventions such as game analysis in order to reduce stress, and positive results were indicated. Furthermore, Douglas (1986) examined adolescent suicide from a TA perspective and suggested that suicides are attempts to gain strokes from others and that parent-child relationships are often dysfunctional.

Communication Skills

Nykodym, Rund, and Liverpool (1986) studied the use of TA as a communication-enhancement tool to improve individuals' involvement in a quality circle program. Results of the study suggest that members' communication skills were improved. Likewise, Spencer (1977) found that employees who received basic training in TA were more productive and communicated more effectively with their coworkers.

Family Counseling

Zerin (1988) wrote about working with families using TA and provided an application of the Karpman (1968) drama triangle to promote change in the multiproblem blended family. TA strategies such as analysis of ego states and transactional changes in the family were cited as effective strategies for counselors and therapists specializing in work with families. In addition, Bredehoft (1986) found that TA offered an effective framework for parent education programs. Participants in this study reported increased adaptability and cohesion among family members. In a later study Bredehoft (1990) found that the use of a TA-based parent education program increased the self-esteem of parents but did not enhance communication.

Finally, Zalcman (1990) reviewed the present status of game and racket analysis and reaffirmed the notion that games tend to destabilize relationships. He also suggested that game and racket analysis should be recognized as a distinct and separate area of TA. Zalcman proposed that a new area of social systems analysis be added to TA to fulfill Berne's goal of a comprehensive theory of social psychology.

■ ■ ■

THE CASE OF JOHN: THE TRANSACTIONAL ANALYSIS APPROACH

A counselor or therapist using TA with John begins with the contract, defined as an explicit bilateral commitment to a well-defined course of action (Stewart & Joines, 1987). The contract is an adult ego state commitment to the self or others to make a change. In TA, contracts specify who the parties are, what they are going to do together, how long it will take, what the goal(s) of counseling will be, and how the counselor and client will know when they have reached the goal(s).

In the case of John, some possible contracts for change include the following:

1. Develop constructive adult confrontation of perceived authority figures (such as his boss) rather than passive adaptive child withdrawal.

2. Improve intimacy with his wife by learning to feel less adapted child guilt about sexual feelings and experience more free child spontaneity.

3. Reduce his amount of leisure reading and understand that this withdrawal mode of time structuring may be a socially acceptable way to avoid intimacy with his spouse and children.

TA-based approaches for John focus on both exploration of past and present behavior. Exploration of the past may be accomplished by the counselor's or therapist's helping John to understand his life script—the notion that present behaviors are influenced by early childhood experiences (permissions or injunctions) with emotionally significant others (usually parents). Based on these early experiences, a child makes unconscious decisions about how to cope with her environment. Later in life, the child-turned-adult may experience emotional difficulties because early subconscious decisions are no longer appropriate responses.

In John's case, it appears that he accepted the following injunctions from his parents: "don't be too close," "don't feel,"; "don't be important," and "don't be well." The "don't be close" injunction is evidenced by John's father, who rarely spent time with him as a child. John currently lives out this injunction by rarely spending time with his wife and two children. The "don't feel" injunction resulted from John's escaping to his room when his parents argued, his rare experience of affection from his father, and the solicitous attention from his mother that he received only when he was ill with stomach problems. John lives out the "don't feel" injunction by working and constantly reading in his leisure time, which in turn results in his having little time for sexual intimacy with his wife and avoiding confrontation. The "don't be important" injunction occurred because neither parent demanded any responsible behavior from John. Now he lives out this injunction by becoming anxious and having stomach problems whenever he has something to do. Finally, the "don't be well" injunction emanated from the attention John received from his mother when he was ill. She promptly took him to the doctor; however, medical reports never revealed any serious illness other than an irritable colon. Today, John visits the doctor for intestinal problems and receives solicitous attention from a wife who carefully watches his diet and keeps the children quiet when he is stressed. He also gets sick whenever things get stressful at work.

The focus on present behavior includes several TA concepts such as parent, adult, and child transactions with others; time structuring and strokes; and games and life positions (self-concept). In the course of treatment, the counselor or therapist spends considerable time helping John understand his parent, adult, and child ego state with the egogram. His egogram might appear as shown in figure 11.9.

The critical parent state is high because of John's early childhood decisions about having genuine feelings of intimacy and having fun. Some of the parent messages may include "don't be too close to others," "don't feel sexual," and "don't let others know how you are feeling." The nurturing parent state is low because John rarely shows any kind of affection toward his wife and children. Furthermore, he probably spends little or no

FIGURE 11.9

John's egogram

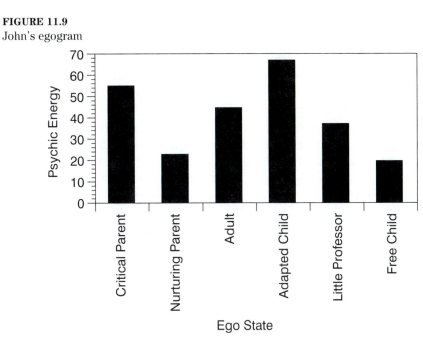

time just taking care of his own needs. The adult state is higher and probably used at work, where John is director of the reference department in the library. The adapted child state is high because John rarely expresses genuine feelings, avoids confrontations, and feel very guilty about sexual feelings. These feelings of guilt may be reinforced by his strong Catholic upbringing. John's little professor state assists the adult state in carrying out the socially acceptable plan of constant reading and sickness to avoid intimacy and confrontations. Finally, the free child state is low because John appears to have little fun in his life other than reading. Further, the episodes of impotency with his wife and the little time he has to enjoy his children suggest little or no spontaneity.

The counselor or therapist also makes John aware of the games he plays that reinforce the early script decisions. In John's case, games include "kick me," or provoking putdowns from his wife or boss; wooden leg, or taking advantage of his stomach problems by avoiding the social responsibility of family life; and "yes, but," or failing to get well despite his wife's concern for his comfort, his mother's offer of special foods for his diet, and the physician's failure to find any significant medical problems. These games justify the racket feelings of guilt and depression that justify the script. They also reinforce the life position of "I'm Not OK–You're OK." This position has a strong critical parent state that turns inward, finds fault, and blames the self for real or imagined mistakes. The free child state is weak because John has little enjoyment, and the nurturing parent state does not provide the care that the personality needs. Finally, the adaptive child state is weak, preferring passivity over assertiveness.

John's methods of time structuring for strokes include withdrawal, or constantly reading at home; games, or constant intestinal stomach sickness; and activity, or working at his job at the library. While the reading is a source of enjoyment, it causes problems with his family. As he did in his childhood, he receives stroke recognition from his mother and wife when he is ill. Finally, transactions with others are probably complementary. He appears to respond from his compliant adapted child state to the parent ego state of significant others in his life, such as his wife, mother, and boss.

In the course of counseling or psychotherapy, John learns how to understand his life script better. Through a script analysis, he becomes more aware of how early childhood decisions contribute to his present unhappiness. Breaking the repetitive patterns of the past is accomplished with the treatment contract.

■ ■ ■

LIMITATIONS

Like other therapeutic approaches, transactional analysis has certain limitations for which it has been criticized. For example, it has been criticized for its dependence on technical terminology to describe the complex behavior patterns of clients. The theory also needs more empirical evidence in support of its effectiveness in various settings and across diverse populations of clients.

Like other major theories, TA has a well-developed jargon. Practitioners of TA may rely too heavily on jargon—those words and phrases that refer to complex behaviors. They include parent, adult, and child ego states, transactions, games, rackets, life positions, strokes, and scripts. By necessity, the counselor or therapist must spend considerable time educating the client about the meaning of these terms before beginning any discussion of how the terms relate to the client's own situation. Typically, clients come to counseling or therapy because of a perceived inability to effectively manage problems. Learning to speak the language of TA before the counseling or therapy begins may lead to frustration on the part of the client.

The complexity of the concepts in TA is another limitation from the practitioner's point of view. For example, assessment of the self and others in terms of one of the ego states (parent, adult, child) can be challenging for the average client. Some clients will have difficulty recognizing the paradigms referenced by the various games identified in TA theory. Yet an understanding of these concepts must occur for TA to work as a therapeutic intervention.

Another major limitation of TA is the lack of empirical evidence concerning its effectiveness. However, past researchers have reported favorable findings. Miller and Capuzzi (1984) reviewed the effectiveness of TA in promoting mental health in educational and clinical settings. According to them, the use of TA resulted in increased self-esteem with elementary school students and improved attendance with high school students. In higher education settings, they found that college students reported more positive feelings and improved academic performance.

As a therapeutic approach, TA is not successful with all types of clients. Although success with schizophrenics was reported by Schiff (1969), Drye (1977) reported mixed results with schizophrenics, certain depressions, phobias, compulsives, and alcoholics. Clearly, more empirically based studies are needed to further validate the use of TA in clinical and educational settings.

SUMMARY

Counselors or therapists use TA's principles to help clients assume autonomy and responsibility in their lives. Those who wish to use transactional analysis in therapeutic settings need to be knowledgeable about the key components of the theory, such as structural analysis, transactional analysis proper, game analysis, script analysis, and basic life positions. The case study of John illustrated the theoretical and practical application of transactional analysis, showing that counselors and therapists can help clients achieve a more balanced and healthier approach to living.

Transactional analysis is a theory that continues to enjoy popularity among counseling and psychotherapy professionals. Through evolution and refinement, it has received widespread application in settings ranging from schools to corporations. Its current status as a major theory is stable, and we expect continued growth and interest in its application.

REFERENCES

Allen, J., & Allen, B. (1989). Stroking: Biological underpinnings and direct observations. *Transactional Analysis Journal, 19*, 26–31.

Berne, E. (1961). *Transactional analysis in psychotherapy*. New York: Grove Press.

Berne, E. (1964). *Games people play*. New York: Grove Press.

Berne, E. (1972). *What do you say after you say hello?* New York: Grove Press.

Bredehoft, D. (1986). An evaluation of self-esteem: A family affair. *Transactional Analysis Journal, 16*, 175–181.

Bredehoft, D. (1990). Self-esteem: A family affair. *Transactional Analysis Journal, 20*, 111–116.

Douglas, L. (1986). Is adolescent suicide a third degree game and who is the real victim? *Transactional Analysis Journal, 16*, 165–169.

Drye, R. C. (1977). The best of worlds: A psychoanalyst looks at TA. In G. Barnes (Ed.), *Transactional analysis after Eric Berne* (pp. 442–457). New York: Harper.

Dusay, J. (1977). The evolution of transactional analysis. In G. Barnes (Ed.), *Transactional analysis after Eric Berne* (pp. 32–52). New York: Harper.

Dusay, J., & Dusay, K. M. (1979). Transactional analysis. In R. J. Corsini (Ed.), *Current psychotherapies* (pp. 374–427). Itasca, IL: Peacock.

Goulding, M. (1987). Transactional analysis and redecision therapy. In J. L. Zeig (Ed.), *The evolution of psychotherapy* (pp. 285–299). New York: Brunner/Mazel.

Goulding, M., & Goulding, R. (1979). *Changing lives through redecision therapy*. New York: Brunner/Mazel.

Harris, T. (1967). *I'm OK–You're OK*. New York: Avon.

Hazell, J. (1989). Drivers as mediators of stress response. *Transactional Analysis Journal, 19*, 212–222.

Horwitz, A. (1982). The relationship between positive stroking and self-perceived symptoms of distress. *Transactional Analysis Journal, 12*, 218–221.

James, M., & Jongeward, D. (1971). *Born to win*. Reading, MA: Addison-Wesley.

Karpman, S. (1968). Fairy tale and script drama analysis. *Transactional Analysis Bulletin, 26*, 39–43.

Klein, M. (1980). *Lives people live: A textbook of transactional analysis*. New York: Wiley.

McClendon, R. (1977). My mother drives a pickup truck. In G. Barnes (Ed.), *Transactional analysis after Eric Berne* (pp. 99–113). New York: Harper.

Miller, C. A., & Capuzzi, D. (1984). A review of transactional analysis outcome studies. *American Mental Health Counselors Association Journal, 6*(1), 30–41.

Nykodym, N., Rund, W., & Liverpool, P. (1986). Quality circles: Will transactional analysis improve their effectiveness? *Transactional Analysis Journal, 16*, 182–187.

Penfield, W., & Roberts, L. (1959). *Speech and brain mechanisms*. Princeton: Princeton University Press.

Schiff, J. (1969). Reparenting schizophrenics, *Transactional Analysis Bulletin, 8*, 49–50.

Spencer, G. (1977). Effectiveness of an introductory course in TA. *Transactional Analysis Journal, 7*, 346–349.

Steiner, C. (1971). *Scripts people live*. New York: Grove Press.

Stewart, I., & Joines, V. S. (1987). *TA today: A new introduction to transactional analysis*. Nottingham, England, & Chapel Hill, NC: Lifespace.

Thompson, C. L., & Rudolph, L. B. (1992) *Counseling children*. Monterey, CA: Brooks/Cole.

Zalcman, M. J. (1990). Game analysis and racket analysis: Overview, critique, and future developments. *Transactional Analysis Journal, 20*, 4–19.

Zerin, M. (1988). An application of the drama triangle to family therapy. *Transactional Analysis Journal, 18*, 94–101.

CHAPTER TWELVE

Rational-Emotive Theory

Hanoch Livneh
Portland State University

Peggy E. Wright
Portland State University

Rational-emotive therapy (RET) is a theory of personality and an integrated method of counseling and therapy that maintains that most human emotions, such as depression and anxiety, are not a direct consequence of an activating environmental event but rather are largely created by the individual's own perceptions or belief system. RET is regarded by its proponents as a comprehensive cognitive-affective-behavioral theory and practice of counseling and therapy.

Albert Ellis, the founder of RET, was born in Pittsburgh, Pennsylvania, in 1913. During his childhood he was frequently beset by illnesses and was hospitalized on several occasions, which interrupted his normal learning and physical activities. He credits these and other family crises with influencing his interest in other people's welfare and his efforts to assist others to solve their problems (Dryden, 1989).

Ellis, who grew up in New York City, received both his masters (1943) and doctoral (1947) degrees in clinical psychology from Columbia University. Early in his career, his clinical practice focused on marriage, family, and sex counseling and therapy. Throughout his professional life he has held several teaching and clinical positions. In 1959, he founded and has directed since its inception the New York-based Institute for Rational Living. He also directs the Institute for Advanced Study in Rational-Emotive Psychotherapy, a clinical training organization that he founded in 1969. In 1974 Ellis received the Distinguished Professional Psychologist award from the American Psychology Association, and in 1985 he was the recipient of the Distinguished Professional Contributions award from the same organization.

The intent of this chapter is to provide the reader with a review of RET. More specifically, it seeks to (1) briefly discuss the historical and philosophical antecedents of RET, (2) review Ellis's perspective on the etiology of both irrational and rational thinking, (3) present the major constructs of RET with a particular emphasis on the ABC model of personality, (4) delineate the process of change as it unfolds during the counseling or therapeutic encounter, (5) list the major goals and intervention strategies typically implemented by RET practitioners, and (6) briefly comment on the research conducted in support of RET's assumptions and therapeutic usefulness. The chapter concludes with he presentation of a case study that provides specific guidelines on how to apply RET principles and techniques to a client manifesting a variety of psychological problems.

HISTORY

The founder of rational-emotive therapy and the principal contributor to its present status was Dr. Albert Ellis. Trained as a psychoanalytically oriented psychotherapist in the late 1940s, Ellis soon became disillusioned with what he perceived to be its inefficiency in treating patients. As a result, during the mid-1950s he embarked upon the development of a more pragmatic and direct approach to treatment, which he termed RET. In addition to his gradual disenchantment with traditional psychoanalysis, Ellis found himself influenced by three schools of thought. The first was the stoic philosophy espoused by Marcus Aurelius and Epictetus (circa A.D. 100), which views people as being disturbed not by things or events but rather by how they perceive them. A second perspective was that of Alfred Adler. Ellis credits Adler with the realization that people's behavior stems from their ideas and thinking modes. Furthermore, Ellis suggests that it was Adler who recognized that human failure and success follow from the meaning assigned to an experience and not directly from the experience as it is perceived. Third, the gradual bridging of behavior and cognitive counseling/therapy during the late 1950s and the 1960s further cemented Ellis's views and influenced his choice of counseling and therapeutic interventions (Burke, 1989: Ellis, 1979b; Ellis, 1989).

Ellis's early experimentation with different counseling and therapeutic methodologies and the gradual evolvement of the rational-emotive system culminated in his book *Reason and Emotion in Psychotherapy* (1962). He further stated that although RET is the convergent product of several schools of thought and therapeutic approaches, it was also a reflection of his own personal experience. In fact, Ellis (1962, 1974) was convinced that his own feelings of inadequacy and shyness, especially around women, had a powerful impact upon his self-perception and his struggle and eventual conquest of these irrational fears.

Based on his personal and clinical experiences during those early days of RET, Ellis gradually came to the realization that individuals are not merely passive recipients of irrational ideas from their social environments (such as family or school), but rather are active pursuers of irrational indoctrinations that they have collected, sustained, and even invented since childhood and are still actively pursuing in the present. He further discovered that these deeply entrenched false and irrational beliefs are not readily amenable to change and require an active-directive and multifaceted assault on the major self-defeating and erroneous ideas and beliefs that create continuous misery in people's lives (Ellis, 1989).

HUMAN NATURE: A DEVELOPMENTAL PERSPECTIVE

Ellis believes that people have the inherent capacity to think and act both rationally and irrationally. In other words, people have the potential toward both healthy functioning (typically defined in terms of rational and logical thinking) and unhealthy or self-defeating functioning (viewed in terms of irrational and illogical thinking) (Ellis, 1962, 1989).

Basic Assumptions

Ellis makes the following basic assumptions about human nature:

- People have vast untapped resources actualizing their potentials and therefore have the capacity to change their destinies (Ellis, 1979a).
- People are naturally hedonistic (pleasure-seeking) (Ellis, 1976; Patterson, 1986).
- People perceive (sense), think (reason), emote (feel), and believe (act) simultaneously. All these basic human functions are interdependently and intricately intertwined in the psyche (Ellis, 1973; Ellis & Harper, 1975).
- People are creative processors of information. They experience, evaluate, and then act upon encountered environmental events (Ellis, 1962, 1973).
- Human beings are essentially verbal animals. They invariably think through the use of language and symbols (Ellis, 1979b; Patterson, 1986).
- Human behavior is only partially determined (self-determinism). Biological tendencies and social climates exert a strong influence on most behaviors. However, people also have at their disposal the element of choice or free will and can, therefore, transcend their pasts (Ellis, 1979b).
- Emotional or psychological disturbances are the result of irrational and illogical thinking (Ellis, 1987, 1989).
- Change in human behavior occurs only when people gain emotional and cognitive insights into their irrational beliefs followed by direct actions to implement these insights (Ellis, 1989).

Irrationality and Rationality

Ellis assumes two core tendencies in his theory of personality (Maddi, 1989). They are "(a) to think irrationally and harm themselves, and (b) to gain understanding of their folly and train themselves to change their self-destructive ways" (p. 153).

From a developmental perspective, the rational-emotive view emphasizes that the newly born has a predisposition toward both healthy and unhealthy functioning. The infant, then, has the capacity to be self-pre-serving, live cooperatively, relate intimately to others, and actualize some of his potentials. The potential for rational and useful living is, however, often compromised not only by the potential for its opposite (that is, irra-tionality) but also by crooked thinking, the origins of which can be traced to early childhood experiences with parental figures and social institutions (such as schools). Contemporary, self-triggered repetitions of this early irrational thinking further cement their influence upon one's cognitive functioning (Ellis, 1962, 1974).

Ellis recognized the source of his notions:

> [the] immense amount of evidence from historical, anthropological, reli-gious, psychological, and biological sources that virtually all humans, indi-vidually and in groups, at all times and places have been exceptionally irra-tional and self-defeating in much of their behaviors and that, in all probability, they have inborn, as well as environmentally acquired, tenden-cies to behave this way. (Ellis, 1974, p. 329)

Antecedents of Rational Thinking

During the course of normal or healthy growing up, the child as a social being seeks to fulfill the need to be cared for and loved. Therefore, she adopts behaviors that are designed to elicit positive responses from those near her. Accordingly, the child evaluates herself on the basis of what oth-ers say or do. The emotionally mature child (and later adult) learns to maintain a delicate balance between her needs and feelings and considera-tion for others' injunctions and evaluations. Inasmuch as the child's inter-actions with parental figures and other adults encourage the development of such a balance, she will proceed to develop rational and effective pat-terns of thinking (Ellis, 1973, 1979b).

Antecedents of Irrational Thinking

As previously discussed, Ellis maintains that emotional and psychological problems are the result of magical, nonempirical, and irrational thinking. Irrational thinking has its origins in early illogical learning that the indi-vidual is both biologically disposed toward and, more important, acquires through the influence of parents, other significant adults, and sociocul-tural institutions. RET, then, asserts the unspecificity of the origin of emo-tional and behavioral disturbances (Ellis, 1979b). Unlike most personality theories, it does not assume any direct link between specific etiological factors (such as early traumas, events, or experiences) and later behaviors. The theory, however, does not deny the possibility that such factors may indeed play a certain role in human development.

In the process of growing up, the child is taught to think and feel certain things about himself and others. Values linked to the idea of *good* become positive emotions. Those associated with the idea of *bad*, on the other hand, become negative emotions with their accompanying distinctions of depression, anger, anxiety, and the like. Ellis maintains that during this rigid enculturation process, and from an early age on, irrational ideas gradually become ingrained or imprinted in the child's mind. Moreover, those irrational ideas, as a result of perceptions of and attitudes toward external events, are incorporated and internalized into the child's language. Once they become a part of the belief system, the individual continues to reindoctrinate them, at the present, through self-verbalization. This self-feeding process leads the individual to behave inappropriately and is the cause of a continued state of emotional disturbance (Ellis, 1973, 1979b).

Ellis argues that these irrational beliefs frequently originate from unconditional "shoulds," "oughts," and "musts" that individuals attach to many events and situations. This type of cognitive rigidity leads to three types of irrational beliefs (Ellis, 1984):

- *Awfulizing*:   "It is catastrophic to be unemployed at my age."
- *Self-damnation*:   "I am not good for anything."
- *I-can't-stand-it-itis*:   "I cannot stand the thought of losing my job."

Irrationality, therefore, consists of blaming oneself; sabotaging one's personal, social, and occupational goals; and, in general, placing continuous obstacles along the path to achieving pleasurable and successful life (Tosi, Leclair, Peters, & Murphy, 1987).

A Dimensional Approach to Rationality-Irrationality

Because families and societies differ in their propensities to encourage crooked or irrational thinking and because individuals also differ in their inherited biological and cognitive tendencies toward acquired irrationality, it follows that the differences between those who are labeled emotionally disturbed and those who are not lie more in the frequency and severity of their disturbances (Prochaska, 1984). In other words, Ellis espouses a dimensional approach of human psychopathology (where emotional disturbances are placed on a continuum and graded according to their degree of severity), unlike most theorists who adhere to the categorical approach (where emotional disturbances are classified as present or absent or at least fall into a small number of well-defined categories).

MAJOR CONSTRUCTS

Ellis has offered little systematic theorizing on the structure of personality. His major emphasis has been placed on the nature of human emotional disturbance and the counseling or psychotherapeutic process to combat these disturbances (Maddi, 1989; Shilling, 1984).

As previously discussed, Ellis makes only a few assumptions about the human condition. These may be summarized as follows:

1. Humans have strong tendencies to think both rationally and irrationally. The latter suggests the propensity toward harming and defeating oneself, which is perceived to be partially innate (that is, biologically determined) and partially learned (that is, socioculturally determined). However, humans are not seen as creatures of instinct but rather as having only certain innate tendencies (Ellis, 1987).
2. Humans are largely responsible for creating their own emotional reactions. Irrational ideas, beliefs, values, and attitudes are directly and causally linked to emotional problems and maladaptive behaviors (Ellis, 1989).

More recently, Ellis (1977, 1979a) has attempted to present his views on personality along three dimensions: a physiological/biological basis, a psychological basis, and a social basis.

Physiological/Biological Basis

Ellis agrees with leading humanistic theorists (for example, Maslow and Rogers) that people possess strong, inborn, self-actualizing capabilities. However, RET emphasizes the biological basis of human personality. This is clearly evident in Ellis's assertion that people have powerful innate tendencies to think irrationally and in the process to cause harm to themselves. The following arguments have been brought forth by Ellis (1976) to support his view on the biological nature of human irrationality:

1. Virtually all people demonstrate major irrationalities.
2. No sociocultural group is immune from behaving irrationally.

3. Irrationality is not necessarily equivalent to stupidity or mental retardation; it is also evident among the bright and the gifted.

4. People often adopt new irrationalities after discarding old ones or even readopt original irrationalities after temporarily mastering them.

Psychological Basis

Ellis's views on the psychological functions of human personality revolve around the distinction between rational and self-enhancing belief systems versus irrational and self-defeating belief systems. As previously suggested, individuals who have developed healthy personalities manifest logical and efficient thinking. Furthermore, they tend to have an internal locus of control (that is, they view themselves as exerting control over their destiny) and have the power to change their thoughts and behaviors (Ellis, 1989; Gilliland, James, & Bowman, 1989). On the other hand, people who have developed emotional disturbances demonstrate illogical and inefficient thinking and condemn themselves, others, and external circumstances for events that they fail to control. In summary, Ellis asserts that emotional and behavioral consequences are largely determined by people's thoughts. The latter partly result from innate processes and partly stem from social conditioning. Ellis's ABC model of personality (to be discussed later) is a further example of his views on the psychological nature of human personality.

Social Basis

Individuals are part of larger social groups. They spend a great portion of their lives trying "to impress, live up to the expectations of, and outdo the performances of other people" (Ellis, 1989, p. 206). They are indoctrinated from an early age to become other-directed and seek the approval and acceptance of others. Successful people develop healthy interpersonal relations and a healthy self-concept. In contrast, people who develop emotional disturbances care excessively about what others think about them. They develop the need for complete approval by others, which, when not met, leads to feelings of anxiety and depression (Ellis, 1962, 1989). Although Ellis has not directly addressed the issue of how personality is structured (that is, the existence of traitlike core characteristics), implicit in his theory is the assumption of the existence of certain cognitive elements (in other words, beliefs or belief systems) that are at the core of all human emotions and behaviors. These cognitive elements can be inferred both from the person's self-verbalizations and from ensuing emotions and overt behaviors.

The ABC Model of Personality

Ellis proposed a simple model to illustrate how cognitions directly affect emotional and behavioral disturbances. He termed this model the ABCs of RET (Ellis, 1974, 1979b). Briefly stated, A (activating event or antecedent) is seen as contributing to C (consequence) via the filtering effect of B (belief system). In other words, it is not the objective event (such as an occurrence or experience) that causes one's emotional reaction (the consequence or response) but rather one's belief (perception or self-evaluative meaning) about that event. Two of Ellis's favorite examples of this notion include the following:

1. It is not the loss of a job that causes an individual to become depressed but rather her irrational belief about it, including self-verbalizations such as "It's awful to lose a job"; "I must be a worthless human being".

2. It is not the termination of a love relationship that leads to feelings of depression, despair, or anger but rather an irrational belief system that upholds notions such as "It's terrible to be rejected" and "I'm so unfortunate."

The following diagram illustrates the nature of irrational versus rational beliefs:

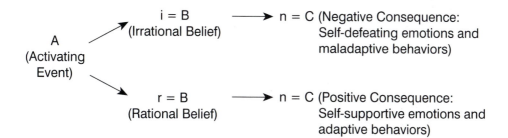

Areas that are particularly susceptible to irrational interferences include academic and occupational success, personal competence, love, approval by others, personal safety, and being treated kindly and fairly by others (Burke, 1989; Ellis, 1979b). Unlike rational beliefs that trigger appropriate and measured emotions of annoyance or sorrow (about losing one's job or love relationship) and inevitably lead to adaptive behaviors (working harder in the future, spending more time with one's mate), irrational beliefs result in inappropriate feelings of anger, depression, or despair, which, in turn, lead to maladaptive behaviors (wasting time, withdrawing socially, refusing to try again in the future, smashing items) (Ellis, 1974).

In his early writings Ellis (1962, 1973) formulated 11 illogical ideas that he viewed as being intimately associated with irrational belief systems that invariably lead to self-defeating emotions and behaviors:

- *It is absolutely essential for a person to be loved or approved of by everyone in his community.* This is an irrational idea because it is an unattainable goal. Furthermore, if one strives for it, he becomes less self-directing, more insecure, and more self-defeating.

- *It is necessary for a person to be completely competent, adequate, and achieving to be considered worthwhile.* This goal is also impossible. To be that compulsive can only result in psychosomatic illness, feelings of inferiority, an inability to live one's life, and a continuous fear of failure.

- *Those people who are bad, wicked, or villainous should be blamed for their wrongdoings and punished.* This idea is irrational because there is no absolute standard of right or wrong. All people occasionally act stupidly or ignorantly, and blaming or punishing them for their mistakes or faults does not necessarily lead to improved behavior.

- *It is terrible and catastrophic when things are not as the person wants them to be.* The idea is illogical because not all situations turn out to be as we would like. Frustration is a normal human experience, but to be severely and persistently upset or depressed is illogical.

- *Unhappiness is caused by outside events and is beyond the control of the person.* In fact, most outside events that we perceive to be harmful are only psychologically harmful and cannot endanger us unless we allow our reactions and attitudes to affect us.

- *If certain things are dangerous and harmful, the individual should continually dwell on and be concerned about them.* This is an irrational idea because simply dwelling on something does not change it. Furthermore, it often leads to worry or anxiety that interferes with objective assessment of the event and, if necessary, dealing with it effectively.

- *It is easier to avoid certain difficulties and responsibilities than to face them.* This belief is irrational because running away from a difficult task does not solve it. Moreover, the situation still exists and may create problems that force the person to deal with them in the future.

- *Persons need to or should be dependent on others and have someone stronger on whom to rely.* While all humans are, to some degree, dependent on others, there is no reason to maximize dependency further. It can only lead to loss of independence, individualism, and self-expression.

■ *Past events in one's life determine present behaviors, and their influence cannot be changed.*   Although the past may influence the present, it does not determine it. The presumed influence of the past may be used as an excuse to avoid changing one's behavior.

■ *A person should be concerned and upset about other people's problems.*   This idea is irrational because one person's problems quite often have nothing to do with those of others. Becoming upset about the problems or behaviors of others can prevent the person from helping others solve their problems.

■ *There is always a correct or perfect solution to every problem, and it is catastrophic if the solution is not found.*   This idea is irrational because there are no perfect solutions to problems. Searching for such solutions leads to anxiety. It can also result in arriving at poor solutions.

Later, Ellis and his coworkers (Ellis, 1977; Ellis & Harper, 1975) reduced these irrational ideas to three main themes:

1. *Condemning self:*   "I must be competent, successful, and must win the approval of virtually all significant persons in my life. It's awful when I don't."

2. *Condemning others:*   "Others must treat me fairly and kindly. It's terrible when they don't, and I can't stand it when they are obnoxious to me."

3. *Condemning the world:*   "I need and must have the things I want. The conditions in my environment and the world around me must be ordered and positive. They must gratify me easily and immediately. It's horrible when the conditions are not the way I want them to be."

THE PROCESS OF CHANGE

According to RET, counseling or therapeutic change in the individual rests on the following assumptions (Ellis, 1979b; Litvak, 1976):

■ It is just as possible to learn new and more rational ways of thinking as it was to learn the older, irrational ways.

■ Because present emotional states and behaviors are controlled by thinking, irrational thinking must first be isolated and corrected in order for affective and behavioral change to occur. More insight into the nature of those original controlling factors, which may have been associated with irrational thinking, is not sufficient to ensure change.

- Learning how to perceive realistically and think rationally leads to a decrease in emotional, interpersonal, and environmental conflicts.

- The quality of the interpersonal relationship between client and counselor or therapist does not need to influence the counseling/therapeutic process or outcome because RET is essentially a self-educative endeavor.

- The client, with the help of the counselor or therapist, decides which emotions and behaviors to change. The client also dictates the pace and duration of the counseling/therapeutic change process.

- Counseling or therapeutic change, as evinced in RET, is essentially an educative, cognitive process involving the client's intellectual mastery of his irrational modes of thinking, followed by practice of new and adaptive behaviors.

According to RET, the essential principles of change include the following:

1. *Direct confrontation* (such as challenging, disputing, contradicting, de-indoctrinating) by the therapist of the client's irrational thinking processes and beliefs. The therapist attacks these irrational thoughts on logico-empirical grounds and then proceeds to teach, train, or model to the client how to change or eliminate these irrational ideas (Ellis, 1974).

2. *Gaining a succession of insights* into the sources (causes) of the disturbance. Several types of insights are stressed (Ellis, 1989; Grieger, 1986):

   - Realizing that the self-defeating behavior is associated with antecedent conditions

   - Understanding that although the client became emotionally disturbed in the past, she is now upset because of continuous self-indoctrination with the same irrational beliefs chosen in the past

   - Realizing that attribution of causes (such as blame) to external events creates and propagates emotional disturbances while assuming responsibility for one's ideas, emotions, and behaviors leads to more effective living

   - Learning how to accept oneself without guilt despite the fact that the client is the cause of the problem

■ Acknowledging that because the irrational beliefs and the tendency to think crookedly are long-standing, habitual, self-reinforced, and powerful, they require continuous hard work to uproot and correct them. Earlier insights (such as emotional ones) are not sufficient to change behavior. It is only when cognitive insights (successful rethinking) and repeated actions to implement the newly gained understanding of one's irrational beliefs are completed that behavioral change is accomplished.

3. After gaining insight, the client must *work actively and energetically*, in the present, to apply the acquired knowledge to the solution of his problems. Active and continuous practice of rational thinking and modes of adaptive behavior ensures the maintenance of successful cognitive and behavioral changes.

The therapeutic change, therefore, is viewed by Ellis as a gradual process that ideally includes the following phases: identifying one's irrational beliefs; gaining insight into how these beliefs are associated with and foster painful emotions and maladaptive behaviors; forcefully confronting these illogical beliefs by demonstrating to oneself their role in creating unhappiness and emotional disturbance; abandoning the irrational, negative, and self-defeating thoughts and replacing them with rational and empirically based thoughts; and developing and maintaining a more rational philosophy of living.

Criteria for Assessing Change

Because RET advocates specific goal setting, counseling or psychotherapy terminates when both counselor or therapist and client agree that goals have been attained. The criteria for evaluating successful outcome include the client's ability to think and behave in rational ways, assume responsibility for thoughts and actions, accept himself fully, demonstrate understanding of RET principles, live independently, show reasonable risk-taking behaviors, and minimize personal and environmental stress (Ellis & Abrahams, 1978; Tosi et al., 1987).

RET counselors or therapists base their judgment of counseling/therapeutic change mainly on the client's self-reports (such as feelings of enjoyment, lack of emotional distress, freedom of choice, effective problem solving) and the counselor or therapist's observations and evaluations of the client's rational thinking and adaptive behaviors. Selected diagnostic instruments and psychological tests are also employed. These are primarily geared toward assessment of irrational-rational ideas (Kassinove, Crisci, & Tiegerman, 1977; Shorkey & Whiteman, 1977).

INTERVENTION STRATEGIES

Counseling/Psychotherapeutic Goals

The overriding goal of RET is to replace irrationality with rationality (Ellis, 1973). More specifically, Ellis continually emphasizes the following goals of RET:

- Teaching the client to analyze, correct, and change introspectively her irrational and illogical views, beliefs, and feelings. In other words, she must be provided with those modes of self-assessment that are incompatible with her irrational beliefs and self-defeating behaviors (Ellis, 1989; Ellis & Harper, 1975)
- Teaching the client how to acquire, internalize, and practice a more rational belief system (Ellis, 1979b, 1989)
- Minimizing the client's self-defeating outlook on life while maximizing a more realistic and tolerant philosophy of life (Ellis, 1979a)

Wallace (1986) succinctly posits the ultimate goal of RET to be "personality change or reorganization through cognitive awareness and philosophic restructuring and the acquisition of a logico-empirical method to maintain that change" (p. 211).

Other goals advocated by Ellis include reducing depression, anxiety, and self-blame; reducing hostility and blaming others and the world (1973); gaining happiness and enjoyment; and assuming self-responsibility (Ellis, 1984; Ellis & Harper, 1975). He has also suggested that RET counselors or therapists should strive to assist their clients to achieve certain goals in order to minimize self-defeating behaviors (Ellis, 1979a; Ellis & Bernard, 1985). These goals, also viewed as values to be internalized by the client, include the following:

- *Self-interest*.   The emotionally mature person recognizes the importance of being concerned about himself as a necessary step toward caring about others. This helps to protect the rights of both self and others.
- *Social interest*.   Stemming from self-interest is the recognition that life is largely social. Hence, one has the responsibility to act socially and protect the rights of others.
- *Self-direction*.   Mature people assume responsibility for their actions and lives. Support of and relying on others are not needed and should not be demanded.
- *Tolerance (of frustration)*.   Highly functioning people are able to accept their own limitations and those of others with only minimal dis-

comfort. They may dislike others' behaviors but do not condemn them as people.

- *Acceptance of uncertainty.*   Mature individuals can accept the fact that we live in a world of probabilities and that absolute certainties do not exist.

- *Flexibility.*   Emotionally mature people are open to change and to viewing the world as being comprised of a wide variety of people, things, and ideas.

- *Empirical or scientific thinking.*   Healthy people practice objective, rational, and empirical thinking. They apply the laws of logic to both external circumstances and to their interpersonal relationships and emotional reactions.

- *Commitment.*   Mature individuals typically maintain at least one creative interest for self-expression. In addition, they often have some interpersonal involvements.

- *Risk taking.*   Emotionally mature people are capable of risk taking. They are adventurous and are willing to accept the thought of a periodic failure.

- *Self-acceptance.*   Healthy individuals accept themselves unconditionally. They do not gauge their value by external standards or achievements; rather, they accept their existence for what it is.

- *Non-utopianism.*   The person realizes that a frustration-free, pain-free, perfect existence is not attainable. However, the experience of negative human emotions can be minimized.

- *Long-range hedonism.*   As an extension of the previous goal, the emotionally mature person seeks pleasure but recognizes the need, when circumstances dictate, to postpone gratification to an appropriate time.

Counseling/Psychotherapeutic Relationships

Ellis asserts that the counseling/therapeutic relationship is not an important aspect of counseling and psychotherapy. Indeed, he frequently argues that a personal relationship characterized by warmth, affection, or love toward the client is neither a necessary nor a sufficient condition for effective counseling and psychotherapy (Ellis, 1979a; Wallace, 1986). However, he maintains that building good rapport with and accepting the client are desirable. Moreover, RET counselors or therapists fully accept their clients as individuals (with all their fallibilities and frailties) and communicate this unconditional acceptance on a regular basis (Patterson, 1986; Wallace, 1986).

The RET counselor or therapist is a highly active and didactic professional and purposefully seeks to persuade, confront, de-indoctrinate, direct, and lead the client toward more rational and adaptive ways of thinking and behaving. He may introject personal views and values into the therapeutic process when such a course is deemed advisable (Ellis, 1962; Ellis & Bernard, 1986). In this model, the client is viewed as a learner (student) while the counselor/therapist is viewed as an educator (teacher, model, expert) who, in order to function effectively, should possess the following characteristics (Ellis, 1980): intelligence, counseling or therapeutic knowledge, empathy, persistence, interest in helping others, and scientific outlook. The RET counselor or therapist must vigorously focus on the client's irrational ideas and have the capability to detect these ideas readily, confront them, and demonstrate to the client that they are at the source of her emotional distress and maladaptive behaviors (Ellis, 1973, 1979a).

The Counseling and Psychotherapy Process

RET is a highly directive, structured, and confrontational counseling or therapeutic intervention (Ellis & Grieger, 1977). Ellis regards counseling or psychotherapy as a reeducative process whereby the client is taught how to discard irrational ideas and acquire and apply logical thinking and problem-solving methods to his life. Accordingly, the counseling or therapeutic process may be visualized as including the following phases (Ellis, 1979a, 1989; Patterson, 1986; Wallace, 1986; Wessler & Wessler, 1980):

- *Establishing rapport with the client.*   This involves gaining the client's confidence in both the counselor or therapist and the counseling or psychotherapy process.
- *Identifying the problem(s).*   This phase involves uncovering those irrational beliefs associated with the client's distressing feelings and distorted behaviors (using the ABC model).
- *Setting goals.*   All RET outcome goals evolve around its principal goal of changing those maladaptive emotional and behavioral consequences (C) that stem from the client's irrational ideas and beliefs. The counselor or therapist should also obtain a commitment from the client to pursue the designated goals actively.
- *Explaining RET to the client.*   The counselor or therapist briefly explains the basic hypothesis underlying the ABC model, with particular emphasis on clarifying the link between irrational beliefs and ensuing emotional and behavioral disturbances.

■ *Showing the client the irrationality of her beliefs.*   The counselor or therapist demonstrates to the client that these beliefs cannot be logically and empirically validated and that they only lead to more self-defeating and distorted behaviors, unhappiness, and emotional disturbances. Clients are challenged to validate their ideas and are subsequently shown that these ideas have no basis in reality.

■ *Showing the client that he is maintaining the disturbance by continuing to think illogically.*   The counselor or therapist provides the client with examples of how his own language contributes to the maintenance of irrational perceptions and thoughts and how the latter, in turn, further fuel the initial emotional disturbance.

■ *Disputing and attacking these irrational beliefs.*   The client is strongly encouraged to abandon illogical ideas and replace them with rational beliefs. Ellis views the disputation of irrational beliefs as a fourth component (D, or disputing) of his ABC(D) model.

■ *Teaching the client how to think logically and empirically.*   By assigning homework, the practitioner coerces a client to put newly acquired rational ideas into everyday practice. When the client can actively and successfully dispute her irrational beliefs, a fifth component is added to the model, ABC(D)(E)—the E signifying an effective new perspective.

■ *Discussing the more general irrational beliefs held by society.*   The client is assisted in developing and practicing a more rational philosophy of living. This rational philosophy of living invariably leads to the elimination and future prevention of emotional disturbances and self-defeating behaviors.

Techniques and Methods of Change

Ellis advocates the use of eclectic therapeutic methods. More specifically, within his cognitive-dynamic framework, he posits a three-mode approach to counseling and psychotherapy. These three modalities include *cognitive, emotive,* and *behavioral* therapies (Dryden, 1984; Ellis, 1973, 1979b, 1985, 1989; Ellis & Bernard, 1985; Gilliland et al., 1989).

Cognitive Methods.   These methods seek to teach and show the client how to separate irrational from rational beliefs; how to give up perfectionism in order to lead a less anxious and a happier existence; how to rid herself of the "shoulds," "oughts," and "musts" that permeate her life; how to employ the logico-empirical methods of thinking successfully; and how to accept reality.

The RET counselor or therapist relies heavily on methods such as *disputation*, which involves confrontation, contradiction, and challenge of the client's irrational self-verbalization and self-destructive beliefs; and *instruction*, which involves advisement, explanation, persuasion, cajoling, and encouragement of the client to use logical thinking, modify irrational self-statements, and reverbalize sentences. Other cognitive techniques may involve the following:

- *Cognitive distraction/diversion procedures*, such as thought stopping or focusing on pleasant images to disassociate oneself from obsessive irrational thoughts
- *Reframing*, in which the counselor or therapist redefines a negative situation and presents it from a positive perspective
- *Referenting*, in which the counselor or therapist assists the client to view events holistically rather than in a fragmented manner
- *Problem solving*, in which counselor or therapist and client identify options for encountered problems and then proceed to rationally analyze them and seek appropriate solutions
- *Presentation of alternative choices*, similar to problem solving, in which clients are made aware of the many choices they have at their command and are assisted in realizing their full range of alternatives
- *Analogies, parables, and stories* used as modes of verbal images to dramatize rational ideas and concretize abstract or unclear notions and beliefs

Emotive Methods.   Using emotive methods (or emotive-evocative techniques), the counselor or therapist attempts to dramatize and demonstrate to the client truths and falsehoods (such as "musts") and how to differentiate between the two; and how to modify basic value systems. The counselor or therapist may use any of several methods:

- *Role playing*, to dramatize the power of false ideas and how they affect relationships with others
- *Modeling*, to show the client how to acquire and develop different ideas and values
- *Humor*, to minimize ideas and self-defeating behaviors that create disturbances and to show the absurdity of these ideas and behaviors
- *Exhortation and persuasion*, to convince the client to relinquish illogical thinking and acquire more efficient and adaptive ideas

- *Shame-attacking exercises*, in which clients are assigned exercises directly related to their fear of being embarrassed or ashamed (such as approaching strangers for purposes of initiating conversation and making requests, performing certain "humiliating" acts, and training themselves to feel unashamed)

- *Paradoxical intention*, in which the counselor or therapist prescribes a symptom (such as anger or depression) and requests that the client practice it or even exaggerate its significance

- *Negative imagery*, in which the client is asked to imagine an extremely unpleasant situation, image the most feared feelings associated with such a situation, implode these feelings, and then imagine changing these fearful feelings into more appropriate ones

- *Future imaging*, in which the client is asked to imagine a feared situation associated with a present event as if it would appear only at a future time, thereby minimizing the dramatic impact of such an event

Behavioral Methods.   These methods are used to assist the client in changing dysfunctional symptoms and actions and in acquiring and maintaining more effective ways of behavior. Methods may include:

- *Homework assignments*, in which clients exercise their written ABCs and practice disputing (D) their irrational beliefs

- *Risk-taking activities*, in which clients are asked to encounter anxiety-provoking situations directly and take the risk of feeling anxious, being rejected, and so on

- *Operant conditioning methods*, such as self- or other-administered positive reinforcement or aversive stimuli, in which clients practice self-management procedures of both emotions and behaviors

- *Assertiveness training*, to teach nonassertive clients to behave more confidently and effectively in social situations

- *Systematic desensitization*, in which homework assignments and counseling/therapeutic practices are combined using imaginary desensitization to assist clients who are fearful, anxious, shy, or nonassertive

- *Relaxation training*, to combat temporarily the deleterious effects of tension, anxiety, and other disturbing feelings

- *Skill training*, to assist the client in acquiring skills in areas such as sexual functioning, communication, and interpersonal relationships

- *Bibliotherapy*, or the weekly assignment of reading books and listening to tapes to assist clients in practicing and reinforcing rational thinking processes

SUPPORTING RESEARCH

Ellis (1979a, 1989) asserts that a large number of outcome studies support the efficiency of RET in treating emotional disturbances. Relying on earlier reviews (such as DiGiuseppe, Miller, & Trexler, 1977; McGovern & Silverman, 1986); meta-analytic studies (such as Smith & Glass, 1977); and his own reviews (Ellis & Whiteley, 1979; Murphy & Ellis, 1979), Ellis observes that "almost all of these studies have shown that groups of individuals who are treated with RET make significantly greater changes in personality adjustment and symptom removal than do control groups who are treated with no therapy or with other forms of counseling" (Ellis, 1979a, p. 211). He further argues that over 90 percent of the many reported controlled experiments support the main personality and clinical hypotheses of RET (Ellis, 1979a, 1989). Ellis also relied on the work of other cognitive (such as Beck) and social learning (such as Bandura) counselors and therapists to argue the structural and clinical validity of RET (Ellis, 1989).

Independent reviews seem generally to agree on the clinical efficacy of RET in reducing various forms of emotional disturbance, such as interpersonal anxiety and depression (Engels & Dieksta, 1987; Haaga & Davison, 1989). In one well-designed study, Lipsky, Kassinove, and Miller (1980) studied the efficiency of three types of RET, as compared to a support and relaxation training program, in decreasing clients' anxiety, depression, and neuroticism and in increasing rational thinking. A control (no-treatment) group was also used. Following treatment, clients who were randomly assigned to any of the three RET groups were found to show significantly higher levels of improvement on all measures than clients who were assigned to either the support and relaxation or control groups.

Ellis's conclusions about RET's unequivocal success and superiority to other forms of counseling and psychotherapeutic treatment, however, are not shared by all. DiGiuseppe et al. (1977), although concluding that studies of the efficacy of RET are increasing in quality and generally appear promising, argue that they still remain far from conclusive. Patterson (1986) suggests that Ellis's claims of 90-percent success are not supported by adequate statistical evidence and that most evidence is usually based on clinical reports. Furthermore, he argues that a factor of selective clinical acceptance to counseling/therapy confounds these findings. Finally, Shilling (1984) maintains that although RET has generated a large number of studies, many of the reported findings are compromised by methodological flaws such as inadequate control or comparison groups, small samples, unsound psychometric measures, and no follow-up studies.

Ellis is also criticized because his theory of personality is not fully developed (Ziegler, 1989) and because it is merely a model of counseling/psychotherapeutic-triggered personality changes. As to its counseling or psychotherapeutic interventions, Ellis's eclectic (or multimodal) approach incorporates highly diverse and even conceptually dissonant methods. This, coupled with an increasingly expanding number of RET hypotheses, has resulted in loss of systematization and dilution of the theory's earlier notions (Mahoney, 1977; Patterson, 1986).

Finally, although results obtained from meta-analytic studies of counseling and psychotherapeutic outcomes generally support the superiority of cognitive-behavioral therapies over psychodynamic and humanistic approaches (such as Shapiro, 1985), the former include a variety of related therapies and are not specifically geared toward the study of the effectiveness of RET. Moreover, other meta-analytic researchers have concluded, from their analyses of the literature, that although cognitive-behavioral therapies are uniformly efficacious, they are not necessarily superior to other psychotherapies (for example, Miller & Berman, 1983).

■ ■ ■

THE CASE STUDY OF JOHN: THE RATIONAL-EMOTIVE APPROACH

The RET approach concentrates on the irrational ideas underlying a client's emotional and behavioral problems, and seeks to assist the client in developing ways to overcome these difficulties. The focus is placed on challenging and correcting irrational beliefs that nourish the client's fears and anxieties. To do so, rational-emotive counselors or therapists use a variety of cognitive, behavioral, and affective techniques. The techniques are designed to facilitate the client's critical examination of present beliefs and behaviors. The counselor or therapist does not typically spend a great deal of time with the client's history or use psychoanalytical techniques such as dream analysis, free association, or the interpretation of the transference relationship between client and counselor or therapist. In working with John, the counselor or therapist's primary target is to reduce feelings of anxiety or fear that appear to be linked to the development of gastrointestinal symptoms and periodic sexual impotency.

Presenting Problems

The application of RET to John's case study begins with an examination of the presenting behavioral problems (John's gastrointestinal symptoms and periodic sexual impotency) and his reported emotional distress (John's feelings of anxiety, fear, depression, and helplessness). In addition, the counselor or therapist looks for possible secondary disturbances (John's perception of his physical and emotional responses). In RET, emphasis is placed on investigating and removing guilt and anxiety associated with the primary problem. The counselor or therapist needs to discover what John is telling himself (his self-verbalizations) that results in feelings of anxiety (for example, it is awful and terrible to have a new director).

Another of John's major problems stems from his social and performance anxieties. He apparently suffers from ego anxiety (feelings of inadequacy), as demonstrated in the past during public speaking and test taking, in addition to discomfort anxiety or low frustration tolerance, as manifested by withdrawal from social interactions.

The ABC Model

Exposing John's Irrational Beliefs.   The counselor or therapist assists John in seeing that his irrational beliefs are the direct cause of his psychological and physiological problems. He is be shown that he is the one who is feeding these irrational and unrealistic assumptions and that he alone is the one who can change his discomfort by changing his illogical beliefs to more rational statements.

John learns that it is not the A's (activating events), such as changing job expectations and the appointment of a new director at work, that cause him to have disturbed C's (emotional consequences), as manifested on both an emotional level through depression and anxiety and on a physiological level through intestinal disturbances. Rather, it is his B's (such as irrational beliefs about having a new director) that are the cause of his misery. The sequence can be portrayed in the following diagram:

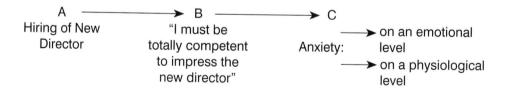

John is shown that if he adopts a rational way of thinking ("It is unfortunate not to be the new director and to be expected instead to follow changing procedures") instead of the irrational belief ("It is horrible and catastrophic to have a new director and to be forced to follow ridiculous instructions), he will make himself feel appropriately concerned and frustrated instead of inappropriately anxious and physically ill. His appropriate response will enable him to cope positively with the new situation at work and with interpersonal problems at home.

A similar ABC model can be developed for the problems of impotence. The counselor or therapist may show John that his view of sexual activity as a test (the need to perform in an absolutely perfect manner) causes his periodic impotence.

Treatment

The three-mode therapeutic approach advocated by RET is applied to John's presenting problems in the following fashion.

Cognitive Interventions.   An important technique in RET is that of teaching the client about absolutistic thinking (self-dialogue about the "musts," "shoulds," and "oughts"). Absolutistic thinking often results in emotional and behavioral disturbances (in the case of John, depression and social and performance anxieties) when the demands are not fulfilled. In essence, John is contributing to his emotional problem by what he is telling himself, by the assumptions he is making, and by his belief system. Together, the counselor or therapist and John identify and write down the "musts," "shoulds," and "oughts" that keep him inappropriately anxious and physically ill. The counselor or therapist helps John see the differences between his absolutistic thinking ("I must perform perfectly" or "I should have been the new director") and his preferences ("I would like to succeed on the job and be the new director"). The counselor or therapist challenges and disputes John's irrational assumptions and teaches him the ABCs of RET.

John's anxieties are preventing him from fully enjoying life due to his fear of failure ("If I fail at something, the results would be catastrophic"). The counselor or therapist teaches him that even if his social behavior has been deemed inept, it does not necessarily mean that he is an inept person. Self-acceptance of personal worth is modeled by the counselor or therapist. John is shown how to refuse to rate his personhood and instead rate only his behavior or performance. He unconditionally rates his personhood as good, just because he exists.

The counselor or therapist strongly disputes John's irrational ideas to show him that in all likelihood he will not lose his job, and that he certainly can perform it successfully as he has done in the past. Philosophical disputation may show John that even if the worst possible scenario occurs and he loses his job, he can survive and look for another job. Because depression was also suggested during the psychiatric evaluation, the irrational beliefs sustaining it also have to be uncovered, understood, and challenged.

Emotive Interventions.   One approach the RET counselor or therapist might pursue with John involves some emotive and behavioral exercises: that is, *rational-emotive imagery,* a form of mental practice in which John thinks, feels, and behaves in exactly the same way be would like to in everyday situations (Maultsby, 1971). The purpose of this technique is to help John learn appropriate emotions and adaptive behaviors (feeling frustrated and concerned rather than extremely anxious). He is asked to imagine, in an intense way, himself feeling and acting exactly as he would like to feel and behave in daily situations. Through rational-emotive imagery, John can explore what he is doing to thwart his getting what he wants to have.

Two additional emotive procedures might include modeling and future imagery. When modeling is applied, the counselor or therapist demonstrates appropriate ways of responding to stressful situations, especially as they relate to John's home and work situations. John is then requested to experience similar situations and role-play different scenarios in which his relationships to others (such as his boss and his wife) have led in the past to negative feelings. Similarly, through the use of future imagery, John is requested to imagine stressful situations (perhaps confrontation with his boss) as if they might occur in a distant, and safer, future. The removal of this potentially fearful experience from the present tends to minimize its impact, thereby allowing John to deal more constructively and rationally with such an event.

Behavioral Interventions.   John is taught that insight alone into his irrational beliefs is not sufficient to change his behavior. He has to work on and practice using these insights and acting on them. Forcefulness is an important principle of RET, used in vigorously challenging irrational beliefs and strongly replacing these beliefs with rational ways of thinking.

Homework assignments might involve having John develop a list of rational beliefs, followed by a review of them on a frequent basis. The completed homework assignments are consistently verified by the counselor or therapist. They are behaviorally practiced in real-life situations in which John further implements the wisdom gained from his cognitive insight (such as openly discussing issues with the new director without fear for his job; viewing sexual activity as an enjoyable, sharing experience rather than an anxiety-provoking, performance-based test).

A number of additional cognitive-behavioral homework assignments and skill-training exercises (such as assertiveness training, muscle relaxation, systematic desensitization, and self-management training) may also be recommended to help John gain self-assurance, reduce anxiety, and practice self-reinforcement of his newly gained skills.

LIMITATIONS

Critics of RET usually point to the following areas, which they see as being deficient:

1. Little systematic theory building has been offered on the process of abnormal and especially normal personality development. Irrational tendencies are attributed to a mixture of biological determinants and social, mainly parental, influences.

2. The theory and its counseling/therapeutic application often neglect the importance of psychodynamic factors, including unconscious motivation, defense mechanisms, and early life experiences.

3. RET has been criticized for simplifying the complexity of the human experience. The ABC model espoused by RET may be elegant at first glance, but it may also be misleading because its linear and simple components may not always fit neatly into the complex emotional and cognitive world that characterizes most people.

4. Clinical acumen and empirical research suggest that direct and indoctrinating methods of persuasion are not effective in changing attitudes and behaviors. In fact, they might even result in resistance to change.

5. RET often ignores the affective dimension of counseling. It focuses almost exclusively on the cognitive and behavioral aspects of the individual.

6. Because of RET's didactic approach, the counselor or therapist may impose his own philosophy of life and personal values upon the client.

7. RET tends to underemphasize the importance of the counseling/therapeutic relationship between the counselor or therapist and the client. Ignoring the establishment of rapport with the client and empathetic responding may undermine future progress.

8. RET neglects to address the issue that many irrational environments in which clients reside and that exist beyond the counseling or therapeutic encounter continue to foster and reinforce irrational thoughts and maladaptive behaviors.

9. RET has not been adequately researched from an empirical standpoint. Most of the studies that support its effectiveness are based on case studies and on nonclinical populations.

10. Powerful human emotions including horror, terror, anger, and bereavement are not irrational and should not be dismissed or reduced to mere self-defeating, illogical beliefs by the unsophisticated counselor or therapist.

SUMMARY

RET was developed by Albert Ellis during the mid-1950s in an effort to confront clients' presenting problems more directly and actively, notably the irrational thought processes believed to be at the core of clients' emotional distress. RET theory views humans as predisposed to think, emote, and behave both irrationally and rationally. These predispositions are determined by biological as well as sociocultural influences.

In order to provide a conceptual framework for how emotional disturbances and maladaptive behaviors are originated and maintained, Ellis developed his ABC theory of personality, which posits that negative emotional consequences (C) stem not directly from noxious, environmental-based activating events (A) but rather from clients' subjective perceptions of these events, as dictated by a client's belief system (B). Consequently, the role of the counselor or therapist is one of a teacher who directly and actively confronts and disputes the client's irrational ideas and beliefs and self-defeating behaviors. Moreover, the RET counselor or therapist functions as an eclectic expert, borrowing from a wide range of cognitive, emotive, and behavioral modes of therapy to enable the client to abandon inefficient and illogical ways of thinking and behaving and adopt a more rational view of life.

Outcome studies of RET generally support its efficacy in alleviating feelings of depression and anxiety. However, more large-scale empirical research must be conducted to study the usefulness of this method as compared to other modes of psychotherapy.

REFERENCES

Burke, J. F. (1989). *Contemporary approaches to psychotherapy and counseling*. Pacific Grove, CA: Brooks/Cole.

DiGiuseppe, A. A., Miller, N. J., & Trexler, L. (1977). Outcome studies of rational-emotive therapy. *Counseling Psychologist, 7*, 64–72.

Dryden, W. (1984). *Rational-emotive therapy: Fundamentals and innovations*. London: Croom Helm.

Dryden, W. (1989). Albert Ellis: An efficient and passionate life (an interview with Albert Ellis). *Journal of Counseling and Development, 67*, 539–546.

Ellis, A. (1962). *Reason and emotion in psychotherapy*. New York: Lyle Stuart.

Ellis, A. (1973). *Humanistic psychotherapy: The rational-emotive approach*. New York: Julian.

Ellis, A. (1974). Rational-emotive theory: Albert Ellis. In A. Burton (Ed.), *Operational theories of personality* (pp. 308–344). New York: Brunner/Mazel.

Ellis, A. (1976). The biological basis of human irrationality. *Journal of Individual Psychology, 32*, 145–168.

Ellis, A. (1977). The basic clinical theory of rational-emotive therapy. In A. Ellis & R. Grieger (Eds.), *Handbook of rational-emotive therapy* (Vol. 1) (pp. 185–202). New York: Springer.

Ellis, A. (1979a). Rational-emotive therapy. In R. J. Corsini (Ed.), *Current psychotherapies* (2nd ed.) (pp. 185–229). Itasca, IL: Peacock.

Ellis, A. (1979b). The rational-emotive approach to counseling. In H. M. Burks & B. Stefflre (Eds.), *Theories of counseling* (3rd ed.) (pp. 172–219). New York: McGraw-Hill.

Ellis, A. (1980). Rational-emotive therapy and cognitive behavior therapy: Similarities and differences. *Cognitive Therapy and Research, 4*, 325–340.

Ellis, A. (1984). Forward. In W. Dryden, *Rational-emotive therapy: Fundamentals and innovations* (pp. i–xv). London: Croom Helm.

Ellis, A. (1985). *Overcoming resistance: Rational-emotive therapy with difficult clients*. New York: Springer.

Ellis, A. (1987). A sadly neglected cognitive element in depression. *Cognitive Therapy and Research, 11*, 121–146.

Ellis, A. (1989). Rational-emotive therapy. In R. J. Corsini & D. Wedding (Eds.), *Current psychotherapies* (4th ed.) (pp. 197–238). Itasca, IL: Peacock.

Ellis, A., & Abrahams, E. (1978). *Brief psychotherapy in medical and health practice*. New York: Springer.

Ellis, A., & Bernard, M. E. (Eds.). (1985). *Clinical applications of rational-emotive therapy*. New York: Plenum.

Ellis, A., & Bernard, M. E. (1986). What is rational-emotive therapy (RET)? In A. Ellis & R. Grieger (Eds.), *Handbook of rational-emotive therapy* (Vol. 2) (pp. 3–31). New York: Springer.

Ellis, A., & Grieger, R. (Eds.). (1977). *Handbook of rational-emotive therapy* (Vol. 1). New York: Springer.

Ellis, A., & Harper, R. A. (1975). *A guide to rational living*. Englewood Cliffs, NJ: Prentice-Hall.

Ellis, A., & Whiteley, J. M. (1979). *Theoretical and empirical foundations of rational-emotive therapy*. Monterey, CA: Brooks/Cole.

Engels, G., & Dieksta, R. (1986). A meta-analysis of rational-emotive therapy outcome studies. In P. Eelen & O. Fontaine (Eds.), *Behavior therapy: Beyond the conditioning framework* (pp. 121–140). Hillsdale, NJ: Erlbaum.

Gilliland, B. E., James, R. K., & Bowman, J. T. (1989). *Theories and strategies in counseling and psychotherapy* (2nd ed.). Englewood Cliffs, NJ: Prentice-Hall.

Grieger, R. M. (1986). The process of rational-emotive therapy. In A. Ellis & R. M. Grieger (Eds.), *Handbook of rational-emotive therapy* (Vol. 2) (pp. 203–212). New York: Springer.

Haaga, D. A., & Davison, G. C. (1989). Outcome studies of rational-emotive therapy. In M. E. Bernard & R. DiGiuseppe (Eds.), *Inside rational-emotive therapy* (pp. 155–197). San Diego: Academic Press.

Kassinove, H., Crisci, R., & Tiegerman, S. (1977). Developmental trends in rational thinking: Implications for rational-emotive school mental health programs. *Journal of Community Psychology, 5*, 266–274.

Lipsky, M., Kassinove, H., & Miller, N. (1980). Effects of rational-emotive therapy, rational role reversal, and rational-emotive imagery on the emotional adjustment of community mental health center patients. *Journal of Counseling and Clinical Psychology, 48,* 366–374.

Litvak, S. (1976). *An outline of rational-emotive therapy.* Unpublished manuscript. University of Wisconsin, Madison.

Maddi, S. R. (1989). *Personality theories: A comparative analysis* (5th ed.). Chicago: Dorsey.

Mahoney, J. A. (1977). A critical analysis of rational-emotive theory and therapy. *Counseling Psychologist, 7,* 43–46.

Maultsby, M. C. (1971). Rational emotive imagery. *Rational Living, 6,* 24–26.

McGovern T. E., & Silverman, M. (1986). A review of outcome studies of rational-emotive therapy from 1977 to 1982. In A. Ellis & R. Grieger (Eds.), *Handbook of rational-emotive therapy* (Vol. 2) (pp. 81–102). New York: Springer.

Miller, R. C., & Berman, J. S. (1983). The efficacy of cognitive behavior therapies: A quantitative review of the research evidence. *Psychological Bulletin, 94,* 39–53.

Murphy, R., & Ellis, A. (1979). *A comprehensive bibliography of materials on rational-emotive therapy and cognitive-behavior therapy.* New York: Institute for Rational Living.

Patterson, C. H. (1986). *Theories of counseling and psychotherapy* (4th ed.). New York: Harper & Row.

Prochaska, J. O. (1984). *Systems of psychotherapy* (2nd ed.). Homewood, IL: Dorsey.

Shapiro, D. A. (1985). Recent applications of meta-analysis in clinical research. *Clinical Psychology Review, 5,* 13–34.

Shorkey, C. T., & Whiteman, V. L. (1977). Development of the rational behavior inventory. *Educational and Psychological Measurement, 37,* 527–534.

Shilling, L. E. (1984). *Perspectives on counseling theories.* Englewood Cliffs, NJ: Prentice-Hall.

Smith, M. L., & Glass, G. V. (1977). Meta-analysis of psychotherapy outcome studies. *American Psychologist, 32,* 752–760.

Tosi, D. J., Leclair, S. W., Peters, H. J., & Murphy, M. A. (1987). *Theories and applications of counseling.* Springfield, IL: Charles C Thomas.

Wallace, W. A. (1986). *Theories of counseling and psychotherapy: A basic issues approach.* Boston: Allyn & Bacon.

Wessler, R. A., & Wessler, R. L. (1980). *The principles and practices of rational-emotive therapy.* San Francisco: Jossey-Bass.

Ziegler, D. J. (1989). A critique of rational-emotive theory of personality. In M. E. Bernard & R. DiGiuseppe (Eds.), *Inside rational-emotive therapy* (pp. 27–45). San Diego: Academic Press.

CHAPTER THIRTEEN

Cognitive-Behavioral Theories

Cynthia R. Kalodner
West Virginia University

Cognitive-behavioral theories are best conceptualized as a general category or set of related theories that have evolved from the theoretical writings, clinical experiences, and empirical studies of behavioral and cognitively oriented psychologists. There is no single definition of cognitive-behavioral theory. The individual theories are tied together by common assumptions, techniques, and research strategies but maintain a diversity of views about the role that cognitions play in behavior change (Kendall & Hollon, 1979; Meichenbaum, 1979). The following statement regarding behavior therapy could be extended to present-day cognitive-behavioral theory and counseling and psychotherapy: "Contemporary behavior therapy is marked by a diversity of views, a broad range of heterogeneous procedures with different rationales, and open debate about conceptual bases, methodological requirements, and evidence of efficacy" (Kazdin & Wilson, 1978, p. 1).

The hyphenated term *cognitive-behavioral* reflects the importance of both behavioral and cognitive approaches to understanding and helping human beings (Garfield & Bergin, 1986). The hyphen brings together behavioral and cognitive theoretical views, each with its own theoretical assumptions and intervention strategies. The amalgamation of cognitive and behavioral theory is described as "a purposeful attempt to preserve the demonstrated efficiencies of behavior modification within a less doctrinaire context and to incorporate the cognitive activities of the client in the efforts to produce therapeutic change" (Kendall & Hollon, 1979, p. 1). This chapter demonstrates how aspects of behavioral and cognitive approaches have blended into cognitive-behavioral counseling and psychotherapy.

Many current theories fit into the category of cognitive-behavioral, including (but not limited to) Albert Ellis's rational-emotive theory (1962), Aaron Beck's cognitive therapy (Beck, 1976; Beck, Rush, Shaw, & Emery, 1979), and Donald Meichenbaum's stress inoculation training (1985) and self-instructional training (1977). Chapter 12 fully describes Ellis's work in rational-emotive theory. Therefore, this chapter highlights the work of Beck and Meichenbaum in the development of cognitive-behavioral approaches to helping people.

HISTORY

To understand cognitive-behavioral theories, it is necessary to study the history of the development of behavioral theory, various cognitive models, and the union of these approaches into cognitive-behavioral theories.

A Brief History of Behavior Theory

Early behaviorism was based on learning theory, the development of clearly defined techniques, and well-designed systematic research (Hayes & Hayes, 1992). The behavioral history of cognitive-behavioral theory began with the behavioral approaches developed by John B. Watson. Behaviorism was formed as a reaction against the Freudian emphasis on consciousness as the subject matter of psychology and introspection as the method of its investigation. Watson (1930) claimed that behavior should be the sole subject matter of psychology and that it should be studied through observation. Furthermore, according to Watson, conscious processes (such as thinking) were determined to be outside the realm of scientific inquiry (Mahoney, 1974).

Using Pavlov's principles of classical conditioning, in which unconditioned stimuli (loud bell) paired with conditioned stimuli (white rat) lead to a conditioned response (startle), Watson trained Little Albert to fear a white rat, white cotton, and even Watson's white hair! This demonstration is important because it indicates that human emotions can be learned and modified using learning principles. There are several other well-known conditioning model behaviorists, including Eysenck, Rachman, and Wolpe, who developed treatments such as systematic desensitization and flooding based on classical conditioning and counterconditioning (Kazdin & Wilson, 1978). The relationship between stimulus and response is essential to these classical behavioral paradigms.

Watson brought a critical contribution to psychology: the methodology for conducting research (Mahoney, 1974). Methodological behaviorism is concerned with procedures for scientific inquiry and data collection. It is characterized by an assumption of determinism, an emphasis on observation of behavior and environmental stimuli, the use of specific operational definitions of independent and dependent variables such that measurement is reliable, the necessity to be able to falsify the hypotheses through research, use of controlled experimentation, and replication of research findings and attempts to generalize findings to other subjects or situations (Mahoney, 1974). Methodological behaviorism continues to have a strong influence on cognitive-behavioral research.

B. F. Skinner and Operant Conditioning   Skinner's work on the principles of reinforcement and operant conditioning further developed the school of behaviorism. His work has been tremendously influential in the field of counseling and psychotherapy. Skinner developed applied behavioral analysis, which is based on operant conditioning. In operant conditioning, reinforcers shape behavior by being contingent on the response (Kazdin & Wilson, 1978; Miller, 1980). He developed contingency explanations for behavior and defined scientific observations as those under the control of some type of contingency (Hayes & Hayes, 1992). Skinner's schedules of reinforcement (1969) defined how different amounts of reinforcement can be delivered to continue to support behavioral changes. Key interventions in applied behavior analysis include reinforcement, punishment, extinction, and stimulus control, each of which involves a search for an environmental variable that will lead to changes in behavior (Kazdin & Wilson, 1978).

In operant conditioning, reinforcement is used to increase behavior. Examples of positive reinforcement include praise or money. Negative reinforcement, which also increases behavior, involves the removal of a negative stimulus, such as an electric shock or a ringing bell. An example of negative reinforcement is turning off a loud bell after a rat presses a bar. Punishment and extinction decrease behavior by the addition of an aversive stimulus or the removal of a positive reinforcer, respectively. An example of punishment involves following cigarette smoking with electric shock. In extinction, a behavior to be decreased is ignored; people who have the habit of interrupting conversation are ignored by friends when they interrupt, but friends listen when comments are made in conversation without interrupting. These and many other applied behavior analysis techniques are included in Miller's (1980) text, which is a programmed learning manual designed to demonstrate the role of behavioral techniques in everyday situations.

John Krumboltz and Counseling.   John Krumboltz popularized behavioral approaches in counseling and psychotherapy (Krumboltz & Thoresen, 1976). He identified behavioral counseling and psychotherapy as "a process of helping people to learn how to solve interpersonal, emotional, and decision problems" (1976, p. 2). This definition emphasizes learning as the method to make change. Further, Krumboltz and Thoresen (1976) indicate that the term *behavioral* is indicative of the way to measure success in counseling and psychotherapy; that is, clients should make changes in behavior as a result of counseling and psychotherapy.

A Brief History of Cognitive Therapy

The cognitive revolution brought about by Ellis, Beck, Bandura, and others began when clinicians found that the available systems of therapy were not satisfactory. Ellis (1962) pointed out that "human beings . . . are not the same as Pavlovian dogs or other lower animals; and their emotional disturbances are quite different from the experimental neuroses and other emotional upsets we produce in the laboratory" (p. 14). He found that the language aspects of neurosis were missing in other theoretical systems, and he believed that individuals have psychological difficulties due to their ability to communicate with others and themselves in a manner different from that available to animals. The basis of Ellis's rational-emotive therapy is that human beings generate psychological disturbances by faulty or irrational thinking.

Aaron Beck Develops Cognitive Therapy.   Beck (1976) also responded with dissatisfaction to psychoanalysis and behavior therapy. He objected to the unconscious aspects of Freud's theory, asserting that people can be aware of factors that are responsible for emotional upsets and blurred thinking. Beck indicated that his work with depressed individuals did not substantiate the psychoanalytic theory (Weinrach, 1988). At the same time, he found the radical behavioral explanation for human emotional disturbance too limited to explain human emotional difficulties adequately. For Beck, psychological disturbances may be the result of "faulty learning, making incorrect inferences on the basis of inadequate or incorrect information, and not distinguishing adequately between imagination and reality" (1976, pp. 19–20).

Cognitive-Behavioral Theory Begins.   Albert Bandura is another influential theorist. He described a social learning theory model that asserts that cognitive processes mediate the development and maintenance of behavior (1977, 1986). He maintained an emphasis on behavioral procedures to change behavior but developed the use of cognitive processes to explain the process of change (Mahoney & Lyddon, 1988). His work was part of a trend away from strict behaviorism, even by those who, like Bandura himself, were leaders in the behavioral movement (Garfield & Bergin, 1986). In his model, principles of classical conditioning and reinforcement are also included; however, the emphasis is on the role of cognitive factors in determining the environmental influences on behavior (Bandura, 1977, 1986). Another unique aspect of Bandura's social learning model is that the relationship between the environment and the individual is described as reciprocal; they influence each other (Mahoney & Lyddon, 1988). Earlier behavioral theories emphasized the role of the environment in shaping behavior but did not include the possibility of the individual's influence on the environment.

After the development of cognitive interventions, many behavior therapists became increasingly concerned with mediational constructs (that is, thoughts); and, at the same time, cognitive therapists developed interest in the research associated with methodological behaviorism (Kendall & Hollon, 1979). For example, in the late 1960s and early 1970s, behaviorists applied operant techniques to thoughts (referred to as coverants). The covert conditioning models assumed that thoughts were covert operants subject to the same rules as behavioral operants. Although many of these techniques have not fared well (Mahoney, 1974), the union between behaviorists and cognitivists is demonstrated.

The union began slowly; and the field was replete with arguments over conceptual models, interventions, and research issues. However, by 1987, 69 percent of the members of the Association for the Advancement of Behavior Therapy (AABT) identified themselves as cognitive-behavioral, while only 26.9 percent and 2 percent selected behavioral or cognitive, respectively, as their theoretical orientation (Craighead, 1990). AABT is a professional group that was formed at the peak of behaviorism, but it has shifted from a focus on strictly behavioral work to cognitive and cognitive-behavioral intervention and research. The convention content of AABT has become much more cognitive, as evidenced by a greater percentage of cognitive and cognitive-behavioral presentations at the annual meeting of the association. Between 1987 and 1990, 39.2 percent of the presentations were primarily cognitive, and 30.7 percent were primarily behavioral (Dobson, Beamish, & Taylor, 1992). In 1990, the greatest percentage (43 percent) of presentations were cognitive-behavioral (Dobson et al., 1992).

HUMAN NATURE: A DEVELOPMENTAL PERSPECTIVE

One wonders what *development* means to behaviorists and cognitive-behaviorists. Early behavioral theory, with its emphasis on learning, seems somewhat antithetical to developmentalism. However, Achenbach (1986) defended the use of learning as a synonym for development when he said that "whether one prefers to think of major changes in behavior in terms of 'development' or 'learning,' concepts of this type help generate testable hypotheses" (p. 118).

The view of the development of human nature for the early behaviorists was limited to the learning concepts of operant and classical conditioning. Individuals born with a tabula rasa (blank slate) develop as they learn to associate stimuli and responses. Development can be seen as the sum total of these associations (Achenbach, 1986). The cognitive paradigm advances from defining development as the acquisition of responses to a definition that includes changes in the structuring of thoughts and behavior (Achenbach, 1986). Further, cognitive approaches include vicarious learning, in which a person may learn through watching a model perform a behavior (Bandura, 1977, 1986).

Cognitive-behavioral theories are not developmental in the same sense that stage theories (such as psychoanalytic) are. There is a stated assumption that behavior is learned (Cormier & Cormier, 1991; Kazdin & Wilson, 1978); this applies equally to the explanation of how problem behaviors and adaptive behaviors are developed. Behavior is assumed to be developed and maintained by external events or cues, external reinforcers, or internal processes such as cognition (Cormier & Cormier, 1991). This assumption expresses the influence of the early behaviorists and the recognition of the importance of cognition in the process of development. Development is based on each individual's different learning history, the unique experiences provided by the environment, and the individual's cognitive understanding of the world.

The use of the here and now, a nonhistorical perspective in cognitive-behavioral therapy, highlights the emphasis on the present in understanding the presenting problems of a client. Childhood learning experiences are not usually the variables that are functionally related to current behavior, and the functional relationship is critical to assessment and treatment. Except as they may relate to present problems, past problems are not attended to in the same way as they might be in other counseling and psychotherapy systems (Beck et al., 1979). However, because current problems are influenced by individual social learning history, past problems are not ignored, although it is clear that there is a relative lack of importance of early childhood experiences.

According to Krumboltz and Thoresen (1976), certain environmental circumstances shape the development of individuals. These include insufficient reinforcement; reinforcement for maladaptive actions; reliance on a single, self-defeating reinforcer; excessive punishment; and insufficient cues to predict consequences. Insufficient reinforcement means simply that an individual may act but not receive a reward. Krumboltz and Thoresen (1976) describe this phenomenon as receiving too few goodies of life. Reinforcement for maladaptive actions refers to the situation that arises when someone is reinforced for behavior that is actually negative. An example is a child who tells the truth about misbehaving and is immediately punished versus the child who lies about bad behavior and avoids punishment.

Reliance on a single, self-defeating reinforcer refers to the use of food, smoking, or other addictive behavior to cope with problems in life. Excessive punishment may be a societal issue based on the use of punishment rather than positive reinforcement to control behavior. Krumboltz and Thoresen (1976) assert that when punishment is used, anxiety and fear may develop. Finally, the environmental problem of insufficient cues to predict consequences occurs when individuals do not know when certain behavior is appropriate. In other words, individuals may be unaware of the effect their behavior may have on others and on themselves. Although these contributors to development explain the way in which individuals are shaped by their environment, individuals are also seen as contributors to their environment; individual behavior and the environment are reciprocally related. This is a strongly behavioral explanation for human development highlighting the role of the environment in explaining human development. Adding a more cognitive and social learning perspective to human development, Bandura (1974) indicated that as individuals mature, they obtain more freedom from reinforcement from others and move toward greater self-reinforcement.

MAJOR CONSTRUCTS

Because cognitive-behavioral theories are an amalgamation of behavioral and cognitive approaches, the cognitive-behavioral theoretical constructs contain aspects of both behavioral and cognitive theory. Considering the separate behavioral and cognitive roots may illustrate the key constructs in cognitive-behavioral theories. Kendall and Hollon (1979) consider the treatment target, treatment approach, and treatment evaluation for behavioral, cognitive, and cognitive-behavioral theories (see table 13.1).

For behavioral interventions, purely behavioral terms such as behavioral excesses or deficits, learning theory, and observed changes in behavior are used. Likewise, the cognitive interventions are based on purely cognitive terms such as cognitive excesses or deficits, semantic interventions (cognitive), and changes in cognitions.

Cognitive-behavioral interventions are considered to be a range of approaches limited by the purer behavioral and cognitive interventions (Kendall & Hollon, 1979). Treatment targets range from behavioral excesses and deficits to cognitive excesses and deficits, and the middle-of-the-road cognitive-behavioral interventions target both cognitive and behavioral excesses and deficits. The treatment interventions also range from an emphasis on behavioral interventions, to an emphasis on cognitive interventions with some behavioral strategies included, to a full integration of cognitive and behavioral strategies. What cognitive-behavioral theories provide, given this amalgamation model, is greater flexibility in treatment targets and interventions with an emphasis on rigorous standards in measurement of change and research evaluation (Kendall & Hollon, 1979).

The Importance of Cognitions

The unifying characteristic of cognitive-behavioral counseling and psychotherapy approaches is the fundamental emphasis on the importance of

TABLE 13.1
General Characteristics of Cognitive-Behavioral Interventions

	Treatment Target	Treatment Approach	Treatment Evaluation
BEHAVIORAL	Behavioral excesses or deficits	Behavioral "learning theory" interventions. Environmental manipulations (e.g., token economies, contingency management)	Observed changes in behavior with rigorous evaluation
COGNITIVE-BEHAVIORAL	Behavioral excesses or deficits	Behavioral interventions. Skills training, information provision (e.g., modeling, role playing)	Observed changes in behavior with rigorous evaluation
	Behavioral and cognitive excesses and deficits	Broadly conceived behavioral and cognitive methods	Observed changes in behavior and cognition with methodological rigor
	Cognitive excesses or deficits	Cognitive interventions with adjunctive behavioral procedures	Examination of cognitive and, to a lesser extent, of behavioral changes
COGNITIVE	Cognitive excesses or deficits	Semantic interventions	Changes in cognitions, "integrative changes," often, but not always, nonempirically evaluated

Source: From Hollon, S. D., & Kendall, P. C. (1979). Cognitive-behavioral interventions: Theory and procedure. In P. C. Kendall & S. D. Hollon (Eds.), *Cognitive-behavioral interventions: Theory, research, and procedures* (pp. 445–454). New York: Academic Press. Copyright 1979 by Academic Press. Reprinted by permission.

cognitive workings and private events as mediators of behavior change (Kazdin & Wilson, 1978; Kendall & Hollon, 1979). The relationship between thoughts and behavior is a major aspect of cognitive-behavioral theory and counseling and psychotherapy. The cognitive-behavioral approaches assume that cognitive processes mediate behavior and experience, that these processes can be studied and altered, and that desired behavior change can be achieved through cognitive change (Dobson & Block, 1988).

The Importance of Learning

The cognitive-behavioral model of psychological disturbance asserts that abnormal behavior is learned and developed in the same way that normal behavior is learned, and that cognitive-behavioral principles can be applied to change the behavior (Cormier & Cormier, 1991). The importance of this statement lies in the focus on learning as the way in which behavior is acquired rather than on the underlying intrapsychic conflicts. It rejects the psychodynamic and quasi-disease models of development, which assume that underlying intrapsychic conflicts cause maladaptive behavior.

The Importance of Operational Definitions and Functional Analysis

In cognitive-behavioral approaches, problems are viewed operationally. The definition of the presenting problem must be concrete, specific, and observable whenever possible. It is assumed that problems are functionally related to internal and external antecedents and consequences. This assumption means that in order to understand behavior, it is necessary to know the events that precede (antecedents) and follow (consequences) the behavior. These events may be external, observable behaviors or internal thoughts and feelings. The functional relationship conceptualization of problems necessitates a clear understanding of the internal and external antecedents that contribute to a problematic behavior as well as the internal and external consequences that maintain behavior. This also means that the causes and treatments of problems should be multidimensional. Causes might include behaviors, environmental circumstances, thoughts, beliefs, or attitudes. Because there is rarely a single cause for a problem, treatments are comprehensive and designed to address the multiple issues. (Treatments are addressed in the intervention section of this chapter.) In summary, cognitive-behavioral theories share a counseling/therapeutic focus, a set of intervention techniques, and research evaluation strategies (Kazdin & Wilson, 1978).

THE PROCESS OF CHANGE

Understanding the process of change means understanding how the theory explains the mechanisms for counseling or therapeutic change. This is particularly important in the cognitive-behavioral arena because there are many different theories and interventions.

Self-efficacy

Bandura's (1977, 1986) self-efficacy theory has been used to provide a cognitive-behavioral theoretical explanation for how people change. It has been proposed as a common pathway to explain how people change even though they use different counseling or therapeutic techniques. Self-efficacy theory asserts that individuals develop expectations for their success in performing specific behaviors and these expectations influence their decision to try new behaviors and maintain behavioral changes (Bandura, 1977, 1986). Self-efficacy may be thought of as a sense of personal competence or feelings of mastery. The degree to which a person feels efficacious influences the amount of effort that will be applied in given situations. Thus, cognitive behavior therapy may work through increasing self-efficacy of clients.

Bandura (1986) described four mechanisms through which self-efficacy can be developed: enactive attainments, vicarious experience, verbal persuasion, and recognition of physiological states. Enactive attainments, the most powerful contributors to self-efficacy development, refer to an individual's own experience with achieving a goal. Vicarious experiences refer to observing others as they succeed or fail. Through the process of observing, individuals are provided with a basis for making comparisons with their own competence to perform the task. Verbal persuasion, in which an individual is told "you can do it," is a less powerful way to influence self-efficacy. The final source of self-efficacy, physiological states, refers to the emotional arousal or degree of apprehension one feels. Feelings of fear may lead to decreased performance, while a moderate amount of anxiety may be helpful when performing a new task.

Examples of how clients learn assertive behavior can be used to apply these sources of self-efficacy. When clients are taught assertiveness skills, they practice making appropriate assertive comments. Enactive attainments are the experience of success that lead clients to feel able to repeat the assertive behavior. In assertiveness training groups, clients watch each other perform new behaviors; this is an example of vicarious experiences. Verbal persuasion is the source of self-efficacy based on telling clients "you can do it"; like encouragement, it might increase self efficacy, but other sources are more powerful. The physiological states mechanism can be used in assertiveness training to inform clients that a moderate amount of anxiety may be helpful as they attempt to make changes in their behavior.

It is important to recognize that when applying the self-efficacy model to how cognitive therapy and other cognitive-behavioral interventions work, all four of the sources of self-efficacy are involved. In the process of learning that cognitions contribute to behavior and affective difficulties, enactive attainments, vicarious experiences, verbal persuasion, and physiological states play major roles.

Does Changing Beliefs Change Behavior?

Addressing the question of how people change, Beck (1976) asserts that behavioral and affective change are hypothesized to occur through the change in cognitions. The assumption is clearly that changing beliefs is the key to helping people. Research has demonstrated that cognitive therapy does indeed change thoughts and that there are reductions in psychological disturbances. However, it has not been clearly demonstrated that changes in cognitions cause changes in behavior or affect. In fact, changes in cognition occur in behavioral programs not designed to change thoughts (DeLucia & Kalodner, 1990) and in pharmacological treatment (Hollon & Beck, 1986). It seems that the mechanism for the relationship between cognitive change and affective or behavioral change is not yet clearly identified (Hollon & Beck, 1986).

INTERVENTION STRATEGIES

There is great variability in the interventions practiced in cognitive-behavioral counseling and psychotherapy. Cognitive-behavioral interventions include various combinations of cognitive and behavioral techniques and are aimed at changing either cognitions, behavior, or both (Hollon & Kendall, 1979) (see table 13.1). Common to cognitive-behavioral interventions is a directive style; structured, goal-directed, and time-limited treatment; use of homework assignments and skills practice; and a focus on problem-solving ability. In addition, the client and the counselor or therapist have a collaborative relationship (Kovacs, 1980). Intervention techniques associated with cognitive-behavioral theory are so varied that there is a *Dictionary of Behavior Therapy Techniques* (Bellack & Hersen, 1987) that contains descriptions of 158 techniques. The title of the book is misleading, however, because cognitive strategies are also included. The techniques range from "alternative incompatible behavior" to "videotape feedback." Further, Mahoney and Lyddon (1988) identified more than 20 different cognitive therapies.

Behavioral Assessment

Counselors or therapists using a cognitive-behavioral theoretical orientation begin work with clients by using a behavioral assessment framework to collect information (Nelson & Barlow, 1981). Behavioral assessment developed along with behavior theory as a reaction against traditional psychological assessment, with an emphasis on developing reliable and valid measures for experimental research (Galassi & Perot, 1992). Behavioral assessment, perhaps now better known as cognitive-behavioral assessment, has evolved from its early emphasis on purely observable behavior to include cognition and cognitive processes. A comprehensive behavioral assessment attends not only to overt behavior, but also to emotional and cognitive behaviors (Galassi & Perot, 1992; Nelson & Barlow, 1981). As a result of the cognitive revolution, assessment strategies have been developed to collect information from clients about their imagery, attributions, beliefs, expectations, and self-statements (Galassi & Perot, 1992).

The triple response mode provides a conceptual framework for counselors or therapists conducting assessment (Nelson & Barlow, 1981). Triple response refers to attention to overt behavior, emotional-physiological, and cognitive-verbal areas (Nelson & Barlow, 1981). It is critical that the counselor or therapist ask questions with the intention of collecting data in the triple response mode to obtain a complete functional analysis of behavior (Nelson & Barlow, 1981). The overt behavior response might be assessed by asking, "If I were watching you, what would I see you do?" Emotional-physiological data could be obtained by asking, "How does your body react?" (Nelson & Barlow, 1981), and the cognitive-verbal area could be questioned with "What statements run through your mind?"

The purposes of behavioral interviewing are to identify the target behavior and the controlling variables and to plan an appropriate intervention (Nelson & Barlow, 1981). Behavioral assessment focuses on the current determinants of behavior and is known for the high degree of specificity (Kazdin & Wilson, 1978). It is concerned with what the client does, feels, and thinks in particular situations. The counselor or therapist works to define the presenting problem concretely and to understand the antecedents and consequences of the problem. Counselors or therapists begin the assessment by asking the client to describe the problem. Nelson and Barlow (1981) warn against assuming that what the client describes initially is the most important problem, for the client may not be ready to reveal the true problem at the beginning of the first meeting. For this reason a global assessment is recommended. There are several structured interviews that assess employment, sleep, stress, and relationships (for example, Lazarus, 1971). The counselor or therapist can then use information derived from the structured interview along with the initial description of the presenting problem to develop a more accurate picture of the problem.

Behavioral assessment may include the use of questionnaires, role playing to assess certain skills (interpersonal, phobias), and interviews with significant others (Nelson & Barlow, 1981). Self-monitoring is an often-used assessment tool in which clients are asked to record their thoughts, feelings, and behaviors as they happen. For example, an individual in treatment for social anxiety might be asked to keep records of attempts to talk to strangers. These records might include the thoughts before trying to say something, pre-approach feelings rated on an intensity scale of 1 to 10, the comment actually made, and the affective reaction to the situation. Open-ended comments may also be helpful in planning interventions.

Behavioral assessment is idiographic (concerned with the individual) in that it attempts to understand the antecedents and consequences of behavior for the individual client (Galassi & Perot, 1992). This is important because such specificity is necessary to develop individualized treatment plans. One of the contributions of the behavioral approaches is the close relationship between assessment and treatment (Galassi & Perot, 1992).

Cognitive-Behavioral Treatment Techniques

Because cognitive-behavioral interventions include aspects of both behavioral and cognitive interventions, this section provides a few examples of some commonly used intervention strategies.

Behavioral Interventions.   Behavioral interventions are those that focus primarily on changing specific behaviors. Examples of purely behavioral interventions include reinforcement, extinction, shaping, stimulus control, and aversive control (Miller, 1980).

Reinforcement is a well-known behavioral strategy. Positive reinforcement is a procedure in which some behavior is increased by following it with something rewarding; for example, children who clean their room are given praise and attention, a gold star, or a new toy. It is most important that the receiver views the reinforcer as positive. Negative reinforcement is the removal of something aversive to increase behavior. The buzz most cars make when the key is put in the ignition is a negative reinforcer designed to increase seat belt usage. Both positive and negative reinforcement can be applied when clients want to increase a behavior.

Extinction is a behavioral intervention designed to decrease a problematic behavior. In this case, a reinforcer that has followed the behavior in the past is removed, and the problem behavior decreases. For example, think about children who repeatedly get out of their seats in a classroom.

When the teacher notices and asks the children to sit down, they may return to their seats. However, the attention of the teacher is reinforcing, and the problem behavior usually continues. Extinction is the procedure by which the teacher ignores the behavior until it stops. Extinction is characterized by response burst, or an increase in negative behavior. In this example, the children may continue to get out of their seats, wander around the classroom, and increasingly engage in negative behavior to get the attention of the teacher. By giving in and attending to the behavior now, the teacher actually reinforces the negative out-of-seat behavior! Response burst is to be expected, and it usually subsides when the individual learns that no amount of negative behavior will get the attention that has been reinforcing.

Shaping is a behavioral intervention used to increase the quality of a behavior gradually. Often used to teach a new skill, shaping works by reinforcing the behavior as it gets closer to the final goal. Shaping is used when there is a clearly identified behavior to be changed and when differential reinforcement (reinforcing the behavior that gets closer and closer to the target while ignoring the other behavior) can be applied to successive approximations of the behavior. For example, in shaping assertive behavior, the counselor or therapist might successively reinforce louder speech, direct eye contact, and other aspects of assertive behavior. This helps the client continue to develop assertiveness speaking skills.

In stimulus control, some event in the environment is used to cue behavior. When a stimulus leads to behavior that is desirable and will be reinforced, the cue is called a discriminative stimulus. For example, seeing exercise shoes in the living room may act as a cue to use an exercise tape to do aerobics. The exercise shoes are a discriminative stimulus for exercise.

One example of aversive control is punishment, which is defined as the addition of an unpleasant event following a negative behavior to decrease the occurrence of that behavior. Punishment is not used often by behaviorists. However, it has been used to eliminate dangerous behavior such as head banging or other self-mutilative behaviors in severely emotionally disturbed children.

Cognitive Interventions.   Cognitive interventions focus on the role of cognitions in the life of clients. Different types of cognitive distortions are identified and changed through the process of cognitive therapy. Some types of cognitive distortions include all-or-nothing thinking, disqualifying the positive, and catastrophizing (Burns, 1980). All-or-nothing thinking is characterized by assuming that things are either 100 percent perfect or absolutely terrible; there is no grey area. Few things are perfect, so all-or-nothing thinking usually leads to depression because everything is viewed as terrible.

Disqualifying the positive is defined as the rejection of any positive experiences (such as compliments) and assuming that these positive events don't really count for some reason. The person using this type of distortion may say, "I only received an A because the test was so easy" or "She is only complimenting me because she wants a ride in my new car." Catastrophizing is the exaggeration of a negative event so that has much more impact than it deserves. A mistake at work or a B on a quiz may be catastrophized into losing the job or failing the course.

Cognitive therapy uses many kinds of procedures to change these negative or maladaptive kinds of thoughts. Thought stopping is a procedure designed to interfere with thoughts that run through the mind of the client and make it difficult to change behavior. For example, thought stopping can be used with a client who thinks that she is too fat. She continues to imagine this troublesome thought running through her mind, and the counselor or therapist shouts, "STOP." While the client may be a bit surprised, the shout does usually stop the thought. The client can then replace the thought with a more adaptive one, such as "I can handle this situation." Clients can learn to stop thoughts on their own and substitute more useful ones.

The use of positive self-statements can go along with thought stopping. Statements such as "My opinion is important" or "I am an assertive person" can be practiced over and over. It is normal if these thoughts do not feel quite right at first. The important point is that what clients tell themselves influences their feelings and behavior. The counselor or therapist may use the self-statements as a way to cue assertive behavior, saying, "If it were true that your opinion was important, how might you behave?" The client might be encouraged to try acting as if the statements were true.

Cognitive-Behavioral Interventions.   The essence of cognitive-behavioral therapies is the union of behavioral and cognitive strategies to help people. Often cognitive-behavioral strategies include the use of treatment manuals or guidelines for the implementation of interventions. Treatment manuals allow counseling and psychotherapy strategies to be operationalized and evaluated. Other advantages of treatment manuals include facilitation of counselor or therapist training and an increased ability to replicate research (Dobson & Shaw, 1988). Beck's cognitive therapy and Meichenbaum's self-instructional training and stress inoculation training have well-developed treatment manuals available for counselors or therapists to use. Although treatment manuals focus on the specific treatment techniques, the relationship between the client and the counselor or therapist is also addressed. Both Beck and Meichenbaum describe the importance of the relationship and include strategies for developing a therapeutic relationship in their manuals.

Beck's Cognitive Therapy.   The primary principle underlying Beck's cognitive theory (CT) is that affect and behavior are determined by the way in which individuals cognitively structure the world. Beck described CT in an interview with Weinrach (1988) as "based on the view of psychopathology that stipulates that people's excessive affect and dysfunctional behavior are due to excessive or inappropriate ways of interpreting their experiences" (p. 160). CT was developed to treat depression; it was later extended as a treatment for anxiety and is now being used to treat other psychological problems such as panic disorder and agoraphobia, drug abuse, and eating disorders (see Scott, Williams, & Beck, 1989; Vallis, Howes, & Miller, 1991). Interested readers are referred to the full description of CT in *Cognitive Therapy of Depression* (Beck et al., 1979) and *Anxiety Disorders and Phobias* (Beck & Emery, 1985).

Beck and Emery (1985) identified the following 10 principles of CT:

1. It is based on the cognitive model of emotional disorders.
2. It is brief and time-limited.
3. It is based on a sound therapeutic relationship, which is a necessary condition.
4. It is a collaborative effort between the counselor or therapist and the client.
5. It primarily uses the Socratic method.
6. It is structured and directive.
7. It is problem oriented.
8. It is based on an educational model.
9. Its theory and techniques rely on the inductive model.
10. It uses homework as a central feature.

The cognitive model of disturbance asserts that cognitions play a central role in human emotional problems. In CT, there is an emphasis on the internal thoughts, feelings, and attitudes, although behavioral techniques are used in conjunction with cognitive therapy to help clients test their maladaptive cognitions and assumptions. Cognitive restructuring is used to identify automatic thoughts, evaluate the content, test the hypothesis, and identify underlying assumptions (Hollon & Beck, 1979).

Unlike some dynamic therapies, CT is time-limited; treatment of anxiety disorders may take from 5 to 20 sessions (Beck & Emery, 1985), and treatment for moderate to severe depression may take 20 sessions over 15 weeks (Beck et al., 1979). The pace of intervention is rapid, and longer-term therapy is viewed as unnecessary to facilitate change. Some guidelines useful for keeping the counseling and psychotherapy process brief include keeping treatment specific and concrete, stressing homework, and developing a brief intervention mental set for both the client and the counselor or therapist (Beck & Emery, 1985).

The therapeutic relationship is highly valued in CT. In order for the cognitive methods to work well, the counselor or therapist must establish good rapport with the client. Accurate empathy and warmth are necessary to enable the client to engage in a relationship with the counselor or therapist so that cognitive techniques can be implemented. Using CT requires a collaboration between the counselor or therapist and the client. It is the counselor or therapist's role to provide structure and expertise in solving the problems presented by the client, but this process is one of teamwork. CT has been described as using collaborative empiricism, which is a continual process used by the counselor or therapist and the client to identify, reality-test, and correct cognitive distortions. Clients are encouraged to be active in the process of learning how maladaptive thoughts interfere with desirable behavior change.

The Socratic method is one in which the counselor or therapist leads the client through a series of questions to become aware of thoughts, identify the distortions in thinking, and find and implement more adaptive replacements for the distortion. Beck et al. (1979) provide the following interaction, which illustrates the use of questions to assist the client to dispute irrational thoughts (pp. 265–266):

Patient: I think anyone who isn't concerned with what others think would be socially retarded and functioning at a pretty low level.
Therapist: Who are the two people you admire most? (The therapist knew the answer from a previous discussion.)
P: My best friend and my boss.
T: Are they overconcerned with others' opinions?
P: No, I don't think that either one cares at all what others think.
T: Are they socially retarded and ineffective?
P: I see your point. Both have good social skills and function at high levels.

It should be clear from this example that the counselor or therapist uses examples and questions to guide the client to the conclusion that the initial statement was inaccurate.

CT is a structured and directive approach to counseling and psychotherapy. Treatment manuals have been developed that are used to structure the counseling and psychotherapy process. Treatment plans are developed for each individual, and each session has an agenda to organize the discussion of specific problems. It is clear that CT is problem-oriented, which means that the focus is on solving present problems. It is based on an educational model; because it assumes that people learn inappropriate ways of coping with life, the process of change involves learning a new way of learning and a new way of thinking. The inductive method is essential to CT because it involves a scientific way of thinking about problems. Clients are encouraged to think about their thoughts as hypotheses that require testing and verification. Counselors or therapists are trained to help the clients disconfirm maladaptive beliefs by confronting individuals with evidence to the contrary. Hypotheses often require behavioral assignments to test assumptions outside of the counseling and psychotherapy session, and clients report on their experiences. In addition, CT requires the client to do regular homework assignments. This involves applying the techniques learned in the counseling and psychotherapy office in the client's world and reporting the results to the counselor or therapist. Homework is used to reinforce the learning and to give the client a place to try out new behaviors.

Meichenbaum's Self-instructional Training and Stress Inoculation Training.   Meichenbaum began his work on self-talk by studying schizophrenia (1969). He found that when individuals with schizophrenia were trained to use *healthy talk* such as "be relevant," they were able to repeat these phrases and behave more appropriately. He continued to consider the role of self-statements in his work with impulsive children (Meichenbaum & Goodman, 1969) and developed the procedures for self-instructional training, which he published in a treatment manual in 1977.

Self-instructional training is a technique in which clients learn to keep track of self-statements (what clients say to themselves) and to substitute more adaptive statements (such as "I know I can do this"). They learn to make these adaptive statements through homework assignments and practice in nonstressful situations. It is important that the statements be phrased in the words of the clients in order to be personally meaningful. Later, the adaptive statements are practiced in increasingly stressful situations to deal with anxiety or phobia. Self-instructional training has been used alone and within the stress inoculation treatment package.

Stress inoculation training (SIT) is a cognitive-behavioral intervention package that combines "didactic teaching, Socratic discussion, cognitive restructuring, problem-solving and relaxation training, behavioral and imaginal rehearsal, self-monitoring, self-instruction and self-reinforcement, and efforts at environmental change" (Meichenbaum, 1985, p. 21). The term *stress inoculation training* highlights the emphasis on stress as the problem; inoculation, an analogy to the medical concept of inoculation against biological disease, as a way to develop the psychological immunities to cope with stress; and training as part of the clinical technique.

SIT consists of three phases: conceptualization, skills acquisition and rehearsal, and application and follow-through (Meichenbaum, 1985). The conceptualization phase focuses on the development of a counseling/therapeutic relationship between the counselor or therapist and the client and provides the client with the background to understand stress and its effects on human life. The second phase, skills acquisition and rehearsal, consists of learning a variety of coping skills and practicing these skills in session and in vivo. In cases in which clients have coping skills they are not using, the counselor or therapist might assist them to understand the intrapersonal and interpersonal issues raised by using the skills and help them remove inhibitors that prevent them from using appropriate coping skills. The final phase, application and follow-through, brings attention to the importance of a booster session, follow-up activities, and relapse prevention.

The specific goals and objectives for each phase of SIT are clearly outlined in Meichenbaum's *Stress Inoculation Training* (1985) and in Meichenbaum and Deffenbacher (1988). The conceptualization phase of SIT is structured to tie assessment of the problematic situation to the development of the counseling or psychotherapy relationship. It is educational and conceptual (Meichenbaum & Deffenbacher, 1988). The counseling and psychotherapy relationship is critical to mediate the behavioral changes; SIT, like Beck's CT, is a collaborative intervention. Meichenbaum (1985) highlights the need for warmth, accurate understanding, and acceptance in order for the client to develop a trusting relationship. The assessment phase consists of a semistructured interview in which the client is asked to describe the problem and provide concrete examples of stressful events. A cognitive-behavioral analysis of stressful reactions is obtained by asking about specific antecedents ("What was going on the last time the problem occurred?") and consequences ("What happened after?"). The assessment phase may include imagery-based recall, a procedure in which clients are guided through an imaginal reexperience of a stressful event to collect information about the thoughts, feelings, and behaviors associated with stress. Self-monitoring and open-ended diaries or stress logs can be used to bring valuable information back to the counseling and psychotherapy sessions. Other sources of information include in vivo behavioral assessments and psychological testing. It should be clear that the conceptualization phase is important because it provides the background necessary for the implementation of coping strategies and helps the counselor or therapist choose the types of coping skills to be introduced in the next phase.

The skills acquisition and rehearsal phase of SIT is designed to ensure that the client learns and can implement various coping skills (Meichenbaum & Deffenbacher, 1988). Clients should complete this phase of counseling and psychotherapy with a repertoire of strategies to cope with stressful situations. Relaxation training is a very commonly used technique. Meichenbaum does not present a single type of relaxation technique; rather, he highlights the need to work with individual clients to assure that the relaxation training procedure will be practiced regularly and used in anticipation of stressful situations. Cognitive restructuring strategies such as Beck's CT may be used to make clients aware of the role that thoughts and feelings have in maintaining stress. Problem-solving training is another intervention that may be implemented. Self-instructional training (Meichenbaum, 1977) is often used to help clients learn to make and use adaptive self-statements.

The third phase of SIT is application and follow-through. The major objective is to facilitate the use of the coping strategies learned in the skills acquisition phase. Clients practice more than one strategy and learn to identify the circumstances under which a particular strategy is likely to work well. Imagery rehearsal is an important part of this phase of SIT. It is used to practice the coping strategies in stressful situations. Clients might imagine themselves becoming stressed and having stressful thoughts and feelings and then using the coping skills they have learned to handle the stress. Behavioral rehearsal, role playing, and modeling can also be used in counseling and psychotherapy sessions to practice the coping skills and to evaluate the effectiveness of the coping skills for specific situations. Greater generalization to the real-life experiences of the clients may be facilitated through the use of homework assignments, in which the clients try out the new strategies and report on the outcomes.

Relapse prevention, based on the work of Marlatt and Gordon (1984), asserts that clients are likely to have slips in their ability to practice new skills. To counter negative effects of relapse, clients are told that it is very likely that they will make mistakes and want to give up trying the coping skills they have learned. This is viewed as a normal part of the process of change. It should be anticipated, and strategies to deal with these events should be planned. Because stress is part of life, clients should expect to continue to face stress; but through the use of coping skills, they can learn to manage the effects. Follow-through is included as a reminder that treatment effects may deteriorate after formal treatment ends. Booster sessions may be helpful to refresh a client's skills and understanding of the principles of SIT.

SIT is a flexible system for conceptualizing and working with clients who have anxiety disorders. Meichenbaum and Deffenbacher (1988) indicate that it may be used along with medication or other interventions to help individuals with various anxiety disorders cope with stress-related problems.

SUPPORTING RESEARCH

There is a great deal of research literature on the effectiveness of various cognitive-behavioral interventions for different types of disorders. This review will be limited to research on the work of Beck and Meichenbaum. Other sources of reviews are available in *Review of Behavior Therapy*, a biennial effort to provide updated information about research on cognitive-behavioral interventions; Kazdin and Wilson's (1978) *Evaluation of Behavior Therapy*; and Hollon and Beck's (1986) chapter "Cognitive and Cognitive-Behavioral Therapies," which appears in Garfield and Bergin's *Handbook of Psychotherapy and Behavior Change*.

Beck's Cognitive Therapy for Depression

The treatment of depression has received a great deal of attention from cognitive-behavioral researchers. Beck's CT, developed for the treatment of depression, has been the subject of numerous treatment outcome studies. CT has been compared to waiting-list controls, nondirective therapy, behavior therapy, and various antidepressant medications, with favorable findings.

Shaw (1977) compared Beck's CT to behavior therapy treatment for depression, which was developed to restore an adequate schedule of positive reinforcement (included activity scheduling, verbal contracts, and communication and social skill development [Lewinsohn, 1974]); nondirective therapy; and a waiting-list control. Those treated by CT had the best outcomes on self-reported measures of depression. In addition, ratings by clinicians unaware of the type of therapy received by individual clients also were more favorable for the CT treatment group.

A meta-analysis of treatment studies comparing cognitive therapy to no-treatment controls yielded the finding that cognitive therapy clients had lower final depression scores than 99 percent of the no-treatment control subjects (Dobson & Shaw, 1988). It is clear that CT is better than no treatment.

The next test involved a comparison of the effects of CT with antidepressant medication. In a now classic study, Rush, Beck, Kovacs, and Hollon (1977) compared the use of CT to pharmacotherapy based on the tricyclic antidepressant imipramine. The clients were moderately to severely depressed individuals seeking treatment for depression. Clients were randomly assigned to CT or drug treatment. CT consisted of no more than 20 sessions in 12 weeks, and the imipramine treatment consisted of 12 weekly sessions. Weekly self-reported depression ratings were obtained. In addition, an independent clinician (unaware of the treatment being received) interviewed the subjects to provide a clinical rating of depression. Although both interventions led to a reduction in depression, the results indicated that CT outperformed medication in client self-reported ratings and in clinician evaluations. Over 78 percent of the clients treated with CT showed marked reductions in depression, and only 22 percent of those treated with medication experienced similar reductions. In addition, there was a greater dropout rate associated with the medication treatment. These results are particularly astounding in light of the fact that many of the therapists were psychoanalytically oriented and were relatively inexperienced in conducting CT. (However, they did follow a specified CT treatment manual and received weekly supervision.) It seems that cognitive therapy is an effective intervention for depression.

Another study that also used medication and CT to treat depression found that the use of drugs and CT were no better than CT alone (Beck, Hollon, Young, Bedrosian, & Budenz, 1985). CT and drug treatment were better than drug treatment alone, leading Beck to conclude that if a client needed antidepressant medication, the person should get CT along with the medication (Weinrach, 1988).

Meichenbaum's Self-instructional and Stress Inoculation Training

Meichenbaum's intervention approaches were developed primarily for the treatment of disorders related to anxiety. The original research conducted using these treatments included treatments for test, speech, and social anxiety; simple phobias; and agoraphobia. However, Meichenbaum and Deffenbacher (1988) list a host of studies that have supported the use of SIT with problems ranging from anxiety-related disorders (test anxiety, performance anxiety, social phobias, generalized anxiety disorder) to anxiety-related medical problems (dental phobias, type A behavior, tension headaches, lower back pain). SIT has also been studied as a treatment for high-stress occupational groups such as teachers, police officers, and nurses. A small sample of the research follows.

In a study that compared the effects of self-instructional training and systematic desensitization on test anxiety, Meichenbaum (1972) found that self-instructional training was more effective in reducing test anxiety and increasing grade-point averages. However, Hollon and Beck (1986) indicate that this finding was not fully replicated in further research on test anxiety. Deffenbacher and Hahnloser (1981) used the separate components of SIT and the entire package to treat test anxiety in college students. Single components were more effective than wait-list controls, and the entire package was more effective than single components.

In a study of social anxiety, Glass, Gottman, and Shmurak (1976) found that male college student volunteers treated with self-instructional training performed better in role-played vignettes than did those exposed to a behavioral skills training. Follow-up data revealed that those exposed to self-instructional training also were able to initiate more telephone calls to females during a six-month follow-up assessment.

A study with interesting results was a comparison of behavioral in vivo exposure, rational-emotive therapy, and self-instructional training with socially anxious outpatients (Emmelkamp, Mersch, Vissia, & Van der Helm, 1985). All of the therapies reduced social anxiety; however, each was most successful in changing the dependent variable associated with the treatment. In other words, RET changed irrational beliefs but not pulse rate. Exposure changed pulse rate but not irrational beliefs. The importance of this study is that it demonstrated construct validity for the interventions; the specific effects of a particular intervention may be seen in measures tied theoretically to that intervention but not in measures unrelated to the intervention.

The work in applying SIT to teachers is original and resourceful (Foreman, 1983). Teachers were trained in six weekly sessions with relaxation training and cognitive restructuring, and they developed stress scripts, which were practiced in role plays and imagery rehearsal. Teachers who participated in this program were less anxious and reported less stress at posttest and in a follow-up assessment conducted six weeks later as compared to no-treatment controls.

Summary of Research

Overall, research based on the use of cognitive-behavioral interventions demonstrates that they are helpful in treating a wide range of problems, including depression and anxiety disorders as well as a large number of other problems faced by clients. Because research on cognitive-behavioral treatment is ongoing, readers may be interested in articles published in journals such as *Behavior Therapy, Cognitive Therapy and Research,* and *Addictive Behaviors.*

■ ■ ■

THE CASE STUDY OF JOHN: THE COGNITIVE-BEHAVIORAL APPROACH

The case study of John can be used as an example of cognitive-behavioral counseling and psychotherapy. To begin, the counselor or therapist conducts a thorough behavioral assessment and then implements one of many possible intervention strategies. How the counselor or therapist decides which intervention is most appropriate for a given client at a specific point in time can be a complicated process. Nezu and Nezu (1989) outline the steps necessary for the clinician to decide how best to help the client. The information in John's case study suggests that Beck's cognitive therapy or either of Meichenbaum's interventions might be appropriate for working with John.

For the assessment, the case study provides bits and pieces of the kind of information necessary to obtain a complete functional analysis. John's presenting problems seem to revolve around stress reactions to changes in his job situation and difficulties in interpersonal relationships, especially with his wife and children. These difficulties are expressed behaviorally in chronic pain (irritable colon) and sexual impotence.

For a complete behavioral assessment, information about John's attributions, beliefs, and self-statements in addition to how he behaves and feels in the problematic situations is necessary. The triple response mode provides guidance for the questioning (Nelson & Barlow, 1981). The case study describes John's problem in terms of behavior (stomach pain and withdrawal from interaction), so it is important to ask John about his thoughts about work (maybe he thinks that if he doesn't obey the new rules, he'll be fired) and at home (he may think that his children prefer spending time with Mom). The counselor or therapist also wants to know how he feels at work (angry, anxious) and at home (inadequate and awkward in his relationship with his children).

It may also be helpful to ask about John's beliefs concerning the cause of his stomach pain and about his thoughts on his forecast for recovery from the pain problem. These beliefs provide valuable information about motivation and may be challenged later in terms of the negative behavioral and emotional consequences of pessimistic beliefs (Miller,

1991). Behavioral assessment may involve role playing to assess John's ability to be assertive and might include interviewing his wife, especially because some of the trouble is seen in the marital relationship.

The counselor or therapist has to establish a good rapport with John. This might be difficult, for John has repeatedly sought medical rather than psychological care for his problem. Individuals who seek counseling and psychotherapy because of chronic pain may view their problems in purely medical terms and try psychological interventions only when medical ones fail (Miller, 1991). John may express ongoing skepticism about the value of cognitive-behavioral interventions, and this may be an ongoing issue in the therapeutic relationship. Accurate empathy and warmth conveyed throughout the assessment and intervention are necessary to engage John in collaborative efforts to test some of the thoughts he identifies and to try new strategies in his work setting and personal relationships. A strong relationship with the practitioner is necessary to allow counseling or therapeutic effects to be maximized.

A cognitive-behavioral counselor or therapist establishes a plan to work with John focusing on developing an understanding of the role his thinking has in his current situation. John is challenged to identify the thoughts that go through his mind at work and at home, especially thoughts that precede his stomach pain. Patterns of thoughts might be classified into general categories of cognitive distortions, such as all-or-nothing thinking, overgeneralization, or disqualifying the positive. As John learns how to identify thoughts, he may also begin to talk about some feelings and see that the thoughts and feelings are related to the stomach pain. It is the primary task of the counselor or therapist to demonstrate that the thoughts, feelings, and behaviors are interrelated and that the counseling or psychotherapy will work by changing the maladaptive thoughts.

In terms of the presenting problem of the irritable colon, it is necessary to ask specific questions to obtain a functional relationship between this problem and antecedents and consequences in terms of other behaviors, thoughts, and feelings. We know from the case study that John's irritable colon is worsened by stressful situations at work and at home; thus stress is acting as an antecedent. It is necessary to define *stress* more specifically. It seems that evaluation anxiety may be contributing to John's difficulties at work and possibly to his withdrawal from social relationships. The cognitive-behavioral counselor or therapist might direct questioning to this topic. What kinds of thoughts does John have about his performance at work? He might ask himself questions like "To what degree is this a test of my competence or acceptability?" "How much do I have to prove myself to others?" (Beck & Emery, 1985, p. 147). The new library director may contribute to this evaluation anxiety. Further, the choice of hiring a new individual rather than promoting John may contribute to his feeling of inferiority, which seems to be making the job environment more difficult.

Once there is an understanding of some of the thoughts that John may be having, the counselor or therapist begins the process of changing the thoughts. Questions such as "What's the evidence?" "What's another way of looking at the situation?" and "So what if it happens?" are useful (Beck & Emery, 1985, p. 201). Faulty logic, hypothesis testing, generating alternative interpretations, and de-catastrophizing are some cognitive strategies that might also be used. Self-monitoring thoughts might become a homework assignment to help John focus on the thoughts and how they affect his behavior and feelings.

We also know that one of the ways in which John copes with stress is to withdraw from interaction with people by reading books. This withdrawal behavior is a consequence of the stomach pain. However, it ultimately increases the stress in his life due to the interpersonal difficulties it creates with his wife. It is likely that this is also tied to the sexual difficulties he is experiencing. Reading acts as an antecedent to additional stress. It seems that John has created a situation in which stress causes his problem, and the strategies he has chosen to cope with the stress cause more stress.

The stress inoculation program might be very helpful for John. Relaxation training is an especially appropriate intervention, and John might be asked to practice progressive relaxation or meditation. He may also be able to use self-instructional training to talk himself through some of the situations in which he would normally withdraw. Self-instructional training could be used at work to help him approach his boss when problems arise. He might be taught to say, "I have good ideas about the way to handle this reference problem" and "I am a good worker" to himself as he prepares to talk to his boss. In addition, he may need skills training to increase his confidence in his ability to spend time with his children. Imagery and rehearsal of these skills may facilitate his ability to use them with his family at home.

It is clear that his wife and mother have "helped" John's irritable colon problem by watching his eating and allowing him to withdraw when his stomach is bothering him. Actually, in terms of reinforcement, this kind of help is providing positive reinforcement for the pain problem, for the attention is pleasant and pain behavior continues. Therefore, the environmental contingencies for pain may need to be changed. Rather than expressing so much concern about John's pain, his family may be encouraged to pay positive attention to him when he is feeling well.

There are certainly other features of John's case study that a counselor or therapist might address, including his sexual difficulties and his marital and family relationships. I have focused primarily on the chronic pain because it seems to be the primary problem, and one for which there is great motivation to seek solutions. As John learns the strategies in SIT and CT, he may be better equipped to address the other problem areas in his life.

■ ■ ■

LIMITATIONS

The union of cognitive and behavioral counseling and therapy into cognitive-behavioral has been able to overcome many of the limitations of either type of therapy alone. However, those individuals who are more inclined toward psychodynamic interpretations continue to object to the lack of attention to unconscious factors in determining behavior and to concepts such as ego strength and insight, which are not included in this approach. In addition, experiential counselors and therapists indicate that cognitive-behavioral strategies do not pay enough attention to feelings. Insight and an emphasis on the past are features of other types of counseling and therapy that do not fit within the purview of cognitive-behavioral theory.

The behavior therapy roots of current cognitive-behavioral theory have been criticized for lack of attention to the role of thoughts and feelings, ignoring the historical context of the present problems, and allowing the counselor or therapist too much power to manipulate the client. Because the origins of behavioral theory emphasized operationally defined behaviors and functional analysis, these are features that define the approach. These are the things that make behavioral counseling behavioral! The idea that behavioral counselors and therapists are manipulative comes from the use of external reinforcers and stimulus-control types of treatments. It seems that this notion is maintained by token economy systems. In individual practice, behavioral counselors or therapists use informed consent to make changes in the contingencies of behavior.

The cognitive therapy roots may be described as too difficult to study empirically. In addition, cognitive therapy has been criticized for paying too much attention to cognitive factors while minimizing affective ones. Cognitive therapies focus to a large extent on internal events (thoughts), which cannot be directly observed. Although the radical behaviorists object to this, most other types of counseling or psychotherapy also fit this criticism. Cognitive therapy researchers have continued to develop thought listing and monitoring strategies to alleviate this criticism. In addition, the cognitive strategies have been challenged for the lack of sufficient attention to affective factors. Some people believe that the emphasis on cognitions may lead to an intellectual understanding of the problem but may not help change the feelings associated with the thoughts. This limitation is related to the fact that the mechanism for understanding how behavior, thoughts, and feelings change is still not understood.

SUMMARY

Cognitive-behavioral interventions target both cognitive and behavioral problems using a full integration of cognitive and behavioral strategies. Cognitive-behavioral research is based on observed changes in behavior and cognition with methodological rigor. Cognitive-behavioral theories provide great flexibility in treatment targets and interventions, sharing a fundamental emphasis on the importance of cognitive workings and private events as mediators of behavior change. Behavioral assessment, operating in the triple response mode, provides a conceptual model of the functional relationships between thoughts, behavior, and feelings as well as the necessary background for clinicians and researchers to implement and evaluate intervention strategies. Currently, cognitive-behavioral theories and counseling and psychotherapy interventions are highly influential. There are many different cognitive-behavioral intervention techniques, and the number is likely to grow as the theories continue to be developed and tested for effectiveness with a variety of psychological problems.

REFERENCES

Achenbach, T. M. (1986). The developmental study of psychopathology: Implications for psychotherapy and behavior change. In S. L. Garfield & A. E. Bergin (Eds.), *Handbook of psychotherapy and behavior change* (3rd ed.) (pp. 117–154). New York: Wiley.

Bandura, A. (1974). Behavior therapy and models of man. *American Psychologist, 29*, 859–869.

Bandura, A. (1977). Self-efficacy: Toward a unifying theory of behavior change. *Psychological Review, 84*, 191–215.

Bandura, A. (1986). *Social foundations of thought and action*. Englewood Cliffs, NJ: Prentice-Hall.

Beck, A. T. (1976). *Cognitive therapy and emotional disorders*. New York: International Universities Press.

Beck, A. T., & Emery, G. (1985). *Anxiety disorders and phobias*. New York: Basic Books.

Beck, A. T., Hollon, S. D., Young, J. E., Bedrosian, R. C., & Budenz, D. (1985). Treatment of depression with cognitive therapy and amitriptyline. *Archives of General Psychiatry, 42*, 142–148.

Beck, A. T., Rush, A. J., Shaw, B. F., & Emery, G. (1979). *Cognitive therapy of depression.* New York: Guilford.

Bellack, A. S., & Hersen, M. S. (Eds.). (1987). *Dictionary of behavior therapy techniques.* New York: Pergamon.

Burns, D. D. (1980). *Feeling good: The new mood therapy.* New York: Signet.

Cormier, W. H., & Cormier, L. S. (1991). *Interviewing strategies for helpers* (3rd ed.). Pacific Grove, CA: Brooks/Cole.

Craighead, W. E. (1990). There's a place for us: All of us. *Behavior Therapy, 21,* 3–23.

Deffenbacher, J., & Hahnloser, R. (1981). Cognitive and relaxation coping skills in stress inoculation. *Cognitive Therapy and Research, 5,* 211–215.

DeLucia, J. L., & Kalodner, C. R. (1990). An individualized cognitive intervention: Does it increase the efficacy of behavioral interventions for obesity? *Addictive Behaviors, 15,* 473–479.

Dobson, K. S., Beamish, M., & Taylor, J. (1992). Advances in behavior therapy: The changing face of AABT conventions. *Behavior Therapy, 23,* 483–491.

Dobson, K. S., & Block, L. (1988). Historical and philosophical bases of the cognitive-behavioral therapies. In K. S. Dobson (Ed.), *Handbook of cognitive-behavioral therapies* (pp. 3–38). New York: Guilford.

Dobson, K. S., & Shaw, B. F. (1988). The use of treatment manuals in cognitive therapy: Experience and issues. *Journal of Consulting and Clinical Psychology, 56,* 673–680.

Ellis, A. (1962). *Reason and emotion in psychotherapy.* New York: Lyle Stuart.

Emmelkamp, P. M. G., Mersch, P. P., Vissia, E., & Van der Helm, M. (1985). Social phobia: A comparison of cognitive and behavioral interventions. *Behaviour Research and Therapy, 23,* 365–369.

Foreman, S. (1983), Occupational stress management: Cognitive-behavioral approaches. *Children and Youth Services Review, 5,* 277–287.

Galassi, J. P., & Perot, A. R. (1992). What you should know about behavioral assessment. *Journal of Counseling and Development, 70,* 624–631.

Garfield, S. L., & Bergin, A. E. (1986). Introduction and historical overview. In S. L. Garfield & A. E. Bergin (Eds.), *Handbook of psychotherapy and behavior change* (3rd ed.) (pp. 3–22). New York: Wiley.

Glass, C., Gottman, J., & Shmurak, S. (1976). Response acquisition and cognitive self-statement modification approaches to dating skills training. *Journal of Counseling Psychology, 23,* 520–526.

Hayes, S. C., & Hayes, L. J. (1992). Some clinical implications of contextual behaviorism: The examples of cognition. *Behavior Therapy, 23,* 225–249.

Hollon, S. D., & Beck, A. T. (1979). Cognitive therapy of depression. In P. C. Kendall & S. D. Hollon (Eds.), *Cognitive-behavioral interventions: Theory, research, and procedures* (pp. 153–203). New York: Academic Press.

Hollon, S. D., & Beck, A. T. (1986). Cognitive and cognitive-behavioral therapies. In S. L. Garfield & A. E. Bergin (Eds.), *Handbook of psychotherapy and behavior change* (3rd ed.) (pp. 443–482). New York: Wiley.

Hollon, S. D., & Kendall, P. C. (1979). Cognitive-behavioral interventions: Theory and procedure. In P. C. Kendall & S. D. Hollon (Eds.), *Cognitive-behavioral interventions: Theory, research, and procedures* (pp. 445–454). New York: Academic Press.

Kazdin, A. E., & Wilson, G. T. (1978). *Evaluation of behavior therapy: Issues, evidence and research strategies.* Lincoln: University of Nebraska Press.

Kendall, P. C., & Hollon, S. D. (1979). Cognitive-behavioral interventions: Overview and current status. In P. C. Kendall & S. D. Hollon (Eds.), *Cognitive-behavioral interventions: Theory, research, and procedures* (pp. 1–9). New York: Academic Press.

Kovacs, M. (1980). The efficacy of cognitive and behavior therapies for depression. *The American Journal of Psychiatry, 137,* 1495–1501.

Krumboltz, J. D., & Thoresen, C. E. (1976). *Counseling methods.* New York: Holt, Rinehart, & Winston.

Lazarus, A. A. (1971). *Behavior therapy and beyond.* New York: McGraw-Hill.

Lewinsohn, P. M. (1974). A behavioral approach to depression. In R. J. Friedman & M. M. Katz (Eds.), *The psychology of depression: Contemporary theory and research.* New York: Wiley.

Mahoney, M. J. (1974). *Cognition and behavior modification.* Cambridge, MA: Ballinger.

Mahoney, M. J., & Lyddon, W. J. (1988). Recent developments in cognitive approaches to counseling and psychotherapy. *The Counseling Psychologist, 16,* 190–234.

Marlatt, A., & Gordon, J. (1984). *Relapse preventions: A self-control strategy for the maintenance of behavior change.* New York: Guilford.

Meichenbaum, D. (1969). The effects of instructions and reinforcement on thinking and language behaviors of schizophrenics. *Behaviour Research and Therapy, 7,* 101–114.

Meichenbaum, D. (1972). Cognitive modification of test anxious college students. *Journal of Consulting and Clinical Psychology, 39,* 370–380.

Meichenbaum, D. (1977). *Cognitive behavior modification: An integrative approach.* New York: Plenum.

Meichenbaum, D. (1979). Cognitive-behavioral modification: Future directions. In P. O. Sjoden, S. Bates, & W. S. Dockens, III (Eds.), *Trends in behavior therapy* (pp. 55–65). New York: Academic Press.

Meichenbaum, D. (1985). *Stress inoculation training.* New York: Pergamon.

Meichenbaum, D. H., & Deffenbacher, J. L. (1988). Stress inoculation training. *The Counseling Psychologist, 16,* 69–90.

Meichenbaum, D., & Goodman, J. (1969). Training impulsive children to talk to themselves: A means of developing self-control. *Journal of Abnormal Psychology, 77,* 115–126.

Miller, L. K. (1980). *Principles of everyday behavior analysis* (2nd ed.). Monterey, CA: Brooks/Cole.

Miller, P. C. (1991). The application of cognitive therapy to chronic pain. In T. M. Vallis, J. L. Howes, & P. C. Miller (Eds.), *The challenge of cognitive therapy: Applications to nontraditional populations* (pp. 3–24). New York: Plenum.

Nelson, R. O., & Barlow, D. H. (1981). Behavioral assessment: Basic strategies and initial procedures. In D. H. Barlow (Ed.), *Behavioral assessment of adult disorders* (pp. 13–43). New York: Guilford.

Nezu, A. M., & Nezu, C. M. (1989). *Clinical decision making in behavior therapy: A problem-solving perspective.* Champaign, IL: Research Press.

Rush, A. J., Beck, A.T., Kovacs, M., & Hollon, S. (1977). Comparative efficacy of cognitive therapy and pharmacotherapy in the treatment of depressed outpatients. *Cognitive Therapy and Research, 4,* 17–37.

Scott, J., Williams, J. M. G., & Beck, A. T. (1989). *Cognitive therapy in clinical practice: An illustrated casebook.* New York: Routledge.

Shaw, B. F. (1977). Comparison of cognitive therapy and behavior therapy in the treatment of depression. *Journal of Consulting and Clinical Psychology, 45,* 543–551.

Skinner, B. F. (1969). *Contingencies of reinforcement: A theoretical analysis.* New York: Appleton Century-Crofts.

Vallis, T. M., Howes, J. L., & Miller, P. C. (Eds.). (1991). *The challenge of cognitive therapy: Applications to nontraditional populations.* New York: Plenum.

Watson, J. B. (1930). *Behaviorism* (2nd ed.). Chicago: University of Chicago Press.

Weinrach, S. G. (1988). Cognitive therapist: A dialogue with Aaron Beck. *Journal of Counseling and Development, 67,* 159–164.

CHAPTER FOURTEEN

Reality Therapy Theory

Robert E. Wubbolding
Xavier University, Cincinnati

William Glasser, M.D., the founder of reality therapy, first used this approach in a correctional institution and a mental hospital. Because it held patients and clients responsible for their behavior, reality therapy provided an alternative to conventional therapy, which Glasser believed had failed to produce behavioral change. Because of its success, reality therapy has been adapted to schools, agencies, parenting, management, and virtually every type of human interaction.

Originally formulated as an eight-step approach, reality therapy now consists of two major components: a friendly, firm, trusting environment and a series of procedures that leads to change. A counselor or therapist using this system establishes an atmosphere of trust and compassion in which clients feel free to self-disclose. The practitioner employs the widely used skills of active listening but adds the skill of questioning in an attempt to help clients explore their motivation and their behavior.

The procedures or more direct interventions used by counselors and therapists can be expressed by the abbreviation *WDEP*. *W* is an explanation of the client's wants, goals, perceptions, and commitment to change. *D* is doing or total behavior, which consists of actions, thinking, and feelings. The heart of the process is *E*—the inner evaluation by the client. Only after a client self-evaluates can change occur. Clients are asked to conduct a searching inner examination of the effectiveness of their behavior and to determine if their life direction as well as their specific actions are helping them fulfill their wants. Similarly, they are asked to evaluate the attainability and the appropriateness of their wants. Finally, they are helped to make specific plans—the *P*—to fulfill their wants. The overall system is free of esoteric language, a fact that sometimes leads counselors or therapists to believe erroneously that it is easily learned and quickly integrated into one's life.

Reality therapy is based on a system of brain functioning known as control theory or control system theory. The source of human behavior is not past conflicts, external stimuli, or rational thinking. Rather, control theory is based on the principle that all human behavior is an attempt to fulfill current human needs: belonging, power or achievement, fun or enjoyment, freedom or independence, and survival. Actions, thoughts, emotions, and even human physiology are continuously generated to fulfill these generic needs and specific wants. Some behavior is helpful and some ineffective or harmful. Through the process of reality therapy a person travels a more effective path to need satisfactions. This journey is a series of choices often unseen by clients in the beginning of therapy. But in a trusting environment in which they can define and express their needs and wants, they self-evaluate and choose alternate plans leading to more effective living.

HISTORY

The founder of reality therapy was William Glasser, M.D., a board-certified psychiatrist who formulated his ideas in a mental hospital and a correctional institution. Trained in the traditional methods of psychiatry, he was taught to help clients gain insight so that after transference was worked through, they could achieve a higher degree of sanity. However, experience provided Glasser with an abundance of data suggesting that even if these goals of the analytic approach were achieved, clients did not necessarily change their behavior. Many clients, understanding their behavior, continued to make unproductive decisions. And so gradually, with support and input from a sympathetic professor named G. L. Harrington, Glasser formulated the early principles of his new treatment modality. The watershed year for reality therapy was 1965 when Glasser published *Reality Therapy: A New Approach to Psychiatry*. In what was then a controversial book, Glasser emphasized that people are responsible for their own behavior. They cannot blame the past or outside forces and at the same time achieve a high degree of mental health. He asserted that behavior is a choice and that there are always options open to most people. Consequently, the objective of counseling and psychotherapy should be measurable behavioral change, not mere insight and understanding of past events or current unconscious drives.

The theory was not greeted enthusiastically by the medical profession but was extremely well received by corrections personnel, youth workers, counselors, therapists, and educators. Because of the practicality and commonsense nature of his theory, Glasser was asked to consult in schools to help students take more responsibility for their behaviors and to blame others less for their plight. Out of this work came his book *Schools Without Failure* (1968), in which he discussed how reality therapy can be used in large groups—what he called "class meetings." While not the same as group counseling or psychotherapy, the meetings have some of the same goals: increased self-esteem, feelings of success, involvement with and respect for each other, and so on.

At this point, reality therapy was seen by many professionals as a method rather than a theory. Then Glasser (1972), formulating what might be called the theory's sociological underpinnings, stated that reality therapy is effective because of the revolution in society that was evident by the 1950s. Three forces contributed to the radical changes in Western civilization: the passage of laws that guaranteed human rights, increased affluence that satisfied the basic need of survival for the majority of people, and the advent of instant communication via the electronic media. These three gradual but important changes facilitated the arrival of the "identity society"—a world in which persons are more focused on their identity needs than on their survival needs. Most people want an opportunity to move beyond economic and political serfdom. Therefore, reality therapy, a theory of human behavior that stresses belonging, self-discovery, involvement with others, positive plans, and self-healing through realistic action, found fertile ground.

Still, this pragmatic and culturally based method needed solid psychological grounding. Such a foundation is provided by a theory of brain functioning not written about to any great extent in conventional university textbooks. Powers (1973) described the brain as an input control system similar to a thermostat that controls the room temperature. Glasser (1984) extended control theory, or control system theory, by incorporating a system of needs to explain human motivation and molded the theory to the clinical setting and the practice of counseling and therapy.

Reality therapy has been further extended to relationships and issues beyond professional counseling and psychotherapy. Ford (1977) states how the principles of reality therapy can be used in raising children; in fact, he has successfully raised his own children using them. He also describes specific ways used by marriage and family counselors and therapists to assist clients to build and maintain relationships (1979, 1983). Wubbolding (1979) and Edelwich (1980) have applied the principles to burnout and suggest that fulfilling needs and making plans are effective alternatives to behaviors that are characteristic of burnout, such as depression, hopelessness, and so on. Extensive applications have been made using reality therapy in schools—for example, in class meetings (Glasser, 1968), in structured groups (Glasser, 1986a), and in school discipline (Gossen, 1992). Special applications to the field of self-help illustrate that both control theory and reality therapy (the terms are often used interchangeably) can be taught to clients, students, and parents (Good, 1987; Wubbolding, 1985a, 1990d). Additionally, according to Wubbolding (1984a, 1990c), the management of employees can be made more successful. He states that the principles of reality therapy, explained in nonclinical terms, have been shown to be useful, practical, and helpful in the plant, office, and factory. Reality therapy, taught in many countries, requires special adaptation to cultures less assertive than those in North America. Such adaptations are beginning to emerge, but much study of multicultural issues remains to be done (Omar, 1990, 1992; Wubbolding, 1990b). Glasser (1990) has recently integrated the ideas of W. Edwards

Deming, pioneer of the total quality management movement and catalyst for the Japanese industrial renewal of the last 40 years, into reality therapy and applied them to schools. He says that every educator is a manager and can more efficiently manage staff and students to produce higher quality work if fear is eliminated, self-evaluation initiated, and an effort is made to meet the students' needs as seen in control theory. Furthermore, if reality therapy is used to counsel and communicate with students and faculty, the instructional system will become effective in reaching the elusive goal of quality.

It is clear that reality therapy has not remained static but has changed and expanded in both its content and applications. Based on the pragmatic principle that if people are treated *as if* they can control their lives, they *will* change them, the theory now explains why and how people can make those changes.

HUMAN NATURE: A DEVELOPMENTAL PERSPECTIVE

Chronological Development

Reality therapy provides a comprehensive explanation of human behavior as well as a methodology for addressing the vicissitudes of the human condition. Control theory explains why and how human beings function; and the WDEP system (Wubbolding, 1989, 1991), as explained in the following paragraph, provides a delivery system for helping oneself and others to remediate deficiencies, make better choices, and become more fully self-actualized.

W implies that the counselor or therapist helps clients explore their wants. *D* means that clients describe the direction of their lives as well as what they are currently doing or how they spend their time. *E* indicates that the counselor or therapist helps in the client's self-evaluation by asking such questions as "Are your current actions effective?" Clients are then helped to make simple and attainable action plans, as implied by *P*. Thus, reality therapy is not a theory of developmental psychology per se. Still, as discussed in detail later, it contains ideas that harmonize with various stages of a person's development.

Fundamental to reality therapy is the principle that human needs are the sources of all human behavior. So an infant as well as a senior adult seeks to control or mold the world around her so that she can fulfill her inner drives. But here the commonality among persons at various stages ends. For as persons grow, they develop specific wants unique to themselves. An infant, child, adolescent, young adult, middle-aged person, or senior adult has formulated a wide range of unique wants, yet they are similar to others of the same age and culture.

Similarly, though the behavior of all human beings is designed to fulfill inner needs, it differs according to age and culture. Consequently, because human behavior determines the impact or perception that one gets from the world, a person's world view (perception) is dynamic, always changing, and it varies from person to person depending on age and culture.

A very special developmental implication of the principles of control theory is that the perceptual system or world view is a storehouse of memories. Because human problems at many levels of development are rooted in relationships, Ford (1979) and Wubbolding (1988) emphasize the necessity of interpersonal quality time as a facilitative component of healthy development. When parent and child, friend and friend, spouse and spouse, or colleague and colleague spend quality time together, they build a storehouse of pleasant and healthy perceptions of each other. In order for quality time to serve as a solid support for effective growth and development, it must include performing activities that have the following characteristics:

- *Effortful.*   The activity requires effort. Watching television and eating together can help, but they are less effective than other activities because they require little or no energy.

- *Awareness.*   The persons are aware of each other. Playing a game or engaging in a hobby is very useful in facilitating the relationship and individual development. Again, watching television without talking to each other qualifies only minimally.

- *Repetition.*   The activity is not an isolated choice; it is performed on a regular basis. Consistent walking with a friend deepens the relationship and enhances the growth of both.

- *Free of criticism and complaining.*   While the activity is being carried out, there should be no criticism of the other person. For instance, child development is enhanced if a parent creates an accepting atmosphere and encourages positive conversation during these important moments.

- *Need fulfilling for all persons.*   The activity is geared to the interest and ability of all concerned. Attending a rock concert with an adolescent might be so painful for the parent that the relationship and therefore the development of both fails to improve.

- *Performed for a limited time.*   Persons of various age levels require various amounts of time to ensure appropriate development. A child obviously requires more quality time than an adult who is more independent.

The phrase *quality time* is a technical term that includes the above characteristics. It is seen as a crucial component of human growth and development. Moreover, the application to various individuals of activities labeled *quality time* is determined by the persons' interests and levels of intellectual functioning as well as their ages and degree of mental health.

Development of Mental Health

Besides looking at development from a chronological point of view, Glasser (1986b) and Wubbolding (1988) have described mental health in terms of both regressive and positive stages.

Regressive Stages.   The stages in which mental health is seen as regressive are not viewed in terms of pathology. Rather, in reality therapy, the stages are seen as ineffective ways to fulfill needs. They are sometimes called failure-directed or irresponsible, but the most useful way to describe them is as a person's best but quite ineffective effort to fulfill human needs.

Stage 1: "I give up."   This person has attempted to fulfill human needs effectively but has not been able to do so. The only alternative that appears reasonable is to cease trying. The person is characterized by behaviors such as listlessness, withdrawal, and apathy. This stage is quite temporary and is followed by the symptoms of the more identifiable second stage.

Stage 2: Negative symptoms.   The following behaviors, like all choices, are seen by clients as their best efforts to fulfill their wants and needs. However, they lead to more frustration. The following behaviors are descriptive of these symptoms:

■ *Actions.*   Someone exhibiting this negative symptom chooses destructive actions harmful to self or others. These range from mildly acting out to severe antisocial behavior such as murder, rape, or suicide.

■ *Thinking.*   Cognitive disturbances are also attempts to fulfill needs. Such efforts often succeed in controlling others; nevertheless, they are self-destructive or harmful to others. The word *disturbance* is used in a wide sense to include negative cognition, ranging from the chronically pessimistic and negativistic thinker to a person with severe psychotic conditions.

- *Feelings.*   Negative emotions include a spectrum ranging from mild to severe depression, from chronic aggravation to habitual anger or rage, and from the "worried well" (Talmon, 1990) to phobic disorders.

- *Physiology.*   Other ineffective attempts to fulfill needs, used when other choices do not appear to be available to a person, include physical ailments. Many such maladies are best treated not only with good medical care but also through counseling or psychotherapy designed to help the client make better choices: that is, to choose positive symptoms.

Stage 3: Negative addictions.   Negative addictions to drugs, alcohol, gambling, and work represent another regressive stage of ineffective behaviors that attempt to fulfill needs.

These three stages of regressively ineffective behaviors are not seen as rigid and exclusive of one another. On the contrary, they provide a way to conceptualize ineffective human behavior related to need fulfillment. They also represent the reverse of effective behaviors.

Positive Stages.   The positive stages of mental health are seen as effective ways to fulfill human needs. They serve to balance the negative stages and can be presented to clients as goals for the counseling or therapy process.

Stage 1: "I'll do it"; "I want to improve"; "I am committed to change."   Such explicit or implicit statements made by clients represent the first stage of effective choices. This stage, like its negative mirror image, is quite temporary.

Stage 2: Positive symptoms.   The following behavioral choices are effectively need fulfilling and lead to less frustration:

- *Actions.*   Effective choices aimed at fulfilling human needs include both assertive and altruistic behaviors. The healthy person knows how to get what he wants, yet he contributes to society through family life, employment, and so on.

- *Thinking.*   The mirror image of cognitive disturbance is rational thinking. Among the many rational thinking patterns implicit in reality therapy are a realistic understanding of what a person can and cannot control, acceptance of what is unchangeable, and knowledge that she is responsible for her own behavior. Therefore, the perception that all early childhood traumas must of their nature continue to victimize a person's adulthood is rejected.

- *Feelings.*   Patience, tolerance, sociability, acceptance, enthusiasm, trust, and hope are among the emotions that are positive behaviors and useful goals in the practice of reality therapy.

■ *Physiology.*   Another symptom of an effective life-style is the effort to attend to one's physical needs. Care of one's body, proper food intake, and reasonable exercise are symbols of effective need fulfillment.

Stage 3: Positive addictions.   Glasser (1976) has identified activities that he calls positive addictions; they enhance mental health and are intensely need satisfying. Included are running and meditation. Such behaviors, as well as others that approach positive addiction, are the opposite of negative addictions. Rather than being self-destructive, positive addictions add to psychological development and increase feelings of self-worth and accomplishment. Such addictions are the result of habitually but noncompulsively choosing the behavior for 12 to 18 months, for a limited time such as 45 minutes per day (or at least on a regular basis), and in a noncompetitive way.

Like the negative stages, the stages of growth are not absolutely discrete categories. Human beings exhibit many characteristics and can float back and forth from the negative to the positive. No one lives entirely in a world of ineffective or effective choices. Even the most disturbed person occasionally chooses effective behaviors. Likewise, even the most well-adjusted person makes unhealthy or ineffective choices at times.

In summary, the principles of reality therapy allow for applications to any stage of a person's chronological and psychological development. The use of quality time, for instance, can be adapted to persons of any age at any stage of development. Furthermore, development is seen as a series of choices leading to stages of regression or the stages of effective need satisfaction.

MAJOR CONSTRUCTS

The underlying theory that justifies the methodology of reality therapy is a system of brain functioning called control theory. While the theory is separate and existed before reality therapy was developed, the two phrases are now sometimes used interchangeably. Norbert Wiener, a Harvard University mathematician, formulated many of the principles that have been subsumed under the name *control theory*. He described the importance of feedback to both engineering and biological systems (1948) as well as the sociological implications for human beings (1950). Insight, intuition, and meditative states were described by Sickles (1976); and Pask (1975) stressed learning models and teaching strategies. However, Wubbolding (1993) has emphasized that the more proximate basis for the clinical applications was formulated by Powers (1973). Powers rejected the mechanism of behaviorism by emphasizing the internal origins of the human control system. Most significantly, however, is the work of Glasser (1980b, 1984, 1986a, 1986b, 1986c), who expanded Powers's work and adapted it to the clinical setting. Human beings, Glasser states, act on the world around them for a purpose: to satisfy their needs and wants. He speaks of "total behavior," which is comprised of action, thinking, feelings, and physiology. All behaviors contain the four elements, although one element or the other is more obvious at a given moment. Such behaviors, negative or positive, are the output generated from *within* a person in order to gain a sense of control or satisfy needs.

Wubbolding (1988) has provided a standard summary of Glasser's control theory as it applies to counseling and psychotherapy:

1. *Human beings are born with five needs:* belonging; power (competence, achievement, recognition, self-esteem, and so on); fun or enjoyment; freedom or independence (autonomy); and survival. These needs are general and universal. Along with wants, which are specific and unique for each person, they serve as the motivators or sources of all behavior.

2. *The difference between what a person wants and what he perceives he is getting (input) is the immediate source of specific behaviors at any given moment.* Thus reality therapy rests on the principle that human behavior springs from internal motivation, which drives the behavior moment to moment (Wubbolding, 1985b). Another consequence of this principle is that human behavior is not an attempt to resolve unconscious, early childhood conflicts. The sources of effective behaviors ("I'll do it," positive symptoms, and positive addictions) as well as ineffective behaviors ("I give up," negative symptoms, and negative addictions) are current, internal, and conscious.

3. *All human behaviors are composed of doing (acting), thinking, feeling, and physiology.* Behaviors are identified by the most obvious aspect of this total behavior. Thus, someone counseled for poor grades in school is seen with a presenting action problem. People are labeled psychotic because the primary and most obvious aspect of their total behavior is dysfunctional thinking. Depression, anger, resentment, and fear are most obvious in other persons, so their behavior is called a feeling behavior. The most obvious component of others' behavior is the physiological element, including heart disease, high blood pressure, and other ailments. Because behavior is total— that is, made up of four components—and because it is generated from within, it is useful to see behavior not as static but as ongoing. Therefore, total behavior is often expressed in "ing" words. Feelings, for example, are described as "depressing," "guilting," "anxiety-ing,"

and so on. Another implication of this principle is that all behavior has a purpose. Human choices are not aimless or random. They are all teleological; in other words, they serve a purpose: to close the gap between the perception of what a person is getting and what she wants at a given moment.

4. *Human behavior, originating from within, means that human beings are responsible for their behaviors.*   In other words, we are all capable of change. This change is brought about by choosing more effective behaviors. The aspect of human behavior over which we have the most direct control is that of acting and secondarily that of thinking. Therefore, in counseling and psychotherapy, the focus is on changing total behavior by discussing current actions along with the evaluation of their effectiveness in fulfilling needs, current wants and the evaluation of their realistic attainability, and current perceptions or viewpoints along with their helpfulness to the individual.

5. *Human beings see the world through a perceptual system that functions as a set of lenses.*   At a low level of perception, the person simply recognizes the world, gives a name to objects and events, but does not make a judgment about them. At a high level of perception, the person puts a positive or negative value on the perception. Exploring the various levels of perception and their helpfulness is part of the counseling process.

THE PROCESS OF CHANGE

To understand how change can occur in the life of a client it is necessary to understand the following implications in the theory and practice of reality therapy.

Present Orientation

Control theory, the theoretical basis for reality therapy, rests on the principle that the human brain functions like a control system—for example, like a thermostat—seeking to regulate its own behavior in order to shape its environment so that the environment matches what it wants. Therefore, human behavior springs from current, inner motivation and is not an attempt to resolve past conflicts or a mere response to an external stimulus. In other words, human beings are not controlled by past history or victimized by the world around them. Rather, they have control over current and future behavior—to varying degrees, to be sure, but they have control nevertheless. To state it another way, human needs and wants that drive human behavior seek satisfaction in the here and now and are quite conscious rather than unconscious.

Emphasis on Choice

One of the goals of counseling and psychotherapy for the practitioner of reality therapy is to help clients make positive choices. Therefore, it is useful to see behavior as a choice, to treat it as such, and to talk to clients as if they have choices. While no human being has total freedom to make better choices easily, it is still helpful to see even severe emotional disturbance as a person's best choice for a given period of time. The work of the counselor or therapist is to open more choices, to help clients see that better choices are possible. Of course, the word *choice* is not used with the exact same meaning for every behavior. To choose to keep an appointment is quite precise and specific. It is more controllable than global choices such as the choice to become free of drugs or the choice to become more assertive. Even though it is empowering to the client to see the latter options as choices, they can also be called goals comprised of many short-range objectives (wants) and more specific steps (choices).

Control of Action

In bringing about change, it is useful to recognize that the component of total behavior over which human beings have the most control is the action element. Although some persons have an amazing amount of direct control over their physiology (some can stop bleeding when they are cut), people seen in counseling and psychotherapy can rarely change their blood pressure, their ulcer condition, or their headaches by simply choosing the opposite. Also, they can rarely change their feelings of depression, guilt, anxiety, or worry merely by choosing to do so. And though they have some control over their thoughts, it is still not easy for them just to begin thinking differently from the way they have in the past.

Because people have most control over the acting element, helping them change actions is more possible than helping them think differently or helping them feel better. It is more realistic to help spouses talk politely to each other than to help them feel better about each other. Increasing self-esteem is possible if a client chooses to act in ways that are different from ways in which he has acted previously. The reason for this is that all four elements of behavior are connected. Total behavior is like a suitcase containing four levels of behavior. The handle of the suitcase is attached to the action. Beneath it are thinking, feeling, and physiology. When the suitcase is moved, it is seized by the handle, the part most easily grabbed. Yet when this occurs, the entire suitcase changes location. So, too, when we help a client change actions, there is a change of all behaviors, though not quite as immediate as when a real suitcase is lifted. Behavior, therefore, is seen as a choice. The most easily changeable component of behavior is action, and when a change in action occurs there is a change in all aspects of behavior.

Importance of Relationship

The specific procedures of the WDEP system are based on the establishment of an empathic relationship. Reality therapy offers specific interventions aimed at helping clients make more effective choices. These are most effective only when there is a genuine relationship established. Counselors and therapists who use reality therapy effectively employ many of the same skills and possess the same qualities as any counselor or therapist: empathy, congruence, and positive regard. As is abundantly clear from research, the relationship between counselor or therapist and client is critical in effecting change. Reality therapy offers specific ways, some unique to reality therapy and some incorporated from general practice, for establishing and maintaining a relationship.

Metacommunication

The procedures of reality therapy are straightforward and direct. Yet when they are used repeatedly, clients seem to gain more than the surface meaning allowed for by the questioning. The art of helping clients define what they want for themselves, examine what they are doing to get it, and make plans is based on an underlying belief that is often heard and incorporated by the client. They get the message that they have the ability inside of themselves to make changes, to feel better, to take better charge of their own lives. They gain self-confidence and a sense of hope, messages that extend beyond the mere asking of questions (see "Intervention Strategies" for more information about specific questioning procedures). Yet it is best for the practitioner to refrain from trying to send a metamessage to clients. Rather, client attitudinal changes will often occur if the WDEP system is skillfully used. Such changes cannot be forced.

Reality therapy developed out of a desire to see change happen in clients rather than have them merely gain insight and added awareness. Contributing to the efficacy of reality therapy is its emphasis on present orientation, choice, action, the relationship, and the underlying message that is communicated through skillful questioning.

INTERVENTION STRATEGIES

The methodology employed in reality therapy consists of establishing an appropriate environment or psychological atmosphere and applying the procedures that lead to change: the WDEP system. Together these constitute the "cycle of counseling." (see figure 14.1).

Environment

An atmosphere that provides for the possibility of change is characterized by specific guidelines and suggestions about what to do and what to avoid. These are designed for use by counselors, therapists, and case managers as well as supervisors and managers in the workplace. They can also be taught to clients, parents, teachers, and others for use in improving their interactions with clients, students, employees, and children. The specific applications vary slightly, but the principles are quite consistent.

Among the behaviors to be avoided is arguing. The counselor or therapist is quite active when applying the procedures; thus there is danger that in helping clients evaluate their behavior, the practitioner will overstep the proper use of reality therapy by arguing about the best choice for the client. This mistake results only in resistance and is counterproductive. Also, belittling, criticizing, demeaning, or finding fault with clients only creates resistance and poisons the atmosphere. In fact, even the oxymoron "constructive criticism" is best avoided in relationships.

One of the most important counselor and therapist behaviors to avoid is that of accepting excuses. Too much empathy or sympathy reinforces the perceived helplessness and powerlessness of clients. For instance, clients often describe how they did something harmful to themselves or someone else not because they made a choice but because of an outside force. For example, the teacher gave an unfair test. Someone rejected me. Another person got me into trouble. They are depressed because of some unfavorable outside event. The alternative to the quicksand of excuses is the effective use of the WDEP system. Asking about wants or goals seems to get quickly beyond the discussion of a perceived external locus of control.

In the early stages of the development of the reality therapy delivery system, the advice was to never give up. A more realistic formulation of this admonition is to stay with the person as a helper past the time she expects to be abandoned. In other words, don't give up easily.

FIGURE 14.1
Cycle of counseling and supervision using reality therapy

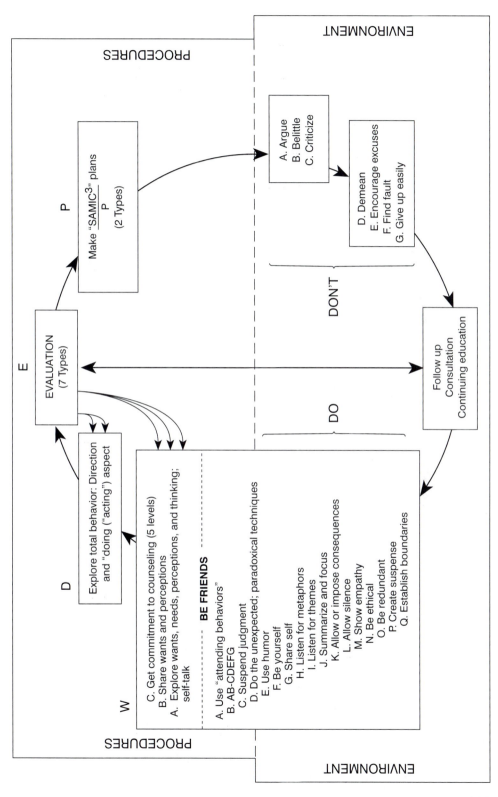

Similarly, the counselor or therapist might be tempted to give up on the WDEP system if it fails to render the desired results immediately. Wubbolding (1986b) emphasizes that this is due to the fact that the principles *appear* to be easy to practice, in view of the fact that the vocabulary is uncomplicated. Yet to be proficient in the practice of the skills, repeated practice and preferably supervision is required.

A positive environment that serves as the basis for the WDEP system is built not only on avoiding the uncongenial behaviors of arguing, criticizing, or giving up, but on the global admonition to be friends. Such efforts to establish an agreeable and harmonious atmosphere are sustained and nourished by the use of the following interventions.

Use Attending Behaviors.   The model of attending behaviors described by Ivey (1980) is especially useful in the practice of reality therapy. Eye contact and facial expression include looking at the client without staring and displaying a genuine interest. Physical posture includes sitting in an open, receptive position. Verbal following includes tracking the client's comments and reflecting in a manner that communicates that the counselor or therapist is listening. Nonverbal behavior includes attending to the client's manner of expression, such as tone of voice. Paraphrasing means restating the client's comments occasionally. These skills serve as an effective foundation for an enhanced relationship between the client and counselor or therapist.

AB-CDEFG.   This abbreviation stands for the following interventions:

■ *Always be courteous.*   Being courteous is a behavior that counseling theory rarely mentions. It is assumed to exist in the counseling or psychotherapy relationship, yet it does not always exist in relationships that could be enhanced by the practice of reality therapy. Authority figures, such as probation and parole officers, are well served by treating the client with respect while refraining from venting anger.

■ *Always be determined.*   The determination of the counselor or therapist is perceived as an explicit and implicit belief or attitude. The metamessage, relayed to the client by the verbal and nonverbal behavior of the practitioner, is simply that no matter what the circumstances of the client's life, no matter how dreadful the past history, a better life is possible.

■ *Always be enthusiastic.*   In this context, enthusiasm is not cheerleading. Nor is it a naive belief about long-standing disturbances and the difficulty in dealing with them. Rather, it is the continuous effort to look at the bright side; to emphasize what the client *can* do; to discuss possibilities, not merely problems; and to take a problem-solving approach. The session thus need not degenerate into an empty ventilation of negative feelings. Thomas Edison, a man who dealt with towering obstacles, once remarked that if we leave our children nothing but enthusiasm, we leave them a legacy of incalculable value.

■ *Always be firm.*   In establishing an empathic environment, the counselor or therapist remains firm. There is no contradiction between seeing the client's point of view and taking a stand for honesty and sobriety while disclosing opposition to dishonesty, drunkenness, or abusive behaviors. Moreover, disclosure that the counselor or therapist supports the policies of the practitioner's employer and applies them unapologetically does not damage the relationship. Rather, it facilitates the establishment of boundaries. On the other hand, firmness is not intended to serve as an excuse for the authoritarian personality to impose her whims on clients.

■ *Always be genuine.*   Personal authenticity and congruence are seen as necessary prerequisites in reality therapy as well as in other helping methods. Those personal qualities are summarized in Glasser's often-repeated statement, "The counselor must be healthier than the client."

The above ABs are intended to serve as guidelines that can be adapted not only by professionally qualified counselors and therapists, but also by anyone who wishes to use the principles of reality therapy. It is important to remember that they constitute an ideal that few people can attain 100 percent of the time. They can be among the personal, internal goals of the counselor or therapist.

Suspend Judgment.   As stated earlier, all behavior is a person's best effort at a given time to fulfill his needs. Consequently, a counselor or therapist who keeps this principle in mind can more easily see quite harmful choices from a low level of perception. They are viewed without approval or disapproval. Balancing such suspension of judgment with "always be firm" is a tightrope on which every counselor or therapist walks daily.

Do the Unexpected.   Unpredictability is a quality that facilitates a helpful counseling or psychotherapy environment. Focusing on a strength, on a success, or on a time when the client felt good often generates the type of discussion that clients do not expect. Nevertheless, clients who are characterized by negative symptoms also choose positive symptoms (Wubbolding, 1981). Therefore, it is good to discuss in detail the circumstances when clients chose effectively, felt good, and remained in effective control of their lives. Wubbolding (1984b) has described other ways for doing the unexpected. He has incorporated paradoxical techniques into reality therapy by showing that reframing, redefining, and relabeling is a helpful way to do the unexpected (Wubbolding, 1988). However, in order to be effective using this and other paradoxical techniques, it is necessary to invert one's thinking. Causes are seen as effects; the objectionable is now a strength (Dowd & Milne, 1986; Fay, 1978; Seltzer, 1986; Weeks & L'Abate, 1982). Wubbolding (1993) states:

> A depressed child is seen as pensive, gentle, and thoughtful. An angry child is outgoing and has deep conviction. The bully is a leader and has ambition, while a submissive child is kind and cooperative. This paradoxical technique is therefore a technique that is useful to establish a relationship and can even serve as a procedure leading to change. However, it is not to be used indiscriminately and manipulatively. Rather, it is a psychological condiment, to be used sparingly. And like the other "guidelines" it is primarily a way to establish a safe counseling environment. (p. 293)

Use Humor.   A healthy and democratic sense of humor is a curative factor for the mental health specialist. Victor Borge once remarked that laughter is the shortest distance between two people. Peter (1982) states that laughter is helpful in dealing with anxiety, depression, and loss. Children learn by having fun. One of Aristotle's definitions of a human being is that she is risible: that is, she can laugh. Consequently, to function fully as a human being, as a person in effective control who is characterized by positive symptoms, it is advantageous to have a sense of humor. Indeed, an effective counselor using the principles of reality therapy can effectively enhance the counseling or psychotherapy environment by laughing *with* the client.

Be Yourself.   Though it is to be expected that students learning counseling and psychotherapy skills will adopt the style of their teachers or that of the leaders in each theory, I hope that they will also adapt the skills to their own personality. Whether they are assertive, placid, exuberant, dispassionate, expressive, restrained, confrontational, or laid-back, they can practice the method effectively. It is a matter of practicing and assimilating the skills and thereby adapting them to a personal style.

Share Yourself.   The creation and maintenance of a trusting relationship is facilitated by appropriate self-disclosure. According to a Swedish proverb, "A joy shared is twice a joy. A sorrow shared is half a sorrow." While self-disclosure by a counselor or therapist can be helpful, a practitioner should be cautious. Cormier and Cormier (1985) warn that there can be a danger of accelerating self-disclosure to the point where the counselor or therapist and the client spend time swapping stories about themselves. As with all the techniques for building a trusting relationship, self-disclosure is best used moderately.

Listen for Metaphors.   Metaphors in this context are figures of speech, analogies, similes, and anecdotes that serve to quantify problems and thereby make them manageable. Barker (1985) states that if properly constructed, stories and other metaphors offer choices to clients. He observes that they are often helpful because "psychotherapy is essentially a process of providing people with more choice in the matter of how they behave, or respond emotionally, in various situations" (p. 17). Also, stories and anecdotes can be humorous and thus help clients perceive their problems and decisions in a different light. Metaphors used by clients are often overlooked by counselors and therapists, or they are paraphrased. It is better, however, to use the metaphor, to extend it, and to return to it in subsequent sessions. The following metaphors might be stated by clients or initiated by counselors and therapists:

"I feel like a floor mat."

"Cleaning my desk is like climbing Mount Everest."

"You sound like you've been on a merry-go-round."

"It sounds like warfare in your house."

"I don't know if I'm going up or down."

"I feel like I'm winning."

"Our relationship has gone sour."

"You seem to be back on track, heading in an upward direction."

Using these metaphors, the counselor or therapist can offer clients specific choices, such as "Would you like to get off the floor?" "Do you want to get off the merry-go-round?" "What would you be doing today if you were on solid ground, away from the merry-go-round?" As with all such techniques used to enhance the counseling and psychotherapy environment, metaphors do not constitute the essence of reality therapy. They do serve, however, to build trust between client and counselor or therapist.

Listen for Themes.   Tying together the ideas, feelings, and actions of clients helps them to gain a sense of direction and control. The counselor or therapist using reality therapy listens carefully for themes such as previous attempts to solve problems, wants that are fulfilled, and what has helped and not helped the client. This technique is not exclusive to the practice of reality therapy, but in using it the counselor or therapist listens for themes that are linked to the WDEP interventions (see "Procedures: The WDEP System").

Summary and Focus.   Similar to the identification of themes, this technique helps the counselor or therapist listen carefully and communicate to clients that they are being heard. Unlike summaries used in other theories, this one concentrates on components of the WDEP system. A counselor or therapist might summarize a client's statements by responding, "You've stated that you've tried to get a promotion at work and been unsuccessful, that you've approached your boss and described what you want, that you've put in extra hours. Nothing so far has gotten you what you want." The counselor or therapist has summarized what the client has done that has not worked and has omitted many other details.

Focusing means to center the conversation on the client rather than on outside forces over which neither involved party has control. Very little can be done to cause changes in other people. Nothing can be done to change the past. Thus, it is most helpful if the counselor or therapist gently and positively assists clients to discuss their own here-and-now wants, total behaviors, plans, hopes, frustrations, and perceptions.

Allow or Impose Consequences.   Professional counselors and therapists have fewer opportunities to use this element of the environment than those who wish to integrate reality therapy into their work. Probation and parole officers, halfway-house workers, and others often function in a supervisory role and are required to impose consequences. It is assumed that the consequence is reasonable and not punitive as well as imposed to help rather than merely control the client.

Even counselors and therapists occasionally impose consequences when life-threatening or evidently dangerous situations are described by the client. The code of ethics of the American Counseling Association states, "When the client's condition indicates that there is clear or imminent danger to the client or others, the member must take reasonable, personal action or inform responsible authorities" (Herlihy & Golden, 1990, p. 10).

Allow Silence.   The appropriate use of silence in reality therapy, if timed properly, allows the client to conduct inner self-evaluation, reassess wants, think about what is controllable and therefore uncontrollable, and in general take responsibility for the direction of the session. Trainees learning reality therapy tend to ask questions nervously in rapid-fire order.

They are well advised to slow down and allow a few incisive questions to reverberate inside the client.

Be Ethical.   The ethical principle concerning clear or imminent danger is one of many that the practitioner of reality therapy practices. A trusting relationship and a professional atmosphere conducive to helping is built around solid ethical principles. Anyone using reality therapy properly knows, understands, and practices the ethical standards of various professional organizations. Professional disclosure is often required, as in the state of Ohio (1984). Thus counselors, therapists, and social workers must provide clients with a written description of their professional qualifications. Wubbolding (1986a) emphasizes that counselors and therapists should provide clients with information about the nature of reality therapy. These details help clarify the boundaries of the relationship as well as the advantages and limitations of the assistance that the practitioner can offer. He also emphasized the importance of knowing how to assess suicidal threats and how this assessment is used in the practice of reality therapy (1987). Informed consent, dual relationships, confidentiality, and proper record keeping are among the many ethical issues impinging on the relationship between counselor or therapist and client.

Be Redundant or Repetitious.   Often the same questions are asked in various ways. When a client is defensive and offering excuses in the form of denial, the counselor or therapist sometimes repeats the same question in a different way. It becomes a theme aimed at helping clients evaluate their own behavior. "When you made that choice, did it help?" "Did it work for you?" "What impact did that action have on you and on others?" "Did it help you enough?" "Was the action the best you were capable of?" Such questions asked at various times become a haunting theme that gradually and supportively lessens denial and facilitates the clients' assumption of responsibility. Yet like the overall art of counseling or therapy, the skill of being redundant is developed through practice and self-evaluation.

Create Suspense and Anticipation.   In a counselor or therapist's effective use of reality therapy there can be an element of drama. A counseling or psychotherapy session should be a significant event in the lives of clients. An authentic buoyancy on the part of the counselor or therapist and a desire to reassure can elicit a feeling of curiosity and a sense of impending success. The ability to communicate a sense of optimism is an advanced skill and is developed with practice and training.

Establish Boundaries.   There are limits within which a counselor or therapist operates, and these should be clarified. The ethical principle of dual relationships, alluded to earlier, is clearly part of boundary classification. Further, the client might wish to shield certain areas from discussion. A useful question for counselors or therapists to ask is, "Is there any topic you do not want me to ask about?" Such questioning empowers clients to choose what they want to work on. If they have numerous topics that are forbidden territory (which they rarely have), the counselor or therapist can ask them if it is helpful for them to conceal or mask potential topics. In any event, the wishes of the client are paramount and are respected.

The above guidelines are designed to help the counselor or therapist using reality therapy establish rapport, mutual trust, and a safe atmosphere by being aware of obstacles and barriers to involvement. They also consist of positive interventions that facilitate the client's expectation that the experience is worthwhile and significant. Moreover, a truly skilled practitioner of reality therapy engages in an ongoing self-evaluation process by means of follow-up with past clients, consultation with peers, and continuing education. These environmental building blocks aimed at establishing and deepening the relationship provide a fundamental prerequisite for what is discernably and essentially the practice of reality therapy: the WDEP system.

Procedures: The WDEP System

The specific interventions that are the essence of reality therapy are based on the trusting relationship described as environment. The procedures or *determinations* (Wubbolding, 1985c) are most appropriately formulated as a system called WDEP (Wubbolding, 1989, 1991). They should not be seen as steps to be used sequentially or mechanically; and although they are described in simple, jargon-free language, they can be difficult to implement. For instance, a counselor or therapist working with a student referred for a school discipline problem would probably not begin with a lengthy discussion of W (wants) but with an exploration of D (doing): in other words, what happened to bring about the referral?

Thus, in conceptualizing the entire process, it is useful to see it as a cycle that can be entered at any point.

W: Discussing Wants, Needs, and Perceptions.   Because human beings are motivated to fulfill their wants and needs, it is important for the counselor or therapist to take the time to explore the specific wants of the client. The questions might include "What do you want from your spouse? school? job? career? friends? parents? children? supervisor? yourself? me? church?" Thus, there are at least 11 generic questions that can be asked. These are multiplied threefold if the counselor or therapist asks more precisely about each category: (1) "What do you want that you are getting?" (2) "What do you want that you are *not* getting?" (3) "What are you getting that you don't want?"

The areas for exploration and clarification become almost endless when the counselor or therapist adds, "How much do you want it?" "What would you need to give up to get what you want?" "What will you settle for?"

All wants are related to the five needs: belonging, power or achievement, fun or enjoyment, freedom or independence, and survival. Therefore, it is useful to help clients link their wants explicitly to their needs by asking, "If you had what you wanted, what would you have?" or "If your wants were met, what would that satisfy inside?" Such questioning of a parent often elicits the following: "I want my child to keep the curfew, get good grades, stay away from drugs, do the house chores, and be pleasant to the rest of the family. If I had that I would have peace of mind. I would know that I am a good parent." The parent has specific wants and has identified the underlying need: achievement or power.

Discussing perceptions is also an important part of W. Questions about clients' perceptions are slightly different from those specifically relating to wants. A parent might be asked, "What do you see when you look at your child?" The answer might be "I see a child who is rebellious at times and cooperative when she wants something from me." Asking about perceptions is especially useful in groups and in family counseling and psychotherapy because arguments can be prevented. A counselor or therapist can intervene by reminding all present that they are discussing their viewpoints, what they see, not what "is."

W: Sharing Wants and Perceptions.   Counselors and therapists using reality therapy share their own wants and perceptions when such disclosure is helpful to clients. They share their wants regarding such issues as how many sessions are necessary and a reminder that the practitioner's role is to help the client make decisions but not to remove responsibility. On occasion the counselor or therapist might even make a specific suggestion about what kind of action would be helpful. In the case of a parent, the counselor or therapist might say, "When I look at your child, I see similar things, but I also see a person struggling to grow up, one who doesn't need lectures but quality time from parents."

A counselor or therapist who shares wants and perceptions does not take responsibility for clients, nor does he lecture or admonish clients. He or she leads but does not coerce.

W: Getting a Commitment.   Change and growth will occur only if the client is committed to making changes in her actions. Thus, it is imperative that the counselor or therapist discuss the client's level of commitment to the process and its outcomes. The question "How hard do you want to work at changing your situation?" gives the client an opportunity to look inward and reflect on the degree of responsibility she wishes to assume.

Wubbolding (1988) has identified five levels of commitment as described by clients:

- *"I don't want to be here."*   This statement clearly illustrates that the client is at best reluctant and resistant. It is even possible that the client has been coerced into counseling or psychotherapy. In fact, this level of commitment is actually no commitment at all, but it is included because it seems to fit an increasing number of clients who are seen by practitioners.

- *"I want the outcome but not the effort."*   This level indicates that the person does want to change and is perhaps at stage 1 ("I'll do it") in gaining effective control and taking personal responsibility. It is a higher commitment than the first level, but it will still result in no change until a higher level is achieved.

- *"I'll try; I might."*   Trying to make a change for the better constitutes the middle level of commitment to change. Still, trying to get out of bed early is not the same as doing it.

- *"I will do my best."*   At this level a person goes beyond trying and commits to specific action. However, such a commitment still allows the possibility of failure.

- *"I will do whatever it takes."*   The highest level of commitment represents an outcome centered on a no-excuses level of commitment. It is the most desirable level from the view of the counselor or therapist.

The levels of commitment are developmental. The higher levels are more helpful than the lower ones. Yet for some clients, "I'll try" is a major improvement. They should not be pushed too vigorously or too quickly to move to a higher level. Rather, the skillful counselor or therapist helps clients to evaluate their level of commitment and gently leads them to the next level.

D: Discussing Behavioral Direction and Doing (Total Behavior).   The counselor or therapist helps the client review his overall direction by inquiries such as "Where do you think you are going if you continue on the same pathway?" A child might be asked, "If you continue to flunk in school, resist your parents' requests, and continue on the same pathway, where will you be in two or three or 12 months?"

The exploration of the overall direction is only the embarkation point for further questioning about current total behavior. More time and effort is needed to help clients examine their specific actions. The counselor or therapist helps the client verbalize exactly what she did for a specific amount of time. The client becomes a television camera, as it were, relating not typical events but what happened that was specific and unique.

Similarly, clients might describe their thoughts and feelings at the time of the actions as well as what they now think and feel about them. Likewise, they could even describe how their overall direction and specific actions are impacting the physiological component of their total behavior.

So important is the generic question "What are you doing?" that a book of reality therapy cases has that name (N. Glasser, 1980). Each word in the question serves as a signpost for the counselor or therapist. Wubbolding (1990a) describes the meaning of each word. "What" implies that the counselor or therapist asks for precise details. When clients take refuge in generalities, they should be encouraged to be more exact. "Are" emphasizes the importance of stressing the present rather than indulging in endless discussions of past behaviors that are out of a client's control. "You" focuses on the client rather than on other people, excuses, and uncontrollable events. Finally, "doing" connotes total behavior: the exploration of direction, specific actions, thoughts, feelings, and physical symptoms accompanying clients' choices.

E: Helping Clients Conduct Evaluations.   In the cycle of counseling and in the WDEP system of procedures, the element of evaluation occupies the central position. Like a keystone in an arch, its pivotal place supports the entire structure. If it is absent, the arch crumbles. The practice of reality therapy is firm and effective to the degree that the counselor or therapist assists clients to evaluate their own behavior, wants, perceptions, level of commitment, and plans.

Because of the prominent place of self-evaluation in the cycle of counseling, reality therapy is properly placed among the cognitive counseling theories. It is here, especially at the cardinal point of self-evaluation, that cognitive restructuring takes place. Clients look inward and examine the effectiveness of their life-style and its specific aspects. Only when they have concluded that some part of their control system (wants, behaviors, perceptions) is not helping them or is not as beneficial as it could be do clients see that a change is necessary.

More specifically, evaluation contains the following elements:

■ *Evaluation of behavioral direction.*   After helping the client describe the overall direction of his life, the counselor assists in evaluating the significance of this direction. Is it the best direction in the mind of the client? Is it helpful or harmful and does the direction have what, for the client, is high quality?

■ *Evaluation of specific actions.*   The questions about specific actions are geared to the descriptions provided in the client's explanation of how a specific segment of her day was spent. Such questions might include "Did sleeping until 10:00 A.M. help or hurt your effort to find a job?" "What were the consequences of hitting your brother?" "When you shout at the kids, do you get what you want?" "Even if they obey for a while, does it help both in the short run and in the long run? Does it help to the degree you were hoping for?" "If you continue to eat a diet of ice cream, sweets, and starch, will you ever attain the weight you said you wanted?"

■ *Evaluation of wants.*   The client is assisted in making judgments about the appropriateness and the attainability of wants. "Is what you want truly good for you?" "How realistic is it for you to get your parents totally off your back?" "How realistic is it for your adolescent child to become 100 percent cooperative or perfect in your own eyes?"

■ *Evaluation of perceptions or viewpoints.*   Perceptions are not very easily changed. Rarely are they changed by a simple decision to view a person, a situation, or an event differently. Yet they can be changed by changing behavior (Glasser, 1980b, 1984; Powers, 1973). But because perceptions are what people want, they occupy an important place in the evaluation process. So even though they are not directly changed, their desirability and appropriateness should be evaluated. More specifically, human beings seek the perception of being adequate, popular, skilled, in control, helpful to others, and comfortable. They also have more specific perceptions relative to each generic perception. Thus, the client is helped to evaluate general and specific perceptions or viewpoints. Evaluative questions for perceptions include "Does it help if you see your son only as rebellious and lazy?" "What is accomplished if you only see the negative aspects of your parents' behavior?" "When you nurse a negative attitude toward your boss, does it help you to improve your situation at work?"

■ *Evaluation of new direction.*   As new possibilities unfold for clients, it is useful to help them determine whether those possibilities are need satisfying. The rebellious student is asked, "How will cooperation at home benefit you and your family?" "If you were to make an effort to learn, do your homework, ask questions in class, and, in general, do what 'successful' students do, would you feel better? What impact would this approach have on your friends and family?"

■ *Evaluation of plans.*   After a new direction is defined, and often even before clients have committed to a change of direction, they can be encouraged to make plans. At first glance, these plans might appear to be meager and insignificant. But they often represent the first steps toward more effective and positive need satisfaction. In working with an adolescent, Wubbolding (1980) was able to help him make a modest, even diminutive plan of action. This high school student had shut himself in his room on the weekends with the curtains and drapes closed. Although resistant at first, he eventually made plans to open the blinds and let the light in. He subsequently developed a healthy social life by making rudimentary changes in his overall direction. Thus, the evaluation of plans is based not on whether they solve the basic problem but on whether they address the problem and aim toward the more effective fulfillment of belonging, power, fun, and freedom.

P: Planning.   According to one saying, "to fail to plan is to plan to fail." Glasser (1980a) states that plans vary. Some are detailed, and some are quite simple. He adds, "There must always be a plan. People who go through life without some sort of a long-term plan, usually divided into a series of small plans to reach larger goals, are like ships floundering without rudders" (p. 52).

The procedure of planning is often mistakenly viewed as the essence of the practice of reality therapy. And though it is important, it is effective only if based on a client's inner self-evaluation.

Plans that are truly efficacious, or at least more likely to be carried out by the client, have at least eight qualities, which can be summarized by the acronym SAMI^{2}C^3. (Wubbolding, 1986b).

S.   **Simple:** The plan is uncomplicated.

A.   **Attainable:** If the plan is too difficult or too long range, the client will become discouraged and not follow through.

M.   **Measurable:** The plan is precise and exact. The client is encouraged to define a clear answer to the question "When will you do it?"

I.   **Immediate:** The plan is carried out as soon as possible.

I.   **Involved:** The helper is involved if such involvement is appropriate. The involvement is, of course, within the bounds of ethical standards and facilitates client independence rather than dependence.

C.   **Controlled by the client:** An effective plan is not contingent on the actions of another person but is, as much as possible, within the control of the client.

C.   **Committed to:** The counselor or therapist helps the client to pledge firmly to put the plan into action.

C.   **Consistent:** The ideal plan is repetitious. A single plan can be a start, but the most effective plan is one that is repeated.

Planning and follow-through are crucial elements in personal growth, enhanced mental health, decision making, and remediation of problems. Helpful plans aimed at achieving these ultimate goals are not forced on clients. Rather, clients are taught that the achievement of their goals will be the result of their own positive choices and plans. Clients are accordingly led to discover within themselves desirable plans aimed at their own need satisfaction.

In summary, the cycle of counseling is a design for understanding reality therapy and an outline for knowing how to apply it. The environment consists of specific recommendations for building a firm but friendly atmosphere in which a client can feel safe and confident while realizing that the counselor or therapist actively seeks to be of help. The WDEP formulation is a system that is not intended to be followed in a mechanical manner. It is, however, to be seen as a system from which the proper intervention is selected at a given time because of its apparent appropriateness.

SUPPORTING RESEARCH

While more research could be conducted to validate the use of reality therapy, the widespread interest in the theory indicates that practitioners have confidence in its efficacy. In 1993, more than 500 persons worldwide completed the 18-month training program and were certified in reality therapy. Anecdotal evidence abounds, which points toward the theory's usefulness with a wide variety of issues, such as eating disorders, child abuse, marriage, aging, elective mutism, career satisfaction, study habits, self-esteem, assertive behavior, and many others (N. Glasser, 1980, 1989).

Glasser (1965) described the dramatic effect of a reality therapy program in a mental hospital, where the ideas were pioneered by Dr. G. L. Harrington. The average stay in a ward of 210 men was 15 years. Within two years, 75 men had been released with only three returning.

A sampling of other empirical studies has shown that the use of reality therapy produced significant results in increasing self-concept and lowering court referrals (Shea, 1973). Gang (1975) showed that the use of reality therapy resulted in change in student behavior in the classroom. The teachers in the study also believed that the relationship skills resulting from the use of reality therapy were essential if change were to result.

The effects of reality therapy in group counseling or psychotherapy with institutionalized adolescents was investigated by German (1975). In relation to a comparative group, the students displayed significantly fewer behaviors requiring disciplinary action. Poppen, Thompson, Cates, and

Gang (1976) found that after reality therapy was used with disruptive students, appropriate behavior increased 18 to 47 percent.

The use of reality therapy as a self-management tool was studied by Atwell (1982). Atwell concluded that the "percentage of time-on-task would significantly increase as a result of the treatment." Yarish (1986) found significant differences in the participants' perceived locus of control. They became aware that they made their own choices rather than being controlled by external forces.

Gorter-Cass (1988) studied the use of reality therapy in an alternative school and stated that the overall trend was toward "less severe behavior" and that there were significant changes in self-worth and self-concept. Elementary school students ages 9 to 11 were studied by Hart-Hester, Heuchert, and Whittier (1989). The students were counseled in groups, and action plans were formulated. The study showed a "pronounced increase in the percentage of time-on-task for each targeted student."

Studying the effects of reality therapy in a therapeutic community in Ireland, Honeyman (1990) found significant changes in the residents' self-esteem, awareness of their inability to control their drinking, and insight into living in a more inner controlled manner. Positive effects have also been shown when reality therapy has been used with teachers (Parish, 1988, 1991; Parish, Martin, & Khramtsova, 1992), undergraduate students (Peterson & Truscott, 1988), graduate students (Peterson, Woodward, & Kissko, 1991), foster parents (Corwin, 1987), and negatively addicted inmates (Chance, Bibens, Cowley, Prouretedal, Dolese, & Virtue, 1990).

In summary, a brief selection of research studies illustrates the value of reality therapy as a reliable tool for counselors and therapists. However, many areas for possible study still remain. Researchers could investigate further the effects of reality therapy on the areas already mentioned as well as on other issues dealt with by counselors and therapists.

■ ■ ■

THE CASE STUDY OF JOHN: THE REALITY THERAPY APPROACH

An important part of writing a diagnosis and treatment plan for John is uncovering more facts relevant to the effective use of reality therapy. The case study as described does not contain all the useful facts that an effective practitioner of reality therapy gathers even in the first session. Such additional details include the following:

■ A detailed description of what the client wants that he is getting and not getting from his wife, family, and job. While it is possible to surmise from the data presented what the client might want, such conjectures remain educated guesses.

■ A detailed description of how John perceives his own need fulfillment. Questions are asked and data gathered about how he sees his own need satisfaction. Does he feel a sense of belonging at home and at work? Is he having as much fun as he needs? Does he have any hobbies? What role does humor play in his personal, family, and professional life? What choices *can* he make at work?

■ A detailed description of past positive symptoms. Such an exploration of John's past behavior is at least as important as the history of his diarrhea and impotence. The description of his college years contains many useful hints. For example, when he was free of the symptoms in college, he seemed to have had his belonging need met. More details on how this was accomplished are gathered by the counselor or therapist using reality therapy.

■ A detailed description of how John perceives his locus of control. The counselor or therapist needs to know to what degree John sees himself as in control and not in control of his life. Does he believe that his current problems are *caused* by the director at the library, his wife, his early childhood, and other forces outside him? To what degree does he believe he can resolve such issues?

A person who uses the WDEP system emphasizes current wants and current symptoms, both negative and positive. The past is important because it shows how clients have attempted to fulfill their needs and get what they want. In the case of John, his past behavior as described in the case history shows that in part he has attempted to fulfill his needs by negative physiological behaviors in times of intense frustration. But a lengthy discussion of this aspect of his past without at least equal emphasis on positive, effective choices leads to client discouragement and feelings of hopelessness. Thus, a discussion of past and present positive symptoms and current fulfilled and unfulfilled wants is also necessary. A counselor or therapist using reality therapy bases a treatment plan on such inner perceptions of the client.

With the limitations just described, the following discussion presents a tentative program of development for John. It is based on his presumed wants and will change as his wants and behaviors change.

John's Strengths: History of Positive Symptoms

It is clear from the limited case history available that when John gets what he wants from the world around him, he more easily chooses positive symptoms. Even at age nine he wanted a kind and nurturing teacher. When his teacher's behavior was not what he wanted, he experienced intense frustration. Among the behaviors that he generated were stomach cramps. When his needs were met by the more flexible behavior of the teacher, he was able to choose more effective behaviors, and his severe cramps became significantly less intense. In other words, his need for belonging as well as other needs were met more satisfactorily.

In John's high school years he received good grades but experienced intestinal problems around exam time. These negative physiological symptoms, in reality therapy terms, were the result of not fulfilling, or believing he would not be able to fulfill, his need for achievement or power. However, of more importance to the reality therapy practitioner is what John did between exam periods that satisfied his needs and enabled him to be free of the negative symptom.

When John went to college, he became quite skilled at meeting his need for belonging. He cultivated male and female friendships, and there is no mention of intestinal problems during his college years. Moreover, he seemed to do well in school; thus his need for power was also met. In reality therapy terms, he had an inner sense of control: that is, his needs seemed to be met, and he got what he desired from the world around him. Even the small amount of negative symptomology he generated, though less desirable than positive choices, served effectively to help him fulfill his need for belonging, for Betty was quite nurturing. It is evident that when he chooses effective behaviors, positive symptoms, and in-control actions, he can relinquish, to some extent, his intensive intestinal problems.

His consistent advancements in his library career were need satisfying both to him and to Betty, who showed her approval. The promotions did not fulfill their needs perfectly, but there was far more positive symptomology than negative. When he subsequently wanted the position of director and did not get it, he again experienced intense frustration. At the same time, he seemed to believe that he was capable of bearing the responsibilities of director, and his career history supports this belief.

While John has many issues that require counseling or psychotherapy, it is important to see his strengths or positive symptoms. Over the years he has made effective choices and has gone through long periods characterized by a need-satisfying life-style. He seems to be capable of getting part of what he wants, as related to belonging, power or achievement, fun or enjoyment, and freedom.

Treatment of John

The goal of treatment is more effective need fulfillment. When John's needs for belonging, power, fun, and freedom are met, he will be able to function as an effective husband and father, a productive and content library administrator, a person who satisfactorily interacts with friends and who contributes to the larger society.

The WDEP System.   After establishing the environment, a friendly atmosphere in which John feels safe to self-disclose—or, to put it another way, once John puts the counselor or therapist in his quality world—the skillful practitioner of reality therapy then applies the WDEP system. The following descriptions display each component of the system. It is important to note, however, that in each counseling or psychotherapy session, the procedures are integrated with one another and flow together.

W: Wants, Perceptions, and Level of Commitment.   John is asked to describe in detail what he wants from his wife, children, job, social life, society in general, and especially himself. He is also asked how important each want is as well as what he is willing to settle for regarding each one. The counselor or therapist explores what John wants that he is getting and not getting. Also included is a disclosure of John's commitment to the helping process: that is, how hard does he want to work at solving the problems?

Let's assume that in the course of such questioning John wants the following:

- From his wife: a continued relationship; nurturance, support, understanding, and acceptance; satisfactory sex; respect
- From his children: pleasant dispositions; obedience; positive behaviors such as getting along with one another
- From his job: cooperative and self-initiating staff; a promotion to director; approval from his present director
- From his social life: deeper friendships; more time spent developing a social life
- From society: security and safety; an opportunity to give of himself to worthy causes

■ From himself: become a better husband; talk more to his wife; spend more quality time with his children; learn how to communicate with his children and enjoy them; be a better sexual partner; be more spontaneous; be free of intestinal problems

In discussions with John it quickly becomes clear that the most urgent and important want is to deal with the stress and the accompanying psychophysiological symptoms. He also puts a high priority on overcoming impotence and in talking about his disappointment at not getting the promotion as well as his resentment of the present director and how she functions without consulting him. When the practitioner explores John's commitment to the counseling or psychotherapy process, John states that he truly wants results and that he is willing to work at achieving his goals.

D: Exploration of Total Behavior.   John is asked to discuss his physiological symptoms and what he has done to lessen their intensity. He describes in detail, not just in a general way, what he feels. He is also encouraged to describe his hurt, anger, resentment, and fears regarding his physiological symptoms, his impotency, his director, and so on. The counselor or therapist links these specific feelings to actions, using questions such as "How did you handle the situation when you felt the resentment toward your director?" While it is acceptable to allow clients to ventilate their feelings, the counselor or therapist encourages more discussion of actions; for actions can be directly changed, and feelings are less under the immediate control of the client. Consequently, the counselor or therapist facilitates a discussion of specific vignettes in which the client felt good or acted satisfactorily and those in which he acted unsatisfactorily or felt inadequate.

E: Discussion of Client's Self-evaluation.   John is asked many evaluation questions. This component of the system is the cornerstone of the practice of reality therapy and requires much more time than is apparent from a written description of it. He is asked to evaluate the realistic attainability of his wants and the effectiveness of his actions. Such questions might include the following:

"Is it realistic for you to have a better relationship with your wife or children?"

"Do you think you will be given the job of director?"

"Do you think it is possible for you to overcome this temporary impotency?"

"Is the overall direction of your life a plus or a minus for you?"

"What impact does it have on your staff when you don't ask them for feedback or input?"

"What helps the relationship with your wife, your children, your director, your friends? What hurts it?"

"What did you do yesterday that helped or hurt any of these relationships?"

At this point, it can be part of reality therapy to teach behaviors that John might want to know: relaxation techniques, assertiveness techniques, communication skills, parenting skills, and, in particular, how quality time can give a major boost to his family life and his marriage.

P: Planning for Change.   After John has made a countless number of evaluative judgments about the attainability of his wants and the effectiveness of his actions, as well as determining to accept what he cannot change (the directorship at the library), he then makes plans. The plans are simple, attainable, measurable, immediate, and controlled by John.

Assuming that John wants to make significant change and to try new behaviors, the following plans might be developed:

- Spend 15 minutes per day reading or playing with his two children without criticizing them.
- Spend 30 minutes a day with his wife doing something enjoyable for both of them: an activity that is noncontroversial and involves effort, such as walking or working on a project in the house.
- Set aside time to ask his staff for ways in which they can improve their work at the library.
- Engage in relaxation activities on a regular basis, such as brief visualization or meditation moments.
- Attempt to develop a relationship with the director by engaging in light conversation with her.
- Ask the director what she wants from him.
- Tell the director what he has to offer her in order to make her job easier.
- Find common activities that his family can do together; schedule them exactly and for protracted periods of time.
- Discuss his fears about impotency with his wife.
- Read materials on sexual response and discuss them with his wife.
- Schedule a session with a sex therapist if necessary. (This will probably be unnecessary if he gets the rest of his life in more effective control.)

The purpose of these plans is more than mere problem solving. They are an attempt to help John increase his storehouse of positive perceptions, thereby changing his view of the world around him. They also help him change what is changeable—his own behavior—and fulfill his needs more effectively. Thus, the more he increases the positive symptoms, the less he will generate the negative destructive behaviors of diarrhea, stress, anxiety, fear, impotency, resentment, withdrawing, and so on.

Working with John will take time, but he will learn that he can take a different and more rewarding path by making plus choices rather than minus choices. Furthermore, he will incorporate the WDEP system as a self-management tool, for he will see that defining what he wants clearly and unambiguously is a major step toward achieving it. He will also realize that settling on what is realistically attainable can ultimately lead to greater happiness and make him a more need-fulfilling person to his wife, family, and friends. The value of direct action to get what he wants will be another lesson that he learns. But most important, he will gain a skill in evaluating his wants and his own actions. "If it is not working, do more of it," the motto of many people, will be a slogan discarded in favor of "If my life is not everything I want it to be, I'll make a positive plan to change it."

■ ■ ■

LIMITATIONS

Reality therapy can be applied to virtually every type of situation presented by clients and in any institution where there is human interaction. Still, there are cautions that the practitioner is advised to keep in mind. Many clients believe that in order to make changes or to feel better they need to gain insight into their past, resolve early conflicts, heal the wounded child, present endless descriptions of the negative aspects of their lives, or at least tell repeatedly how they arrived at their present state. Many can be quickly and successfully encouraged to emphasize their present behavior because it is more controllable than past history. But some therapy-wise clients have been led to believe that no change can result without somehow dealing with past pain, and "dealing with" means endless discussion. For them, reality therapy will appear to avoid the real issues.

Part of this limitation resides in the skill of the counselor or therapist rather than the theory, but in the minds of clients it is often difficult to separate the theory from the practitioner. For such a client, the practitioner needs to adjust the therapy rather than blindly cling to the principle of discussing current behavior. Counselors or therapists who have been trained to emphasize a discussion of feelings as the true test of effective counseling or therapy find the quick emphasis on clients' actions premature if not hasty. On the other hand, a skillful reality counselor or therapist is aware of all aspects of clients' behavior, actions, thinking, and feelings and responds to them as a unit rather than as disconnected from one another. Still, if feelings such as anger are seen as the root cause of problems rather than as feelings caused by unmet needs, the counselor or therapist will probably be less effective when using the WDEP system of reality therapy.

The language of reality therapy is, in a sense, a reverse limitation. There is little jargon or technical terminology. The theory and practice employ words like belonging, power, fun, freedom, wants, plans, self-evaluation, effective control, and so on. Because the language of reality therapy is easily understood, its practice can appear to be easily implemented. Nevertheless, the effective use of reality therapy requires practice, supervision, and continuous learning.

Because reality therapy is straightforward and deals with the present issue, its subtlety is often obscured. The discussion of current and future actions and plans is often the most obvious part of the counseling or therapy process. Still, the most important components are the clarification of clients' wants and their self-evaluation. The exploration of these elements is central to any desired change. In learning reality therapy, counselors or therapists who are in a hurry to see results frequently proceed too rapidly to action planning. Such efforts to help clients make decisions, solve problems, or take more effective control of their lives result in resistance due to the inappropriate use of reality therapy principles.

Reality therapy should be seen as an open system that will grow and change. It is not a narrow theory that is rigidly applied. Yet as a freestanding theory and practice of counseling and therapy, it has limitations. Some of these are inherent in the theory, and some reside in the skill of the practitioner.

SUMMARY

Reality therapy is a practical, down-to-earth system designed for use with virtually any kind of client. It began in a mental hospital and a correctional institution and has since spread to schools, addictions programs, agencies, private practice, hospitals, and other settings. Persons seeking training in reality therapy come from every discipline represented in the helping professions: counselors, therapists, teachers, social workers, psychologists, probation and parole officers, managers, supervisors, and others.

Control theory, a theory of brain functioning, serves as the basis of the delivery system. Viewed from the perspective of control theory, human beings generate total behavior (actions, thinking, feelings, and physiology) to get what they want from the external world. Their wants are related to five needs; belonging, power or achievement, fun or enjoyment, freedom or independence, and survival. Thus all human behavior is purposeful. Yet it can be effective or ineffective, helpful or hurtful, plus or minus in fulfilling wants and needs. The goal of the counselor or therapist using the WDEP system is to help clients define and clarify what they want and examine what they are doing. The cornerstone of the WDEP system is the effort of the counselor or therapist to help clients conduct a searching and consistent evaluation of their behavior, wants, level of commitment, and perceptions. Action planning follows this fearless personal inventory of the value, adequacy, and effectiveness of the direction of clients' lives. Counselors and therapists are careful to recognize that even seemingly trivial plans are initial steps toward a lofty goal, so they help clients make plans that they can realistically carry out.

Finally, one of the striking characteristics of reality therapy is that it is taught and explained in simple language. However, even though it is easily understood, it is more difficult to put into action and to use with clients. In short, it is deceptively simple. Therefore, an 18-month training program has been designed to help interested people gain added skill (*Programs, Policies, Procedures, and Materials Manual*, 1990). The program consists of attendance at skill-building workshops and a realistic amount of supervision between the sessions.

REFERENCES

Atwell, B. (1982). A study of teaching reality therapy to adolescents for self-management. *Dissertation Abstracts International, 43*, 699.

Barker, P. (1985). *Using metaphors in psychotherapy*. New York: Brunner/Mazel.

Chance, E., Bibens, R., Cowley, J., Prouretedal, M., Dolese, P., & Virtue, D. (1990). Lifeline: A drug/alcohol treatment program for negatively addicted inmates. *Journal of Reality Therapy, 9*, 33–38.

Cormier, W., & Cormier, L. (1985). *Interviewing strategies*. Monterey, CA: Brooks/Cole.

Corwin, N. (1987). Social agency practice based on reality therapy/control theory. *Journal of Reality Therapy, 7*, 26–35.

Dowd, E., & Milne, C. (1986). Paradoxical interventions in counseling psychology. *The Counseling Psychologist, 14*(2), 237–282.

Edelwich, J. (1980). *Burn-out*. New York: Human Sciences Press.

Fay, A. (1978). *Making things better by making them worse*. New York: Hawthorne.

Ford, E. (1977). *For the love of children*. New York: Doubleday.

Ford, E. (1979). *Permanent love*. Minneapolis: Winston.

Ford, E. (1983). *Choosing to love*. New York: Harper & Row.

Gang, M. (1975). Empirical validation of a reality therapy intervention program in an elementary school classroom. *Dissertation Abstracts International, 35*(8B), 4216.

German, M. (1975). The effects of group reality therapy on institutionalized adolescents and group leaders. *Dissertation Abstracts International, 36*, 1916.

Glasser, N. (Ed.). (1980). *What are you doing?* New York: Harper & Row.

Glasser, N. (Ed.). (1989). *Control theory in the practice of reality therapy*. New York: Harper & Row.

Glasser, W. (1965). *Reality therapy*. New York: Harper & Row.

Glasser, W. (1968). *Schools without failure*. New York: Harper & Row.

Glasser, W. (1972). *The identity society*. New York: Harper & Row.

Glasser, W. (1976). *Positive addiction*. New York: Harper & Row.

Glasser, W. (1980a). Reality therapy. In N. Glasser (Ed.), *What are you doing?* (pp. 48–60). New York: Harper & Row.

Glasser, W. (1980b). *Stations of the mind*. New York: Harper & Row.

Glasser, W. (1984). *Control theory*. New York: Harper & Row.

Glasser, W. (1986a). *Control theory in the classroom*. New York: Harper & Row.

Glasser, W. (1986b). *Control theory-reality therapy workbook*. Los Angeles: Institute for Reality Therapy.

Glasser, W. (1986c). *A diagram of the brain as a control system*. Los Angeles: Institute for Reality Therapy.

Glasser, W. (1990). *The quality school*. New York: HarperCollins.

Good, P. (1987). *In pursuit of happiness*. Chapel Hill, NC: New View.

Gorter-Cass, S. (1988). Program evaluation of an alternative school using William Glasser's reality therapy model for disruptive youth. *Dissertation Abstracts International, 49*, 1702A.

Gossen, D. (1992). *Restitution*. Chapel Hill, NC: New View.

Hart-Hester, S., Heuchert, C., & Whittier, K. (1989). The effects of teaching reality therapy techniques to elementary students to help change behaviors. *Journal of Reality Therapy, 8*(2), 13–18.

Herlihy, B., & Golden, L. (1990). *Ethical standards casebook*. Alexandria, VA: American Association for Counseling & Development.

Honeyman, A. (1990). Perceptual changes in addicts as a consequence of reality therapy based on group treatment. *Journal of Reality Therapy, 9*(2), 53–59.

Ivey, A. (1980). *Counseling and psychotherapy*. Englewood Cliffs, NJ: Prentice-Hall.

Omar, M. (1990, January). Counseling Moslems residing in Western societies: Omar model of religious approach. *Omar Psychological Series*.

Omar, M. (1992, Winter). Omar and el-Kadi model for counseling and treating individuals with AIDS. *Omar Psychological Series*.

Parish, T. (1988). Helping teachers take more effective control. *Journal of Reality Therapy, 8*(1), 41–43.

Parish, T. (1991). Helping students take control via an interactive voice communications system. *Journal of Reality Therapy, 11*(1), 38–40.

Parish T., Martin, P., & Khramtsova, I. (1992). Enhancing convergence between our real world and ideal selves. *Journal of Reality Therapy, 11*(2), 37–40.

Pask, G. (1975). *The cybernetics of learning and performance*. London: Hutchinson.

Peter, L. (1982). *The laughter prescription*. New York: Ballantine.

Peterson, A., & Truscott, J. (1988). Pete's pathogram: Quantifying the genetic needs. *Journal of Reality Therapy, 8*(1), 22–32.

Peterson, A., Woodward, G., & Kissko, R. (1991). A comparison of basic week students and introduction to counseling graduate students on four basic need factors. *Journal of Reality Therapy, 9*(1), 31–37.

Poppen, W., Thompson, C., Cates, J., & Gang, M. (1976). Classroom discipline problems and reality therapy: Research support. *Elementary School Guidance & Counseling, 11*(2), 131–137.

Powers, W. (1973). *Behavior, the control of perception*. New York: Aldine.

Programs, policies, procedures, and materials manual. (1990). Los Angeles: Institute for Reality Therapy.

Seltzer, L. (1986). *Paradoxical strategies in psychotherapy*. New York: Wiley.

Shea, G. (1973). The effects of reality therapy oriented group counseling with delinquent, behavior-disordered students. *Dissertation Abstracts International, 34*, 4889–4890.

Sickles, W. (1976). *Psychology: A matter of mind*. Dubuque, IA: Kendall/Hunt.

State of Ohio. (1984). Counselor and Social Worker Law (chap. 4757, rev. code). Columbus, OH: Author.

Talmon, M. (1990). *Single-session therapy*. San Francisco: Jossey-Bass.

Weeks, G., & L'Abate, L. (1982). *Paradoxical psycho-therapy*. New York: Brunner/Mazel.

Wiener, N. (1948). *Cybernetics*. New York: Wiley.

Wiener, N. (1950). *The human use of human beings: Cybernetics and society*. Boston: Houghton Mifflin.

Wubbolding, R. (1979). Reality therapy as an antidote to burn-out. *American Mental Health Counselors Association, 1*(1), 39–43.

Wubbolding, R. (1980). Teenage loneliness. In N. Glasser (Ed.), *What are you doing?* (pp. 120–129). New York: Harper & Row.

Wubbolding, R. (1981). Balancing the chart: Do it person and positive symptom person. *Journal of Reality Therapy, 1*, 4–7.

Wubbolding, R. (1984a). Reality management: getting results. *Landmark: Indo-American Society, 11*, 6–8.

Wubbolding, R. (1984b). Using paradox in reality therapy: Part I. *Journal of Reality Therapy, 4*(1), 3–9.

Wubbolding, R. (1985a). *Changing your life for the better*. Johnson City, TN: Institute for Sciences & the Arts.

Wubbolding, R. (1985b). Characteristics of the inner picture album. *Journal of Reality Therapy, 5*(1), 28–30.

Wubbolding, R. (1985c). Counseling for results. *Not Out of Sight, 6*, 14–15.

Wubbolding, R. (1986a). Professional ethics: Informed consent and professional disclosure in reality therapy. *Journal of Reality Therapy, 6*(1), 30–35.

Wubbolding, R. (1986b). *Reality therapy training*. Cincinnati: Center for Reality Therapy.

Wubbolding, R. (1987). Professional ethics: Handling suicidal threats in the counseling session. *Journal of Reality Therapy, 7*(1), 12–15.

Wubbolding, R. (1988). *Using reality therapy*. New York: Harper & Row.

Wubbolding, R. (1989). Radio station WDEP and other metaphors used in teaching reality therapy. *Journal of Reality Therapy, 8*(2), 74–79.

Wubbolding, R. (1990a). Evaluation: The cornerstone in the practice of reality therapy. *Omar Psychological Series, 1*(2), 6–27.

Wubbolding, R. (1990b). *Expanding reality therapy*. Cincinnati: Real World.

Wubbolding, R. (1990c). *Managing people: What to say when what you say doesn't work*. Cincinnati: Real World.

Wubbolding, R. (1990d). *A set of directions for putting (and keeping) yourself together*. Cincinnati: Real World.

Wubbolding, R. (1991). *Understanding reality therapy*. New York: HarperCollins.

Wubbolding, R. (1993). Reality therapy. In T. Kratochwill (Ed.), *Handbook of psychotherapy with children* (pp. 288–319). Boston: Allyn & Bacon.

Yarish, P. (1986). Reality therapy and locus of control of juvenile offenders. *Journal of Reality Therapy, 6*(1), 3–10.

CHAPTER FIFTEEN

Ecosystems Theory

Peter A. D. Sherrard
University of Florida

Ellen S. Amatea
University of Florida

Ecosystems counseling and therapy enlarges the field of inquiry and intervention from the individual to the couple, the family, and the larger sociocultural contexts that constitute the individual's environment. Ecosystems theory helps us look at the patterns of communication and relationship that connect people to each other and to their social and physical environments. Ecosystemic thinking articulates the underlying currents of a "movement toward holism, toward understanding the system as a system and giving primary value to the *relationships* that exist among seemingly discrete parts" (Wheatley, 1992, p. 9). This "movement toward holism" constitutes a shift in epistemology—that is, a shift in understanding "the necessary limits" of the "processes of knowing, thinking and deciding" (Bateson, 1979, p. 228)—a shift made possible by the advent of the one-way mirror (Hoffman, 1981).

The one-way mirror and the subsequent use of the video camera gave clinicians and participants two places to sit: "One could take a position, and have somebody else take a position commenting on or reviewing that position" (Hoffman, 1981, p. 4). The resultant contrast in views confronted clinicians with the limitations of a monocular view and the benefits of the binocular view. Bateson (1979) declared, "It is correct (and a great improvement) to begin to think of the two parties to the interaction as two eyes, each giving a monocular view of what goes on, and, together, giving a binocular view in depth" (p. 133). For example, the benefits of a binocular view can be shown when two drawings of a cube, each taken from the perspective of a monocular view, are fused by a stereoscope into a double view of a higher logical type. "Both two-dimensional drawings are combined to generate a three-dimensional view" (Keeney & Ross, 1985, p. 20). The synthesis of two descriptions produces a sense of depth that is the bonus gained when the brain registers the differences between what the two eyes see (de Shazer, 1982a). By synthesizing the "double descriptions" gained from the two places to sit, clinicians pursue the bonus of depth, the vision of "differences that make a difference," the construction of "patterns that connect"—a pursuit made possible by binocular vision (Bateson, 1972, 1979).

This chapter will introduce the reader to the ecosystemic views generated by observations through the one-way mirror. The chapter will explore the foundations on which the various forms of ecosystemic family counseling and therapy rest and will outline representative applications of ecosystemic epistemology to understanding and impacting couples, families, and other human systems. The chapter follows the definition of family counseling, family therapy, or ecosystemic therapy proposed by Stanton (1988):

Family therapy—perhaps more appropriately, systems therapy—is an approach in which a therapist (or a team of therapists), working with various combinations and configurations of people, devises and introduces interventions designed to alter the interaction (process, workings) of the interpersonal system and context within which one or more psychiatric/behavioral/human problems are embedded, and thereby also alters the functioning of the individuals within that system, with the goal of alleviating or eliminating the problems. (p. 9)

All models of family counseling and therapy are ecosystemic in orientation: they recognize the interconnectedness of the individual, family, and sociocultural context. By expanding the field of inquiry and intervention, clinicians and participants gain the benefit of multiple description and depth perception, which can lead to productive change.

HISTORY

Helping troubled individuals by including family members in the helping conversation was unworkable before the 1950s, despite an early emphasis in the social work movement on dealing with the family as a whole (Richmond, 1917). The idea gained momentum in the 1950s as a serious treatment alternative when curious clinicians shifted their attention from the lone individual to the familial context within which the individual operated. They began to view people with problem behaviors in their natural habitat—the family—rather than in a clinician's office (Hoffman, 1981). These curious clinicians went beyond the dominant counseling and psychotherapy paradigms of their day in search of a new vision. They borrowed the participant-observation methods of anthropology to gain exposure to suffering persons as they lived at home (Henry, 1965). They also borrowed the new concepts of cybernetics (Ashby, 1956; Wiener, 1948) and general system theory (Bertalanffy, 1968) to make sense of the interactions observed (Haley, 1976a).

These forays into other disciplines led to the formulation of what was hailed as a new paradigm (Barker, 1992; Cottone, 1992) of clinical practice: family systems therapies (Ferber, Mendelsohn, & Napier, 1972; Guerin, 1978). Hoffman (1981) notes that there was no father or mother of family therapy and no first family interview; rather, "like Topsy, the movement just growed" (p. 17).

This new movement generated a distinctly different way of looking at and thinking about human behavior (Ackerman, 1958; Handel, 1967). It shifted focus from the behavior of one family member to transactions involving the family as a whole; individual behavior was seen as inseparable from its social context, and emphasis was placed on the relationships among family members rather than on the individual family members alone (Ferber et al., 1972). Donella Meadows, a systems thinker, quotes an ancient Sufi teaching that captures this shift in focus: "You think because you understand *one* you must understand *two*, because one and one makes two. But you must also understand *and*" (1982, p. 103). Ecosystems theory generates a language for understanding the *and*.

This new way of thinking was very difficult, as Jackson (1965) confessed:

> Despite our best intentions, clear observations of interactional (transactional) process fade into the old, individual vocabulary, there to be lost indistinguishable and useless. To put the problem another way, we need measures which do not simply sum up individuals into a family unit, characteristics for which we presently have almost no terminology. We can only use this rule of thumb: the whole is more than the sum of the parts, and it is the whole in which we are interested. (p. 4)

Jackson and his associates sought a language that made visible the invisible network of interrelationships that constitute a family.

An Introduction to Systems Concepts

"Systems thinking is a discipline for seeing wholes. It is a framework for seeing interrelationships rather than things, for seeing patterns of change rather than static snapshots" (Senge, 1990, p. 68). Bertalanffy (1968) defined systems as "complexes of elements standing in interaction" (p. 33) and asserted that systems thinking required one to "think interaction" rather than "reduction," to concentrate on the relationships among elements rather than the elements themselves. It is this characteristic (that is, the concentration on relationships among elements and their attributes) that stands out in the classic definition of a system advanced by Hall and Fagen (1968): "A system consists of a set of objects together with relationships among the objects and between their attributes" (p. 81).

For Hall and Fagen (1968), the *objects* that make up a human system are specified by the way in which boundaries are drawn; every entity inside the specified boundary is an object of the system, and everything outside the specified boundary constitutes the system's environment. Individual persons are the most obvious objects of human systems, while couples, families, work groups, and organizations represent more abstract examples. *Attributes* refer to the characteristics ascribed to objects. Human objects generate such attributes as body type, culture, ethnicity, gender, personality, race, religion, skin color, temperament, and timing; and they afford different, unequal biological and social expectations, privileges, and rewards to their holders (Breunlin, Schwartz, & Kune-Karrer, 1992). The *relationships* to which Hall and Fagen refer are those that "tie the system together"; human systems communicate, organize, and reorganize as they accommodate themselves to the transactions between action (sequences of behavior) and the meanings (patterns of belief) attributed to the action (Breunlin et al., 1992; Keeney, 1983). System elements are so tightly interrelated that they constitute an irreducible totality that is distinct from the sum of its parts: change in any element of the system triggers changes in the system as a whole.

As previously indicated, systems are specified by the drawing of a boundary that distinguishes a system from its environment. The boundaries of a human system (or subsystem) are determined by "the rules defining who participates, and how" (Minuchin, 1974, p. 53). Boundaries regulate the flow of information and energy required by a living system in order for it to maintain a harmonious balance with its environment. "Without permanent boundary activity, no structure would form; there would only be endless sequences of new behaviors. The function of boundaries is to protect the differentiation of the system and to allow the emergence of structure" (Umbarger, 1983, p. 23).

Systemic structure is the byproduct of consistency: "consistent elements are related to each other in a consistently describable or predictable fashion" (Steinglass, 1978, p. 305). Consistency and redundancy enable one to construct sets of procedures specifying how the various parts of the system are interrelated, to identify the rules by which the various subsystems and the system itself operate, and to specify the tasks (roles) that components fulfill in carrying out system rules and procedures. Human systems are considered rule-governed systems because their members exhibit such consistent and redundant patterns of relationship that they appear to "follow the rules." The procedures, rules, and roles together constitute systemic *structure*, which Gottman (1979) defines as "constraint determined by the reduction of uncertainty in temporal patterns" (p. 290).

Family structure reflects "the invisible set of functional demands that organizes the ways in which family members interact" (Minuchin, 1974, p. 5). Thus, structures are constructed by the predictable routines of the family and are differentiated from processes by the persistence of these routines over time:

> The expression of a process over time gives that process the status of structure. If mother and son *repeatedly*, over time, join forces against the father's effort to direct a decision, then one may speak of a mother-son

> *coalitional structure*. Where such an arrangement does not persist over time, then the observer has simply witnessed a brief, transitional process . . . and not an enduring structure. (Umbarger, 1983, p. 13)

Bertalanffy (1968) noted that "structures are slow processes of long duration" (p. 27); by contrast, "processes are structural arrangements of very short duration" (Umbarger, 1983, p. 14).

A system's environment, also designated as the system's suprasystem, includes all those objects and their attributes that are outside the system's boundary and that perturb (precipitate changes in) the system and are perturbed by it (Hall & Fagen, 1968). These perturbations/constraints challenge homeostasis and elicit the feedback processes that provoke stability (first-order change) and change (second-order change). Those systems that are receptive to environmental perturbation are said to be *open* systems; those systems that are insulated or isolated from direct environmental influence are said to be *closed* systems.

The practice of systems thinking starts with the concept of feedback. The tracing of feedback loops reveals how actions can amplify or counteract each other and leads to the recognition of patterns of stability/change and types of structures that persist over time. The *aesthetic* emphasis in systems thinking consists of giving attention to overall *patterns* of organization—"interlocking circuits of contingency"—and situating those patterns in the larger contexts (environments) within which they are occurring (Keeney, 1983). The approach relies on eliciting multiple descriptions of what is going on, constructing circular rather than lineal representations of interrelationship, transforming redundant sequences of behavior into transactional patterns, identifying the consistent reciprocal and recursive nature of these patterns, and generating hypotheses regarding the contextual meaning and value of these patterns. By contrast, the *pragmatic* emphasis in systems thinking consists of giving attention to immediate sequences of interaction and their reciprocal impact on participants (Watzlawick, Beavin, & Jackson, 1967).

Human systems evolve over time, constantly changing to adapt to new information while maintaining sufficient stability to protect their integrity. They develop identifiably different levels of complexity and a cybernetic hierarchy of control (Powers, 1973). In this multilevel hierarchy, smaller units or levels are nested within and are subject to larger units even while retaining their own integrity. Koestler (1967) coined the term *holon* to name these semiautonomous units; Minuchin and Fishman (1981) attributed the following characteristics to them:

> A holon exerts competitive energy for autonomy and self-preservation as a whole. It also carries integrative energy as a part. The nuclear family is a

holon of the extended family, the extended family of the community, and so on. Each whole contains the part and each part also contains the "program" that the whole imposes. Part and whole contain each other in a continuing, current, and ongoing process of communication and interrelationship. (p. 13)

In human systems, some holons have more influence than others, but systems are healthiest when they are balanced. "This state exists when each holon of a multilevel system (1) has the degree of influence, the access to resources, and the responsibility appropriate to its [function] and to its level in the system and (2) is equal to other holons at the same level" (Breunlin et al., 1992, p. 41). For family counselors and therapists, "the unit for intervention is always a holon (Minuchin & Fishman, 1981, p. 13).

Early Beginnings: The Role of Gregory Bateson

Gregory Bateson is acknowledged by many as a pioneer in applying cybernetic systems thinking to human interaction.[1] He gained exposure to cybernetics at the Josiah Macy Conferences in the 1950s, which were attended by Wiener and other cyberneticians. Bateson saw that cybernetic systems thinking provided a powerful alternative language for explaining behavior, one that did not resort to descriptions of the internal workings of mind or instinct (Segal, 1991). He began to use these ideas to understand social interaction (Ruesch & Bateson, 1951), retrospectively applying cybernetic principles to his study of the Iatmul headhunters of New Guinea (Bateson, 1958) and then extending cybernetic principles to the study of families of schizophrenics (Haley, 1976a).

In his study of the Naven ceremony, Bateson discovered that social differentiation follows two patterns: "Either the differences between two individuals or groups are emphasized or their similarities are emphasized" (Simon, Stierlin, & Wynne, 1985, p. 346). The emphasis on difference was

---

[1] *Cybernetics* was defined by Wiener (1948) as the science of control and communication. Ashby (1956) called it the art of steersmanship. Cybernetics "treats not things but ways of behaving"; it does not ask, "What is this thing?" but "What does it do?" (Ashby, 1956, p. 1). It refers to the study of self-regulation as it occurs in both natural systems (such as the homeostatic regulation of the body) and manufactured systems (such as the heating system in one's home); it deals with problems of control, recursiveness, and information (Bateson, 1979). Like Keeney and Ross (1985), we define *cybernetics* as "the study of a particular recursive complementarity concerned with the interrelation of stability and change" (p. 50). Cybernetic systems are "patterns of organization that maintain stability through processes of change" (p. 51). Cybernetic systems rely on feedback, "a method of stabilizing a system by recycling into it the changes of its past performance" (p. 51).

called the *complementary* pattern, while the emphasis on similarity was named the *symmetrical* pattern. Bateson (1958) gave this "process of differentiation in the norms of individual behavior" the name *schismogenesis* and asserted that it occurs over time as "each party reacts to the reaction of the other" (p. 189).

For example, in the complementary pattern of relating, the emphasis of each party is on acting differently from the other while retaining connection to the other: one may give, the other receive; one may move toward, the other move away; one may assume a "one-up" position exercising authority and control, while the other may assume a "one-down" position submitting to that exercise of authority and control (Haley, 1963). By contrast, in a symmetrical pattern of relating, the behaviors of the two (or more) partners oscillate between mutuality and escalation: when each agrees to the equality of the relationship, mutuality, trust, and respect prevail; however, when the two parties each attempt to gain or maintain a dominant position (as in competition where each party strives to be a "little more equal" than the other), escalation prevails and the existing relationship is threatened (Simon et al., 1985).

Bateson (1958) originally believed that these two patterns of behavior represented two kinds of forces in Iatmul society: destructive forces, which could propel the participants into a pattern of escalating antagonisms leading to the possible secession of a splinter group, versus positive forces that supported accommodation and social cohesion. But when he reexamined his data through the lens of cybernetics and the concepts of circular causality, feedback, and self-corrective circuits, he revised his beliefs. Symmetrical escalation, once seen as destructive, was now seen as expressive of the dynamics of change generated by positive feedback, while complementary patterns were now seen as expressive of the stabilizing impact of negative feedback. He realized "that an excess of symmetrical rivalry triggered complementary rituals, and conversely" (Simon et al., 1985, p. 310). Bateson (1958) concluded that "this oscillation between the symmetrical and the complementary" prevented the social disintegration that he had predicted in his earlier lineal view of schismogenesis. These constructs were later used to account for the stability/change mechanisms inherent in family communication binds (Watzlawick et al., 1967).

The Palo Alto Group: Homeostasis and the Double Bind

Bateson considered pattern, process, and communication to be the fundamental elements of description and explanation and believed that by observing human systems he could formulate rules that could explain the dynamics of human interaction. In 1952, Bateson received a grant from the Rockefeller Foundation to investigate the general nature of communication and was joined by Jay Haley, John Weakland, William Fry, and Don D. Jackson (the Palo Alto group). The group defined the family as a cybernetic, homeostatic system whose parts (family members) co-vary with each other to maintain equilibrium by means of error-activated negative feedback loops (Jackson, 1968a, 1968b). For example, whenever deviation-amplifying information is introduced (such as an argument between two family members or the challenge of a new stage in the family life cycle), a designated family member initiates a counterdeviation action (that is, exhibits symptomatic behavior) so that the family's existing equilibrium is restored and threatened changes are defeated. This emphasis on homeostasis and its companion, morphostasis, prevailed in family counseling and therapy theory into the 1980s.

The recognition of the symptomatic double bind as a homeostatic maneuver regulating family patterns of relationship is considered to be the definitive contribution of the Palo Alto group. An oft-quoted example of the symptomatic double bind stems from the interaction between a mother and her son who had "fairly well recovered from an acute schizophrenic episode."

> [The son] was glad to see her and impulsively put his arm around her shoulders, whereupon she stiffened. He withdrew his arm and she asked, "Don't you love me any more?" He then blushed, and she said, "Dear, you must not be so easily embarrassed and afraid of your feelings." The patient was able to stay with her only a few minutes more, and following her departure, he assaulted an aide and was put in the tubs. (Bateson, Jackson, Haley, & Weakland, 1976, pp. 14–15)

The Palo Alto group noted both the incongruence of the mother's message and the fact that the son could not clearly and directly comment on it. They concluded that the son's craziness was his "command" commentary on his mother's contradictory behavior.

Command messages define the relationship among the communicators as either complementary or symmetrical, and they are usually expressed through paraverbal and nonverbal behaviors. Command messages are differentiated from *report messages*, which refer to the verbal content. Command (or analogic) messages have multiple referents—there is no one response to analogic communication because of the ambiguity present—and the meaning of the message depends on the context within which it took place. By contrast, report (or digital) messages have a specific referent (Ruesch & Bateson, 1951; Watzlawick et al., 1967). In the example of the mother and son, the report and command messages contradicted each other, thereby creating a crisis situation.

Double-bind theory specifies circumstances that are necessary for such "crazy" provocations and proposes that a symptomatic double-bind situation exists when the following conditions are met (Bateson et al., 1976):

1. Two or more persons are involved.
2. The situation is a replication of prior experience so that the double-bind structure becomes a habitual expectation.
3. A primary negative injunction is involved that uses one of the following forms: (a) "Do not do that, or I will punish you," or (b) "If you do not do that, I will punish you."
4. A secondary injunction conflicts with the first at a more abstract level. Like the first, it is enforced by punishments or signals that threaten survival; and it is usually communicated to the child by nonverbal means.
5. A tertiary negative injunction prohibits the victim from escaping from the field.
6. The complete set of ingredients is no longer necessary when the victim has learned to perceive her universe in double-bind patterns.

In the mother-son example, the son is the victim and the mother is the binder in what was confirmed as a repeated experience. The primary negative injunction was conveyed by her body movement (the command message), which implied that she did not want his affection. The secondary injunction (the report message) contradicted the first by implying that he *should* express his love. The tertiary negative injunction (an additional command) implied that he was not free to comment on his mother's incongruence directly—hence, his "crazy" behavior. The theory proposes that the son will act crazily in all situations after he has learned to perceive his relationships in double-bind patterns. The theory later emphasizes that the pattern of interaction has generated the craziness. Neither participant is more to blame than the other for the unfortunate outcome; rather, they mutually contributed to the perpetuation of the pattern so that family homeostasis was maintained (Weakland, 1976).

Watzlawick et al. (1967) asserted that the power of symptomatic double binds can only be broken by counter double binds, called therapeutic double binds: "In other words, what has been found to drive people crazy must ultimately be useful in driving them sane" (p. 240). The researchers proposed the following conditions for a counter double bind:

> Structurally, a therapeutic double bind is the mirror image of a pathogenic one. . . .

1. It presupposes an intense relationship, in this case, the psychotherapeutic situation. . . .
2. In this context, an injunction is given which is so structured that it (a) reinforces the behavior the patient expects to be changed, (b) implies that this reinforcement is the vehicle of change, and (c) thereby creates paradox because the patient is told to change by remaining unchanged. . . .
3. The therapeutic situation prevents the patient from withdrawing or otherwise dissolving the paradox by commenting on it. (Watzlawick et al., 1967, p. 241)

The purpose of the therapeutic double bind is to put the client in an untenable position in relation to his pathology. In a pathogenic double bind, the patient is "damned if he does and damned if he doesn't"; but in a therapeutic double bind, he is "changed if he does and changed if he doesn't" (Watzlawick et al., 1967, p. 241).

The double-bind theory freed family therapy from the constraints of psychodynamic theories and the language of pathology (Anderson & Goolishian, 1988). It has been subjected to much theoretical and experimental scrutiny and criticism (see Olson, 1972). Whereas inconsistent messages (single binds) are quite common and easily identified, true double binds are quite rare (Guttman, 1991). Dell (1980) observed that the double-bind theory, properly understood, epitomizes the ecosystemic shift to observing transactional patterns (the relationships among components) rather than substance (the components themselves). It is this shift that constitutes the novel contribution of cybernetic systems thinking to the exercise of family counseling and therapy (Keeney, 1983; Keeney & Ross, 1985).

Milton Erickson: Elicitation and Pattern Intervention

The Palo Alto group drew on the therapeutic wisdom of Milton Erickson, an innovative psychiatrist and hypnotherapist from Phoenix, Arizona. Erickson demonstrated remarkable sensitivity to the subtleties of human communication, a sensitivity gained as a consequence of his own experiences with polio and paralysis. He turned this sensitivity into an approach to counseling and therapy that emphasized the positive and focused on the strengths and resources that existed for the client in the present or that could be developed and used in the future. Whatever the client presented was used, including symptoms, anxieties, pessimism, resistance, rigidity, or delusions. He believed that each person was unique and that counseling and psychotherapy theory and practice should be adapted to meet the uniqueness of the individual's needs rather than be used to force the client to adapt to its demands (O'Hanlon, 1987).

Erickson was both direct and indirect in communicating his messages. He was willing to take responsibility and make decisions for his clients when it was necessary (Haley, 1963). He got his clients to act, often by directing them to behave in the symptomatic way while adding a novel twist: the symptom might be relabeled, the ritual sequence might be reorganized, or an ordeal might be prescribed as a means of blocking the symptomatic activity. Erickson's approach focuses on the present and on social interactions; symptoms are metaphoric communications, and awareness or insight is unnecessary for change (rather, change and the persistence of that change are the by-products of rearranging the client's situation) (Haley, 1967). Change happens in response to counselors or therapists: they create an intense relationship with their clients and then use that relationship to get a client to cooperate or therapeutically rebel to prove the counselor or therapist wrong (O'Hanlon, 1987). Erickson encouraged resistance, provoked a response by frustrating it, encouraged a relapse, provided a worse alternative, amplified a deviation, and used anecdotes and metaphors to anchor ideas or make a previously unacceptable possibility acceptable (Haley, 1973). His counseling and therapy approach exemplified the interpersonal impact of the counselor or therapist on the unconscious of the client.

HUMAN NATURE: A DEVELOPMENTAL PERSPECTIVE

Family systems theory situates individual development within the context of the family life cycle and multigenerational patterns of connection (Boszormenyi-Nagy & Spark, 1971). Individuals benefit (and sometimes suffer) from the legacy of successes and failures, conflicts and resolutions passed on to them by their parents, grandparents, great-grandparents, and other family members. The family life cycle identifies the challenges and tasks that "normal" families confront over time (see table 15.1). Symptoms and dysfunctions appear when there is a dislocation or disruption in the anticipated "natural" unfolding of the life cycle. "The symptom is a signal that a family has difficulty in getting past a stage in the life cycle" (Haley, 1973, p. 42). The goal of counseling or therapy is to help reestablish the family's developmental momentum so that family members can resolve developmental crises and move on to the next stage of the family life cycle. Family therapy "frames problems within the course the family has moved along in its past, the tasks it is trying to master, and the future toward which it is moving" (Carter & McGoldrick, 1988, p. 4).

TABLE 15.1
The Stages of the Family Life Cycle

Family Life Cycle Stage	Emotional Process of Transition Key Principles	Second-order Changes in Family Status Required to Proceed Developmentally
1. Leaving home: Single young adults	Accepting emotional and financial responsibility for self	a. Differentiation of self in relation to family of origin b. Development of intimate peer relationships c. Establishment of self through work and financial independence
2. The joining of families through marriage: The new couple	Commitment to new system	a. Formation of marital system b. Realignment of relationships with extended families and friends to include spouse
3. Families with young children	Accepting new members into the system	a. Adjusting marital system to make space for child(ren) b. Joining in child rearing, financial, and household tasks c. Realignment of relationships with extended family to include parenting and grandparenting roles
4. Families with adolescents	Increasing flexibility of family boundaries to include children's independence and grandparents' frailties	a. Shifting of parent-child relationships to permit adolescent to move in and out of system b. Refocus on midlife marital and career issues c. Beginning shift toward joint caring for older generation
5. Launching children and moving on	Accepting a multitude of exits from and entries into the family system	a. Renegotiation of marital system as a dyad b. Development of adult to adult relationships between grown children and their parents c. Realignment of relationships to include in-laws and grandchildren d. Dealing with disabilities and death of parents (grandparents)
6. Families in later life	Accepting the shifting of generational roles	a. Maintaining own or couple functioning and interests in face of physiological decline; exploration of new familial and social role options b. Support for a more central role of middle generation c. Making room in the system for the wisdom and experience of the elderly; supporting the older generation without overfunctioning for them d. Dealing with loss of spouse, siblings, and other peers and preparation for own death; life review and integration

Source: From B. Carter & M. McGoldrick (Eds.), *The Changing Family Life Cycle*. © 1988 by Gardner Press. Reprinted by permission.

The Family Life Cycle

The first detailed description of the family life cycle from a systemic point of view was presented by Jay Haley (1973), who organized and applied the counseling and therapeutic techniques of Milton Erickson to six stages of the life cycle stretching from courtship to old age. Haley emphasized the idea that symptoms are most likely to occur at points of transition between stages of the life cycle and that counseling and therapy's purpose is to help people move past the crisis and on to the next stage of family life. Carter and McGoldrick (1988) developed this emphasis further by observing that family stress is most intense during these transition points in family development. Following Bowen (1978), they assert that the escalation, intensity, and duration of family anxiety are the significant factors in provoking disturbed family transitions and that these factors vary in response to both vertical and horizontal pressures (see figure 15.1). The vertical pressures emanate from the family's multigenerational patterns of

FIGURE 15.1
Horizontal and vertical stressors

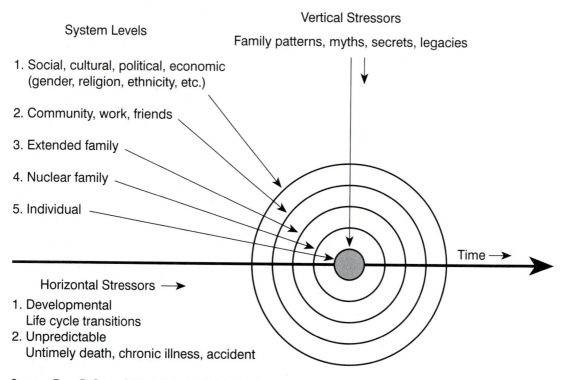

Source: From B. Carter & M. McGoldrick (Eds.), *The Changing Family Life Cycle.* © 1988 by Gardner Press. Reprinted by permission.

connection and include all the family attitudes, taboos, expectations, labels, and loaded issues that are passed from one generation to another; the horizontal pressures emanate from the nuclear family's passage through time and its response to the challenges and changes of life. According to Carter and McGoldrick (1988), these horizontal pressures include "the predictable developmental stresses and those unpredictable events, 'the slings and arrows of outrageous fortune' that may disrupt the life cycle process (untimely death, birth of a handicapped child, chronic illness, war, etc.)" (p. 8). When horizontal stressors coincide with vertical stressors in areas of family vulnerability, there is a quantum leap in anxiety in the immediate family, which makes it more likely that various family members will manifest the stress in disturbing ways.

The Family Life Spiral

Combrinck-Graham (1985) offers a different view of the family life cycle. She observes that it "is not a linear event; it does not begin with a stage, nor does it end with the deaths of members of a particular generation" (p. 142). Rather, she conceptualizes the life cycle as an evolving helix and superimposes the developmental tasks of three generations in the family to yield a family life spiral (see figure 15.2). Each family member's developmental issues are situated in relation to every other family member's developmental issues so that the relationships prone to especially intense mutual reciprocal influence are more visible. For example, Erik Erikson's (1963) stage of generativity coincides with childbearing and child rearing on the one side and grandparenthood on the other. The birth of a child pushes the older generations along the time line, whether or not they are ready. Similarly, the "40s crisis" (Levinson, Darrow, Klein, Levinson, & McKee, 1978), which involves the reconsideration of status, occupation, and marital state, may coincide with adolescent identity struggles on the one side and grandparent plans for retirement on the other; in either case, family members tend toward a preoccupation with self rather than with family.

The spiral is compact at the top to illustrate the family's closeness during centripetal (CP) periods and spread out at the bottom to represent centrifugal (CF) periods of greater distance among family members. The close periods are designated as centripetal to indicate "the predominance of forces in the family system that hold the family together" (Combrinck-Graham, 1985, p. 143). CP stages are those with an inner orientation requiring intense bonding and cohesion (early childhood, child rearing, grandparenting), and during CP periods both the individual and the family life structure emphasize internal family life. External boundaries are tight-

FIGURE 15.2
Family life spiral model

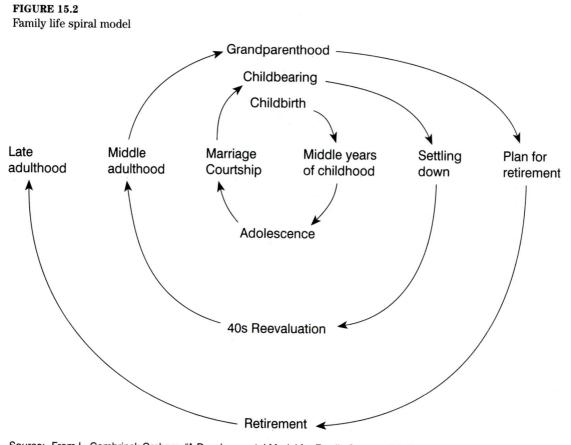

ened while internal boundaries may be more diffuse to enhance teamwork. By contrast, the distant or disengaged periods are designated as centrifugal to indicate the predominance of forces that pull the family apart. CF stages are those with an outer orientation and focus on developmental tasks that emphasize personal identity and autonomy (adolescence, midlife, retirement). The external family boundary is loosened, old family structures are dismantled, and distance between family members increases.

Families oscillate between centripetal (CP) and centrifugal (CF) forces, depending on the developmental tasks required of them at various stages of the family life cycle (see figure 15.2). Typically, an individual will experience three oscillations in a lifetime, spanning six developmental stages of the family life cycle: one's own childhood (CP) and adolescence (CF), the birth (CP) and adolescence (CF) of one's children, and the birth

(CP) and development (CF) of one's grandchildren. Each oscillation is approximately 25 years in length, producing a new generation with each full oscillation. These oscillations appear to provide opportunities within the family context for family members to work and rework issues of intimacy and generativity in the CP stages and identity and self-actualization in the CF stages (Harvey, 1993).

Neither CP nor CF directions of movement define a pathological condition; they only describe the relationship styles of the family at particular stages of the family life spiral. Symptom formation, however, often occurs when the family is confronted with an event that is out of phase with the anticipated development of the family life spiral, such as when a child dies. Whatever the event, throughout the life spiral and the life cycle, "the central underlying process to be negotiated is the expansion, contraction, and realignment of the relationship system to support the entry, exit, and development of family members in a functional way" (Carter & McGoldrick, 1988, p. 13). Thus, the family life cycle and the family life spiral conceptualize the temporal context within which the family system and its members evolve.

The Family Genogram

Mapping the progression of a particular family through the life cycle over three or more generations is greatly enhanced by the family genogram, "a format for drawing a family tree that records information about family members and their relationships over at least three generations" (McGoldrick & Gerson, 1985, p. 1). Genograms can map birth order and complex family developmental patterns in a way that provides a rich source of hypotheses about the way current concerns are connected to the family context and how concerns and context have evolved over time. Taken together, the family life cycle, the family life spiral, and the genogram are valuable assessment tools for the family counselor or therapist.

MAJOR CONSTRUCTS

The major constructs of family counseling and therapy are rooted in the debate about epistemological foundations. Bateson (1977) believed that a family counselor or therapist cannot avoid an epistemology: "You cannot claim to have no epistemology. Those who so claim have nothing but a bad epistemology. And every description is based upon, and contains implicitly, a theory of how to describe" (p. 147). Epistemology is, according to Bateson (1979), "always and inevitably personal. The point of the probe is always in the heart of the explorer: What is my answer to the question of knowing?" (p. 98).

Held and Pols (1985) suggest that the question of knowing in family counseling and therapy theory oscillates between two different meanings attributed to the concept of epistemology: Meaning 1 concerns itself with "the nature of knowledge—both with what knowledge is as distinct, say, from mere belief or prejudice, and with how we know" (p. 510). By contrast, meaning 2 is "more concerned with what we know (or think we know)"—that is, "with what philosophers call metaphysics or ontology: inquiry into the nature of the world as it is" (p. 510).

Keeney (1982) clearly intended meaning 1 when he defined *epistemology* as "the process of knowing, constructing, and maintaining a world of experience" (p. 165). By consciously reflecting on how we know, family counselors and therapists are attending to how they edit the universe and to how they participate in the "social construction of reality" (Berger & Luckmann, 1966). "The fundamental act of epistemology is to draw a distinction—distinguishing an 'it' from the 'background' that is 'not it'" (Keeney, 1982, p. 156). Bateson referred to this activity as *punctuation*. A particular punctuation organizes (that is, patterns) events in a certain way:

> Punctuating or mapping a world follows from how an observer *chooses* to see. . . . In cybernetics, seeing a world follows from how we draw it. It is as if one's hand draws outlines on one's own retina. The process is recursive— what one draws, one sees, and what one sees, one draws. (Keeney, 1982, p. 157)

The act of punctuating involves everyone—husband and wife, son and daughter, teacher and student, counselor or therapist and client—in the construction and reconstruction of experience. Family counseling and therapy constitute a specific invitation to repunctuate experience within the safety of the counseling or therapeutic encounter. As Keeney (1982) puts it, "A world of experience is carved and known by the mental process we habitually call 'therapy.' Therapy, in other words, becomes epistemology" (p. 167).

The Ecosystemic View: A Choice of Lenses

The act of punctuating can produce distinctions that reflect the different positions occupied by the observer/epistemologist: is she inside or outside the system observed? Wiener (1948) was keenly aware of the two positions and their implications for cybernetic theory. He believed that looking at the whole picture meant including the observer:

> Essentially your ecosystem, your organism-plus-environment, is to be con-
> sidered as a single circuit . . . and you're not really concerned with an input-
> output, but with the events within the bigger circuit, and you are part of the
> bigger circuit. (Brand, 1976, p. 37)

Bateson demonstrated Wiener's point of view and distinguished between the two positions by drawing figure 15.3, which summarizes the two cybernetic epistemologies that have evolved. First-order cybernetics (or simple cybernetics) refers to the observer as occupying a position (labeled *engineer* in figure 15.3) on the outside of the system observed. From this outside position, an observer is inclined toward mechological inquiry, lineal description, either/or choices, and disciplined objectivity (Auerswald, 1990). In the other position, called second-order cybernetics (or cybernetics of cybernetics), the observer becomes a participant, occupying a position (labeled *Wiener, Bateson, Mead* in figure 15.3) on the inside of the system observed. As an insider, an observer is inclined toward ecological inquiry, circular description, both/and choices, and disciplined subjectivity. Bateson believed that the views from both positions were significant and valuable, as shown by his observation regarding a projected study of dolphins: "There are at least *two levels* to be studied all the time, dolphin events, relationships, and meanings, and events, relationships, and meanings involving *scientist and dolphin*" (M. C. Bateson, 1977, p. 72). His caveat regarding the disciplined subjectivity required by the second relationship was summarized in this declaration: "The problem is *not* to resist falling in love. The problem is to fall in love and be the wiser thereby" (p. 72).

FIGURE 15.3
Two cybernetic views

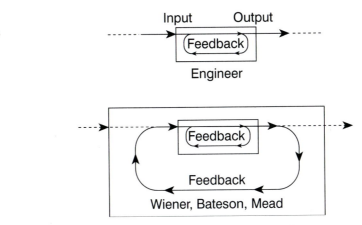

Source: From Stewart Brand, "For God's Sake, Margaret: Conversation with Gregory Bateson
and Margaret Mead," in *The Co-evolution Quarterly, 10.* © by *The Co-evolution Quarterly.*
Reprinted by permission.

Second-order cybernetics acknowledges the involvement of the observer as constituting a second level of analysis, one that expands the base of information to include the unique, phenomenological perspectives of all participants, including the observer. The exclusivity of first-order thinking is enlarged and humanized by the inclusiveness of second-order thinking (Auerswald, 1987). Andersen (1991) suggests that we are all constantly moving in our thinking back and forth between first-order and second-order views. It is easier to take the second-order position "when we have some distance on the issue in question, e.g., when we are 'calm' in relation to it." On the other hand, the first-order view seems "more natural" when "we are very eager in dealing with an issue or emotionally disturbed by it, e.g., angry or sad or fearful" (p. 65). Therefore, we do not have to choose one or the other; rather, it is helpful to know which position we are taking when making distinctions and asking questions.

A Second-order Ecosystemic View: Cybernetics of Cybernetics

An increasing number of family counselors and therapists (Andersen, 1991; Anderson & Goolishian, 1988; Daniels & White, 1994; Hoffman, 1990) describe the process of family counseling and therapy from the inside position: they consider themselves part of the "problem-determined linguistic systems" that become the agents of change (Daniels & White, 1994). They consider therapy to be a linguistic event that takes place in a counseling or therapeutic conversation wherein the participants together move from a position of not knowing to knowing, from helplessness to empowerment. The role of the family counselor or therapist is that of conversation facilitator for the "problem-organizing, problem-dis-solving" therapeutic system (Anderson & Goolishian, 1988, p. 379).

They recognize that they cannot influence others without being influenced; therefore, they include themselves as part of what must change. As coequal participants, family counselors and therapists use circular questions that elicit perceptions and events that, when taken together, construct the patterns that connect all the participants, including the counselor or therapist (Tomm, 1988). In addition, the counselor or therapist respects all members of the ecosystem as autonomous individuals functioning as self-organizing agents of stability and change. They invite members of the ecosystem to reflect upon the implications of their current perceptions and actions and to consider new meanings and alternative actions; what the members decide, however, is up to them. Family counselors and therapists behave like guides or facilitators who encourage participants to mobilize their own problem-solving resources and to cocreate solutions they can implement. One major presupposition undergirding these ways of working is that the counseling and therapeutic system is coevolutionary: what family counselors and therapists do is to initiate reflexive activity among those sharing the ecosystem's existing belief system. Thus, ecosystemic family counselors and therapists endeavor "to interact in a manner that opens space for the members of the ecosystem to see new possibilities and to evolve more freely of their own accord" (Tomm, 1988, p. 9).

THE PROCESS OF CHANGE

The ecosystemic theory of change begins with the recognition that "a system is any unit structured on feedback" (Campbell, Draper, & Huffington, 1988, p. 26). To understand ecosystemic change, one must understand the cybernetic control processes involving information and feedback. In ecosystemic theory, change is presumed to be constant and continuous (see figure 15.4). The impact of change on systems is a function of feedback. Information in the form of feedback precipitates shifts that either amplify (positive feedback) or counteract (negative feedback) the direction and outcome of changes already in progress.

All systems must change to stay the same, and they do so by using the cybernetic principle of negative feedback: information about system performance is used to stabilize the system (morphostasis) by decreasing deviation from existing forms and restoring homeostasis. Keeney (1982) suggests that "homeostasis is a way of describing how change leads to stability and how stability embodies change" (p. 159). This kind of change, called first-order change, is essentially "change without change" because it does not produce a change in the structure of the system (Lyddon, 1990, p. 123). By contrast, movement toward a qualitatively different state (morphogenesis) requires a change of change using the cybernetic principle of positive feedback: information about system performance is used to increase the system's deviation from its original morphostatic phase toward new forms of interrelationship (Elkaim, 1990). This kind of change, called second-order change, is a "type of change whose occurrence alters the fundamental structure of the system" (Lyddon, 1990, p. 123).

Each type of feedback generates change: while positive feedback amplifies the direction of movement and generates novel arrangements and forms, negative feedback limits amplification to oscillation around a predetermined reference point. Positive feedback fosters the discontinuities and transformations in the structure and internal order of a system to

FIGURE 15.4

A plan for structural change in a normal adaptive system

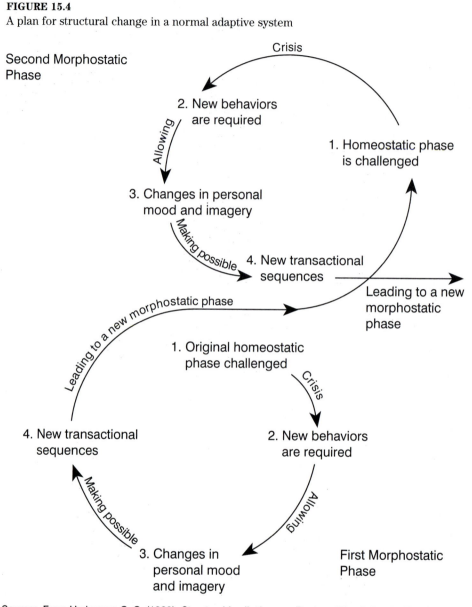

Source: From Umbarger, C. C. (1983). *Structural family therapy*. Boston: Allyn & Bacon. Reprinted by permission.

produce new forms. Negative feedback enables a system to maintain itself by assimilating small adjustments into its existing structures.

Both types of feedback are emphasized by family counselors and therapists. Lyddon (1990) suggested that an emphasis on helping clients solve problems by using existing structures without disrupting them (the pragmatic preference) constitutes a first-order intervention focus; any second-order change is seen as serendipitous within this emphasis (see de Shazar, 1988; Haley, 1976b; Segal, 1991; Watzlawick et al., 1974). By contrast, an emphasis on understanding historical, developmental, and organizational themes and patterns (the aesthetic preference) is characteristic of a second-order intervention focus in which qualitative structural change is expected (Boscolo et al., 1987; Bowen, 1978; Keeney, 1983; Minuchin, 1974). The former leads to small change, the latter to big change.

Whichever focus is adopted, family counselors and therapists implement a binocular theory of change (de Shazar, 1982a). The counselor/therapist system initiates a change of change by joining with the client system to form a suprasystem that generates multiple descriptions of the disturbing situation and directs attention to exceptions to the rule of problem or pattern. Each system is environment for the other, and their interaction alters the ecology of mind that they share (Bateson, 1979). The counselor/therapist system contributes a vision from a different angle that perturbs the client system in such a way that new possibilities of meaning and action emerge to transform the suprasystem in unpredictable ways.

When counselors and therapists cooperate with client systems to formulate frames for understanding and action that fit client aspirations, the client system usually cooperates by changing its way of changing (de Shazar, 1982a); but when counselors or therapists promote frames that don't fit client aspirations or otherwise fail to cooperate, negative feedback loops are activated, and the new ways of changing are rejected (Senge, 1990). Thus, the direction of change is influenced by timely information or news of differences that can make a difference in system functioning. The counselor or therapist's job is to create a new context where new possibilities emerge that afford the client system opportunity to solve troublesome problems and to experience alternative patterns of communicating and relating.

INTERVENTION STRATEGIES

Initially, cybernetic thinking and the negative feedback principle led clinical researchers to shift their attention from a search for the causes of human problems, as in the psychodynamic and behavior therapies, to a search for what maintains human problems (Watzlawick et al., 1974). More recently, the positive feedback principle has led clinical researchers to shift their attention again—from what maintains problems to what solves them (Walter & Peller, 1992). The first shift occurred when clinicians at the Mental Research Institute (MRI) in Palo Alto traced feedback loops in order to learn what perpetuates the problem; the problem state was seen as a steady state that was maintained by the equilibriating influence of negative feedback. The second shift occurred when the clinicians at the Brief Family Therapy Center of Milwaukee (BFTC) decided to ignore problem analysis and direct client attention to the search for solutions that fit their situation, preferably something they were already doing (de Shazar & Molnar, 1984). They found that the search for exceptions to a problem occurrence offered clues to action that, when amplified, dissolved the problem.

The First Shift: What Maintains the Problem?

In the spring of 1967 the MRI program began to pursue three goals: (1) to find a quick and efficient means for resolving client complaints, (2) to transform therapy from an art into a craft that could be taught, and (3) to study change human systems (Segal, 1991). They synthesized the thinking of Gregory Bateson, Milton Erickson (Haley, 1973), and Heinz von Foerster (Segal, 1986) to formulate a counseling and therapy approach for problem resolution (or re-solution).

The MRI team focused on observable behavioral interaction in the present: "We try to base our conceptions and our interventions on direct observation in the treatment situation of *what* is going on in systems of human interaction, *how* they continue to function in such ways, and *how* they may be altered most effectively" (Weakland et al., 1974, p. 150). The team members hypothesized that persistent problems begin as a mishandling of everyday events; the problems are then maintained by the very efforts people make to resolve them. They concluded that once a difficulty begins to be seen as a problem, the continuation and often the exacerbation of this problem results from initial solution attempts. They concluded further that complaints are maintained by the clients' idea that what they decide to do about the original difficulty is the only right and logical thing to do; therefore, clients (and helpers) persist in doing more of the same (the chosen solution), and "the solution becomes the problem" (Watzlawick et al., 1974, p. 31). Choosing the right path necessitates rejection of all alternatives as wrong: the client follows the either-or logic of the Aristotelian or positivist epistemology (Johnson, 1946). Thus, the problem is maintained by the attempted solution.

Consider, for instance, a common pattern between a depressed patient and his family. The more they try to cheer him up and make him see the positive sides of life, the more depressed the patient is likely to get: "They don't even understand me." The action meant to *alleviate* the behavior of the other party aggravates it; the "cure" becomes worse than the original disease. (Weakland et al., 1974, p. 149)

Solutions become problems in one of three ways (Watzlawick et al., 1974):

1. Action is necessary to solve a problem but is not taken: the problem is denied.
2. Action is taken when it should not be: the difficulty is unchangeable.
3. Action is taken at the wrong level: a first-order change is initiated when only a second-order change will do, or vice versa: the solution becomes the problem.

Inadequate solution attempts tend to follow four patterns (Fisch, Weakland, & Segal, 1982):

1. Demanding that self or others spontaneously correct the behavior, as in the directive "cheer up"
2. Seeking a no-risk method when some risk is inevitable, as in a person's attempts to avoid rejection
3. Attempting to reach accord through opposition, as in "you shouldn't feel that way"
4. Confirming the accuser's suspicions by defending oneself

The brief counselor or therapist uses four criteria to differentiate a difficulty from a problem (Segal, 1991). For a concern to qualify as a problem, a person must say:

I am in pain or distress.

I attribute my pain to the behavior of others or myself.

I have been trying to change this behavior.

I have been unsuccessful. (p. 174)

Clinical intervention proceeds on the basis that the client's initial complaint is the problem; it is not a symptom of something else. Furthermore, the complaint is seen as a function of interaction with other people, especially significant others. Often what perpetuates complaint behavior is the behavior of other people in relation to the complaint. The counselor or therapist's primary task involves "taking deliberate action to alter poorly functioning patterns of interaction as powerfully, effectively, and efficiently as possible" (Weakland et al., 1974, p. 145). However, the deliberate action is usually clothed in an indirect, nonauthoritarian style.

The attempted solution begins with the clinician's answer to these questions: "What is the complaint? What solutions has the client attempted? What is the client's goal? What are the client's positions on the problem and treatment?" (Amatea, 1989, p. 100). After the answers have been formulated, the clinician must plan how to interrupt the attempted solutions that perpetuate the problem and decide who should be seen, what directives will be used, and how the directives should be framed. Specifically, the clinician will answer the following five questions (Segal, 1991):

1. What is the attempted solution?
2. What will be a 180-degree shift from the attempted solution?
3. What specific behavior will put the shift into motion?
4. Given the client's positions, how can the counselor or therapist sell the behavior?
5. What can the client report that will signal that the intervention has been successful and that the case is ready for termination?

In table 15.2, Amatea (1989) offers some examples of brief therapy directives, their intended impact, and the rationale that accompanies the directive

The Second Shift: What Will Solve the Problem?

Steve de Shazer's solution-focused ideas are "historically rooted in a tradition that starts with Milton H. Erickson and flows through Gregory Bateson and the group of counselors/therapists-thinkers at the Mental Research Institute" (de Shazer, 1982a, p. ix). He developed his ideas in concert with Insoo Kim Berg and James F. Derks at BFTC in Milwaukee in the late 1970s and early 1980s. Focusing on a noncritical approach that sought to understand client systems on their own terms, he used *the death of resistance* as a useful description of client behavior and suggested that it more often described the behavior of the counselor or therapist. He emphasized simplicity, brevity, and cooperation with the client:

> Each family (individual or couple) shows a unique way of attempting to cooperate, and the therapist's job becomes, first, to describe that particular manner to himself that the family shows and, then, to cooperate with the family's way and, thus, to promote change. (de Shazer, 1982a, p. 10)

TABLE 15.2
Strategic Shifts in Coercive and Avoidance Solution Efforts

Characteristics of the Problem/Solution Cycle	Nature of Proposed Solution Shift	Intended Impact	Rationale Presented
Trying to coerce a spontaneous performance from oneself	Having the person try harder to fail in his performance	Creating a no-contest structure that interrupts the original effort	Either explain that it is important to bring on the problem behavior for diagnostic purposes or explain that it is the first step to eventual control
Coercing a particular response from another that can only occur voluntarily	To interrupt the response of one-up demandingness, vague requests, or overstatement of one's power by directing person to take one-down position, making requests in casual and nonauthoritarian manner	To give the other person nothing to fight against	Agree person is correct but that he has become too predictable and thus is losing the battle
Denying another's accusations by defending oneself	Direct defender to agree with the accusations but for reasons hard for accuser to agree with; or confuse the accuser by deciding when and when not to perform behavior	Create a no-contest situation and confuse accuser	Can end the game if you can make the accuser see how mistaken he is; can do this by agreeing with accusations
Attempting to master a feared event by postponement	Direct person to expose himself to feared task but under conditions of nonmastery, and restrain person from trying to improve	To provide a worse alternative that the person will defy	Need to become more appreciative of real dangers involved. To do this must get back into the situation and bring these on only to accept them, not to improve
Attempting to gain compliance through voluntarism	Directing person who suggests compliance indirectly to make requests direct even if they are arbitrary	To make the avoidance of a direct request worse than the direct request	Describe the indirect stance as harmful and the direct stance as beneficial

Source: Amatea, E. S. (1989). *Brief strategic intervention for school behavior problems.* San Francisco: Jossey-Bass. Reprinted by permission.

Basing his ideas on the premise that "any response to any task that the family reports can be described as defining the family's unique way of attempting to cooperate" (p. 14), de Shazer (1982a) developed a decision tree to help clinicians cooperate with their clients (see figure 15.5). After client response to the first task or clue given by the counselor or therapist is identified, all subsequent clues or tasks are offered in a way that allows for a client response style similar to that demonstrated in the first response. For example, if clients report that they have done the opposite of the given task (for example, fought when the counselor or therapist suggested that they not fight), then future tasks are given in anticipation that clients may continue to do the opposite of what is suggested (the counselor or therapist may suggest they fight at least once this next week, which allows for the possibility that they might do the opposite and not fight at all).

Every counseling or therapeutic intervention is constructed in such a way that a compliment and a clue are embedded within a story line that is congruent with the client's world view yet approaches that view from a different angle. The compliment is designed to build the first steps of a "yes set" that communicates and elicits cooperation: "Some positive statements with which the family can agree are used to facilitate its acceptance of the clues (suggestions or tasks) that follow the compliment" (de Shazer, 1982a, p. 43). The compliment recognizes and acknowledges the family's current experiences, places these experiences within a framework of positive connotation, and creates an opening for a clue designed to trigger awareness of differences that can make a difference. When clients and families accept the compliment, there is an increased likelihood that the associated clue (task or suggestion) will be accepted as compatible with their manner of cooperating. If, on the other hand, clients and families do not accept the compliment, then they are not likely to find a way to cooperate with the clue. Whatever the response, counseling or therapeutic efficacy will depend on the clinician's ability to recognize the type of client response and adjust subsequent interventions accordingly (de Shazer, 1982a).

Experience with shaping the counseling or therapeutic message (the compliment and the clue) according to anticipated client response patterns (figure 15.5) led de Shazer (1988) to differentiate among three types of counseling and therapeutic contracts: visitor, complainant, and customer. A visitor contract exists when the counselor or therapist "has been unable to help the client describe a complaint" or when the counselor or therapist "has been unable to help the client develop even a minimal expectation of change" (p. 41); the counselor/therapist should only give compliments when this contract defines the therapeutic situation. A

FIGURE 15.5
The cooperation decision tree

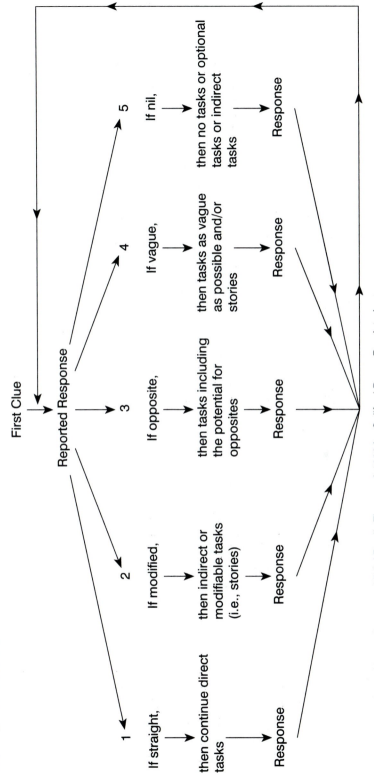

Source: From S. de Shazer, *Patterns of Brief Family Therapy.* © 1982 by Guilford Press. Reprinted by permission.

complainant contract describes "a client-therapist relationship built on the client's having developed an expectation of change as a result of the interview" (p. 42), although the client may be expecting someone else to change. When such a situation occurs, the counselor or therapist should give only observation tasks (no action tasks). A customer contract describes a client-therapist relationship that, as a result of the interview, "is built on the client's wanting to do something about building a solution" (p. 42). The client is now ready to change, so an action task is appropriate.

The search for solutions follows a planned sequence of choice points and relevant tasks. When presented with a concern, the counselor or therapist first asks himself, "Is there a joint work project? That is, is this someone who has a complaint and who wants to do something about it?" If not, the relationship fits the visitor designation, and the client is complimented for her conscientiousness and whatever else can be offered. If yes, or if the situation is vague and the client expects change, the counselor or therapist should use the following formula first-session task: "Between now and next time we meet, we (I) would like you to *observe*, so that you can describe to us (me) next time, what happens in your (pick one: family, life, marriage, relationship) that you want to continue to have happen" (de Shazer & Molnar, 1984, p. 298). This observation task directs client attention toward what she wants: toward solution talk rather than problem talk.

The orientation to solution talk can be advanced further by focusing on five types of questions (Berg & Miller, 1992). First, use questions and tasks that highlight pre-session change. For example, "It is our experience that many people notice that things are better between the time they set up an appointment and the time they came in for the first session. Have you noticed such changes in your situation?" (p. 72). Second, join the client in the search for exceptions to the rule of the problem. For example, ask clients to describe whatever is happening when the complaint is not (de Shazer, 1985). Third, ask "the miracle question": "Suppose that one night, while you were asleep, there was a miracle and this problem was solved. How would you know? What would be different? How will your husband (wife, friend) know without your saying a word . . . about it?" (de Shazer, 1988, p. 5).

A fourth way to advance solution talk is to invite comparative estimates from clients: ask clients to put their problems, priorities, successes, emotional investments in relationships, and level of self-esteem on a numerical (1–10) scale and explore the significance of various shifts over time and how they were achieved (Berg & Miller, 1992). Finally, clues to solutions can often be found in inquiries into coping behavior. Acknowledge the client's "terrible experiences" and "discouraging situation" and ask, "How do you keep going everyday?" (Berg & Miller, 1992). By using such inquiries, the counselor or therapist and the client can create as clear a picture as possible of what a solution will look like, even when the original complaint is vague, confused, or otherwise poorly described.

"A solution-focused brief therapy is a consumer approach. We endeavor to help clients get what they want" (Walter & Peller, 1992, p. 52). And getting what they want is easier when their goals are well defined. Berg and Miller (1992) identify seven qualities of well-formed treatment goals:

1. Goals must be important to the client, and the client must view the achievement of each goal as personally beneficial.
2. The goals that the client sets must be small enough to be achieved.
3. Goals must be precise and stated in concrete, specific, and behavioral terms.
4. Goals must state the presence of something rather than the absence of something; they must state in positive, proactive language what the client will do instead of what the client will not do.
5. Goals must specify the beginning rather than the end of something— the first small steps the client will take toward the desired outcome.
6. Goals must identify what is realistic and achievable within the context of the client's life.
7. Goals must be perceived as requiring hard work. Acknowledging the hard work involved in making changes promotes (and protects) the client's sense of self-worth and dignity as he advances toward an uncertain future.

When goals are clearly formulated, progress can more easily be determined. If clients do not reach all their goals right away, small successes can be complimented and reminders given that slow, steady progress is normal and more hard work remains to be done.

After goals have been established, the counselor or therapist concentrates on action tasks interrelating goals and solution possibilities. For example, a specific goal-focused task can be given to start clients on their way. Or when exceptions to the rule of the complaint are recognized as already happening, a "do something different" task can be offered as impetus to generating additional exceptions. If the exceptions are spontaneous and not within client control, a prediction task can be assigned. First, clients are asked to predict whether or not the exception will occur during the next 24 hours. Then they are to record whether the prediction was correct, at which time a new prediction will be made for the next 24 hours. Predictive efficacy often leads the client to a new sense of control over exceptional behavior. When the exceptions are deliberate and within client control, the client is invited to do the exception pattern more often. In each case, the presumption is that solutions can be built by getting the nonproblematic patterns to happen with greater frequency (de Shazer, 1988). When clients have reached their goal or figured out how to reach their goal and are well on their way, it is time to terminate.

SUPPORTING RESEARCH

Outcome research has treated family therapy as a treatment modality rather than as a conceptual framework and has sought answers to Paul's (1967) questions, "What therapy is most effective for what problems, treated by what therapists, according to what criteria, in what setting?" (p. 111). Many authors have reviewed the research answers to Paul's question, the most notable being Gurman and Kniskern (1978, 1981); Gurman, Kniskern, and Pinsof (1986); Pinsof (1981); Todd and Stanton (1983); and Szapocznik and Kurtines (1989). Gurman et al. (1986) summarize the overall impression in their conclusion that "reassuringly, . . . when family therapy methods have been rigorously tested, they have been found to be effective without exception" (p. 58).

Gurman et al. (1986) drew the following conclusions based on their review of the research:

- With family related issues, many different family therapies are more effective than individual psychotherapy.
- In both behavioral and nonbehavioral marital counseling or therapy, improved couple communication seems to be the key to successful outcome.
- For marital problems, conjoint couples counseling or therapy is clearly better than individual counseling or therapy.
- Negative outcomes are twice as likely to occur if marital problems are treated with individual counseling or therapy rather than conjoint counseling or therapy.
- Positive outcomes occur in family counseling or therapy and individual counseling or therapy in the same proportion of cases.
- Deterioration in counseling or therapy is associated with a counselor or therapist style that involves "little structuring" and "confrontation of highly effective material" (p. 572). If the therapist promotes interaction and gives support, the probability of deterioration is reduced.

- Co-counseling or therapy has not been demonstrated to be superior to marital or family counseling/therapy by one practitioner.

- Higher-level counselor/therapist relationship skills appear to be necessary for positive outcomes in therapy. Basic technical skills may prevent worsening of the problem and maintain the precounseling or therapy status of the family.

- When compared to no treatment, nonbehavioral marital and family counseling or therapy is effective in about two-thirds of cases.

- Whether the identified patient is a child, an adolescent, or an adult is not associated with treatment outcomes.

- Successful outcomes occur in relatively few (one to 20) sessions in both behavioral and nonbehavioral marital and family counseling or therapy.

- The preferred treatment for alcohol-involved marriages is conjoint couples treatment in groups. Such treatment may be superior to individual counseling or therapy with the alcoholic spouse.

- Nonbehavioral conjoint marital counseling or therapy may be more effective than individual counseling or therapy for marital problems.

- Improvement can be expected in about 71 percent of childhood or adolescent behavioral problems when any one of a variety of family counseling or therapy methods is used.

- Clinicians tend not to use family counseling or therapy research. However, the research that is most likely to be used by clinicians relates to process issues regarding how to handle problems encountered in counseling or therapy.

Piercy and Sprenkle (1990) reviewed the marriage and family counseling and therapy research of the 1980s and identified certain trends, which have been summarized by Becvar and Becvar (1993, pp. 1120–1122):

- A move away from "global comparative questions to specificity questions," which includes studying specific presenting problems with an eye to which method is most appropriate with a particular problem or type of client

- A move away "from hubris to 'mellowing,'" as systems purists become open to alternative explanations

- A trend "from design weakness to design strength"; more studies now employ "rigorous controls, careful execution, and a variety of reliable and valid measures" and "diligent attempts to raise and eliminate the possibility of alternative explanation for their findings" and provide "excellent models of long-term follow-up and attention to attrition and relapse"

■ A move "from statistical to clinical significance" by increasing use of meta-analysis

■ A move from quantitative to both qualitative and quantitative research methodologies. Qualitative research is seen as complementing quantitative research, particularly in the "'discovery' of relationships among variables, understanding complex events and interactions in the natural context"

Piercy and Sprenkle also provide recommendations for family research in the 1990s, as does Wynne (1988).

Both Gurman et al. (1986) and Keeney (1983) suggest that we need not give up our historical traditions; however, we do need more inclusive approaches to research. The crux of the matter seems to be that "the realization that the map is not the territory does not require that we throw away all our old maps. We must, however, keep in mind that a map is a map" (Kniskern, 1983, p. 61).

■ ■ ■

THE CASE STUDY OF JOHN: THE ECOSYSTEMS APPROACH

Using the case study of John, we will briefly sketch the outlines of a response from the following frames of reference: MRI brief therapy and solution-focused brief therapy.

The MRI Approach

An MRI brief strategic counselor or therapist attends first to what is defined by the person experiencing the problem (or by others involved with him) as the "nature of the problem," and second, to how those persons respond in an attempt to resolve the problem. The counselor or therapist assumes that it is often the very ways in which persons are defining a problem and responding to it that may unknowingly keep the vicious problem-solution cycle going.

The MRI counselor or therapist's goal is to assist John and the others involved with him to respond differently to the problem. This approach—doing something different to resolve the problem—depends on helping people to act in ways that they often fear are exactly the wrong things to do. It also requires that their current solution efforts be interrupted so that new options can evolve. Helping people to see the problem differently often allows them to respond differently to it.

John presents with a problem of a severe nervous stomach and occasional sexual impotence, and he describes his stomach ailment as a problem of longstanding duration. His counselor or therapist wants to hear his story (as well as the story of each family member vis-à-vis the problem) in order to understand the nature of the problem-solution cycle(s) in which he and others may be entangled. In particular, this method involves finding out how big a problem John's complaints are for him (that is, how much of his life is taken up by it, how unresolvable it feels, what specific forms it takes, what he believes is the cause of the problem, what he has tried to do to resolve it, how others have been involved with him in the problem and its resolution, and what he believes is the best way to deal with it). During this information-gathering time it is very important to not fall into the same ways of responding to John and his difficulty as others in his social system have done. If the counselor or therapist acts in ways that parallel the solutions offered by others, she cannot offer John an opportunity to respond differently.

There are two distinctive problem-solution patterns that are of interest: the first involves how John responds to his difficulties; the second concerns how others respond to John and his difficulties. It appears that when John confronts a stressful, fear-inducing situation, such as dealing with an interpersonal conflict or a performance challenge, he gets highly anxious, his stomach acts up, and he retreats and avoids the situation. Over time John has curtailed many possible activities to keep himself from being anxious. It appears that the more John perceives a situation as fear-inducing, the more anxious and fearful he feels, the more upset he becomes (as shown by his stomach upsets and sexual performance difficulties), the more he either avoids the situation or tries to avoid the impact of his fears by medicating himself. The result is that he never experiences being in the situation and he never learns how to master it. To alter this response of avoidance as the major solution to overcoming fear, it is necessary to transcend John's belief that he must not engage in an activity until he can succeed at it and his corresponding action of avoiding the situation as the prelude to learning how to manage it.

The second problem-solution pattern, which reinforces the first, concerns how the well-intentioned efforts of others to assist John in resolving his difficulties actually make them worse. It appears that key people in his life (his mother and his wife) respond to John and his fears either by accommodating them and agreeing they are not manageable or voluntary, or by becoming exasperated and denying that they are unmanageable or involuntary—often with the suggestion that if he could just handle the situation, he would stop being so anxious about it. These various solution efforts of involved others have probably had the unforeseen negative effect of either further confirming John's belief that the problem is unmanageable or his belief that others do not fully appreciate the scope of the difficulties of his situation and are foolishly suggesting he try something that will only make his situation much worse.

In order to avoid falling into these traps that others have gotten into when responding to John, the counselor or therapist empathizes with him about the seriousness and magnitude of the difficulty he has been experiencing. The counselor or therapist does not minimize the difficulty or indicate that it is something that John can get over immediately. A useful way this approach might be framed is to talk with John about the way in which he has been oppressed by his fears, to search for a label for his fears that enables him to separate himself from them, and to examine how these fears have cramped his life-style and his ability to live the way he wants. The talk can be expanded to include an examination of how others (his wife and children, his fellow workers) might have been fellow sufferers with him in his oppression. This might lead to a consideration of what can change and what can stay the same if these constraints are removed. By taking his problems seriously and examining the dangers inherent in change, the counselor or therapist prepares John for the possibility that he can learn to contain (not eliminate) his problems so that they do not dominate so much of his life and the life of his loved ones.

When John is ready, he might be asked to do an experiment, something that seems crazy to him: to put himself into one of the fear-inducing situations—not for the purpose of mastering his anxiety, but rather to observe specifically how it oppresses him, to see just how big it is. Thus, he will put himself into a fearful situation not for the purpose of succeeding at it, doing it perfectly, but for the purpose of failing at it, doing it imperfectly, in order to learn more about what distresses him. He is asked to build an outline of action steps he might take in order to fail and to enact them slowly so that he can observe himself in action. The actions taken occur within the flexible frame of experimentation and learning rather than the rigid frame of performance and perfection. His family is encouraged to join the experiment by listening carefully to his observations each time so that they, too, can learn about the details of his distress. They are cautioned, however, to offer no advice or judgment, only wonder at his rigor. The experiment continues with the counselor or therapist's applauding John's efforts; framing his efforts as ways in which he is learning about what distresses him so that he can keep his fears in their proper place; reminding him that because his fears were used to taking up all his life, they would surely try to trick him into retreating again; urging vigilance so that he can observe the retreat carefully; and cautioning him to be deliberate in his continual experimentation so that he can continue to learn.

The Solution-focused Approach

A brief solution-oriented counselor or therapist is also interested in getting John and his family to do something different. Therefore, rather than analyzing the problem in detail, the counselor or therapist directs her attention elsewhere. She searches for exceptions to the rule of John's struggles with sex and a nervous stomach: When does he not have these difficulties? When do his wife and mother respond differently to him? When does John do something different? When is the problem not a problem? Are these exceptional moments related to the goals John and his family want to pursue? If so, the counselor or therapist builds on and expands them by encouraging John and his family to engage in these exceptional activities more frequently. This expands John's arena of competence and comfort.

The steps involved are similar to those spelled out earlier in this chapter: compliment John for his sensitivity and his attention to detail, his family for their care and persistence; offer them a progressive series of clues, beginning with an observation task and moving (in step with John's progress) to prediction tasks and action tasks. For example, family members might be asked to observe what is happening in their lives that they want to keep happening, to predict whether tomorrow is going to be a bad-stomach day or a good-stomach day, to notice their predictive efficacy, to do something (anything) different and to do it again if it works to enhance responses that are compatible with their goals. As the self-generated solution activity grows, the complaint is likely to recede into the background where it can be contained

■ ■ ■

LIMITATIONS

Ecosystems counseling and therapy has been criticized primarily for four shortcomings. First, the early language chosen for describing family systems was "combative and bellicose, often suggesting willful opposition: double bind, identified patient, family scapegoat, binder, victim, and so on" (Nichols, 1987, pp. 18–19). The choice of language emphasized the destructive power of families and contributed to an assault on the family by several pioneers in family therapy (Cooper, 1970; Laing, 1969). It is this background that marks the significance of de Shazer's (1984) declaration of the death of resistance—that is, the dissolution of the opposition between counselor or therapist and family.

Second, family counselors and therapists "found the family, but lost the self." Early family counselors and therapists used the concepts of general systems theory and cybernetics as a metaphor for family functioning as well as a model of it and described the family as "a coherent composite that behaves as an irreducible unit" (Nichols, 1987, p. 24). In so doing, the early clinicians forgot that thinking of families as a system is just one way of thinking: that is, the map is not the territory (Held & Pols, 1985). The result is the attribution of an inflated sense of power to the family system and the neglect of individual autonomy (Nichols, 1987).

Third, family counselors and therapists have ignored the different socializing processes for men and women; therefore, they have ignored the way in which these socialization processes disadvantage women (Goldner, 1985; Hare-Mustin, 1987). Seeing family members "as individuals instead of a reified family forces an acknowledgement that the individuals in the family are not equal—not in status, resources, or power" (Goodrich, Rampage, Ellman, & Halstead, 1988, p. 5). Walters, Carter, Papp, and Silverstein (1988) call for family counselors and therapists to analyze all family counseling and therapy concepts through the lens of gender socialization in order to eliminate the dominance of male assumptions and promote the "recognition of the basic principle that no intervention is gender-free and that every intervention will have a different and special meaning for each sex" (p. 29).

Fourth, family counselors and therapists have been divided over the importance and design of research for the practice of family counseling and therapy. Clinical writings abound, as do countless workshops and conferences demonstrating family counseling and therapy interviewing and proclaiming its merits. But the research has not kept up in quantity or quality; with some exceptions, it is piecemeal and not cumulative, and it has not kept pace with clinical practice and theorizing in the field (Wynne, 1988). Efforts have been made in recent years to reverse this trend (Liddle, 1991; Williams, 1991; Wynne, 1988).

SUMMARY

Ecosystemic thinking enables the thinker to see wholes rather than parts, to see interrelationships rather than isolates, to see patterns of change rather than static snapshots (Senge, 1990). It provides conceptual tools for mapping and modeling a specified territory. The map produced is not the territory itself but a way of representing the territory (Held & Pols, 1985; Keeney, 1982).

The practice of ecosystemic thinking starts with the concept of feedback, which shows how actions can amplify or counteract each other and leads to the construction of patterns of stability and change (Keeney, 1983). In ecosystemic thinking, feedback refers to any reciprocal flow of influence: every influence is seen as both cause and effect, and nothing is ever influenced in one direction alone. Cause and effect are not closely related in time and space; there is always a delay between actions initiated and feedback received (Senge, 1990).

The key to describing reality ecosystemically is to construct circles of influence rather than straight lines (Keeney 1983; Senge, 1990). Over time, feedback loops generate redundant sequences of information that become identified as patterns that connect (Bateson, 1979). A system is any specified set of relationships structured on information and feedback and differentiated from a context that is the system's environment (Campbell et al., 1988). Meaning and behavior can be described as having a recursive or circular relationship. In other words, human systems voluntarily act as they do because they have certain beliefs about the context within which they operate that help them anticipate (the feed-forward dimension [Penn, 1985]) the consequences of their actions. These beliefs change or persist according to the system's assessment of information elicited by its action (the feedback dimension [Keeney, 1983]). Negative feedback loops (that is, change without change) restore and maintain system stability; positive feedback loops (or change of change) amplify the direction of change to generate new patterns that connect (Keeney, 1983; Lyddon, 1990).

No pattern exists without an observer (the counselor or therapist) who punctuates events in such a way that patterns are constructed (Keeney, 1982). Observers can exclude themselves by punctuating events from the outside (Silvern, 1972) or include themselves by punctuating events from the inside (Daniels & White, 1994).

Aesthetic description is holistic: it acknowledges the interlocking circuits of contingency that transcend conscious awareness. Pragmatic description, on the other hand, attends to immediate outcomes—the behavior elicited by oscillating sequences of interaction (Watzlawick et al., 1967). The pragmatic meaning of a message is the response it elicits independent of intention (Bandler & Grinder, 1979).

Both structural and process explanations are generative: they address the underlying sequences of behavior at a level that stimulates creative reorganization (Minuchin, 1974; Senge, 1990). By contrast, event explanations (that is, immediate, short-term explanations) doom us to reactivity because they blind us to accurate anticipation of future consequences (Senge, 1990).

Change is serendipitous. It occurs all the time, so expect the unexpected (Walter & Peller, 1992). Small change is generative of larger change because of the ripple effect. Therefore, problems large or small can be solved one step at a time (Walter & Peller, 1992). As time progresses, systems (such as persons and families) and the contexts they create and are constrained by dynamically change each other (Massey, 1986). Changing patterned arrangements of either long or short duration can produce different sequences of behavior—novel patterns that are responsive (rather than reactive) to our situation in life because they help us anticipate consequences (Senge, 1990).

A counselor or therapist should meet each person or family at their map or model of the world (de Shazer, 1982a). Remember that people choose the best alternatives available at any given moment (Cameron-Bandler, 1985). Cooperation can be inevitable; clients are always cooperating (that is, there is no resistance). They show attentive counselors and therapists how they think change takes place and invite practitioners to understand their thinking and act accordingly (de Shazer, 1982a, 1982b, 1985, 1988). However, if counselors and therapists choose not to cooperate, they will discover that the harder they push, the harder the client system pushes back (Senge, 1990).

People are resourceful: they have all they need to solve their problems when given help to access their resources and strengths (O'Hanlon & Weiner-Davis, 1989). Complaints or problems invite people to develop new understandings of the patterns of meaning and organization that connect them so that more productive changes (that is, a better fit) can happen (Campbell et al., 1988; Keeney, 1983; Keeney & Ross, 1985).

Counselors and therapists are enlisted by clients who recognize that changes are happening and who want help changing the way things are changing (Campbell et al., 1988; de Shazer, 1988). The aim of ecosystems counseling or therapy is to create a context in which all participants can think differently about the problem: soliciting multiple descriptions of the situation, noting differences (exceptions) that make a difference, and generating new possibilities for understanding and action (de Shazer, 1985, 1988; Keeney & Ross, 1985).

The referring person, the family members, interested parties (clergy, friends, neighbors, school personnel), and the counselor or therapist, together with the members of his team, are all a potential part of the problem-organizing, problem-dissolving counseling or therapeutic system (Anderson & Goolishian, 1988). The counselor or therapist should respect all messages from each member of the problem-determined, problem-dissolving therapeutic system; together, they offer the benefit of depth perception (Daniels & White, 1994).

The counselor or therapist should remember that there is no blame. Rather than searching for scapegoats, ecosystemic thinking directs us to search for differences that make a difference in leveraging changes of change (Senge, 1990). In the same way, there is no failure, only feedback (Bandler & Grinder, 1979).

The person(s) with the broadest repertoire of behaviors and choices will be the controlling element(s) in the counseling or therapeutic system (Sherrard, 1991). This principle is based on Ashby's (1956) law of requisite variety and reminds us of the survival value inherent in flexibility and variety. It offers a skeleton key to counseling and therapeutic efficacy and the changing of change.

Finally, the central philosophy (and simplest statement) of ecosystemic practice is contained in the following rules of thumb (Berg & Miller, 1992, p. 17):

If it ain't broke, don't fix it!

Once you know what works, do more of it!

If it doesn't work, then don't do it again. Do something different!

REFERENCES

Ackerman, N. W. (1958). *The psychodynamics of family life*. New York: Basic Books.

Amatea, E. S. (1989). *Brief strategic intervention for school behavior problems*. San Francisco: Jossey-Bass.

Andersen, T. (1991). *The reflecting team: Dialogues and dialogues about dialogues*. New York: Norton.

Anderson, H., & Goolishian, H. (1988). Human systems as linguistic systems: Preliminary and evolving ideas about the implications for clinical theory. *Family Process, 27*, 371–393.

Ashby, W. R. (1956). *An introduction to cybernetics*. London: Chapman & Hall.

Auerswald, E. H. (1987). Epistemological confusion in family therapy and research. *Family Process, 26*, 317–330.

Auerswald, E. H. (1990). Toward epistemological transformation in the education and training of family therapists. In M. P. Mirkin (Ed.), *The social and political contexts of family therapy* (pp. 19–50). Boston: Allyn & Bacon.

Bandler, R., & Grinder, J. (1979). *Frogs into princes*. Moab, UT: Real People Press.

Barker, J. A. (1992). *Future edge*. New York: Morrow.

Bateson, G. (1958). *Naven: A survey of the problems suggested by a composite picture of the culture of a New Guinea tribe drawn from three points of view* (2nd ed.). Stanford: Stanford University Press. (Original work published in 1936)

Bateson, G. (1972). *Steps to an ecology of mind*. San Francisco: Chandler.

Bateson, G. (1977). The thing of it is. In M. Katz, W. Marsh, & G. Thompson (Eds.), *Explorations of planetary culture at the Lindisfarne conferences: Earth's answer* (pp. 142–155). New York: Harper & Row.

Bateson, G. (1979). *Mind and nature: A necessary unity.* New York: Dutton.

Bateson, G., Jackson, D. D., Haley, J., & Weakland, J. G. (1976). Toward a theory of schizophrenia. In C. E. Sluzki & D. C. Ransom (Eds.), *Double bind: The foundation of the communicational approach to the family* (pp. 3–22). New York: Grune & Stratton.

Bateson, M. C. (1977). Daddy, can a scientist be wise? In J. Brockman (Ed.), *About Bateson* (pp. 57–74). New York: Dutton.

Becvar, D. S., & Becvar, R. J. (1993). *Family therapy: A systemic integration* (2nd ed.). Boston: Allyn & Bacon.

Berg, I. K., & Miller, S. D. (1992). *Working with the problem drinker: A solution-focused approach.* New York: Norton.

Berger, P., & Luckmann, T. (1966). *The social construction of reality.* Garden City, NY: Doubleday.

Bertalanffy, L. (1968). *General system theory.* New York: Brazillier.

Boscolo, L., & Cecchin, G. (1982). Training in systemic therapy at the Milan centre. In R. Whiffen & J. Byng-Hall (Eds.), *Family therapy supervision: Recent developments in practice* (pp. 153–164). London: Academic Press.

Boscolo, L., Cecchin, G., Hoffman, L., & Penn, P. (1987). *Milan systemic family therapy.* New York: Basic Books.

Boszormenyi-Nagy, I., & Spark, G. M. (1971). *Invisible loyalties.* New York: Harper & Row.

Bowen, M. (1978). *Family therapy in clinical practice.* New York: Aronson.

Brand, S. (1976). For God's sake, Margaret: Conversation with Gregory Bateson and Margaret Mead. *The Co-evolution Quarterly, 10,* 32–44.

Breunlin, D. C., Schwartz, R. C., & Kune-Karrer, B. M. (1992). *Metaframeworks.* San Francisco: Jossey-Bass.

Cameron-Bandler, L. (1985). *Solutions.* San Rafael, CA: Future Pace.

Campbell, D., Draper, R., & Crutchley, E. (1991). The Milan systemic approach to family therapy. In A. S. Gurman & D. P. Kniskern (Eds.), *Handbook of family therapy* (Vol. 2) (pp. 325–362). New York: Brunner/Mazel.

Campbell, D., Draper, R., & Huffington, C. (1988). *Teaching systemic thinking.* London: Karnac.

Carter, B., & McGoldrick, M. (1988). Overview: The changing family life cycle—A framework for family therapy. In B. Carter & M. McGoldrick (Eds.), *The changing family life cycle* (2nd ed.) (pp. 3–28). New York: Gardner.

Cecchin, G. (1987). Hypothesizing, circularity and neutrality revisited: An invitation to curiosity. *Family Process, 26,* 405–414.

Combrinck-Graham, L. (1985). A developmental model for family systems. *Family Process, 24,* 139–150.

Cooper, D. (1970). *The death of the family.* New York: Pantheon.

Cottone, R. R. (1992). *Theories and paradigms of counseling and psychotherapy.* Boston: Allyn & Bacon.

Daniels, M. H., & White, L. J. (1994). Human systems as problem-determined linguistic systems: Relevance for training. *Journal of Mental Health Counseling, 16.*

Dell, P. F. (1980). Researching the family theories of schizophrenia: An exercise in epistemological confusion. *Family Process, 19,* 321–326.

de Shazer, S. (1982a). *Patterns of brief family therapy: An ecosystemic approach.* New York: Guilford.

de Shazer, S. (1982b). Some conceptual distinctions are more useful than others. *Family Process, 21*, 71–84.

de Shazer, S. (1984). The death of resistance. *Family Process, 23*, 79–93.

de Shazer, S. (1985). *Keys to solution in brief therapy*. New York: Norton.

de Shazer, S. (1988). *Clues: Investigating solutions in brief therapy*. New York: Norton.

de Shazer, S. (1991). *Putting differences to work*. New York: Norton.

de Shazer, S., & Molnar, A. (1984). Four useful interventions in brief family therapy. *Journal of Marital and Family Therapy, 10*, 297–304.

Elkaim, M. (1990). *If you love me, don't love me*. New York: Basic Books.

Erikson, E. (1963). *Childhood and society* (2nd ed.). New York: Norton.

Ferber, A., Mendelsohn, M., & Napier, A. (Eds.). (1972). *The book of family therapy*. New York: Science House.

Fisch, R., Weakland, J., & Segal, L. (1982). *The tactics of change*. San Francisco: Jossey-Bass.

Goldner, V. (1985). Feminism and family therapy. *Family Process, 24*, 31–47.

Goodrich, T. J., Rampage, C., Ellman, B., & Halstead, K. (1988). *Feminist family therapy: A casebook*. New York: Norton.

Gottman, J. M. (1979). *Marital interaction: Experimental investigations*. New York: Academic Press.

Guerin, P. (Ed.). (1978). *Family therapy: Theory and practice*. New York: Gardner.

Gurman, A. S., & Kniskern, D. P. (1978). Research on marital and family therapy: Progress, perspective and prospect. In S. Garfield & A. Bergin (Eds.), *Handbook of psychotherapy and behavior change: An empirical analysis* (2nd ed.) (pp. 817–902). New York: Wiley.

Gurman, A. S., & Kniskern, D. P. (1981). *Handbook of family therapy*. New York: Brunner/Mazel.

Gurman, A. S., Kniskern, D. P., & Pinsof, W. M. (1986). Research on the process and outcome of marital and family therapy. In S. Garfield & A. Bergin (Eds.), *Handbook of psychotherapy and behavior change* (3rd ed.) (pp. 525–623). New York: Wiley.

Guttman, H. A. (1991). Systems theory, cybernetics, and epistemology. In A. S. Gurman & D. P. Kniskern (Eds.), *Handbook of family therapy* (Vol. 2) (pp. 41–62). New York: Brunner/Mazel.

Haley, J. (1963). *Strategies of psychotherapy*. New York: Grune & Stratton.

Haley, J. (Ed.). (1967). *Advanced techniques of hypnosis and therapy: Selected papers of Milton H. Erickson, M.D.* New York: Grune & Stratton.

Haley, J. (1973). *Uncommon therapy*. New York: Norton.

Haley, J. (1976a). Development of a theory: A history of a research project. In C. E. Sluzki & D. C. Ransom (Eds.), *Double bind: The foundation of the communicational approach to the family* (pp. 59–104). New York: Grune & Stratton.

Haley, J. (1976b). *Problem-solving therapy*. San Francisco: Jossey-Bass.

Haley, J. (1980). *Leaving home: The therapy of disturbed young people*. New York: McGraw-Hill.

Haley, J. (1987). *Problem-solving therapy* (2nd ed.). San Francisco: Jossey-Bass.

Hall, A. D., & Fagen, R. E. (1968). Definition of a system. In W. Buckley (Ed.), *Modern systems research for the behavioral scientist* (pp. 81–92). Chicago: Aldine.

Handel, G. (Ed.). (1967). *The psychosocial interior of the family* (2nd ed.). Chicago: Aldine/Atherton.

Hare-Mustin, R. T. (1987). The problem of gender in family therapy theory. *Family Process, 26,* 15–28.

Harvey, E. A. (1993). *The differential impact of death on family stress levels as determined by stage of the family life cycle.* Unpublished manuscript.

Held, B., & Pols, B. (1985). The confusion about epistemology and "epistemology" and what to do about it. *Family Process, 241,* 509–516.

Henry, J. (1965). *Pathways to madness.* New York: Random House.

Hoffman, L. (1981). *Foundations of family therapy.* New York: Basic Books.

Hoffman, L. (1990). Constructing realities: An art of lenses. *Family Process, 29,* 1–12.

Jackson, D. D. (1965). The study of the family. *Family Process, 4,* 1–20.

Jackson, D. D. (1968a). Family interaction, family homeostasis and some implications for conjoint family psychotherapy. In D. D. Jackson (Ed.), *Therapy, Communication and Change* (pp. 185–203). Palo Alto, CA: Science and Behavior Books.

Jackson, D. D. (1968b). The question of family homeostasis. In D. D. Jackson (Ed.), *Communication, family and marriage* (pp. 1–11). Palo Alto, CA: Science and Behavior Books.

Johnson, W. (1946). *People in quandaries.* New York: Harper.

Keeney, B. (1982). What is an epistemology of family therapy? *Family Process, 21,* 153–168.

Keeney, B. P. (1983). *Aesthetics of change.* New York: Guilford.

Keeney, B. P., & Ross, J. M. (1985). *Mind in therapy.* New York: Basic Books.

Kniskern, D. P. (1983). The new wave is all wet. *The Family Therapy Networker, 7*(4), 60–62.

Koestler, A. (1967). *The ghost in the machine.* London: Hutchinson.

Laing, R. D. (1969). *Self and others* (2nd ed.). New York: Pantheon.

Levinson, D. J., Darrow, C. N., Klein, E. B., Levinson, M. H., & McKee, B. (1978). *The seasons of a man's life.* New York: Knopf.

Liddle, H. A. (1991). Empirical values and the culture of family therapy. *Journal of Marital and Family Therapy ,17,* 327–348.

Lyddon, W. J. (1990). First and second order change: Implications for rationalist and constructivist cognitive therapies. *Journal of Counseling and Development, 69,* 122–127.

Madanes, C. (1981). *Strategic family therapy.* San Francisco: Jossey-Bass.

Madanes, C. (1984). *Behind the one-way mirror.* San Francisco: Jossey-Bass.

Madanes, C. (1991). Strategic family therapy. In A. S. Gurman & D. P. Kniskern (Eds.), *Handbook of family therapy* (Vol. 2) (pp. 396–416). New York: Brunner/Mazel.

Massey, R. F. (1986). What/who is the family system? *The American Journal of Family Therapy, 14,* 23–39.

McGoldrick, M., & Gerson, R. (1985). *Genograms in family assessment.* New York: Norton.

Meadows, D. (1982). Whole earth models and systems. *Co-evolution Quarterly, 10,* 98–108.

Minuchin, S. (1974). *Families and family therapy.* Cambridge: Harvard University Press.

Minuchin, S., & Fishman, C. (1981). *Family therapy techniques.* Cambridge: Harvard University Press.

Nichols, M. P. (1987). *The self in the system: Expanding the limits of family therapy.* New York: Brunner/Mazel.

O'Hanlon, W. H. (1987). *Taproots: Underlying principles of Milton Erickson's therapy and hypnosis.* New York: Norton.

O'Hanlon, W. H., & Weiner-Davis, M. (1989). *In search of solutions.* New York: Norton.

Olson, D. H. (1972). Empirically unbinding the double bind: A review of research and conceptual formulations. *Family Process, 11,* 69–94.

Paul, G. (1967). Outcome research in psychotherapy. *Journal of Consulting Psychology, 31,* 109–188.

Penn, P. (1982). Circular questioning. *Family Process, 21,* 267–280.

Piercy, F. P., & Sprenkle, D. H. (1990). Marriage and family therapy: A decade review. *Journal of Marriage and the Family, 52,* 1116–1126.

Pinsof, W. M. (1981). Family therapy process research. In A. S. Gurman & D. P. Kniskern (Eds.), *Handbook of family therapy* (pp. 669-674). New York: Brunner/Mazel.

Powers, W. T. (1973). *Behavior: The control of perception.* Chicago: Aldine.

Richmond, M. E. (1917). *Social diagnosis.* New York: Sage.

Ruesch, J., & Bateson, G. (1951). *Communication: The social matrix of psychiatry.* New York: Norton.

Segal, L. (1986). *The dream of reality: Heinz von Foerster's constructivism.* New York: Norton.

Segal, L. (1991). Brief therapy: The MRI approach. In A. S. Gurman & D. P. Kniskern (Eds.), *Handbook of family therapy* (Vol. 2) (pp. 171–199). New York: Brunner/Mazel.

Selvini-Palazzoli, M., Cecchin, G., Prata, G., & Boscolo, L. (1980). Hypothesizing-circularity-neutrality. *Family Process, 19,* 3–12.

Senge, P. M. (1990). *The fifth discipline: The art and practice of the learning organization.* New York: Doubleday/Currency.

Sherrard, P. A. D. (1991). Neurolinguistic programming and family therapy. In A. M. Horne & J. L. Passmore (Eds.), *Family counseling and therapy* (2nd ed.) (pp. 347–382). Itasca, IL.: Peacock.

Silvern, L. C. (1972). *Systems engineering applied to training.* Houston: Gulf.

Simon, F., Stierlin, H., & Wynne, L. (1985). *The language of family therapy: A systemic vocabulary and sourcebook.* New York: Family Process Press.

Stanton, M. D. (1988). The lobster quadrille: Issues and dilemmas for family therapy research. In L. C. Wynne (Ed.), *The state of the art in family therapy research: Controversies and recommendations* (pp. 7–31). New York: Family Process Press.

Steinglass, P. (1978). The conceptualization of marriage from a systems theory perspective. In T. J. Paolino & B. S. McCrady (Eds.), *Marriage and marital therapy* (pp. 298–365). New York: Brunner/Mazel.

Szapocznik, J., & Kurtines, W. M. (1989). *Breakthroughs in family therapy with drug abusing and problem youth.* New York: Springer.

Todd, T., & Stanton, M. (1983). Research on marital therapy and family therapy: Answers, issues and recommendations for the future. In B. Wolman & G. Stracker (Eds.), *Handbook of family and marital therapy* (pp. 91–115). New York: Plenum.

Tomm, K. (1988). Interventive interviewing. Part II: Intending to ask lineal, circular, strategic, or reflexive questions? *Family Process, 27,* 1–15.

Umbarger, C. C. (1983). *Structural family therapy.* Boston: Allyn & Bacon.

Walter, J. L., & Peller, J. E. (1992). *Becoming solution-focused in brief therapy.* New York: Brunner/Mazel.

Walters, M., Carter, B., Papp, P., & Silverstein, P. (1988). *The invisible web: Gender pat-

terns in family relationships. New York: Guilford.

Watzlawick, P., Beavin, J. H., & Jackson, D. D. (1967). *Pragmatics of human communication.* New York: Norton.

Watzlawick, P., Weakland, J., & Fisch, R. (1974). *Change: Principles of problem formation and problem resolution.* New York: Norton.

Weakland, J. M. (1976). The "double-bind" hypothesis of schizophrenia and three-party interaction. In C. E. Sluzki & D. C. Ransom (Eds.), *Double Bind: The foundation of the communicational approach to the family* (pp. 23–38). New York: Grune & Stratton.

Weakland, J., Fisch, R., Watzlawick, P., & Bodin, A. (1974). Brief therapy: Focused problem resolution. *Family Process, 13,* 141–168.

Wheatley, M. J. (1992). *Leadership and the new science.* San Francisco: Berrett Koehler.

Wiener, N. (1948). *Cybernetics.* Cambridge, MA: Technology Press.

Williams, L. M. (1991). A blueprint for increasing the relevance of family therapy research. *Journal of Marital and Family Therapy, 17,* 355–362.

Wynne, L. C. (Ed.). (1988). *The state of the art in family therapy research: Controversies and recommendations.* New York: Family Process Press.

CHAPTER SIXTEEN

Developmental Counseling and Therapy: Integrating Individual and Family Theory

Sandra A. Rigazio-DiGilio
University of Connecticut—Storrs

Oscar F. Gonçalves
University of Minho, Portugal

Allen E. Ivey
University of Massachusetts—Amherst

This chapter presents an alternative, developmental, and integrative model of counseling and therapy. Developmental counseling and therapy (DCT) offers a comprehensive method for the treatment of individuals from a nonpathological, positivistic perspective (Ivey, 1986, 1991). Systemic cognitive-developmental therapy (SCDT), an extension of the DCT model, applies the same developmental paradigm to working with families and larger social units (Rigazio-DiGilio, 1991d, 1993b, 1994a, 1994c, in press). Both models also provide an organizational framework for practitioners to use to select strategies and interventions from a variety of counseling and therapy approaches (see Ivey, 1986, 1991; Ivey & Rigazio-DiGilio, in press; Kunkler & Rigazio-DiGilio, 1994; Rigazio-DiGilio, 1991d, 1993a, 1993b, 1994a, 1994c; Rigazio-DiGilio & Ivey, 1991, 1993).

Before using a case study to demonstrate the clinical and counseling utility of the developmental perspective, this chapter frames the work of counselors and therapists within a facilitative paradigm. DCT and SCDT reject the pathological view of symptom manifestation and instead embrace a developmental interpretation of client difficulties. At the very center of DCT and SCDT models is knowing how to help individuals and families move beyond constricted experiences, thoughts, and actions regarding their issues. This chapter also elaborates the process of change and the developmental interventions that are considered to be easily taught, learned, applied, and researched (Borders, 1994).

It is appropriate that the DCT chapter concludes this book's discussion of major models of counseling and therapy. Once readers have obtained a working knowledge of the various models of counseling and therapy, they can use this chapter as one path toward integrating strategies and interventions to construct developmentally tailored treatment plans for those individuals, couples, and families seeking their services.

HISTORY

Counseling and psychotherapy are replete with theories and treatment models that clinicians can draw upon to understand and work with individuals and families seeking service. There may be a problem, however, not only in terms of number and variety, but also in terms of the weak links that exist between developmental theory and clinical practice (Ivey & Rigazio-DiGilio, 1991c; Liddle & Saba, 1983; Rigazio-DiGilio & Ivey, in press) and between individual and systemic perspectives and approaches (Rigazio-DiGilio, in press; Rigazio-DiGilio & Ivey, in press; Snyder, 1989). Today's clinician is faced with the task of integrating this multitude of perspectives and approaches in an organized fashion that connects individual and systemic developmental processes to counseling and psychotherapy methods and procedures.

Developmental counseling and therapy is an integrative model that represents one of the first attempts to organize theories and approaches within a developmental framework (Ivey, 1986, 1991; Ivey & Gonçalves, 1988; Ivey, Gonçalves, & Ivey, 1989; Ivey & Rigazio-DiGilio, in press; Rigazio-DiGilio & Ivey, 1991). DCT provides an important connection between developmental theories and clinical practice and offers a framework for assessment and treatment planning that is broader in scope than any one model.

A reader can surmise from the previous statement that DCT values the ability to see clients from multiple perspectives and to access a wide range of treatment approaches to meet the needs of diverse clientele. Only in this way can we enter the unique worlds constructed by our clients, understand the developmental processes and cultural contexts influencing their interpretations, and join with them to co-construct developmentally appropriate and culturally sensitive treatment plans. This chapter presents a model that represents a coherent approach to treatment and also establishes guidelines for the integration of interventions and techniques from other theories of counseling and psychotherapy.

Background

DCT grew out of a need to connect the explanatory power of developmental theories with the solution-focused strength of clinical practice. Although DCT was officially conceived in 1986, the basic assumptions and constructs that support the model transcend any one psychological perspective or approach.

DCT was built on a synthesis of several philosophical, developmental, and psychological perspectives. Philosophically, it is based on a reinterpretation of Plato (see Conford, 1982/1941) and Hegel (see Miller, 1807/1977). DCT suggests that the ways clients understand and operate in the world are both facilitated and constrained by two main interacting systems. The first is the level of cognitive development the client has achieved. The second is the cultural implications of the larger social units in which the client is involved (such as family, community, society, and culture). As such, client world views are co-constructed due to the constant interactions that occur between persons and environments (see Harland, 1987; Harre, 1983). The clinical reality that arises out of the counseling and psychotherapy process is generated in a parallel fashion. The clinician and the client work together to co-construct the reality that will guide treatment. Each influences and is influenced by the other.

DCT's psychological foundation is based on an adaptation of Piagetian constructivism (Piaget, 1954, 1923/1955, 1965) and the discovery that the basic cognitive-developmental stages of childhood are repeated throughout the entire life span and are directly represented in the counseling and psychotherapy process. Even though DCT is rooted in traditional Piagetian theory, the model moves beyond Piaget's linear, stage-oriented framework by defining a holistic cognitive-developmental process. It rejects hierarchical notions of development and values instead the concept of *multiperspective thought*. Using this alternative understanding, DCT (and its systemic extensions described later) bring together linear and hierarchical (Haley, 1973; Kohlberg, 1981; Loevinger, Wessler, & Redmore, 1970; Perry, 1970; Piaget, 1954), cyclical and relational (Carter & McGoldrick, 1989; Erikson, 1963; Gilligan, 1982), and spiraling (Breunlin, 1988; Combrinck-Graham, 1985; Kegan, 1982) theories of development within a spherical framework.

Other theorists who have had a direct impact on DCT include Guidano (1987), Kelley (1955), Lacan (1977), and Mahoney (1991), all of whom reinforce the co-constructivist–developmental nature of DCT. The writings of theorists and practitioners in other fields have also been applied to the model. The systemic theories and approaches of Attneave (1969, 1982), Basseches (1984), Minuchin (1974), Reiss and Oliveri (1986), and others; the cultural identity theories of Brooks (1990), Jackson (1975), and others; and the multicultural theories of Cheatham (1990), McGoldrick, Pearce, and Giordano (1982), and others have paved the road toward the integration of DCT within the family domain, as shown by the systemic cognitive-developmental therapy model (Ivey & Rigazio-DiGilio, 1991a; Rigazio-DiGilio, 1991d, 1993a, 1993b, 1994c; Rigazio-DiGilio & Ivey, 1991, 1993), the network domain (Ivey, 1991; Rigazio-DiGilio, 1994a, in press), and the supervisory domain (Rigazio-DiGilio, 1994b; Rigazio-DiGilio & Anderson, 1991, in press).

DCT assessment and treatment strategies evolved from Ivey's previous work in the skills and structure of counseling and psychotherapy (Ivey, 1971, 1983a, 1983b; Ivey & Authier, 1978; Ivey, Ivey, & Simek-Morgan, 1993). Based on this accumulated body of knowledge, developmental theory was brought into practice with the anticipation of predictable results due to specific interventions. DCT's metatheoretical framework depends on multiple theories and approaches to describe a holistic developmental perspective. This integrative model shows us how to use traditional methods and theories more effectively while staying in tune with client constructions of the world.

DCT was developed by a multicultural, multinational team, all of whom remain active in the advancement of the model.[1] This collaborative effort indicates Ivey's commitment to co-constructing a broad, culturally sensitive model that is continually subject to change, challenge, and modification.

HUMAN NATURE: A DEVELOPMENTAL PERSPECTIVE

The work of Piaget figures predominantly in the DCT conception of human nature. Piaget found that children construct knowledge at four different cognitive-developmental levels, and he suggested that movement to the higher, more complex levels of thinking was a sign of positive development. Ivey (1986, 1991) and others (Basseches, 1984; Commons, Richards, & Armon, 1984; Kegan, 1982; Rosen, 1985) have found that analogues of Piagetian thinking also exist in adolescent and adult cognitions. Building on this concept, DCT provides a reinterpretation of Piagetian levels and developmental processes to explain individual development from a holistic life-span perspective. SCDT extends this idea to define holistic family development over the life span (Ivey & Rigazio-DiGilio, 1991a; Rigazio-DiGilio, 1993b, 1994a, 1994c; Rigazio-DiGilio & Ivey, 1991, 1993).

DCT postulates an unending process of development in which individuals and systems continually recycle themselves through the four Piagetian levels (redefined in DCT as *cognitive-developmental orientations*) as they move through their life tasks. DCT suggests that each orientation represents a different way to view and understand the world. Therefore, each facilitates unique ways to see, feel, and act along life's journey. The ability to work within several orientations affords clients the opportunity to take multiple perspectives and to construct expanded life choices as they adapt to and influence their worlds.

By rejecting hierarchical notions of development in favor of this holistic world view, DCT suggests that no one orientation is more adaptive than any other. Rather, development depends on clients' abilities to function within and between all orientations, "being able to act and feel [sensorimotor], to operate on their actions and feelings [concrete], to think about these operations [formal], and to think about systems of thinking [dialectic/systemic]" (Ivey & Gonçalves, 1988, p. 412).

---

[1]This team includes Machiko Fukuhara, Tokiwa University, Japan; Oscar Gonçalves, University of Minho, Portugal; Allen Ivey and Mary Bradford Ivey, University of Massachusetts; Sandra Rigazio-DiGilio, University of Connecticut; and Koji Tamase, Nara University of Education, Japan.

DCT posits that individuals build theories about the world as they interact with their environment (family, community, society, culture). These theories continually influence how individuals approach the environment and their life tasks. It is also true that when individuals join together to form relationships, the interactions that occur between them lead to collective theories. These collective theories affect how individuals and families give meaning to their relationships and their world as well as how they operate within them. Thus, every client enters treatment with a way of seeing the world that has developed in relation to significant others, family, and culture. DCT defines these theories as *cognitive-developmental structures* and suggests that clients who have broad and adaptive structures actually have access to all four of the cognitive-developmental orientations (sensorimotor, concrete, formal, and dialectic/systemic).

Both individuals and families rely on their cognitive-developmental structures to work through life tasks. As their efforts to master each life task are rewarded, rebuffed, reframed, or retarded, their cognitive-developmental structures are also correspondingly altered. Therefore, the interactive relationship between the individual, the family, and the environment is constant and pervasive. As it occurs, it continually affects all levels of understanding, experiencing, and behaving for the individual and family who, in turn, affect many aspects of the environment.

DCT views growth as a continuous mastery of life tasks that leads individuals and families to develop increased competence in the use of all four cognitive-developmental orientations. Conversely, it views development as delayed or arrested when individuals or families are unable to master life tasks. In these instances, cognitive-developmental structures can become too restricted or disorganized. When this occurs, individuals and families cannot access the unique resources inherent in each orientation, leaving them with a limited range of thoughts, feelings, and actions to draw upon to adapt to their world.

These assumptions about human and systemic development establish the primary objectives of the counseling and therapy process:

1. To assist clients to develop well integrated and organized cognitive-developmental structures; that is, to help them access the unique resources available within each of the cognitive-developmental orientations so that they have a wider range of alternatives to draw upon

2. To empower clients to use these orientations to view their issues from multiple perspectives

3. To co-construct solutions with clients that are appropriate to their developmental and environmental needs

MAJOR CONSTRUCTS

The Developmental Sphere

A multidimensional sphere was adopted to symbolize the major constructs of DCT and its extension to family (SCDT) and network counseling and psychotherapy (see figure 16.1). The sphere indicates the four cognitive-developmental orientations and provides a graphic understanding of the concepts of cognitive-developmental structures, dialectic interactions, and cognitive-developmental adaptation and change.

FIGURE 16.1
A spherical model of development

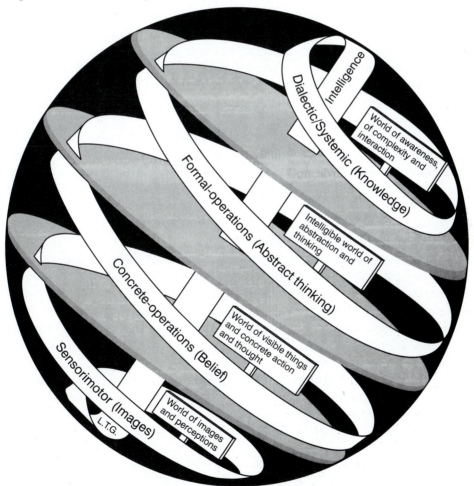

Source: Originally drawn in 1985 by Lois T. Grady of the University of Massachusetts. Reprinted by her permission.

Cognitive-Developmental Orientations

The visual model illustrates how individuals receive data through sensory modalities of seeing, hearing, and touch (sensorimotor) and organize the data into a way of understanding that permits them to operate predictably in the environment (concrete-operational). They can reflect on their feelings, actions, and thinking through abstract thought (formal-operational) and can also look at the total process and outcome of their interaction (dialectic/systemic).

The developmental sphere also describes how collective ways of understanding develop in relationships. As the sensory worlds of individuals merge, they share perspectives, emotions, and behaviors (system exploration/formation). Repetitive experiences evolve into a collective way of understanding the relationship that serves to organize predictable ways of thinking, feeling, and acting (system maintenance/consolidation). Within the formal orientation, members can reflect on and enhance this understanding (system enhancement/modification), while the dialectic/systemic orientation promotes awareness of how and in what contexts this way of understanding was constructed and how it might be transformed (system transformation).

A client's way of making sense of the world is influenced by the unique perspectives of each orientation. Although any orientation may have potential influence, it is also true that at any given point, or regarding any given issue, individuals and systems[2] primarily operate within one of the four orientations. This primary orientation is defined as the *predominant cognitive-developmental orientation* and frames the meanings, emotions, and actions dominating the client's world view.

Clients experiencing psychological distress are often either overrelying on one particular orientation that is out of sync with their environment or are unable to access any orientation fully enough to provide facilitative assistance toward effective adaptation. Therefore, it would be clinically useful to assess the predominant cognitive-developmental orientation being used by clients. This is one of the tasks of DCT assessment and is discussed later in the chapter.

DCT and SCDT suggest that a client's primary orientation can be identified in the natural language of the interview. Table 16.1 briefly illustrates the patterns of individual and systemic thoughts, feelings, and

---

[2]Although families and larger social systems are composed of many individuals, each operating from within her own predominant orientation, the entire group of individuals tends to perceive and respond to issues from a dominant, collective orientation. This unifying orientation may be a combination of all the represented perspectives or one that only reflects some subsystem of the family or network (such as the dominant or most central family members or a network's administrative body).

behaviors unique to each orientation, along with corresponding limits and potentials. The orientations, as defined for larger social systems, can be found elsewhere (Ivey & Rigazio-DiGilio, in press; Rigazio-DiGilio, 1994a).

Cognitive-Developmental Structures

Building a solid understanding and use of the cognitive, affective, and behavioral ranges within each orientation (horizontal development) allows individuals and families to move to other orientations (vertical development) and to construct a unified use of the entire sphere. Adaptive use of the sphere is optimized for individuals and families who can move within (horizontal) and among (vertical) all orientations.

Horizontal Development.   Horizontal development refers to an exploration, mastery, and elaboration of the attitudes, emotions, and behaviors that correspond to one orientation. This is the process used to ensure the construction of strong foundations. There are three processes of horizontal development that an individual or system can engage in: basic, intermediate, and deep.

Many clients require a counseling or psychotherapy arena focused on horizontal movement so they can build a firm foundation within a particular orientation before exploring other, less familiar orientations. It is also true that once movement to a new orientation is achieved, all clients require a horizontal focus that allows them to "practice" the alternative perspectives, feelings, and behaviors available to them at the new orientation. At this time, horizontal movement helps clients develop a certain degree of automaticity with the alternative options available within the less familiar orientation.

Vertical Development.   Moving vertically among orientations provides access to multiple perspectives and behaviors. For example, clients predominantly operating within sensorimotor or concrete orientations need facilitative assistance to move to more abstract orientations in order to see the pattern (formal) and origins (dialectic/systemic) of the thoughts, feelings, and behaviors that are maintaining the presenting problem. Conversely, clients predominantly operating within the abstract contexts representative of formal or dialectic orientations need facilitative assistance to move to concrete or sensorimotor orientations in order to directly feel, actively participate, and effectively determine appropriate solutions. Again, it is important to emphasize that higher is not necessarily better. What is considered most adaptive is for clients to be able to access the unique resources within each of the orientations.

TABLE 16.1
The Four Cognitive-Developmental Orientations of DCT and SCDT: Individual and Family Functioning

Individual	Family
Sensorimotor: Focusing on the Elements of Experience	
Individuals functioning predominantly within this orientation rely on their sensory experience—what they directly see, hear, and feel—to make sense of their world. They may show randomness in their conversation and incongruent nonverbal behaviors. Strengths of this style include an awareness of the here-and-now and a willingness to directly experience life and emotions. Weaknesses and issues that may promote treatment include difficulties in cognitive organization, inability to self-reflect, irrational or magical thinking, inability to act effectively because of confusion, and a tendency toward reactive behaviors dominated by affect, images, and impressions.	Families operating within this orientation tend to function chaotically and are prone to interactions guided by affect rather than reason. Family strengths include a willingness to collectively participate in a full range of emotions and to respond to the feelings of others. Families who over-rely on this orientation may have difficulty organizing their world, are easily overwhelmed by events, and often overreact to variations or disruptions. At such times, they have difficulty sustaining any coherent sense of family identity or of events, and they may require assistance to structure their lives.
Concrete-Operational: Searching for Situational Descriptions	
These individuals act in their world with some predictability. They focus mainly on actions and observable events and describe their life situations with great detail. Strengths of this style include the ability to descriptively attend to the world and to plan and implement actions, a willingness to take a position, and the ability to develop linear models of causality. Weaknesses include a predominant reliance on a narrow range of beliefs and behaviors, an inability to recognize mixed or ambivalent feelings, the inability to see others' perspectives, difficulty in conserving and transferring learning, and the inability to reflect on self, situations, or emotions.	Families within this orientation rely on a predictable set of beliefs and behaviors to give meaning to and operate in their world and to sustain a sense of family identity. They use linear reasoning to explain variations and count on solutions that maintain continuity. Functioning is adaptive when "tried and true" thoughts and behaviors are sufficient to deal with changing circumstances. Because they do not recognize the parameters of their meanings and actions, they have difficulty revising thinking and behavior patterns, considering options, and generalizing to novel situations. They may continue to use outdated interactions, even when these become ineffective.

TABLE 16.1 *continued*

Formal Operational: Examining the Nature of the Self-in-Context

Individuals functioning within this orientation tend to reflect on self and situation by analyzing information from multiple perspectives. They like to think about their patterns of thinking, feeling, and acting. Strengths include the ability to examine problems from a distance, to generate multiple perspectives, and to recognize others' perspectives. Individuals who over-utilize this orientation, however, become so involved in self-reflection that they detach from sensorimotor experiences and concrete actions and events. They cannot challenge their basic assumptions, so they are prone to develop rigid representations of the world that are not in sync with their direct experience.

These families identify and analyze their communication and behavior patterns. They interpret events and generate alternative solutions. They find various ways to work within their meaning and action structures (first-order change) but are not able to challenge the assumptions basic to these structures. Over-reliance on this orientation may promote logic-tight assumptions about family identity and continuity that are not in sync with changing circumstances. Families analyze issues in ways that do not promote effective action and are apt to analyze rather than actually experience their feelings.

Dialectic/Systemic Operational: Integrating Self-in-Context

These individuals reflect on reflections and can work with comfort on systems of operations. They are usually quite skilled intellectually and able to see self-in-context and identify how environmental pressures affect them. They can recognize the influence of family and cultural systems, can see the complexity and variability of emotions and thoughts, can challenge their own assumptions, and can transform their thinking in response to changing circumstances. Those same strengths can simultaneously be weaknesses when too much thinking interferes with engaging in sensorimotor experiences and concrete actions when required.

These families recognize the effects of intergenerational, intrafamilial, and extra-familial influences on their cognitive, affective and behavioral patterns. They can challenge their basic assumptions, which allows them to deconstruct and reconstruct their worldviews and actions in response to changing circumstances (second-order change). Predominant functioning at this orientation can lead to a diffuse, abstract sense of family identity that hinders the ability to deal effectively with sensorimotor experiences and concrete actions and events.

Source: From "Developmental Counseling and Therapy: A Framework for Individual and Family Treatment." by S. A. Rigazio-DiGilio and A. E. Ivey, 1991, *Counseling and Human Development, 24*, pp. 5 and 6. Copyright 1991 by Love Publishing Company. Reprinted by permission.

Types of Cognitive-Developmental Structures.   The degree of organization and integration that clients achieve within the developmental sphere can be categorized by four types of cognitive-developmental structures: flexible and varied, diffuse, underdeveloped, and rigid.[3]

Flexible and varied cognitive-developmental structures are typical of adaptive individuals and systems. Individuals and the systems they create possess the ability to move within and across all orientations without sacrificing their sense of self, family, community, or culture.

Diffuse and *underdeveloped structures* resemble the nonintegrated, underorganized thinking patterns of young children and newly forming or transitional relationships and systems. Individuals and the systems they create are highly reactive to changes in the environment. Attempts to adapt usually appear chaotic and represent an ineffective use of any of the available orientations.

Rigid cognitive-developmental structures are representative of people and systems who rely predominantly on one orientation, sacrificing the multiple perspectives and options available within other orientations. These individuals and systems have usually gained a certain level of adaptation using their narrow cognitive-developmental structure but can easily experience difficulty when attempting to deal with unfamiliar internal or external demands for change.

Clients entering treatment are usually relying on rigid, diffuse, or underdeveloped structures. A second task of DCT assessment is to determine which type of structure is active in the co-construction process. This is discussed later in the chapter.

Dialectic Interactions: A Multicultural Perspective

The potential of any cognitive-developmental structure is bound within the dialectic relationship between intrapersonal contexts (existing individual cognitive-developmental structures), intrafamilial contexts (existing collective cognitive-developmental structures), and interpersonal contexts (the sociocultural-historical environment). This view also extends to the counseling or therapeutic relationship and affects how practitioners should look at theoretical perspectives, counseling/therapeutic approaches, and the client/clinician relationship.

Basically, all counseling and psychotherapy is a multicultural experience. The counselor or therapist should work to provide an environment

---

[3]The first three types of cognitive-developmental structures correspond to the permeable, rigid, and loose personal constructs defined by Kelley (1955).

that can, at times, be in sync with the developmental and sociocultural constructions of the client (horizontal movement) and that can, at other times, facilitate creative and viable alternative constructions (vertical movement).

Traditionally, most theories have emerged from a Eurocentric perspective. This single lens has dominated the field since Freud. Recently, increased awareness of the diversity of our society has pushed practitioners to augment case conceptualizations within a cultural context. DCT assumes that all clients carry with them specific sociocultural and historical backgrounds that influence the course of treatment. Furthermore, the practitioner's own sociocultural-historical context affects the counseling or therapy relationship. Ivey, Ivey, and Simek-Morgan (1993) contend that within the helping partnership, there are really four participants: the clinician and his sociocultural-historical background and the individual or family client and their sociocultural-historical background.

DCT emphasizes the cultural boundaries of our cognitive-developmental structures and suggests that treatment planning should account for the client's sociocultural-historical background. The term *co-construction* is analogous to the self-in-relation concepts of feminist therapy (see Goldner, 1988; Luepnitz, 1988) and holistic Afrocentric theory (see Cheatham, 1990; Jackson, 1975). By accepting a co-constructive frame of reference, the counselor or therapist moves toward a more egalitarian client/clinician partnership.

THE PROCESS OF CHANGE

DCT uses Piaget's concept of *equilibration* to explain the change process. Cognitive-developmental change is brought about by the interaction between accommodation and assimilation.

Accommodation

Accommodation refers to the process by which cognitive-developmental structures are altered as a result of environmental interaction. The ease with which individuals and families adapt to the thinking of others, their willingness to see patterns that don't align with preconceived ideas, or their openness to learning from experience signifies their degree of accommodation. Overaccommodation is usually associated with dysfunctional adaptation. These clients possess diffuse cognitive-developmental structures and hold loose personal constructs about the world and their relation to it. It is not unusual for these clients to bring new world views to each session or to assume mannerisms and attitudes of significant others, including the counselor or therapist.

Assimilation

Assimilation is the imposition of an existing point of view on the environment. Through the use of assimilative reasoning, individuals and families attempt to alter the perceptions of others. The tenacity of their beliefs indicates the degree of assimilation they are capable of using for any given issue. Overassimilation is typical of clients who are dealing with substance abuse problems, compulsive disorders, and depressive disorders. These clients rely on the mechanisms of denial, distortion, and reaction formation in order to preserve their world view.

Co-construction and Adaptation

The co-constructive process is inherent in the relationship between accommodation and assimilation. When there is an adaptive balance between the two, an appropriate integration of new ideas from the environment coexists with the reinforcement and validation of existing constructs. This is labeled as a state of equilibration.

The co-constructive process extends to the counseling and therapeutic relationship. The clinician is the environment of the client, and the client is the environment of the clinician. Through the accommodative and assimilative processes of both client and clinician, counseling or therapeutic change occurs.

Most clients present in treatment when the relationship between accommodation and assimilation is out of balance. They might be overaccommodators with diffuse or underdeveloped cognitive-developmental structures. Or they might be overassimilators with rigid cognitive-developmental structures. Clients who are overaccommodators require a clinical relationship that initially supports and strengthens their cognitive-developmental structure and then moves to expand their structure without promoting a loss of their sense of self, family, or culture. For overassimilators, the counselor or therapist needs to adopt an assimilative style that facilitates clients to loosen rigid structures and exercise accommodative skills. In other words, DCT recommends that both horizontal and vertical development be attended to for as many cognitive-developmental and emotional issues as are feasible to assist clients to construct a balance between accommodation and assimilation.

INTERVENTION STRATEGIES

DCT assessment and treatment strategies have three primary aims:

1. To access and assess client constructions of the world, the presenting problem, and the treatment process
2. To design interventions that initially match a client's predominant cognitive-developmental orientations
3. To co-construct expanded (horizontal) and alternative (vertical) perspectives and options with the client that are more in tune with adaptive functioning within the client's unique sociocultural environment

Developmental Assessment and Conceptualization

Counseling and psychotherapy should be developmentally and culturally matched to the client. Therefore, the task is to assess client constructions and to match the counseling or psychotherapy style with the cognitive-developmental necessities and possibilities of the client.

The first objective is to assess the predominant cognitive-developmental orientation being used by the client as well as the range and flexibility found within the client's cognitive-developmental structure. Additionally, across their developmental history, psychologically distressed clients are frequently unable to master some of the tasks of each developmental orientation, thus limiting the theory they use to understand, act, and experience their worlds. Therefore, DCT suggests that a full assessment of the client's *developmental profile*, or the developmental issues that adversely affect growth within each orientation, is warranted if the initial assessment reveals deeper-level problems (Gonçalves & Ivey, 1992).

Assessing Cognitive-Developmental Orientation and Structure.   In order to identify the client's predominant orientation and to determine the degree of range and flexibility found in the client's cognitive-developmental structure, practitioners use the standard cognitive-developmental interview (Ivey & Rigazio-DiGilio, 1991b) and its classification system (Rigazio-DiGilio & Ivey, 1991) with individuals, and the systemic cognitive-developmental interview (Rigazio-DiGilio, 1991b) and its classification system (Rigazio-DiGilio, 1991c) with families. (See table 16.2 for an abbreviated version of DCT and SCDT questioning strategies. The types of questions used to assess larger social networks can be found elsewhere [Ivey & Rigazio-Digilio, in press; Rigazio-DiGilio, 1994a]). Both interviews are structured and are divided into two sections.

TABLE 16.2
Developmental Questioning Sequence for Individual (DCT) and Family (SCDT) Assessment and Treatment Planning

Goals	Sample DCT Individual Questioning Strategies	Sample SCDT Family Questioning Strategies
	Opening Presentation of an Issue for Preliminary Assessment	
1. To obtain understanding of presenting problem, as organized by individual or family, with minimal interference from counselor or therapist. 2. To assess cognitive-developmental orientation currently exerting the most influence on individual's or family's perspective of presenting problem.	1. Can you tell me what has brought you here? 2. What occurs for you when you focus on these issues and your family and/or other significant systems?	1. Can you talk together and come to consensus about what occurs in your family and/or other significant systems when you focus on the issues that brought you to treatment?

Comments: Use paraphrasing and reflection of feelings to bring out data, but try to impact the story minimally. Then summarize key facts and feelings before moving on.

Goals	Sample DCT Individual Questioning Strategies	Sample SCDT Family Questioning Strategies
	Sensorimotor/Elemental Explorations (Key words: see, hear, feel; believe)	
1. To elicit *sensory-based dialogue*, related to how they experience presenting problem. 2. To elicit their understanding of this sensory-based experience.	1. Can you think about one visual image that occurs to you in relation to this issue? What are you seeing? Hearing? Feeling? 2. As you make this image, hear these sounds, and feel these feelings, what one thing stands out for you?	1. [Ask the family to agree on an image generated by most members when they focus on the presenting problem. Once an image is chosen, ask the following questions:] What does the image look like? Sound like? What feelings are generated as you discuss this? What does this image and the feelings it generates say about your family and/or wider network?

Comments: Before moving on, summarize key *sensory realities* as provided by individual or family.

Concrete/Situational Explorations
(Key words: do; if/then)

1. To elicit description of concrete details of representative situation in linear, sequential form, with major emphasis on *facts versus interpretation.*
2. To facilitate understanding of this event, usually with if/then dimension.

1. Could you give me a specific example of this problem including all the people involved?
2. [Ask behavioral tracking questions such as:] What did you do? How did she react? What did you say then? What happened just before you did that? What happened afterward?
3. [After this description, ask:] Given the way you have figured out these facts, what do you think causes or triggers what? How do you think you influence one another?

Comments: Before moving on, summarize the key *descriptive facts* and if/then interpretations.

Formal/Pattern Exploration
(Key words: patterns; self; relationship; family roles)

1. To facilitate examination of individual, intrafamilial and extrafamilial *roles and the patterns* of thoughts, feelings, and behaviors that influenced described situation.
2. To facilitate understanding of how these same *roles and patterns* occur in other *similar situations.*

1. Can you give me a specific example of another situation where you seem to take on this same role? Where you and/or significant others seem to take the same positions?
2. Do you think/feel/act this way in other situations? Is this a pattern for you?

Comments: Before moving on, summarize key *roles and patterns* and *similar situations* mentioned.

Concrete/Situational Explorations
(Key words: do; if/then)

1. [Ask the family to choose an example. Once members agree, ask behavioral tracking questions such as:] Who is involved? What happened next? What did your parents do then? What happened just before the children started yelling? Who steps in then? What happened afterwards?
2. [After this description ask:] Given the way these facts emerged, what do you think causes or triggers what? What did you learn about how you influence one another?

Formal/Pattern Exploration

1. Can you describe other things that happen that seem to require each of you to take similar positions/roles?
2. Can you describe other situations that seem to generate the same kinds of thoughts, feelings, and behaviors?

TABLE 16.2 *continued*

Goals	Sample DCT Individual Questioning Strategies	Sample SCDT Family Questioning Strategies
	Dialectic/Systemic Explorations	
	(Key words: integrate, challenge, change patterns and roles-in-context)	
1. To help individual or family identify *assumptions* and *rules* underlying roles and patterns that provide them with a sense of identity and continuity.	1. *Integration:* How do you put together/make sense of all that you have told me today?	1. *Integration:* How would all of you organize all that you have discussed together with me today?
2. To facilitate their understanding that such assumptions and rules are *co-constructed* and to help them explore how this occurred.	2. *Co-construction:* What rules are you operating under? Where did these rules that influence how you think, feel, and act come from? Where do you think you learned these rules? Who taught you these rules? What role does your religion, ethnicity, etc. play in the way you develop and hold onto these rules?	2. *Co-construction:* How would you define the rules that influence how your family thinks, feels, and acts when you are together or when you interact in the wider context? Where did these rules come from? How did your family come to determine that these would be the rules to live by at home? What role does your religion, ethnicity, etc. play in the way you develop and hold onto these rules?
3. To help them identify *parameters* of these assumptions and rules, and to elicit *multiple perspectives* that challenge these parameters.	3. *Multiple perspectives:* How might someone else describe the situation? How could we describe this from another point of view or framework?	3. *Multiple perspectives:* Are there other ways to look at the rules your family lives by? How might another family see things differently?
4. To help them explore *alternatives* that will promote *modifications* in or *transformations* of these assumptions and rules, and that will facilitate new ways of thinking, feeling, and acting.	4. *Deconstruction and action:* Do you notice any flaws or constraints in these rules—ways that these rules do not get you what you need? How might you change these rules? Given these possibilities, what action might you take right now to work on the issues that brought you to treatment?	4. *Deconstruction and action:* Can you identify any ways your rules might not be working effectively for you right now? If you could add to or change these rules, how would you do it? Based on all this, is there anything that your family could do differently to work on the issues that brought you here?

Source: From "Developmental Counseling and Therapy: A Framework for Individual and Family Treatment" by S. A. Rigazio-DiGilio and A. E. Ivey, 1991, *Counseling and Human Development*, 24, pp. 12 and 13. Copyright 1991 by Love Publishing Company. Reprinted by permission.

The assessment phase is designed to elicit the client's predominant interpretation of the presenting problem. The treatment phase is designed to determine how skilled the client is at conceptualizing the problem from the various orientations. The assessment phase consists of an open-ended question designed to elicit a presentation of the issues that promoted treatment. For individuals, the client's natural language provides evidence of the primary cognitive-developmental orientation. For example, the language of individuals predominantly functioning within the sensorimotor orientation is spontaneous and emotionally laden. The language of dialectic individuals is analytic and devoid of emotion.

As family members discuss the open-ended question, they eventually come to a concise statement that clarifies their collective interpretation of the presenting problem. The communication process used to construct the response as well as the resultant content provides the counselor or therapist with data to classify the family's collective predominant orientation. This process can also point to the primary orientations of individual members.

As with individuals, the language used by the family to frame the presenting problem indicates the orientation centrally involved in the family's understanding of the presenting problem. For example, concrete families describe situations, tell stories, and use linear thinking to define the issues that have brought them to treatment. Families primarily operating within a formal orientation may elaborate rationalizations for problematic patterns of behavior but present little evidence of the emotionality underlying the issues (sensorimotor) or of adequate responses to the situation (concrete).

The treatment phase includes four sets of questions designed to determine the degree to which specific questioning strategies can promote client explorations within each orientation. This phase yields data about the range and flexibility of the client's cognitive-developmental structure while also facilitating the co-construction of alternative perspectives on the problem. The alternative views that evolve help form the initial reframe (mutually constructed, expanded definition of the problem) that guides treatment.

In individual treatment, clients are asked to respond to specific questions while the counselor or therapist uses basic attending skills to facilitate exploration (Ivey & Gluckstern, 1982). In family settings, members are asked to talk together within each of the orientations to determine their collective ability to understand and act on the presenting issues from the multiple perspectives within each orientation. The interview allows the counselor or therapist to enter the constructed world of the client. This is important in the co-construction of a frame for treatment. It also helps to identify a firing order for treatment. This refers to the co-construction of a developmentally appropriate, culturally sensitive, sequential order of treatment based on both horizontal and vertical movement.

Assessing Developmental Profiles.   A comprehensive assessment of the client's organization and symptomatic expression within each orientation can also be completed. For individuals, this process facilitates the design of an *intrapersonal* developmental profile, while for families it facilitates the design of an *interpersonal* developmental profile. This profile constitutes a cognitive-developmental conceptualization of the individual's or family's functioning over the life span (Gonçalves & Ivey, 1992).

An individual's or family's organization within each orientation is identified by obtaining a detailed developmental history. For individuals, this involves a reconstruction of the client's organization of self and reality during infancy (sensorimotor), childhood (concrete), adolescence (formal), and adulthood (dialectic/systemic) (Guidano, 1987). For families, this history reconstructs the family's organization of its system during family exploration/formation (sensorimotor), family consolidation/maintenance (concrete), family enhancement/modification (formal), and family transformation (dialectic/systemic) (Rigazio-DiGilio & Ivey, 1991, 1993).

Having obtained an understanding of the historical evolution of the client's constructions, the counselor or therapist proceeds to identify the resultant symptomatic expression within each orientation. The sensorimotor assessment evaluates modes of experiencing the world within sensorial and emotional domains. Concrete assessment is intended to identify specific patterns of interaction with the environment within motor and operational domains. Formal assessment is aimed at identifying specific cognitive operations through self- or family statements, automatic thoughts assessment, and irrational beliefs analyses. Finally, dialectic/systemic assessment is aimed at evaluating core cognitive processes, personal constructs, and tacit processes. Special attention is given to the client's cognitive ability to examine self-in-context, particularly in relation to person-environment issues, intergenerational family issues, and multicultural issues.

It is important to recall the dialectic nature of the counseling/therapeutic relationship during assessment—practitioner and client co-constructing together a different understanding of the presenting problem, the nature of the relationship, and the objectives for treatment. Simply conducting the interview and the developmental profile facilitates clients to gain new perspectives on the issues promoting treatment (see Rigazio-DiGilio & Ivey, 1990).

Treatment Planning

A treatment plan is designed for each client based on the assessment process. Two major phases constitute this treatment process: developmental matching and developmental mismatching. They are accomplished within specific counseling/therapeutic environments.

Counseling/Therapeutic Environments.   Counselors and therapists should provide different environments for clients functioning within different cognitive-developmental orientations. For example, an *environmental structuring style* is more adaptive to the needs of sensorimotor clients. A *coaching style* provides the ideal environment for concrete clients. A consulting style is a good match for formal clients. Finally, a *collaborative style* is suited to work with dialectic/systemic clients. (See table 16.3 for descriptions of each counseling/therapeutic environment.)

Developmental Matching.   The identification of the primary orientation used at any point in the counseling or psychotherapy process is fundamental for designing interventions well adapted to the client's current mode of experiencing reality. During developmental matching, the objective is to work with the client within the predominant orientation. This lends itself to horizontal development.

The matching environment is seen as a safe harbor. It initially allows for the formation of the counseling or therapeutic relationship and assists clients to participate in problem definition and treatment planning from a position of adequacy and equality. During the treatment process, matching environments are also used after mismatching strategies have promoted vertical movement to less familiar orientations. In this way, clients are given the opportunity to anchor new perspectives and to practice the alternative options available.

Developmental Mismatching.   By assessing a client's cognitive-developmental structure, the practitioner can design a developmentally appropriate sequence of interventions to promote both horizontal and vertical development.

By shifting styles, strategies, and language, the counselor or therapist provides facilitative assistance to move the client toward the direction of other orientations. This helps clients to explore resources and overcome symptomatic obstacles within each orientation.

The mismatching process has a dual focus. The first focus concerns the target of the counseling or therapeutic intervention. Here, the practitioner is concerned with setting the intervention within the most appropriate cognitive-developmental orientation. The counselor or therapist draws on specific strategies, depending on the particular issues and the cognitive-developmental structure presented by the client.

TABLE 16.3

Counselor Styles, Approaches, and Strategies Specific to Each Cognitive-Developmental Orientation

Counseling Style/Objectives	Approaches/Strategies	
	Individual	Family
Sensorimotor environmental structuring: Used to assist clients to explore issues at the sensorimotor level. A highly directive approach, it provides the structure for clients to be in contact with here-and-now sensory experience. Interventions are organized not to facilitate thinking about emotional and physical sensations but to experience these directly.	Gestalt empty chair Relaxation training Guided imagery Medication Community intervention Modeling	Family sculpting Spatialization Family choreography Conjoint family drawing Unbalancing reframes Heightening intensity Free association Unbalancing
Concrete operational coaching: Helps clients to understand their thoughts, feelings, and behavior from a concrete, linear perspective. The clinician assumes the role of coach and encourages clients to move and act in certain ways and to identify concrete aspects of their situations.	Assertiveness training ABC analysis of rational-emotive therapy Adlerian logical consequences Microskills Applied behavioral analysis Systematic desensitization Social-skills training Problem-solving training	Family puppet interviews Role playing There-and-then techniques Behavioral parent training Caring days Conjoint sex therapy Enactments Homework assignments Extended reframes

Formal operational consultation: Used to facilitate reflections about actions, thinking, and emotions. The clinician assumes the role of consultant, and the client takes the lead in mobilizing formal means of cognition and metacognition. Recognizing patterns and cycles is the basic objective.

Pattern search
Genogram-pattern analysis
Rogerian examination of self
Life-review techniques
Psychodynamic dream analysis
Analysis of transference
Adlerian early recollection analysis

Genogram-pattern analysis
Cycles of interaction analysis
Interpretation
Family life chronology
Cognitive restructuring techniques of structural family therapy
Enhancing reframes
Circular questioning

Dialectic/systemic collaboration: Focuses on system operations with two central objectives: (1) to facilitate the identification of underlying epistemological and ontological issues so that new constructs of self and reality are made possible, and (2) to introduce a dialectic interaction between the client and the environment.

Intergenerational analysis
Feminist consciousness raising
African-American consciousness raising
Network therapy
Analysis of projective identification
Examination of family rules

Multigenerational transmission analysis
Transforming reframes
Family reconstruction
Cultural analysis
Contextual analysis

Source: From "Developmental Counseling and Therapy: A Framework for Individual and Family Treatment" by S. A. Rigazio-DiGilio and A. E. Ivey, 1991, *Counseling and Human Development, 24*, p. 11. Copyright 1991 by Love Publishing Company. Adapted by permission.

The second focus concerns the objectives of treatment, or the level at which the clinical intervention is aimed. DCT argues that interventions can be targeted at three different levels of restructuring: basic, intermediate, and deep. Therefore, besides proposing specific counseling and therapeutic strategies for each of the four basic orientations, DCT advances treatment aimed at different levels of restructuring.

The DCT Metatheoretical Framework.   Beyond the specific DCT strategies of assessment and matching/mismatching, the model also provides clinicians with an organizational framework to integrate strategies and techniques representative of other counseling and psychotherapy theories into a coherent, developmentally oriented treatment plan (see, for example, Ivey, 1986, 1991; Ivey & Rigazio-DiGilio, in press; Kunkler & Rigazio-DiGilio, 1994; Rigazio-DiGilio, 1993a, 1993b, 1994a; Rigazio-DiGilio & Ivey, 1991, 1993). To illustrate this point, table 16.3 correlates the four primary counseling or therapeutic styles with corresponding individual and family treatment approaches and strategies.[4]

SUPPORTING RESEARCH

Clinical Findings

The DCT model has been used successfully to treat children and families with transitional difficulties (Ivey & Ivey, 1990), agoraphobics (Gonçalves, 1988, 1989; Gonçalves & Ivey, 1992), anxiety disorders (Gonçalves & Machado, 1987), victims of physical accidents (Kenny & Law, 1991), Japanese university students (Fukuhara, 1984), students preparing to enter the workplace (Mailler, 1991), men who batter and their partners (Lanza & Rigazio-DiGilio, 1994; Rigazio-DiGilio, Lanza, & Kunkler, 1994), and inpatient depressives (Rigazio-DiGilio & Ivey, 1990). All the above studies have demonstrated that the cognitive-developmental orientations represented in client language can be accessed and assessed throughout the course of treatment and that these data can be used to design and

---

[4]It is important to note that many strategies and approaches lend themselves to multiple orientations and that the intentionality of their use determines the impact on the client (Kunkler & Rigazio-DiGilio, 1994; Rigazio-DiGilio, 1994a, in press; Rigazio-DiGilio & Ivey, 1991, 1993). For example, even though reality therapy is associated with the coaching style (concrete), specific reality therapy techniques that require the client to evaluate the effects of certain behaviors may be approached from a formal or a dialectic perspective. Similarly, by helping clients experience the natural consequences of their actions, the counselor or therapist is working within a sensorimotor orientation. The same is true with many of the family counseling and therapy models. For example, restructuring techniques focused on behavioral change are best suited to concrete families, while cognitive restructuring toward enhancement fits best with families working within a formal orientation.

monitor developmentally appropriate and culturally sensitive treatment plans. Fukuhara's work also demonstrates the actual differences that occur in cognitive processing before, during, and after treatment.

Allen and Mary Ivey (1990) have demonstrated the practical implications of the DCT model in the treatment of child abuse. They further illustrate that grade school children are capable of both horizontal and vertical movement. Their clinical findings indicate that DCT can be used successfully with adults, children, and families to bring about counseling and therapeutic change.

Rigazio-DiGilio and Ivey (1991) have demonstrated the clinical use of DCT and SCDT in the treatment of a family dealing with a father's terminal illness, a mother's depressive symptomatology, and a son's substance-abusing behaviors. Rigazio-DiGilio (1994a) demonstrates the practical implications of both DCT and SCDT in the treatment of a first-generation Italian family dealing with the delayed entry of their seven-year-old son into the American school system following his leukemia remission. This case study makes clear how these models can be used with individuals, families, and larger social and treatment networks.

Lanza has used a semistructured, developmentally oriented, open-ended group format for men who batter and has demonstrated the usefulness of DCT for increasing the range and flexibility of group members' feelings, thoughts, and behaviors. Clinical application of DCT has resulted in group members' remaining in the groups longer and reporting deeper and more lasting change than typically described (Lanza & Rigazio-DiGilio, 1994; Rigazio-DiGilio, Lanza, & Kunkler, 1994).

Empirical Findings

Using an inpatient depressive population, Rigazio-DiGilio and Ivey (1990) empirically validated the existence of DCT constructs and the viability of the DCT questioning strategies to facilitate patient explorations within each of the cognitive-developmental orientations.[5] They found that interviewers can access an individual's predominant orientation in language that can be reliably classified by independent raters (0.90). Further, they found that the DCT questioning strategies designed to promote patient explorations within each of the orientations actually accomplishes this objective with a high degree of predictive validity (89 percent of the

---

[5]This research actually used an extended version of the standard interview, with early and late components corresponding to each of the four primary cognitive-developmental orientations. The questions were highly predictive in helping subjects view their issues from within each of the resulting eight orientations.

responses). All patients involved in the study were able to develop alternative perspectives on their problems and to commit to try a new behavior that they designed during the interview process. This is, in fact, basic to the dialectic nature of the counseling or therapeutic encounter; that is, if we can expand the contexts within which clients operate, the net result will be enhanced understandings and wider ranges of alternative options to choose from (Rigazio-DiGilio, 1991a; Rigazio-DiGilio & Ivey, 1990).

This research provided the basis for several current projects that focus on the adaptation of this model to family systems. Presently, two long-term research projects are underway to empirically validate the SCDT constructs and questioning strategies. The first study, which is being conducted by Rigazio-DiGilio, is investigating the construct validity of the four basic orientations as each is manifest in family communication. She is determining the type of relationship that exists between a family's collective predominant orientation and the individual orientations of key family members. Rigazio-DiGilio is also conducting a second research project designed to investigate the predictive validity of the sequential set of SCDT questioning strategies and to determine if family members can collectively explore their issues within each of the cognitive-developmental orientations using language that can be reliably identified by independent raters. Both studies are considered crucial to the continued adaptation of DCT to the treatment of families and larger social systems.

Three ancillary research projects are also underway. The first is being conducted by Rigazio-DiGilio and Sabatelli at the University of Connecticut and involves the development of a measure for individuation based on the holistic and developmental conceptualizations of the DCT model. The second, which is being conducted by Rigazio-DiGilio, Anderson, and Meth at the same university, involves the measurement of cognitive complexity in marital and family therapy graduate students, again using the holistic, developmental conceptualizations of DCT. Finally, a third study, conducted by Lanza, Rigazio-DiGilio, Anderson, and Meth, involves the evaluation of DCT groups for men who batter.

The DCT framework is the newest of the theories presented in this book. While early clinical and research data are promising, much more research and clinical trials are necessary to both validate and enrich the model. Fortunately, DCT was designed as a system open to change and modification. In fact, it is the only system that had, at its origin, specific suggestions for how to clinically and empirically examine the validity of DCT constructs and the viability of the counseling and therapy model. Specific suggestions for investigating DCT assessment and treatment strategies are outlined in Ivey's first book, *Developmental Therapy: Theory into Practice* (1986). His *Developmental Strategies for Helpers:*

Individual, Family, and Network Interventions (1991) lists specific examples for future investigation in each chapter.

In summary, the clinical and empirical bases for DCT is growing. While the research will add important confirming data, the clinical applications of DCT and SCDT have already been positively received by practitioners seeking more integrative, developmental, and egalitarian models of treatment (see Borders, 1994; Ivey, Bradford-Ivey, & Rigazio-DiGilio, 1989; Ivey & Rigazio-DiGilio, 1989; Rigazio-DiGilio, Lanza, & Kunkler, 1994).

■ ■ ■

THE CASE STUDY OF JOHN: THE DEVELOPMENTAL APPROACH

Assessing Cognitive-Developmental Orientation and Structure

Even though it would be difficult to present a secure statement on John's or his family's primary orientation or structure without the help of the standard and systemic cognitive-developmental interviews, we can hypothesize about both from the information given in the case summary.[6]

John appears to be primarily operating from within the sensorimotor orientation, characterized by a concentration on the sensory aspects of his experience. He seems overwhelmed by the sensory, physical, and physiological dimensions of his experience and marginally aware of the concrete, formal, and dialectic aspects of his problems. We speculate that the treatment phase of the standard interview would indicate that John has an overassimilative style and that he relies primarily on the sensorimotor and concrete orientations of his cognitive-developmental structure. This is illustrated by his somatic experiences (gastrointestinal difficulties), his concrete repetitive behaviors (withdrawal into reading), and his cognitions (listening to others but rationalizing to do what he wants) when faced with demands for performance or change.

Based on the clinical data presented in the case study, we can infer certain dynamics about the marital relationship. The primary systemic ori-

---

[6]We will illustrate SCDT assessment and treatment strategies by focusing on John's family of procreation. In the actual treatment process, SCDT would also develop a family-of-origin profile for both John and Betty. These profiles would be used to gain an in-depth understanding of the intergenerational patterns and cultural dynamics affecting the current system. However, in light of the absence of sociocultural and historical data about Betty, we cannot provide the reader with a balanced interpretation of how each member's history affects the system.

entation appears to be concrete, in that the couple is operating within a very narrow range of behaviors and cognitions (work roles, parenting functions, interactions around John's somatic experiences and complaints). The couple appears to be working within a rigid cognitive developmental structure. While John moves between concrete and sensorimotor, Betty moves between concrete and formal. This is a significant point of stress for the system. For example, when Betty reflects on the nature of the relationship between John and his children, John manifests gastrointestinal problems. This recalibrates the system back to concrete, and previous roles of identified patient and care giver are reestablished.

The case summary identifies several points where both John and his family of procreation have not mastered developmental tasks. This affects both their cognitive constructions and symptomatic expressions.

Assessing the Intrapersonal Developmental Profile

Sensorimotor Organization.   Within this orientation, John was the object of an ambiguous attitude. His father was mainly absent and affectionless and tended toward an aggressive attitude when he was present. His mother was affectionate and overprotective. The combination of both converged to a similar end point. By his absence and aggressiveness, John's father was instrumental in restricting exploratory behavior. His mother's attention and overprotection also restricted John's exploratory behavior.

As noted by Guidano (1987, 1991), this configuration of attachment patterns lends itself to the development of a cognitive organization characterized by an image of personal weakness in the face of any reality pressure. John's deep sense of personal weakness has been, since early childhood, externally expressed via intestinal problems when facing school difficulties and social pressure.

John's early somatic symptoms helped to construct several important meanings. First, he was able to prevent excessive pressure from the environment, thus reducing perceived threats (for example, when the physician called the school requesting a more flexible attitude from the teacher). Second, his symptoms awarded him secondary gains from an overconcerned and solicitous mother. Third, by finding a physical expression for his psychological vulnerabilities, John could maintain an acceptable level of self-esteem.

Sensorimotor Symptomatic Expression.   The symptomatic outcome of this organization is represented by difficulties in identifying, recognizing, discriminating, and accepting feelings related to the problematic situations (school, family, marriage, work). As a consequence of these difficul-ties, all John's reactions are going to be subsumed under a somatic expression (gastrointestinal problems).

Concrete Organization.   John's first cognitive organization was further reinforced through the school years. The intestinal problems kept prevent-ing him from dealing with difficult situations. This time, however, he found another effective tool that ended up as a functional organizer for his life: reading. Social situations, which have been necessarily unpredictable (school) and difficult (arguments between parents), were again avoided, but this time by using reading as a protective territory.

This attitude was very compatible with the traditional tasks of con-crete operations, and it helped John keep up with school requirements (highly valued in German culture), thus preserving his self-esteem and protecting him from environmental conflicts and pressures. John is well adapted to the requirements of school life, and his books constitute an island, reinforcing the attitude of motor control and the limitations of his exploratory behavior (reading instead of playing with other youngsters).

Concrete Symptomatic Expression.   The concrete structural organi-zation is currently expressed in John's difficulties with decentering from somatic reactions. Additionally, he seems unable to recognize, conceptual-ize, and solve problematic situations, primarily those of a social nature. He avoids confrontations (family duties, social activities, marital interac-tions, job confrontations) using strategies he developed in childhood: somatic problems and reading.

Formal Organization.   Although we don't have enough data on John's inner thoughts, it seems apparent that with the attainment of formal thought, he began to formulate a personal theory of self and reality that gave personal meaning to his defensive organization. Majoring in library science seemed an ideal outcome for his difficulties in dealing with social problems. This formal theory contributed to the preservation of self-esteem and helped to establish a necessary base from which his first tenta-tive social adventures were attempted (small group of friends, first dates with Carol, beginning relationship with Betty).

Formal Symptomatic Expression.   The features of John's formal orga-nization are currently expressed in his difficulties with gaining awareness of his thoughts and thought patterns. From the case description, we get the impression that John is his own thoughts—that he is unable to decen-ter and operate on propositional thoughts. This situation is illustrated by his response to Betty's concern about his absent relationship with the children, to which he responds that "his own father had spent very little time with him, but he cared for his father nonetheless." This kind of response shows that John is facing difficulties in gaining access to his own internal processes, avoiding them through the operation of defensive maneuvers.

Dialectic/Systemic Organization.   John's developmental history culminates in a personal ontological (theory of existence) and epistemological (theory of knowledge) organization of an absolutist nature characterized by a set of core assumptions regarding dependence, autonomy, and control. He avoids threats to his personal system through personal isolation, escaping through his books and doing what he thinks is best regardless of other opinions, but never confronting. Paradoxically, his sense of weakness, symptomatically expressed through his somatic problems, reinforces an absolute dependence without threatening psychological self-esteem.

Dialectic/Systemic Symptomatic Expression.   Within this orientation, John's symptoms are evident in his difficulties with identifying, decentering, and introducing more flexibility on his major ontological and epistemological assumptions regarding dependency, autonomy, and control.

Assessing the Interpersonal Developmental Profile

System Exploration/Formation.   The early years of his relationship with Betty were marked by limited social exchange, limited intimate bonding, and an overdependence on the themes constructed in John's family of origin. While John appeared to interact reluctantly with Betty's family, Betty and John's mother developed a caretaking team in the service of John's illness. As a result of all these factors, the system's early identity was vested in both John's success and frailties. This set in motion the blueprint for a predictable and narrow range of interactions, where John's symptoms would be used as a regulator for intrafamilial and extrafamilial closeness and distance. Given the German heritage of an intense work ethic and a restrained emotional style, this pattern is not surprising.

System Maintenance/Consolidation.   The period after their marriage and before the birth of Michael seemed to be happy years for the couple. The themes embedded in the couple's relationship during system formation, combined with a clear division of labor (typical of traditional German families), were the two forces governing the relationship at this time. All external (extrafamilial, work, and social) and internal (marital) interactions remained centralized around the meaning structure established about John in his family of origin. The couple established predictable routines that settled John's nervous stomach, while Betty went out of her way to maintain John's good humor.

The one flaw in this "reasonably good" marriage was the increased expectation from Betty that John pay more attention to her and less to his reading. However, during this phase Betty did not challenge in a way that was sufficient to overpower John's defenses, so symptoms were not noticeable.

It should be noted that it is difficult to determine, beyond the reasons associated with her Catholic upbringing, why Betty accepted her role. We might hypothesize that it had something to do with a caretaker/accommodative position she had constructed or learned about in her family of origin, but this history was not provided for us.

System Enhancement/Modification.   The arrival of children significantly altered the comfortable balance that Betty and John had established in the previous stage. As Betty's role changed from caretaker and wife to caretaker, wife, and mother, the intimacy between the couple waned. John has noticed the withdrawal and now characterizes Betty as nagging. With Betty's increased demands that John put down the books and spend time with his family and with John's cultural and familial experiences that it is the mother's role to be emotionally involved with the children, it's not surprising that his intestinal troubles have increased and that episodic impotence has been noted. Both can be considered strong maneuvers to regain a sense of familiarity in his family and marital relationships. Even John's mother reentered the marital domain (a typical response of the paternal grandmother in a predominantly German family), a move that constricted the couple's ability to work through their issues and helped to ensure the preservation of the predominate themes and, therefore, of interactional behaviors that were familiar for both John and Betty.

System Transformation.   Given the facts of the case, we can only surmise about the nature of this stage of system development. Two possible scenarios might happen without counseling or therapy. First, the symptoms may continue to intensify as the needs of the children increase (Michael is entering preadolescence, and Karen will be exploring the world of school). System regulation may result in a hospitalization. The second outcome might be that Betty's challenges intensify to the point of separation or divorce. However, without intervention, the system will more than likely present challenges and counterchallenges for change, only to return to the same state of affairs unless and until a normative or nonnor-mative developmental demand can break the cycle (such as the continued development of the children or the death of John's mother).

Developing an Individual Treatment Plan

The counselor or therapist uses the previous individual assessment to design a developmentally organized treatment plan that addresses both horizontal and vertical development and targets basic, intermediate, and deep levels of restructuring.

Basic Level Objectives.   DCT suggests four objectives for John:

1. Decrease the level of somatic symptoms through the development of relaxation and coping skills
2. Improve action schema and social skills through assertiveness training
3. Decenter John from familiar concrete actions by facilitating the identifi-cation of thoughts and cognitions
4. Promote self-knowledge development by facilitating John's identifica-tion of the internal and external determinants of his experiences

Basic Process.   In order to accomplish these objectives, DCT uses developmental matching and mismatching, starting in John's primary ori-entation and then moving vertically to each of the other orientations. The following strategies are suggested for work at this level:

1. *Sensorimotor*:   coping skills of relaxation (see Goldfried, 1980; Gonçalves, 1990)
2. *Concrete*:   assertiveness and social skills training (see Gonçalves, 1990)
3. *Formal*:   identification of patterns of internal dialogue (see Beck & Emery, 1985; Gonçalves, 1992)
4. *Dialectic/systemic*:   cognitive-behavioral functional analysis (see Gonçalves, 1986; Weinstein & Alschuler, 1985)

Intermediate Level Objectives.   At the end of the basic-level work, John is expected to have reduced his symptomatic reactions and to have applied his newly learned social skills to improving his relationships with his wife, children, and coworkers by being able to confront and to deal with conflictual situations. Once John is able to accomplish these objectives, we can move to an intermediate level of work based on the following objectives:

1. Facilitate the ventilation and identification of primary feelings
2. Improve John's perceptions of self-efficacy through the development of problem-solving skills
3. Facilitate the development of more relativistic and functional cognitions
4. Facilitate the identification of patterns in personal history

Intermediate Process.   Several strategies are suggested to deal with these objectives:

1. *Sensorimotor*:   focusing exercises to identify primary feelings that occur in problematic and conflictual situations (see Gendlin, 1978)
2. *Concrete*:   problem-solving training (see D'Zurilla, 1986)
3. *Formal*:   propositional combinatory exercises with the critic as well as disputation and exercises to identify alternative cognitions (see Gonçalves, 1992; Joyce-Moniz, 1985)
4. *Dialectic/systemic*:   analysis of personal developmental history with the identification of ontological and epistemological patterns (see Basseches, 1984; Gonçalves & Machado, 1989; Moshman & Hoover, 1989)

Deep-level Objectives.   At the end of the intermediate work, we expect that the somatic symptoms will have disappeared as well as the patterns of behavioral avoidance. Additionally, problem-solving skills and attitudes have promoted a more confronting and effective attitude in the face of life events, thus bringing additional improvements to John's perceptions of self-efficacy. Finally, John has gained some awareness of his thoughts, improving simultaneously his ability to act on them.

Assuming that John has progressed at the intermediate level, we suggest the following objectives to guide counseling and therapeutic work at the deep level:

1. Facilitate the recognition, emergence, acceptance, and synthesis of complex emotions
2. Promote more effective dealings with failure and frustration in highly demanding problematic situations
3. Promote the identification of core cognitive processes

4. Increase the flexibility of ontological/epistemological representations

Deep-level Process.   To accomplish these strategies, the following counseling and therapeutic strategies are suggested:

1. *Sensorimotor*:   emotional work through evocation, synthesis, restructuring, and modification of emotional experiences (see Greenberg & Safran, 1984, 1987, 1989)
2. *Concrete*:   self-exposures to highly demanding situations with attempts at dealing with potentially more difficult outcomes both cognitively and behaviorally (see Trower, Casey, & Dryden, 1988)
3. *Formal*:   identify and challenge core cognitive schema through the analysis of common themes (see Safran, Vallis, Segal, & Shaw, 1986; DeRubeis & Beck, 1988)
4. *Dialectic/systemic*:   metaphor and drama counseling to analyze the foundations of his ontological/epistemological patterns of absolutist nature and to experience alternative, more flexible patterns (see Gonçalves & Craine, 1990; Gonçalves & Machado, 1987, 1989; Joyce-Moniz, 1988, 1989)

Developing a Family Treatment Plan

The main objectives of a concurrent family treatment plan for John's family include:

1. Promoting horizontal movement to assist the couple to extend the narrow range of cognitions, emotions, and behaviors that are currently maintaining symptomatic expression
2. Promoting vertical and horizontal development to increase proficient use of all four cognitive-developmental orientations within a collective structure in a way that is more in tune with a "couple and family identity" and less enmeshed with preexisting family-of-origin constructs

Promoting Horizontal Movement.   The first objective of SCDT is to introduce change in a way that is accepted and hopeful yet somewhat unfamiliar. This is accomplished by using language and strategies associated with the system's predominant orientation. SCDT relies on refocusing techniques to co-construct an alternative view of the problem that facilitates the recognition of more viable solutions within the predominant orientation.

The reframing process, behavioral enactments, and homework assignments associated with structural family therapy provide the types of facilitative assistance conducive to concrete family functioning. Extending this couple's reality through reframe provides a platform for the couple and clinician to address issues of differentiation, individuation, bonding, and team building—all tasks related to the first developmental hurdle that the couple mismanaged: system formation. A segment of this reframe might include the following: "This marriage has not yet left the safety of its parents. We could focus on developing a marriage less in need of parents." From here, enactments (such as facilitating the couple to discuss a plan for mutually agreed-upon family-of-origin involvement and for mutually agreed-upon family-of-procreation goals) and assignments (such as placing the husband in charge of somatic symptoms by regularly attending his individual sessions) might serve to anchor the developmental objectives inherent in the reframe.

Promoting Vertical and Horizontal Development.   The intent of the first objective is to expand awareness and competencies at the primary orientation to help systems deal with their changing circumstances. Using both cognitive and behavioral restructuring techniques ensures system consolidation around the extended focus. Once this occurs, the family constructs a firmer, more adaptive foundation within the concrete orientation, which is more reflective of the current developmental tasks and needs. At this point, the focus can shift to other orientations, depending on the need. After any vertical movement, an accommodative environment is necessary to ground new perspectives into the worlds of action and experience.

Within the sensorimotor orientation, SCDT questioning strategies might be used along with systemic methods (such as Gestalt techniques, family sculpting, unbalancing, and heightening intensity) to facilitate the experience and discussion of the couple's worries about the domineering and restrictive nature of the symptoms, their upcoming normative and nonnormative life events, and their own level of sexual and emotional intimacy.

Within the formal orientation, SCDT questioning strategies and several systemic techniques (such as genogram pattern discussion, discussion of cycles of interaction, interpretation, challenging reality, family-life chronology focused on family of procreation) can be used to help the couple identify the recurrent patterns of thoughts, feelings, and interactions that are constricting their full potential. Horizontal reinforcement might include in-session role plays or enactments aimed at facilitating alternative patterns of communication while blocking less adaptive patterns. Homework assignments may include practicing these new patterns with the children and with family-of-origin members, particularly John's mother.

Within the dialectic/systemic orientation, SCDT questions and systemic methods (such as family reconstruction, genogram multigenerational transmission discussion, identification of cultural themes, family-life chronology focused on family of origin, feminist therapy techniques) may be used to facilitate the identification of and individuation from multigenerational, cultural, and gender patterns and themes.

This treatment plan began by using the couple's primary orientation to help John and Betty revisit and master developmental tasks that they had not successfully worked through during the system formation stage. Using this new foundation as a point of departure, the couple has been assisted to revisit each orientation using these expanded resources. New cognitions and skills are constructed at each orientation, leading to continued mastery of developmental tasks.

LIMITATIONS

As an alternative theory of counseling and psychotherapy, the application of DCT is limited in three ways. First, while the clinical and empirical indications of the model are quite positive, more specific investigations need to be undertaken. Both process and outcome studies should be designed to test the counseling and therapeutic efficacy of the model. At the individual level, do certain developmental history patterns respond better to a particular sequence of horizontal and vertical interventions? Are certain types of presenting problems more associated with certain cognitive-developmental structures? What are the outcome effects of DCT, and do these compare favorably with other cognitively based treatment results?

The basic construct reliability and predictive validity aspects of SCDT are currently being examined. Investigations that go beyond the basic psychometric properties of the model also need to be initiated. Questions concerning the relationship between the predominant collective family cognitive-developmental orientation and individual members' primary orientation need to be empirically explored. Are particular family types or ethnic backgrounds more associated with particular orientations? Studies need to be designed that compare duration of treatment, client and clinician satisfaction, and effects of SCDT treatment with other forms of family counseling and therapy.

The second limitation concerns the degree of training that clinicians require to implement the full range of DCT/SCDT interventions. As is evident in our case analysis, clinicians require an understanding of a variety of treatment models and firm grounding in developmental theory. At the basic level, counselors- or therapists-in-training can begin by using the questioning strategies to ascertain the predominant cognitive-developmental orientation of others. At the intermediate level, beginning counselors and therapist can use the concepts of matching and mismatching to stimulate client movement through the sphere. At this stage, clinicians should have mastered at least two schools of counseling or psychotherapy and be branching out to understand and integrate other approaches. Finally, at the deep level of integration, practitioners will possess a full range of interventions strategies so that the most appropriate, developmentally oriented treatment plan can be co-constructed with each client. The learning curve implicit in counselor or therapist development can be accelerated if the supervisor adopts a cognitive-developmental approach to supervision (Rigazio-DiGilio & Anderson, 1991, in press).

While not a limitation of the model, it should be noted that the DCT/SCDT clinician must become familiar with the cultural and gender implications of treatment. Strong training in the areas of multicultural and gender-awareness counseling or psychotherapy is a prerequisite before effectively adopting DCT and SCDT methods. Truly engaging an individual or a family in the co-constructive process outlined in this chapter requires empathic practitioners who can gently enter the world of the client. Proficiency in these areas is not just relevant to the DCT/SCDT model but is, in fact, fundamental for effective practice using any counseling or psychotherapy model.

The third limitation of the model concerns attitudes. DCT/SCDT evolved within a developmental paradigm. As such, it rejects the psychological model of helping that places the clinician in a superior position to the client and labels dysfunctional behavior in pathological terms. This model seeks to restore the dignity of the client by acknowledging the co-constructive nature of practice and by viewing psychological distress as a symptom of developmental delays or impasses, not as personality disorders or characterological flaws that must be healed. This shift in perspective is the limitation that is most difficult to overcome because it directly challenges established views of the professional identity of counselors and therapists.

SUMMARY

DCT offers practical methods to integrate developmental theory in counseling and psychotherapy practice. By using specific questioning strategies, it is possible to access and assess the primary orientation, the range and flexibility of the cognitive-developmental structure, and intra- and interpersonal developmental profiles for individuals and families seeking treatment. It is also possible to use this data to assist in the co-construction of developmentally appropriate, culturally sensitive treatment plans.

DCT's concepts of equilibration, vertical and horizontal development, developmental matching and mismatching, counseling/therapeutic environments, and target restructuring levels specify the DCT strategies, counseling and therapy models, and techniques that can be used to facilitate multiple perspective taking and the use of a wider range of cognitive, behavioral, and affectual options. DCT is the first major treatment model to describe in detail specific clinical tools based on developmental theory.

The world is multifaceted and multidimensional; and the greater the range and depth of cognitive orientations we use to understand and operate within our environment, the greater our adaptive potential will be. Our comprehensive understanding of situations leads to more viable emotional, behavioral, and cognitive functioning in our world. DCT provides one path toward enhancing our own and our client's multidimensional understanding.

REFERENCES

Attneave, C. (1969). Therapy in tribal settings and urban network interventions. *Family Process, 8,* 192–210.

Attneave, C. (1982). American Indian and Alaska native families: Emigrants in their own homeland. In M. McGoldrick, J. Pearce, & J. Giordano (Eds.), *Ethnicity and family therapy* (pp. 55–83). New York: Guilford.

Basseches, M. (1984). *Dialectical thinking and adult development.* Norwood, NJ: Ablex.

Beck, A. T., & Emery, G. (1985). *Anxiety disorders and phobias: A cognitive perspective.* New York: Basic Books.

Borders, L. D. (1994). Potential of DCT/SCDT in addressing two elusive themes of mental health counseling. *Journal of Mental Health Counseling, 16*(1), 75–78.

Breunlin, D. (1988). Oscillation theory and family development. In C. Falicov (Ed.), *Family transitions.* New York: Guilford.

Brooks, E. (1990, October). *Levels of emotional display in cultural identity theory: The Brooks model.* Paper presented at the North Atlantic Regional Association of Counselor Education and Supervision, Southington, CT.

Carter, B., & McGoldrick, M. (1989). *The changing family life cycle.* Boston: Allyn & Bacon.

Cheatham, H. (1990). Empowering black families. In H. Cheatham & J. Stewart, (Eds.), *Black families* (pp. 373–393). New Brunswick, NJ: Transaction.

Combrinck-Graham, L. (1985). A developmental model for family systems. *Family Process, 24*(2), 139–150.

Commons, M., Richard, F., & Armon, C. (Eds.) (1984). *Beyond formal operations.* New York: Praeger.

Conford, F. (1982). *The republic of Plato.* London: Oxford University Press. (Originally published in 1941)

DeRubeis, R. J., & Beck, A. T. (1988). Cognitive therapy. In K. S. Dobson (Ed.), *Handbook of cognitive-behavioral therapies*. New York: Guilford.

D'Zurilla, J. (1986). *Problem solving therapy: A social competence approach to clinical interventions*. New York: Springer.

Erikson, E. H. (1963). *Childhood and society* (2nd ed.). New York: Norton.

Fukuhara, M. (1984). *Is love enough?—From the viewpoint of counseling adolescents*. Paper presented at the 42nd annual conference of the International Association of Psychologists, Mexico City.

Gendlin, E. T. (1978). *Focusing*. New York: Bantam.

Gilligan, C. (1982). *In a different voice: Psychological theory and women's development*. Cambridge: Harvard University Press.

Goldfried, M. L. (1980). Psychotherapy as coping skills training. In M. J. Mahoney (Ed.), *Psychotherapy process*. New York: Plenum.

Goldner, V. (1988). Generation and gender: Normative and covert hierarchies. *Family Process. 27*(1), 17–33.

Gonçalves, O. F. (1986). Consulta psicológica e desenvolvimento do autoconhecimento: Uma perspectiva cognitivo-construtivista [Counseling psychology and self-knowledge development: A cognitive-constructivist approach]. *Cadernos de Consulta Psicológica, 2*, 35–45.

Gonçalves, O. (1988). *Developmental counseling and therapy: Treatment strategies for agoraphobia*. Presented at the 1988 Conference on Counseling Psychology, University of Southern California, Los Angeles.

Gonçalves, O. (1989). *Cognitive representation of self-narratives and self-knowledge development of agoraphobic clients*. Presented at the First European Congress of Psychology, Amsterdam.

Gonçalves, O. F. (1990). *Therapia comportamental: Modelos teóricos e manuais terapêuticos [Behavior therapy: Theoretical models and therapeutic manuals]*. Porto: Ediçoes Jornal de Psicologia.

Gonçalves, O. F. (1992). *Terapias cognitivas: Teoria e prática [Cognitive therapies: Theory and practice]*. Porto: Afrontamento.

Gonçalves, O. F., & Craine, M. (1990). The use of metaphors in cognitive therapy. *Journal of Cognitive Therapy, 4*, 135–150.

Gonçalves, O., & Ivey, A. (1992). Developmental therapy: Clinical applications. In K. T. Kuehlwein and H. Rosen (Eds.), *Cognitive therapy in action: Evolving innovative practice*. San Francisco: Jossey-Bass.

Gonçalves, O. F., & Machado, P. P. (1987). A terapia como co-construçao: Das metáforas do cliente às metáforas do terapeuta [Therapy as co-construction: From client's metaphors to therapist's metaphors]. *Jornal de Psicologia, 6*, 14–20.

Gonçalves, O. F., & Machado, P. P. (1989). Do pensamento absolutista ao pensamento dialéctico através da terapia cognitiva [From absolutist to dialectical thought through cognitive therapy]. In J. F. Cruz, R. A. Gonçalves, & P. P. Machado (Eds.), *Psicologia e educaçao*. Porto: APPORT.

Greenberg, L. S., & Safran, J. D. (1984). Integrating affect and cognition: A perspective on the process of therapeutic change. *Cognitive Therapy & Research, 89*, 55–578.

Greenberg, L. S., & Safran, J. D. (1987). *Emotions in psychotherapy*. New York: Guilford.

Greenberg, L. S., & Safran, J. D. (1989). Emotion in psychotherapy. *American Psychologist, 44*, 19–29.

Guidano, V. F. (1987). *Complexity of the self: A developmental approach to psychopathology and therapy*. New York: Guilford.

Guidano, V. F. (1991). *The self in process: Toward a post-rationalist cognitive therapy.* New York: Guilford.

Haley, J. (1973). *Uncommon therapy: The psychiatric techniques of Milton H. Erikson.* New York: Norton.

Harland, R. (1987). *Superstructuralism.* London: Methuen.

Harre, R. (1983). *Personal being.* Cambridge: Harvard University Press.

Ivey, A. (1971). *Microcounseling: Innovations in interviewing training.* Springfield, IL: Charles C Thomas.

Ivey, A. (1983a). *Intentional interviewing and counseling.* Monterey, CA: Brooks/Cole.

Ivey, A. (1983b). *Three approaches to counseling.* North Amherst, MA: Microtraining Associates.

Ivey, A. (1986). *Developmental therapy: Theory into practice.* San Francisco: Jossey-Bass.

Ivey, A. (1991). *Developmental strategies for helpers: Individual, family, and network interventions.* Pacific Grove, CA: Brooks/Cole.

Ivey, A., & Authier, J. (1978). *Microcounseling* (2nd ed.). Springfield, IL: Charles C Thomas.

Ivey, A. E., Bradford-Ivey, M., & and Rigazio-DiGilio, S. A. (1989). *Integrating counseling and development: Implications of the developmental therapy model.* A full-day institute for the American Association for Counseling and Development, annual national convention, Boston.

Ivey, A., & Gluckstern, N. (1982). *Basic attending skills.* North Amherst, MA: Microtraining Associates.

Ivey, A., & Gonçalves, O. F. (1988). Developmental therapy: Integrating developmental processes into the clinical practice. *Journal of Counseling & Development, 66,* 406–413.

Ivey, A., Gonçalves, O., & Ivey, M. (1989). Developmental therapy: Theory and practice. In O. Gonçalves (Ed.), *Advances in the cognitive therapies: The constructive-developmental approach.* Porto: APPORT.

Ivey, A., & Ivey, M. (1990). Assessing and facilitating children's cognitive development: Developmental counseling and therapy in a case of child abuse. *Journal of Counseling & Development, 68,* 299–305.

Ivey, A., Ivey, M., & Simek-Morgan, L. (1993). *Counseling and psychotherapy from a multicultural perspective* (3rd ed.). Englewood Cliffs, NJ: Prentice-Hall.

Ivey, A., & Rigazio-DiGilio, S. A. (1989). *Adapting developmental theory to individual and family therapy.* A full-day institute for the North Atlantic Regional Association for Counselor Education and Supervision, regional convention, Newport, RI.

Ivey, A., & Rigazio-DiGilio, S. (1991a). Development over the life span. In A. Ivey, *Developmental strategies for helpers: Individual, family, and network interventions* (pp. 119–156). Pacific Grove, CA: Brooks/Cole.

Ivey, A., & Rigazio-DiGilio, S. (1991b). The standard cognitive-developmental interview. In A. Ivey, *Developmental strategies for helpers: Individual, family, and network interventions.* Pacific Grove, CA: Brooks/Cole.

Ivey, A., & Rigazio-DiGilio, S. (1991c). Toward a developmental practice of mental health counseling: Strategies for training, practice, and political unity. *Journal of Mental Health Counseling, 13,* 21–36.

Ivey, A., & Rigazio-DiGilio, S. A. (in press). Developmental counseling and therapy: Can still another theory be useful to you? *The Journal for the Professional Counselor.*

Ivey, A., Rigazio-DiGilio, S., & Ivey, M. (1991). The standard cognitive-developmental classification system. In A. Ivey, *Developmental strategies for helpers: Individual, family, and network interventions*. Pacific Grove, CA: Brooks/Cole.

Jackson, B. (1975). Black identity development. *Journal of Educational Diversity and Innovation 2*, 19–25.

Joyce-Moniz, L. (1985). Epistemological therapy and constructivism. In M. J. Mahoney & A. Freeman (Eds.). *Cognition and psychotherapy*. New York: Plenum.

Joyce-Moniz, L. (1988). Self-talk, dramatic expression and constructivism. In C. Perris, I. Blackburn, & H. Perris (Eds.), *Cognitive psychotherapy: Theory and practice*. Heidelberg: Springer.

Joyce-Moniz, L. (1989). Structures, dialectics, and regulation of applied constructivism: From developmental psychopathology to individual drama therapy. In O. F. Gonçalves (Ed.), *Advances in the cognitive therapies: The constructive-developmental approach*. Porto: APPORT.

Kegan, R. (1982). *The evolving self*. Cambridge: Harvard University Press.

Kelley, G. (1955). *The psychology of personal constructs* (Vols. 1 & 2). New York: Norton.

Kenny, D., & Law, J. (1991). Developmental counseling and therapy with involuntary midlife career changers. *Journal of Young Adulthood and Middle Age, 3*, 25–39.

Kohlberg, L. (1981). *The philosophy of moral development*. New York: Harper & Row.

Kunkler, K. P., & Rigazio-DiGilio, S. A. (1994). Systemic cognitive-developmental therapy: Organizing structured activities to facilitate family development. *Simulation and Gaming: An International Journal of Theory, Design, and Research, 25*, 75–87.

Lacan, J. (1977). *Écrits*. New York: Norton.

Lanza, A., & Rigazio-DiGilio, S. (1994). *Developmental counseling and therapy: An integrated approach for working with men who batter*. Manuscript submitted for publication.

Lanza, A. S., Rigazio-DiGilio, S. A., & Kunkler, K. P. (1993a). *A cognitive-developmental framework for working with men who batter: Organizing group intervention strategies*. Two-day seminar for research preparation, Connecticut Superior Court/Family Division, Willimantic, CT.

Lanza, A. S., Rigazio-DiGilio, S. A., & Kunkler, K. P. (1993b). *Developmental therapy: An integrative approach to battering*. Paper presented at the 51st annual conference of the American Association for Marriage and Family Therapy, Anaheim.

Liddle, H., & Saba, G. (1983). Clinical use of the family life cycle: Some cautionary guidelines. In J. C. Hansen (Ed.), *Family therapy collection* (Vol. 7) (pp. 161–175). Rockville, MD: Aspen Systems.

Loevinger, J., Wessler, R., & Redmore, C. (1970). *Measuring ego development* (Vols. 1 & 2). San Francisco: Jossey-Bass.

Luepnitz, D. (1988). *The family reinterpreted: Feminist theory in clinical practice*. New York: Basic Books.

Mahoney, M. J. (1991). *Human change processes: The scientific foundations of psychotherapy*. New York: Basic Books.

Mailler, W. (1991, October). *Preparing students for the workplace: Personal growth and organizational change*. Paper presented at the North Atlantic Regional Association for Counselor Education and Supervision, Albany.

McGoldrick, M., Pearce, J., & Giordano, J. (1982). *Ethnicity and family therapy*. New York: Guilford.

Miller, A. (Ed. & Trans.). (1977). *Phenomenology of spirit* by G. W. F. Hegel. Oxford:

Oxford University Press. (Original work published by Hegel, 1807)

Minuchin, S. (1974). *Families and family therapy.* Cambridge: Harvard University Press.

Moshman, D., & Hoover, L.M. (1989). Rationality as a goal of psychotherapy. *Journal of Cognitive Psychotherapy, 3,* 31–51.

Perry, W. (1970). *Forms of intellectual and ethical development in the college years.* New York: Holt, Rinehart, & Winston.

Piaget, J. (1954). *The construction of reality in the child.* New York: Basic Books.

Piaget, J. (1955). *The language and thought of the child.* New York: New America Library. (Originally published in 1923)

Piaget, J. (1965). *The moral judgment of the child.* New York: Macmillan.

Reiss, D., & Oliveri, M. (1986). Sensory experience and family process: Perceptual styles tend to run in but not necessarily run families. *Family Process, 22,* 289–308.

Rigazio-DiGilio, S. A. (1991a). *Developmental therapy and depressive disorders.* Paper presented at the second annual International Conference on Constructivism in Psychotherapy, Braga, Portugal.

Rigazio-DiGilio, S. (1991b). *The systemic cognitive-developmental classification system.* Available from author.

Rigazio-DiGilio, S. (1991c). *The systemic cognitive-developmental interview.* Available from author.

Rigazio-DiGilio, S. A. (1991d). *Systemic cognitive-developmental therapy.* Paper presented at the second annual International Conference on Constructivism in Psychotherapy, Braga, Portugal.

Rigazio-DiGilio, S. A. (1993a, November). Developmental counseling and therapy and systemic cognitive developmental therapy: An intensive approach to treatment for individuals, couples, and families. Two-day confer-

ence at Johns Hopkins University. (Assisted by A. S. Lanza & K. P. Kunkler).

Rigazio-DiGilio, S. (1993b). Family counseling and therapy: Theoretical foundations and issues of practice. In A. Ivey, M. Ivey, & L. Simek-Morgan. *Counseling and psychotherapy* (3rd ed.). Englewood Cliffs, NJ: Prentice-Hall.

Rigazio-DiGilio, S. (1994a). A co-constructive-developmental integration of treatment for individuals, families, and networks. *The Journal of Mental Health Counseling, 16,* 43–74.

Rigazio-DiGilio, S. A. (1994b). Systemic cognitive-developmental therapy: Training practitioners to access and assess cognitive developmental orientations. *Simulation and Gaming: An International Journal of Theory, Research, and Design, 25,* 61–74.

Rigazio-DiGilio, S. A. (1994c). *Systemic cognitive-developmental therapy: A therapeutic model and metatheoretical framework for working with partners and families.* Paper presented for the International Round Table for the Advancement of Counseling, München, Germany.

Rigazio-DiGilio, S. A. (in press). Beyond paradigms: The multiple implications of a co-constructive–developmental model. *Journal of Mental Health Counseling.*

Rigazio-DiGilio, S., & Anderson, S. (1991). Supervisee-focused supervision: A cognitive-developmental model. Presented at the 49th annual American Association for Marriage and Family Therapy Conference, Dallas.

Rigazio-DiGilio, S. A., & Anderson, S. A. (in press). A cognitive-developmental model for marital and family therapy supervision. *The Clinical Supervisor.*

Rigazio-DiGilio, S., & Ivey, A. (1990). Developmental therapy and depressive disorders: Measuring cognitive levels through patient natural languages. *Professional Psychology, 21,* 470–475.

Rigazio-DiGilio, S., & Ivey, A. (1991). Developmental counseling and therapy: A framework for individual and family treatment. *Counseling and Human Development, 24*(1), 1–20.

Rigazio-DiGilio, S., & Ivey, A. (1993). Systemic cognitive-developmental therapy: An integrative framework. *The Family Journal: Counseling and Therapy for Couples and Families, 1*(3), 208–219.

Rigazio-DiGilio, S. A., & Ivey, A. (in press). Professional counseling as development: Implications for training. *Guidance and Counseling.*

Rigazio-DiGilio, S. A., Lanza, A. S., & Kunkler, K. P. (1994). A co-constructive-developmental approach for the assessment and treatment of relationship violence. *Family Counseling and Therapy, 2*(2), 1–27.

Rosen, H. (1985). *Piagetian dimensions of clinical relevance.* New York: Columbia University Press.

Safran, J. D., Vallis, T. M., Segal, Z. V., & Shaw, B. F. (1986). Assessment of core cognitive processes in cognitive therapy. *Cognitive Therapy & Research, 8,* 333–347.

Snyder, D. (1989). Introduction to the special series. *Journal of Consulting & Clinical Psychology, 57,* 3–4.

Trower, P., Casey, A., & Dryden, W. (1988). *Cognitive-behavioral counseling in action.* London: Sage.

Weinstein, G., & Alschuler, A. S. (1985). Educating and counseling for self-knowledge development. *Journal of Counseling & Development, 64,* 19–25.

PART THREE

Additional Perspectives for Counseling and Psychotherapy

■ ■ ■ CHAPTERS

A textbook focused on the topic of counseling and psychotherapy would not be complete without the perspectives contained in part 3. Chapter 17, "Nontraditional Approaches to Counseling and Psychotherapy," provides the reader with ideas for approaches to individual work with clients that do not rely as much on verbal communication as do some of the more traditional theoretical orientations. As noted by the chapter's author, many mental health professionals are questioning the limitation of verbal-based orientations, especially with clients who have difficulty expressing themselves, and are advocating alternative therapies that focus on nonverbal strategies. This chapter describes the use of hypnosis, hypnotherapy, the creative arts, play therapy, multimodal therapy, and transpersonal approaches to counseling and psychotherapy. We think readers will find this chapter both interesting and informative.

For the past three decades, writers, researchers, and professionals have been espousing the need for multicultural and crosscultural strategies and approaches to individual counseling and psychotherapy. Traditional counseling and psychotherapies were developed for white middle- and upper-middle-class clients. These theories were developed by white practitioners who were enmeshed in Western cultural values; and the applicability of these theories, without modification, to multicultural populations is questionable. We agonized over the issue of whether to ask each contributing author to include discussion of multicultural and crosscultural variations or to include a chapter focused solely on this topic and written by individuals known for their expertise in this area. We decided on the latter in order to avoid repetition throughout the text and to ensure content of the highest quality. We think you will find chapter 18, "Counseling and Psychotherapy: Multicultural Considerations," extremely pertinent to your work with racial, cultural, and ethnic minorities. We recommend that you reevaluate the strengths and weaknesses of each of the theories presented in this text after you finish reading chapter 18.

The authors of chapter 19, "Counseling and Psychotherapy: An Integrative Perspective," pose the possibility that the profession may be moving away from an idealistic adulation of a "grand master" or a "grand therapy" toward a greater personal responsibility in creating clinicians who use an integrative approach in the process of counseling and psychotherapy. The authors discuss three models for integrative work with clients: atheoretical, which emphasizes commonalities or techniques to the exclusion of theory; technical, which emphasizes a single theory base but uses a wide variety of techniques from other orientations; and synthetic, which stresses a blending of two or more theories and a variety of techniques. A discussion of the strengths and weaknesses of an integrative approach along with guidelines for developing one gives readers some thought-provoking ways to begin assessing their own theoretical orientations. We think this chapter provides appropriate closure for the book and will help readers carefully think through their perspectives about individual work with clients.

CHAPTER SEVENTEEN

Nontraditional Approaches to Counseling and Psychotherapy

Ardis Sherwood-Hawes
Clark College

The majority of current approaches to counseling and psychotherapy (such as cognitive-behavioral, client-centered, and psychodynamic) rely on interventions that require an ability to communicate information about thoughts and feelings. Many mental health professionals are questioning the limitations of verbal-based orientations, especially with clients who have difficulty expressing themselves, and are advocating alternative therapies that focus on nonverbal strategies for counseling (Allan & Clark, 1984; McBrian, 1990). Recent studies indicate that when treatment strategies are adapted to acknowledge the individual qualities, resources, and special needs of clients, counseling and therapeutic interventions are more effective. Counselors are currently becoming more aware of the tremendous impact that preferred modalities for learning have on the outcome of therapy (Griggs, 1991; Otani, 1990). Griggs (1991) maintains that when counseling or therapy approaches are selected to match the representational systems of clients (such as auditory, visual, tactile, kinesthetic), the counseling or therapeutic process is enhanced; and she suggests that mental health professionals make assessments of clients' perceptual strengths and combine existing theoretical models with strategies that are compatible with clients' learning preferences.

This chapter describes three alternative approaches to verbal-oriented therapies: hypnotherapy, arts therapy, and play therapy; multimodal therapy; and a systematic model of eclectic interventions. It concludes with a brief overview of transpersonal psychology, a group of perspectives that is concerned with the study of humanity's highest potential. These orientations can be used as adjuncts to other theoretical systems or can serve as primary approaches to counseling and psychotherapy.

HYPNOSIS

According to *Webster's New World Dictionary* (1984), *hypnosis* or *trance* is a "sleeplike condition psychically induced, usually by another person, in which the subject is in a state of altered consciousness and responds, with certain limitations, to the suggestions of the hypnotist" (p. 691). Many people imagine that hypnosis involves a helpless, mesmerized person who is controlled by an outside influence. In reality, people often experience the dissociated state of trance when they block external stimuli by becoming totally immersed in a daydream or music, engrossed in a television program, or fixated on an activity (such as drumming or artwork) (Carich, 1990b).

Hypnosis is thought to be linked to the right brain hemisphere and is believed to be the key to unlocking experiences and emotions that are not in the conscious level of awareness (Erickson & Rossi, 1981). Although a trance produces minimal enhancement of the memoric recovery of recently stored material, it seems to facilitate the recall of long-term memories. This phenomenon might be due to the reduction of emotional barriers to those memories during a trance (Page, 1992). A person who is experiencing a trance becomes more relaxed, has increased accessibility to unconscious data, is more receptive to external and internal suggestions, and benefits from an augmented ability to assimilate new material (Carich, 1990a; Fairchild, 1990). Studies indicate that according to individual motivation, hypnotic responding can improve with practice and will eventually reach a stable plateau (Page, 1992).

Stages of Hypnosis

Traditionally, the process of hypnosis involves five phases: trance induction, trance preparation, trance deepening, working stage, and reorientation stage.

Trance Preparation and Induction.   Counselors and therapists carefully prepare clients for the experience of hypnosis. The purposes of trance preparation are to develop rapport between practitioners and clients; foster close counseling or therapeutic relationships; and discuss the functions, purposes, and goals of hypnotic interventions (Carich, 1990a). When clients are comfortable with the process of hypnosis, they are invited to go into a light trance. Trance induction can be natural or orchestrated by the counselor or therapist. Examples of direct or formal trance induction techniques include deep muscle relaxation, imagery, eye fixation, and hand levitation. Indirect or informal techniques can include accessing naturalistic and spontaneous trance states through indirect suggestions, self-focus on breathing, imagery, use of metaphors, and story telling.

Trance Deepening.   The depth of the trance experience ranges on a continuum from a light trance, in which clients are relaxed, comfortable, alert, open to simple and posthypnotic suggestions, and able to nonjudgmentally perceive and experience sensations and messages from the unconscious, to a stuporous or plenary trance with feelings of timelessness, unawareness of physical sensations, significantly decreased respiration and pulse rate, and abatement of spontaneous mental activity. Professionals can facilitate trance deepening through counting techniques, changing vocal tone and inflection, encouraging a focus on pleasant memories that create a positive alliance between conscious and unconscious processes, and using words and images that imply depth or gentle exploration.[1]

Working or Intervention Stage.   This is the stage in which counselors and therapists promote change by using individually tailored strategies of hypnotic interventions. Practitioners may use direct or indirect questions and suggestions to explore naturalistic patterns and unconscious resources as well as the way in which internal experiences influence the life-style of clients. Hypnotic techniques include the following:

■ *Subconscious questioning.*   The hypnotic process allows counselors and therapists to communicate more directly with the unconscious realm (Fairchild, 1990). When clients communicate with the right hemisphere of the brain, practitioners can obtain additional information about clients' unique beliefs, goals, and methods of motivation; understand ways in which clients perceive themselves and their worlds; and facilitate discovery of clients' available yet unrecognized resources (Otani, 1990).

■ *Hypnotic suggestions.*   Hypnotic suggestions can be direct (that is, straightforward or intentional) or indirect (subtle or floating). Direct suggestions can range from authoritative ("You will feel more relaxed") to a more persuasive style that provides alternatives and choice ("You might choose to feel yourself becoming more and more relaxed"). Gunnison (1990) asserts that the use of implied directive language during the treatment process gives control and personal power to clients and encourages self-responsibility and independent behavior. Indirect suggestions optimally are formulated using clients' own language and meaningful experiences and appeal to their unconscious processes through the use of interventions such as metaphors, stories, analogies, fantasy, reframing, and paradoxical suggestions. Fairchild (1990) proposes that many messages are ineffective when communicated directly because they may increase client resistance, become blocked at the conscious level, tap into clients' feelings of guilt, or exacerbate sources of shame. In addition, because alteration of symptomatic behavior is not considered to be a sufficient condition for enduring change, Otani (1990) recommends that counselors and therapists simultaneously use goal-oriented directives to elicit specific behavioral changes and indirect suggestions to promote psychological growth and a reorganization of the cognitive and experiential world of the client.

---

[1]Research indicates that the attainment of deeper levels of trance is not necessary for hypnotherapy to be effective (Carich, 1990b).

- *Age regression.*   Age regression, in which clients recall and experience past events, has two purposes. First, it encourages clients' recall of conscious material so they can experience it in new ways; and second, it uncovers knowledge that is unavailable to conscious memory (Carich, 1990b).

- *Posthypnotic suggestions.*   Posthypnotic suggestions are proposals that counselors and therapists give to clients for use after they reorient from the trance. For example, clients may be told, "When I [the practitioner] count back from 5 to 0, you will feel increasingly more relaxed, more powerful, and more confident" (Carich, 1990b). Posthypnotic suggestions can be homework assignments, paradoxical suggestions, or proposed changes for actions and emotions.

- *Reorientation stage.*   During the reorientation stage of hypnosis, clients are gradually awakened to more conscious states of awareness. The reorientation phase is the most important stage of the hypnotic process; for here clients can contemplate their own wisdom, understand that self-generated solutions are real and attainable, acknowledge their own personal power, and transform acquired insight and the expectation for change into workable strategies that elicit the desired behavior (Fairchild, 1990).

HYPNOTHERAPY

During the past few years, the traditional approach to hypnotism—the induced trance and the focus on the authority and ability of the hypnotist—has shifted to a new form of hypnosis in which the formal trance is not induced and an emphasis is placed on equality in counseling or therapeutic relationships (Sperry, 1990). Milton H. Erickson's valuable research on the use of hypnosis in the mental health field has had a tremendous impact on the current direction of hypnotherapy (Gunnison, 1990). Erickson believed that the unconscious is an untapped reservoir of valuable and accessible knowledge and that hypnosis can provide a passageway to this knowledge. He considered the unconscious wisdom of past experiences to be a counseling or therapeutic force, a source of growth and movement, and a powerful influence on behavioral and personality changes (Otani, 1990). Erickson maintained that hypnosis, when used as a tool or an adjunct to a theoretical model of counseling or therapy, created a counseling/therapeutic situation in which practitioners could simultaneously communicate with the unconscious and conscious dimensions of clients. He originally espoused strategies that used formal trance induction, but he became uncomfortable with the formal trance phenomena and evolved toward advocating hypnotherapy without trance induction (Gunnison, 1990). Erickson concluded that all hypnosis is self-induced, that practitioner is merely a guide to unconscious resources. The role of the counselor or therapist in hypnosis is to enable clients to transcend their conscious limitations and access their own wisdom. Throughout the process of hypnotherapy, Erickson promoted personal mastery, competence, and clients' beliefs that they were responsible for changes. He maintained that this self-belief was vital to the enduring success of the mental health process (Otani, 1990).

Hypnotherapy is an eclectic intervention that combines hypnosis with other counseling or therapeutic strategies, and it can be used successfully with a multitude of counseling/therapeutic models (for example, insight-oriented, creative arts, cognitive-behavioral, and multimodal) (Friedrich, 1991; Otani, 1990; Rhue & Lynn, 1991; Sperry & Carlson, 1990). This combination of techniques is effective in treating a variety of human conditions (such as depression, reduction of pain, posttraumatic stress disorder, dissociative disorders, global amnesia, traumatic grief, trauma of rape, and childhood sexual abuse) in a diverse range of populations (Cochrane, 1991; Friedrich, 1991; McBrian, 1990; Rhue & Lynn, 1991). Hypnotherapy is predicated on the Ericksonian style of hypnosis in which a trancelike state is not considered necessary for corrective change. The unconscious is viewed as a storehouse for past learning and experiences where individuals spontaneously find the answers to solve problems, change negative experiences, and achieve positive growth (Fairchild, 1990; Gunnison, 1990). This intuitive change or unconscious self-regulation of behavior can transcend conscious efforts of self-control and can result in profound changes to the basic structure of personality (Otani, 1990).

The goal of the hypnotherapist is not to induce a trancelike state in clients but rather to create, with the permission and cooperation of clients, a state in which they are more receptive to hidden resources and movement toward positive behavioral growth (Fairchild, 1990; Gunnison, 1990). People do not passively receive information but creatively, actively, and distinctly process external data to form internal realities (Cochrane, 1991). Therefore, hypnotherapy is more effective when treatment strategies are tailored to acknowledge and incorporate the unique resources, qualities, and special needs of clients and reflect their preferred modality for learning (visual, auditory, kinesthetic) (McBrian, 1990; Otani, 1990). In addition, these techniques may empower clients and foster a sense of autonomy and commitment to positive growth because empirical evidence implies that corrective changes are more enduring when clients believe that modification spontaneously emerges from internal sources (Otani, 1990).

Techniques

There are many techniques from which counselors and therapists can choose to create an individualized, empowering hypnotic atmosphere where clients become more sensitive to external and internal stimulations for changes in perception, action, cognition, and emotion. These hypnotic forms do not require the induction of a formal trance, and most can be incorporated into strategies for counseling and psychotherapy with little or no formal training for hypnosis (Sperry, 1990). It is imperative, however, that practitioners and clients candidly and openly discuss all aspects of the process of hypnosis before using techniques that can induce an informal hypnotic state. The following represents a sample of these techniques:

Use of Language.   Erickson maintains that language is a powerful agent for change. Subtle variations in the use of language (such as tone, grammar, structure, tempo, timbre, syntax) and interspersals, or the emphasis of provocative words, humor, metaphors, and paradoxical suggestions, can create hypnotic patterns that allow clients access to unconscious processes and increase the impact of the counseling or therapeutic experience (Erickson & Rossi, 1981).

Reframing.   Reframing is the creation of more positive visualizations of unwanted personal qualities, problematic situations, and dysfunctional behaviors (overt and covert). This technique encourages clients to perceive problems differently and facilitates their ability to change their responses to difficulties (Gunnison, 1990). For example, unhealthy patterns of behavior can benefit clients in obscure ways, and reframing can help them recognize payoffs or reinforcers to behaviors. Once clients become aware of the hidden advantages of their behavior, resistance to change can be reduced (Sperry, 1990).

Metaphor and Analogy.   Metaphors and analogies can act as bridges between right- and left-brain hemispheres and can connect the rigid thinking processes of the left brain to the expanded patterns, perceptions, and psychological movement of the right brain (Mays, 1990). These forms of communication work best when they match the representational or preferred learning modality of clients (Gunnison, 1990). Metaphors allow clients to perceive and understand phenomena in different ways, and they can be gentle, nonintrusive hints about possibilities for change. For example, the counselor or therapist might tell a depressed client, "It sounds like you feel you are falling into a deep, dark, empty, cold, and lonely hole. There are steps out of that hole. I wonder when you will start climbing those steps?" Metaphors can also create shared bonds between practition-ers and clients and become shorthand symbols for referring to the coun-seling or therapeutic process (Mays, 1990). When the client who is depressed achieves a movement toward change, the counselor or therapist might merely state, "Ah, I see you are using the steps."

Story Telling.   Story telling is a naturalistic method of hypnosis that promotes the use of imagery, client absorption, and spontaneous contem-plation of the ideas presented by the story (Friedrich, 1991; Rhue & Lynn, 1991). Counselors and therapists can encourage right-brain imagery and discourage resistance by presenting parables or short stories that relate uniquely to the needs of clients. Stories or metaphoric messages contain implicit strategies for change; and when practitioners tell stories with ani-mated casualness, clients generally listen attentively and do not intellectu-alize or attempt to analyze stories (Sperry, 1990).

Story-telling techniques are especially well suited for children and for adults who have experienced trauma. Research suggests that the ability to be hypnotized is increased in adults who have sustained trauma and that children in general are usually more able to be hypnotized than adults (Friedrich, 1991; Page, 1992). Studies also indicate that there is an asso-ciation between measures of fantasy and imagination and the ability to be hypnotized. Adults and children often use imagination and fantasy to regu-late their internal processes and to dissociate and distance themselves from the pain and negative effects of traumatic experiences (Rhue & Lynn, 1991). The naturalistic trance induced by story-telling techniques can allow clients to reduce the emotional turmoil that often surrounds trauma and problems and enable them to view their difficulties from other per-spectives. In addition, story telling can creatively combine direct and indi-rect proposals for change, foster perceptions of control and mastery over problems and trauma, facilitate an awareness of unexpressed emotions, relieve feelings of guilt and anxiety, and reconnect the unconscious and conscious parts of self (Fairchild, 1990; Mays, 1990; Rhue & Lynn, 1991). It works best when counselors and therapists do not try to process stories and, after completing narratives, proceed to other subjects (Sperry, 1990).

Autogenic Training.   McBrian (1990) advocates clinical uses of self-hypnosis as an effective strategy for treating clients who are depressed.[2] Self-hypnosis, when correctly taught and regularly practiced, can facilitate the achievement of client goals and thus move clients away from the quag-

---

[2]*Self-hypnosis* is generally defined as a autogenic (self-directed) hypnotic state during which an indi-vidual makes self-directed hypnotic suggestions (Cochrane, 1991).

mire of depression and toward the action patterns that promote psychological growth. McBrian (1990) recommends that mental health professionals assume a role of educator and teacher instead of the traditional nonauthoritarian role of counselor or therapist. He suggests:

> Since the focus is on training the client to harness thoughts, images and mental rehearsal in order to become goal-directed and more satisfied in daily achievement, a teaching-learning attitude is required. The goals for self-hypnosis are simple: (a) to experience and enjoy the meditative, altered state of consciousness some refer to as trance; (b) to develop a positive mind-set that desired goals are being realized; (c) to accept and process unconsciously the direct and indirect suggestions which describe goal achievement; and (d) to mentally rehearse strategies for realizing the specific positive changes agreed on during counseling. (p. 483)

The use of collaboratively planned hypnotic interventions can promote a global extension of the effectiveness of the counseling or therapeutic process;[3] and Cochrane (1991) suggests the use of audiotaped interventions as an adjunct to counseling and psychotherapy strategies. Audiotapes can be commercially produced or can be created through the joint endeavor of the client and practitioner. Cooperatively planned interventions that coincide with a client's perception of the situation can offer a sense of personal empowerment. Counseling or therapeutic impact is enhanced when clients are willing to participate, have a sufficient capacity for absorption, are able to respect and acknowledge their own contribution to the audiotape, and regularly use the audiotape outside the counseling or therapeutic setting.

Conclusion

Mental health professionals whose approach to counseling and psychotherapy is predicated on the establishment of a cooperative, collaborative relationship and the promotion of client autonomy and self-worth have tended to avoid the incorporation of traditional hypnosis techniques into their mental health strategies (Sperry, 1990). Dreikurs (1962) views hypnosis as an interpersonal relationship between a dominant and a submissive person. He maintains that in a counseling or therapeutic situation,

---

[3]There are circumstances in which collaboratively planned hypnotic interventions are of limited value or even detrimental to the counseling and psychotherapy process. Collaborative hypnotic interventions work best with clients who are more advanced in the counseling or therapeutic process and have gained enough ego strength to experience confidence in their ability to fully participate in the process (Cochrane, 1991).

hypnotism is a manipulative misuse of power, creates a climate in which clients are extremely malleable, and represents a direct threat to the essential component of an effective counseling/therapeutic relationship: equality between practitioners and clients. During hypnosis, clients usually refrain from using their own critical-thinking processes and irrevocably accept and believe the ideas formulated by mental health professionals. In addition, Dreikurs (1962) warns that people who are hypnotized may not have a sense of their own accomplishments. Even when counselors and therapists merely mobilize the internal forces responsible for all the client transformations and beneficial effects achieved during sessions, clients are not likely to believe themselves to be the initiators of these changes and may attribute their positive growth to the expertise and power of mental health professionals.

Proponents of hypnosis maintain that individuals who are hypnotized are in total control of their trance experiences. They will not respond to hypnotic suggestions that contradict their personal value system and will only divulge information that they feel comfortable sharing with other individuals (Carich, 1990b). They argue, however, that professionals who use hypnotherapy in an authoritarian manner are also likely to be subtly controlling in their approach to counseling. Furthermore, they say that in any counseling or therapeutic situation, it is impossible for a practitioner's wishes not to have a tremendous impact on clients. It is extremely important for every mental health professional to consistently work at maintaining equality in the counseling or psychotherapy relationship. Whether or not practitioners include hypnosis in their strategy for treatment, the scales that balance power are weighted in favor of counselors and therapists. To achieve equality, practitioners must persistently promote counselor-client relationships that are based on mutual respect, self-determination, and autonomy.

ARTS IN COUNSELING AND PSYCHOTHERAPY

The use of arts in counseling and psychotherapy is probably the most ancient model of mental health intervention, yet it is only in recent years that art therapy orientations have begun to gain gradual acceptance in the mental health profession and receive recognition as distinct disciplines or primary counseling/therapeutic models (Rubin, 1988). Historically, as civilizations became more advanced and complicated, the use of art forms as sources for psychological healing gradually subsided. Models for mental health began to place more value on objective rather than subjective aspects of counseling and psychotherapy and rely on reaching the mind and effecting behavioral changes through verbal-oriented interventions (Seligman, 1985). During the past 20 years, creative arts disciplines have experienced renewed acceptance for two reasons. First, current literature indicates that verbal approaches to counseling and psychotherapy are often ineffective (Vernon, 1991); and second, it shows that the healing language of psychology is more effectively communicated through the arts, not through the logic of scientific reason (Hale, 1990).

Creative arts therapy is a coalition of diverse disciplines (for example, visual arts, dance, drama, and writing) that promote "the powers of creativity and nonverbal modes of expression as a means of healing" (Johnson, 1991, p. 1). Art counselors and therapists use art modalities in a counseling or therapeutic setting to encourage clients to express inner thoughts and feelings (Rubin, 1982). The focus on art forms is beneficial because artistic endeavors are relaxing, and clients become more receptive to interventions that promote insight into internal conflicts and mastery over difficult situations. These innovative methods of counseling and psychotherapy are especially effective with resistant clients, clients who are nonverbal, or those who have difficulty talking about their needs, emotions, and predicaments (Allan, 1991).

Many art therapy disciplines predominately base their theoretical framework on Jung's (1964) concept of human nature. His theory places less emphasis on maturational and developmental processes and focuses on the recurrence of mystical themes common to all humankind (Allan, 1991; Hale, 1990; Johnson, 1991; Pendzik, 1988). According to Jung, the personality is formulated from conscious and unconscious forces. He expanded Freud's concept of the unconscious to include two levels: the personal unconscious, which houses all repressed and forgotten material, and the collective unconscious, which is inherited and shared by all individuals. The collective unconscious is the repository of all common knowledge and experience accumulated by humans over the span of their existence. The archetypal self is the organizing principle of the collective unconscious, and knowledge of the self is expressed through images, symbols, and metaphors. The ego is postulated to emerge from the archetypal self, and a balanced communication between the logical ego and the intuitive self is necessary for psychological growth. "In order for the Ego to survive stress and to grow, it needs to maintain its connection with the instinctual roots of the psyche. Damage to this Ego-Self axis leads to feelings of alienation from the Self" (Allan, 1991, p. 5). The voice of the self relates original remembering that comes from the source, or collective unconscious; and when humans acknowledge, accept, and understand the images and symbols of the psyche, their inner life flourishes and grows. Jung (1964) believed that mandalas (such as circles, squares, triangles) were manifestations of the source that promotes ego growth and strength (Pendzik, 1988). Mandalas represent the psyche's effort to grow and restore itself, and tremendous healing powers are attributed to these symbols.

The first goal of art counselors and therapists is to create an accepting, safe atmosphere that will nurture remembering and a connection to the inner wisdom of the unconscious realm. Clients generally repress memories to protect themselves, and practitioners need to respect their rhythms of growth and follow their lead. Expressive-oriented mental health professionals listen attentively, support, and encourage disclosure without interpreting or judging the images and memories that emerge during the counseling and psychotherapy process. Art therapists are asking clients not only to remember personal dreams, childhood memories, and family history, but also to gather memories from the source of all wisdom—the collective unconscious—and translate those memories into experience (Hale, 1990).

One of the basic functions of arts counseling and psychotherapy is to facilitate this symbolic communication by making it manifest through art activities. The art modalities of music and poetry can be used to illustrate this principle. Music is effective in stimulating specific images because of the close proximity of the auditory cortex with the visual cortex and other sensory areas of the brain. When hearing music, clients often visualize colorful images or remember odors that trigger suppressed memories and emotions. Hale (1990) advocates the use of guided imagery and music (GIM) to promote the recollection of forgotten memories. GIM professionals assess the essence of clients (for example, their rhythm, voice tone, or mood) and play classical music designed to match the clients' own music. GIM differs from other guided imagery techniques because the music, not the practitioner's narrative, is used as the stimulus to awaken buried memories and wisdom. Counselors and therapists quietly guide the GIM process and interactively facilitate a counseling or therapeutic exploration of clients' disclosures. Similarly, poetry also cultivates the reminiscent process, the expression of intense emotions, and insight into past events and future possibilities (Getzel, 1983). A poetry-based treatment strategy can enable clients to transform images of dreams into colorful reality, give tangible form to longings and hopes, and musically write about their future potentialities (Emunah, 1990).

Numerous effective counseling and therapeutic disciplines are predicated on the use of arts, and most art modalities are easily adapted to other orientations (such as developmental models or psychoanalysis) (Landreth, 1987; Ornstein, 1985). In fact, bibliotherapy, role playing, and journaling are so commonly incorporated into other counseling and psychotherapy systems that professionals tend to forget that these interventions are actually creative arts modalities.

Creative arts are also appropriate with a variety of mental health models (such as group, individual, marriage, and family) and are effective with all age groups. For example, Getzel (1983) proposes that a poetry-focused group approach can assist people to encounter and work through the pervasive and painful losses associated with growing older. Nevertheless, because of space restrictions in the chapter, I have decided to use the rest of this section to focus on selected therapy applications for children and adolescents. The most common of these strategies are visual arts and writing, music, drama, and dance.

Visual Arts and Writing

Visual arts and writing are nonthreatening mediums through which clients can safely express fantasies and repressed emotions by creating analogies, symbols, and images that represent their unconscious turmoil (Allan, 1991). Artistic creations are often derived from remembrances and imagination; and as memories stimulate art, art kindles memories (Hale, 1990). Symbolic communication is generated through a wide array of sensory experiences that activate associations and conscious awareness of repressed memories and emotions. For instance, when clients work with various art forms, they are exposed to sounds, colors, textures, odors, and different body movements, and they are visually stimulated by their work (Hale, 1990). As clients reproduce their fantasies in a tangible form, their psychological growth is encouraged (Allan, 1991; Vernon, 1991).

Art counseling and psychotherapy is an excellent method of intervention for children and adolescents. Art activities can be soothing and relaxing to distraught youth, and the expression of art can facilitate the communication process between young people and adults. Most professionals recommend an open, nondirective approach to art counseling and psychotherapy with young clients (Allan, 1991; Rubin, 1988). The establishment of a trusting, egalitarian relationship is an essential component of effective counseling and psychotherapy, and practitioners can convey their respect for children by permitting them the right to choose art materials and the way these materials will be used in the counseling or therapeutic process. Moreover, young clients are often connected to their own curative processes and instinctively know what art forms will benefit them (Allan, 1991). When children are able to choose their medium of expression as well as what they will produce, they can determine what will be dealt with during sessions. As a result, they are in charge of their own healing process, feel autonomous, become self-responsible, and view the counselor or therapist as a helper rather than a director or a fixer (Rubin, 1988).

Serial Approaches.   John Allan (1991) incorporated the principles of Jung (1964) to develop a serial approach to creative arts therapy. Jung proposed that the unconscious is the source of psychological growth and that the healing potential of the psyche is activated when fantasy material is tangibly symbolized over time. The expression of art forms over time also allows counselors and therapists to obtain a clearer and more accurate understanding of clients' unconscious processes (Allan, 1991). Many mediums for art expression work well with the serial approach (for example, sand play, drama, writing, and sculpture), and the art form chosen should reflect preferred learning modalities of clients. Allan (1991) uses the art form of drawing to illustrate the serial art therapy format.

Serial drawing is a creative arts therapy approach that creates conditions that facilitate the unconscious drive toward psychological wellness. This intervention, in which young clients are requested to draw a picture during their weekly sessions, promotes a safe environment where children can systematically express internal pain and move toward the resolution of painful experiences. Counselors and therapists refrain from analysis and interpretation of drawings and encourage clients to create images and allow those images to direct their unique path toward healing. The themes of these drawings often denote overwhelming feelings of hopelessness and lack of control over situations, and they can reflect clients' perceptions of themselves and their world. Young people's distinctive patterns for healing are revealed through the serial approach. They often choose one symbolic theme during serial drawing to move themselves toward healthier modes of coping with traumatic situations, and practitioners can use this theme to systematically track psychological growth. Serial drawing can be used in a wide variety of settings and is especially suitable for working with children in the educational system.

Cox and Price (1990) advocate a highly structured serial arts therapy program for people who are chemically dependent, family members of substance abusers, adult children of alcoholics, and individuals with eating disorders. Their approach, which combines creative arts therapy with 12-step work, is particularly suitable for adolescent substance abusers. These adolescents are typically resistant to treatment programs, enjoy using chemicals, and emphatically deny that their behavior is problematic. Adolescents express themselves through music, drama, dance, and art; and resistance to treatment programs can be reduced when counseling or therapeutic interventions appeal to clients' creative propensities. This program uses *incident drawings* to break through the denial, engage adolescents in the counseling process, facilitate the acceptance that the addiction is a disease, and encourage adolescents to participate fully in the treatment program. The intervention is based on the concept of incident writing as it is used in trauma resolution therapy (Collins & Carson, 1989). In incident writing, clients are requested to write about a situation that occurred while they were drinking or using drugs. They must personalize their narrative (that is, use *I* or *me*), describe the experience in the past tense, limit discussion to the incident, and be as accurate as possible in recalling the event. As they write, clients are asked to describe their emotional reactions, invited to orally share the essay, and receive feedback about their experience. Incident drawing follows much the same format. Adolescents are instructed to draw or paint a picture that illustrates an incident that happened while they were "using" and are encouraged to be aware of what they are feeling as they draw. This technique facilitates understanding of how addiction is connected to previous losses and pain and how substance abuse directly contributes to further traumatic experiences. It also enables adolescents to work through developmental issues that may have been impeded by the use of drugs.

Although the incident drawing technique is powerful when used individually, Cox and Price (1990) recommend that this intervention be combined with the principles of group counseling and psychotherapy. When clients share memories with a group, they are "able to see more objectively the devastating effects substance abuse has had on others, as well as get feedback on the 'incidents' from their peers" (p. 335). The group interaction promotes the concept that drug or alcohol dependency is a disease and that outside assistance is necessary to recover from its debilitating influences.

Drama, Music, and Dance

Adolescence is a time of tremendous upheaval, and the normal course of adolescence can create sources of unmanageable distress for young people. During this transitional state from childhood to adulthood, adolescents are faced not only with new challenges, but also with the reemergence of unresolved conflicts from earlier developmental states (Golden & Sherwood, 1991). Adolescents need a release for their inner turmoil, and the creative arts can provide a constructive and acceptable means for expressing inner explosiveness typical of this developmental period (Allan, 1991).

Emunah (1990) maintains that creativity is an intrinsic function of the adolescent developmental stage. She suggests that counselors who work with adolescents can take advantage of this natural propensity by eclectically incorporating various modes of art expression into their strategies for intervention. A flexible approach to art therapy seems to work best with adolescents when distinct developmental tasks are paired with specific art modalities that reflect the emotions and struggles encountered during different stages of psychological growth. For example, the process of separation and identification of self often includes mourning the loss of childhood and dependence on parents; and adolescents can use the internal or solitary arts of painting, writing, poetry, or journaling to work through the trauma of grieving and loss. The more external and collaborative arts, such as dance and drama, can be employed to encourage peer socialization and satisfactory interpersonal relationships. In addition, music can reduce psychological tensions and can be used to express emotional states, drama can facilitate the development of self-identity, and movement and dance can help clients explore an awareness of self (Bowman, 1987; Emunah, 1990). Goldman (1986) advocates a similar integrated creative arts approach for children and adolescents. Her school-based group intervention program for young people who are experiencing trauma related to parental separation and divorce incorporates the art modalities of photography, drawing, journaling, and drama to help young people master feelings of anxiety, anger, rejection, and loss that are frequently associated with the crisis of divorce.

Dramatic Approach.   "Drama therapy is the intentional use of the dramatic medium for the purpose of healing, integration and growth" (Pendzik, 1988, p. 81). This art modality facilitates a sense of mastery and inner control by providing an arena where clients can symbolically act out aggressive impulses; work through and integrate unresolved developmental and psychological issues; gain insight into interpersonal distortions and maladaptive behaviors; experiment with behavioral changes and future roles; and learn, practice, and master alternative responses and adaptive ways of coping with life situations (Allan, 1991; Emunah, 1990; Irwin, 1987). Dramatic presentations encourage clients to take behavioral risks because playing a role in a drama allows them to separate partially from their ego selves, and the make-believe context of drama creates a distance that facilitates the expression of unacceptable feelings or unwanted aspects of personality. Although players become immersed in their roles, they still must retain a connection with reality so they can interact with other performers on the stage (Pendzik, 1988). Drama is the art form that most closely resembles daily life; and because of this link, insights and skills acquired during dramatic rehearsals can be easily generalized to real-life situations (Emunah, 1990).

The expression of self through drama is an excellent intervention strategy for adolescents and children (Irwin, 1987). This modality allows them to channel excessive sources of energy into more creative pursuits; undergo catharsis of undesirable emotions; and symbolically play out confusing dreams, memories, conflicts, fantasies, and experiences. In addition, drama-based group counseling or psychotherapy promotes cooperation and self-responsibility when group members are allowed to write, direct, and produce their own plays. Adolescent creations are characteristically autobiographical, and dramatic themes will typically include common adolescent developmental dilemmas such as narcissism, aggressiveness, and exhibitionism; conflicts with family members and authority figures; and issues related to morality, dependence-independence, and the development of self-identity (Allan, 1991).

During dramatic enactments, counselors and therapists can devise interventions that promote the healing potential of drama. For example, clients can change their perceptions about problems and acquire more effective methods of responding to difficulties when scenes are frozen, discussed, and played out with different endings. Clients can also gain new perspectives on situations by enacting roles of significant others with whom they are in conflict, watching other thespians impersonate their character, or witnessing a mirror (mimic) of their performance (Emunah, 1990; Pendzik, 1988).

The mirroring technique is a tool that is often used to interface drama with counseling and psychotherapy. This technique echoes conflicts back to clients and allows them to maintain a distance between themselves and distressful situations. Mirroring can be used in a variety of ways. Actors can improvise dramas based on personal experiences that have been submitted by members of an audience, counselors and therapists can dramatize clients' unspoken emotions, or performances can be videotaped and played back to clients or group members. When mirroring is combined with constructive feedback from professional leaders or group members, it facilitates innovative methods of coping and creative problem-solving skills. In addition, the production of artwork (such as painting, sculpture, or videotape), when reflected back to clients, contributes to their sense of mastery, achievement, completion, and self-esteem (Rubin, 1988).

Conclusion

Creative arts are making significant contributions to all aspects of the field of mental health. Art modality interventions are especially effective in working with people who are traumatized, disabled, or have special needs (Vernon, 1991).

Art therapy is distinguishing itself in the treatment of sexual abuse and trauma by helping patients access their hidden memories. Dance therapy is discovering new pathways into the treatment of eating disorders and traumatic brain injuries. Music therapy is now well established as critical in the treatment of dementias and Alzheimer's disease, and truly exciting discoveries are on the horizon in the treatment of chronic pain and auto-immune diseases. Drama and poetry therapy are being used extensively in the treatment of post-traumatic stress disorder and substance abuse. (Johnson, 1991, p. 3)

Art provides clients with an outlet for internalized emotions; but, more important, it allows them to spend time with those feelings, and gain mastery over them (Allan, 1991). Through art activities, clients connect their intrinsic sources of wisdom to real-life events, discover their own solutions to difficulties, and use self-originated mechanisms to control inner impulses and turmoil. Changes and growth are perceived as belonging to the self rather than being caused by external forces, and this internalization process contributes to clients' sense of achievement and self-esteem (Emunah, 1990).

PLAY THERAPY

The development of inner resources necessary to cope with life experiences is a graduated process beginning in infancy and continuing throughout the entire life span (Bettleheim, 1977). During childhood, play is the process humans use to accomplish these developmental goals (Allan, 1987). Unfortunately, circumstances can occur during childhood that reduce or inhibit the ability to learn and grow through the natural maturation process of play.

Children have an intrinsic need to be nurtured and protected by significant others. Unconditional love and healthy structure enables children to thrive and grow (Clarke & Dawson, 1989). Conversely, young people who encounter neglect, abuse, losses, or other detrimental environmental conditions often experience diminished capacities to enjoy and explore their internal and external worlds, and they can manifest developmental delays or arrests or can revert to earlier developmental levels to obtain comfort and avoid intolerable frustrations (Chess, 1988). People who have experienced childhood deficiencies often protect themselves from overwhelming emotions by withdrawing, numbing themselves, or manifesting aggressive and acting-out behaviors. They view the world as an unsafe place and build impenetrable barriers to ward off further assaults to their psyche (Miller & Boe, 1990).

Play therapy is recommended as an effective strategy for children. It gives children the opportunity to resolve trauma by encouraging them to externalize their fears, emotions, and fantasies; develop a sense of mastery over feelings and events; and subsequently increase control over their inner turmoil (Allan & Berry, 1987). The primary objective of play therapy is not to solve specific problems but to facilitate healthy developmental growth. This aspiration is achieved through the following goals (Landreth, 1987):

- The initiation of a protective and loving counseling or therapeutic relationship that nurtures the capacity to bond and form healthy attachments to adults

- The development of an unconditionally safe, liberated, and empathetic atmosphere in which children can autonomously explore and learn about themselves and their world

- The provision of alternate forms of communication that promote expression of experiences, thoughts, and emotions

- The unconditional acceptance and promotion of children's efforts to express their underlying thoughts and feelings

- The facilitation of conditions that foster self-determined problem-solving and coping skills

The History and Development of Play Therapy

Play approaches are grounded on the principles of developmental psychology (Landreth, 1987) and relationship therapy (Moustakas, 1959); and they draw heavily from the theoretical maxims of Jung, Freud, Adler, and Piaget (Ornstein, 1985). The first documented case of the use of play in counseling or therapy was the classical child analysis of Little Hans by Sigmund Freud in 1909 (Landreth, 1987). Within five years, Hermine Hug-Hellmunth began to emphasize a psychoanalytic play approach to child counseling and therapy, and Melanie Klein and Anna Freud elaborated on the use of play for analysis and treatment of young clients (Conn, 1989). Klein advocated interpretation as the vital component of the treatment process and maintained that counseling or therapeutic gains would not be accomplished until practitioners enabled children to consciously and unconsciously understand the true meaning behind their play behaviors. Anna Freud believed there were other factors involved in the healing process and made a significant contribution to child counseling and therapy when she introduced the concept that the emerging client-practitioner relationship was also an important contingency in the counseling/therapeutic process (Ornstein, 1985).

In the early 1930s, David Levy introduced the experimental play method that focused on the abreactive effects of play, and Jacob Conn (1989) developed the play interview method.[4] Later in the decade, therapists such as Fred Allan, Otto Rank, Jesse Taft, Frederick Allen, and Cuthbert Rogerson introduced the relationship approach, which de-emphasized analysis and interpretations and promoted the relationship between counselors or therapists and clients as the major curative factor for psychological healing (Conn, 1989; Moustakas, 1959). The following decades were periods of advancement and refinement for the emerging field of play therapy. Virginia Axline (1947) applied nondirective counseling and therapeutic principles to play therapy, and Moustakas (1959) made important amplifications on the theory, practice, and applications of the relationship approach. Play therapy was now advanced as an effective strategy for mental health prevention and intervention, and it was promoted as a method to address the developmental needs of children. In fact, many professionals maintained that until children attained more advanced verbal and cognitive developmental levels, meaningful communication between children and adults could only occur through expressive play activities (Landreth, 1987).

Contributions of Relationship Approaches to Play Therapy.   The major focus of relationship counseling and psychotherapy centers on the relationship that emerges during the counseling/therapeutic process. Proponents of this orientation maintain that the counseling or psychotherapy relationship is the essential factor in determining whether or not treatment strategies will benefit clients. They also maintain that psychological growth will only occur when a genuine and fundamental relatedness exists between counselors or therapists and clients. Clients of all ages are regarded as unique individuals with internal resources to determine their own path of self-development, and this capacity for self-actualization is nurtured and encouraged through unconditional love, acceptance, and respect. Relationship-oriented practitioners relate to clients in the present, begin where clients begin, and deal with here-and-now feelings rather than the investigation and interpretation of underlying causes for symptomatic behaviors. The main goal of relationship counseling and psychotherapy is not to change clients, but to allow them to discover and develop innate

---

[4]During play interview therapy, children are provided with dolls that represent themselves and significant others, and they are encouraged to dramatize dialogues that symbolically express their thoughts, fears, and conflicts. The goal of play interview therapy is the resolution of difficulties through children's realizations of their contribution to problematic situations and the development of new strategies for coping and dealing with problems (Conn, 1989).

methods of coping with adversity, solving problems, adapting to life situations, and achieving psychological equilibrium (Moustakas, 1959).

Relationship-based counseling and therapy are advocated as effective methods of treating the emotional and behavioral problems of childhood (Brenner, 1988). When relationship and play orientations are combined, children are further empowered and given a sense of value and self-worth. Relationship-based counselors and therapists use play to encourage autonomous exploration and grant children the right to determine how they themselves will initiate the healing process, get in touch with their feelings, recognize their unique potentiality, and orchestrate their own positive growth (Allan, 1987). This nondirective play approach is especially useful for children who have experienced trauma (Miller & Boe, 1990).

Contributions of Developmental Approaches to Play Therapy. Counseling and therapeutic strategies for adolescents and children are more effective when they are formulated from a developmental perspective (Landreth, 1987). Children are not miniature adults, and they process experiences differently during their course of growth because of the continuous changes in their physical, cognitive, social, and emotional skills (Brandell, 1988). These developmental processes (such as mental operations, communication skills, and perception of rules) have a direct impact on symptoms manifested by children and can determine whether counseling or therapeutic interventions will be beneficial, useless, or even injurious to their psychological health. For example, intervention strategies based on the use of abstract rules for behavioral control will generally be confusing, overwhelming, and detrimental to the self-esteem of children who are in the preoperational phase of their development (Kendall, Lerner, & Craighead, 1984). In addition, children and adolescents are more vulnerable to developmental disturbances due to their rapid cognitive and emotional growth, and their ability to cope is dependent on the availability of consistent, stable, nurturing, protecting, and healthy attachment figures. When children perceive the world as an unsafe place and are not offered protection by significant others, their capacity to think, feel, and cope is significantly diminished; they become increasingly more vulnerable to stressful life events (Campos, 1988; Miller & Boe, 1990). According to developmental counselors and therapists, necessary life-sustaining skills are germinated and rehearsed through children's play (Ornstein, 1985). Developmental play therapy provides an appropriate means of expression and communication for children, addresses their individual needs, and assists them in resolving developmental and environmental dilemmas (Landreth, 1987).

The Process of Play Therapy

According to Landreth (1987), play therapy

> is a way of being, a way of relating, a vehicle of communication, and a form of personal expression. Through spontaneous and self-generated play activities, children express and explore their fears, frustrations, concerns, and hopes. Through the process of acting out a living relationship with the counselor, children experience the meaning of self-responsibility, explore alternative behaviors that are more satisfying, and discover new dimensions of themselves that result in revised self-images and new behaviors. (p. 259)

Play therapy is generally conducted in a playroom that is stocked with a diverse variety of play materials. This is the children's place, a sanctuary from the outside world where they learn to love, trust, and explore; discover the healing potential of interpersonal relationships; and become aware of their unique intrinsic capabilities (Allan, 1987). The room and the counselor or therapist become constants in children's lives. Outside the playroom, children have little control over changes, but within this space, they are in charge (Moustakas, 1959).

The toys and play materials are selected according to the possible contribution they will make to the objectives of play therapy. For example, family dolls and puppets are useful in creating dramas and play activities that reflect fears, conflicts, and difficulties with significant others; and punch dolls can encourage the release of hostility and aggression in socially acceptable ways. Although the collection of toys should be eclectic, it is not necessary to have toys that represent every experience children may encounter. Children have powerful imaginations and tremendous capacities for projection, and they can make almost any object represent what they want (Campos, 1988). It is also important to include an assortment of generic toys (such as cars, boats, paper, and pencils) that children can use for noncommittal play activities while they become comfortable with the counseling or psychotherapy setting (Moustakas, 1959). Play materials should be uncomplicated and in good condition. Highly structured (that is, mechanical) or broken play objects may inhibit children's ability to express themselves (Landreth, 1987).

Through the structuring statements of counselors or therapists, children are granted the freedom to use their own capacities and skills and be autonomously responsible for their actions and decisions (Moustakas, 1959). Healing comes through expression and play. Although practitioners consistently facilitate developmental growth by being actively, unconditionally, and empathetically present for children, the direction and pace of the healing process is set by young clients (Allan, 1991; Miller & Boe, 1990).

Children's road to recovery can often seem confusing and uncertain to mental health professionals, and patience is an important quality in those who work with children. Practitioners indicate their unconditional respect and regard for young clients by allowing them to direct their own path toward psychological growth. As Moustakas (1959) says:

> Waiting is a positive force, a commitment of faith actively expressed by the therapist. This is in direct contrast to the psychoanalytic approach in which the therapist quickly establishes himself as a powerful person as quickly as possible in order to direct the therapeutic process and to involve the child in a dependency relationship. (p. 2)

Conjointly, Ornstein (1985) warns that professional overinvolvement in children's play activities (for example, interpretation) can be disruptive to the natural play process. Nondirective treatment strategies enable children to immerse themselves hypnotically in play activities and tap into essential life forces. In addition, refraining from interpretation can enable children to maintain a safe distance from the original trauma, freely express psychological distress through the use of metaphors, and gain a sense of ownership over discovered insights and new methods of coping (Miller & Boe, 1990).

Although the atmosphere of the playroom is permissive, the setting of limits is one of the most important components of play therapy. Limits are necessary to the counseling or therapeutic process and provide the boundaries and structure in which growth occurs. Moreover, relationship bonds are formed when children accept the limits established by counselors or therapists. Aside from the time limit of sessions and the mandatory health and safety limits, the boundaries that evolve out of the counseling or psychotherapy relationship depend on the uniqueness of the child, the practitioner, and the situation. Typically, children accept these boundaries, but occasionally they will refuse to comply with the requests of counselors or therapists. These resistant behaviors represent a break in relationship bonds, and counselors and therapists must determine how they can simultaneously enforce rejected limits and reestablish counseling or therapeutic connections with young clients (Moustakas, 1959).

Sand Play Approach to Play Therapy.   Sand play, an intervention formulated from the principles of Jungian psychology, was initiated by British pediatrician Margaret Lowenfeld (Allen & Berry, 1987) and further developed by Swiss psychologist Dora Kalff (Carey, 1990). Sand play is also strongly linked to the theories of developmental psychology. It is a nondirective, projective treatment strategy that offers clients the opportunity to project traumatic internal and external experiences metaphorically onto containers filled with sand. This versatile intervention has no age barriers and has been effective in treating a variety of diagnostic categories (such as affective disorders, eating disorders, schizophrenia, autism, and post-traumatic stress disorders) (Carey, 1990; Miller & Boe, 1990).

Sand trays are containers, usually 20 by 30 by 4, in which clients use miniature objects to create their own sand worlds. The size of the tray is important because clients need ample space to work, yet they should be able to examine the entire sand world in a single glance. Clients are generally offered two sand trays, one containing wet sand and the other dry sand, and they are invited to select freely from a repertoire of miniature toys and objects and to play in the sand.

Sand play is an excellent intervention for children. Young people understand and trust the language of metaphor (Bettleheim, 1977), and their unconscious conflicts are quickly illustrated by the emerging sand pictures (Carey, 1990). Although children are unique in the expression of their inner strife, sand play therapy typically follows a movement from chaos to struggle to resolution. Initially, children tend to introduce chaotic conditions into their sand worlds. This stage generally lasts two to three sessions and reflects the emotional upheaval and overwhelming turmoil children are experiencing. Pandemonium is eventually replaced by struggle, and during this phase children create many different types of battles and events of annihilation. Over time, these clashes become more organized and balanced, heroes emerge, and death is less likely to occur. The sand drama gradually evolves into the resolution stage and begins to resemble the natural order of the universe. Animals may graze contentedly in fields protected by fences, people may live in houses, and automobiles may run smoothly on roadways that wind evenly through the countryside. In this phase, children's feelings of completion and resolution are often symbolically manifested through the introduction of squares, rectangles, and circles (Allan & Berry, 1987).

Conclusion

Observations of natural play have provided professionals with insight into the hidden windows of the mind and have revealed valuable information about the development and function of the psyche. Ornstein (1985) maintains that in many ways, play enactments resemble counseling or therapeutic dream work. Play and dreams both serve as connections between conscious behaviors and the healing powers of the psyche, and they both provide major sources for psychological growth. Play is similar to dreams in that it offers counselors and therapists a glimpse into the inner essence of clients; however, play can give practitioners additional opportunities to promote the healing process. Dreams ordinarily occur when clients are alone, and they may not be able to accurately remember or report the content of their dreams. Conversely, counselors or therapists are present during play and can observe, respond, and interact with the here-and-now process. Therefore, they can more fully encourage psychological healing.

MULTIMODAL THERAPY

Arnold A. Lazarus (1986) describes multimodal therapy (MMT) as "an overall *approach* that endeavors to use state-of-the-art technology and clinical acumen to enhance the broad enterprise of psychotherapy and to provide a systematic and comprehensive model for problem solving in various settings, systems, and agencies" (p. 102). This orientation, which he developed in 1981, is based on the assumption that clients are typically troubled by a multitude of specific and idiosyncratic problems. Therefore, an eclectic strategy for treatment should be formulated to deal with each individual problem. During his practice as a clinical psychologist, Lazarus discovered that the prognosis for enduring corrective change was significantly greater when a wider range of specific problems were systematically discharged during the counseling and psychotherapy process. Lazarus's original theoretical orientation was behavior therapy.[5] He became dissatisfied with this circumscribed form of treatment when 10 years of secondary posttreatment investigations indicated that clients who initially manifested positive outcomes to counseling and psychotherapy had high rates of relapse. He hypothesized that a broader-based approach would produce more enduring counseling and therapeutic changes, and he began advocating a broad-spectrum method of counseling and psychotherapy (1981). He described this approach as "systematic eclecticism" and called it MMT (Greenburg, 1982, p. 134).

Theoretically, this approach is formulated on principles from social learning theory but also draws heavily from systems theory and group and communication theory (Greenburg, 1982). The orientation is essentially behavioral, in that empirical methods of research are valued. However, MMT does not identify with any specific school of psychological thought, nor does it propose a new theory of counseling and psychotherapy (Weikel, 1990). MMT has a strong humanistic component because the uniqueness and self-determination of the individual is valued (Weed & Hernandez, 1990). It is also holistic because the approach is presumed to

---

[5]In 1958, Lazarus introduced the terms *behavior therapy* and *behavior therapist* into professional literature.

encompass the entire spectrum of complex human experiences and behaviors. MMT is flexible and adaptable, and practitioners of this approach are encouraged to incorporate counseling and therapeutic procedures from many epistemologically incompatible systems without necessarily subscribing to the underlying principles or beliefs of those systems (Lazarus, 1986). Thus, practitioners may elect to combine cognitive and behavioral techniques with Gestalt and Rogerian approaches to counseling and psychotherapy. Interventions are chosen according to their probability of effectiveness in dealing with individual qualities of clients, specific types of problems, and unique situations (Greenburg, 1982). Therefore, to employ the multimodal perspective successfully, professionals should be thoroughly knowledgeable about a variety of current counseling and therapeutic strategies (Weikel, 1990). The methods used will depend on the skills and background of the counselor or therapist; and when clients' needs require skills, training, and education outside practitioners' realm of expertise, they are expected to refer those clients to more appropriate mental health professionals (Ponterotto & Zander, 1984). The purpose of MMT "is to equip the client with as many prosocial, adaptive, coping responses as possible, based on the premise that lasting change calls for the implementation of a wide rage of techniques and strategies" (Lazarus, 1986, p. 96).

The Multimodal Approach

The multimodal orientation provides an integrative assessment and strategy for treatment that considers the whole person (Weed & Hernandez, 1990). Most problems are assumed to arise from deficits in the social learning process. However, this method recognizes that genetic endowment, physical environment, and social learning history interactively contribute to the unique complex patterns of behaviors manifested by individuals (Lazarus, 1981).

> Lazarus believes personality is formed, maintained and altered through many processes; classical and operant conditioning, modeling and vicarious learning, unobservable occurrences such as thoughts, feeling, images, and sensations; unconscious processes such as interpersonal distortions and avoidances and metacommunications. (Greenburg, 1982, p. 134)

Furthermore, individuals have different degrees and levels of awareness, idiosyncratic responses to environmental stimuli, and distinct unconscious processes that influence conscious actions, thoughts, and feelings (Lazarus, 1981). Lazarus proposed that there was a need for an approach that placed primary emphasis on the uniqueness of the individual and formulated a framework of seven specific and interrelated modalities to extensively examine clients' special sensory, imagery, cognitive, and interpersonal factors. This precise and comprehensive model for the assessment and treatment of behavior, affect, sensation, imagery, cognition, interpersonal relationships, and biological factors is represented by the acronym *BASIC-ID*.

BASIC-ID.   The BASIC-ID is presumed to incorporate all aspects of the human personality (Greenburg, 1982); and it is assumed that all behaviors (such as emotions, actions, thoughts) that are attributable to individuals can be accounted for by examining the components and interactions within their BASIC-ID (Lazarus, 1986). It is also considered essential for the counselor or therapist to recognize and include factors that are not addressed by the BASIC-ID, such as sociocultural, political, and other microenvironmental events (Lazarus, 1981).

B	**Behavior:** observable habits, activities
A	**Affect:** feelings and emotional responses
S	**Sensation:** senses, physical concerns
I	**Imagery:** internal visualizations, fantasies
C	**Cognitions:** thoughts, beliefs, goals, philosophies
I	**Interpersonal relationships:** interactions with others
D	**Drugs/biology:** diet, exercise, sleep habits, recreational, and therapeutic use of drugs

Comprehensive Multimodal Life History Questionnaire.   Typically, assessment begins with an initial interview and the comprehensive multimodal life history questionnaire (CMLHQ). This 12-page self-assessment inventory is an analysis of current behavior in the seven modalities of the BASIC-ID. It provides counselors and therapists with explicit information about past history, interpersonal relationships, important events, and specific problems in each modality; it examines the interaction among modalities; it indicates intervention strategies that are tailored to address clients' unique needs and styles of learning; and it investigates clients' expectations regarding the counseling or psychotherapy process (Weed & Hernandez, 1990; Weikel, 1990). During the initial session, practitioners use the BASIC-ID format to gather information about ongoing problems, antecedent events, and factors that maintain difficulties. Counselors and therapists generally focus on two interlocking questions: "What led to the present situation?" and "How is the problem being supported?" (Lazarus, 1981). Although the initial session is also used to foster rapport, it is not unusual for interventions to begin with this session. The CMLHQ is generally given to clients at the end of the first session to complete and bring to the second session.

Modality Profile.   MMT practitioners use the accumulated information from interviews and CMLHQ to complete a modality profile, or list of specific problems in each modality of the BASIC-ID. This profile, which can be modified throughout the course of treatment, serves as a blueprint for specific behavioral goals and ensures that all significant issues receive proper attention (Lazarus, 1986). A collaborative construction of the modality profile can facilitate movement and commitment in clients, and it is recommended that clients and practitioners interactively explore profile data, outline specific interventions that can ameliorate problems, and plan general strategies for treatment (Brunell, 1990).

Structural Profile.   Counselors and therapists can gain additional quantitative information about personality functioning by administering structural profiles. This questionnaire is based on a seven-point scale, and clients self-rate themselves in each dimension of the BASIC-ID by answering the following questions (Lazarus, 1986):

- *Behavior*.   How active and energetic are you? Do you keep busy? How much of a doer are you?
- *Affect*.   How deeply do you feel things? How emotional are you?
- *Sensation*.   How attuned are you to your five senses? How much do you focus on the pleasures and pains derived from your body?
- *Imagery*.   Do you engage much in daydreaming and fantasies? Do you have a vivid imagination?
- *Cognition*.   Do you analyze things thoroughly? How much of a thinker are you? Do you tend to mull things over?
- *Interpersonal*.   How important are other people to you? How much of a social being are you? Do you gravitate to people?
- *Drugs/biology*.   Are you physically healthy? Do you avoid overeating, ingestion of excessive alcohol, unnecessary drugs?

After clients complete self-rating scales, counselors or therapists can construct a bar diagram or graph to indicate personality preferences more clearly. Structural profiles are especially useful in couples counseling and psychotherapy because the profile can demonstrate areas of compatibility and noncompatibility. Clients may also complete the questionnaire according to how they believe their partner will rate them. This separate assessment can provide clients with valuable data about perceptions regarding self, partner, and interpersonal interactions (Lazarus, 1986).

Modality Firing Order.   Counselors and therapists can further individualize treatment strategies by helping clients systematically trace the modality (such as cognition or affect) sequence that precipitates emotional distress (Lazarus, 1986). The modality firing order is revealed as practitioners and clients explore the interaction among modalities and how clients contribute to their own emotional upheavals. The sequence is ranked, and the triggering modality indicates the starting point and the direction of treatment strategies (Weikel, 1990). "It is logical that the sequence of intervention follow the sequence in which clients create and maintain their problems" (Greenburg, 1982, p. 137). For example, anxiety can be precipitated by negative thoughts (C) and adverse images (I), which elicit feelings of fear (A) and trigger the physiological manifestations of anxiety. Firing orders are not always fixed, and response patterns can differ according to situations. However, most people tend to respond to and organize their world according to their favored representational system (for example, visual or sensory) and have a fairly well-established sequence of modality interaction (Lazarus, 1986).

Second-order BASIC-ID.   When counseling and psychotherapy methods prove ineffective or resistance to certain behavioral changes occurs, a second-order BASIC-ID helps professionals devise more appropriate strategies of intervention and overcome the treatment impasse. This procedure uses the BASIC-ID format to assess specific problem areas. Counselors and therapists might encourage clients to visualize how they would like to behave and how they would feel (emotionally and physically) if they behaved that way, vividly imagine themselves in the new behavior, fully explore their thoughts and emotions that are connected to this imagery, review how significant others will respond to this new behavior, and connect this total experience to their biological difficulties (Lazarus, 1986).

Application and Research

The behavioral component in the multimodal approach is reflected in the emphasis on concrete specification of problems, goals, and treatment strategies and systematic measurement of pre- and posttreatment differences in BASIC-ID. Lazarus (1986) conducted a thorough outcome assessment of MMT clients and determined that over an eight-year span, more than 75 percent of the clients achieved major treatment goals. Consistent, positive, and enduring outcomes have been reported in individual, group, family, and couple counseling and psychotherapy formats (Lazarus, 1981, 1986; Weed & Hernandez, 1990) and for specific problems such as agoraphobia, depression, mental retardation, anorexia nervosa, anxiety disorders, posttraumatic stress disorders, alcoholism, psychosomatic disorders, sexual dysfunction, and childhood disorders (Brunell, 1990; Keat, 1979; Lazarus, 1986; Ponterotto & Zander, 1984; Weed & Hernandez, 1990; Weikel, 1990).

Studies also indicate that the multimodal approach is especially effective in promoting and maintaining corrective changes in clients who have undergone long-term, unsuccessful attempts at counseling and psychotherapy; are resistant to treatment; or experience difficulties that are particularly unyielding to change. Lazarus (1986) suggests that the multimodal method can succeed in cases where less comprehensive and systematic approaches have failed. Follow-up data on clients who had an unfavorable prognosis for success indicate that over 50 percent of these "difficult" clients maintain or surpass their counseling or therapeutic goals.

This versatile, flexible, multidimensional approach can easily be adapted to address the needs of a multitude of professions, populations, situations, and settings. For example, the multimodal orientation is recommended as an approach to counselor or therapist education programs (Greenburg, 1982) and counselor or therapist supervision (Ponterotto & Zander, 1984). It is projected to be successful in many environments (such as classrooms, institutions, rehabilitation centers, and industry) (Lazarus, 1986; Weed & Hernandez, 1990); is appropriate for a wide range of populations (including children, adolescents, and adults who are older) (Keat, 1979; Weikel, 1990); and is used by many different professional fields (such as counseling, psychology, social work, education, and psychiatry).

Conclusion

The multimodal approach differs from other multifaceted methods in the level of systematic consideration given to each dimension of the client's BASIC-ID. Traditional counseling or therapy approaches tend to be limited in focus and only direct interventions toward a portion of the seven human modalities. For example, Gestalt therapy emphasizes affect, sensation, and imagery (Ponterotto & Zander, 1984), and rational-emotive therapy centers on how cognitive distortions influence emotions and behaviors (Weikel, 1990). According to Weikel (1990), "the major benefit of the multimodal approach is that it allows the mental health professional the freedom to work on any or all modalities in a systematic fashion" (p. 319). Other benefits include the following (Brunell, 1990; Lazarus, 1986):

- The BASIC-ID expedites the counseling or therapeutic objective to formulate systematically an eclectic strategy for treatment that appreciates the unique and special needs of clients.

- The framework of systematic evaluation immediately engages the interest, participation, and commitment of clients.

- The interaction among the modalities enables clients to gain insight through perceptions, emotions, or cognitions into how they choose to behave in certain ways and how these actions affect every phase of their lives.

- The development of specific interventions for identified difficulties reduces overwhelming global problems into distinct workable units and makes problems seem less insurmountable. Clients feel more hopeful when they experience small successes while working toward larger goals and are encouraged to use creative problem-solving processes to find workable solutions to difficulties. As progress occurs, clients begin internalizing a sense of control over their lives and manifesting more self-responsible behaviors.

TRANSPERSONAL PSYCHOLOGY

During recent years, there has been an increased interest in the theories and practices of transpersonal psychology (Walsh, 1992). This perspective, which emerged from the humanistic orientation of psychology as the fourth force in psychology (Sutich, 1969), is based on the assumption that humans possess the potential to ascend beyond the ordinary limits of the ego and attain higher levels of consciousness (Lajoie & Shapiro, 1992). According to the basic premise of transpersonal psychology, the discovery and exploration of the self is only one step toward mature development, and this perspective integrates the philosophies of Eastern traditions with Western psychologies to study states of higher consciousness (including mystical experiences, ecstasy, transcendence of self, altruism, wonder, cosmic awareness, and integration) and how these experiences relate to optimal psychological well-being (Koltko, 1989; Lajoie & Shapiro, 1992).

Eastern Philosophies

Eastern disciplines are based on a body of knowledge accumulated during several thousand years of human history (Muzika, 1990). This ancient epistemology is predominately concerned with experiences, teachings, and techniques that address issues such as the interrelatedness of all things in the universe, human suffering, spiritual awareness, and methods of achieving peacefulness and harmony with internal and external phenomena (Atwood & Maltin, 1990).

Typically, Eastern philosophical thought proposes that objects in the universe, including the self, are not separate and absolute but are connected and interwoven, fluid and ever-changing. While most Western mental health approaches focus on the reconstruction and growth of the ego as a prerequisite for psychological health, many Eastern traditions maintain that the ego can never be healthy, that very presence of the self is the root of all psychological problems. Furthermore, Eastern philosophers assume there are two realities—the human interpretation of reality and reality beyond human knowledge—and consider the concept of self to be an illusion created by human perception (Atwood & Maltin, 1991; Bogart, 1991). Humans are believed to be severely constricted in the ways in which they comprehend and encounter life. They perceive phenomena from a personal position and only come to know the surface of experience. When humans can detach themselves from idiosyncratic emotions, perceptions, body experiences, and a directedness toward their pseudo-self, they become more open to expanded feelings, ideas, memories, and somatic sensations. This new awareness is attained without intent and enables humans to adapt an altered sense of identification and consciousness (Atwood & Maltin, 1991; Muzika, 1990).[6]

> The highest aim for followers of Eastern traditions is to become aware of the unity and mutual interrelation of all things, to transcend the notion of an isolated individual self, and to identify themselves with the ultimate reality. The emergence of this awareness—known as Enlightenment—is not only an intellectual act, but an experience involving the whole person and is religious in its ultimate nature.[7] (Atwood & Maltin, 1991, p. 369)

Eastern traditions are centered around the acquisition of mindfulness or an intense focus on here-and-now situations, sensations and movements, transcendental experiences, and transcendence into states of enlightenment. Transcendence is often first experienced when people begin to question their basic belief systems and, through intuitive flashes, become more aware of the many different planes of reality and how the

---

[6]The intellect is not viewed as the source of knowledge but rather a tool to analyze and interpret experiences, and humans gain pure understanding through detached observation devoid of cognitive interference (Atwood & Maltin, 1991).

[7]Religion is considered to be a state of global awareness, a knowledge of one's place in the universe (Atwood & Maltin, 1991).

duality of cognitive processes (for example, thoughts created by the mind versus pure thoughts achieved by sudden awareness, insight, and intuition) contribute to the different grades of reality (Alexander, Rainforth & Gelderloos, 1991). Enlightenment or transcendental consciousness is a recognition of what already exists before it is obscured and distorted by inconsequential and constricted surface perceptions (Tart & Deikman, 1991). Most Eastern disciplines consider the development of mindfulness to be a precursor to the ultimate goal of transcendental consciousness and have developed specific techniques, such as meditation, that promote mindfulness and enlightenment (Bogart, 1991; Tart & Deikman, 1991).

Meditation.   Although meditation is a fairly new phenomena to Western psychological orientations, it is one of the oldest traditions of counseling and psychotherapy (Walsh, 1992). Meditation enhances the processes of attending and memory, promotes total absorption in an activity, and inspires action to complete goals. In addition, this acquired mindfulness allows people to attend to internal processes from a distance and thus facilitates control over thoughts and emotions (Atwood & Maltin, 1991; Muzika, 1990). Current research has indicated the existence of a positive correlation between meditation and healthy mental states (Koltko, 1989). Studies show this act of reflective contemplation can promote deep relaxation combined with states of heightened alertness; reduce anxiety; and increase perceptual sensitivity, empathy, longevity, and tolerance for pain (Walsh, 1992). Although meditation does not automatically improve psychological difficulties, it does facilitate an awareness of mental and emotional processes, mastery over compulsive behaviors, effective coping skills, insight into realities about internal and external phenomena, altruism, and the development of transcendental consciousness (Atwood & Maltin, 1991; Bogart, 1991; Koltko, 1989; Wilber, 1989b).

Transcendence and Human Development

Models of human development are based on the premise that humans mature through an interrelated sequence of developmental stages. Many mental health professionals are now suggesting that the full realization of higher states of consciousness also naturally unfold through a progression of stages and that the scheme of human development should be expanded to include an advanced component of human growth: spiritual development (Alexander et al., 1991; Atwood & Maltin, 1991; Muzika, 1991; Wilber, 1989a, 1989b). This extended theory of human development suggests "that what we may have thought as normality may be a form of arrested development" (Walsh, 1992, p. 25).

Alexander et al. (1991) advocate a model of human growth that surpasses the basic stages of cognitive development suggested by traditional developmental models. They hypothesize that an entirely new mode of knowing exists for humans—a higher state of consciousness that can naturally emerge at the postrepresentational tier of development. Their model proposes that it is not necessary for humans to reach a mature, well-integrated level of functioning before they can achieve transcendence. Conversely, the development of higher states of consciousness is made possible through a systematic model (for example, the transcendental meditation [TM] program) that strengthens the ego and teaches and promotes transcendental levels of consciousness.

> The capacity to transcend may not just be available to a privileged few but the birthright of all which can be reclaimed through use of an appropriate technology of consciousness such as the TM program. Cultivation of transcendence through such a technique appears to make a critical contribution to alleviating psychological distress, promoting self-actualization, and ultimately, developing higher states of consciousness far beyond the ordinary endpoint of human growth. (Alexander et al., 1991, p. 239)

Unfortunately, stressors of daily living can inhibit the natural ability to achieve transcendence, and certain socialization practices discourage the freedom to explore, understand, and express feelings; to be spontaneous and creative; to use intuitive abilities; and to be unique. Therefore, human development generally becomes arrested at the concrete or abstract reasoning stages (Alexander et al., 1991).

Wilber has incorporated the developmental stages of child, adult, and spiritual into a single continuum model of development and suggests that the latter stages of adult psychological growth merge into the lower levels of spiritual maturation (Wilber, Engler, & Brown, 1986). Transcendence contributes to all stages of growth (that is, child through spiritual), and all higher stages include the basic needs and concerns of the lower stages. The highest stages are not finite but are beginnings of an unending process toward boundless, ever-changing developmental growth (Wilber, 1989a).

Conclusion

The purpose of transpersonal psychology is not to displace traditional models of psychology but to advance existing theories by assimilating them into an expanded visualization of human potentiality. This orientation proposes that all perspectives on human nature are partial and that no single theory, including transpersonal, represents the whole truth.

Rather than fighting for the exclusive dominance of one perspective over others, transpersonal psychology suggests that apparently conflicting schools may address different perspectives, dimensions, and stages and may therefore be partly complementary. For example, Freudian psychology and object relations theory may address important issues of early development, and existential psychology and therapy may speak particularly to universal issues confronting mature adults. Behavior therapy may point to the importance of identifying specific environmental reinforcers that maintain appropriate and inappropriate behavior, and cognitive therapies may help us appreciate the power of unrecognized thoughts and beliefs. Likewise, multidimensional schools such as Jungian psychology and psychosynthesis point to, among other things, the possibility of transpersonal development and the therapeutic power of images and symbols. Asian systems such as Buddhist, Yogic, and Vedantic psychologies may compliment Western approaches by, for example, pointing out the therapeutic and transpersonal developmental power of ethic, meditation, and attentional training. (Walsh, 1992, p. 26-27)

SUMMARY

Most of the traditional approaches to counseling and psychotherapy rely on interventions that require an ability to comprehend and communicate information orally about mental and emotional processes. These forms of therapy can be unproductive with clients who do not fully acknowledge, sense, or understand overt and covert behaviors, thoughts, and feelings. Recent studies indicate that treatment strategies are more effective when they are tailored to address individual qualities, embrace unique resources, and reflect special requirements and preferred learning modalities of clients. Mental health professionals can better accommodate specific needs of clients when alternative approaches to counseling and psychotherapy are incorporated into treatment strategies. This chapter focuses on five nontraditional approaches to counseling and psychotherapy: hypnotherapy, nonverbal-oriented therapies (such as art therapy and play therapy), multimodal therapy, and transpersonal psychology.

Hypnotherapy is an eclectic intervention that can be successfully used with a variety of counseling and therapeutic models and is effective with a wide range of mental health difficulties. Hypnotherapists emphasize equality in counseling and therapeutic relationships; do not consider a trance to be a necessary condition for corrective change; and endeavor to create a collaborative, individualized, and empowering hypnotic atmosphere in which clients can transcend conscious limitations and access their own untapped reservoir of internal wisdom and personal experiences. Hypnotherapy can help reduce emotional barriers to unconscious memories and motivations and facilitate receptive states in which clients

spontaneously discover their own solutions to problems, change negative experiences, and autonomously achieve positive growth. The ultimate goal of hypnotherapy is personal mastery, competence, and self-responsibility.

Creative arts therapy includes a variety of disciplines (visual arts, dance, drama, writing) that use art modalities in a counseling or therapeutic setting to promote autonomous healing, integration, and growth. Art allows clients to symbolically externalize and express emotions, memories, and thoughts; spend time with their own experience; gain mastery over their inner processes; and reconnect with their inner sources of wisdom, courage, and power. Creative arts therapy is effective as a primary approach to counseling and psychotherapy or as an adjunct to other theoretical orientations. It is useful for all age groups and with a variety of mental health models (group, individual, family, marriage). Art modality interventions are especially appropriate for children and adolescents, clients who have been traumatized, clients who are nonverbal, or clients who have difficulty connecting with and expressing their thoughts and feelings. The effectiveness of creative arts therapy is further enhanced when treatment strategies are designed to reflect and complement issues unique to individual developmental stages of growth.

The natural maturation process of childhood play advances the development of inner resources necessary for the ability to cope with life experiences. Circumstances can occur during childhood that impede or circumvent this intrinsic right to learn and grow through play. Play therapy is recommended as an effective strategy for children. The approach is grounded in the principles of developmental psychology and relationship therapy. By providing a safe, protective, accepting, and predictable environment in which children can express and explore their fears, anger, sadness, pain, and personal needs, play therapy re-creates necessary conditions of unconditional love and healthy structure that enable children to thrive and grow. The primary objective of play therapy is to facilitate healthy developmental growth; and the combination of the counselor-client relationship, metaphoric communication, and unstructured play promotes healing and the development of self-determined, life-sustaining skills.

Multimodal therapy is based on the assumption that clients are typically troubled by a multitude of specific, individual problems and that prognosis for enduring corrective change is significantly greater when these problems are systematically addressed during the counseling or therapeutic process. This versatile, flexible approach advocates a multidimensional model for assessment and treatment: the BASIC-ID. This precise and comprehensive treatment strategy encompasses the entire range of human experience and behavior and examines seven separate yet interrelated dimensions of overt and covert behavior, interpersonal data, and

biological factors. Interventions are eclectic and chosen according to individual needs, qualities, situations, and learning styles. The multimodal approach is appropriate for numerous professions, populations, situations, and settings. It adapts well to most counseling and psychotherapy formats (group, individual, family, couple) and is effective with a diverse range of specific problems (anxiety disorders, eating disorders, depression, posttraumatic stress disorder, drug or alcohol abuse, and childhood disorders). The ultimate goal of multimodal therapy is to promote the realization that behavior is self-determined and to encourage self-responsibility and adaptation of healthier modes of coping and solving problems.

Transpersonal psychology is grounded on the premise that humans possess an inherent potential to transcend the ordinary limits of the ego and attain higher levels of consciousness. This perspective integrates the philosophies of Eastern traditions and Western psychologies to study higher states of consciousness and how these experiences relate to mental well-being. Transpersonal psychology advances the traditional models of human development to include elevated components of human growth. This spiritual dimension of development surpasses the basic stages of cognitive development and represents a higher state of consciousness and a new mode of knowing for humans. Transcendence is made possible through systematic meditation and is considered to be a natural stage in the cycle of human development.

REFERENCES

Alexander, C., Rainforth, M., & Gelderloos, P. (1991). Transcendental meditation, self-actualization, and psychosocial health: A conceptual overview and statistical meta-analysis. *Journal of Social Behavior and Personality, 6*(5), 189–247.

Allan, J. (1987). Counseling with expressive arts: Overview. *Elementary School Guidance & Counseling, 21*(4), 251–252.

Allan, J. (1991). *Inscapes of the child's world: Jungian counseling in schools and clinics.* Dallas: Spring.

Allan, J., & Berry, P. (1987). Sandplay. *Elementary School Guidance & Counseling, 21* (4), 300–306.

Allan, J., & Clark, M. (1984). Directed art counseling. *Elementary School Guidance and Counseling, 14,* 39–46.

Atwood, J., & Maltin, L. (1991). Putting Eastern philosophies into Western psychotherapies. *American Journal of Psychotherapy, 45*(3), 368–381.

Axline, V. (1947). *Play therapy.* New York: Ballantine.

Bettleheim, B. (1977). *The uses of enchantment: The meaning and importance of fairy tales.* New York: Random House.

Bogart, M. (1991). The use of meditation in psychotherapy: A review of the literature. *American Journal of Psychotherapy, 45*(3), 383–412.

Bowman, R. (1987). Approaches for counseling children through music. *Elementary School Guidance & Counseling, 21*(4), 284–289.

Brandell, J. (1988). Narrative and historical truth in child psychotherapy. *Psychoanalytic Psychology, 5*(3), 241–247.

Brenner, A. (1988). From acting out to verbalization. *Journal of Contemporary Psychotherapy, 18*, 179–192.

Brunell, L. (1990). Multimodal treatment of depression: A strategy to break through the "strenuous lethargy" of depression. *Psychiatry in Private Practice, 8*(3), 13–22.

Campos, L. (1988). Empowering children II: Integrating protection into script prevention work. *Transactional Analysis Journal, 18*(2), 137–140.

Carey, L. (1990). Sandplay therapy with a troubled child. *The Arts in Psychotherapy, 17*, 197–209.

Carich, M. (1990a). The basics of hypnosis and trancework. *Individual Psychology, 46*(4), 401–410.

Carich, M. (1990b). Hypnotic techniques and Adlerian constructs. *Individual Psychology, 46*(2), 166–177.

Chess, S. (1988). Child and adolescent psychiatry come of age: A fifty-year perspective. *Journal of the American Academy of Child and Adolescent Psychiatry, 27*(1), 1–7.

Clarke, J., & Dawson, C. (1989). *Growing up again: Parenting ourselves, parenting our children.* San Francisco: Harper & Row.

Cochrane, G. (1991). Client-therapist collaboration in the preparation of hypnosis: Case illustrations. *American Journal of Clinical Hypnosis, 33*(4), 254–262.

Collins, J., & Carson, N. (1989). *Trauma resolution therapy.* Houston: Self-published.

Conn, J. (1989). Play interview therapy: Its history, theory and practice—A fifty-year retrospective account. *Child Psychiatry and Human Development, 20*(1), 3–13.

Cox, K., & Price, K. (1990). Breaking through: Incident drawings with adolescent substance abusers. *The Arts in Psychotherapy, 17*, 333–337.

Dreikurs, R. (1962). The interpersonal relationship in hypnosis: Some fallacies in current thinking. *Psychiatry, 25*, 219–226.

Emunah, R. (1990). Expression and expansion in adolescence: The significance of creative arts. *The Arts in Psychotherapy, 17*(2), 101–107.

Erickson, M., & Rossi, E. (1981). *Experiencing hypnosis: Therapeutic approaches to altered states.* New York: Irvington.

Fairchild, B. (1990). Reorientation: The use of hypnosis for life-style change. *Individual Psychology, 46*(4), 451–458.

Friedrich, W. (1991). Hypnotherapy with traumatized children. *International Journal of Clinical and Experimental Hypnosis, 39*, 67–81.

Getzel, G. (1983). Poetry writing groups and the elderly: A reconsideration of art and social group work. *Social Work with Groups, 6*(1), 65–76.

Golden L., & Sherwood, A. (1991). Counseling strategies for children and adolescents. In D. Capuzzi & D. Gross (Eds.), *Introduction to counseling: Perspectives for the 1990s* (pp. 275–298). Boston: Allyn & Bacon.

Goldman, R. (1986). Separation and divorce. In T. Fairchild (Ed.), *Crisis intervention strategies for school-based helpers* (pp. 22–69). Springfield, IL: Charles C Thomas.

Greenburg, S. (1982). Using the multimodal approach as a framework for eclectic counselor education. *Counselor Education and Supervision, 22*(2), 132–137.

Griggs, S. (1991). Learning styles counseling. *ERIC Clearinghouse on Counseling and Personnel Services.* (ERIC Document Reproduction Service No. ED 333308).

Gunnison, H. (1990). Adler, Erickson, and hypnocounseling. *Individual Psychology, 46*(4), 411–422.

Hale, S. (1990). Sitting on memory's lap. *The Arts in Psychotherapy, 17*(3), 269–274.

Irwin, E. (1987). Drama: The play's the thing. *Elementary School Guidance & Counseling, 21*(4), 276–283.

Johnson, D. (1991). On being one and many. *The Arts in Psychotherapy, 18*(1), 1–5.

Jung, C. (1964). *Man and his symbols*. Garden City, NY: Doubleday.

Keat, D. (1979). *Multimodal therapy with children*. New York: Pergamon.

Kendall, P., Lerner, R., & Craighead, W. (1984). Human development and interventions in childhood psychopathology. *Child Development, 55*, 71–82.

Koltko, M. (1989). The humanized no-self: A response to Schneider's critique of transpersonal psychology. *Journal of Humanistic Psychology, 29*(4), 482–492.

Lajoie, D., & Shapiro, S. (1992). Definitions of transpersonal psychology: The first twenty-three years. *Journal of Transpersonal Psychology, 24*(1), 79–98.

Landreth, G. (1987). Play therapy: Facilitative use of child's play in elementary school counseling. *Elementary School Guidance & Counseling, 21*(4), 253–261.

Lazarus, A. (1981). *The practice of multimodal therapy*. New York: McGraw-Hill.

Lazarus, A. (1986). Multimodal psychotherapy: Overview and update. *International Journal of Eclectic Psychotherapy, 5*(1), 95–103.

Mays, M. (1990). The use of metaphor in hypnotherapy and psychotherapy. *Individual Psychology, 46*(4), 423–430.

McBrian, R. (1990). A self-hypnosis program for depression management. *Individual Psychology, 46*(4), 481–489.

Miller, C., & Boe, J. (1990). Tears into diamonds: Transformation of child psychic trauma through sandplay and storytelling. *The Arts in Psychotherapy, 17*, 247–257.

Moustakas, C. (1959). *Psychotherapy with children*. New York: Ballantine.

Muzika, E. (1990). Evolutions, emptiness and the fantasy self. *Journal of Humanistic Psychology, 30*(2), 89–108.

Ornstein, A. (1985). The function of play in the process of child psychotherapy: A contemporary perspective. *The Annual of Psychoanalysis, 12–13*, 349–366.

Otani, A. (1990). Characteristics of change in Erickson hypnotherapy: A cognitive-psychological perspective. *American Journal of Clinical Hypnosis, 33*(1), 29–39.

Page, R. (1992). Clark Hull and his role in the study of hypnosis. *American Journal of Clinical Hypnosis, 34*(3), 178–184.

Pendzik, S. (1988). Drama therapy as a form of modern shamanism. *Journal of Transpersonal Psychology, 20*(1), 81–92.

Ponterotto, J., & Zander, T. (1984). A multimodal approach to counselor supervision. *Counselor Education and Supervision, 24*(1), 40–50.

Rhue, J., & Lynn, S. (1991). Storytelling, hypnosis and the treatment of sexually abused children. *International Journal of Clinical and Experimental Hypnosis, 39*(4), 198–215.

Rubin, J. (1982). Art therapy: What it is and what it is not. *American Journal of Art Therapy, 21*(2), 57–58.

Rubin, J. (1988). Art counseling: An alternative. *Elementary School Guidance & Counseling, 22*(3), 180–185.

Seligman, L. (1985). The art and science of counseling. *American Mental Health Counselor Association Journal, 7*, 2–3.

Sperry, L. (1990). Incorporating hypnotherapeutic methods into ongoing psychotherapy. *Individual Psychology, 46*(4), 443–450.

Sperry, L., & Carlson, J. (1990). Hypnosis, tailoring and multimodal treatment. *Individual Psychology, 46*(4), 459–465.

Sutich, A. (1969). Some considerations regarding transpersonal psychology. *Journal of Transpersonal Psychology, 1*(1), 11–20.

Tart, C., & Deikman, A. (1991). Mindfulness, spiritual seeking and psychotherapy. *Journal of Transpersonal Psychology, 23*(1), 29–52.

Vernon, A. (1991). Nontraditional approaches to counseling. In D. Capuzzi & D. Gross (Eds.), *Introduction to counseling: Perspectives for the 1990s* (pp. 205–229). Boston: Allyn & Bacon.

Walsh, R. (1992). The search for synthesis: Transpersonal psychology and the meeting of East and West, psychology and religion, personal and transpersonal. *Journal of Humanistic Psychology, 32*(1), 19–45.

Webster's New World Dictionary of the American Language. (1984). New York: Simon & Schuster.

Weed, R., & Hernandez, A. (1990). Multimodal rehabilitation counseling. *Journal of Applied Rehabilitation Counseling, 21*(4), 27–30.

Weikel, W. (1990). A multimodal approach in dealing with older clients. *Journal of Mental Health Counseling, 12*(3), 314–320.

Wilber, K. (1989a). God is so damn boring: A response to Kirk Schneider. *Journal of Humanistic Psychology, 29*(4), 457–469.

Wilber, K. (1989b). Reply to Schneider. *Journal of Humanistic Psychology, 29*(4), 493–500.

Wilber, K., Engler, J., & Brown, D. (1986). *Transformations of consciousness: Conventional and contemplative perspectives on development.* Boston: New Science Library/Shambhala.

CHAPTER EIGHTEEN

Counseling and Psychotherapy: Multicultural Considerations

G. Miguel Arciniega
Arizona State University

Betty J. Newlon
University of Arizona

Although a significant amount of research and writing has addressed the impact of culture on counseling and therapy, very few mainstream textbooks have incorporated multicultural themes into their discussions of counseling and therapeutic theory. Multicultural counseling and therapy is at a crossroads; and in spite of the increased attention it has received, it is still considered to be in its infancy (Ponterotto & Sabnani, 1989).

The existence of cultural bias in counseling and therapy has been documented by many authors (Atkinson, Morten, & Sue 1989; Katz, 1985; LeVine & Padilla, 1980; Pedersen, Draguns, Lonner, & Trimble, 1989; Ponterotto & Casas, 1991; Sue & Sue, 1990). Wrenn (1962) first introduced the concept of the culturally encapsulated counselor by pointing out how counselors protect themselves from the reality of change by "surrounding [themselves] with a cocoon of pretended reality—a reality which is based upon the past and the known, upon seeing that which is as though it would always be" (p. 446). More than 20 years later Wrenn (1985) again addressed the issue of the encapsulated counselor with a broader view that dealt with counselors who denied the reality of change.

The history and legitimacy of multicultural counseling and therapy has paralleled the sociopolitical movements in the United States. The civil rights efforts of the 1960s, 70s, and 80s produced a racial and cultural pride among minority groups, which in turn stimulated their demand for recognition and equality. This movement has pushed mental health professionals to consider cultural issues.

For the past three decades, writers, researchers, educators, and professionals in the counseling and therapeutic fields have espoused the need for multicultural and crosscultural awareness, knowledge, strategies, and approaches in order to serve the increasing number of racial, cultural, and ethnic minorities throughout the nation. The need for a minority perspective in counseling and therapy has become one of the most important topics in journals. Between 1983 and 1988, the major counseling and counseling psychology journals (*The Counseling Psychologist, The Journal of Counseling Psychology, The Journal of Counseling and Development,* and *The Journal of Multicultural Counseling and Development*) published 183 conceptual and empirical articles in this area (Ponterotto & Casas, 1991). More recently *The Journal of Counseling and Development* published a special issue called "Multiculturalism As a Fourth Force in Counseling" (American Association for Counseling and Development, 1991).

Wehrly (1991) stated, "In spite of the fact that the United States has been (and is) a nation of immigrants whose values differ, a major theme of Euro-American individualistic psychology seems to have been that of assimilation" (p. 4). She proceeded to point out that writers in the fields of counseling and therapy have been slow to recognize the cultural impact of American ethnic minorities. They have not broadened the theoretical base of counseling or therapy beyond Western thought. Consequently, most training institutions, while they might offer a course on multicultural counseling or therapy, still use theory texts that expound a monoethnic, monocultural theory.

We need to acknowledge that traditional theories are based on Western Euro-American assumptions that are considered to be morally, politically, and ethnically neutral. This foundation has also been perpetuated as culturally fair and unbiased. Atkinson et al. (1989) and Ivey (1981) have noted that counseling or therapy approaches and theories were developed for the white middle class and traditionally conceptualized in a Western individualistic framework.

To clarify this point, Katz (1985) presented a paradigm for viewing cultural dimensions of traditional therapy in terms of white values and beliefs. Katz concluded that the "similarities between white culture and the cultural values that form the foundations of traditional counseling theory and practice exist and are interchangeable" (p. 619). These monocultural-based theories assume applicability to all populations regardless of minority, racial, and cultural experiences. While these theories may be well intentioned, they have not systematically integrated the current sociopolitical nature of the multicultural populations they address.

NATIVE AMERICANS, AFRICAN AMERICANS, HISPANIC AMERICANS, AND ASIAN AMERICANS/PACIFIC ISLANDERS

Because it is not possible to provide a descriptive overview of all American minority groups, we have selected the following four groups because they have been identified for special attention by the American Psychological Association and the American Counseling Association: native Americans, African Americans, Hispanic Americans, and Asian Americans/ Pacific Islanders. In order to understand the current experience of these populations, it is essential that counselors or therapists understand the groups' historical, educational, social, political, and economic development and climate in addition to their basic family characteristics and values. For a more thorough presentation and understanding of these groups, see LeVine and Padilla (1980), Pedersen et al. (1989), and Sue and Sue (1990).

It is not our intent to provide a comprehensive analysis of all of the factors impinging on counseling and therapeutic theories but to introduce the multiplicity of social, ethnic, and cultural issues and considerations that counselors or therapists must take into account when applying theory.

This chapter addresses the following as they relate to the four previously mentioned racial, ethnic, and cultural groups: definitions, counselor and therapist self-awareness, Euro-American mainstream assumptions, acculturation, demographics, racial and ethnic cultural considerations, and racial and ethnic cultural components. In addition, we present a discussion of counseling and therapeutic theories and their appropriateness or adaptability to traditional minority groups. The chapter concludes with a discussion of how multicultural considerations can add breadth to prevailing theories.

DEFINITIONS

For the purpose of this chapter, we propose the following terms and definitions (Krogman, 1945; Linton, 1945; Rose, 1964):

- *Race*: a group of people who possess a definite combination of physical characteristics of genetic origin that distinguishes them from other groups of humans
- *Ethnicity*: a group classification in which members are believed, by themselves and others, to have a common origin and share a unique social and cultural heritage such as language, religious customs, and traditions that are passed from generation to generation
- *Culture*: the configuration of learned behavior whose components and elements are shared and transmitted by the members of a particular society

It is necessary to point out that these terms (*race*, *ethnicity*, and *culture*) have often been used interchangeably in the literature and are often misunderstood. Race refers to a biological concept, while ethnicity and culture refer to shared and uniquely learned characteristics. Ethnic groups within races differ in their cultural specificity, and people of the same racial background and same ethnic group may differ in their cultural specificity. For example, African Americans may be part of a Hispanic ethnic group but may identify with a number of cultural groups from their country of origin.

Here are some other important terms and definitions (Katz, 1985; Pedersen, 1988):

- *Minority*: a group of people who, because of their physical or cultural characteristics, receive differential and unequal treatment due to collective discrimination

■ *Multicultural counseling or therapy*: a situation in which two or more people with different ways of perceiving their social environment are brought together in a helping relationship

■ *Stereotype*: rigid preconceptions about members of a particular group without regard to individual variations

■ *White culture*: the synthesis of ideas, values, and beliefs coalesced from descendants of white European ethnic groups in the United States

COUNSELOR AND THERAPIST SELF-AWARENESS

The implementation of a counseling or therapeutic theory that is more responsive to racial and cultural groups requires practitioners to determine the appropriateness or inappropriateness of their approaches. They must have knowledge of the demographics of these groups and an awareness of their history, sociopolitical issues, communication styles, culture, class, language factors, world views, acculturation, and identity. In addition, practitioners must have an awareness of their own biases and beliefs. This requires critically examining themselves and their theoretical frameworks in order to provide effective and ethically appropriate services.

As the previous list implies, this process is not an easy task. It also requires a paradigmatic shift in thinking—broadening personal realities with other world views and integrating them into counseling and therapeutic theory and practice. Midgette and Meggert (1991) propose such a paradigmatic shift for multicultural counseling or therapy. Their paradigm gives the counselor or therapist conceptual clarity and provides a framework of thought to explain various aspects of reality (Kuhn, 1962). They state, "Multicultural instruction represents an emergent synthesis—a somewhat new systematic outlook that benefits from knowledge of previously developed philosophies but is not an eclectic composite" (p. 136). Ibrahim (1985) states that effectiveness in crosscultural counseling or therapy is determined by how well the helpers are aware of their world view and can understand and accept the world view of the client. The power of a dominant, preset paradigm can block the pursuit of knowledge through alternative approaches and thereby create major limitations by closing the system and not allowing further development. These paradigms are the source of basic beliefs and attitudes that are difficult to modify. However, if counselors or therapists are to act with integrity and commitment, they must begin to take steps in shifting their theoretical paradigms to include racial and cultural world views.

This paradigmatic shift requires one to assess his or her personal values and beliefs and determine how others' views can be integrated into our own. Newlon and Arciniega (1992) proposed a process of cultural integration involving the following (p. 286):

1. Confronting and challenging personal stereotypes held about cultural groups
2. Acquiring knowledge about the groups' cultures and, even more important, about heterogeneous responses of the groups
3. Understanding the traditional institutional interaction between the dominant society and minorities, and vice versa
4. Understanding the effects of institutional racism and stereotypes
5. Acquiring firsthand experience with focus minority groups
6. Challenging normative counselor and therapist approaches and understanding their cultural implications
7. Knowledgeably using a culturally pluralistic model

Sue and Sue (1990) posited similar observations in the form of characteristics of a culturally aware counselor or therapist. These characteristics included "being aware and sensitive to their own values and biases; comfortable with differences between themselves and their clients in terms of race and beliefs; sensitive to circumstances dictating referral; and aware of their own racist beliefs and feelings" (p. 160). This shift offers an opportunity to expand theoretical frameworks (not necessarily to replace them) and to integrate a more comprehensive view of our world.

ACCULTURATION

Acculturation is an important phenomenon to be considered in light of counseling/therapeutic theory and practice. It is composed of numerous dimensions, such as cultural values, ideologies, ethnic identity, beliefs, attitudes toward self and majority, language use, cultural customs, practices, and ethnic interaction. It has been often confused with the concept of assimilation. For the purpose of this chapter, *acculturation* is defined as the degree to which an individual who is a racial or ethnic minority uniquely incorporates, adds to, and synthesizes the values, customs, language, beliefs, and ideology of the dominant culture in order to survive and feel a sense of belonging. *Assimilation*, on the other hand, refers to a "process of acculturation in which an individual has changed so much as to become disassociated from the value system of his/her group or in which the entire group disappears as an autonomously functioning system" (Teske, 1973, p. 7907a).

Each racial or ethnic group has its own distinct acculturation process, even though they all manifest similar concerns. Native Americans, who were here before the white settlers, were forced onto reservations and only later entered the majority mainstream. They differ from the Hispanics and Asians, who came from another country. The history of African-American acculturation also has unique characteristics, including slavery and economic and racial oppression.

Acculturation is not continuous from traditional to mainstream; rather, its origin might be best understood as a multidimensional, multifaceted phenomenon. An individual may learn how to become Americanized, but this does not imply that the person incorporates society's values. These values may be additive and not supplantive. Persons can retain their culture-of-origin values and still operate within the mainstream values simultaneously. Minority individuals who have retained their identity and who still incorporate American values in a healthy way are those who have come to an understanding of self without losing their cultural self-concept.

DEMOGRAPHICS

A century from now, the population of the United States is expected to be closer to the world balance: 57% Asian American/Pacific Islander, 26% white, 7% African American, and 10% Hispanic (Edmunds, Martinson, & Goldberg, 1990; Ibrahim, 1991). Judging from information gathered in 1989, 1990, 2000, and 2010, researchers believe that the white population will have marginal overall growth, while African-American and Hispanic populations will grow at an accelerated rate. By the year 2010, whites will represent 76.6% of the total population, down from 80.7% in 1989; African Americans will represent 13% of the population, up from 11.8% in 1989; and Hispanics will represent 10.3% of the total population, up from 7.5% in 1989 (U.S. Bureau of the Census, 1989).

The most up-to-date age-related racial and ethnic group data stem from 1987 and are summarized in the recent *Statistical Abstract of the United States* (U.S. Bureau of the Census, 1989). Whites are the most highly represented group in the age 45–65 cohort (19.3%) and in the 65-years-and-over age group (12.4%). Whites are followed by African Americans and then Hispanics in terms of "older group" representation.

Hispanics are the highest-represented group among the two youngest age groups. Almost 11% of Hispanics are under 5 years of age, while 9.4% of African Americans and 7.3% of whites fall in this category. In the age 5–14 category, Hispanics have the highest relative percentage at 19.6, followed by African Americans (18.3%) and whites (13.6%). Unfortunately, recent age-related data on Asian American/Pacific Islanders and native Americans are not available.

In terms of median age, native Americans are the youngest, with a median age of 23, followed closely by Hispanics at 23.2 years. Interestingly, when looking across age-group categories, we note that more than 50% of African Americans, Hispanics, and native Americans are under the age of 25.

Some additional demographic information follows.

Native Americans

The term *native Americans* includes American Indians, Eskimos, and Aleuts (Alaska natives). American Indians are geographically dispersed throughout the United States. There are 511 federally recognized native entities and an additional 365 state-recognized American Indian tribes with 200 distinct tribal languages (LaFromboise, 1988). Theory application must be sensitive to the tremendous heterogeneity and diversity existing among native Americans. The 1980 national census reported the native American population as roughly 1.5 million (U.S. Bureau of the Census, 1982), but a more recent estimate places the current population between 1.5 and 1.8 million (LaFromboise & Low, 1989). States with relatively high native American populations include California, Oklahoma, Arizona, New Mexico, North Carolina, and Alaska (Dillard, 1985). According to LaFromboise (1988), only 24% of the population lives on reservations, and that segment is remarkably young, with a median age of 20.4 compared to the U.S. median age of 30.3.

In terms of educational, economic, and political power, native Americans are at the lowest end of the spectrum. More often than not, they have little influence over what happens in the United States or in their own lives (LaFromboise, 1988).

African Americans

African Americans constitute the nation's largest racial and ethnic minority group. They represent 12.1% of the total U.S. population and number close to 30 million. The African-American population is growing at a faster pace than the white majority, with an annual growth rate of 1.87% as compared to a 0.06% growth for whites (Rogler, Malgady, Constantino, & Bluenenthall, 1987). The African-American population is spread throughout the United States: 11.3% in the Northeast, 10% in the Midwest, 18.8% in the South, and 5.6% in the West (U.S. Bureau of the Census, 1988).

African Americans as a racial group are represented by numerous diverse ethnic and cultural groups, including Spanish-speaking populations from Cuba, Puerto Rico, and Panama; groups from the Caribbean Islands and Northern Europe; and native American/African Americans (Wehrly, 1991). It is important for counselors and therapists to acknowledge and understand the tremendous diversity within the African-American population in the United States.

The African-American experience in America is unique. This group first arrived in the United States in the 1600s and, unlike immigrant groups who followed, came involuntarily as slaves. The group as a whole, because of its darker skin, has been subjected to continuing majority-group oppression. In no case has the sheer brutality and evil of racism, prejudice, and penetrating hate been so evident and salient as in the white majority's treatment of African-Americans throughout U.S. history.

Hispanic Americans

Hispanics comprise a large diverse group composed of Mexican Americans, Puerto Ricans, Cuban Americans, South and Central Americans, and others. There is also a great deal of heterogeneity within each specific subgroup. Mexican Americans who have recently arrived in the United States may be quite different in values, behaviors, attitudes, and counseling and therapeutic needs from Mexican Americans who are third-generation citizens and more acculturated. Further, internal diversity among groups of Mexican Americans can also be attributed to geographic region and socioeconomic status.

Hispanics are the fastest-growing racial and ethnic group in the United States, and they make up the second largest minority group. Of the many Hispanic groups in the United States, the Central and South Americans experienced the greatest growth rate during the 1982–1987 period: 40%. Given the overall high growth rate of Hispanics in general, it is expected that by the year 2035 they will surpass African Americans as the largest racial and ethnic minority group in the United States (Ponterotto & Casas, 1991).

Hispanics of Mexican origin are the largest segment of the Hispanic population, accounting for 63% of the total Hispanic population. Other Hispanic subgroups are represented as follows: Puerto Ricans at 12%, Central and South Americans at 11%, and Cubans at 5%. A majority of Mexican Americans reside in the Southwest. Puerto Ricans reside primarily in and around New York City. A majority of Cuban Americans live in South Florida and in the vicinity of New York City. A number of Central American groups are located in the New York City, Los Angeles, and San

Francisco areas (Ponterotto & Casas, 1991). Overall, the Hispanic population is younger, less educated, poorer, and more likely to live in inner-city neighborhoods than the general population (Rogler et al., 1987).

Asian Americans/Pacific Islanders

Asian Americans/Pacific Islanders are represented by a number of major subgroups, including Japanese, Chinese, Filipinos, Koreans, Guamians, Malays, Samoans, and Southeast Asians. This collective heterogeneous group represents the third largest racial and ethnic minority group in the United States. Asian-American/Pacific Islander groups are growing in rapid numbers, and some projections expect this total population to number more than 9.8 million by the year 2000 (Ponterotto & Casas, 1991).

The Chinese and Japanese were the first Asians to settle in the United States in large numbers; and like other minority groups, they arrived in the hopes of improving their economic conditions, life-styles, and social and political life (Dillard, 1985). Today Asian Americans/Pacific Islanders are dispersed throughout the United States. A large percentage are located in urban areas in large cities on the West and East coasts. Although some Asian-American/Pacific Islander groups have been portrayed as "model minorities" in terms of significant educational and economic success, we emphasize that large percentages of these groups live in poverty and suffer high levels of psychological stress (Sue & Sue, 1990).

Asian Americans/Pacific Islanders also differ from group to group. Again, varying levels of acculturation attest to marked internal heterogeneity within groups. The tremendous heterogeneity both between and within various Asian-American/Pacific Islander groups defies categorization and stereotypic description. This group has been subjected to continuing societal oppression, discrimination, and misunderstanding.

RACIAL AND ETHNIC CULTURAL CONSIDERATIONS

Each of the specific racial and ethnic groups that we have addressed have cultural considerations that must be taken into account by counselors and therapists. These considerations should be evaluated with respect to minority groups needs, values, and level of acculturation. Newlon and Arciniega (1983) addressed these considerations as "factors" to be considered by counselors and therapists when gathering information and integrating them into counseling and therapeutic theory and process. Racial and ethnic cultural considerations include language, cultural identity, generation, cultural custom styles, geographical location and neighborhoods, family constituency, psychohistorical and religious traditions, and individuality (Newlon & Arciniega, 1983).

Language

When working with minority clients who still use their language of origin, understanding the language is not enough; the practitioner must consider both content and contextual meaning. In addition, the counselor or therapist must be able to assess the language of the various minority groups: all members may not have the same degree of fluency in the language of origin or in English. Counselors or therapists must be cognizant of the fact that the language of origin is where much of the affect is first learned. Although some minority clients may be fluent in English, the affect of the English words may have a different meaning from that of the language of origin.

Cultural Identity

Counselors or therapists must be aware of the self-referent labels that clients choose. Self-referent labels are a sensitive issue for many clients and may be different even for various members within the family. For example, to individuals of Mexican or Latin American descent, the identifiers may be Mexican American, Hispanic, Chicano, Americans of Mexican descent, or Latinos. For clients of African descent, these may be African American, Negro, black, or West Indian. For native Americans, identifiers may be American Indian, red, or important tribal names. For Asian Americans/Pacific Islanders, the identifiers may be Asian, Asian American, Oriental, or specific countries of origin.

Generation

The clients' generational factors—that is, first, second, or third generation in this country—should be assessed by the counselor or therapist to assist in judging the degree of acculturation. First-generation clients may have more ties to the traditional culture, and these ties may be reflected in the nuclear and extended family dynamics. The acculturation process is unique for each minority group and individual. Contrary to some current beliefs, as clients become acculturated they do not drop their former cultural ways but rather add new ones and synthesize both the new and the old in a creative manner.

Cultural Custom Styles

In addition to the obvious cultural customs of food, dress, and traditions, several cultural styles of responsibility and communication have to be considered. For example, the Mexican, Indian, and Asian cultures emphasize the responsibility an oldest child has for younger siblings. An Asian family's expectations for unquestioning obedience may produce problems when family members are exposed to American values emphasizing independence and self-reliance.

The style of communication in traditional native American and Mexican-American clients stresses patience and personal respect. Clients from traditional families may show respect by looking down and not making eye contact with authority figures. With African-American clients, verbal interaction moves at a faster pace; sensitive confrontation is accepted more readily than with traditional Hispanic, native American, or Asian families.

Geographical Location and Neighborhoods

Ethnic groups from different geographical locations exhibit distinct geo-cultural traditions and customs. Counselors or therapists cannot assume that the same customs apply to seemingly similar cultural groups. They should also note rural and urban influences in the client's present situation within the family history.

Neighborhoods where the minority clients reside have a great deal to do with how clients see themselves. Minority clients living in a totally ethnic area have a different view than clients living in an integrated neighborhood or clients residing in a neighborhood where they are the only minority family.

Family Constituency

In most minority families, kinship networks help to satisfy important cultural needs for intimacy, belonging, and interpersonal relations. Extended families, where more than one generation lives in the same household and where formalized kinship relations exist, are common among minority groups. In many Hispanic and native American families, significant adults may extend to uncles, grandparents, cousins, close friends, and godparents. Family holds a special place for most minority clients. Love, protection, and loyalty to the family are pronounced, creating an environment where members can develop strong feelings of self-worth despite the lingering effects of discrimination and racism.

Psychohistorical and Religious Traditions

The history of the ethnic group along with the history of the ethnic group in the United States is information that counselors or therapists need. Minority clients reflect the psychohistory of the family through child-rearing practices. Many facets of child rearing are rooted in the history of minority groups and are distinct from the dominant culture in which the clients presently live. For example, Hispanics and native Americans have been raised in a cooperative mode rather than the competitive mode of the dominant culture.

Spiritual and religious practices traditionally have been strong within most minorities. Religion provides the medium through which minority clients deal with forces and powers beyond their control. It also provides a basis for social cohesion and support. Historically, the church has been a resource for personal counseling or therapy and a refuge from a hostile environment. For example, African Americans have traditionally gone to church leaders for advice and direction.

Individuality

The concept of individual responsibility is viewed differently by minority groups. Native Americans, for instance, judge their worth primarily in terms of whether their behavior serves to better the tribe. Tribal culture places a high value on the harmonious relationship between an individual and all other members of the tribe. This concept of cooperation within certain ethnic groups has been documented (Kagan & Madsen, 1971). Responsibility to the family is a major value found in African-American, Hispanic, native American, and Asian-American clients and should be considered and encouraged. Individual responsibilities are of secondary value, after the family.

RACIAL AND ETHNIC CULTURAL COMPONENTS

Specific racial and ethnic cultural components that are common to the four racial cultural groups should be clarified as they are uniquely important to these respective groups. These components have been identified as critical in assessing minority relationships to the various counseling and therapeutic theories. It is important to have knowledge of these components in order to determine whether theories directly or indirectly address these factors and, if not, whether they can be modified or adapted to their theoretical framework.

These components are related to some of the cultural considerations discussed in the previous section. However, they are presented here in light of counseling and therapeutic theory variables as opposed to counselor or therapist variables. This distinction is important in determining whether a theory allows for the extenuating manifestations inherent in each component. In addition, because these components and considerations manifest a holistic view, they have descriptive overlaps.

Language

Aside from the obvious fact that minority groups may retain their language of origin, use black English, or use code switching (words from English combined with another language), there are other considerations that need to be taken into account. Counselors or therapists must be competent in the languages of the particular diverse populations, but they must also be cognizant of the fact that affect is learned in the culture of origin through presymbolic and symbolic language at an early age. This affect reflects the minority member's world view philosophy and the inherent assumptions of the culture. Therefore, the counseling and therapeutic theoretical framework must be able to allow for these considerations directly or indirectly.

Family and Social Relationships

The importance of family is a major consideration for all four groups. Extended family kinship ties, respect for elders, defined gender roles, emphasis on the nurturing of children, hierarchical nature of family structure, primary responsibility to family, and identity are closely linked through strong family ties in all four groups. A counseling and therapeutic theory that does not incorporate this multifaceted component has limited value. The theory must be able to address this component in a familial holistic sense because of the minority group's strong sense of belonging and identity to the family group.

Time Focus

For these four groups the dimension and concept of time are distinct from the majority view in which the focus is the future: you sacrifice for tomorrow and postpone gratification. The concept of rigid adherence to time is an artifact of Euro-American culture. For the four groups discussed in this chapter, the present and past may be more important than the future, due to cultural or socioeconomic factors. World views that are based on past cultural history still operate in the present. For these minority groups, time is viewed contextually as an artificial concept of mainstream society. Future predictions and time specificity are placed in context of a possibility, not a fact. Social relations and obligations often have a higher priority than specific time-clock appointments. Theories that incorporate a planning of individual's future behavior may be counterproductive if this is not taken into consideration. In addition, those theories that impose the "fifty-minute hour" at a specific time take a mainstream cultural view that is not responsive to the cultural world view of these groups. Events or situations that happen to these groups are often viewed as more important than being on time and, consequently, may be misinterpreted as client resistance by a majority theoretical view.

Nature-People Relationships

The relationship of people to nature has a distinct and unique value orientation for these four minority groups. Life may be determined by external forces such as fate, God's will, or "that's the way it is." Acceptance (not subjugation) and harmony with nature coexisting without control are part of an inherent cultural view for these groups. People are a reality, and relationships are important and primary. This view is often at cross-purposes with the majority view that operates in terms of overcoming, controlling, or conquering nature and environment, including self-behaviors. Counseling and therapeutic theories that assume that the individual is greater or separate from nature and the environment have limited effectiveness with these groups.

Holistic View

A holistic view for these groups encompasses both a particularistic cultural perspective and a universal view. These groups operate from the interaction of their environment and themselves as a whole. Support of the interrelationship between individual and environment has been documented extensively (Katz, 1985). Therefore, this holistic component has both universal and particularistic (edic and emic) aspects for these minority groups. Life is based on a totality of this interaction and does not fragment and separate. Counseling and therapeutic theories that only address this component from either a universal view or a particularistic view have limitations in their theoretical application.

Human Activity and Cooperation

Common to all four minority groups is the cultural component of cooperation, which includes connectedness and loyalty to their respective groups. This component is part of the groups' socialization and child-rearing patterns, which are manifested in unique complementary roles and tasks in the family and community. These focus groups emphasize the concept of "being" as sufficient, not of having to become better in order to have status with one's own group. Contribution is seen from a collective view, with members having value simply because of who they are. Counseling and therapeutic theories that emphasize only the growth of the individual, regardless of how it affects a minority individual's group, will meet with obstacles and confusion.

Identity

For these four groups, self-identity cannot be separated from the cultural identity with which each member contends. Theories that address the universal self or identity development alone bypass a very important cultural component. The process of minority identity has been addressed extensively by Sue and Sue (1990). Hall, Cross, and Freed (1971) have elaborated further on minority identity models. Each minority member may have distinct self-referent labels that vary even within each group, and these labels are related to both negative and positive identity. Additionally, most members struggle with imposed stereotypes from the majority culture, which affect self-esteem and self-worth of each group member. The psychological costs of racism in identity cannot be stressed enough. Counseling and therapeutic theory and process need to be able to address these complex identity components.

Mental Health

Counseling and therapeutic theories address the concept of mental health from the assumption of a universal (emic) Euro-American point of view, to the exclusion of a culture-specific (edic) view. The four minority groups have similarities in their world view of what constitutes normality and abnormality, a view that is different from mainstream society. Current theories rarely take into account the cultural mental health views of these groups, who may not separate the physical from their mental states. The goals and processes of a theory are intimately linked with the theoretical frame of reference that assumes all populations are the same. This issue should be one of the most complex and important concerns when practitioners view theory and process as they apply to these groups.

Spirituality

Each of these four groups deals with unique and distinct spiritual issues as part of their daily lives. Spirituality and religion are an integral part of every group and its members. They have been a source of stability and hope for these groups for many generations and are part of their socialization. Few counseling and therapeutic theories address this component and consequently omit a major mainstay and refuge used by these groups in hostile environments.

Responsibility

The concept of responsibility in these four groups is different from the American majority view. For them, a concept of collective responsibility is prioritized: first to family, then to their own group or community, and finally to self. Most theories deal with responsibility according to the reverse priority: first to individual, then to family, and some to group and community. Neither approach implies a wrong or right; but when theories operate from the development of responsibility to self and do not consider the consequences of those implications to members of minority groups, they will meet with confusion and resistance. Individually centered theories, with their goal of individual responsibility, work in counterproductive ways and are apt to discount the values of these groups. While some theories may espouse the concept of universal responsibility, they often fail to address cultural specificity.

Oppression and Racism

All four groups have experienced a history of oppression and racism that has impacted them in terms of identity, alienation, and devaluation of their worth. While other American minority groups have experienced oppression, these four groups have distinct physical traits that are more readily identifiable. This factor alone has kept the differentness on the surface, no matter what may transpire within. Because of the United States's melting-pot philosophy, which is still in existence despite the culturally pluralistic views and values of cultural diversity being professed, racism continues to persist and affect these groups. Few counseling and therapeutic theories address this component in their frameworks, and this omission appears to discount their cultural reality.

The following chart presents a framework to view diagrammatically whether the 12 theories presented in this book address the proposed racial ethnic components. It vertically lists the 12 theories and identifies racial and ethnic components horizontally at the top, with their respective intercepting boxes marked as follows: (+) theory responds in the positive; (-) theory responds in the negative; (0) theory does not address; (P) theory responds partially.

Note that the diagrammatic chart has been proposed as an outline to view how the various identified components correspond to the theories. We interject a note of caution here, pointing out that this chart is not intended to be definitive and closed but to facilitate the understanding of the relationship among the theories and the racial and ethnic components. Arbitrary assessments were made after reviewing theories and are subject to different interpretations.

For the purpose of this chart, we have given consideration to *traditional* racial and ethnic groups where *survival* is primary and where educational level may be lower than the general white population. For many groups, a major segment of the population has less than a high school education. In addition, many of these minority groups still hold on to the culture and language of origin and therefore still reflect different world views.

CHART SUMMARY AND CRITIQUE OF THEORIES

In light of the racial and ethnic components that we proposed, our results indicate that very few of the theories discussed in this book address those components effectively. Our purpose is not to show the limitations of these theories with racial or ethnic minorities, but to point out that when the theories were developed, populations with differing and complex world views were not taken into consideration.

Individual psychology ecosystems and developmental theory appear to address the components more effectively than the others, due to their basic assumptions about the importance of world views, family, sociocultural systems and equality, cooperation, social interest, and the fact that they incorporate culture as a major consideration. These assumptions have enough flexibility to address several of the components we have described. This is not to say, however, that theories do not have limitations; we will discuss those limitations later in the section.

FIGURE 18.1
Counseling and therapy theories in terms of racial and ethnic components

THEORY		RACIAL AND ETHNIC COMPONENTS										
	Language	Family and Social Relations	Time Focus	Nature-People Relationships	Holistic View	Human Activity and Cooperation	Identity	Mental Health	Spirituality and Religion	Responsibility	Oppression and Racism
Psychoanalytic	–	–	0	–	–	–	0	–	0	–	–
Jungian analytical	0	–	P	0	P	P	0	0	P	–	0
Adlerian individual	0	+	P	P	+	+	P	+	+	+	+
Existential	0	–	P	0	+	+	P	+	P	P	0
Person-centered	0	–	+	P	+	+	P	P	P	–	0
Gestalt	0	–	P	–	+	–	0	P	–	–	0
Transactional analysis	0	P	0	0	P	0	–	0	0	–	0
Rational-emotive	0	P	+	0	P	0	P	P	0	–	0
Cognitive-behavioral	0	P	+	0	0	0	P	+	0	–	0
Reality therapy	0	P	+	P	0	–	P	0	0	0	0
Ecosystems	P	+	0	0	+	+	0	P	0	+	0
Developmental	P	+	P	+	+	P	+	+	P	0	P

+	Theory responds positively	0	Theory doesn't address
–	Theory is contrary	P	Theory responds partially

Existential and person-centered theories, with much interpolation, could possibly respond to specific components. However, such a response would result from counselor or therapist interpretation that is not necessarily inherent in the theory. It could be argued that existential theory, which is part of person-centered theory, has much leeway in the universal sense; therefore, important components could be addressed with adaptations. Philosophically, there may be merit in this approach. However, in relation to the specificity of these components, both theories appear to be lacking.

The appropriateness of cognitive-behavioral theories is subject to a counselor or therapist's awareness and sensitivity rather than inherent in the theory itself. For the most part, the rest of the theories have little relevance when dealing with these minority populations.

Psychoanalytic Theory

One of the main limitations of Freudian psychoanalytic theory is its focus on intrapsychic conflict as the source of all dysfunction and its failure to consider interpersonal and sociocultural variables. It ignores social class, culture, ethnicity, and race as variables in the developmental process. The consequences of racism on the intrapsychic process are not addressed and do not acknowledge differential experiences or the values of being different in a white-dominated society. Psychoanalytical theory is individualistic and does not deal with cultures that are group or family centered. Stage developments are based on a two-parent family, which is not always the case in many minority groups. The theory also involves a process in which clients are expected to be verbal and disclosing, which can be counterproductive and alien when used with such groups as Asian Americans, native Americans, and Hispanics, who are socialized not to disclose (Okum, 1990). In addition, the anonymous role the counselor or therapist assumes can be restrictive for minority clients and is in direct conflict with minority clients' social framework and environmental perspective.

Most minority clients cannot afford to devote 5 years to intensive treatment when what they want is immediate response to specific issues. The goals of psychoanalytic therapy are not appropriate for minority clients when dealing with the practical concerns in their social environments. This theory with modification could have some application with diagnosed (borderline minority clients) if they were examined from a sociocultural and developmental perspective. Additionally, the diffused sense of ethnic identity could be addressed but, again, would bring up the issue of long-term therapy. Intrapsychic processes, stages of development conflict, and the lack of interpersonal and family importance does not make this model appropriate for the racial and ethnic groups we have discussed (Corey, 1991; Ivey, Ivey, & Simek-Morgan, 1993).

Jungian Analytical Theory

Like Freudian theory, Jungian theory offers similar limitations for racial and ethnic minority groups. It is an intrapsychic process and does not address racism and discrimination as variables in the developmental process. Consequently, all the problems lie within the individual. Jung's mystical approach, with its collective unconscious, archetypes, and unconscious factors, would have little appeal to those minority groups struggling to survive. It also emphasizes a single model of healthy functioning—one that would take years of counseling and therapy and much money. In addition to using impersonal treatment modalities, counselors or therapists are subject to their own beliefs about and interpretations of the symbols.

The racial and cultural groups we have discussed may have distinct symbols and are not socialized to deal with abstract symbolic articulation as required by this model. The theory does not deal with the influence of either social class or institutional oppression and thus can be misinterpreted by counselors or therapists. The methodology of this model is inappropriate and does not provide a reality base congruent with these minority groups. While it is a holistic model and deals with spirituality, it is not culturally specific to these groups. The model would not be very relevant to or effective with these traditional groups.

Adlerian Individual Theory

Strict Adlerian individual theory would have some limitations for minority clients who want quick solutions, for the clients would have little interest in exploring early childhood, early memories, or dreams. These clients may not see the purpose of dealing with life's problems by going through details of life-style analysis. However, of all the theories this one holds the great promise because of several characteristics. It focuses on the person in a familial and sociocultural context; it is involved in developing social interest and in contributing to others; and it emphasizes belonging, which supports the value system of these minority groups. In addition, its emphasis on the role of the family and culture fits well with the values of these focus minority groups. Adlerian assumptions that people are equal, social and goal centered, that they seek cooperation, contribute to the common good of the group, and are holistic are congruent with the cul-

tural values of these racial and ethnic groups. The individual's unique subjective interpretation and perception are part of Adlerian theory, and the
clients' values and views are honored and accepted. Adlerian goals are not
aimed at deciding for clients what they should change about themselves.
Rather, it works in collaboration with clients and their family networks.
This theory offers a pragmatic approach that is flexible and uses a range
of action-oriented cognitive techniques to explore personal problems
within their sociocultural context. It has the flexibility to deal both with
the individual and the family, making it very appropriate for racial and ethnic groups. (Sherman & Dinkmeyer, 1987).

Existential Theory

Existential theory is based on the understanding of the individual and
allows the freedom to use other systems and techniques that can be made
applicable to racial and ethnic groups. The existential notion of freedom
and control can be helpful in assisting clients to clarify their cultural values, identity, and meaning. Ibrahim (1985) has pointed out that an existential approach provides for the concept of "cultural relativity" and "relative objectivity" (p. 635). It is essential in this approach to understand
one's own cultural heritage and world views so that a practitioner can
more effectively help people with other world views.

A major criticism of this approach is that it is excessively individualistic; freedom of choice is a reality. Minority clients may not feel they have
much choice because of their environmental circumstances. These client
groups often seek counseling or therapy for specific direction. Therefore,
reflecting on freedom of choice and meaning may create frustration and
misunderstanding. Lack of direction in terms of specificity and the concept of individual responsibility can be counterproductive to these focus
minority groups (Corey, 1991; Yalom, 1988).

Person-centered Theory

In many ways person-centered theory has made significant contributions
to practice in multicultural settings. Until his death, Carl Rogers used this
approach in several countries throughout the world. The theory emphasis
is on humanness and the core conditions that place an egalitarian concept
into the model. On the other hand, these core conditions are difficult to
translate into the cultural framework of Hispanic, native American,
African-American, and Asian-American/Pacific Islander racial and ethnic
groups. It is incumbent on the counselor or therapist to go beyond core
conditions of humanness and deal with the cultural relatedness of these

minority groups. Because the theory originated in a white, middle-class milieu, it has inherent limitations unless counselors or therapists carefully look at their own beliefs and their understanding of otherviews.

A limitation of person-centered theory is that many racial and ethnic groups want more structure and direction than is inherent in this theory. Person-centered theory values internal focus, while minority groups may still operate on the value of external evaluation—that of the family and group identity. This theory emphasizes self and real self, which can be counterproductive because it obscures relational and broader environmental issues that are a priority with these minority groups. These clients may focus more on the real world than the ideal (Corey, 1991; Ivey, Ivey, & Simek-Morgan, 1993; Rogers, 1980; Sue & Sue, 1990). In addition, the focus on individual development can be at odds with cultural values that stress the common good and cohesion of a person's group. This model provides a foundation for a relationship to be developed if the counselor or therapist integrates cultural factors. Thus, the theoretical framework alone is not important but rather how it is used by the counselor or therapist.

Gestalt Theory

Because of its emphasis on individual responsibility and techniques that may be too confrontational or out of the realm of reality for these minority groups, Gestalt theory has several limitations. Confrontation and the techniques used may produce intense feelings that minority clients are not ready for or that are not culturally appropriate. Responsibility focuses on the self without connecting to the group relationship, which may have a higher priority for these minority groups. Native Americans, Asian Americans, and Hispanics have strong cultural characteristics that prohibit them from expressing strong negative emotions about their parents and family. Where cooperation is a heavy cultural injunction, these individuating directions for self-responsibility might meet with opposition. Another theoretical characteristic in Gestalt theory is that of "being in the present." This may not be understood by groups in which connectedness with the past is important to their world view. Again, the application of the model depends on its sensitive use by the counselor or therapist (Corey, 1991; Okum, 1990; Perls, 1973; Sue & Sue, 1990).

Transactional Analysis Theory

Transactional analysis theory has limited value for these focus racial and cultural groups for a number of reasons:

1. The use of terminology and structure is from a white perspective and requires too much interpolation to reach these defined groups effectively

2. It may not be meaningful because of its complexity and its emphasis on the techniques itself

3. It has the inherent capacity to be primarily an intellectual experience without regard to the effect of the sociocultural milieu that is part of the group

Transactional analysis does not take into account the feelings or acknowledge the cultural issues that these groups present. To be fair, it does focus on cultural and familial injunctions, which, if practitioners are able to reach these clients, might have some relevance. However, these injunctions can be counterproductive if they disregard family and loyalty to the group (Berne, 1961; Corey, 1991).

Rational-Emotive and Cognitive-Behavioral Theories

We discuss these two theories together because they are closely related. Although there are some differences in techniques, both hold to the basic concept of belief systems. Rational-emotive theory does not deal with past history. It does address the client's view of the problem, yet only the cognition of specific events or incidents. This has the danger of devaluing the minority group members' feelings of frustration and self-cultural concept. The theory can be confrontational and dismiss the story around the event or incident that is part of the minority's holistic view, thereby devaluing integrity and values.

Inherent in this theory is the tenet that rational and irrational beliefs are the basis of client problems. These beliefs are based on white, middle-class values; what is rational or irrational for the counselor or therapist may not be for the minority client. The issue of how much power counselors or therapists have may be intimidating or even negatively challenging, creating a retreat from the counselors or therapists or, even worse, an acquiescence to their ideas.

This theoretical framework has a firm set of beliefs that are not culturally relevant and could create confusion. The beliefs the minority client holds may be interpreted as blame and further exacerbate feelings of insecurity. Unless the counselor or therapist deals carefully and sensitively with the client's cultural beliefs and world view, this model will meet with disaster.

The theory challenges dependency, which to these groups may be counterproductive to their concept of interdependency, an important part of their cultural values and one they view as essentially healthy. The theory does not deal with such factors as racism, sociocultural experience, and family roles, which are conditioned by the groups' culture (Corey, 1991; Okum, 1990).

There are other cognitive-behavioral theories that do not take such a dogmatic approach as Ellis. Beck (1976) and Meichenbaum (1979) considered the sociocultural determinants more closely. Yet their approach is basically the same, with the problem being defined as the client sees it. However, Beck and Meichenbaum's approach looks at the cultural milieu before determining faulty beliefs and involves the client in mutually acceptable goals that can be culturally relevant. Structure is still primary; and once goals are determined, the model proceeds on its own. Nevertheless, it still leaves little room for people who do not possess mainstream ideas and are less articulate in majority logic. Behaviors and thoughts deemed culturally acceptable by the dominant culture may have unique and different meanings for these focus groups. Such values and meanings are not accounted for in cognitive-behavioral theory (Okum, 1990). Casas (1988) pointed out that cognitive-behavioral theory does not address racial ethnicity and culture in the development of research paradigms. He points out that the basic assumption of this model is that people are responsible for their own anxiety, contribute significantly to it, and can decide responsibly to act. This view may not be congruent with the life experiences of minorities. Casas further stated, "Racism, discrimination and poverty may have created a cognitive mind set antithetical to any self-control approach" (1988, p. 109). The counselor or therapist's value systems concerning race and class are eminently important. If they are incompatible with those of a minority group member, they may be imposed on the client and consequently affect him inappropriately. "The theory implies that the dominant therapist's value system is the correct one" (Okum, 1990, pp. 200–201).

Reality Therapy Theory

The principles of this model, which incorporate care, respect, and rejection of the medical model, are that behavior is purposive and geared to fulfilling needs; and the model has much potential depending on its application. In this model counselors or therapists can demonstrate their respect for cultural values and assist minority clients to explore how satisfying their current behavior is and collaboratively form realistic plans that are consistent with their cultural values. The focus is on acting and thinking rather than identifying and exploring feelings. It focuses on positive steps that *could* deal with cultural specificity, which would appeal to these minority groups. However, in this theory the responsibility lies totally with the individual. The counselor or therapist does not seek out the support systems and cooperation values that are part of these groups. The model itself does not address the very real aspects of discrimination and racism that limit these groups. If counselors or therapists do not accept these environmental restrictions as real, minority group members may resist and feel misunderstood. Additionally, many minority group members may be reluctant to state what they need to an institutional counselor or therapist because of real paranoia or because their socialization has not reinforced self-assertiveness. Their socialization has been to think more in terms of what is good for the group than of their individual needs. Again, as in other approaches, the effectiveness of reality therapy is based on the counselor or therapist's ability to be sensitive to cultural aspects rather than on the theory itself (Corey, 1991; Glasser, 1965).

Ecosystems Theory

Ecosystems theory incorporates several of the leading family systems theorists and principles of holistic thinking. This theory considers the family as the basic social system and that understanding the system's environment is paramount to be an effective practitioner. By definition a system's environment (institutional, societal, cultural) includes all that affects the basic family system. Consequently, this theory has great implications in its application to minority populations. However, in order for the theory to be effective, practitioners have to have a strong training base in multicultural counseling. It is surprising that this theory which has such an inherent ability to extend itself to racial and ethnic populations does not specifically address any of the cultural issues or considerations.

The basic premises of ecosystems theory deal with the individual, whole family system in their sociocultural contexts. It addresses extended family kinships and respects the concepts of cooperative functioning, an approach that would have much appeal to the racial and ethnic groups we have discussed. It sees the family as the basic unit of development and examines the alliances, subsystems, relationships, and crossgenerational issues in their relationship to the larger whole. The authors include Minuchin's structural approach that has been implemented with several minority groups, therefore making it culturally adaptable. Minuchin and Fishman (1981) and Aponte and Van Dusen (1981) in particular have emphasized the reciprocal influences of the family and community and have focused on interventions that address this interdependence. They incorporate a broad world view and a knowledge that different cultural systems do impact the function of the family and individuals. The structural approach within the ecosystems approach can be used with an individual or family yet still deal with the extended family system. However, this approach does not address the concept of racism and discrimination in the larger sociocultural content.

In general, ecosystems theory has been criticized because it does not specifically address the larger institutional issues that harbor racism, class discrimination, and specificity in culture. Often problems that are embedded in the larger social systems are improperly assessed as dysfunctional in nuclear family systems. However, because of the very nature of the theory, it uses a comprehensive and holistic approach that could be culturally sensitive and shows much promise in addressing the issues faced by these racial ethnic groups (Aponte & Van Dusen, 1981; Minuchin & Fishman, 1981; Okum, 1990).

Developmental Counseling and Therapy Theory

The developmental counseling and therapy theory is one of the rare theoretical models that directly and indirectly address the comprehensive importance of culture, family systems, and world view of clients. It is one that shows the greatest promise in addressing cultural issues because of its inherent assumptions, characteristics, and processes. It stresses the importance of the larger sociocultural context of the clients and the family that is congruent to the value system of the minority groups presented. The theory assumes an egalitarian posture in relationship to clients and more importantly, presents a schema that the practitioners and clients cooperatively co-construct the client's world view. Psychological distress is seen not as a personality disorder but as a developmental impasse which, in terms of mental health, would be very appropriate to minority cultural populations, who experience institutional racist distress. The theory assumes that all counseling is cross-cultural and provides a methodology for assessing multiple perspectives that lead to a holistic view.

While the theory does not specifically address all of the cultural components presented in this chapter, by implication and its process it has the potential to get an assessment of most of the components. However, the application of this model assumes that the practitioner be well trained in multicultural counseling. This assumption is a major concern in that some may assume that the use of this theory could access all of the multicultural information needed. The theory does address this issue but in a limited way.

Another concern centers around the universal application of a modified Piagetian organizational framework that may or may not be applicable to the four minority groups discussed. The model assumes that this conceptual framework is applicable to all groups. It also is not clear about what is required of the clients in terms of time and length of sessions. Considering the defined traditional low-income and less educated minority populations discussed, several questions arise. What level of cognitive functioning does the model require? How does the model factor in the orientation to formal counseling that is not a part of these minority groups' world view? It seems an assumption is made that the process will be effective with these groups. What if the practitioner cannot speak the language or understand its philosophical metaphors? These are a few questions that arise about this, albeit culturally sensitive, theory.

SUMMARY

This chapter discusses some of the multicultural issues facing our profession, in particular the racial and ethnic considerations impinging on current counseling and therapeutic theories. The complexity of multiculturalism in theory has many facets that must be considered, including demographics, definitions, racial and ethnic cultural considerations, acculturation, and socioeconomic and cultural distinctions. These considerations do not provide a prescriptive analysis for integration into existing theories but have been included in this chapter because of their importance to the four focus minority groups. The chart in figure 18.1 should facilitate your understanding of this complex interacting phenomenon. We hope our critique of the chart and the general discussion of the theories will provide insight into the dilemma of how theories must be viewed in light of our changing population. Counseling and therapeutic theories are fundamental to the way in which counselors and therapists deliver services, but they carry inherent assumptions that we rarely question. Nevertheless, we need to critically evaluate them in light of minority concerns.

Current counseling and therapeutic theories reflect the Zeitgeist of the era and region in which the theorists lived. Therefore, traditional counseling and psychotherapies were developed for white, middle- and upper-middle-class clients (Atkinson et al., 1989). As Katz (1985) noted, these theories were developed by white practitioners enmeshed in Western cultural values, and the applicability of these theories to multicultural populations is questionable.

The onus for the development of cultural awareness and applicability has been shouldered by counselors and therapists. Only recently have training institutions begun to provide crosscultural training, but those counselors or therapists already out in the field have had to rely on workshops or their own readings and experiences to obtain this awareness.

Many of them have developed theoretical frameworks and have tried to integrate cultural factors, usually by looking for a "prescription."

In addition to the cultural milieu in which theories were developed, one also has to consider the theoretical framework that reflects practitioners' own Zeitgeist. Theory cannot be considered apart from the context of its original background and filtered through a counselor or therapist's interpretation. This may provide an even more distorted view, not only of the theory but also of its applicability to different cultural groups. Each of the major models of counseling and therapeutic theory has this unexamined assumption: it is true and therefore correct. But at best, theory can only lay a foundation from which to view client behavior and development. There is no one *fully acceptable model* that is considered unassailable in today's world.

Counseling and therapeutic theories in their perfect form do not specifically address the racial, ethnic, and cultural considerations of American minority groups. However, it is possible to adapt some theories if certain cultural considerations are taken into account. So before one "throws the baby out with the bath water," it is essential to take a critical look at significant cultural components in relation to theory.

Counselors and therapists are facing a critical impasse in the profession. Pedersen (1991) called multiculturalism the fourth force. Perhaps this fourth force will require a redefinition of current theories and a major integration of multicultural considerations into our current theories. A paradigm shift in our thinking about how to deliver services based on a theoretical framework that incorporates multicultural aspects is no longer just an idea but a reality. As counselors and therapists, we cannot wait for the evolution of a new theory because we need to proceed now with what we know. The reality of the changing demographics of our clientele presents our greatest challenge to integrate into our own theory these multicultural components.

REFERENCES

American Association for Counseling and Development. (1991). Special issue: Multiculturalism as a fourth force in counseling. *Journal of Counseling and Development, 70,* 4–76.

Aponte, H., & Van Dusen, J. (1981). Structural family therapy. In A. S. Gurman & D. P. Kniskern, *Handbook of family therapy* (pp. 310–360). New York: Brunner/Mazel.

Atkinson, D., Morten, G., & Sue, D. W. (1989). *Counseling American minorities: A cross-cultural perspective.* Dubuque, IA: Brown.

Beck, A. (1976). *Cognitive therapy and emotional disorders.* New York: New American Library.

Berne, E. (1961). *Transactional analysis in psychotherapy.* New York: Grove.

Casas, M. (1988). Cognitive behavioral approaches: A minority perspective. *The Counseling Psychologist, 16*, 106–110.

Corey, G. (1991). *Theory and practice of counseling and psychotherapy*. Pacific Grove, CA: Brooks/Cole.

Dillard, M. (1985). *Multicultural counseling: Ethnic and cultural relevance in human encounters*. Chicago: Nelson-Hall.

Edmunds, P., Martinson, S. A., & Goldberg, P. F. (1990). *Demographics and cultural diversity in the 1990's: Implications for services to young children with special needs*. Washington, D.C.: Office of Special Education Programs, U.S. Department of Education.

Glasser, K. (1965). *Reality therapy: A new approach to psychiatry*. New York: Harper & Row.

Hall, W., Cross, W. E., & Freed, W. R. (1971). Stages in the development of black awareness: An exploratory investigation. In R. L. Jones (Ed.), *Black psychology* (pp. 156–166). New York: Harper & Row.

Ibrahim, F. A. (1985). Effective cross-cultural counseling and psychotherapy: A framework. *The Counseling Psychologist, 13*, 625–638.

Ibrahim, F. A. (1991). Contribution of cultural worldview to generic counseling and development. *Journal of Counseling and Development, 70*, 13–19.

Ivey, A. (1981). Counseling and psychotherapy: Toward a new perspective. In A. J. Marsella & P. B. Pedersen (Eds.), *Cross-cultural counseling and psychotherapy*. New York: Pergamon.

Ivey, A., Ivey, M. B., & Simek-Morgan. (1993). *Counseling and psychotherapy: A multicultural perspective*. Boston: Allyn & Bacon.

Kagan, S., & Madsen, M. (1971). Cooperation and competition of Mexican, Mexican/American and Anglo children of two ages under four instructional sets. *Developmental Psychology 5*, 32.

Katz, J. (1985). The sociopolitical nature of counseling. *The Counseling Psychologist, 13*, 615–624.

Krogman, W. M. (1945). The concept of race. In R. Linton (Ed.), *The science of man in world crisis* (pp. 38–61). New York: Columbia University Press.

Kuhn, T. (1962). *The structure of scientific revolution*. Chicago: University of Chicago Press.

LaFromboise, T. D. (1988). American Indian mental health policy. *American Psychologist, 43*, 388–397.

LaFromboise, T., & Low, K. G. (1989). American Indian children and adolescents. In J. T. Gibbs & L. N. Huang (Eds.), *Children of color: Psychological intervention with minority youth* (pp. 114–147). San Francisco: Jossey-Bass.

LeVine, E. S., & Padilla, A. M. (1980). *Crossing cultures in therapy: Pluralistic counseling for the Hispanic*. Monterey, CA: Brooks/Cole.

Linton, R. (Ed.). (1945). *The science of man (woman) in the world crisis*. New York: Columbia University Press.

Meichenbaum, D. (1979). *Cognitive-behavioral modification*. New York: Plenum.

Midgette, T., & Meggert, S. (1991). Multicultural counseling instruction: A challenge for faculties in the 21st century. *Journal of Counseling and Development, 70*, 136–141.

Minuchin, S., & Fishman, H. (1981). *Techniques of family therapy*. Cambridge: Harvard University Press.

Newlon, B. J., & Arciniega, M. (1983). Counseling minority families: An Adlerian perspective. *Counseling and Human Development, 16*, 1–12.

Newlon, B. J., & Arciniega, M. (1992). Group counseling: Cross cultural considerations. In D. Capuzzi & D. Gross (Eds.), *Introduction to group counseling* (pp. 286-306). Denver: Love.

Okum, B. (1990). *Seeking connections in psychotherapy*. San Francisco: Jossey-Bass.

Pedersen, P. B. (1988). *A handbook for developing multicultural awareness*. Alexandria, VA: American Association for Counseling and Development.

Pedersen, P. (1991). Multiculturalism as a generic approach to counseling. *Journal of Counseling and Development, 70*, 6–12.

Pedersen, P., Draguns, J. G., Lonner, W. J., & Trimble, J. E. (Eds.). (1989). *Counseling across cultures* (3rd ed.). Honolulu: University of Hawaii Press.

Perls, F. (1973). *The Gestalt approach and eyewitness to therapy*. New York: Bantam.

Ponterotto, J., & Casas, M. (1991). *Handbook of racial/ethnic minority counseling research*. Springfield, IL: Charles C Thomas.

Ponterotto, J., & Sabnani, H. (1989). Classics in multicultural counseling: A systematic five-year content analysis. *Journal of Multicultural Counseling and Development, 17*, 23–37.

Rogers, C. (1980). *A way of being*. Boston: Houghton Mifflin.

Rogler, L. N., Malgady, R., Constantino, G., & Bluenenthall, R. (1987). What do culturally sensitive mental health services mean? The case for Hispanics. *American Psychologist, 42*, 565–570.

Rose, P. I. (1964). *They and we: Racial and ethnic relations in the United States*. New York: Random House.

Sherman, R., & Dinkmeyer, D. (1987). *Systems of family therapy: An Adlerian integration*. New York: Brunner/Mazel.

Sue, D. W., & Sue, D. (1990). *Counseling the culturally different: Theory and process*. New York: Wiley.

Teske, R. (1973). An analysis of status mobility patterns among middle-class Mexican Americans in Texas. *Dissertation Abstracts International, 42*, 7907a.

U.S. Bureau of the Census. (1982). *Census of the population: Supplemental report. Race of the population by states*. Washington, DC: U.S. Government Printing Office.

U.S. Bureau of the Census. (1988). *Census of the population: Supplemental report. Race of the population by states*. Washington, DC: U.S. Government Printing Office.

U.S. Bureau of the Census. (1989). *Census population totals for racial and Spanish origin groups in U.S.* Washington, DC: U.S. Government Printing Office.

Wehrly, B. (1991). Preparing multicultural counselors. *Counseling and Human Development, 24*, 1–23.

Wrenn, C. G. (1962). The culturally encapsulated counselor. *Harvard Educational Review, 32*, 444–449.

Wrenn, C. G. (1985). Afterward: The culturally encapsulated counselor revisited. In P. B. Pedersen (Ed.), *Handbook of cross-cultural counseling and therapy*. Westport, CT: Greenwood.

Yalom, I. D. (1988). *Existential psychotherapy*. New York: Basic Books.

CHAPTER NINETEEN

Counseling and Psychotherapy: An Integrative Perspective

Loretta J. Bradley
Texas Tech University

Gerald Parr
Texas Tech University

L. J. Gould
Texas Tech University

In previous chapters of this book, the authors discuss a number of discrete theories. Proponents of each psychotherapeutic theory maintain that with a wide range of client problems, the philosophy, principles, and interventions of that theory are preferable and more effective. Despite the many positive contributions of each theory, research has not shown that any one theory is superior to any other (Smith & Glass, 1977). Further, no theory is an island. Beutler and Clarkin (1990) state that the practice of psychotherapy is evolutionary, extending through the realms of experience and knowledge that are incorporated into the still-developing field. They state:

> Every theory is, in reality, an amalgamation of previous viewpoints. When we speak of one theory or another as "a different perspective," we forget that it is derived developmentally from others. When a "new theory" is developed and compared with an old one, the comparison dims one's awareness of the fact that the new theory has incorporated some of the common knowledge to which the earlier theory contributed. (p. 6)

As more theories and research appear, it becomes increasingly difficult for counselors and psychotherapists to defend a strictly separatist view. The search for a more comprehensive therapy often leads to integration. Smith (1982) captures the essence of the search for a more integrative approach:

> Counselors and psychotherapists who consider single-theory orientations too provincial in both theoretical concepts and methodological options tend to seek an eclectic alternative. Eclecticism promises the possibility for a comprehensive psychotherapy that is based on a unified and well-organized body of knowledge and strategies. (p. 802)

The main purpose of this chapter is not to judge the merits of the theories described in previous chapters; rather, it is designed to help you translate information from various counseling or psychotherapy knowledge bases into a counseling or psychotherapy approach that best fits your style. Specifically, this chapter will assist you in your search for a counseling or psychotherapeutic model that integrates your beliefs, experiences, values, and personal characteristics. The integrity of your personal model depends, in part, on your ability to explicate the beliefs and assumptions that underlie your approach. You should be prepared to answer any of the following questions:

> Are there common, curative factors that have universal applicability, regardless of the client's background or presenting problem?

What roles should the counselor or psychotherapist be willing to assume as a helper: a teacher, a mentor, a technical expert, an empathic listener, an informed consultant, a role model, or a wise advisor?

Are problems solved in the same way in which they are developed?

Another step toward professional integrity is understanding how your personal experiences have influenced your beliefs. Perhaps a counselor or psychotherapist helped you at one time, and you want to offer to others the same ingredients that you found helpful. Perhaps you respect a counselor, educator, psychotherapist, or supervisor and want to incorporate some of that person's ideas into your approach. Becoming aware of your values and their role in your learning is important too. Your values filter and focus your experiences. Those who value family will seek out approaches—systemic approaches, for example—that feature family as the focal point of intervention; those who value concrete results may be drawn to cognitive-behavioral approaches, which emphasize specific behavior change. Finally, being aware of your personal needs and personality style can help illuminate why certain approaches appeal to you. A person-centered approach, for example, might argue with a dominant personality style. Likewise, a rational-emotive approach might not be the best fit for an individual who avoids conflict.

In this chapter, we will define integrative theory and address its history and its various types. Additionally, we will focus on the development of a personal integrative approach, including personal philosophy, clients, treatment goals, and theory constructs.

INTEGRATIVE COUNSELING AND THERAPY DEFINED

Integrative counseling and psychotherapy evolved from a need. Basically, it began with the assumption that a single theory is too limiting. Proponents advocate that each counselor or psychotherapist should be able to construct her own model by taking portions from other theories. This approach allows the counselor or psychotherapist to create a model by synthesizing existing theory and practice. In essence, integrative counseling and psychotherapy operates on the premise that the counselor or psychotherapist can choose the best from among the various theories.

Young (1992) defines *eclecticism* (integration) as a theory that selects what is best from among many theoretical stances. Implied in this definition is the assumption that the counselor or psychotherapist has a thorough knowledge of existing theories, including both strengths and limitations as well as the knowledge of the necessary ingredients for effective theory building. Young also writes that what is best in counseling or psychotherapy is that which works, and integrative counseling and psychotherapy is a pragmatic approach devoid of a single viewpoint.

Gilliland, James, and Bowman (1989) describe this integration as a broad-based approach that makes systematic and appropriate use of the best interventions from all theories. Garfield (1982, 1988) cautions that the integrative approach cannot be simply a combination of existing theoretical views or the addition of some interventions from one therapy to another. Instead, it denotes a conceptual synthesis and pragmatic blending of diverse theoretical systems into a superordinate or metatheoretical model that includes philosophy, theory, principles, and interventions (Halgin, 1985; Kelly, 1988, 1991; Norcross, 1985, 1990; Patterson, 1989b; Wolfe & Goldfried, 1988).

In chapter 2 of this book, the authors discuss the importance of developing a personal theory. The counselor or psychotherapist develops his theory based on study, research, and experience in the field in addition to his personal values and view of human nature. The integrative perspective allows counselors and psychotherapists to create models that reflect their unique personalities, talents, and experiences. Typically, this approach represents a synthesis of selected constructs and practices espoused by major theories. It offers the counselor or psychotherapist several advantages. First, ownership is high when counselors and psychotherapists expend the effort to develop and explicate their own paradigms, which often result in an enhanced commitment to ongoing model refinement. Second, this approach encourages authenticity and congruence, which is not fostered by unreflective imitation. Third, integrative counseling and psychotherapy allows counselors and psychotherapists the flexibility to tailor their approach to best fit the population and problems that characterize their practice. To illustrate, counselors and psychotherapists who provide short-term, crisis-oriented assistance, as many school counselors do, may want to rely more heavily on problem-solving models, such as the cognitive-behavioral approaches discussed in chapter 13, than would counselors and psychotherapists in private practice, who treat intra- and interpersonal problems over 10 to 20 sessions.

Conversely, the integrative perspective presents challenges that, if unmet, could become disadvantageous to counselors and psychotherapists. Those who fail to develop, articulate, and define a model of counseling and psychotherapy can fall prey to the "lazy eclecticism" that Eysenck (1970) has so forcefully denounced. Single-theory adherence suits some counselors and psychotherapists, and an attempt to be integrative may argue against their needs. Some may find that only single-theory adherence can impart the confidence that they need. Others, especially inexperienced counselors and psychotherapists, may lack the courage of their convictions or may find it too demanding to invent a model when ready-made approaches are so readily available. Single-theory adherence can be very alluring when it is formalized with institutes and certification because these trappings can impart a sense of belonging, power, and direction to its devotees. Neophytes often want the security of a well-defined, widely endorsed road map as they launch their professional careers.

HISTORY

Orthodoxy dominated the early spirit of the counseling and psychotherapy movement. However, early on, Sigmund Freud experienced much controversy both from within and outside his theory base of psychoanalysis. Influenced by psychoanalysis, many theorists, such as Jung (chapter 6) and Adler (chapter 7) soon began developing or seeking other models of counseling and psychotherapy. With the rise of schools of therapy that were independent from psychoanalysis, orthodox psychotherapy was challenged. Schools of therapy, including cognitive-behavioral (chapter 13), Gestalt (chapter 10), rational-emotive (chapter 12), person-centered (chapter 9), and transactional analysis (chapter 11), emerged as the preeminence of the analytic paradigm waned. Developmental counseling and therapy (chapter 16) and ecosystems theory (chapter 15) have also contributed to new perspectives in counseling and psychotherapy.

With the development of new paradigms, an increase in innovative methods and interventions emerged and were quickly shared by practitioners from the various schools, a group more likely to use the tools of other orientations and less likely to adhere blindly to one theory (Smith, 1982). Beutler and Clarkin (1990) describe the role of borrowing from other therapies:

> Given the role of borrowing and assimilation occurring in the natural course of theory development, the exponential increase in the number of discrete theories of psychotherapy, and the necessity of defining both the similarities and differences among applied theories in order to conduct empirical research, the eventual and formal acceptance of eclecticism may have been inevitable. (p. 10)

Historical Antecedents

Historically, integrative counseling and psychotherapy first appeared when the constructs and principles of one paradigm were used to explain those of another. Dollard and Miller (1950), for example, drew upon learning theory to explain psychoanalytic theory. The principle of reinforcement replaced Freud's pleasure principle. Transference was explained as a special case of generalization. Thorne (1950), frustrated by the ideological confusion of the psychological sciences, wrote *Principles of Personality Counseling* in which he espoused an integrative approach that he hoped would promote a standardization of counseling and psychotherapy practice similar to that of the medical profession. Borrowing heavily from the medical model, Thorne's approach was reeducative. It emphasized rational-intellectual factors and launched the integrative movement.

MAJOR CONSTRUCTS

Integration is a broad-based approach that makes systematic and appropriate use of the best interventions from all theories. A fundamental assumption of the integrative approach is that counseling and psychotherapy involve a relationship that, as with other theories, stresses the importance of the rapport between counselor or psychotherapist and client. A basic inference of this model is that the counselor or psychotherapist is a genuine human being willing to and capable of establishing a working alliance with the client. As stated in chapter 1, this working alliance best begins through the practice of the core conditions of counseling and psychotherapy. The practitioner must show the client empathic understanding, respect and positive regard, genuineness and congruence, concreteness, warmth, immediacy, and cultural awareness. Without these core conditions, counseling and psychotherapy is extremely difficult, if not impossible. Further, the practitioner must recognize that the process of counseling and psychotherapy is developmental. The stages of counseling and psychotherapy, like the stages of human development, often do not follow in a one-two-three order; but they most often occur in the order of relationship development, extended exploration, problem resolution, and termination and follow-up. A second assumption is that the counselor or psychotherapist is cognizant of the strategies and methods used in a variety of theories and can differentiate and selectively use them to meet the needs of the client. A third assumption is that the counselor or psychotherapist will keep current on new developments in the field so that she continually extends and develops her theory base.

In reviewing research on integrative theory, researchers have concluded the following (Brammer, 1969; Dryden, 1986; Garfield, 1973, 1980; Palmer, 1980; Thorne, 1967):

- The counselor or psychotherapist must assume that the primary need of the client is to achieve and maintain his highest level of functioning; thus, the practitioner must deal with the client's current psychological state.

- The counselor or psychotherapist's approach must be scientific, systematic, and logical without an identification with a single orientation.

- The counselor or psychotherapist's orientation should be constantly evolving and changing to incorporate new ideas, concepts, interventions, and research. The counselor or psychotherapist should not operate on faith, guesswork, emotion, popularity, or special interest; nor should she consider ideological consistency to be an end in itself.

- The theory should be broad enough to organize, comprehend, integrate, resolve, and use the contributions, consistencies, and inconsistencies of all other counseling and therapy approaches.

- The counselor or psychotherapist must have a repertoire of concepts, skills, competencies, and strategies from which to draw and thus avoid narrow and simplistic treatments.

- The counselor or psychotherapist must deal directly with the client as a person (including his world view, developmental level, culture, social interactions, values, and goals). Counseling and psychotherapy should focus directly on the client's behavior, goals, and problems as opposed to merely talking about them. Counseling and psychotherapy should also deal with problems outside client control (for example, poverty or prejudice).

- The counselor or psychotherapist must function in a variety of roles as needed, including counselor or psychotherapist, teacher, consultant, facilitator, mentor, advisor, and coach.

There are three main thrusts in integrative therapy. First, the counselor or psychotherapist helps the client become aware of the problem situation. Following awareness, he encourages the client to choose consciously—and, to the extent possible, intentionally—to exercise control over her problem behavior. Finally, he assists the client in developing a higher level of personal integration through proactive choice.

INTEGRATIVE MODELS

Norcross (1986) describes three types of models in integrative counseling and psychotherapy: atheoretical models, models that emphasize commonalties or interventions above theory; technical models, or models with a single theory base but using a wide variety of interventions from other orientations; and synthetic models, or models emphasizing a blending of two or more theories and a variety of interventions.

Atheoretical Models

Common Factors Model.   The common factors model is an example of an atheoretical model emphasizing specific common factors responsible for success in counseling and psychotherapy regardless of theoretical orientation. In fact, Karasu (1986) states that it is the nature of psychotherapy to have commonalties. All orientations use some combination of affective, experiential, cognitive, and behavioral regulations as agents of change. Frank (1981) posited that six common curative factors are shared by all therapeutic orientations: the strength of the client and counselor or psychotherapist relationship, methods that increase motivation and expectations of help, the enhancement of the client's sense of mastery or self-efficacy, the provision of new learning experiences, the arousal of emotions, and the enhancement of opportunities to practice new behaviors. Frank concluded that these six factors exist to varying degrees in different orientations. Beutler and Clarkin (1990) suggest that common treatment ingredients are created and enhanced by (1) the specific and controllable communication patterns inherent in caring counselors or psychotherapists, (2) the interventions chosen by caring counselors or psychotherapists, (3) the sensitive use of interventions, and (4) the reasonable amount of control that the counselor or psychotherapist maintains over the counseling or psychotherapy experience.

Building on Frank's common factors model, Young (1992) developed the REPLAN model, which is an example of a specific application of the common factors model. Young's model is based on curative factors (megafactors), which are dimensions of the therapeutic process underlying all counseling or psychotherapy approaches (Frank, 1981; Yalom, 1985). The curative factors in REPLAN are relationship (R), efficacy and self-esteem (E), practicing new behaviors (P), lowering or raising emotional arousal (L), activating expectations of help and motivation (A), and providing new learning experiences and changing perceptions (N). The model assumes that treatment planning should be organized and structured so that coherent concepts are presented to the client and reasonable and defensible plans for therapy may be developed. Therapeutic goals are defined by the client and counselor or psychotherapist, and the treatment plan uses the curative factors to achieve the goals. Interventions are chosen on the basis of client characteristics. Counseling or psychotherapy is structured around specific goals in each session to help the client stay on task. REPLAN is a systematic and pragmatic approach suitable for counselors or psychotherapists who have single-theory orientations or multiple orientations.

Even in the context of the same theoretical orientation, diversity exists in therapeutic outcomes (Lieberman, Yalom, & Miles, 1973; Luborsky, Singer, & Luborsky, 1975), thus suggesting that common factors are responsible for success in counseling and psychotherapy rather than the theoretical orientation. While there is agreement that common factors exist, agreement ends and debate begins about the degree to which common factors can become basic ingredients of therapy (Frank, 1973; Garfield, 1973; Lambert, 1986; Parloff, 1986; Wilkins, 1984). Likewise, Fiedler (1950b) and Sloane, Stapels, Cristol, Yorkston, and Whipple (1975) report that inconsistencies exist between the counselor or psychotherapist's stated theory and in-therapy behaviors, thus suggesting that individuals with differing theoretical assumptions may behave similarly and use common factors in therapy sessions.

Phase Models.   The basic assumption underlying the phase model, another type of atheoretical model, is that the therapy process is characterized by marked phases or stages that clients experience during therapy. Common phases include resistance, action, and change. Phases-of-change models attempt to identify characteristic phases (stages) of treatment that are linked to a variety of theories. In phase models, counseling and psychotherapy interventions are dependent on the phase (stage) of treatment.

Prochaska (1984) and Prochaska and DiClemente's (1984, 1986) transtheoretical model, an example of a phase model, is based on a comprehensive study of phases and principles of change prevalent in a variety of theories. Ten processes of change obtained from client self-reports on personal problem solving were described: consciousness raising (interventions that make clients aware of problems), self-liberation (improving self-efficacy and client involvement in the change process), social liberation (freedom from social obligations), counterconditioning (reframing negative situations or outcomes into positives), stimulus control (learning triggers of negative behaviors, feelings, and thoughts), self-reevaluation (methods for evaluation of values and client-action potential), environmental reevaluation (evaluation of environmental demands), contingency management (controlling rewards and punishments), dramatic relief (removal of symptoms), and helping relationships (use of methods committed to client well-being). Within the counseling and psychotherapy process, there are three stages of change that are based on the client's awareness of his problem: precontemplation—the client is unaware of problems; contemplation—the client, through consciousness raising, becomes aware of problems and begins thinking about them; and action and maintenance—change processes occur. Change occurs on five distinct but interrelated levels: symptom or situational, maladaptive cognitions, current interpersonal conflicts, family or systems conflicts, and interpersonal conflicts. In the stages-of-change model, the client and counselor or psychotherapist work together to determine the level on which interventions will be focused.

Thorne's Model.   Thorne's (1967, 1968) model is a rigidly empirical scientific approach that avoids giving priority to any theoretical viewpoint. Because all existing methods are included, Thorne described his model as the only truly scientific model. Although not a new model, it does present a collection of methods applied rationally according to their indications and counterindications. Because Thorne's model posits a specific treatment method for specific disorders, it has been called a medical model of counseling and psychotherapy and is an example of another atheoretical model. In operational terms, Thorne's model first requires a compilation of all known counseling or psychotherapeutic interventions. Next, operational definitions are determined by an experimental analysis of the dynamics of each method, with each method being evaluated to establish its indications and contraindications as well as its relation to psychopathology. Therapeutic effects of each method are then determined, and criteria are established. Statistical analysis is conducted on large-scale data to determine validation through prognosis.

Technical Models

Technical Model.   The technical model emphasizes the importance of the counselor or psychotherapist as a technician, a skilled master of interventions successful on a practical level without a well-articulated guiding philosophy or theory. In this model, the counselor or psychotherapist applies systematic and planned logic to the assignment of treatment for a client. A technical model is not the idiosyncratic and undefined blend that in the past has often been called eclectic counseling or psychotherapy. It is, rather, a decision-making process for selecting interventions based on the client's symptoms and goals (Beutler, 1983; Frances, Clarkin, & Perry, 1984; Goldstein & Stein, 1976; Held, 1984; Lazarus, 1976, 1981; Norcross, 1986).

BASIC-ID Model.   Lazarus's (1967, 1973, 1976, 1981) BASIC-ID is an example of a technical model. This multimodal approach is broad-spectrum, both in terms of the battery of interventions Lazarus employs and in terms of how he assesses clients' problems. His interventions range from the creative, intuitive use of imagery (1984) to more standard behavioral interventions, such as aversion therapy (1971). Lazarus's multimodal BASIC-ID profile provides a good example of a technical model. This is a pragmatic approach that focuses on who or what is best for the client and methods for resolving problems. The theory base is behaviorist, although a variety of interventions are applied to client treatment without regard for their theoretical origins. The behavioristic basis of the model suggests that client problems have a triggering sequence and that effects in one mode are transferred to other modalities. Thus, interventions are designed for each modality (B = behavior, A = affect, S = sensation, I = imagery, C = cognition, I = interpersonal, D = drug or alcohol) and are implemented simultaneously in a shotgun approach to interrupt the cycle. Lazarus's assessment procedure addresses the areas denoted by the acronym BASIC-ID and includes an innovative inquiry into potential transference phenomena. For example, he asks his clients to imagine what it would be like to be shipwrecked with him on a desert island for six months (1971). Lazarus asserts that clients' responses to this projective intervention help him identify their expectations and clarify their concerns. In our review of Lazarus's publications, it is apparent that he stresses the importance of designing individual strategies for the client and closely monitoring the progress of the interactive efforts in therapy.

Prescriptive Model.   The prescriptive model is a specific problem-solving treatment approach addressing various levels of human functioning (biological, intrapsychic, interpersonal) in both theoretical and applied (practical) terms. According to Diamond, Havens, and Jones (1978), the prescriptive model requires "a framework that permits flexibility in the process of individualizing treatment yet does not lose the benefits of information from theory and research in psychotherapy" (pp. 239–240). It is a systematic effort to provide a specific set of treatment procedures for each of several conditions (neurotic disorders, psychopathology, sexual dysfunction, habit disorders, and psychosis) by delineating the relationship between symptom presentation and treatment. The clinical process includes five steps: theory or conceptual superstructure, assessment, goal setting, intervention, and evaluation. The prescriptive model emphasizes the importance of research in the clinical decision-making process and focuses on the client and counselor or psychotherapist relationship rather than theoretical positions, although theory is given more importance than in the purely technical model (Diamond & Havens, 1975; Diamond et al., 1978; Goldstein & Stein, 1976; Held, 1984; Norcross, 1990).

Differential Therapeutics Model.   The differential therapeutics model combines clinical wisdom from experienced counselors and psychotherapists with a variety of clinical examples to define counseling or therapeutic practice. Diagnostic, character, and environmental variables help define contraindicators and enabling factors for predicting treatment outcome. This model is less specific than other technical models and depends on the use of a cookbook approach to effective intervention (Beutler & Clarkin, 1990; Frances et al., 1984; Perry, Frances, & Clarkin, 1985).

Synthetic (Systematic) Models

Synthetic (Systematic) Model.   Allport (cited in Lewis, 1985) captured the essence of the synthetic model when he insisted that counselors or psychotherapists should be systematic rather than syncretic in client treatment, and that each component of the system should be critically evaluated according to coherence and the available evidence. Further, the counselor or psychotherapist must avoid dogmatism and have a flexible theory base.

Allport's model focuses on both technical integration and social persuasion theory (Brehm, 1976; Brehm & Brehm, 1981; Brehm & Smith, 1986; Goldstein, 1966; Strong, 1978). It is difficult to develop decision criteria for assignment of treatment procedures independent of the theories on which the procedures are based. There are three client/problem dimensions (symptom complexity or severity, defensive style, interpersonal resistance level), which are matched with three complementary aspects of counseling or psychotherapy interventions (treatment focused on symptoms or conflicts; on cognitive, behavioral, or affective procedures; and on the degree of directiveness from the counselor or psychotherapist). The systematic model stresses the importance of the relationship between the client and the counselor or psychotherapist and of matching the needs of the client with interventions that enhance acceptance of change. Six areas of intervention are considered after assessment: insight enhancement, emotional awareness, emotional escalation, emotional reduction, behavioral control, and perceptual change. Treatment is adjusted as client/problem status changes (Beutler, 1983, 1986; Beutler & Mitchell, 1981; Calvert, Beutler, & Crago, 1988).

Biopsychosocial Model.   The biopsychosocial model has its origins in psychiatry. It is pluralistic and maintains that disorders have determinants from biological, psychological, and social arenas. This model suggests that the best treatment for mental disorders must combine interventions from all three areas (Abroms, 1983).

Frey's Model.   Frey's model is a synthesis of two continua for describing counseling or psychotherapy theory: a rational-affective dimension conceptualizing the process and an action-insight dimension conceptualizing the goals. Counselors or psychotherapists may use the model as a means for integrating goals and classifying differing theories according to client needs (Frey, 1972). The model possesses four quadrants: action-rational, insight-rational, insight-affective, and action-affective. For example, Gestalt therapy emphasizing both the affective and action dimensions is classified as a quadrant 2 therapy.

Functional Model.   The functional model, another example of the synthetic model, advocates the use of an implicit metatheory (integration of several theories) to interrelate different interventions and concepts. It is a pragmatic method that endorses the use of any tools that may help the counselor or psychotherapist in her work with clients. The method gives equal attention to behavior, thoughts, feelings, and social circumstances. It gives more attention to cognitions and behaviors under conscious control rather than to unconscious determinants and automatic behaviors (Hart, 1983).

Interpersonal Style Model.   Using Leary's interpersonal diagnosis model, Andrews (1989) analyzed the therapeutic world views and intervention styles of several counseling and psychotherapy theories. Viewed from Leary's typology, which is depicted as a circle, Andrews characterized psychoanalysis as hostile-submissive; humanistic-Rogerian therapy as friendly-submissive; and behavioral and cognitive-behavioral therapy as friendly-dominant. Similarly, Andrews used Leary's typology to classify leading counselors or psychotherapists. Perls, for example, exemplifies a hostile-dominant therapeutic stance. What is especially relevant about Andrews's article is the thesis that a flexible, integrative approach avoids the limitations of a single vision of reality. More specifically, Andrews states:

> To be fruitful, therapeutic interactions must not complement too exactly the client's interpersonal style, or else that style—and the problems associated with it—will be reinforced. . . . When we structure a personal style or therapeutic outlook around a single vision, we risk becoming single-dimensional caricatures. (pp. 806–812)

Thus, the integrative counselor or psychotherapist modifies his interpersonal behavior to challenge the client and to offer an alternative view of reality.

Redecision Model.   Goulding and Goulding's (1978, 1979) redecision therapy is an excellent example of synthetic integration. Combining transactional analysis and Gestalt, the Gouldings use a group format in a ranch setting to have individuals revisit early childhood decisions. Imagined dialogues allow group participants to rework dysfunctional, childhood script decisions. The Gouldings' approach promotes intellectual understanding, cathartic release, and behavioral change by mixing the conceptual framework and interventions of an experiential perspective (Gestalt) with a rational-educative perspective (transactional analysis).

Strategic Model.   The strategic model is based on two primary concepts: constructivism, which states that individuals do not discover reality but rather invent it; and the systems view of the process, which states that individuals are open to variation that stimulates interaction. Interventions are matched to the client by examination of her construction and process orientations. Three components are paramount to the strategic model: (1) viewing the client's problem from various theory perspectives that address his level of problematic functioning; (2) choosing and applying the theory or theories that best conceptualize the problem in service of counseling or psychotherapy goals (theory, client, counselor or psychotherapist); and (3) incorporating strategic interventions into therapy to enhance change. The strategic model is a systematic and problem-solving approach that provides multiple theories and methods for understanding the client's problem and interventions needed to maximize change (Duncan, Parks, & Rusk, 1990; Held, 1984).

In summary, the atheoretical, technical, and synthetic (systematic) models account for most of the integrative models; however, other examples of responsible integration abound (Beutler, 1983; Diamond & Havens, 1975; Garfield, 1980; Held, 1984; Prochaska, 1984), which is not surprising, because research supports its popularity and effectiveness. Studies illustrate that integration is the most common theoretical preference of counselors or psychotherapists (Garfield & Kurtz, 1977; Jayartne, 1982; Norcross & Prochaska, 1982; Smith, 1982). Smith and Glass (1977), using meta-analysis, provided indirect support for the importance of curative factors in counseling and psychotherapy when they concluded that although no one theoretical school is better than any other, counseling or psychotherapy benefits about 80 percent of those who receive it. Lambert (1986) amplifies this by identifying three common curative factors that account for counseling or therapeutic gains: support, learning, and action. Fiedler's historical research (1950a, 1950b), which suggested that experience rather than theoretical adherence accounted for differences among counselors or psychotherapists, may have been the forerunner of these contemporary studies.

DEVELOPING AN INTEGRATIVE APPROACH

Before a counselor or psychotherapist decides to use an integrative approach in the practice of counseling and psychotherapy, she must have a clear understanding of the process involved. First, she must recognize the diversity of ideas available in the theories of counseling and psychotherapy. She must read, study, and understand the philosophy, constructs, and goals of the various theories so that an informed and systematic choice may be made with regard to their inclusion or exclusion in her theory base. Second, the counselor or psychotherapist must know his own personal agenda: values, beliefs, and perceptions about humanity. Without this knowledge, he cannot properly judge the fit of a theory to his own philosophy. Third, the counselor or psychotherapist must know the types of clients she will see and where (agency, private practice, school, etc.) she will be working with these clients. Finally, the counselor or psychotherapist should recognize that combining some theories and interventions may be problematic; thus, he should find alternative ways of achieving the intended goals.

In the process of developing an integrated theory approach, the first area of consideration is the theory's philosophy. After examining the basic philosophy of the various theories, the counselor or psychotherapist should move to an examination of the constructs inherent in each theory. These constructs include the focus of the theory, goals for counseling or psychotherapy, counselor or psychotherapist and client relationship, and applications. Finally, the counselor or psychotherapist should examine the interventions of each theory and her comfort level in using them with clients.

Philosophy

In searching the basic tenets of the various theories, the counselor or psychotherapist should consider his personal belief system. For example, if his basic belief about human nature is that humankind is self-determining, then he will have difficulty integrating psychoanalytic theory, which emphasizes the importance of psychic energy, unconscious motives, and impulses, as well as early experiences determining human behavior. However, depending on other personal beliefs, he might be capable of integrating parts of individual psychology, existential, Gestalt, or person-centered theories, which stress the importance of self-determination in the change process. A counselor or psychotherapist who believes that problems arise from poor choices made by individuals might integrate transactional analysis (TA), rational-emotive therapy (RET), and reality therapy. Depending on her cognitive bias and attitude toward learning theories, the counselor or psychotherapist might also consider behavioral therapy and cognitive-behavioral approaches.

Constructs

Within the various theories, several constructs are considered. This section includes discussions of the following: focus on the present or the past, on insight or action, on feelings or cognitions, on counseling and psychotherapy goals, on counseling and psychotherapy interventions, and on the counseling or therapeutic relationship. An important issue to consider is whether it is more important to focus on the client's present problems or past experiences. Psychoanalytic and analytical psychotherapy stress the importance of the past to the present problems. Gestalt, which is firmly based in the here and now, uses interventions to bring past or unfinished business into the present. Behavioral, cognitive-behavioral, TA, and reality therapy are concerned with present behavior and needed change. Existential and person-centered theories are concerned with the present and future growth of the individual.

Should counseling or psychotherapy focus on insight or action? In psychoanalytic theory the focus is on insight; the client is helped to examine his ego defenses and unconscious processes that have resulted in inadequate resolution of psychosexual stage development. Analytical psychotherapy stresses the importance of developing self-knowledge by integrating the conscious and unconscious through the use of archetypes and other symbols within the psyche. Obviously, the insight theories will be difficult to integrate with the action-oriented theories. However, the theories that focus on action—individual psychology, Gestalt, TA, behavioral, cognitive-behavioral, RET, and reality therapy—may not be entirely compatible. Individual psychology with its cognitive perspective on motivation and goals would not blend well with Gestalt, which emphasizes feelings and unfinished business. However, behavioral, cognitive-behavioral, and reality therapy, all with strong emphasis on learning new behaviors, might integrate easily.

Does the counselor or psychotherapist focus on feeling (emotion) or thinking (cognition)? Person-centered, Gestalt, psychoanalytic, and analytical psychology theories are highly focused on feelings and emotional states. Other theories, such as RET and TA, attempt to consider both emotions and cognitions. Behavioral, cognitive-behavioral, and reality therapy focus on faulty learning and behavior. Another problem concerns the client's preferred way of looking at the world. A client who "thinks" may be unprepared to deal with feelings in the beginning of counseling and psychotherapy. If the counselor or psychotherapist moves too quickly into feelings, the client may terminate counseling or psychotherapy because of fear. Therefore, the practitioner must follow the client's lead and use a more cognitive approach initially and, as appropriate, move to a more feeling-oriented approach.

What are the goals of counseling or psychotherapy and what type of change is to be accomplished? Many clients come to counseling or psychotherapy in a quest for self-knowledge. Analytical, person-centered, Gestalt, and existential theories focus on this issue. Analytical psychology provides self-knowledge through the understanding of the conscious and unconscious by investigation of dreams and introspective examination of personal symbols of archetypes. Person-centered theory provides a safe haven for self-exploration that allows the client to become more open, spontaneous, and trusting of herself and others. Both existential and Gestalt stress moment-to-moment awareness and responsibility for change. Change in behavior, the goal of reality therapy, RET, TA, behavioral, and cognitive-behavioral theories, may be accomplished by connecting thoughts, feelings, and behaviors; or change may be accomplished by focusing on problem-solving and retraining by systematic methods exemplified by behavioral theory. Change in decisions and decision-making processes is found in TA, RET, and reality therapy.

The counseling or therapeutic relationship is important in all theories. Most accept the core conditions of counseling and psychotherapy as being essential to building a good client and counselor or psychotherapist relationship, but other issues in the therapeutic relationship must be considered. First, what role does the counselor or psychotherapist play in the process of counseling and psychotherapy? In psychoanalytic theory, where the counselor or psychotherapist is the object of projection and transference, he is not as open as in existential or person-centered theories, where the practitioner is a partner in a human-to-human encounter. The counselor or psychotherapist is a catalyst for helping the client explore her unconscious processes in psychoanalytic and analytical psychology. The counselor or psychotherapist plays the role of teacher-trainer in behavioral, cognitive-behavioral, TA, and RET.

Finally, the counselor or psychotherapist must consider the applications of the various theories. It is important to recognize that the setting in which she will be working and the types of clients that she will be seeing affect the choice of theory. For example, a school counselor would not use psychoanalytic or analytical psychology because both theories are more suited for adults who are interested in intensive, long-term counseling and psychotherapy. The school counselor would be better served by individual psychology, reality therapy, behavioral, cognitive-behavioral, or person-centered theories, depending on the problems of the clients. Counselors or psychotherapists who specialize in crisis intervention might consider combining existential, Gestalt, and cognitive-behavioral theories because of the importance each places on personal responsibility and coping mechanisms. Most theories can be applied equally well to individual, group, and family therapy.

Interventions

Integrative approaches have often been criticized on the grounds that interventions are chosen haphazardly by the counselor or psychotherapist. Before using any intervention, the counselor or psychotherapist should ask himself three questions: What will be accomplished by the use of this intervention? Am I comfortable with the intervention's methodology? Is the client psychologically prepared for the possible results? Some interventions are used by virtually all theories—questioning, paraphrasing, summary, clarification, confrontation, and so on. Other interventions are goal specific. For example, behavioral interventions such as operant conditioning, systematic desensitization, and reinforcement would not be useful for a client interested in self-knowledge. However, contracting, cognitive restructuring, modeling, and rehearsal, all of which are behavioral interventions, might help the client in her quest.

Finally, the counselor or psychotherapist must keep in mind that the client is the prime concern in counseling or psychotherapy: it is the client who must be served, not the counselor or psychotherapist's personal agendas. To be successful, the counselor or psychotherapist must calibrate her interventions to account for the developmental and cognitive levels of her clients. Essentially the counselor or psychotherapist serves as a pacer. Additionally, she must know and abide by the ethical boundaries of the profession, always keeping in mind that the welfare of the client is paramount. The counselor or psychotherapist must recognize and affirm the client as a human being.

As stated earlier in this chapter, the counselor or psychotherapist should not operate on faith, guesswork, emotion, popularity, or special interest. His theory base should organize, comprehend, integrate, resolve, and use the "best from the best." Further, the counselor or psychotherapist must have a repertoire of skills, competencies, strategies, and interventions that he is comfortable with using in order to avoid simplistic and narrow treatments.

STRENGTHS AND WEAKNESSES

The integrative approach to counseling and psychotherapy has deep roots in tradition and equally deep roots in controversy. Accordingly, this part of the chapter presents the strengths and weaknesses associated with integrative counseling and psychotherapy.

Strengths

One of the many strengths of integrative counseling and psychotherapy is its broad-based, integrated system capitalizing on the selection of interventions and strategies for their effectiveness rather than for their membership in a particular theory base. Similarly, integrative counseling and psychotherapy advocate selectively applying interventions and strategies to meet the specific needs of clients rather than selection based on counselor or psychotherapist comfort. Accordingly, Young (1992) concluded that the focus on common factors and the development of specific interventions maximizes the effectiveness of integrative counseling and psychotherapy. Researchers describe the integrative approach as especially effective when a specific treatment is recommended for a specific problem and further stress the value of the counselor or psychotherapist's acquaintance with a variety of theories and interventions (Halgin, 1985; Held, 1984; Lambert, 1986; Nelson-Jones, 1985; O'Leary, 1984; Rubin, 1986; Winter, 1985). Another positive feature of the integrative approach is its assumption that counselors or psychotherapists are competent individuals capable of selecting, integrating, and applying either part or whole theories appropriately. Because a single theory has not been identified as the best theory, the integrative model has proven as effective as any single-orientation theory (Lambert, 1986).

Other advantages offered by the integrative approach include its flexibility of choice of methods and its multiagency application. Further, it forces each counselor or psychotherapist to develop her personal style. The very core of integrative counseling or psychotherapy requires the practitioner to evaluate and develop her personal view continually, thus avoiding stagnation or dependence on a single theory. A purely separatist viewpoint can preclude a comprehensive vision of client care and can produce a polarization in counseling and psychotherapy approaches (Garfield, 1982; Karasu, 1986). In contrast, the integrative approach conceptualizes counseling and psychotherapy as evolving from a variety of established theories, thus avoiding polarization. Finally, a primary advantage of the integrative approach is that it allows the counselor or psychotherapist to develop an internally consistent, coherent rationale for his counseling or psychotherapy behavior. Implied in this description is the assumption that he will study various approaches and thus make a theory selection based on critical analysis. Another implication is that the counselor or psychotherapist will be forced to consider the whole person in counseling or psychotherapy sessions. A further strength, and perhaps one often overlooked, is that the integrative approach can build bridges between incompatible viewpoints (Norcross, 1990).

Weaknesses

While defenders of the integrative approach list its numerous strengths, it also receives its share of criticism. Researchers have described integrative counseling and psychotherapy as a haphazard clinical approach (Garfield, 1982; Norcross, 1990; Wolfe & Goldfried, 1988), an approach with little theoretical purity (Omer & London, 1988) or research support (Patterson, 1989a). In a later article, Patterson (1989b) maintains that integrative counseling or psychotherapy consists of disparate interventions from many approaches with little attempt at systematic organization or the formation of guiding principles to regulate their use. Eysenck (1970) has referred to integrative counseling and psychotherapy as an undisciplined hybrid of systems likely to breed confusion. Eysenck categorizes it as a "mish-mash of theories, a hugger-mugger of procedures, a gallimaufry of therapies, and a charivaria of activities having no proper rationale and incapable of being tested or evaluated" (p. 140). Kottler and Brown (1992) and Patterson (1986) liken integrative counseling or psychotherapy to a technician approach. They state that counselors or psychotherapists operating without the philosophy and assumptions of theory are like technicians who can fix what is broken but do not have the in-depth knowledge to understand why. Abroms (1983) concluded that clients are viewed as problems instead of people. Additionally, Kottler and Brown (1992) contend that integrative counselors or psychotherapists often use a shotgun approach that is unduly concerned with symptom alleviation rather than with resolving underlying problems. Karasu (1986) has asserted that without belief in one's own school or orientation, an element of success in counseling or psychotherapy is missing that builds confidence and professional identity. McBride and Martin (1990) concluded that the integrative approach does not provide the counselor or psychotherapist with the information needed to operate in new and different situations. Patterson (1989b) has said that it demonstrates little concern for compatibility or orderly integration of theories; instead, it attempts to include as many methods and interventions as possible. Linden (1984) stated that without a clear grounding in theory, it is difficult to establish goals, provide encouragement, or measure results.

The question of efficacy has surfaced in regard to integrative counseling and psychotherapy. Chessick (1985), Linden (1984), Russell (1986), and Stall (1984) concluded that efficacy is diminished by lack of its fundamental bases in theory, concepts, and empiricism. Similarly, Patterson (1989a) criticized the integrative approach because he believes it lacks a metatheory necessary to guide and implement counseling or psychotherapy practice and principles. Abroms (1983) described the integrative approach as having connotations of superficiality. Finally, in their discussion of integrative counseling and psychotherapy, Kottler and Brown (1992) concluded that there is an inherent difficulty in expecting counselors or psychotherapists to learn the technology of all systems and to keep current with the constant changes in the field. They stated that this leads to mediocrity and to generalists who know a little about everything and a lot about nothing.

CONCLUSION

The integrative approach has many factors in its favor. It advocates a wide-based approach with a large selection of interventions and strategies that have proven effective. It assumes that counselors or psychotherapists are capable of the appropriate use of interventions and strategies. Further, it forces the counselor or psychotherapist to develop a personal style and theory. However, there is no doubt that there are problems inherent in the use of an integrative approach. If not carefully considered, it can lack guiding principles to regulate the use of interventions and strategies. Too often, it has been a shotgun approach—fixing what is broken without knowing why. Further, for less experienced counselors or psychotherapists, an integrative approach may not inspire the confidence or professional identity of a single theory.

Despite the controversy and criticism surrounding integrative counseling or psychotherapy, counselors and psychotherapists are continuing to opt for the integrative approach, one that provides flexibility of choice from any and all existing theories. In the 28 years between 1961 and 1989, researchers reported that between 32 percent and 65 percent of practitioners indicate multiple school allegiance or designate themselves as eclectic or integrationists (Garfield & Kurtz, 1976, 1977; Goldfried, 1980; Jayartne, 1982; Kelly, 1961; Kelly, Goldberg, Fiske, & Kokowski,

1978; Larson, 1980; Norcross & Prochaska, 1982; Smith, 1982; Swan, 1979; Swan & MacDonald, 1978; Watkins, Lopez, Campbell, & Himmell, 1986). Hart (1983) captures the invasion of integrative counseling and therapy when he writes:

> Modern psychotherapists are becoming more eclectic in their approach. Schools still exist, but psychotherapists are less likely to have a life-long membership in just one school, and even psychotherapists who affiliate with a single school are likely to borrow ideas and interventions from other schools. (p. 6)

Perhaps this trend toward integration (eclecticism) reflects a maturation within the profession that parallels human growth and development. The profession may be entering its early adolescence where individuation takes precedence over dependence on a grand master or a grand theory. Perhaps the profession is moving away from those with idealistic adulations toward a greater acceptance of personal responsibility and agency in creating effective counselors or psychotherapists. No doubt, like adolescents, counselors and psychotherapists attempting to find their integrative identity go through periods of awkwardness and uncertainty. Grand masters and grand theories are vital, as are parents; and unlike many adolescents, we acknowledge their contributions to the development of the profession. At the same time, however, this chapter has celebrated the individual counselor or psychotherapist who dares to discover her own identity through integrating the ideas of others, through personal experience, and through personal exploration. To achieve this integration, the counselor or psychotherapist must struggle, take risks, experiment, model, and reflect. This professional development is no less tumultuous than being an adolescent, and it is also no less exciting, rewarding, and meaningful.

REFERENCES

Abroms, E. M. (1983). Beyond eclecticism. *American Journal of Psychiatry, 140,* 740–745.

Andrews, J. (1989). Integrating visions of reality: Interpersonal diagnosis and the existential vision. *American Psychologist, 44,* 803–817.

Beutler, L. E. (1983). *Eclectic psychotherapy: A systematic approach.* New York: Pergamon.

Beutler, L. E. (1986). Systematic eclectic psychotherapy. In J. C. Norcross (Ed.), *Handbook of eclectic psychotherapy* (pp. 94–131). New York: Brunner/Mazel.

Beutler, L. E., & Clarkin, J. F. (1990). *Systematic treatment selection: Toward targeted therapeutic interventions.* New York: Brunner/Mazel.

Beutler, L. E., & Mitchell, R. (1981). Psychotherapy outcome in depressed and impulsive patients as a function of analytic and experiential treatment procedures. *Psychiatry, 44,* 297–306.

Brammer, L. M. (1969). Eclecticism revisited. *Personnel and Guidance Journal, 48,* 192–197.

Brehm, S. S. (1976). *The application of social psychology to clinical practice.* New York: Wiley.

Brehm, S. S., & Brehm, J. W. (1981). *Psychological reactance: A theory of freedom and control.* New York: Academic Press.

Brehm, S. S., & Smith, T. (1986). Social psychological approaches to psychotherapy and behavior change. In S. L. Garfield & A. E. Bergin (Eds.), *Handbook of psychotherapy and behavior change* (3rd ed.) (pp. 69–115). New York: Wiley.

Calvert, S. J., Beutler, L. E., & Crago, M. (1988). Psychotherapy outcome as a function of therapist-patient matching on selected variables. *Journal of Social and Clinical Psychology, 6,* 104–117.

Chessick, R. D. (1985). The frantic retreat from the mind to the brain: American psychiatry in mauvaise foi. *Psychoanalytic Inquiry, 5,* 369–403.

Diamond, R. E., & Havens, R. A. (1975). Restructuring psychotherapy: Toward a prescriptive eclecticism. *Professional Psychology, 6,* 103–200.

Diamond, R. E., Havens, R. A., & Jones, A. C. (1978). A conceptual framework for the practice of prescriptive eclecticism in psychotherapy. *American Psychologist, 33,* 239–248.

Dollard, J., & Miller, N. (1950). *Personality and psychotherapy.* New York: McGraw-Hill.

Dryden, W. (1986). Eclectic psychotherapies: A critique of leading approaches. In J. C. Norcross (Ed.), *Handbook of eclectic psychotherapy* (pp. 353–378). New York: Brunner/Mazel.

Duncan, B. L., Parks, M. B., & Rusk, G. S. (1990). Strategic eclecticism: A technical alternative for eclectic psychotherapy. *Psychotherapy, 27,* 568–577.

Eysenck, H. J. (1970). A mish-mash of theories. *International Journal of Psychiatry, 9,* 140–146.

Fiedler, F. E. (1950a). A comparison of therapeutic relationships in psychoanalytic, nondirective, and Adlerian therapy. *Journal of Consulting Psychology, 14,* 435–445.

Fiedler, F. E. (1950b). The concept of an ideal therapeutic relationship. *Journal of Consulting Psychology, 14,* 239–245.

Frances, A., Clarkin, J., & Perry, S. (1984). *Differential therapeutics in psychiatry: The art and science of treatment selection.* New York: Brunner/Mazel.

Frank, J. D. (1973). *Persuasion and healing: A comparative study of psychotherapy* (rev. ed.). Baltimore: Johns Hopkins University Press.

Frank, J. D. (1981). Therapeutic components shared by all psychotherapies. In J. H. Harvey & M. M. Parks (Eds.), *Psychotherapy research and behavior change* (pp. 175–182). Washington, DC: American Psychological Association.

Frey, D. H. (1972). Conceptualizing counseling theories: A content analysis of process and goal statements. *Counselor Education and Supervision, 11,* 243–250.

Garfield, S. L. (1973). Basic ingredients or common factors in psychotherapy? *Journal of Consulting and Clinical Psychology, 41,* 9–12.

Garfield, S. L. (1980). *Psychotherapy: An eclectic approach.* New York: Wiley.

Garfield, S. L. (1982). Eclecticism and integration in psychotherapy. *Behavior Therapy, 13,* 610–623.

Garfield, S. L. (1988). Commentary on Omer and London. *Psychotherapy, 25,* 180–182.

Garfield, S. L., & Kurtz, R. (1976). Clinical psychologists in the 1970s. *American Psychologist, 31*, 1–9.

Garfield, S. L., & Kurtz, R. (1977). A study of eclectic views. *Journal of Consulting and Clinical Psychology, 45*, 78–83.

Gilliland, B. E., James, R. K., & Bowman, J. T. (1989). *Theories and strategies in counseling and psychotherapy* (2nd ed.). Englewood Cliffs, NJ: Prentice-Hall.

Goldfried, M. R. (1980). Some views on effective principles of psychotherapy. *Cognitive Therapy and Research, 4*, 271–306.

Goldstein, A. P. (1966). Psychotherapy research by extrapolation from social psychology. *Journal of Counseling Psychology, 13*, 38–45.

Goldstein, A. P., & Stein, N. (1976). *Prescriptive psychotherapies*. New York: Pergamon.

Goulding, R., & Goulding, M. (1978). *The power is in the patient: A TA/Gestalt approach to psychotherapy*. San Francisco: TA Press.

Goulding, R., & Goulding, M. (1979). *Changing lives through redecision therapy*. New York: Brunner/Mazel.

Halgin, R. P. (1985). Teaching integration of psychotherapy models to beginning therapists. *Psychotherapy, 22*, 555–563.

Hart, J. (1983). *Modern eclectic therapy: A functional orientation to counseling and psychotherapy*. New York: Plenum.

Held, B. S. (1984). Toward a strategic eclecticism: A proposal. *Psychotherapy, 21*, 232–241.

Jayartne, S. (1982). Characteristics and theoretical orientations of clinical social workers: A national survey. *Journal of Social Service Research, 4*, 17–30.

Karasu, T. B. (1986). The specificity versus nonspecificity dilemma: Toward identifying therapeutic change agents. *American Journal of Psychiatry, 14*, 687–695.

Kelly, E. L. (1961). Clinical psychology—1960: Report of survey findings. *Newsletter, Division of Clinical Psychology, 14*, 1–11.

Kelly, E. L., Goldberg, L. R., Fiske, D. W., & Kokowski, J. M. (1978). Twenty-five years later: A follow-up study of the graduate students in clinical psychology assessed in the V.A. selection research project. *American Psychologist, 33*, 746–755.

Kelly, K. R. (1988). Defending eclecticism: The utility of informed choice. *Journal of Mental Health Counseling, 10*, 210–213.

Kelly, K. R. (1991). Theoretical integration is the future for mental health counseling. *Journal of Mental Health Counseling, 13*, 106–111.

Kottler, J. A., & Brown, R. W. (1992). *Introduction to therapeutic counseling* (2nd ed.). Pacific Grove, CA: Brooks/Cole.

Lambert, M. J. (1986). Implications of psychotherapy outcome research for eclectic psychotherapy. In J. C. Norcross (Ed.), *Handbook of eclectic psychotherapy* (pp. 436–462). New York: Brunner/Mazel.

Larson, D. (1980). Therapeutic schools, styles, and schoolism: A national survey. *Journal of Humanistic Psychology, 20*, 1–20.

Lazarus, A. A. (1967). In support of technical eclecticism. *Psychological Reports, 21*, 415–416.

Lazarus, A. A. (1971). *Behavior therapy and beyond*. New York: McGraw-Hill.

Lazarus, A. A. (1973). Multimodal behavior therapy. *Journal of Nervous and Mental Disease, 156*, 404–411.

Lazarus, A. A. (1976). *Multimodal behavior therapy*. New York: Springer.

Lazarus, A. A. (1981). *The practice of multimodal therapy*. New York: McGraw-Hill.

Lazarus, A. A. (1984). *In the mind's eye*. New York: Guilford.

Lewis, T. T. (1985). Gordon Allport's eclectic humanism: A neglected approach to psychohistory. *Psychohistory Review, 13,* 33–41.

Lieberman, M. A., Yalom, I. D., & Miles, M. B. (1973). *Encounter groups: First facts.* New York: Basic Books.

Linden, G. W. (1984). Some philosophical roots of Adlerian psychology. *Individual Psychology: Journal of Adlerian Theory, Research, and Practice, 40,* 254–269.

Luborsky, L., Singer, B., & Luborsky, L. (1975). Contemporary studies of psychotherapies. *Archives of General Psychiatry, 32,* 995–1008.

McBride, M. C., & Martin, G. E. (1990). A framework for eclecticism: The importance of theory to mental health counseling. *Journal of Mental Health Counseling, 12,* 495–505.

Nelson-Jones, R. (1985). Eclecticism, integration, and comprehensiveness in counseling theory and practice. *British Journal of Guidance and Counseling, 13,* 129–138.

Norcross, J. C. (1985). Eclecticism: Definitions, manifestations, and practitioners. *International Journal of Eclectic Psychotherapy, 4,* 19–32.

Norcross, J. C. (1986). Eclectic psychotherapy: An introduction and overview. In J. C. Norcross (Ed.), *Handbook of eclectic psychotherapy* (pp. 3–24). New York: Brunner/Mazel.

Norcross, J. C. (1990). Commentary: Eclecticism misrepresented and integration misunderstood. *Psychotherapy, 27,* 297–300.

Norcross, J. C., & Prochaska, J. O. (1982). A national survey of clinical psychologists: Affiliations and orientations. *The Clinical Psychologist, 35,* 4–6.

O'Leary, K. D. (1984). The image of behavior therapy: It is time to take a stand. *Behavior Therapy, 15,* 219–233.

Omer, H., & London, P. (1988). Metamorphosis in psychotherapy: End of the systems era. *Psychotherapy, 25,* 171–180.

Palmer, J. O. (1980). *A primer of eclectic psychotherapy.* Monterey, CA: Brooks/Cole.

Parloff, M. B. (1986). Frank's "common elements" in psychotherapy: Non-specific factors and placebos. *American Journal of Orthopsychiatry, 56,* 521–530.

Patterson, C. H. (1986, Summer). Counselor training or counselor education? *Spectrum Newsletter,* pp. 10–12.

Patterson, C. H. (1989a). Eclecticism in psychotherapy: Is integration possible? *Psychotherapy, 26,* 157–161.

Patterson, C. H. (1989b). Foundations for a systematic eclectic psychotherapy. *Psychotherapy, 26,* 427–435.

Perry, S., Frances, A., & Clarkin, J. F. (1985). *A DSM-III casebook of differential therapeutics: A clinical guide to treatment selection.* New York: Brunner/Mazel.

Prochaska, J. O. (1984). *Systems of psychotherapy: A transtheoretical analysis* (2nd ed.). Homewood, IL: Dorsey.

Prochaska, J. O., & DiClemente, C. C. (1984). *The transtheoretical approach: Crossing the traditional boundaries of therapy.* Homewood, IL: Dow Jones-Irwin.

Prochaska, J. O., & DiClemente, C. C. (1986). The transtheoretical approach. In J. C. Norcross (Ed.), *Handbook of eclectic psychotherapy* (pp. 163–200). New York: Brunner/Mazel.

Rubin, S. S. (1986). Ego-focused psychotherapy: A psychodynamic framework for technical eclecticism. *Psychotherapy, 23,* 385–389.

Russell, R. L. (1986). The inadvisability of admixing psychoanalysis with other forms of psychotherapy. *Journal of Contemporary Psychotherapy, 16,* 76–86.

Sloane, R. B., Stapels, F. R., Cristol, A. H., Yorkston, N. J., & Whipple, K. (1975). *Psychotherapy versus behavior therapy.* Cambridge: Harvard University Press.

Smith, D. S. (1982). Trends in counseling and psychotherapy. *American Psychologist, 37,* 802–809.

Smith, M. L., & Glass, G. V. (1977). Meta-analysis of psychotherapy outcome studies. *American Psychologist, 32,* 752–760.

Stall, R. (1984). Disadvantages of eclecticism in the treatment of alcoholism: The "problem" of recidivism. *Journal of Drug Issues, 14,* 437–448.

Strong, S. R. (1978). Social psychological approach to psychotherapy research. In S. L. Garfield & A. E. Bergin (Eds.), *Handbook of psychotherapy and behavior change* (2nd ed.) (pp. 101–135). New York: Wiley.

Swan, G. E. (1979). On the structure of eclecticism: Cluster analysis of eclectic behavior therapists. *Professional Psychology, 10,* 732–734.

Swan, G. E., & MacDonald, M. L. (1978). Behavior therapy in practice: A national survey of behavior therapists. *Behavior Therapy, 9,* 799–807.

Thorne, F. C. (1950). *Principles of personality counseling: An eclectic approach.* Brandon, VT: Clinical Psychology Publishing.

Thorne, F. C. (1967). *Integrative psychology.* Brandon, VT: Clinical Psychology Publishing.

Thorne, F. C. (1968). *Psychological case handling: Establishing the conditions necessary for counseling and psychotherapy* (Vol. 1). Brandon, VT: Clinical Psychology Publishing.

Watkins, C. E., Lopez, F. G., Campbell, V. L., & Himmell, C. D. (1986). Contemporary counseling psychology: Results of a national survey. *Journal of Counseling Psychology, 33,* 301–309.

Wilkins, W. (1984). Psychotherapy: The powerful placebo. *Journal of Consulting and Clinical Psychology, 52,* 570–573.

Winter, D. A. (1985). Personal styles, constructive alternativism, and the provision of a therapeutic service. *British Journal of Guidance and Counseling, 58,* 129–135.

Wolfe, B. E., & Goldfried, M. R. (1988). Research on psychotherapy integration: Recommendations and conclusions from an NIMH workshop. *Journal of Consulting and Clinical Psychology, 56,* 448–451.

Yalom, I. (1985). *Theory and practice of group psychotherapy* (3rd ed.). New York: Basic Books.

Young, M. E. (1992). *Counseling methods and techniques: An eclectic approach.* New York: Macmillan.

Name Index

Subject Index